THE PELICAN HISTORY OF ART

EDITOR: NIKOLAUS PEVSNER

ASSISTANT EDITOR: JUDY NAIRN

Z30

PREHISTORIC ART IN EUROPE

N. K. SANDARS

Details of shield from the river Witham, England.
Third-second century (?). Bronze with coral studs.
London, British Museum

N. K. SANDARS

PREHISTORIC ART IN EUROPE

PUBLISHED BY PENGUIN BOOKS

Penguin Books Ltd, Harmondsworth, Middlesex
Penguin Books Inc., 3300 Clipper Mill Road, Baltimore, Maryland, 21211, U.S.A.
Penguin Books Australia Ltd, Ringwood, Victoria, Australia

*

Text printed by Richard Clay (The Chaucer Press) Ltd, Bungay, Suffolk
Plates printed by Balding & Mansell Ltd, London
Made and printed in Great Britain

*

Copyright © N. K. Sandars, 1968
First published 1968

TO MY SISTER

BRIDWELL LIBRARY
SOUTHERN METHODIST UNIVERSITY
DALLAS, TEXAS 75222

CONTENTS

BRIDWELL LIBRARY
SOUTHERN METHODIST UNIVERSITY
DALLAS, TEXAS 75275

LIST OF FIGURES

The following Figures were drawn or re-drawn by Miss Sheila Gibson: 2–8, 11D, 14, 19, 22, 25, 26, 28–9, 31, 33, 35–44, 45, B and C, 46, 48–51A, 52, 53D, 54, 56C, 57, 59, A and B, 60, 61, 65, 66, B and C, 67, 68, 69, 71–3, 75–9, 80–6, 88–91, 95B, 96, 97, 101, 102, 103C.

LIST OF PLATES

Where credit for a photograph does not appear, the source is the museum quoted as the location. Objects of Paleolithic art are now displayed in the new Anthropos Museum at Brno.

Frontispiece: Detail of shield from the river Witham, England. Third-second century (?). Bronze with coral studs. L. of whole 44 in : 1·10 m. *London, British Museum* (photo British Museum)

1 Solutrian 'laurel leaf'. Flint. H. *c.* 9⅓ in : 23·9 cm. *Paris, Musée de l'Homme*

2 Man from Brno, Czechoslovakia. Gravettian. Ivory. H. 8 in : 20·5 cm. *Brno, Moravian Museum* (Poulík and Forman, *Prehistoric Art*)

3 Woman from Willendorf, Lower Austria. Gravettian. Limestone. H. 4⅓ in : 11 cm. *Vienna, Naturhistorisches Museum* (Courtesy Dr Kromer)

4 Animals from the Vogelherd cave, Württemberg, Germany. Gravettian. Bone and ivory. L. of lion 3⅗ in : 9·2 cm. *Tübingen, Institut für Vor- und Frühgeschichte* (Courtesy Professor Kimmig and H. Hell, *Vorzeit an Rhein und Donau*)

5 Woman's torso from Ostrava Petřkovice, Czechoslovakia. Gravettian, *c.* 25,000. Haematite. H. 1¾ in : 4·5 cm. *Brno, Academy of Sciences, Archaeological Institute* (Courtesy Dr Klíma)

6 Woman's head from Dolní Věstonice, Czechoslovakia. Gravettian, *c.* 23,000. Ivory. H. 2 in : 4·8 cm. *Brno, Moravian Museum* (Courtesy Dr Valoch)

7 Bear from Dolní Věstonice, Czechoslovakia. Gravettian, *c.* 23,000. Baked clay. L. 3 in : 7·5 cm. *Brno, Moravian Museum* (Courtesy Dr Valoch)

8 Woman from Dolní Věstonice, Czechoslovakia. Gravettian, *c.* 23,000. Baked clay. H. 4½ in : 11·5 cm. *Brno, Moravian Museum* (Courtesy Dr Valoch)

9 Breasts from Dolní Věstonice, Czechoslovakia. Gravettian, *c.* 23,000. Ivory. H. of larger 3½ in : 8·7 cm. *Brno, Moravian Museum* (Courtesy Dr Valoch)

10 Woman's head from Grotte du Pape, Brassempouy, Landes, France. Gravettian, *c.* 22,000 (?). Ivory. H. 1⅓ in : 3·5 cm. *Saint Germain-en-Laye, Musée des Antiquités Nationales* (Hurault)

11 Woman's torso from Sireuil, Dordogne, France. Gravettian. Calcite. H. 3⅗ in : 9·2 cm. *Saint Germain-en-Laye, Musée des Antiquités Nationales* (Éditions Arthaud)

12 Woman's torso from Savignano, Italy. Gravettian. Serpentine. H. 8⅔ in : 22 cm. *Rome, Museo Pigorini* (Deutsches Archaeologisches Institut, Rome)

13 Woman from Lespugue, Haute-Garonne, France. Final 'Perigordian' or Gravettian (?). Ivory. H. 6 in : 15 cm. *Paris, Musée de l'Homme*

14 Engraved vulvae from La Ferrassie, Dordogne, France. Aurignacian. Rock. L. 26½ in : 67·5 cm. *Musée des Eyzies* (Courtesy S. Giedion, photo Herdeg)

15 Engraved 'macaroni' at Pech-Merle, Dordogne, France. Solutrian (?). Hardened mud (Centre d'Études et Documentations Préhistoriques, Montignac-sur-Vézère, photo Windells)

16 Bison engraved in the cave of La Grèze, Dordogne, France. Gravettian. L. 2 ft : 60 cm. (Centre d'Études et Documentations Préhistoriques, Montignac-sur-Vézère, photo Windells)

17 Horses engraved in the cave of Pair-non-Pair, Gironde, France. Proto-Magdalenian (?). L. of right-hand horse 29½ in : 75 cm. (Courtesy S. Giedion, photo Weider)

18 Relief of a man from Laussel, Dordogne, France. Gravettian, *c.* 19,000 (?). Stone. H. 18½ in : 47 cm. *Bordeaux, Charon Collection* (Courtesy S. Giedion, photo Herdeg)

19 Relief of a woman from Laussel, Dordogne, France. Gravettian, *c.* 19,000 (?). Stone. H. 18 in : 46 cm. *Paris, Musée de l'Homme* (René Pasquino)

20 Bison at Tuc d'Audoubert, Ariège, France. Magdalenian, after 15,000. Modelled clay. L. 25 and 24 in : 63 and 61 cm. (Yan, Toulouse)

21 Relief of cows at Fourneau du Diable, Charente, France. Solutrian (?). L. of right-hand cow 14 in : 36 cm. (Courtesy S. Giedion, photo Herdeg)

135 Pot with graphite paint from Karanovo, Bulgaria. Karanovo VI, fourth millennium. Clay. *Sofia, National Museum* (Courtesy Professor Mikov)

136 Cucuteni pot, Rumania. Cucuteni B, third millennium. Painted clay. H. 14⅕ in : 36 cm. *Bucharest, National Museum of Antiquities, Institute of Archaeology* (Courtesy Dr V. Dumitrescu)

137 Tarxien temple, Malta. Late third millennium (Valetta Archaeological Museum, Malta; courtesy Dr J. Evans)

138 Figure from Hağar Qim, Malta. Late third millennium. Clay. H. 5 in : 12·7 cm. *Malta, Valetta Archaeological Museum* (Courtesy Dr J. Evans)

139 Impressed pot from Comiso, Sicily. Fifth–fourth millennium. *Syracuse, Museo Nazionale* (Soprintendenza alle Antichità, Syracuse)

140 Painted pot from Megara Hyblaea, Sicily. Stentinello, fifth–fourth millennium. D. 7½ in : 19 cm. *Syracuse, Museo Nazionale* (Soprintendenza alle Antichità, Syracuse)

141 Stentinello pot from Matrensa, Sicily. Fifth–fourth millennium. *Syracuse, Museo Nazionale* (Courtesy Professor B. Brea, photo Soprintendenza alle Antichità, Syracuse)

142 Diana style pots from Paternó, Sicily. Late fourth–third millennium. *Syracuse, Museo Nazionale* (Soprintendenza alle Antichità, Syracuse)

143 Serra d'Alto pot handle from Paternó, Sicily. Late fourth millennium. Maximum girth *c.* 11 in : 28 cm. *Syracuse, Museo Nazionale* (Soprintendenza alle Antichità, Syracuse)

144 Castelluccio painted pot from Monte Tabuto, Sicily. Third–second millennium. *Syracuse, Museo Nazionale* (Soprintendenza alle Antichità, Syracuse)

145 Monochrome red-ware cup from Malpasso, Sicily. Third millennium. H. *c.* 8 in : 20 cm. *Syracuse, Museo Nazionale* (Soprintendenza alle Antichità, Syracuse)

146 Woman from Senorbí, Sardinia. Ozieri culture, late third–early second millennium. Marble. H. 17⅓ in : 44 cm. *Cagliari, Museo Archeologico Nazionale* (Courtesy Dr Pesce)

147 Bossed plaques from the Cava della Signora, Castelluccio, Sicily. Third–second millennium. Bone. H. of largest 6½ in : 16·5 cm. *Syracuse, Museo Nazionale* (Soprintendenza alle Antichità, Syracuse)

148 Tomb door slab from Castelluccio, Sicily. Third–second millennium. H. 39⅜ in : 1 m. *Syracuse, Museo Nazionale* (Soprintendenza alle Antichità, Syracuse)

149 Woman from S'Adde, Macomer, Sardinia. Neolithic (?). Basalt. H. 5½ in : 14 cm. *Cagliari, Museo Archeologico Nazionale* (Courtesy Dr Pesce)

150 Tomb chamber of passage-grave at Maes Howe, Orkney. *c.* 2000 (Crown Copyright; reproduced by permission of the Ministry of Public Building and Works)

151 Ball from Glas Towie, North-East Scotland. Late third millennium (?). Stone. D. *c.* 2–3 in : 5–8 cm. *Edinburgh, National Museum of Antiquities* (Courtesy Mr R. Stevenson)

152 Stone tomb slabs at Gavr'inis, Brittany. Passage Grave, third millennium (?) (Belzeaux-Zodiaque)

153 Stele from Mas Capelier, Aveyron, France. *c.* 2000 (?). Stone. H. *c.* 2½ ft : 76 cm. *Saint Germain-en-Laye, Musée des Antiquités Nationales* (Belzeaux- Zodiaque)

154 Decorated grave slab from Leuna-Göhlitzsch, Merseburg, Germany. Saale Corded Ware, end of third millennium. Stone. L. 6½ ft : 2 m. *Halle, Landesmuseum für Vorgeschichte* (Courtesy Dr H. Behrens)

155 Face-pot from Svinø, Denmark. Passage Grave Period, third millennium. H. 4¾ in : 12 cm. *Copenhagen, National Museum* (Elswing)

156 Axe with elk's head from Alunda, Uppland, Sweden. Neolithic, third millennium (?). Stone. L. 8¼ in : 21 cm. *Stockholm, Museum of National Antiquities* (Antikvarisk Topografiska Arkivet, courtesy Dr B. Schönbäck)

157 Flask from Mokrin, Yugoslavia. Perjamus, early second millennium. Clay. H. 7¼ in : 18·5 cm. *Belgrade, National Museum* (Josephine Powell)

158 Cup from Ruma, Yugoslavia. Baden culture, *c.* 2000. Clay. H. 2¼ in : 5·5 cm. *Zagreb, Archaeological Museum* (Josephine Powell)

159 Funeral vase from Patince, Slovakia, Czechoslovakia. Pannonian Crusted Ware, first half of the second millennium. Clay. H. 6 in : 15 cm. *Nitra, Archaeological Institute of the Slovak Academy of Sciences* (Courtesy Dr A. Točik, photo J. Krátky)

160 Three white-encrusted pots from Sarvaš, Yugoslavia. Vučedol, early second millennium. Clay. H. of tub-shaped pot 7 in : 17·5 cm. *Zagreb, Archaeological Museum* (Josephine Powell)

161 Amphora from Omoljica, Yugoslavia. Vattina type, second millennium. Clay. H. 5½ in : 14 cm. *Belgrade, National Museum* (Josephine Powell)

162 Funeral vase from grave 54, Cîrna, Oltenia, Rumania. Mid second millennium. Clay. H. 7¼ in : 18·3 cm. *Bucharest, National Museum of Antiquities, Institute of Archaeology* (Courtesy Dr V. Dumitrescu)

163 Funeral vase from grave 48, Cîrna, Oltenia, Rumania. Mid second millennium. Clay. H. 6 in : 15·6 cm. *Bucharest, National Museum of Antiquities, Institute of Archaeology* (Courtesy Dr V. Dumitrescu)

164 Handled pot from Barca, Slovakia, Czechoslovakia. Otomani culture, mid second millennium. *Nitra, Archaeological Institute of the Slovak Academy of Sciences* (Courtesy Dr A. Točik, photo J. Krátky)

165 Base of cup from Hungary. Füzesabony type. Clay (Courtesy Professor J. Banner)

166 High-necked pot from Barca, Slovakia, Czechoslovakia. Otomani culture, mid second millennium. Clay. H. 11 in : 28 cm. *Nitra, Archaeological Institute of the Slovak Academy of Sciences* (Courtesy Dr A. Točik, photo J. Krátky)

167 Figure from Kličevac, Yugoslavia (destroyed). Mid second millennium. Clay. H. 12⅝ in : 32 cm. (Belgrade National Museum, courtesy Dr D. Garašanin)

168 Figure in wheeled vehicle from Dupljaja, Yugoslavia. Mid second millennium. Clay. H. *c.* 4 in : 10 cm. *Belgrade, National Museum* (Josephine Powell)

169 Woman from grave 10, Cîrna, Oltenia, Rumania. Mid second millennium. Clay. H. *c.* 7 in : 17·6 cm. *Bucharest, National Museum of Antiquities, Institute of Archaeology* (Courtesy Dr V. Dumitrescu)

170 Lunula from Ireland. Early second millennium. Gold. W. 9⅙ in : 23·3 cm. *London, British Museum*

171 Sword from Hajdusámson, Hungary. Second millennium. Bronze. L. *c.* 21 in : 53 cm. *Debrecen, Déri Museum* (Courtesy Dr A. Mozsolics, photo Susits László)

172 Butt of axe from Apa, Rumania. Second millennium. Bronze. L. 3¼ in : 8 cm. *Bucharest, Museum of Antiquities, Institute of Archaeology* (Courtesy Dr V. Dumitrescu)

173 Axe from Hajdusámson, Hungary. Second millennium. Bronze. L. 10 in : 25 cm. *Debrecen, Déri Museum* (Courtesy Dr A. Mozsolics, photo Susits László)

174 Axe from Hajdusámson, Hungary. Second millennium. Bronze. L. 10 in : 25 cm. *Debrecen, Déri Museum* (Susits László)

175 Bracelet from Bellye, Hungary. Second millennium. Gold. L. *c.* 4⅓ in : *c.* 11 cm. *Vienna, Naturhistorisches Museum* (Courtesy Dr K. Kromer)

176 Tubes and disc from Nitriansky-Hrádok, Slovakia, Czechoslovakia. Mid second millennium. Bone. *Nitra, Archaeological Institute of the Slovak Academy of Sciences* (Courtesy Dr A. Točik, photo J. Krátky)

177 Lid from Surčin, Croatia, Yugoslavia. Mid second millennium. Marble. D. 2⅓ in : 5·8 cm. *Zagreb, Archaeological Museum* (Courtesy Dr Z. Vinski)

178 Swords from Stensgård and Torupgårde, Denmark. Period I/IIa, mid second millennium. Bronze. L. of former 26⅗ in : 67 cm. *Copenhagen, National Museum* (Elswing)

179 Axe from Fårdrup, Denmark. Period I/IIa, mid second millennium. Bronze. L. 7⅗ in : 19·5 cm. *Copenhagen, National Museum* (Elswing)

180 'Scimitar' with incised boat from Rørby, Denmark. Period I/IIa, mid second millennium. Bronze. L. 23¼ in : 58·8 cm. (detail). *Copenhagen, National Museum* (Elswing)

181 Dagger from Hindsgavl, Denmark. Mid second millennium. Flint. L. 10¾ in : 27·5 cm. *Copenhagen, National Museum* (Elswing)

182 Tutulus from Langstrup, Denmark. Period IIbc, second half of the second millennium. Bronze. D. *c.* 11¼ in : 28·5 cm. *Copenhagen, National Museum* (Elswing)

183 Axe from Brondsted, Denmark. End of second millennium. Bronze. L. *c.* 11 in : 28 cm. *Copenhagen, National Museum* (Elswing)

184 Gorget from Gleninsheen, Co. Clare, Ireland. Dowris Phase, eighth century (?). Gold. W. 12 in : 30·5 cm. *National Museum of Ireland*

185 Horse and car with 'sun-disc' from Trundholm, Denmark. Thirteenth century (?). Bronze and gold. L. of horse 11½ in : 29·3 cm. *Copenhagen, National Museum* (Elswing)

186 Horse and car with 'sun-disc' from Trundholm, Denmark. Thirteenth century (?). Bronze and gold. L. of car 2 ft : 60 cm. *Copenhagen, National Museum* (Elswing)

H. of handle 6⅝ in : 17 cm. *Jena, Vorgeschichtliches Museum der Friedrich-Schiller-Universität* (Courtesy Professor G. Neumann)

244 Flagon from Dürrnberg, Austria. *c.* 425. Bronze. H. 18⅓ in : 46·5 cm. *Salzburg, Carolino Augusteum* (Courtesy Professor K. Willvonseder)

245 Flagon from Dürrnberg (detail) (Courtesy Professor K. Willvonseder)

246 Flagon from Basse-Yutz, Lorraine, France. Early fourth century (?). Bronze, coral, and enamel. H. 15¼ in : 38·7 cm. *London, British Museum*

247 Brooch with heads from Oberwittighausen, Baden, Germany. Fifth–fourth century (?). Bronze. W. 1¾ in : 4·4 cm. *Karlsruhe, Badisches Landesmuseum* (Courtesy Professor Kimmig and H. Hell, *Vorzeit an Rhein und Donau*, photo Hell)

248 Brooch from Parsberg, Oberpfalz, Germany. Fifth–fourth century (?). Bronze. W. 3½ in : 8·8 cm. *Nuremberg, Germanisches National-Museum*

249 Openwork ornament from Cuperly, Marne, France. Late fifth century. Bronze. H. 2⅓ in : 6 cm. *Saint Germain-en-Laye, Musée des Antiquités Nationales* (Belzeaux-Zodiaque)

250 Wooden stand or platter from Høstad, Norway. Fifth century (?). *Trondheim, Videnskapsselskapets Oldsaksamling* (Courtesy and photo Professor S. Marstrander)

251 Cast of pot from La Cheppe, Marne, France. Fifth century (?). H. 13⅓ in : 34 cm. *Saint Germain-en-Laye, Musée des Antiquités Nationales* (Belzeaux-Zodiaque)

252 Discs from Saint Jean-sur-Tourbe, Marne, France. Late fifth century (?). Bronze. D. 9½ in : 24 cm. *Saint Germain-en-Laye, Musée des Antiquités Nationales* (Belzeaux-Zodiaque)

253 Busts from Waldalgesheim, Rhine, Germany. Mid fourth century. Bronze. H. 3½ and 3 in : 8·9 and 7·5 cm. *Bonn, Rheinisches Landesmuseum*

254 Necklet and bracelets from Waldalgesheim, Rhine, Germany. Mid fourth century. Gold. D. of necklet 7¾ in : 19·9 cm. *Bonn, Rheinisches Landesmuseum*

255 Handle with bulls' heads on cauldron from Brå, Jutland, Denmark. Third century (?). Iron and bronze. D. of ring 8 in : 20 cm. *Aarhus, Museum* (Elswing)

256 Owl from Brå cauldron. W. 2 in : 4·8 cm.

257 Spout with back-to-back heads from Dürrnberg, Austria. Third century (?). Bronze. L. 5⅓ in : 13·7 cm. *Salzburg, Carolino Augusteum* (Courtesy Professor K. Willvonseder, photo E. Penninger)

258 Openwork ornament from Brno-Maloměřice, Czechoslovakia. Third century (?). Bronze. H. of animal head *c.* 2⅓ in : 6 cm. *Brno, Moravian Museum*

259 Openwork ornament from Brno-Maloměřice, detail of Plate 258

260 Two heads from openwork ornament from Brno-Maloměřice. *Brno, Moravian Museum*

261 Linch-pin from Champagne, France (?). Third century (?). Iron plated with bronze. L. 3⅓ in : 8·5 cm. *Saint Germain-en-Laye, Musée des Antiquités Nationales* (Belzeaux-Zodiaque)

262 Tube with faces from Champagne, France (?). Third century (?). Iron plated with bronze. L. 2¾ in : 7 cm. *Saint Germain-en-Laye, Musée des Antiquités Nationales* (Belzeaux-Zodiaque)

263 Bracelet from Tarn, France (?). Third century (?). Bronze. D. 2 in : 5 cm. *Saint Germain-en-Laye, Musée des Antiquités Nationales* (Belzeaux-Zodiaque)

264 Bracelet from Aurillac, Tarn, France. Third century (?). Gold. D. 3 in : 7·8 cm. *Paris, Bibliothèque Nationale*

265 Detail of Aurillac bracelet

266 Head from Heidelberg, Germany. Fourth century (?). Sandstone. H. 12 in : 30 cm. *Karlsruhe, Badisches Landesmuseum* (Courtesy Professor Kimmig and H. Hell, *Vorzeit an Rhein und Donau*, photo Hell)

267 Pillar from Pfalzfeld, Rhineland, Germany. Fourth century (?). Stone. H. 4 ft 10 in : 1·48 m. *Bonn, Rheinisches Landesmuseum*

268 Pillar from Waldenbuch, Württemberg, Germany. Fourth–third century. Sandstone. H. 4 ft : 1·25 m. *Stuttgart, Württembergisches Landesmuseum* (Courtesy Professor Kimmig and H. Hell, *Vorzeit an Rhein und Donau*)

269 Figure from Holzgerlingen, Württemberg, Germany. Third–second century (?). Stone. H. 7½ ft : 2·3 m. *Stuttgart, Württembergisches Landesmuseum* (Courtesy Professor Kimmig and H. Hell, *Vorzeit an Rhein und Donau*)

270 Janus heads from Roquepertuse, Provence, France. Fourth–second century. Stone. H. 8¼ in : 21 cm. *Marseille, Musée Borély* (Belzeaux-Zodiaque)

271 Seated figure from Roquepertuse, Provence, France. Fourth century or later. Stone. H. 5 ft : 1·50 m. *Marseille, Musée Borély* (Belzeaux-Zodiaque)

FOREWORD

A BOOK *written about prehistoric art is neither art history nor prehistory, but it is something of both, and it has to meet the difficulties of both. Writers on this subject have been constructing systems ever since curiosity was roused by the first discoveries of objects and monuments. As long ago as 1898 Hoernes set out his three periods, each dependent on an economic stage. There was first the realistic picture-making of primitive hunters, that is to say Paleolithic art; then the schematic geometric idealistic art of agriculturalists and pastoralists, the Neolithic; and finally a higher artistic development that went with trade and industry. There have been other systems like that which sees a parallel between Impressionism and Paleolithic art, Expressionism and Spanish Levantine painted rock-shelters, and between Cubism and the art of the Neolithic and Bronze Ages. But the authors of all these schemes select for their own purposes and do not take account of enough of the facts as we have them. So for example Old Stone Age art bursts the strait-jacket of all aesthetic theories, for it is naturalistic and impressionist; there are extremes of stylization and a complex use of patterns and symbols. It is at one time strong and assured and at another refined and decadent or merely incompetent; while the Neolithic, which should, according to the rules, be schematic and geometric,* is *indeed both sometimes, but is also naturalistic, expressionist, and classical. I have on the whole avoided systems and labels drawn from recent and contemporary art, and the reader will be disappointed who looks in the pages that follow for yet another self-sufficient evolutionary scheme.*

Today a healthy suspicion attaches to those attempts, very popular not so long ago, to formulate grandiose theories of beginnings and of universal characteristics of 'primitive' religion or art; but although criticism can be levelled at any and every particular *theory of beginnings, beginnings there were, and if for reasons that will appear in my first chapter they must remain unknowable, we can still be sure that they were as different from any 'primitive' or traditional society that exists today as from ourselves. If art history has sometimes claimed too much, prehistorians more often reiterate the theme of the inescapable limitations of their subject. Professor Childe wrote in 1925, 'our material is only the skeleton of an organism which once was clothed with flesh and which still is immanent in every moment of our lives'; and very recently Professor Piggott, 'What we have at our disposal as prehistorians is the accidentally surviving durable remnants of material culture, which we interpret as best we may, and inevitably the peculiar quality of this evidence dictates the sort of information we can obtain from it'. These warnings should be pondered by everyone who approaches the prehistoric past from whatever direction and towards whatever end they work. Yet a study of prehistoric art, if it is to be more than a catalogue or graph of sites, influences, and developments, must grope beyond these limits and enter this forbidden country.*

I have to admit at once that in the pages that follow I shall not limit myself to the skeleton, 'the fraction of a society's behaviour [that] fossilises'. The study of prehistoric art allows, if it does not actually demand, a much greater freedom than does prehistory itself. There is in the nature of the subject and the monuments an absence of classificatory machinery, a lack of definition, a something ambivalent, in addition to the usual, and quite shocking, barrier of distance and decay, which justifies the use of whatever help can be got from neighbour arts and sciences: metallurgy, nuclear physics for dating, the history of religion, and ancient literary tradition.

In the first two chapters I shall draw on studies, necessarily speculative, of the genesis of language and of religio-mythical consciousness, and of 'primitive' conceptions of time and of human and divine action, beside the close scrutiny of the monuments themselves and the archaeological data. In later chapters we move on to relatively firmer ground, but even here I cannot promise any sure footing nor an escape from the problematic and speculative; but since contemporary and recent art has eluded definition, and since our own ideas of what art is are continually changing, it is not to be expected that the art of several thousand years ago can be understood and defined. But, while allowing this, we must still treat it as though it could be described, manipulated, and compared, even when the task is not unlike building a snowman in the path of a slow avalanche. If at the end it should be found that some light has been thrown on a small part of the way which the human consciousness has taken from what Ernst Cassirer described as 'the stupor of material existence' towards greater realization of itself, then the proceedings are justified.

The scheme followed is chronological with chapters divided according to well-worn categories – 'Neolithic', 'Bronze Age', and so on – which, although now to some extent superseded, still have a value, perhaps more value, because of that lack of precision which is, in a strict regional prehistory, their disadvantage. The results of the Carbon 14 method of dating have been used as far as possible where appropriate, but all dates are very approximate and may be revised. Geographically we will be concerned until about 8000–6000 B.C. with the whole of Europe, after which new 'Neolithic' ways of life appear and we take leave of peninsular Greece and the Greek islands. Again during the last millennium B.C. we will leave Italy to the Etruscans and Greek colonists, and rather later Spain to Carthaginians and Iberians, none of whom are our concern. The eastern boundary through Russia is not well defined. We include the Paleolithic of the Ukraine and the 'Neolithic' rock-engravings of the far north, but are not concerned with the copper-working and bronze-using people of the Caucasus nor, except briefly when they impinge on Central Europe, with Scyths and their relatives. In the west the lower limit is the conquest, first of Gaul and then of Britain, by Rome.

Some general subjects are treated more fully on their first occurrence, but what is said then continues to apply to later times; for example, much that is said of potting in general in Chapter 4 applies also to potting throughout the Neolithic and Bronze Age, and the account of metallurgical processes in Chapter 6 does not cease to apply to bronzesmithing of the last thousand years B.C., but these accounts will not be repeated.

Even within a span that omits every sign of art before the Upper Paleolithic, we still have some 30,000 years and a sub-continent to cover, and this being so, fair treatment and justice to all are impossible. To refer to all the art even of the European Bronze Age would mean a mere cataloguing of names; I have therefore attempted to find what is most significant either for itself, what it is, or for what will come after. There are large, and I believe unavoidable, lacunae. It has seemed occasionally less of a distortion to omit completely than to describe inadequately; but while the Upper Paleolithic on the one hand with its carvings and painted caves, and Celtic

La Tène art on the other, tempt by their quality and quantity to a greater expansion and far more detailed discussion, I have tried to show how the intervening arts of the Mesolithic, Neolithic, and Bronze Age must not be ignored and are in their way also 'immanent in every moment of our lives'.

Within the given chronological limits there is a peculiar disparity, for whereas in the Upper Paleolithic we are looking at an art that is relevant to the wider history of man and the world, later on interest contracts to a purely European scale. From around 8000 Europe, though never insulated from the rest of the world, seems to lag where once it led, until with the La Tène art of the last centuries B.C. *we meet something that is very new, very individual, and completely European.*

The question will arise of how far a description of prehistoric art in Europe is also a prehistory of European art. Is it possible to recognize in these long centuries any consistent traits, to isolate characteristics and say, 'these are European, they are unlike what is found anywhere else'; or is everything fortuitous and contingent, all the prehistoric arts random responses to stimuli which from time to time have been directed into Europe? The reader will have to judge which alternative agrees best with the evidence.

I owe a profound debt of gratitude to scholars here and in many other countries whose advice and help has carried me forward in a sometimes daunting and perhaps rash undertaking. They cannot all be named, though the kindness of all is remembered; but I must especially express my thanks to Professor Stuart Piggott of Edinburgh; Mr Terence Powell of Liverpool and Mr John Cowen of London, whose counsel, conversation, and criticism on many occasions, at home in England, and abroad in diverse parts of Europe, have saved me from errors, made difficulties lighter, and pointed the way to new problems.

I have also profited by advice, conversations, and material help from Mr John Boardman of Oxford; Mr John Brailsford of the British Museum; Dr J. Campbell of Oxford; Mr Humphry Case and Dr Hector Catling of the Ashmolean Museum, Oxford; Professor Graham Clark of Cambridge; Dr Ian Cornwell of the Institute of Archaeology, London; Mr V. R. d'A. Desborough of Manchester; Mr R. C. Arnold; Professor J. D. Evans of the Institute of Archaeology, London; Professor C. F. C. Hawkes of Oxford; Professor George Huxley of the Queen's University, Belfast; Mr Sinclair Hood; Mr David Jones; Dr C. B. M. McBurney of Cambridge; Mrs K. R. Maxwell-Hyslop; Mr James Mellaart of the Institute of Archaeology, London; Mr R. B. K. Stevenson of the National Museum of Antiquities of Scotland; and Professor T. Sulimirski of London.

Dr S. Foltiny of the Institute for Advanced Studies, Princeton; Professor Marija Gimbutas, University of California; and Dr H. O'N. Hencken of the Peabody Museum, Harvard.

Miss Dorothy Garrod and Mlle de Saint-Mathurin; Monsieur A. Varagnac, formerly Musée des Antiquités Nationales, Saint Germain-en-Laye; and Monsieur Roger Grosjean, Centre de Préhistoire, Corsica.

Professor L. Bernabò-Brea, Museo Nazionale, Syracuse; Professor P. Graziosi of the University of Florence; Mrs L. Guido of Syracuse; Dr G. Pesce of Cagliari; Dr S. Tinè (formerly Museo Nazionale, Syracuse); and Dr Vicenzo Tusa of Palermo.

Dr J. J. Butler of the Biologisch-Archeologisch Institute, Groningen.

Dr H. Behrens, Landesmuseum für Vor- und Frühgeschichte, Halle; Dr O.-H. Frey of the Vorgeschichtliches Seminar, Mainz; Professor W. Kimmig, Institute für Vor- und Frühgeschichte, Tübingen; Professor H. Kühn of Mainz; Professor V. Milojčić, Institut für Ur- und Frühgeschichte, Heidelberg; Dr G. Neumann, Vorgeschichtliches Museum der Friedrich-Schiller Universität, Jena.

Dr Karl Kromer of the Naturhistorisches Museum, Vienna; Professor K. Willvonseder, Carolino Augusteum, Salzburg.

Professor O. Klindt-Jensen of Risskov, Denmark; Mr E. Lomborg of the Institute of Prehistoric Archaeology, Copenhagen.

Professor R. Indreko of Stockholm; Dr L. Kaelas and Professor C.-A. Moberg of the Archaeological Museum, Göteborg; Dr B. Schönbäck, Museum of National Antiquities, Stockholm; Dr B. Sternquist and Dr M. Strömberg of the Historical Museum, Lund.

Dr S. Marstrander of the Kongelige Norske Videnskabers Selskabs Museum, Trondheim.

Professor J. Filip, Institute of Archaeology, Prague; Dr V. Hrubý of the Moravian Museum, Brno; Dr B. Klíma of the Institute of Archaeology, Brno; Dr L. Kraskovská, National Slovak Museum, Bratislava; Dr J. Neustupny, the National Museum, Prague; Professor J. Poulík of the Archaeological Institute, Brno; Professor B. Svoboda, Institute of Archaeology, Prague; Dr K. Tihelka, Archaeological Institute, Brno; Dr A. Točík, Institute of Archaeology, Nitra.

Professor J. Banner of Budapest; Dr I. Bognár-Kutzián, Institute of Archaeology, Budapest; Dr J. Csalog, Koszta József Museum, Szentes; Dr A. Mozsolics, National Museum, Budapest; Dr O. Trogmayer, Móra Ferenc Museum, Szeged.

Professor A. Benac, Zemaljski Museum, Sarajevo; Dr S. Gabrovec, National Museum, Ljubljana; Dr D. Garašanin, National Museum, Belgrade; Professor M. Garašanin, Institute of Archaeology, Belgrade; Dr M. Grbíc, Archaeological Institute, Belgrade; Dr J. Todorovic, Zemun and Belgrade; Dr Z. Vinski and Mrs Vinski-Gasparini of Zagreb.

Professor D. Berciu, Mr E. Comşa, Professor E. Condurachi of the Institute of Archaeology, Bucharest; Professor C. Daicoviciú of the Historical and Archaeological Institute, Cluj; Dr V. Dumitrescu of the Institute of Archaeology, Bucharest; Mr A. Florescu and Mrs Florescu of the Historical Museum of Moldavia, Iaşi; Professor K. Horedt of the Historical and Archaeological Institute, Cluj; Professor I. Nestor, the Institute of Archaeology, Bucharest; Dr M. Petrescu-Dimboviţa, the Historical Museum of Moldavia, Iaşi; Dr D. Popescu, the Institute of Archaeology, Bucharest; Mr M. Rusu, the Historical and Archaeological Museum, Cluj; Professor R. Vulpe and Mr A. Vulpe of Bucharest.

Dr P. Detev of the National Archaeological Museum, Plovdiv; Mrs I. Jandova of Sofia and Professor V. Mikov of the Institute of Archaeology, Sofia.

I am exceedingly glad to record my gratitude to the Principal and Fellows of St Hugh's College, Oxford, who, through the grant of the Elizabeth Wordsworth Studentship for three years, gave me the opportunity for far more extensive travel than would otherwise have been possible, especially in Eastern Europe, Scandinavia, and the Mediterranean. I must also thank the Board of Management of the Gerald Avery Wainwright Fund for Near Eastern Archaeology for grants which enabled me to broaden considerably the background to prehistoric art in Europe.

The names of Authors and Institutions who have most kindly supplied material for illustra-

tions is acknowledged in the lists. A number of photographs have been taken specially for this volume by Miss Josephine Powell. Miss Sheila Gibson has given much skill and understanding to the text-figures, most of which have been specially drawn or redrawn.

I am most grateful to Professor Pevsner for his forbearance and encouragement; also to Mrs Judy Nairn for her vigilance and patience over the text and to Mr Nicholas Usherwood for his tenacity and enthusiasm in the hunt for illustrations. To my sister, who has had to live with Prehistoric Europe for so long, I owe more than to anyone, while her reading of the text has led to many improvements.

MAPS

MAP 1. Map for Chapters 1 to 2 showing distribution of two-dimensional (linear) and three-dimensional (plastic) art between approximately 30,000 and 8000 B.C.; also the more important carved reliefs. Note that the division between very deep engraving and low relief is not exactly definable; nor is that between three-dimensional objects and cut-out contours with engraved details.

MAP 2. Map of principal sites referred to in Chapters 3 to 5.

MAP 3. Map of principal sites referred to in Chapters 6 to 9.

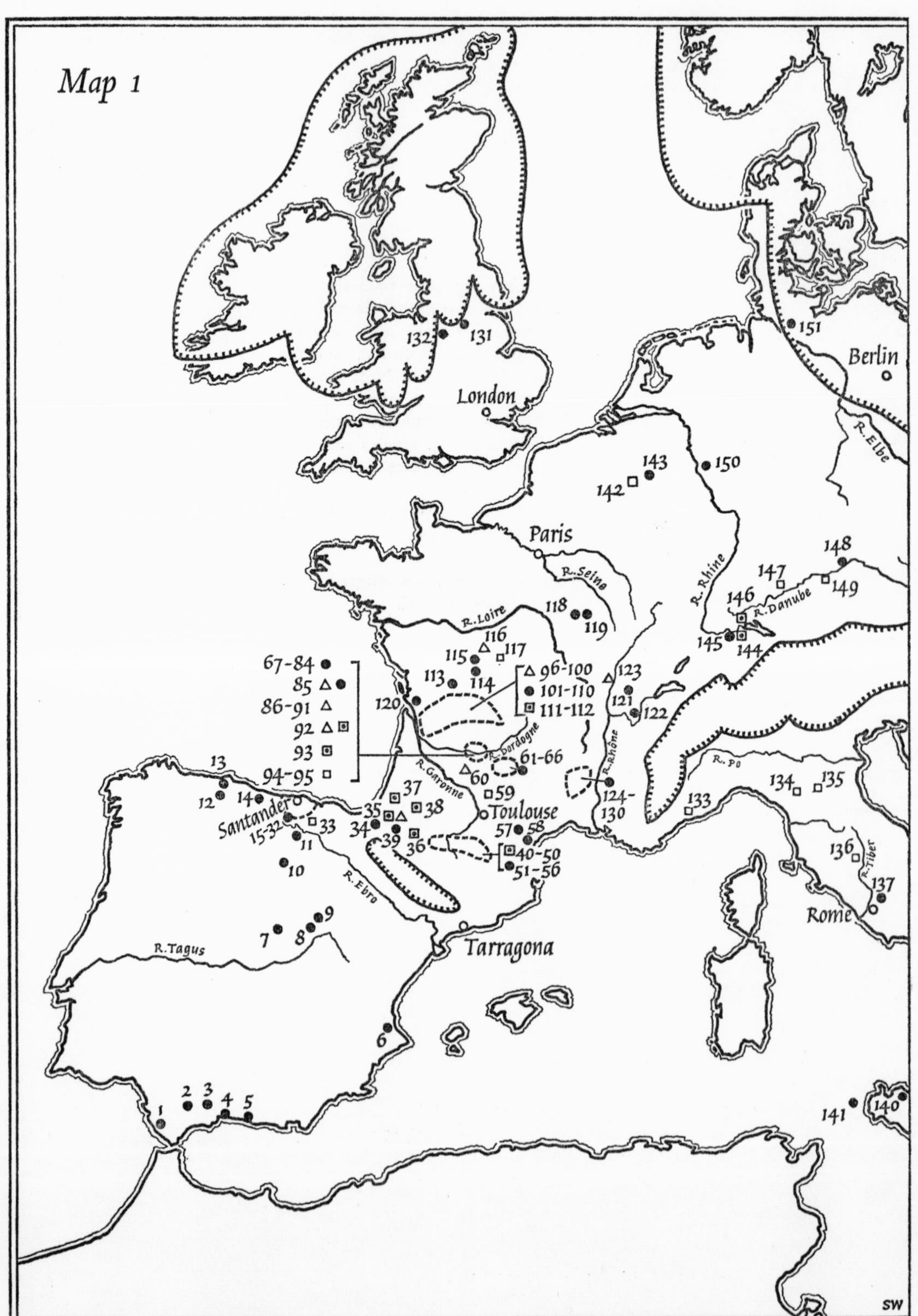
Map 1
London
Paris
Berlin
Santander
Toulouse
Tarragona
Rome
R. Elbe
R. Rhine
R. Seine
R. Loire
R. Danube
R. Dordogne
R. Garonne
R. Rhône
R. Po
R. Tiber
R. Ebro
R. Tagus
67-84
85
86-91
92
93
94-95
96-100
101-110
111-112
124-130
40-50
51-56
61-66
15-32
SW

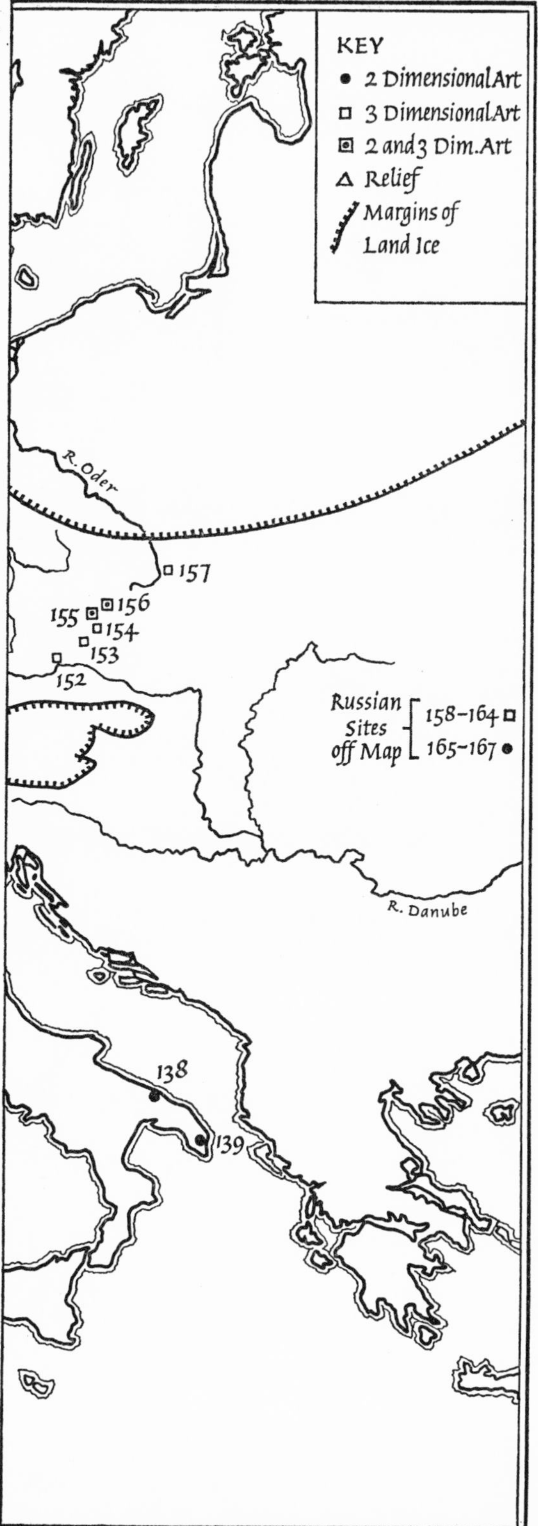

Site List Map 1

SPAIN
1 Las Palomas
2 La Pileta
3 Ardales
4 La Cala
5 Nerja
6 El Parpallò
7 El Reguerillo
8 La Hoz
9 Los Casares
10 Atapuerca
11 Penches
12 Las Mestas
13 La Peña de Candamo
14 El Buxu
15 Pindal
16 La Loja
17 La Meaza
18 Las Aguas de Novales
19 Clotilde de Santa Isabel
20 Altamira
21 Santian
22 Monte Castillo, La Pasiega, El Castillo, Las Chimeneas, Las Monedas
23 El Pendo
24 Hornos de la Peña
25 Salitré
26 Covalanas
27 Venta de la Perra
28 La Haza
29 Santimamiñe
30 Sotarizza
31 El Valle
32 La Callalvera
33 El Rascaño
34 Berroberria

FRANCE
35 Isturitz
36 Arudy
37 Duruthy
38 Brassempouy
39 Etcheberriko-Karbia
40 Lourdes
41 Lortet
42 Labastide
43 Gourdan
44 Le Tuc d'Audoubert
45 Les Trois Frères
46 Le Mas d'Azil
47 Le Portel
48 Bédeilhac
49 La Vache
50 Lespugue
51 Gargas
52 Tibiran
53 Montespan
54 Niaux
55 Ussat
56 Marsoulas
57 Sallèles-Cabardès
58 Aldène
59 Bruniquel
60 La Magdeleine
61 Pech-Merle
62 Cantal
63 Marcenac
64 Sainte-Eulalie
65 Cougnac
66 Rocamadour
67 Jean-Blancs
68 La Roche-Lalinde
69 La Ferrassie
70 Bara-Bahau
71 La Croze à Gontran
72 La Mouthe
73 Font-de-Gaume
74 Les Combarelles
75 La Calévie
76 Bernifal
77 Beyssac
78 Abri Labatut
79 Abri Blanchard
80 Abri Castanet
81 Belcayre
82 Limeuil
83 Les Eyzies, Le Bout-de-Monde
84 Péchialet
85 Terme-Pialat
86 Gorge d'Enfer, Oreille d'Enfer
87 Commarque
88 La Grèze
89 Cap Blanc
90 Laussel
91 Abri Reverdit
92 Laugerie-Basse, Laugerie-Haute
93 La Madeleine
94 Sireuil
95 Tursac
96 Abri Poisson
97 Champs-Blancs
98 Le Fourneau du Diable
99 La Chaire à Calvin
100 Le Roc de Sers
101 Les Fées
102 Puy de Lacan
103 Teyjat: La Mairie, Abri Mège
104 Montgaudier
105 Lascaux
106 Raymonden
107 Saint-Cirq
108 Le Gabillou
109 Abri Cellier
110 Villars
111 Pair-non-Pair
112 Le Placard (Roche-bertier)
113 Chaffaud
114 La Marche
115 Laraux
116 Angles-sur-l'Anglin
117 Saint-Marcel
118 Le Trilobite
119 Arcy-sur-Cure
120 Saint Germain-la-Rivière
121 La Colombière
122 Les Hoteaux
123 Solutré
124 Le Colombier
125 Ebbou
126 Oulen
127 Chabot
128 Le Figuier
129 La Baume-Latrone
130 Bayol

ENGLAND
131 Creswell Crags
132 Robin Hood's Cave

ITALY
133 Balzi Rossi
134 Chiozza
135 Savignano
136 Trasimeno
137 Tivoli
138 Monopoli
139 Romanelli
140 Monte Pellegrino
141 Levanzo

BELGIUM
142 Trou Magrite
143 Trou de Châleux

SWITZERLAND
144 Kesslerloch
145 Schweizersbild

GERMANY
146 Petersfels
147 Vogelherd
148 Klausenhöhle
149 Weinberg
150 Oberkassel
151 Ahrensberg

AUSTRIA
152 Willendorf

CZECHOSLOVAKIA
153 Dolní Věstonice
154 Brno
155 Pekarna
156 Předmostí
157 Ostrava Petřkovice

Off Map

RUSSIA
158 Mezin
159 Kostienki
160 Gagarino
161 Andeevo
162 Yelisevici
163 Buret
164 Maltá
165 Choulgan-Tache (Kapova)
166 Sishkino
167 Terpen (Rostov)

Map 2
Maes Howe
Vingen
Landsverk
Kløfterfoss
New Grange
Resen
Egemarke
Ystad
Rymarksgård
Stonehenge
R. Elbe
R. Oder
Radewell
Göhlitzsch
R. Rhine
Coizard
R. Marne
R. Seine
Gavr'inis
Domäne-Viesenhäuserhof
R. Danube
Cortaillod
L. Neuchâtel
R. Saône
R. Garonne
Mas Capelier
R. Rhône
R. Po
R. Douro
R. Ebro
Vila Nova de San Pedro
Las Carolinas
Cogul
Levantine Art
R. Tagus
Morella
Albarracín
Valltorta
Elba
RIPOLI
Alcalá
Fuencaliente
Alpera
Dos Aguas
Carmona
Romeral
Minateda
Ozieri
Macomer
Mesas de Asta
Almerian Neolithic Culture
Senorbí
CAPRI
Tajo de las Figuras
Almizaraque
Los Millares
Egadi Is.
Lipari Is.
Levanzo
SICILY & AEOLIAN IS.
Castelluccio
Stentinello
Gozo
Malta
MILES 0 100 200 300 400 500

KEY
'CUCUTENI' ETC. Painted Pottery Cultures
Almerian Neolithic Culture
Spanish Levantine Art
Arctic Hunters' Art
White Sea
Zalavruga
Nämforsen
L. Onega
Bessov-Noss
Alunda
R. Volga
R. Don
R. Dniepre
R. Dniestre
R. Bug
Abrahám
MORAVIA
Hluboké-Mašůvky
Střelice
Lang-Enzersdorf
Lengyel
Zengö-varkony
R. Tisza
Trușești
TRIPOLYE
Șipeniț
Cucuteni
Traian
Valea Lupului
CUCUTENI
Szegvár-Tüzköves
Hódmezövásárhely-Kökénydomb
Ariușd
Starčevo
Vinča
Butmir
Vidra
Gumelnița
GUMELNIȚA
Hamangia
Cernavoda
Maikop
Danilu Is.
Hvar Is.
DALMATIA
Predionica
Karanovo
Yassa Tépé
Vršnik
APULIA
Nea Nikomedeia
GREEK PAINTED WARES
ANATOLIAN PAINTED WARE
Hacilar
Catel Hüyük
SW

Map 3
Bohuslän
see Inset
Broighter
Lisnacroghera
Torrs
Gleninsheen
Cerrig-y-Drudion
Roos Carr
R. Witham
Snettisham
Lord's Bridge
Marlborough
Billericay
Glastonbury
Battersea
Wandsworth
Aylesford
Trundholm
Aukamper Moor
Jastorf
R. Rhine
R. Elbe
Borsch
Mšecké-Žehrovice
Champagne
Basse-Yutz
Pfalzfeld
Waldalgesheim
PARIS
Saint-Jean-sur-Tourbe
Rodenbach
R. Marne
Rheinheim
Heidelberg
Parsberg
Neuvy-en-Sullias
Euffigneix
Klein Aspergle
Vix
Waldenbuch
R. Danube
Nebringen
Holzgerlingen
Heuneburg
Lac de Neuchâtel
Erstfeld
La Tène
Dürrnberg
Hallstatt
Vače
R. Garonne
R. Tarn
R. Rhône
Este
R. Po
Tarbes
Roquepertuse
Marseilles
Bologna
Spina
Tartessos
Sant' Anastasia
Barumini
Pantalica
MILES
0 100 200 300 400 500

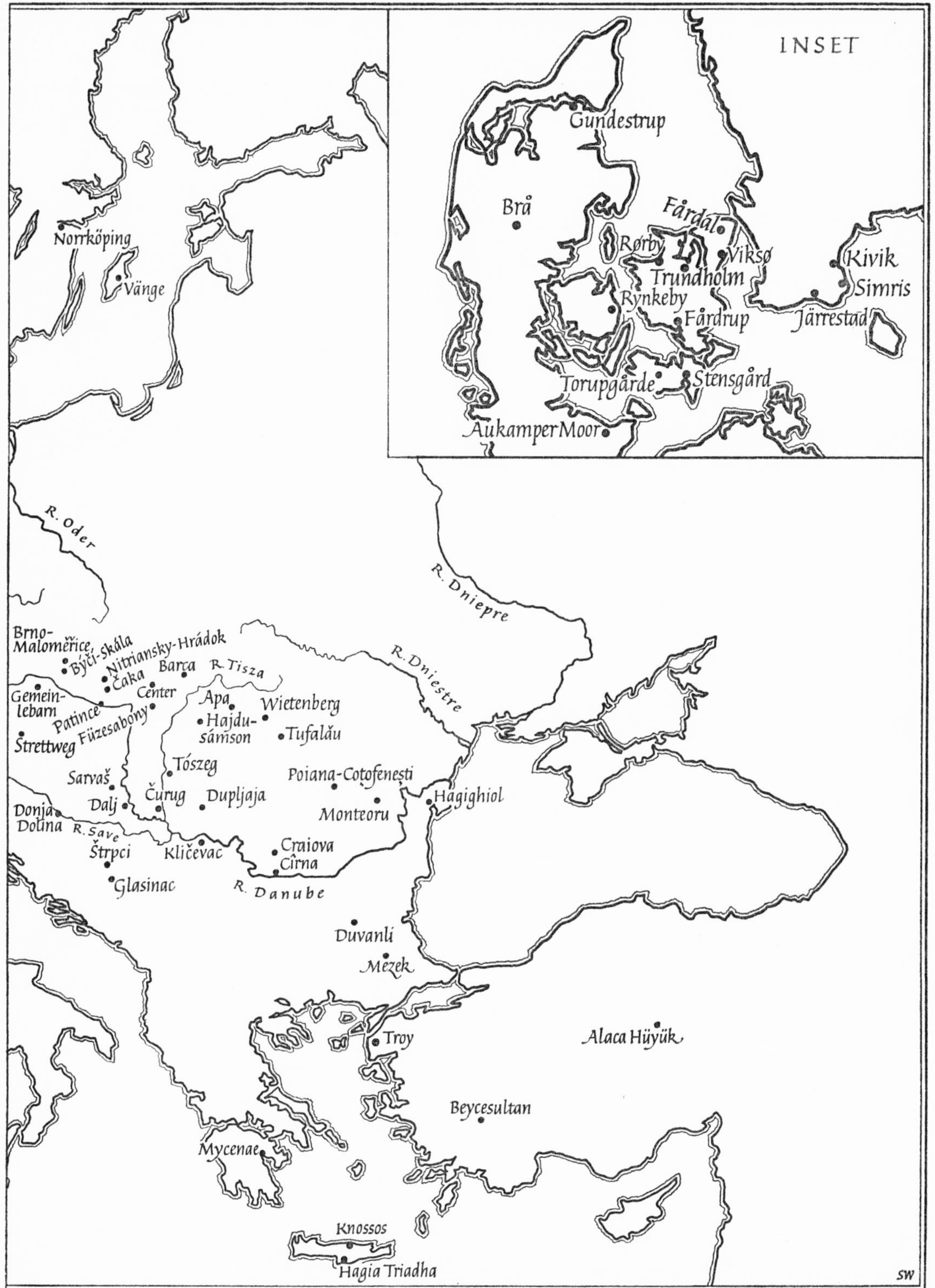
INSET
Gundestrup
Brå
Fårdal
Rørby
Viksø
Trundholm
Kivik
Simris
Rynkeby
Fårdrup
Järrestad
Torupgårde
Stensgård
Aukamper Moor
Norrköping
Vänge
R. Oder
R. Dniepre
Brno-Maloměřice
Býčí-Skála
Nitriansky-Hrádok
Čaka
Barca
R. Tisza
R. Dniestre
Gemeinlebarn
Center
Apa
Wietenberg
Patince
Füzesabony
Hajdusámson
Tufalău
Štrettweg
Tószeg
Sarvaš
Poiana-Coţofeneşti
Čurug
Dupljaja
Hagighiol
Dalj
Monteoru
Donja Dolina
R. Save
Štrpci
Kličevac
Craiova
Cîrna
Glasinac
R. Danube
Duvanli
Mezek
Troy
Alaca Hüyük
Beycesultan
Mycenae
Knossos
Hagia Triadha
SW

TABLES

TABLE I. TO *c.* 9000 B.C.

YEARS B.C.	*Climate (Europe)*	*Cultures and human and hominid types*	*Carbon 14 dates sites with art only*	*Sites and principal categories of art*
				Addaura
		EPI-GRAVETTIAN (Italy)	9010 Romito II	Levanzo
10,000	Allerød oscillation warmer	MAGDALENIAN V–VI		
	cool		10,590 La Vache (final Magdalenian)	La Mairie à Teyjat, *fine engraving*
	warmer Bøllins			
12,000		MAGDALENIAN III–IV; MAGDALENIAN (East)	Angles-sur-l'Anglin 12,210	La Magdeleine *relief*
				Cap Blanc *relief*
		MAGDALENIAN I II	13,540 Altamira (Magdalenian III)	Trois Frères, etc., *fine engraving*
14,000	LAST GLACIATION (Würm III)			
				Lascaux *painting*
			15,240 Lascaux	
16,000		SOLUTRIAN		
				Fourneau-du-Diable? Roc de Sers, *relief* Pech-Merle 'macaronis'? *Use of Deep Caves*
18,000	very cold	PERIGORDIAN (West Gravettian); EAST GRAVETTIAN (PAVLOVIAN)	Laugerie-Haute (Lower Solutrian) 18,940	
20,000		V PROTO-MAGDALENIAN (France)		Laussel *reliefs?* Belcayre, etc., *deep engraving*
				Pair-non-Pair
21,000				Upper Kostienki I? Brassempouy?
		AURIGNACIAN	21,230 Abri du Facteur, Tursac	Castanet
		IV		Abri Cellier } *deep engraving* La Ferrassie }
			22,970 Pavlov Hills site	Předmostí *engraving?*
23,000	colder		Dolní Věstonice 23,820	Dolní Věstonice *clay modelling* and carving, houses
	Paudorf oscillation	III		
25,000				Ostrava Petřkovice
	warmer			Vogelherd level V? Brno-Francouzská? Willendorf? *Sculpture in the round*
27,000		II		
	cold and wet			
28,000	Mid Würm Glaciation	I Homo Sapiens		
30,000	Gottweig Interstadial Mild Early Würm	LATE Châtel perronian? MOUSTERIAN Neanderthaloid types		*Cup marks* *Ritual burial*

	GREECE, NEAR EAST	ITALY, SICILY, MALTA, SARDINIA	BULGARIA	YUGOSLAVIA	HUNGAR
1200	Land and sea raids in Near East; Hittite and Mycenean break-up	PANTALICA I SUB-APENNINE Filitosa (Corsica)			PILINYI *Urnfields* *Tumuli* *Tells ending*
1400	Mycenae dominant in Aegean Hittite Empire	APENNINE CULTURE, TERREMARE Barumini (Sardinia)	Mycenean influences	Dupljaja Dubovac-Žuto Brdo	*Bone hors* FÜZESABO Hajdusámson hoards
1600	Mycenae shaft-graves Crete dominant in Aegean	Mycenean contacts with Lipari		VATTINA	Tószeg II HATVAN
1800	Troy VI	Early nuraghi Tarxien cemetery		PERJAMOS	
	Troy V	*Beakers*		Sarvaš VUČEDOL	Tószeg I. *Tells* NAGYRÉV
2000					
	Troy III–IV Maikop Troy II Ur (Sargonid) Alaca Hüyük	OZIERI (Sardinia) CASTEL-LUCCIO (Sicily)		BADEN	Center. BADE *Ox-wagons*
2500	Ur (Royal Cemetery) Troy I EARLY MINOAN I *Writing*	TARXIEN (Malta) *Temples*	GUMELNIŢA B Karanovo VII?	PROTO-BADEN	
3000	JEMDET NASR GERZEAN Hierokonpolis	Ġgantija (Malta) SAN CONO		Hvar I BUTMIR Predionica	BODROG-KERESZTU *Copper shaft-h axes*
3500	EARLY URUK	DIANA *Copper?* SERRA D'ALTO	Karanovo VI GUMELNIŢA A	VINČA-PLOCNIK	
4000	NAQADA I (Egypt) *Copper axes Near East*	Malta Early Neolithic Ripoli	Karanovo V Karanovo IV	*C O* DANILU	LENGYEL TISZA-POL *P P E*
4500	Dhimini (Greece		Karanovo III Karanovo II	VINČA-TORDOS	TISZA-THEISS BANDKERA
5000	Hacilar I GREEK PAINTED POTTERY CULTURES	STENTINELLO painted pottery	*Tells* Karanovo I	STARČEVO	KÖR
5500	Catel Hüyük II–VIA Hacilar VI	STENTINELLO impressed pottery MOLFETTA			
6000	Nea Nicomedeia				

• 1200 B.C.

MANIA, OUTH USSIA	CZECHO-SLOVAKIA, AUSTRIA, SOUTH GERMANY	SCANDINAVIA, NORTH GERMANY	FRANCE, LOW COUNTRIES, SWITZERLAND	BRITISH ISLES	IBERIA	
A	HALLSTATT AI Urnfields Tumuli	Period III Kivik Trundholm Period II (II/IIbc)	Urnfields (Eastern France)			1200
wheels – carts ı .SSIC 'OMANI .TENBERG	OTOMANI MAĎAROVCE VĚTĚROV Tumuli	*Danubian imports* Period I (I/IIa) DAGGER GRAVES	BRETON TUMULI	MIDDLE BRONZE AGE	EL ARGAR	1400
:LY 'OMANI	LATE UNĚTICE Patince	Late Neolithic (Scandinavia)		Stonehenge III WESSEX CULTURE		1600
III HNECK- 'BERG •er-graves aine)	EARLY UNĚTICE LATE CORDED WARE *Beakers*	LATE CORDED WARE	MARNE CHALK-CUT GRAVES	*Battle-axes*		1800
IRE AVES *'le-axes*	CORDED WARE	SINGLE GRAVES *Battle-axes* Late Neolithic	Lébous BEAKERS (France)	BEAKERS Maes Howe? BOYNE CULTURE Stonehenge I	Los Millares	2000
:UTENI B POLYE B :UTENI	BELL BEAKER RIVNAČ	Dolauer Heide PASSAGE-GRAVES Mid-Neolithic Salzmünde Dysser	BELL BEAKER (Low Countries)	BELL BEAKER	ALMERIAN	2500
:GANS POLYE A :UTENI A MELNIȚA			Mid-Neolithic PASSAGE-GRAVES (Brittany)	MEGALITHIC CULTURES		3000
MANGIA avoda)	FUNNEL BEAKER	FUNNEL BEAKER Early Neolithic	MICHELS-BERG	WINDMILL HILL Neolithic	EAST SPANISH HUNTERS' ART	3500
UŞD •ASTRA *P P E R*	MORAVIAN PAINTED WARE RÖSSEN				Impressed pottery	4000
AN D- RAMIK *pots*	BAND-KERAMIK	MESOLITHIC	BAND-KERAMIK Egolzwil III ? Early Neolithic CHASSEY CORTAILLOD (early) ?	MESOLITHIC	Early Neolithic impressed pottery?	4500
						5000
						5500
		MAGLE-MOSIAN				6000

TABLE 3. FROM 12

		WESTERN AND NORTHERN EUROPE				EAST
	Styles and Periods: Europe	*South Germany, Austria*	*France, Switzerland, Low Countries*	*British Isles*	*Scandinavia, North Germany*	*Central a Eastern Eu*
700	*Geometric and orientalizing* Hallstatt C1	Tumulus burials *Hallstatt Geometric*		DOWRIS PHASE till 200 B.C. (Ireland)	Rock-engravings	*Orientalizing bronzes*
	Hallstatt B3	Horse-gear hoards	Urnfields spread to southern France	Compasses, gold-work LATE BRONZE AGE	Cast bronzes Fårdal *Razor art*	Horse-gear hoards
	Razor art Northern Period V	Beginnings of effective iron-working			Viksø *Boss-style bronzes imported*	Iron-workin
800	Hallstatt B2					
900		Urnfields			Rock-engravings	
	Hallstatt B1					
1000	Northern Period IV Hallstatt A2		Urnfields (eastern France, Switzerland)	Beaten gold	*Boss-style gold-work* Darup razor	
1100	Hallstatt A1	*Boss-style bronzes*		Gold–copper alloy (Ireland)		Wheeled ca drons
	Northern Period III	Early cart-graves				*Beaten bronz boss-style*
	Boss style	Urnfields				
	Bronze Period D	Urnfields RIEGSEE (tumuli)		MIDDLE BRONZE AGE		Urnfields 'Pyre-grave
1200						

IRST CENTURY B.C.

OPE	MEDITERRANEAN					
Balkans	*Italy*	*Sicily, Sardinia Malta*	*Iberia, North Africa*	*Greece and the Near East*	*Styles and Periods: Greece*	
urazzo ded foundations hrace			Greeks exploring west Mediterranean	Scyths in Asia Minor Cimmerians sack Gordion. Greek imports to Bug, Don, Donetz	Archaic sculpture Daedelic bronzes *Orientalizing*	
nište early k imports	*Orientalizing* Etruscan expansion	Phoenicians in Sicily and Malta	Catalan urnfields	Cimmerians in Asia Minor		700
			Carthage founded		*Proto-Corinthian*	
SINAC	BENACI I 750 Cumae founded	733 Syracuse founded Bronzes (Sardinia)	Phoenician explorations, 'Tartessos' trade	745 Urartians defeated by Assyria in Syria Greeks at Al Mina		
		Full nuragic to 500 B.C. (Sardinia)		Urartians expanding	*Figured Geometric*	
						800
					Plain Geometric	
ns	Pithekoussai VILLA-NOVANS Urnfields			Phrygian power growing		
						900
		Phoenicians reach Sardinia?				
						1000
	APPENINE CULTURE			Dorians in Greece (cist-graves)	*Proto-Geometric*	
						1100
Y SINAC	LATE TERREMARE	Early nuraghi		Depopulation and outward migration from central Greece	Late Helladic IIIC	
	Peschiera	PANTALICA Sea-raiders?		1190 Defeat of Sea Peoples by Rameses II in the delta	Late Helladic III B/C	
						1200

TABL

	Styles and Periods: Europe		WESTERN AND NORTHERN EUROPE				EAST
			South Germany, Austria	*France, Switzerland, Low Countries*	*British Isles*	*Scandinavia, North Germany*	*Central a Eastern Eu*
0	La Tène D = 3				Snettisham		
					Aylesford	Rynkeby	
	La Tène C = 2b			58–51 Caesar conquers Gaul	55–54 Caesar's raids		
100							
			113 Cimbri and Teutones	109 Cimbri in Aquitaine	Belgic invasions	Gundestrup?	113 Cimbri Teutones
							Great Oppi
	La Tène C = 2a		Oppida	124 Romans conquer Provence		Cimbri moving south	
	Sword Style						
200			Helvetii move to Switzerland	Votive swords at La Tène			
	La Tène B = 1c						
					Wandsworth, Witham Torrs		Celts in Dobrogea
300	*Plastic style*			Provençal sanctuaries start	Continental settlers to Yorkshire 'Arras', and perhaps south-west England	Brå	Brno Maloměřic
	Waldalgesheim style		Waldalgesheim				Celts and Illyrians fi ing
	La Tène B = 1b			Basse Yutz			
			Rheinheim				Parsberg, et
400			GREAT CELTIC EXPANSION			JASTORF	GRE
	Northern Iron Age		Weisskirchen, etc.	Marnian graves			
			Klein Aspergle	Somme-Bionne			
	La Tène A = la	overlapping	Rich Rhenish graves				
	Early Style Hallstatt D3		East Alpine route and Etruscan imports				Vače situla Magdalensk Gora
500							
	Hällstatt D 2/3		Heuneburg V	Vix	Settlers to England from the Continent		
	Hallstatt D2		Kappel-Vilsingen rich graves, gold, imported flagons	Grächwil			Scyths and Dacians on Danube
	Northern Period VI			Rhône route and west alpine passes			
	Hallstatt D1						
600	Hallstatt C2			*c.* 600 Massilia founded	Hallstatt imports		
	Hallstatt C1/2		Gemeinlebarn Strettweg?	Some Greek imports	Bronze cauldrons		

NTINUED

.OPE	MEDITERRANEAN					
Balkans	*Italy*	*Sicily, Sardinia, Malta*	*Iberia, North Africa*	*Greece and the Near East*	*Styles and Periods: Greece*	
						0
	82 Gallia Cisalpina to Rome					
						100
	Cimbri					
Romans on Drave driven from ace	Celts forced north of Alps 192 Boii defeated		133 Romans in Spain 146 Carthage destroyed by Rome			200
Celts defeated Antigonas atas	266 Rome supreme in Italy	Rome takes Sicily		270 Galatians settled on Halys		
k	Celts driven out of Tuscany			279 Celts sack Delphi		300
				336 Accession of Alexander the Great		
				369 Celts in Peloponnese	'*Kerch*' *Style and Italiote*	
	387 Celts at Rome					
.TIC EX	PANSION					400
;, Strpči belts						
nli		Sardinian decline		478 Persians withdraw from Europe	*Classical*	500
arius's raid	*c.* 520 Spina founded	510 Carthaginian invasion of Sardinia	Celts in Spain from Algarve to Catalonia	513–12 Darius's Scythian expedition	*Red Figure* (till 300 B.C.)	
nište rich es erians and es?	CERTOSA					600
	ARNOALDI First situlae ESTE II		Greeks excluded by Phoenicians 609 Phoenicians circumnavigate Africa	Scythians expelled through Caucasus Lydians defeat and expel Cimmerians	*Black Figure* *Corinthian*	

D

CHAPTER I

THE BEGINNING

Irritante, mais essentielle fragilité des origines. . . . Par un mécanisme dont le détail, dans chaque cas, paraît évitable et accidentel, mais dont l'universalité prouve qu'il reflète une condition fondamentale de notre connaissance, embryons, pédoncules, phases initiales de croissance quelle qu'elles soient, vont s'évanouissant en arrière à nos yeux.

Teilhard de Chardin

A STUDY of prehistoric art ought to begin at the beginning, but by its nature a beginning is what we cannot have. All early stages of growth possess this irritating fragility, they recede into the past, vanish from sight: everything seems to have burst into the world ready-made, and history appears a discontinuous succession of levels.[1] This is as true of art as of embryos; not only at the most remote stages but again and again throughout its history we will find levels and discontinuities. The more radical and far-reaching the change, the more abrupt it will appear. The conclusion of Dr Jacobsthal's immense study was that Early Celtic art has no genesis, the La Tène style 'flashes up' mature, perfect, and puzzling; and when we are faced with phenomena such as the creation of a system of writing we hear of the extraordinary difficulty of the inquiry into first causes.[2] These things are respectively no more than two and a half thousand and five thousand years old, but the early stages of art carry us back some thirty thousand years, and that is still not the beginning but only the first that it is profitable to study of these discontinuous levels. It is therefore the less surprising that what we find is neither crude nor tentative but an ivory figure, a female torso, and a woman's head (Plates 2, 5, and 6), which are, I think, works of art by any standard.

It is important at the start not to underestimate these artists, and ancestors of ours. The sculptors of the Brno II man and the Ostrava Petřkovice woman were indistinguishable from ourselves, physically, and in mental capacity. They had not yet experienced our history, and that is the measure of the difference between us. Before exploring some of the corollaries of this simple fact it may be of use to go a little farther back, if only to have some sort of scale against which to measure the art of the Upper Paleolithic, of which we get a partial and arrested vision across the last advances of the great European ice-sheet. Attempts to recreate the strange landscape of those times, and the extinct animals, only add to their remoteness, but measured against our longer human and pre-human ancestry they move up surprisingly close.

On Plate 1 is an object quite different from the carvings in ivory and bone. It is a flint artifact, called from its shape 'laurel-leaf', made by removing flakes from a core by pressure with a second tool, which gives much greater control, regularity, and precision than the older percussion method. The laurel leaf belongs to the short-lived Solutrian culture of Western Europe between roughly 19–18,000 and 15,000 B.C., so considerably later than the ivories of Brno and Ostrava Petřkovice. Whether or not it served a practical purpose, it shows aesthetic sensibility, as well as great manual dexterity. It can also be taken as a point of departure for a probe into the more remote past, because from it a continuity in technique runs back to the earliest yet known tools and weapons of about a million years ago (see Table I, pp. xlii–xliii). These are pebbles that have been found in Tanganyika, along with the bones of ape-like creatures which anthropologists and archaeologists recognize as pre-men, very probably in the direct ancestral line of *homo sapiens*. From the rough chipped tools or weapons of the lower Oldovai beds we pass on to a series of 'hand-axes': large nodules of flint or allied stones, from which flakes have been removed by light blows with a wooden punch to give them a cutting edge. Vast numbers have been found; the earlier are clumsy and irregular, the later stereotyped, regular, and with an obvious leaning to symmetry (Figure 1A).

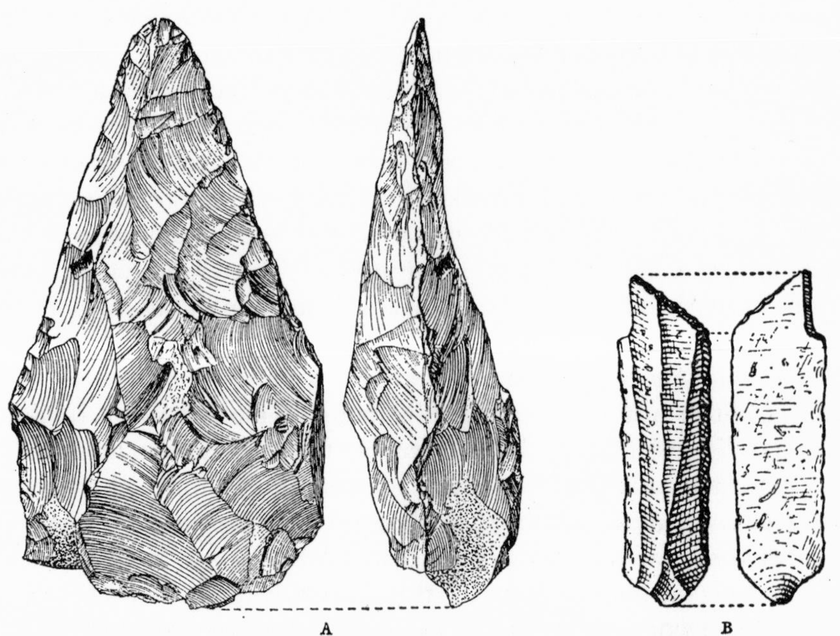

Figure 1. A Middle Acheulian flint hand-axe from Swanscombe, Essex
B Flint angle-burin from Liège, Belgium, used to engrave bone and stone

The question one would like to ask, but without any hope of an answer, is at what point in this series some craftsman manipulating flint and wood went beyond what was strictly necessary for utility and removed a flake, or reserved a scar just for the appearance, giving it an agreeable but unnecessary symmetry; so performing a gratuitous act which changed a tool or weapon, an artifact pure and simple, into a tool or weapon that was also a work of art. All we know is that this probably happened some time during the Middle Pleistocene, a quarter of a million years ago. It is unlikely to have been in Europe and was certainly not by the hand of modern sapient man, who had not yet emerged. The real beginning, like writing and Early Celtic art, can only be recognized in the light of what it would become; it is itself irrecoverable. But although this is so, it may be worth while to ask questions about the physical and cultural milieu in which art began; the pre-requisites without which it never could have arisen, but which because of their more general and durable character are, within limits, easier to answer.

It has taken something between ten and forty million years for the genetic line which was to culminate in sapient man to emerge from its monkey-like (pro-simian) ancestry; while something that may be called a 'culture' – tools of stone and bone, quantities of sorted and collected bones of 'prey', occupation sites – only appeared about one million years ago. This estimate comes from the new 'potassium-argon' method of dating, which has nearly doubled the conjectured age of *australopithecus*, the pre-man of South and East Africa, who was the first it seems to walk upright, and who made the tools or weapons of the lower fossil beds at Oldovai in Tanganyika.[3] The upright carriage may have become necessary when these ape-like creatures left the forests in a desiccating continent to live in open country. It both freed the hands for tool-making and made tools and weapons essential to survival, digging roots and killing prey. The skull of *australopithecus* is not much larger than that of our contemporary apes, but it has some quite unape-like characteristics, particularly the teeth, which are those of a flesh-eater. Like all other primates, he had stereoscopic vision. Fossil hands of great age are even rarer than skulls, but a child's hand was found not long ago at Oldovai, below undoubted remains of *australopithecus*. At this very early stage it is impossible to separate tools from weapons, but it certainly looks as though *australopithecus* was a killer.

Both tool- and weapon-making show that this ape-man had crossed the threshold of reflection. This is the most elusive and probably the most essential of all the prerequisites of art. Consciousness of self, reflection, is the touchstone of humanity, 'no longer merely to know but to know that one knows'.[4] This threshold at which our million-year-old ancestors had arrived was already behind the *pithecanthropus* group of pre-men who lived about 500,000 years ago, and among whom was *sinanthropus*, the so-called Pekin man with a brain capacity of up to twice that of *australopithecus*, though still by the same amount less than our own. *Pithecanthropus* is almost certainly in the direct ancestral line of *homo sapiens*; he also made better tools and used fire. In spite of his smaller brain he was culturally almost as advanced as some modern 'primitive' races, and he may have been a cannibal.

Cannibalism is practically unknown among the higher animals; and among the various 'primitives' who practise it today it often seems to have the sacramental motive of eating the life-matter, so that we can please ourselves as to whether we interpret Paleolithic cannibalism as depraved or as a groping spirituality. Fire-making, however, was one of the climacteric leaps forward the memory of which was burnt into the human psyche. Other such leaps have occurred from time to time in our history, and echo in our myths. With fire man was no longer the victim of his environment; he had begun to change, and, in a limited degree, to control it. Caves, from which the great carnivores were driven, were made safe by fire at night, and fire for cooking flesh reduced the time needed for eating. The point is vital in man's cultural development. Vegetarian gibbons must spend half their waking lives eating in order to survive; with knowledge of cooking the time needed for the whole process, cooking and eating, can be reduced to around two hours in the day.[5] Just as walking upright freed the hands of the tool-maker, and ultimately the artist, so fire and cooked food gave to the hunter and tool-maker leisure to discover in himself the artist and thinker.

It is not certain that Pekin man *made* fire as well as capturing and preserving it, but it is quite certain that the pre-men of the last interglacial[6] did. Before this, perhaps a quarter of a million years ago, among the makers of 'Acheulian' hand-axes, we may expect to find our first artists (Figure 1A). The tool or weapon had advanced in complexity far beyond that made by Pekin man, and towards the end of the Middle Pleistocene objects were being produced from stone cores so fine, and with so fragile a cutting edge, that it is believed that they were never used as tools but were sacred and ceremonial objects like the 'churingas' of Australian aborigines. Fashioning a tool to make a tool in order to meet unknown future needs implies consciousness of biological time, of past, present, and future; it implies differentiation of object and subject, 'I' and world, and for its diffusion, and survival as a technique, the employment of language. It is the extraordinary uniformity of hand-axes from England to Palestine and from South Africa to India that has led to this conclusion.

Speech, more even than fire, must have increased the speed of cultural evolution, and *cultural* evolution was much more rapid, even at that remote time, than biological. With speech, culture is learnt and transmitted regardless of biological descent. If so much can be inferred from the uniformity and spread of hand-axes towards the end of the Mindel-Riss Interglacial and in the succeeding major glaciation, speech too has much older roots. A pre-requisite is right-handedness, since the left roof-brain is the seat of speech and to be right-handed is to be left-brained. Handedness came before speech, and as there is no obvious superiority in right-handedness it must have conferred some now unrecognized evolutionary advantage.[7] Pekin man is thought to have had some sort of language, and even possibly *australopithecus*, for he was already right-handed as a tool-maker, whereas chimpanzees and other primates use either hand indiscriminately.

It is not our business to ask how language came about, but there is one corollary of this invention which does concern us: language implies the mental capacity for making symbols. Without this capacity there is no created art. An ape will scream when it sees a lion; the scream conveys to other apes that there is danger, it is the 'sign' of a lion instantaneously communicated to them. The great step from sign to symbol came when an ape used the sound, which before had only been used in the *presence* of 'a' lion, to stand for 'lion' when none is there. This symbol detached from its object and standing for it in its absence is the word, and with words not only absent objects can be brought to mind, but relationships between them can be discussed, and so eventually every abstract idea.[8]

A different approach to the genesis of language and of symbol led Ernst Cassirer to observe that an important stage in the development from animal to man is the transition from grasping to pointing. The hands are so closely bound up with the intellect that they appear almost to form part of it; so that both genetically and actually there may be a continuous transition from physical to conceptual grasping; from grasping the thing within reach (which we share with the animals), to grasping at a distance or pointing. The interpretation through the senses that accompanies physical grasping leads to the higher interpretation expressed in language.[9] When word is substituted for gesture something that started as imitative expression becomes analogical expression, and the way is opened to universal symbols. So we find that manual dexterity and certain sorts of tools imply language, and language implies the capacity for making symbols. There is interplay and a subtle relationship between artifact, language, and art; and the capacity which allows a speaker to 'grasp at a distance' or point *intellectually*, allows an artist to grasp at a distance *imaginatively*. In some such way as this the capacity to create and manipulate symbols is added to the make-up of the Paleolithic artist.

The early history of our pre-human ancestors has shown them gradually acquiring powers and faculties necessary for the appearance of the artist. Some, like cooking, seem very humble but nevertheless had important consequences, no less important than stereoscopic vision, clever hands, means of communication, conceptual thought, symbol-making, and aesthetic instinct. We should probably add mythology and religion, but I will return to them when we come to look at the higher arts of Upper Paleolithic man, his sculpture and paintings. Aesthetic *instinct* is not the least important, for it is this that must have controlled the actual form of the first work of art. The removal of a few small flakes, more or less, from a heavy flint object is not a very impressive beginning, but the gratuitous nature of the action, and its direction, which always seems to be towards pattern and symmetry – this is again the difference between man, or near-man, and animal.

The symmetry is less important or novel than the gratuitous quality of the action, the motive behind rather than the object itself (which could as well have been of bone or stick). Honeycombs and some birds' and insects' nests are wonderfully constructed according to pattern and symmetry. This aesthetic instinct I have left till last, but it may in fact be the oldest of all; and it is of set purpose that I call it an instinct, not a gift or sense. A search for its source and for reasons might carry us many times farther back than we have already travelled, through our animal ancestry, to impossibly remote regions. Archaeologists make a root distinction between *using* a tool, which we share with a great many animals, and *making* a tool for use hereafter, with all that that implies of foresight, memory, and reflection. The same sort of distinction should be drawn between a jackdaw-like collecting of *objets trouvés* to satisfy the rudimentary aesthetic instinct which we share with animals, and the voluntary fashioning of a pleasing object solely to satisfy that instinct, or altering a useful object for the appearance rather than utility. These aesthetic reasons are buried beyond reach in our pre-rational animal past. All that we know is that they are there, and from the beginning have been there. They cannot be put to the question, but something can be learnt from zoological theories still very speculative. The painting chimpanzees provide one line of approach, particularly in what have been called their self-rewarding actions: unusual in animals because performed for their own sake rather than to attain any basic biological goal. Most are very simple gymnastic feats, often rhymically performed: play, a curiosity in which any strange object is opened, rearranged, shaken, rhythmically tapped, or moved in a repetitive pattern. These activities usually belong only to young animals whose serious needs are looked after by their families and among species 'which have their survival problems under control and that have a fund of surplus nervous energy requiring some outlet'.[10] When the animal grows older they are abandoned for the immediate problems of survival. It is just possible that these self-rewarding activities, of young and comparatively leisured apes, are in some way related to the gratuitous act which turns a simple stone artifact into a work of art. More basic and more universal is the evidence among animals of preference for pattern and order over muddle and chaos. Experiments in the selection of ready-made visual patterns show that steadiness, symmetry, repetition, rhythm are the factors that govern choice with birds as well as apes and monkeys, though not apparently fishes.[11] So too with the paintings and drawings of different apes that are thought to show a distinct tendency to pattern, and a preference for order and organization rather than confusion. If this is so, the aesthetic sense that makes *us* prefer one hand-axe to another will be of the same kind as that which originally dictated the axe's form.

We are very much in the dark, but it is possible that this is somehow related to those instincts towards pattern and order in behaviour which seem to be tied together in a bundle, and whose purpose is the survival of the species. The bundle includes the instincts, as strong in animals as in men, to hierarchy through dominance, territorial possessions, care of the young, and social survival. An understanding of animals, free and in their natural habitat, teaches that time and again when social survival comes into conflict with the instincts, equally deep-seated but selfish and anarchic in character, of hunger, sex, survival of the individual, the former will conquer.[12] This is the primordial dichotomy between cosmos and chaos, the tension of which is seated deep in the heart of our mythologies and religions. Cosmos and chaos, gods and giants, lapiths and centaurs are older than the first work of art. They are there in the early ice age; and so too apparently is the Apollonian gesture, ensuring that in this 'debate of the instincts' order is stronger than anarchy. The primitive work of art, with the aesthetic instinct that formed it, was on the side of order, symmetry, cosmos; though more than purely intellectual activities, and sometimes to its peril, it has trafficked with chaos. Visual, constructed pattern will be considered in later chapters; at this point only a suggestion might be made, that what is active and creative in man, giving an irregular object of utility unnatural symmetry, regularity, and beauty, has in animals a receptive, passive aspect which is connected with such involuntary phenomena as protective colouring, bright plumage, the chameleon's ability to change its colour; while an equally involuntary movement towards pattern, expressed in the rituals of birds and animals, courtship and threatening display, in human beings becomes consciously creative and is one of the links connecting all the arts.[13]

Another two hundred thousand years and the disappearance of the *pithecanthropus* group of pre-men separate our first sapient sculptors from the makers of the hand-axe (Figure 1A). Another glaciation and another shorter interglacial, and finally the confused beginning of the last great ice age occupy this span of time, during which our ancestors were growing into more complex, more self-conscious, and more gifted beings. Physically the emergence of *homo sapiens* was a long-drawn-out process, and there are still many gaps in our knowledge concerning it. It seems at present most likely that during this long period there were several physically distinguishable populations, including the immediate ancestor of *homo sapiens*, all of which, with the one exception, are now extinct.[14] Neanderthal man was the last to disappear, and the nature of the relationship between his race and ours is still very obscure. There is fair agreement that the European branch of Neanderthal man, whose lowering physiognomy, heavy brows, receding chin, and stooping carriage are so often illustrated, was a highly specialized end-product, having only a very distant collateral connexion with modern man. Even so, he was less beastly and retarded than we used to think.[15]

The relics of this long period are still almost entirely stone tools and weapons, hearths and broken bones; with towards the end of the period and among Neanderthal groups the immensely important addition of formal burial and monumental markings as well as undoubted cannibalism; moreover, hand-axes tend to be superseded by lighter, more adaptable tools made by trimming large flint flakes and cores. At more than one site in Europe and the Near East bodies were placed carefully in prepared graves, lying in traditionally stereotyped attitudes with funeral gifts of food and weapons.

Once, at the cave of La Ferrassie in France, the body of a child was covered with a large stone on the underside of which deep pits or 'cup-marks' had been pecked out in roughly placed pairs. They are not a very impressive monument but cup-marks exactly like them were being made during the comparatively recent Neolithic, and are still objects of superstitious veneration in remote places; bodies too were daubed with red ochre.

Belief in life after death, and in the efficacy of a visual sign, can now be added to the growing complexities of man. In the words of a contemporary poet, 'We are with beasts of a sort, but not it would seem perishing beasts'.[16] Most of the Neanderthal remains come from the early part of the last ice age, when there were a number of changes from greater to lesser cold. There is fairly general agreement on the last two advances of this ice, but for the earlier, when Neanderthal man was in possession of Europe, much is still in doubt – see Table I. Compared with later advances, this first phase was one of less extreme, rather damp cold; and an average estimate would bring it to an end about 40,000 B.C., with its greatest intensity around 55,000 B.C.[17] Neanderthal man lived on into the beginning of the warmer interstadial after 40,000 B.C., while *homo sapiens*, completely evolved with chin and high smooth forehead, appears in Europe during the same temporary retreat of the ice.

There are minor variations in the skulls and bones of *homo sapiens*, and the particular branch that established itself in Europe probably came from Western Asia by way of the Balkans, and from there moved across to the Atlantic coast and to Britain, which was of course part of the Continent. The specialized European branch of Neanderthal man that had survived in caves through intense cold, was soon after this extinct. Since the climate and the physical environment were at first less, rather than more, hostile, it is reasonable to presume that his disappearance was to some extent the work of the

BRIDWELL LIBRARY
SOUTHERN METHODIST UNIVERSITY
DALLAS, TEXAS 75275

new men. Nevertheless there must have been a considerable time, several thousand years, when both lived side by side in Europe. Sapient man was familiar with the physiognomy and habits of the Neanderthal race. Alongside the now extinct animals which were to be the subjects of the Upper Paleolithic artist, there was the unforgettable image of that other creature, not quite true man, not animal. We may wonder how long that image lived on in the consciousness of modern man, and whether we will ever find it modelled in clay or carved in bone, or looking at us from a cave wall. Indeed we may have already seen it.

With the disappearance of the Neanderthalers, and the spread of *homo sapiens* over the globe, we are back at the point where this probe into the more distant past began – back with the sculptors of Plates 2 and 5. It has taken us a long way from our starting point, but there is less danger now of underrating their capacity as men and artists. Identical with us in brain, they still had no history. This does not mean that their minds were an intellectual void, a *tabula rasa* waiting to be filled with the experience of civilization. The mind of the artist was already stored with the million years of his life as a reflective being. Most of this is now beyond our reach. Interpretations that are based on comparison with modern primitives have been found of little help when not actually misleading, and the art of young children is even more misleading than primitive art. There is no recapturing what we have lost through progressive blunting of the senses; but when we have subtracted that part of Upper Paleolithic man's make-up which came from his superior sight, hearing, smell (apart from any extra-sensory perceptions that may have been accessible to him as they appear to be to modern 'primitives'), there is still a residuum of which we can say it is altered, not obliterated, and through which we may hope ourselves to gain access to some few, even if not the most important, aspects of his art.

The First Sculpture (30,000–15,000)

A man's head and body carved from mammoth ivory was found at Brno in Moravia (Plate 2).[18] A portion of the neck is missing and the legs are broken off. There once were arms and part of one survives, but whether the legs were ever complete is not known. If they were, and were long in proportion, then the figure would have stood some 17 inches (42 cm.). In spite of the ravaged condition of the face, enough survives to show that it was no caricature: the hair was cropped, the brow rather low but straight, the eyes deep-sunk. The body is too damaged to judge its degree of naturalism but it seems more schematic than the head. Both head and body are pierced lengthwise. The figure was found with the burial of a man who wore, in his prepared grave, a headdress or necklace made up of some 600 slivvers of *dentalia* shells, roundels cut from bone, and cut and polished beads of mammoth tooth, and finally a stone disc with a central hole, probably used in drilling and possibly connected with fire-making.

According to a recent re-examination of the material and of the site, the man who had owned these personal treasures was of a rather primitive physical type: robust, with unusually heavy brow-ridges very slightly hollowed between the eyes, and approximating to the so-called Combe Capelle type. It seems possible that some of his ancestors belonged to the less specialized Neanderthal-like race known to have lived in the eastern part of Europe. The same robust type has been traced into the Late Bronze Age and even the Middle Ages. This is in marked contrast to other burials from Czechoslovakia. The date, within broad limits, is early in the middle phase of the last glaciation, when the dry cold was increasing after a fairly long milder interlude.[19] This is very much the same as part of the site at Willendorf in Lower Austria from which a small female figure, the so-called Venus, has come, and only a little earlier than the carved ivory figures of animals from the Vogelherd in the Lontal in Württemberg (map on pp. xxxiv–xxxv).

The lady from Willendorf is probably the best known of all these 'Venus' statuettes. Found as long ago as 1908, she has been illustrated countless times (Plate 3), and although many other figures are known now from Italy to Siberia, she remains in a way unique. Carved from limestone, once coloured red, of which traces remain, she is fat, faceless, and preoccupied; collected into herself and the fecundity of which she seems the total embodiment, she has a quite unformalized vitality. Compared with the mother-goddesses, if such they are, of the ancient civilizations of Asia, she does not impress us as an abstraction, an idea or ideal of the female and the fecund; rather one feels, in spite of facelessness and gross exaggeration, that this is actual woman. Carbon 14 dates for the Willendorf sites suggest perhaps 30,000–25,000 B.C. for the statuette.[20]

The animal carvings from the Vogelherd cave are naturalistic (Plate 4).[21] The wild horse with arching neck from Level 5 is a quite different conception, and possibly a different animal, from the stocky beasts with short neck and characteristically low-hung head which we know from the much later paintings in the caves.[22] The break at the legs is ancient. There is very little decoration on the surface, only a hair-fine hatching at the base of the crupper (not visible in the photograph). Eye, nose, and mouth are shown by a single line. Spirited and graceful, it fits comfortably into the hand like so many of the smaller carvings, and like the animals Eskimos carve to carry with them on their journeys. In spite of great injury the panther, with its ears laid back, still has admirable tension. The line of jabs on the flank and shoulder may stand for wounds. The cave lion is rather later in date, coming from Level 4. The ears are again laid back, and the heavy, slack body has been deeply marked with a net or lattice pattern.

This Gravettian sculpture corresponds to the late Aurignacian culture in the West. In the earliest Aurignacian there is no higher art, but there is an ample use of bone, sometimes with rudimentary decoration, and there are finer, more versatile stone tools. It was these, in particular the flint burin (Figure 1B), which made the carving possible. Flint shatters easily on bone, but the burin with notch and point does not; it is the bone- and ivory-workers' tool *par excellence*. Bone needles were also made, and these in turn imply the wearing of clothes: primitive tailoring. Coverings of a sort may have been worn before, but in this last-but-one advance of the last glaciation, the great cold was faced for the first time by hunters able to come away from the fire, and stay warm on the long hunting forays needed to follow and slaughter mammoth and other migrating herds.[23] Just as earlier the invention of cooking had freed the human animal from the tyranny of incessant eating, now warm clothes gave him greater freedom and a new weapon against starvation. The hairy rhinoceros and most of the old primigenious species of animals still existed in large numbers; and the enormous cave bear, which could stand up to ten feet, was much to be respected. All were models for the carver.

At this point the lack of an agreed framework of relative dates and of cross-datings becomes most embarrassing. Systems adopted for different areas – Central and Eastern Europe, the Alps, the Rhineland, Kurdistan, the Ukraine – have not yet been brought together into a single framework.[24] On the whole recent studies have reduced the high dates once believed in, and this has been pure gain, lessening the immense tracts of time during which the art of the caves and hearths of Paleolithic man had to survive as a single tradition or set of connected traditions. The 'four hundred centuries of cave art' that once seemed probable would now be reduced by most archaeologists to fifteen thousand years or less; stretching back from the latest art of reindeer hunters about 10,000 B.C. (or a little later) to the last warm or Paudorf Interstadial,[25] for the beginning of which 25,000 B.C. is suggested by Carbon 14 tests, while a study of soils and sites may add another 5,000 years for the Brno, Willendorf, and Vogelherd Level 5 carvings.[26]

The mature work of the first phase of Paleolithic sculpture is extraordinarily scarce. It is the more fortunate that between them these sites give us man, woman, and beast. But as well as being a long time ago, this art was produced in a physical environment which was extremely hostile to man and which, in spite of fire, clothes, and food, he was still very poorly equipped to endure.

The men who lived during the Paudorf Interstadial, a period of less bitter cold from roughly 27,000 to 24,000 B.C., have left us much information about themselves. They also added to bone-carving the art of modelling in clay, and probably a little rather tentative engraving and painting. Although the times were relatively milder, they were not unlike southern Greenland or the Canadian barrens today. At Dolní Věstonice in Czechoslovakia, one of the important sites of this period, the landscape varied from cold, sparse forest with pine, spruce, willow, and birch and many clearings, to open moorlike country with sedges and grasses. The contorted soils are still evidence of that violence of nature, subject to alternating frost and thaw, the rendings and the uncontrollable power of the rivers in the annual break-up, which have been described by people with experience of the arctic north today.[27] Mammoth, reindeer, wolf, horse, arctic fox, arctic hare, wolverine, and willow-grouse were all hunted, and their bones are found in the middens near the living-places. The mammoth was the great provider of food, along with the reindeer. Bones of rhinoceros are not found in middens, but woolly rhinoceros is portrayed along with boars and the large predators.

The hunters who lived in this violent world had already gathered, for at least part of the year, into settled communities and traces of their houses have been found. They probably trekked between regular seasonal quarters. The enormous accumulations of bones on some sites show them to have been occupied for several hundred years. At Dolní Věstonice the hunters had gone beyond a mere dragging together of branches for shelters (which in any case would leave no trace), and lived in huts with clay walls on stone footings; large bones of mammoth were also convenient building material. These settlements in the Pavlov hills near Dolní Věstonice are perhaps the most completely studied of the older Upper Paleolithic sites. Four distinct phases are connected in an unbroken development; and there are fifteen such sites, with at least thirty huts, known from Czechoslovakia alone. The huts are generally near springs, and have from one to five hearths inside them. With five or six huts occupied at the same time in a settlement, a community of a hundred to a hundred and twenty persons has been calculated; numbers well suited to the organized mammoth hunts which furnished the massive spoils of the middens.[28] These hunters were of the local East Gravettian culture which extends into southern Russia. They were gifted artists, and among their huts are special workshops in which ivory and bone were carved and clay was modelled and roughly baked.

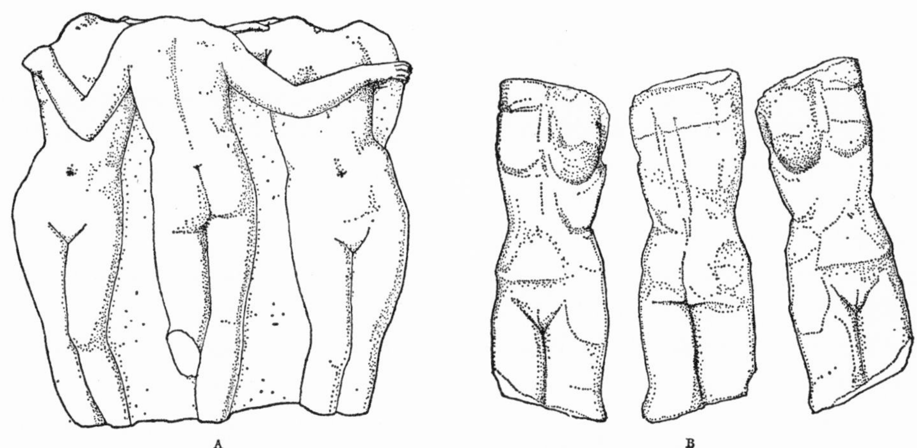

Figure 2. A Late classical relief of the Three Graces
B Haematite carving from Ostrava-Petřkovice, Czechoslovakia (three views)

A site at Ostrava Petřkovice on the left bank of the Oder in northern Moravia is a little older than Dolní Věstonice, and here three oval huts have been excavated.[29] Each hut had two hearths on which coal fires burnt through the long glacial winter, and Hut III had a workshop for making stone and flint tools, among which were lumps of half-baked haematite, to be used as pigment, like the red ochre used by Neanderthal man and by men of the Neolithic and Bronze ages, and indeed contemporary primitives, to decorate the living and give the colour of life to the recent dead. A small figure was found at the side of one of the hearths under a mammoth molar (Plate 5). It is a carved female torso and it measures only $1\frac{3}{4}$ inches ($4\frac{1}{2}$ cm.). Apart from minor damage (thigh and one breast) it is very nearly perfect. In a setting that gives a weird foretaste of the Industrial Revolution with its coal and iron, the artist has produced a figure of a touching naturalism and truth. The rugged quality in the work is probably due to the material, but the slim youthful figure has the proportions, and even the equilibrium (the weight on the right leg), of a late classical Venus or of the three Graces. Three views taken together in Figure 2 show how well the proportions and even the pose of this tiny figure fit the classical canon. The only real divergence from naturalism is the rigid line of the buttocks; otherwise this pose, which has been claimed as a 'beautiful invention of fifth-century Greece', is strangely prefigured by our Upper Paleolithic artist.[30]

At Dolní Věstonice three finds are especially important: a woman's burial, a small ivory head (Plate 6), and a primitive kiln. Hut II was found to have a prepared floor, clay and stone foundation walls, and around the hearth the clay vault of a kiln-like structure inside which were portions of modelled animals (Plate 7); while thousands of clay pellets, some with impressions of the artists' fingers, lay ready for use along with broken-off legs, and human and animal heads: bears, foxes, and others uncertain, and some fine completed animals. The 'kiln' was evidently used for firing the small figures; its vault overhangs the soot-stained hearth and the underside is burnt red. More figures, mostly animals, have been found on a slightly later site in the Pavlov hills. Local clay and loess with backing of bone and small stones was used. Some animals are 'wounded'.[31]

One of the comparatively rare human figures (Plate 8) belongs to a totally different climate (we cannot yet speak of tradition) from the Ostrava Petřkovice torso. It is of baked clay and was found in 1925. At that date huts had not been identified, but the position of the large hearth where it lay, in the centre of the settlement, makes it virtually certain that this figure too had been left inside a building. Like Willendorf, it is faceless; it also lacks arms and hair, and it is more schematized, though the collar-bone is shown realistically; the buttocks are flat, and an arbitrary line is continued round the front of the figure. This gives it an odd likeness, which may be quite fortuitous, to the elbow joint of the human skeleton (the end of the humerus above and proximal ends of ulna and radius below). If such bone idols ever existed they have not been recognized, but neither are they likely to be. This figure lacks the living quality of the Willendorf woman; it is already becoming less a representation than the tool of a cult. The modelled animals found on the hearth of another hut – rhinoceros, bear, mammoth – are naturalistic, with an admirable bulkiness, and in the case of the bear an appearance of lumbering movement which has been reproduced with great skill (Plate 7). I do not think they would ever be mistaken for toys. The clay of the figures again shows traces of kneading and of the use of a broad implement, perhaps a bone or wooden spatula. One carefully modelled mammoth from the Pavlov hills is represented without the usual obscuring curtain of hair; either it is a young beast, or it may be that the hunter's intimate knowledge of his prey looks behind the appearance.[32] This skill in the portrayal of animals proves that the artist knew his business and did what he wanted to do. The peculiarity of the Dolní Věstonice woman is not due to artistic ineptitude but to causes which must be investigated later.

The small face carved in mammoth ivory (Figure 3A) was found in 1952 in another hut at Dolní Věstonice.[33] It is an expressive sketch, very inferior to the face on Plate 6, also from Dolní Věstonice but found in 1936, and one of the masterpieces of early carving. Though only 2 inches (48 mm.) high, this shows a fine structure and thoughtful expression. The long nose has a convincing bump at the tip. The only odd feature is the crooked line of the brow, which affects the entire left side of the face including the slightly drawn-up mouth, exactly as in the 'sketch' (Figure 3B). A natural deformation like this could have been caused by injury to the nerve of the left cheek. The third important discovery at Dolní Věstonice is a woman's skeleton found in 1949, the skull of which had a defect on the left side which would probably have brought about a corresponding deformation of the soft parts, curiously like that shown on the two ivory faces. The skeleton is that of a small and elegantly built woman, 5 feet 3 inches, and about forty years old, which is very old for those days.[34] She had been given an elaborate burial inside one of the huts, laid in a prepared hollow on the left side in a contracted position, facing west. Body and head were covered with red ochre and protected by two shoulder-blades of mammoth, one of which had a network of irregular lines incised on its surface. With the woman were placed her stone tools, and close to her left hand the paws and tail of an arctic fox, with the teeth in her other hand.[35] The ceremonial of crouched burial and the westward-facing position of the body were already part of the rite of Neanderthal burial, and during the later part of the last ice age the rite is known from as far east as Maltá near Lake Baikal.

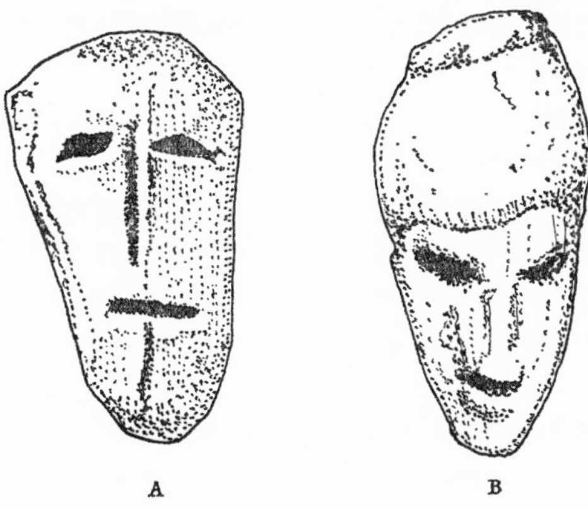

Figure 3. Mammoth ivory heads from Dolní Věstonice, Czechoslovakia: A found in 1952, B found in 1936 (cf. Plate 6)

Great spiritual or intellectual power must have belonged to the slight old woman who had been singled out for such careful burial. The coincidence of the same physical defect in three distinct fossils from the same locality, two of them within 25 feet of each other, belonging to the same culture, and not far separated in time, is, to say the least, odd, and added to the evidence of the Brno man with his robust physique and rugged carving it raises a doubt as to whether the early art of Upper Paleolithic sapient man was not in some way concerned with portraiture.[36] On the other hand, the distortion of the carving may be due to the need to avoid the completed perfection of symmetry.

The Dolní Věstonice woman (Plate 8) concentrated attention on the breasts and belly; also from Dolní Věstonice comes a small ivory in which the body has been reduced to a mere stick supporting the breasts; while another suppresses the body altogether and represents the breasts alone (Plate 9). Such objects are truly instruments of a cult, 'tool-like minimum images' for the production of which we do not have to wait till the settled communities of the Neolithic.[37] In them the idea of nourishment is represented in as nearly impersonal a form as the artist could compass.

The largest number of carved human figures of the Upper Paleolithic, perhaps over two-thirds of the whole, are in Russia. At Kostienki, near Voronezh on the Don, forty-three figures have been found, and at Maltá in Siberia twenty, and there are other important sites, among them Gagarino on the Don and Yelisevici (Eliseevichi). Most are permanent or semi-permanent settlements of hunters living in houses. They hunted the mammoth more than all other animals and, as in Czechoslovakia, used its bones to build the houses, since timber was scarce on the tundra and on the slightly more genial *taiga* or barren lands. Again, as in Czechoslovakia, the figures are usually found inside the huts. One structure at Yelisevici was curiously long and narrow. The walls were formed of shoulder-blades and long-bones of mammoth, and it may have been a shrine rather than a dwelling. It may also be rather late in date; an ivory woman's figure found inside is unusually long and cylindrical, rather reminiscent of Neolithic figures. Some figures from Maltá are extremely stylized, and the feet are pierced, probably to be hung from a narrow cord or sinew and worn on the person like the charms of later ages. Figures from the great sites of Gagarino and Kostienki are both slender and obese. Some almost look like rougher versions of the Willendorf lady. A woman's figure from Kostienki I is more carefully carved in mammoth bone (Figure 6c).[38] She wears a wide girdle, perhaps of fur, seen at the back but hidden in front by the enormous breasts. She appears to be pregnant, and like Willendorf is faceless, but the flat-backed, long-limbed physique is quite different. A female figure from Buret is unusual because dressed in what looks to be a thick fur robe with fur hood, very much like the Eskimo 'parka'. The figure is slender, with arms held tight to the sides, and seems to belong to a different set of needs and interests.[39] It underlines the really exceptional nature of the naked figures of which we have so many. Nakedness is itself a powerful magic. Celtic warriors stripped for battle, for this gave them supernatural immunity; and Australian aborigines still strip to perform sacred ceremonies. There is no agreed synchronism between Russian and other European sites, and this makes it particularly difficult to correlate the carvings from Russia and from Central and Western Europe. The upper level at Kostienki I, from which the figures came, was probably a little later than the Paudorf Interstadial; and they are not likely to be any earlier than the dated one from Czechoslovakia. The East Gravettian culture which produced them may have lasted locally to as late as 10,000 B.C.[40]

The same difficulty regarding dates, though not for the same reasons, applies to many of the small figures from French and Italian sites which, on stylistic grounds, are usually grouped with those of Eastern Europe. The Russian finds belong to recognized cultural 'horizons', and a lot is known about the way of life of their makers, but many of the western figures were found before excavation techniques had advanced sufficiently for proper records to have been kept. Others are chance finds without any context of information. Where evidence does exist, it may be hard to interpret; nevertheless the carvings are of great intrinsic interest, and one recent find *can* be dated.[41]

The first known figure was found in 1892 in the Cave du Pape at Brassempouy in the Landes, in the west of France. It is an ivory woman's torso, and in spite of being a mere fragment it lacks neither skill nor subtlety. The date is usually given as 'Mid-Aurignacian', which in the west corresponds to the Gravettian of Dolní Věstonice, but it may be even earlier.[42] Several other small figures were found at Brassempouy; the best preserved are a slender, rather rudimentary, type which is known also in the later Magdalenian of France (Laugerie Basse) and at Siberian Maltá. Finally there is a small ivory head of a woman with an elaborate coiffure (Plate 10). It is one of the rare heads on which the features are shown, but it lacks the refined carving and characterization of Plate 6, the element, if such it is, of portraiture. This is a young smooth face that looks directly outwards, not sunken, blank, or brooding like the obese and pregnant women. The perfect oval of the head has been disturbed only just enough to define brows and nose. The rest is left in its geometric purity. Neck and chin join naturalistically. It is possible that the face was once coloured, like the Willendorf stone, so that, as with antique marble, the coolness may be accidental.

A figure from Sireuil in the Dordogne is again quite different (Plate 11). It was found by itself not far from the entrance to a small cave which had been used by Middle Aurignacian men, but this cannot be taken as evidence of its date, which remains uncertain. It is carved from hard calcite. The head is lost and the limbs are oddly stunted, but the proportions of the elongated torso and large buttocks are those of young bushmen girls of today, among whom a sway-backed, fat-hipped posture and steatopygy are not infrequent. With bushmen, hottentots, and some other peoples the extra fat stored in the buttocks is considered both useful and beautiful.[43] The feet are pierced, and the diminished limbs may have been due to convenience in carrying: the need for a compact whole without breakable extremities. A serpentine figure found at Savignano near Modena, Italy, has more extreme steatopygy (Plate 12). It is an unflattering but very realistic carving of a particular physical condition; some sort of high, pointed headdress seems to be worn. A number of other female figures have been found in Italy, at Balzi Rossi, Chiozza, and Trasimeno. A small stone figure found not long ago at Tursac (Dordogne) comes formally between Sireuil, with its vestigial limbs, and Trasimeno. It could be androgynous, if such a category does exist, or more probably the form was dictated by the nature of the stone and the needs of touch and portability. The date 'final Perigordian' is about 18,000, and since it is archaeologically vouched, it supports that of other figures like Sireuil and Trasimeno (see Table 1). The last, in steatite, with its suppression of every feature beyond a congregation of spheres and half-circles, seems to have been expressly designed for holding in the hand; it looks equally convincing whichever end is uppermost.[44]

An ivory woman from Lespugue (Haute-Garonne) is sometimes given an Upper Aurignacian date, around 20,000–18,000 B.C., but the evidence is far from conclusive.[45] The site is a shallow cave that overlooks a gorge from a height of 260 feet, and the figure is said to have been found in a hearth inside the cave. In this carving stylization has been taken a stage further, not through ineptitude or failing artistic impetus, but by choice (Plate 13). The flatness of the back may be due in part to the shape of the ivory. A kind of apron worn at the back can be seen in rear views. The pose is that of the

Willendorf lady, with hands on breasts, head sunk forward, neglect of face and feet; but the contrast in other respects could not be more complete. In the one, in spite of exaggeration, the figure is natural and alive; the other is remote, elegant, almost abstract, built up by a geometry of circles, ovoids, and cones. The globular shapes are not slack but combined and concentrated into their own logic of construction. Lespugue is an entirely original conception which convinces, just as much as Willendorf, in spite of the hint of cleverness. It is so far removed from the brutal vitality of the other that the millennia separating them are no surprise at all.

The First Drawings (23,000–15,000)

So far as we know, sculpture precedes drawing, but not by very much. The real beginning of drawing, even more than sculpture, is as fugitive as the soft mud, the sand and melting snow in which it was traced. If drawings are to survive at all a durable medium is necessary, and the earliest we have were scratched on stone at the beginning of the last re-advance of the ice about 23,000 B.C., roughly contemporary with the modelled animals of the Pavlov hill sites in Moravia, and a little later than the Dolní Věstonice carvings. They are found in the floor deposits of caves and shelters, among the tools and weapons that serve to date them. Some are on loose pebbles, some on stone

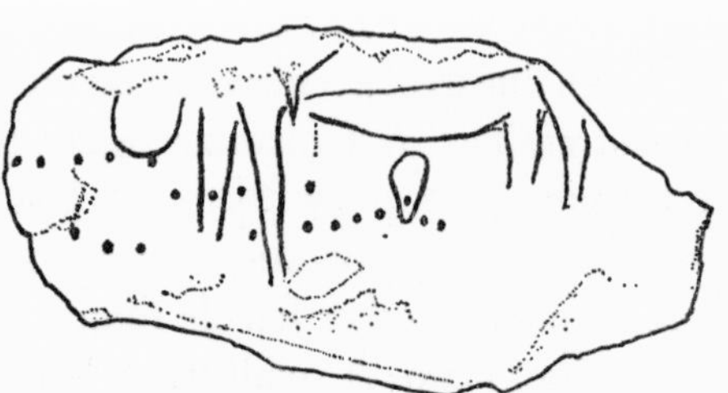

Figure 4. Rock engraved with vulvae and an animal from La Ferrassie, France (cf. Plate 14)

that has flaked from the side of the rock wall. A flint burin was the artist's pencil or stylus, and with it almost hair-fine line was possible. Among the oldest are probably deeply engraved vulvae from the Abri Cellier, Castanet, and La Ferrassie, all three in the Dordogne (Plate 14 and Figure 4). There are also animals with thick pecked and engraved outlines and, at La Ferrassie, four legs, while at Abri Belcayre there could be two legs or four. At Abri Cellier there are only heads.[46] The vulvae, concrete primitive signs, like Neanderthal cup-marks, outlived much more complicated images, for the same sign was used for 'woman' by the Sumerians in the pictographic precursor of cuneiform script during the fourth millennium B.C. Rather later, but still extremely early, there are hands stencilled in colour – red, black, or yellow – on cave walls at Gargas, and also, less early or undatable, in many other caves 'macaronis' – meandering patterns made by trailing the fingers through soft mud which later hardened and so preserved them. At Gargas again they are probably early, around 18,000 or at least before 15,000; but though technically primitive, they are not easy to date, and those at Pech-Merle may be Solutrian or even Early Magdalenian (Plate 15).[47]

Many of the animals drawn on stone, or (less often) bone, or painted in outline, show a grasp of the essential character of the subject even when they are far from accurate transcriptions.[48] There is a fine and monumental bison which is still in position on the wall of the cave of La Grèze in the Dordogne (Plate 16). It is seen in absolute profile, the line of sight at right angles to the centre; only two legs appear, but the head and horns are full face so that it does not look absolutely flat. A painted stag from the Abri Blanchard, also in the Dordogne and also a profile, has antlers viewed from the front. Both these are early examples of the 'twisted perspective' which was to be used so much in the caves. Horses from Pair-non-Pair (Gironde) have the elongated head and

Figure 5. A Bone with engraving of a horse from Isturitz, France
B Engraving of a horse in the cave of Gargas, France

pinched muzzle which is also a recurring stylistic peculiarity (Plate 17). This shelter had a composite drawing, or rather consecutive drawings of an ibex and a horse, using some of the same lines for both subjects.[49] Another horse, scratched on a stone from a floor deposit in the Pyrenean cave of Isturitz, has the arched neck and broad muzzle of the carved ivory one from Vogelherd (Plate 4).[50]

Also from Isturitz there is part of a bone javelin that was found in a Late Aurignacian or Upper Gravettian level of probably a little before 20,000 B.C., on which is engraved a horse (Figure 5A). The back and neck are drawn in with a single strong, confident line like the goats and horses of Pair-non-Pair, but the line is interrupted at the muzzle and the long, sensitive hairs of the chin have been rendered impressionistically (though much simplified) by detached strokes.[51] Later again, rather after 20,000, a bâton from Laugerie Haute in the Dordogne has two engraved mammoths facing each other with the tails and the long hair of the coat in fine impressionist strokes. The same device was used at Gargas on the walls of a small side-chamber in the innermost and darkest part of the cave (Figure 5B). The strokes are long, and do not so much mask a known but invisible contour as give a general impression of the hairiness of a horse's mane, cheek, and fetlocks, or of the throat and neck of bison and goat. Gargas is particularly difficult to date, as it was frequented much later by Magdalenian hunters as well as during the later Aurignacian or Gravettian.[52] However this may be, a number of animal stereotypes, including those for mammoth and bull, were already established now.

Returning again to Central Europe, there is one extraordinary object which, though 'drawn' and representing a human being, is quite outside the West European tradition. The people of Předmostí in Moravia were mammoth-hunters like those of Dolní Věstonice not far away, and some artist among them has taken a section of tusk about a foot long and engraved on it a female figure[53] (Plate 23). Reduction of the human body to a pattern of lines and dashes could not have been taken much farther. We have already seen the body, or its parts, treated in a highly impersonal and schematic manner at Dolní Věstonice (Plate 9), and now, hardly if at all later than the drawings at Belcayre or even at Pair-non-Pair (Plate 17), this need to turn *things* into concepts, and to generalize, is asserted in a very downright fashion.

All other very early drawings, whether of man or animal, give the profile view; only antlers and heads are occasionally seen from the front in twisted perspective. The difficulty of rendering a three-dimensional object as a two-dimensional outline is great enough, but the frontal view is infinitely more difficult and was very seldom attempted by Paleolithic artists. For the human figure there may have been some particular sanction upon it, as there was in Egypt much later. The Předmostí construction is based on natural shapes; the proper proportions of the body are at least suggested, though as a formalized symmetrical pattern. The outline of the breasts is a two-dimensional projection of Dolní Věstonice (Plate 9), and the third dimension is suggested by a sort of contouring; or else the five-fold outline may be due to the habit of tracing patterns in mud with fingers and thumb like the 'macaronis' of the French and Spanish caves. It remains a constant technique, re-appearing in the Celtic Iron Age and even in the Middle Ages. The face, though schematic, has features: eyes, nose, and mouth are suggested as though on a mask; or possibly tattooing or painting of the face are to be understood. With the Předmostí engraving the wish to imitate nature has been dropped as completely as with the Lespugue statuette. This is an image to which any or every woman *could* conform, and which stands equally aloof from them all.

The number of securely dated early engravings and paintings, even if enlarged to include, on stylistic grounds, a certain number of animals in twisted perspective, makes a comparatively insignificant prelude to the great years of cave art after 15,000 B.C.[54]

The Beginning of Relief (23,000–15,000)

Theoretically, the art of relief might be expected to appear between sculpture in three dimensions and drawing or engraving; but in fact a mastery of naturalistic representation in relief entails mastering almost all the problems that confront the draughtsman. In his tools and manner of working this artist may be closer to a sculptor in the round, but he must also have resolved the intellectual problems of drawing. A two-dimensional pattern lies embedded in the two and a half dimensions of the relief. The first steps towards relief were taken at much the same time that engraving was gaining in assurance; for, with very few and doubtful exceptions, relief did not appear until after about 18,000. But there are borderline cases, like Terme-Pialat in the Dordogne, where the engraving is so deep as to be virtually relief; and a block fallen from the roof of the shelter at Belcayre, also Dordogne, has a reindeer (or ibex?) in a mixture of deep engraving and pecking that is probably Late Aurignacian.[55]

In spite of these early beginnings, monumental carving in low and medium relief on rock faces, often in the open or under the shelter of an overhanging cliff, probably begins with the Solutrian of France. This was a short interlude of some 4,000 years, when a technical revolution in flint-working spread rapidly through the west among different groups of hunters. At this time the wild horse was the favourite prey. Though careless with bone, the hunters were superb flint-workers; the laurel leaf (Plate 1) shows their standard, which equals the best work from Early Dynastic Egypt or Early Bronze Age Denmark.

The first of the true reliefs, and the only one that might be pre-Solutrian, was found in the rock-shelter of Laussel in the Dordogne.[56] The site had been used at various times during the last glaciation, and though the excavators claimed the reliefs to be Aurignacian and only a little later than Dolní Věstonice, the stratigraphy could allow a later date. Laussel is a rock shelter with a spring, above the valley of the Beune. Most of the reliefs are on blocks of fallen rock, but the best preserved is also the only one found upright *in situ*. This is the figure often called the 'Laussel Venus' (Plate 19). At first glance she appears to be seen from the front, with head turned to her right. No features are shown; the left hand is on the belly, but the right is not, as usual, placed symmetrically, but holds the horn of a bison which she has raised to her face. The hips are bulging and deformed, and she is usually described as pregnant. The outline was sketched in by pecking and the hollows then joined into a single line. Originally she was coloured, like the Willendorf statue, and a little red pigment has survived.

More than any other *relief*, this figure is like the carved and modelled statuettes, particularly from Kostienki I. There is the same bumpy outline, the same knock-kneed stance and overall proportions; but I believe that the likeness goes deeper and that there is an explanation for the anatomical distortion of the hips. If the figure is bisected and the left side compared, not with a front view of Kostienki, but with the side views, we have the normal profile of a rather plump and possibly pregnant woman (see Figure 6, B–D, where both are drawn to a similar scale).[57] If the artist of Laussel had not yet mastered the complicated conventions of relief, he may still be one of the great

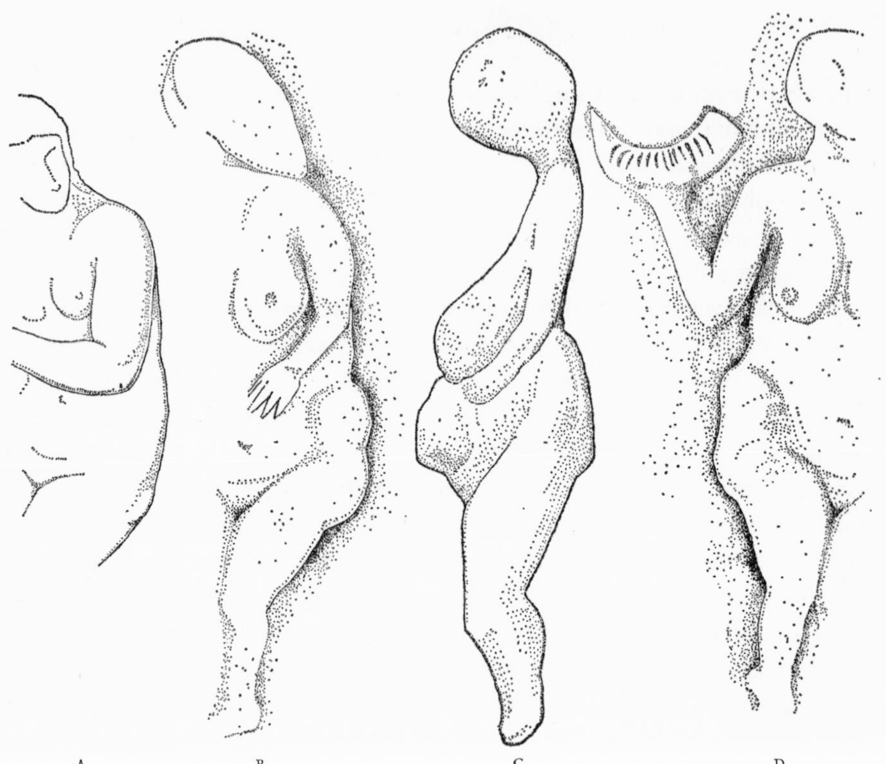

Figure 6. A Detail from the 'Ellesmere Venus' by Titian
B Relief of a woman from Laussel, France (right side; cf. Plate 19)
C Small ivory figure from Kostienki, South Russia
D Left side of Laussel relief

innovators; and if he was already a master in the tradition of sculpture in the round, he was accustomed to turn and view the block with the emerging figure from a variety of angles. In many statuettes the side view is the most striking and characteristic, and so it would not be surprising if he attempted to combine in his relief everything, or as much as possible, that belonged to the three-dimensional figures. It is this which gives the breadth of belly and the extraordinary conformation of the hips, quite unlike the usual shape, which tapers from a single area of maximum breadth down to the knees. Perhaps we could go a step farther and compare the left side of the bisected figure with the outline of a Renaissance Venus Anodyomene – such as the Titian in the Ellesmere Collection (Figure 6A). Comparison of the two finished works is ludicrous; but if outlines only are taken, there is a surprising likeness of proportion and of pose. The Titian has been called 'one of the most complete and concentrated embodiments of Venus in post-antique art', anticipating 'the whole conception of the subject which ended, for our generation, in the nudes of Renoir'.[58] Is it possible that these too are anticipated by an infinitely older 'Venus'? Though her claim to that title may be dubious, she must be allowed a place as a 'concentrated embodiment of woman' that is much older than the antique.

If the Laussel lady marks a stage in the development of relief, the man from the same site shows that more problems are on the way to solution (Plate 18). Neither head nor right arm exists, and there is something rather awkward about the left thigh. The legs are in profile, but the upper part of the body is turned to the front; and this is already the profile convention that lasted in Egypt from the fourth millennium to the fourth century B.C. and that was sometimes used, but less strictly, in ancient Mesopotamia.[59] This figure is in lower relief than the lady. He wears a belt round the waist, and the gesture is that of a man poised to hurl a spear. Finally there are three much smaller women, all seen from the front. The workmanship is poor, but one holds an object in one hand that may be a horn, and another has been thought to represent either a birth or copulation. The condition of the stone is poor, however, and the evidence inadequate.

Deep engravings from Terme-Pialat were mentioned above. One is really a very low relief of two women. It is sometimes dated as early as 23,000 B.C., the same as the Dolní Věstonice clay figure, to the side view of which there is some resemblance. Like the statuette, the better figure lacks arms and face and has a very simplified body. Compared to Laussel, Terme-Pialat is rudimentary, but it *is* a true profile.[60]

If, at Laussel, doubts remain in the mind concerning date and interpretation, other sites such as Fourneau du Diable (Plate 21) are certainly later and perhaps Solutrian. The site at Roc de Sers is large and complicated; it has a small cave, a shelter, a working area, and burials. When they were found, a number of carved blocks lay where they had fallen, face downwards, in the working area. When raised they provided a continuous frieze of animals which once followed the line of the overhanging rock wall above the river bank.[61] The animals vary from 28 to 12 inches (70 to 30 cm.); there are horses, some of them probably mares in foal, bison, ibex, deer, a bird, and perhaps a badger. Older carvings of bison have been transformed, like the engraved ibex of Pair-non-Pair, into horses, and one has been turned into an odd monster with the head of a boar. Two blocks are especially interesting. The first is in too poor condition for reproduction, but a scene has been deciphered which shows two small horses and perhaps a badger advancing towards the left, with a naked man in profile in front of them. The other half of the block has a large and extremely well conceived bison or bull, head lowered, menacing another naked man, who may be in flight, for the legs are bent sharply at the knees. Both front legs of the animal are shown, and the head between them is in true perspective. The carver has used the natural relief of the rock-face to increase the depth of the animal's shoulder.[62] Another block has a pair of ibexes, head to head as though butting or, more likely, as a deliberately formal antithetical group, like the mammoth of Laugerie Haute (Plate 22).

Open-air sites, like Laussel, Roc de Sers, La Chaire à Calvin, and a few others with less important carvings, were used also in the later centuries of Magdalenian art alongside the painted caves (see below), but though reliefs and paintings overlap geographically, they seem to belong to different artistic traditions or to a different set of needs and uses. The reliefs are all in daylight, or at least in half-light, on the walls of rock shelters or at the entrance to shallow caves. At Isturitz, a cave in the Basses Pyrénées, carving ceases at exactly the point where daylight fails. The difficulty and labour of pecking-out the stone background from an engraved outline, in dark and cramped conditions, might be thought a sufficient cause, but there are grounds for suspecting less material reasons. An attempt has recently been made to separate an entire cycle of daylight art, either in relief or *deep* engraving, centred on western France, from the much more widespread paintings and *fine* engravings, found in the total dark of caves which are on the whole more southerly, clustered in the Pyrenees and the Cantabrian mountains. In the Dordogne both overlap. The daylight art is often near, or even part of, the sites where men lived in the shelter of cliffs or at the entrance to the cave on or near a river bank. An arrangement of large blocks or of heaps of stones may suggest withdrawal from the actual living-place with its hearths and débris; so that, although closely linked with everyday affairs, there may have been something there of the special character of a sanctuary. Another difference between this art and that of the caves is that animals are not portrayed wounded, but there are sometimes curious and unexplained artificial ring-holes bored in the rock, on or beside the carvings. More important still, human beings are portrayed very much as in life. Masked and semi-human figures do not appear, and there are more female representations than male; but, dealing in such small numbers, these observations must be treated with caution.[63]

Once it had been so far perfected, the art of relief remained in the repertoire, to be used occasionally and with great success by the later Magdalenian artists (see below, p. 40); but in spite of this, relief was always rare in prehistoric Europe compared to carving and modelling in the round.

Divine Image and Magic Drum

The sculpture illustrated on Plates 2 and 6 comes to us as the two crests of a single wave; even with the reliefs and drawings of Plate 19 and Figure 5 it is not very impressive. The important point is that here, rather than in the famous caves with their multitude of paintings and engravings, is the beginning of the European higher arts. It is on the strength of this small collection that we must test the large assumptions of the art historians. Have we got at the beginning the 'aim at a likeness' or the 'attempt to rival creation'? Historically does 'making come before matching'? Who were the artists and who or what are portrayed in the ivory man from Brno, the haematite torso from Ostrava Petřkovice, the Předmostí construction, and the rest? Can we find an answer in terms of what the art of sculpture and painting was to become?[64]

Unlike the flint hand-axe, the human and animal figures serve no obvious purpose, they take their shape from no obvious tool; only in a metaphorical sense are they 'tools of a cult', and even then is this really an accurate description? The invention of the Acheulian hand-axe could be explained to some extent from a practical need, to hit or dig or scrape, standardized by the mind at its concept-forming, symbol-making games and given final definition by a basic aesthetic instinct. But for the engraved, sculptured, and modelled figures there is no equally compelling explanation. The practical need may still be there, since needs are few and permanent: food, shelter, warmth, increase, propitiation, dominance, and the object may mediate these needs. But if we are going to accept this, it is necessary to accept a number of religious and metaphysical propositions, and with them we move on to very treacherous ground. Two quotations underline the difficulty: '. . . Science did not germinate and grow in an open and healthy prairie of ignorance, but in a noisome jungle of magic and superstition, which again and again choked the seedlings of knowledge', and 'modern man is irremediably identified with history and progress . . . history and progress are a fall, both implying the final abandonment of the paradise of archetypes and repetition'.[65] These opposing statements really tell us next to nothing about ancient man but, like some biographies, tell us more about the authors. They are a measure of the confusion of mind which we bring to the early records of our past. There are no answers to our question; but if it is true that 'out of uninterrupted sense experiences science cannot be distilled, no matter how industriously we gather and sort them. Bold ideas, unjustified anticipations and speculative thought are our only means of interpreting nature'; then let them all come unashamed to assist the interpretations of art.[66]

We have been warned against ethnological comparisons, and this applies to art as much as to sociology and religion. So great a time separates the few remaining primitive societies from the Upper Paleolithic hunters that analogies must not be pressed, but they can *sometimes* point a direction even when they lead us to no goal. The more universal they are, the more likely to be vestiges of a common human experience. Above all, let us remember that it is our own forebears at whom we are looking.

Between ourselves and the Lapps, Finns, Siberian hunters, and reindeer herdsmen still, or till recently, living on the perimeter of the western world, there may be a very distant blood-relationship, so that the shared Paleolithic ancestry opens the way to a limited understanding of our common past; at the same time the literate and articulate people of the Mediterranean and ancient Near East open yet another. In spite of errors and misinterpretations, ancient no less than recent, in spite of so much changed and lost, enough remains to provide another bridgehead. For in important ways, and prejudices to the contrary notwithstanding, a sixth-century Greek was as close to an Upper Paleolithic hunter as to man in this atomic age. Finally there are language and psychology to help us. It may be a trick of mental vision, but the impression is inescapable that the lines running back into the past are lines of increasing uniformity.

It is likely that there was at some time, probably before the emergence of language and reflection, a stage when things existed for the 'I' only if and as they affected it emotionally. The creature experienced an indeterminacy of feeling in which certain impressions are set off from the common background of feeling by their special intensity. To these, and not to conscious reflection, probably correspond the first mythological images. This stage preceded the personification and worship of natural objects, or universal forces, itself hardly possible before the emergence of language. Out of it grew the 'little gods' of later ages: nature gods and demons born of an instantaneous impression, a momentary tension.[67] Among the songs of some of the most primitive people still living, the aboriginals of Arnhemland, there are already many which express an accurate, sensitive perception of the natural world, as well as the underlying awe at the presence of mysterious powers.[68] Again, before he was aware of his own personality as separated from the whole of nature, man felt himself as a link in the chain of life joining every individual creature and thing, so that continuous transition or metamorphosis of one being into another appeared both possible and necessary. According to this view, objects are grouped into species and genera by outward appearance, or as they affect the individual, through sensations and impressions, rather than by rational knowledge and inference. Instead of known rules of heredity, things that look or feel alike are brought mythologically or actually into the unity of one genus. Through such an order of relationship or 'sympathy' man and animal can belong to the same family. It must be admitted that terms like 'animism' or 'totem' often mystify more than they enlighten; for instance an infinite number of gradations are possible in the so-called totemic and totemistic relationships, and even among very primitive contemporaries some are at a spiritual level which distinguishes perfectly between the material totem, a natural species or class of objects, and the spirit of which it is the symbol.[69] In earlier anthropological writings all would have been confused; but though these subtle distinctions are a great advance, it is still possible, and even probable, that at a much earlier stage in the life of man the confusion was real.

Fluidity of living (and sometimes even inanimate) categories lies behind the shape-shifting of the shaman and his power of conversing with birds, animals, and spirits; and it survives long enough to give an impetus and direction to later religions and to a much later art. There are even traces of it in the art of the Celts. For Upper Paleolithic man (as for many contemporary 'primitives') it greatly complicated the business of hunting, eating, and the, to us, humdrum routine of living. Animals, more than insensate objects, have magical or spiritual powers, and hunting and killing animals entails a magical or spiritual, as well as a physical, relationship between the man and his prey. We see this consciousness not only in the painted caves, but already in the 'wounded' bear and rhinoceros of the Pavlov hills.

It is quite possible that Neanderthal man had a mythology as well as a ritual – since the cannibal feast, with its eating of brain matter, is likely to be the repetition of some mythical act.[70] Ritual and the celebration of culture heroes have a common source in the remembrance of those dramatic and free acts through which the human race made one of its periodic leaps forward. All, or nearly all, known mythologies have traces of remote benefactors, bringers of fire, great hunters, originators of this or that special tool or weapon, builders, or founders of settlements. Sometimes they are human or animal ancestors and fathers of the race, gods or heroes, or strangers who appeared mysteriously bringing their gifts. These originators lingered as symbols of great potency into the late classical world – Prometheus, Apollo, Orpheus – but they also go back to the beginnings of whatever art they practise. The capture of fire, invention of the chemistry of cooking, domestication of grasses and animals, building a house, each achievement was at first regarded with terror. These were revolutionary, historical and profane acts that must be made safe and acceptable by shifting the responsibility on to supernatural beings, through the performance of ritual and repetition of myth. When man is aware only or chiefly of biological time, the present moment of any ritual can be felt to coincide with the mythical moment of 'the beginning', and the human act acquires effectiveness exactly as it repeats the exemplary act performed by the god, hero, or ancestor. The dances, the great huntings, and the ritual of their preparation, making a weapon, marrying, giving birth, and dying; these are never merely human but, as they repeat a sacred event, they too are sacred, part of the transformation of chaos into cosmos – from the beginning. In this lies the force of sympathetic magic, a far richer and more complex thing than is often assumed by prehistorians trying to 'explain' the rituals of early man. They cannot, any more than the great historical religions, be 'explained' in a sentence. Sympathetic magic also operates on different levels. A mere rehearsal could exert no power over tomorrow's event unless by its means the actors enter the primordial world of 'other days' and 'once upon a time'.

Although this may explain the long survival of ritual (and it applies in the Neolithic and Iron Age and today), it does not account for its origin. There is another possible explanation. Now that we are beginning to understand so much more about the real nature of animals by studying them in the wild, and not in captivity, what impresses most is the rigid formality of their behaviour, bound by strict laws of hierarchy, territory, group responsibilities, compared to which the lives of 'primitive traditional' peoples seem actually spontaneous and free, though, compared with ourselves, so rigid and enclosed. It is as though it were exactly the formality and the rigidity that is the animal inheritance; while it is the breaks in the tradition, the great innovations, above all the sense of history that are human. Ritual transformed the more elaborate, instinctive actions of animals, and myth explained what the ritual transformed. However we account for it, each new advance creates a new environment, the impact of which on the human being is like experiencing the terrors of a metamorphosis such as we feel today from the impact of sub-atomic physics.[71] The first creation of the work of art is itself such another break with traditional ways, and possibly a source of terror, until it has been brought into the safe formality of ritual, or locked up in a conventional image. Professor Gombrich calls one of his chapters 'Pygmalion's Power', because of the awe in which the act of creation and the created image were held in the classical world. The need for protection against that 'too much life' which the artist's skill could confer gave rise to all the stories of images that come to life if not chained down, or which are left imperfect in some detail. The conventional, the stylized, the unfinished figure is safer than a too life-like imitation. Willendorf and Kostienki are faceless, Ostrava Petřkovice has neither head nor legs. This may be the real reason why the Dolní Věstonice faces are crooked.

Not the least important question is what kind of people the artists were who tried to use this dangerous power. We know that they were gifted with great manual dexterity, and also that they were capable of the detachment and the sustained effort necessary to turn a mental image into an object wholly independent of themselves. I think we also know where to look for them. In those inaccessible or inhospitable places where primitive hunting societies survive today we find that they have their wise men, medicine-men, shamans. Wherever they are found, these specialists have much in common: they hold positions of authority or superior prestige, and they mediate between ordinary people and the surrounding powers, natural and supernatural. Most to the purpose of this study is the particular shamanism of the northern hunters and fishers: the Yakuts, Buriats, and Samoyeds of Siberia, and also the Lapps and Eskimo. As the character of the shaman will recur fairly often in the following pages, he must be briefly described.

The name comes from Siberia, where he is also called *tabid*. The Eskimo have their *angekok*, and the Lapps their *noi'de*, but in Siberia there were also women who were *shamankas*. The climate, the landscape, and the life of these northern hunters, with whom we may include the Ainu of northern Japan, is probably closer to that of Upper Paleolithic man in Europe during the last ice age than any other today; only the great animals have disappeared, the mammoth, rhinoceros, and cave-bear. It has been said of the Lapp religion that it belongs to the 'archaic residue of a once coherent Eurasian, perhaps circumpolar, hunting culture', which implies an unbroken tradition from the Upper Paleolithic, and there is purely archaeological evidence for such a tradition. Moreover, all the circumpolar religions have in common the shaman's techniques of ecstasy, the soul-flight, the activities of guardian spirits, the use of drums as a means to exaltation, the companionship and conversation with birds and animals in a special language, the healing powers and the mastery of fire.[72] During his initiation, the shaman has generally met an animal, or some object, which reveals to him its language. The shamanic session begins with an appeal to the guardian spirits and conversation in the secret language; then follows drumming and dancing, in which movements of animals and birds are imitated; and it culminates with the deep trance of the shaman when the soul is believed to have left the body. In the old Lapp religion myths are said to be of less importance than the religious life that revolves around the *noi'de*, who alone has access to the spiritual powers, and in the veneration shown to certain places where men have felt themselves to be in touch with mysterious forces.

The man buried at Brno with such exceptional ceremony and with precious objects, including one that may be connected with fire-making, looks suspiciously like a precursor of the shaman; the fragile old woman ceremonially buried at Dolní Věstonice in a grave under mammoth bones, with the arctic fox, fastest of all the animals, in her hands, was perhaps a precursor of the *shamanka*, and both precursors of the professional artist, just as among the Eskimo shaman and medicine man are the artists. The mental equipment of these primitive people of today, though so different from our own, is exceedingly rich, and there is no reason to think that Upper Paleolithic man was poorer.

In this chapter I have had to select, isolate, and perhaps over-emphasize four strands, which are in practice closely interwoven with many others, but which more than others may help to restore the background that we need. The sense of a diffused sacredness which may erupt into everyday life and which leads eventually to the recognition of nature gods and spirits; an order of relationships the categories of which take no account of genetic barriers and which will lead to ideas of metamorphosis inside and outside this life so that it is often difficult to decide whether transmigration is meant or metamorphosis;[73] unhistorical time with its returning cycles and its corollary in 'once upon a time', milieu for the actions of ancestors, culture heroes, and gods, which will lead to sophisticated literary myth and rituals; and finally the character and position of the medicine man or shaman, which we thought we saw prefigured in Moravia. It is the same composite being that hovers on the verge of history: prophet, poet, musician, sage, healer, divine leader of men, and guardian of popular religious tradition and of legends, united in one divine man whose supernatural prestige still enveloped a Pythagoras or Empedocles, and who at some point in his descent had joined hands with culture heroes like Orpheus, Musaeus, and the Hyperborean Apollo. Except for Prometheus and Daidalos, the classical tradition has not retained that one of his functions most important to us – his powers as artist – but other civilizations have.[74]

It is now time to return to the questions with which this section opened; questions concerning not 'the beginning of art', which is unknowable, but the earliest art that we actually know. There is a very ancient theory according to which representation began as the projection of a mental image on to some natural formation which had suggested it: a rock surface, lump of earth, or tree-trunk.[75] This could possibly be said of the engraved and painted caves, but we now know that the paintings are much later than the sculpture which has been the subject of this chapter. The theory *could* be extended to some sculpture in the round. A stick or stone may suggest a face and, with only a little added or subtracted, be turned into something more convincing; but it is a much bigger step from such an *objet trouvé* to Plates 4 and 5; and the earliest drawings, apart from hypothetical scrawlings in sand, snow, or mud, seem in fact to have been very small, very formal scratched outlines on pebbles and flakes of stone which are almost as remote from the cave paintings as the sculpture (Plate 14). I suspect that this will prove to have been a false scent.

It has been said that the Greeks were the first to overcome 'the psychological pull towards the distinctive conceptual image that dominated representation' before them.[76] This fits very well the Dolní Věstonice clay lady and the breast idols, and still more the ivory from Lespugue and the schematic engraving from Předmostí; but it does not fit the leopard from the Vogelherd, which is as early, nor the lumbering bear from the Pavlov hills. It takes no account of the Dolní Věstonice ivory face, which is neither an ideal head nor a caricature but is closer to a likeness than anything else. The same may be suspected of the Brno II man, but the fragmentary condition hinders judgement. We have seen that the Ostrava Petřkovice torso prefigures in its proportions and pose those of a classical Venus and the Graces; and that, with a little cheating, a hint of a Renaissance Venus can be surprised in one of the Laussel reliefs. There will be other such coincidences, but because of the great age of these figures they are perhaps the most significant.

I think that we must admit that our Upper Paleolithic sculptors, possessing in full 'Pygmalion's Power' and a consciousness of its perils, went a long way beyond the presentation of a conceptual image and towards direct imitation of nature. Nor can there have been anything merely instinctive or automatic in the imitation. The preparation and carving of mammoth tusks, and still more of hard haematite, was concentrated, cold-blooded labour compared with tracing a line on a wall or in a cave floor. It entails not only making fine tools and preparing materials, but also refining and preserving a consistent image, the result of truthful observation of the world, all of which presuppose certain immensely complicated psychological processes which must be essentially the same as those experienced by artists everywhere and in all ages.

So up to a point the aim at a likeness comes before, or as soon as, attempts to rival creation; matching is as old as making. But, so much allowed, we also know that the Willendorf statuette and the Laussel relief were coloured with red ochre, like the bodies of prehistoric, and even some contemporary, dead; the Ostrava Petřkovice woman was carved out of red haematite, the colour of blood and so of life. Painting the image, like painting the dead body, gave it life and was an act of an order similar to the 'feeding' of images (see below), and the crushing of bone and fat said to have been used with the clay of modelled animals. Here the artist is imitating nature, not in her appearances only, but in the manner of her workings. Perhaps we can draw a parallel from the far more ancient genesis of language. In language there is no such thing as wholly passive reproduction, for reproduction presupposes an inner production; this never consists in tracing, line for line, a specific content, but in selecting some pregnant motif and producing a characteristic outline of its form. Imitation is becoming representation. In language, as in creative art, the image of the object is more freely formed than in mere mechanical imitation; mimetic or analogical expression gives way to purely symbolic, which again by virtue of something 'other' in itself becomes the vehicle for a new and deeper spiritual content.[77] This is the same as 'making before matching'. The making takes place within the mind of the artist; the motifs are suggested by the world around him. The observing, selecting, producing, and representing of the Upper Paleolithic artist are only conceivable in terms of the observing, selecting, producing, and representing brought into use in the creation of language, and to some extent in the shaping of a regular stone hand-axe a quarter of a million years before. We must be content to do without intermediate stages.

The last question put to this small collection of sculpture and drawing concerns whom, or what, the figures portray. It is no easier to answer, and the temptation to make ethnographic comparisons is strong but can only be indulged with the greatest caution; here again the Lapps and Siberian hunter-fishers may be the least misleading.

Among the Lapps there is an ancient cult of gods or spirits called *seite* which served the community and the family. Some were represented in the form of small wooden statues; others inhabited natural rocks or the tops of mountains that were holy places of the cult. The *seite* is widely thought to be a relic of prehistoric hunting and fishing cultures, preserved by the intervening reindeer-nomads. The sacred statues and rocks are at the same time the dwelling of the spirit, the spirit itself, and its visual manifestation.[78] There is a 'great spirit' linked with a wooden pillar which is thought of as the world's axis, and this belief is so widely held that it too may be inherited from the old circumpolar culture. There was also an order of beings called *saivo* living under the earth, often in sacred mountains, whose existence parallels that of men and who are associated with the land of the dead, transmigration of souls, and reincarnation. There are Lapp bear-hunting rites and bear-graves, and this bear cult spread round the polar north to the

Ainu of Japan; a memory has lingered in Europe in Artemis Brauron and in Pyrenean bear-dances and mimes. Finally the Lapps had mother- and birth-goddesses. Ostiaks and Yakuts living in Siberia make female figures of larch and aspen wood called *Dzuli*, who they believe were the originators of mankind and protectors of the family and the race. When the hunters leave the hut it is given into the guardianship of the *Dzuli*, and when they return they feed it with gristle and fat, the fruits of the successful hunt, while they repeat 'make us stay healthy, make us catch more game'.[79]

It is unfortunate that the nude female figures have been indiscriminately labelled 'Venuses', concentrating attention on their erotic or fertility aspect, and reducing something much more complex and less well defined to the inappropriate categories of a later mythology. Some look pregnant and may be concerned with the risks and anxieties of child-bearing, which, in the severe conditions of the ice age, must have been very great. Infant mortality will have been high, the bearing of healthy children of prime importance, and the employment of supernatural aids, among which were perhaps the statuettes, not surprising. But other figures certainly are not pregnant, and an answer to their meaning may lie in the sedentary life of the carvers, which gave a new solidarity to the family and to blood relationship through the mother. Life in houses with its returns to hearth and home enhanced the standing of the mother as woman, and perhaps as 'wise-woman' or *shamanka*. In Siberia, through her spiritual powers the *shamanka* aids the hunt, although she does not take part in it.

It could be argued that the number of statues found in houses – Kostienki, Gagarino, Mezin, Maltá, Dolní Věstonice, Předmostí, Mainz – has no other significance than their better chance of survival and discovery, and that the practice of burying the dead inside the houses was yet another factor; but the number of female figures found in or near the hearth may also be significant. Among them are the Dolní Věstonice clay figure, Ostrava Petřkovice, and some from Kostienki and Lespugue. Among primitive people it is often the women who are the fire-makers and who 'possess' fire, a role of even greater importance before the discovery of fire-*making*. The occasional wildfire captured by men and carried back to the camp is kept alive by the women. The woman guarding the fire protects the family and becomes the centre of the social gathering; later she begins to explore the chemistry of cooking.

Among the Ainu, whose relationship to Paleolithic hunters is much the same as that of the Lapps, the goddess of the hearth is supremely respected. She is regarded as a loving old woman; her symbol, a stick with wood-shavings, stands by the hearth; and so, living in the house, she knows the personal affairs of the family and attends to their prayers. Hestia, according to Herodotus, was one of the older gods, older than Prometheus.[80]

Some of the smaller figures with holes through them were probably carried about on the person, but the Brno II man would have been too large and may have stood in a 'shrine' like figures from Russian sites. The old woman of Dolní Věstonice, buried with her fox in her hands, reminds us of the Anatolian 'mistress of animals' with her leopards. It was from Anatolia that the Cretan *potnia theron* probably came, the Bronze Age goddess who was also Eileithyia the divine midwife, 'who brings forth the young both of beasts and men into the light of day and she fosters them'.[81] As Artemis she lived on into classical antiquity, keeping her bears at Brauron.

This brings us back to the Laussel lady with a bison horn (Plate 19). The horn makes her a much more complex symbol than the single figures that preceded her. The Neanderthal men of La Chapelle-aux-Saints buried mammoth tusks in a trench, and at Brno tusks were laid in a bed of ochre by men of *sapiens* race. These were the early manifestations of a belief concerning tusks, horns, and antlers according to which the head contained the procreative element, a source of fertilizing liquid, and horns were a concentration of the life substance or psyche. Ideas like this were common to Scandinavia, Iran, Greece, Palestine, and Celtic lands. From them there stem the altar horns of Israel and Crete, the gilding of the horns of the sacrificial ox, the Iranian belief in an ox's horn as the tree of life, and the horned tiaras and helmets of gods and warriors everywhere[82] (Plates 200 and 207). In addition, hunters and farmers must have known that the growth of horns and antlers is connected with the sexual cycle of animals. From this set of ideas we have the horn of plenty, the cornucopia, a source of all new-born creatures and of fruits, and itself an embodiment of procreative power and the fertilizing rain. So at Laussel two very potent symbols make contact, the naked lady and the horn of plenty, not forgetting the unicorn. It is too early at this date to look for altars and altar horns, but the Laussel site certainly bears some of the marks of a sanctuary.

These can only be regarded as hints towards, not a single identity, but many connected identities: the huntress, guardian of animals, guardian of fire, midwife, mother, lover. It is the same with the animals; we would be unwise to take *them* quite at their face value either. Some may have been used in the hunters' rituals when the death of the victim was re-enacted, but this victim was sometimes a profane source of food, sometimes a supernatural being, and then it was the death of a god.

These are not concepts only, and not imitations only; they are symbols in another and more advanced order of symbolism than that of conventional signs and language. We will never know who or what Willendorf was, still less Předmostí, but we can apply to them, as to Christian or Buddhist art, a three-fold division into the material of the image, the parts of the image (or imagery), and a transcendent idea (the reality symbolized).[83] At Willendorf stone is the material, the exaggerated physical characteristics are the imagery; only the transcendent idea (to us that of a grossly fat brooding pregnant woman) is beyond our reach. Předmostí is much more intellectualized, and is so unlike the objects of every day life that it would be impossible to mistake it for anything but an image in the sense of the New Testament ikon, 'the very essence of a thing made visible in its image'. As the Emperor Julian says in a letter: '. . . our fathers established statues and altars, and the maintenance of undying fire, and generally speaking everything of the sort as symbols of the presence of the gods, not that we should regard such things as gods, but that we may worship the gods through them. . . . Therefore, when we look at the images let us not indeed think they are stones or wood, but neither let us think they are the gods themselves. . . . He who loves the gods delights to gaze on the images . . . he feels reverence and shudders in awe of the gods who look at him from the unseen world.'[84] The symbols in any language will inevitably die when their images are treated as ends in themselves, and this is as true of Paleolithic art as of any other.

Before turning to the infinitely richer and more prolific art of the caves, and the small art of the reindeer hunters, we can summarize this chapter as showing that, contrary to accepted ideas, the higher art of Europe begins neither exclusively with obese female figurines, which have been dismissed as 'little more than symbols of fertility', nor with imaginary projections on the stalagmite of cave walls, but with a quite large, naturalistically carved man, with animals carved or modelled naturalistically in the round, with carved human heads that may be portraits of living models, and with a young female nude whose proportions are those of the classical Mediterranean ideal of woman. The others of course exist: the minimum tool-like images, breast idols, patterns and constructions. Because of their immense age and rarity, we tend to regard all as of equal merit; but as well as the masterpieces there were no doubt many run-of-the-mill products, popular versions, and personal fetishes. We have sometimes over- as well as under-estimated the scant relics of the past. Paleolithic artists established two poles of art: on the one hand an irregular object of utility was given unnatural regularity and beauty – the symmetry of the stone tool; on the other a regular object, tusk or ball of clay, was given naturalistic, imitative, irregularity and beauty – the modelled and carved figure or head.

CHAPTER 2

UPPER PALEOLITHIC ART: 15,000–8000

> ... the glitter
> Of glaciers, the sterile immature mountains intense
> In the abnormal day of the world, and a river's
> Fan-like polyp of sand.
>
> W. H. Auden

WHEN the ice advanced for the last time to its southern limit, between 18,000 and 16,000 B.C., it covered the whole North European plain as far as Dresden in the south. The Alpine and Pyrenean glaciers also spread lower into the valleys; all over Europe it was a time of biting dry cold. Only in the extreme west near the Atlantic and in sheltered valleys in Spain, the Dordogne, and even on the west coast of Denmark, did milder, wetter oceanic weather prevail, allowing a richer growth of trees and plants. Generally the landscape was cold tundra, or only a little less bleak *taiga*; trees were scrubby and stunted, growing only in valleys near the ice, but grasses, sedges, and flowers abounded in the summer months, springing up over a permanently frozen subsoil. The white *dryas octopetela*, artemisia, and rumex made sweet summer browsing for reindeer. It was in fact a landscape excellently suited to the support and movement of large herds of grazing animals: wild cattle and horse, bison and mammoth.

When the final retreat of the ice began about 16,000 it was very slow, and there were several temporary halts, reversals, warmer interludes, and 'oscillations'. One of these came about 15,000, and at about this time the paintings of Lascaux in the Dordogne were begun; as this is also the most studied and perhaps the finest of the caves, it is a good moment to start a new chapter. There were later oscillations around 11,000 and 9500, and from at least 12,000 forests were spreading up from the Mediterranean coast into Central and Northern Europe. This was to be a massive invasion that swallowed the grasslands, bringing forest animals, elk and red and roe deer, to supplant those of the tundra, the barrens, and the steppe. Between 12,000 and 8000 the level of the ocean and of the North Sea rose rapidly as water was released from the melting ice, rivers were swollen, the old shore-line submerged, and another new epoch began.[1]

The recent lowering of dates for the later phases of the Upper Paleolithic has brought the need to reconsider the great pioneering systems, classifications, and 'cycles' of art. Most archaeologists now believe that the greater part of the work in the caves and shelters falls between Late Solutrian and Magdalenian IV, a period spanning some four to five thousand years (see Table 1).[2] Naturalistic sculpture, as we have seen, had achieved maturity almost with its first appearance, and even seemed to be declining into formalism at Lespugue and Maltá. There was to be a remarkable renaissance during our period, but, instead of the image of man, it is now the animals about him that we see. Some of the later Magdalenian carving is extremely delicate, even exquisite, and much of the best was produced in Magdalenian IV, before 12,000, but it continued till Magdalenian VI (10,000–9000), when it was in full decline.

Relief sculpture, after a much later start, did not reach its finest expression till some time in the Early Magdalenian, but it is to graphic art above all that the major systems of classification were applied, and in graphic art reassessment is most necessary. Carbon 14 dates, used with proper safeguards (see above, Chapter 1, Note 17), along with stratigraphical work are helping to amplify and correct the stylistic criteria. Up to the present most of the new work has been destructive. Dating by superpositions of paintings and engravings no longer carries much weight, since there is no means of telling how long (or short) a time separates the upper from the lower subject; and the persistence of identical 'stereotypes' for long periods reduces the value once given to the likeness, sometimes very striking, between a 'sketch' of a subject found buried in an archaeologically dated level and the finished work on the wall of a cave.[3] The fine engravings, like the paintings to which they are often joined, usually lie far away from the places where men lived. They are rare before about 15,000, but increase at the same time as new and more refined tools in bone and antler begin to appear, that is to say, the typical Magdalenian equipment. To some extent in Italy and the Alps and very much in Eastern Europe, including Russia, the old Gravettian cultures with their traditional small carved figures in the round and their domestic and funerary customs lasted longer.

The importance of the climatic phase beginning around 16,000 as a turning-point is shown therefore by the new tools, weapons, and techniques of the hunters, as well as by new developments in art. While the open country still teemed with animals, man also could travel easily great distances, following the herds and pitching his camp on migration routes between summer and winter grazings. The summer camps were probably lightly built shelters and wind-breaks in valleys down which flowed the melt-water from the glaciers. A little before 13,000 reindeer hunters, some of them perhaps from South-East Europe, were going as far north as Schleswig Holstein. Among the animals whose bones are found in their summer camps many were calves of one or two summers, and from these and other bones it seems that the hunters were only there from June to September. On the other hand animal bones found in shallow caves and shelters used by Middle Magdalenian men in western France include hinds and young deer carrying their antlers, the buck alone having lost theirs, and this agrees with occupation during the winter months. The fragile bones of arctic grouse tell the same story, for when snow is on the ground these birds prefer running to flying and are easy to trap. At least one is shown in an engraving from the Pyrenean cave of Isturitz, and not a few of the Lascaux painted ponies have their long winter coats (Plate 54).

In numbers man himself was still a comparatively rare animal, but the open grassland with wooded sheltered valleys allowed him not only to travel easily between summer and winter hunting grounds, but also to have the sort of occasional encounters with other groups of men that would stimulate his development, the growth of intellect and complexity of manners; qualities also valuable to the artist. All that we know of later history corroborates the belief that isolation is fatal, contact essential to a creative civilization and arts. Climate and landscape very like this had existed at other times during the Upper Paleolithic, but apparently, except in a few places in Eastern Europe, the human creature was not yet ready to take advantage of them. They existed less and less towards the end of this five-thousand-year-long period; and finally they did not exist at all, when forest had colonized the whole of the European plain. When this happened the great herds disappeared, for there was less room for free ranging, and less food. Men took to hunting in smaller parties after smaller game, using different techniques. They too were cut off from many of their old haunts. Farther east there was less alteration and more continuity.

Studies of Late Paleolithic art nearly always divide it into two distinct bodies, large and small; cave-paintings with the large reliefs, and portable objects; 'parietal' and 'mobiliary'. Under different labels the division is much the same.[4] The plan adopted here is rather different, for it takes its two main divisions first from art in three dimensions – sculpture and modelling – and then in two dimensions – painting and engraving, irrespective of the size of the work. If we think in the first place of the artist in his craft, instead of the work of art as it is 'received' and 'used', then we see on the one hand the draughtsman or painter and his problems, his experiments in perspective and two-dimensional representation, and on the other the sculptor and modeller with a quite different set of problems.

Two-dimensional art may be 'large' on walls or ceilings, or 'small' on bone antler and loose stones. The earliest drawings show the artificiality of the mobiliary–parietal division; for most are very small and scratched on stone that has flaked from the walls to become embedded in the floor and ultimately dug out among tools of stone or bone, but because of scale and accident of discovery this is classified as 'mobiliary'. In the map on pp. xxxiv–xxxv, carving in the round is spread over a greater area than two-dimensional work, with a concentration in France and Spain; even so the difference is not so marked as on maps made according to the usual division. In fact graphic art is almost as extended as sculpture, especially if we include paintings in the Urals.[5] Engravings from Germany, Switzerland, and Czechoslovakia are not inferior to, or different in style from, those in the great centres in Spain and France. The plodding horse with frozen matted coat, engraved according to true perspective on a bone from Schweizersbild on Lake Constance, belongs to the same style, one could almost say the same 'school', as the head of a horse at Lascaux, another at Los Casares in eastern Spain, or the painted horses of Niaux (Ariège) (Plates 34, 35, and 36).[6] It is the same with reindeer from Petersfels in Baden and Les Combarelles in the Dordogne, or mammoth from Maltá in Siberia and from the Dordogne. One curious example of similarity is the jawbone of a horse found in a Magdalenian level in the Pekarna cave in Moravia, on which are engraved three horse-heads, back to front in a sort of whirligig, which is very nearly the same arrangement as the three horse-heads carved in the round from Mas d'Azil (Ariège) (Plate 29 and Figure 7). The same techniques, the same stereotypes are common from the Carpathians to the Atlantic and from the northern plain to the Mediterranean; but if quality is equal, quantity is not. Although there are caves, and good limestone, in other parts of Europe (for instance in Czechoslovakia) and the search has been as intense, the results have been meagre. It is not the artist who is limited, tied down to a few square miles in the 'Franco-Cantabrian zone', but only the monuments, the painted caves and carved shelters, that are limited. These regions, crowded with sites, are the Athens, the Byzantium, the Île de France of their age. The particular climate and ecology of Europe may itself be responsible for these great concentrations. The annual return, following the game on its customary routes, would ensure the same neighbourhoods being frequented with enough regularity for the formation and continuation of 'styles' and 'traditions' which can now be recognized as particular to a neighbourhood, or even to one cave. At the same time this movement, repeated and regular, would prevent the segregation of special clans or tribes who alone, greatly gifted, produced the great paintings and drawings. I prefer to think, therefore, that this was an art of Upper Paleolithic man in Europe as a whole, although its monuments are confined to a comparatively small hilly and mountainous region. The five thousand odd years of this great phase of art is a very long time, though far shorter than that allowed in the older systems. But it is not too long for the continuance of a single tradition. There is as little alteration in three thousand years of Egyptian art.

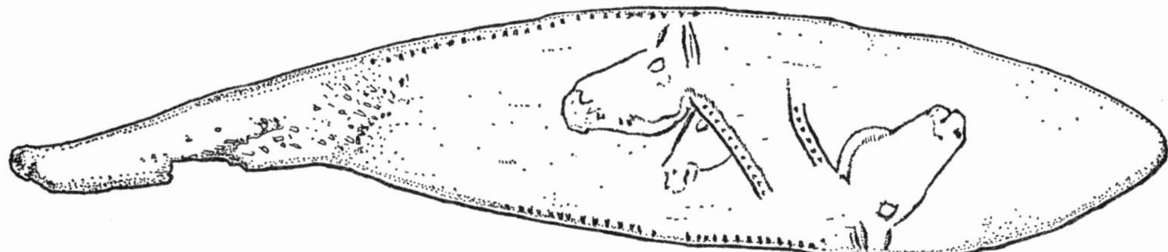

Figure 7. Engraved bone from Pekarna, Czechoslovakia

The engravings, and still more the paintings, that have survived are a small part of what must have existed, even in those caves that have been well explored. Atmospheric and water action were at their work of destruction from the beginning. Water oozing through limestone causes the face of walls and ceilings to flake away, or concretions of calcite form over paintings and engravings. Lichens, mosses, and algae eat into them, or they are buried under stalagmite, and where the surface has remained dry, chemical action may change the colour of the background and confuse the outlines so that what is left is still only a fragment. Lascaux is a comparatively small, shallow cave, which an accidental sealing-off may have helped to preserve; but on the whole it is the deepest, least accessible places which have suffered least from time. At Les Combarelles in the Dordogne, which stretches horizontally for 260 yards (237 m.), any paintings there once were in the first hundred yards from the entrance have been completely destroyed. In a limestone cave a constant temperature of 50° F day and night and 96–97° air moisture actually preserves painting, but this can only be found at great depths. Hot air in summer condensing on the walls, and in winter the cold air pouring in to take its place, are equally destructive. The irruption of the twentieth century into Lascaux almost brought disaster, and has led to intense research into the particular balance of temperature and humidity that had preserved the paintings so long.[7] Their future, it seems, can only be assured by virtually excluding the world. Many more paintings no doubt lie invisible under formations of calcite, the *mal blanc* that has appeared recently also at Lascaux.

All these agents of destruction, at work over many thousands of years, may account for the absence of paintings; they do not explain why paintings are found at great depths and vast distances from the outside world, and sometimes in positions extremely difficult to reach and even to see; nor the apparently arbitrary choice of one rather than another passage or gallery. This question of situation belongs to a different order of problems from the purely mechanical; it is an aspect of prehistoric art that immediately and powerfully impresses everyone who has visited the caves, especially the tortuous labyrinths like Tuc d'Audoubert, where earlier visitors crawled, waded, and groped the 700 odd yards of the approach to the 'bison hall', or the 900 yards between daylight and the *salon noir* at Niaux.

The drive to enter the darkness of deep caves is probably too ancient for explanation. It may have its beginnings long before the capture of fire had made them safe to live in. Many animals, including monkeys and apes, that normally would not enter a cave, when sick or dying creep away from the band and hide in deep clefts or far down cavernous passages. Perhaps the cool, moist darkness eased the fever of wounds and disease, and this early role of caves, linked at a deep level with the circumstances of illness, death, and sometimes recovery, may still have acted, even if subconsciously, on men of the Upper Paleolithic.[8]

Most studies of Paleolithic art have been more concerned with interpretation, with the possible religious, magical, mythological, and social aspects of what is portrayed, than with the portrayal itself.[9] For the moment it is this last that I want to explore, in spite of the great difficulty. At the point in time at which we have now arrived, 15,000 B.C., the Paleolithic artist, as much as any later, was working within a tradition. This means that he was subject to all the forces of tradition, the burden and ballast as well as the stimulus and inspiration; the repetitions of conventional *schemata* and their infinitesimal alterations. We find the same rhythm of *schema* and correction that can be followed throughout the art of Europe in historical ages. But here the student of prehistoric art at once runs into difficulties due to the rarity of chronological signposts and the great lapse of time that must be bridged between them. The gaps, though much fewer than before, are still great enough to make perilous any description according to strictly stylistic evolution. They are not of millennia, but neither are they yet of decades and half-centuries. Shortening of the time-scale allows us, for example, to see the whole series of Lascaux paintings as very possibly falling within a few generations (omitting some of the palpably later engravings).[10] All the same, when using 'tradition' in this context it is better to think of the dividing and interlacing of connected branches than of a single stem; of overlapping continuities rather than a single continuum.

The same experiments and discoveries may have been made in different places at different times, but there *is* a recognizable connexion between them. The individual works of art are no longer isolated like the unique and, for the most part, indecipherable landmarks of earlier ages, the Brno carving or the Předmostí drawing, but we still cannot place them in the irreversible sequences of historical schools.

Sculpture and Modelling

Of *large* sculpture in the round there is extremely little in the caves and none outside them. The little that does exist is modelled, not carved. The reason often given, and it is probably correct, is the great difficulty of pecking and cutting hard rock with crude stone hammers and fragile flint burins. At any time this was laborious, stubborn work, but in the cramped conditions of the caves, in darkness lit by poor lamps of hollowed stone with wicks of moss, it was out of the question. The painter and the engraver using a fine sharp line could achieve clear results in a short time, but the sculptor must stay outside in the daylight, as in fact he did. The exceptions, the animals modelled in clay, are in two of the deepest and most intricate caves, Tuc d'Audoubert (Ariège) (Figure 23) and Montespan (Haute-Garonne). The clay must have been soft when the end gallery at Tuc d'Audoubert, 750 yards from the entrance, was in use, for it has preserved in it many footprints, and where it was wettest there are little collapsed heaps that may have been clay figures; but in a dryer part of the gallery were found two almost perfect clay bison, 25 and 24 inches (63 and 61 cm.) long, a bull following a cow (Plate 20). In front and on the ground lay a much smaller bison. The two large ones are half supported by a block of stalagmite. The modelling is quite accomplished, particularly the head, with nostril, eye, and horns; the hairy crest is marked by incision in the clay, and the pose has a stiffness that is not unnatural to the animal. These are not completely three-dimensional figures, and there is some flattening. Concentration on a profile pose suggests an artist more used to relief than to sculpture in the round. The sides of the animals have been deeply dented in several places, perhaps with deliberately inflicted wounds.

At Montespan the work is very inferior. Several lumps of clay have been roughly shaped into the bodies of bears. There are no heads, but bony fragments from the skull of a real bear were found lying in front of the best preserved of the bodies, that of a life-size animal crouching with paws on the ground. The skull and the stabbed clay suggest that the bodies were dummies over which was thrown a bearskin mantle with the head attached. This is not art in any real sense, but rather another of those tools of cult, meaningless without the clothing of furs, mystery, and ceremonies. They are, however, in their limited way, free-standing, three-dimensional figures.

If there was ever a flourishing school of modelling within the caves, its monuments have long ago dissolved into shapelessness with damps and time. As far as we know today, large sculpture in the round was never to be attempted by Upper Paleolithic artists; any desire for the monumental found expression in relief. The large models of Montespan cannot compare with the older, but far smaller clay bears of the Pavlov hills (Plate 7). Yet Magdalenian artists *did* attempt to represent the plastic quality of matter in relief, in painting, and in the small carvings in bone and antler. In this small-scale work the sculpture of the older period had its sequel. It achieved great refinement, and sometimes a degree of standardization that is almost industrial.[11] Objects are conceived so as to be viewed from two sides, like two reliefs cut out and stuck back to back (Plate 26). One reason may be the limitations of the material, the plate-like surfaces of the antler palm, the narrow rods and tubes of bone and tine. No carving in wood has survived, and there may have been more freedom in using the softer and more amenable material.

Many of the small carvings are also meant for use as tools or weapons, like the spear-thrower from Mas d'Azil (Ariège) carved with a fawn or young ibex (Plate 24). The fawn is well observed and lovingly portrayed, particularly the head with the strained muscle of the neck, though there is a purely formal inner line incised from fore- to hind-leg, which shows that even this was a conventional rendering, an often repeated *schema*; and there is in fact another fawn, from Bédeilhac, just like it, except that the legs are tucked up in an attitude natural to the animal and convenient to the carver. It was to be repeated untold times throughout the later history of animal art. Here there is perfect adaptation of the natural animal to the limitations of the material – a shaft and palm of reindeer antler. The full-grown ibex, also from Mas d'Azil (Plate 25), is so skilfully evolved out of the antler haft that, if viewed from directly in front, it gives the illusion of seeing the whole animal. The horns embracing the stem of antler are a decorative invention that was also used by Achaemenian and Celtic gold- and bronze-smiths. The essential requirement of a spear-thrower is that it have a hook at one end (the evacuation of Plate 24) against which the shaft of spear or javelin rested. Holes at the other end may have been for finger pegs or for a crossbar. When, as here, the palm of antler is kept and carved, this also has the practical purpose of weighting the spear-thrower, by which means the missile can be sent farther with less effort. Only fast bounding or flying creatures were chosen for spear-thrower carvings.[12]

In work on so small a scale, limitation of pose and the representation of *pars pro toto* may have been forced on the artist. A whole animal, leggy and long-necked, could be and was engraved on narrow bone or antler (Plate 34 and Figure 11D), but those fragile extended limbs, if carved in the round, would never have survived day-to-day use. So the artists became adapters and opportunists. Reindeer and horses have their legs tucked under them, or the hind-legs are stretched back, almost in the vertical plane along the shaft (Plate 27). The proportions remain true, but the limbs look dislocated, which is not surprising remembering the artists' familiarity with dead and dismembered beasts. But against the number of whole animals carved there are many simple heads. There is a group of twenty-one spear-throwers, all decorated with a horse's head, all very alike, though some are from the Pyrenees, others from the Dordogne and Lake Constance: a geographical dispersal which accords with the mobility of hunters and artists, or rather hunter-artists. The three horse-heads on a very heavy spear-thrower already referred to in another connexion (Plate 29) are carved in the round, but the third, engraved on the antler shaft, shows the herbivorous teeth which naturally would be hidden by the cheek. The drawing of the fleshy ear and nose-tip show that this is not meant for a naked skull, and it is in fact one of those curious X-ray drawings which we shall meet again. The other side of the shaft has an engraving of a horse's leg on a smaller scale.

The use of *pars pro toto* on separate throwers, and on a number of still unexplained objects, so-called bâtons, is new, and in itself important. Many of the tiny clay figures from the Pavlov hills were incomplete, but there the leg of an animal or a human arm was as likely to be pinched out as the head, and at Dolní Věstonice it was breasts. In contrast, it seems that for the Magdalenian carver the head *was* the animal, just as for us the head on a coin or a stamp *is* the sovereign. This is one of those cases, and there are many others, in which the mode of working of the Paleolithic artist is so like our own and seems so natural to us that we easily overlook what is really astonishing. Other peoples at other times add a diminutive or a distorted body to the larger head, or slight the face for some other feature (like those earlier sculptors of Central and Eastern Europe). But although the animals on the spear-throwers were probably selected because of their speed, it was the head, and not the hoof or leg, that was chosen (the leg on the Mas d'Azil thrower may have had this significance); but the simpler shorthand that seeks to convey the essence of a sound by depicting an ear was also known.

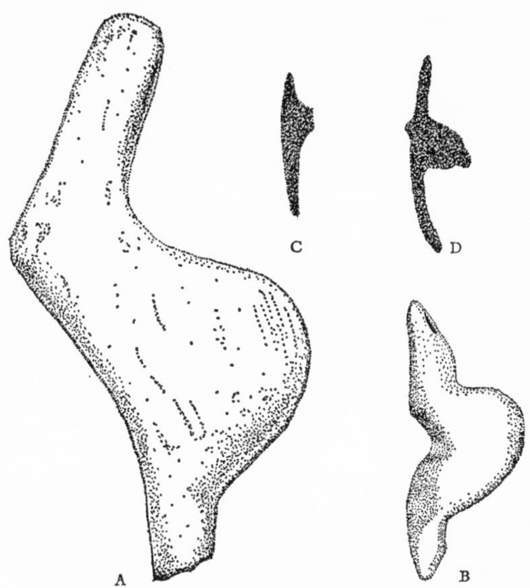

Figure 8. Simplified carvings of a woman: A bone, from Pekarna, Czechoslovakia, B jet, from Petersfels, Germany; C and D painted 'signs' at Altamira, Spain

The small carvings are far easier to date than paintings inside caves or reliefs outside them, for many lay in the débris of old fires and on camping sites in use in one or another phase of the predominating culture. Rather simple spear-throwers, for instance, are found in Magdalenian III, but the finely carved ones almost always come from Magdalenian IV. So much good carving was done in those centuries, with such an exuberant rifling of the animal world for subjects, that it is possible to speak of an 'explosion'. Thereafter quality and quantity fall away, though carvings of a sort were still done in the tenth millennium.[13]

Among subjects carved, it is useless to look for the image of man. The Lespugue lady, perhaps the latest of the older body of sculpture, may be very little earlier than the animal carving of Magdalenian III and IV (see above); but although she was found in the Haute-Garonne surrounded by the work of Magdalenian painters and carvers, she comes from a different world. There is one sort of small objects, hardly works of art, that have rather the same relation to the female figure as the breast idols of Dolní Věstonice, but now the buttocks are chosen for emphasis, while legs and body are mere prolongations. Several come from Pekarna in Moravia, but others very like them, carved in jet, were found in Magdalenian IV (possibly VI?) levels of the Petersfels cave in Baden (Figure 8, A and B). These had string-holes and were no doubt worn as pendant-amulets. The stone being soft, they are beautifully polished by use. The same shorthand applied to the engraved silhouette appears on a piece of rock in the cave of La Roche in the Dordogne, also probably Magdalenian, and still more abbreviated it becomes a 'sign' at Altamira and elsewhere (Plate 28 and Figure 8C–D). A small headless stone figure from Mauern in Bavaria is a possible point of departure for these images, and at the other end of Europe, at Mezin in the Ukraine, there are a number of small ivory figures of the same sort but covered with an elaborate engraved meander pattern (Figure 9).[14]

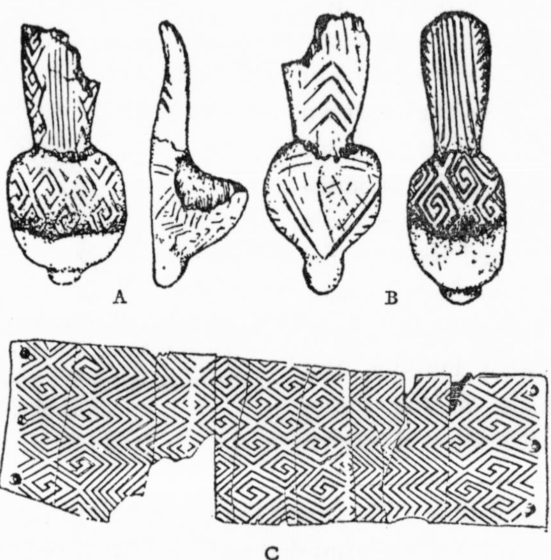

Figure 9. A and B Carved and engraved ivory figures from Mezin, Russia
C Development of pattern engraved on bone ring from Mezin, Russia

It is dangerous to generalize when a single new find may alter the entire balance, but at present it seems that Magdalenian artists were not interested in depicting the human figure in the round, though they owned fetishes ultimately derived from it.

Magdalenian Relief

Some early relief has been described. Unlike sculpture in the round there is no real break, and Early Magdalenian reliefs like Cap Blanc, Chaire à Calvin, and Angles-sur-l'Anglin carry on the same styles and techniques, though adding new subjects and more skilful handling. This art is still closely connected, by situation and subject, to deep engravings, and sometimes both techniques are used in the same place. The implications of this, and the contrast with painting and fine engraving, have been described (p. 22). Deep engraving dies out after Magdalenian III (*c.* 13,000) and no relief is *certainly* later than this, so that the end of both may possibly coincide with the beginning of fine engraving in the deeper caves. If so, the dichotomy described in the last chapter is of time as well as space.

The Roc aux Sorciers near Angles-sur-l'Anglin (Vienne) is very like other sites with reliefs, being a 160-foot-long ledge above a stream at one end of which is a small cave. Some time between 12,000 and 9000 B.C. there was a tumble of rock which brought large boulders down on top of the hearths of the Middle Magdalenian people who lived on the ledge and whose tools of bone and stone were found scattered beneath them (Trench 1). Many of the blocks are carved, and on some there are traces of paint. At the other end of the ledge, some 100 feet distant, towards the fallen boulders, excavation has uncovered carvings *in situ*.[15] At this end the ledge was still occupied in Late Magdalenian (VI) times. The reliefs are of two sorts: life-size ibexes and women, and small horses and bison. The bison are partly obliterated by the larger figures and so should be earlier. The horses are well-carved, solid little animals, and one has turned its head and is looking back over the off-side shoulder, a very rare attitude indeed.

There is great accomplishment in the carving of animals, some ibex being in especially high relief. Of great interest, because of its rarity, is a life-size bust of a man found on one of the fallen boulders.[16] It is a profile in medium relief with engraved and painted detail. Several shades of ochre have been used, a purplish red for cheeks and a brick red for the chest. Some sort of (unpainted) garment is worn over the shoulders; the hair, beard, and pupil of the eye are manganese black. This eye is shown full-face, as in the Egyptian and Cretan convention. Hair and eyelashes are engraved, and there is a criss-cross of scorings on the cheek, the same as we often find on the body of animals; some stone has flaked from the nose and lips, spoiling the profile. But apart from the peculiarity of the eye, this is a realistic portrayal of a man, neither idealized nor quite a caricature. Compared with the Dolní Věstonice head the features are coarse, but it is quite unlike the monster of Plate 71. In fact the physiognomy is very like that of some 'primitive' tribes in South-East Asia and could be a portrait from the life.

Between a group of horses and bison and another with ibexes is the most remarkable subject of the site: three life-size women's figures. They are carved from the waist downwards in low relief round a buttress of rock, while above the waist the body melts into the rocky overhang; neither heads nor feet were ever worked (Plate 33). The left-hand figure is turned slightly to the left in a three-quarter pose; the centre one is almost full-face and in higher relief, but the legs have broken away from the knees; and the third is completely frontal. A small stylized head that can be made out on the overhang does not, according to the excavators, belong to the group. Two small bison are tangled with the right-hand figure, but are probably part of an earlier design.[17] The figures are slender; the pubic triangle is emphasized, but the strong impression is of a natural, harmonious, and fluid composition. The carving of the legs, close together and slightly bent, may give the bodies their weightless, floating quality, half-materialized and billowing out from the rock face. The erotic concentration in this trio of graces, nymphs, or goddesses does not obscure the existence of an aesthetic purpose not unlike that which binds the classical and Renaissance trios of graces, goddesses, *Deae Matres*, however overlaid with sophistication, domesticity, or philosophy. But by far the

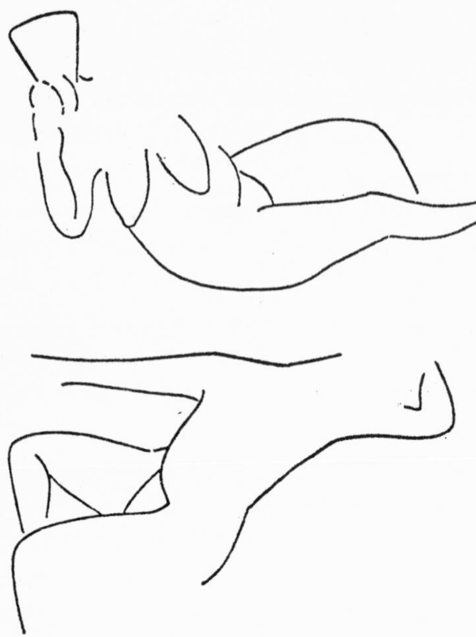

Figure 10. Outline of two relief figures at La Magdeleine, France (cf. Plates 30 and 31)

most extraordinary thing about the figures is the mastery of perspective and the three-quarter view as they half turn, like dancers in line, ready one by one to peel off and join the movement. If this seems to force too much into the thinly worked rock-face, it is fair to add that remains of paint found on other reliefs justify a suspicion that the bodies would have been coloured and the illusion of life much greater.

A hundred and twenty-five miles farther south, at La Magdeleine near Penne (Tarn), there are two reclining female nudes (the term is justified here if nowhere else), carved in deeper relief and of more assured workmanship than the Angles-sur-l'Anglin women, but only half life-size. There is not the same direct evidence for their date as at the other site, though Magdalenian man has left signs of his presence.[18] At La Magdeleine there are three shallow caves, one over the other, known since 1900, but the reliefs in the middle one of the three were only discovered in 1950. First of all on the right-hand side, 15 feet from the entrance, but still near enough to be clearly visible by the light of day, there is a horse carved in the style of those of Angles-sur-l'Anglin and other sites. At the same height, 6 feet above the ground, and another 6 feet farther in, is the reclining figure of a nude woman with her head resting on her hand (Plate 30 and Figure 10); on the opposite wall of the cave, carved in slightly higher relief, is a second reclining nude with one arm outstretched (Plate 31 and Figure 10), and under it a deeply engraved and poorly preserved bison. Both female figures have suffered a good deal of surface damage. The legs are best preserved, and the right arm of the right-hand figure. The heads can barely be made out and may never have been finished.

The reliefs have caused a good deal of astonishment because of the mastery of perspective and easy freedom of pose with its foreshadowing of classical and Renaissance art. But it is more than ever necessary here to clear our minds of preconceived ideas about the brutishness of early man, and the crudity of the Paleolithic image of man. We must forget the fat women of Willendorf, Savignano, and Gagarino, and the diminutive, half human, half animal simulacra scratched on bone or stone, or lost in the smother of animals on the walls of caves, and think instead of the classical proportions of the Ostrava Petřkovice torso, the harmony of the Angles-sur-l'Anglin group, and the sober, simplified animals of Cap Blanc.

Compared with the earlier work at Laussel, we can see the extraordinary advance in the mastery of perspective, particularly in the disposition of the legs (Plates 18 and

19). The left-hand La Magdeleine figure has the same change of direction, with front view of shoulders and side or three-quarter view of legs, as the Laussel man, but the awkwardness and the appearance of 'twist' have gone. The problem of delineation that had been too much for the Laussel artist is solved at La Magdeleine in a manner that foreshadows the whole train of reclining banqueters and river gods of classical art, Dionysus and 'Kephisus' of the Parthenon, the 'Dusk' of the Cappella Medici, and a host of others. The outstretched arm at Laussel is a male gesture that probably comes from the dart- or spear-thrower and will become the hurler of the thunderbolt, or the gesture of authority of Apollo at Olympia. The right-hand nude also owes something to Laussel, this time to the lady with the bison horn; not, that is to say, directly to Laussel, but to that state of development in bas relief of which Laussel is the only surviving example. The sharply bent arm is the same, the heavy breast and the line of the right leg. But here again the confused perspective and the clumsiness have vanished. The stiff and tortured pose is relaxed, and the perspective of the legs solved in a manner that points forward to the reclining Aphrodite or Hesperid of the Parthenon, or Michelangelo's 'Dawn', and a host of nymphs and Venuses, in which the open, relaxed pose and the arm bent back on itself are constant.

Though superficially similar, these two figures are in fact as different as 'Dawn' from 'Dusk'. The one half rising with raised arm has the same latency of action as the Angles-sur-l'Anglin figures. Moreover, in spite of careful carving of the pubic triangle, it is severe in character and almost sexless. The right-hand figure, on the contrary, if we had her whole, would probably remind us more, in her pose of sleepy abandonment, of Bellini's Demeter in the 'Feast of the Gods', or a Titian Venus, of whom she is a not discreditable forerunner.

What has happened seems to be that, between the time of Laussel and Angles-sur-l'Anglin, there was a great deal of experiment by draughtsmen exploring three dimensions in terms of two, without which, and the degree of success achieved by them, the portrayal of such complicated poses as those of La Magdeleine would be unthinkable.

The standing nude has been with us from the first as a completely realized conception, whether classical and ideal as at Ostrava Petřkovice, or realistic at Gagarino and Savignano. The reclining nude may be only half as old, and the clumsier work of Laussel shows one of the steps by which these great conventional attitudes were achieved.[19]

Twenty-five sites have been listed in South-West France where reliefs are known, either on cliffs in the open, or near the entrance of a shallow cave, or on large loose blocks; but of the twenty-five only six have human figures, and of these Roc de Sers, Laussel, Angles-sur-l'Anglin, and La Magdeleine are the most ambitious. One of the finest of the animal friezes is Cap Blanc in the Dordogne. The situation is quite typical: a terrace above a river sheltered by a limestone bank. Tools and small carved objects were found, showing occupation of the site more or less contemporary with Angles-sur-l'Anglin. The frieze is 40 feet long and shows seven large horses, some smaller bison, and other indeterminate quadrupeds, either cattle or reindeer. The horse is life-size (Plate 32), measuring 7 feet (2·15 m.) from head to tail, and the relief is exceptionally high, 12 inches (30 cm.) on the body and 4 inches (10 cm.) at the nose. The lower legs were carved in a band of inferior rock and have flaked away. The lighting of the photograph does not do justice to the modelling of the neck and body, which is sensitive without detracting from the monumentality of the whole animal. The eye is slightly hollowed, and the mane represented by hatching. Traces of red paint show that the animals were coloured as well as carved. Here and at La Chaire à Calvin (Charente), horses are the dominating animal, and their proportions and build suggest a larger beast than the 'ponies' painted at Lascaux and carved at Roc de Sers. At Commarque in the Dordogne there is perhaps the most sensitive treatment of a horse's head in all Paleolithic art. Use has been made of the irregularities of the natural rock, and the result is rightly called 'a beautiful horse'.[20] Cap Blanc, Chaire à Calvin, La Magdeleine, Angles-sur-l'Anglin and the rest would be noble monuments in any age; as it is, they are outstanding representatives of a single vigorous artistic tradition.

Line – Shading – Pattern

The earliest drawings, as we have seen, were few in number and tentative in execution. At one time a single groove was sufficient to outline an animal and present it in its natural proportions, but flat, devoid of volume, two-dimensional (Plates 16 and 17). It is a large step from this to the representation of softness, where edges are blurred by fur or hair. Yet this, as we have seen, was done at Gargas, which *may* be pre-Magdalenian, and at Isturitz and Laugerie Haute, which certainly are so (p. 18). This impressionist device was carried much further and implies real advance in the psychology of perception as well as in draughtsmanship. The artist had discovered that he need only supply enough visual clues to leave no doubt of his intention and other men's eyes would complete the image. The means employed are of the simplest, but none the less interesting because they show us that artist and beholder were using their visual experience in exactly the same way that we ourselves do when we create and accept the illusion of a three-dimensional body.

A flint burin was still the engraver's tool throughout the Upper Paleolithic, for the finest work on bone and antler, and for coarser grooves on stone. The line may be as much as 1¼ inches (3 cm.) deep, especially in the earlier work, and enormous quantities of burins must have been used up on the rock walls. Every artist had to be a skilled flint-knapper in order to keep himself supplied with his tackle.

Some of the most accomplished drawing comes from a rock shelter at La Colombière (Ain).[21] The drawings are on river pebbles, one of which has both its sides engraved with animals, one on top of another (Plate 38). One side has a shaggy horse and, upside down, a reindeer with shed antlers, an ibex, and perhaps two bears (Figure 11, A–C); the other has an excellent woolly rhinoceros with the head drawn twice and, only partly decipherable, another horse and a deer. Pebbles from the earlier excavations add a well-drawn bear, a horse, and a reindeer pierced with winged darts or, according to an interpretation referred to below, sexual symbols, and a likewise 'wounded' rhinoceros. All the animals are drawn with great assurance and life-like proportions; they are realistic and satisfying representations of their subject. These are in fact the same stereotypes that have appeared countless times in the art of the caves: the horse with thick mane, the rhinoceros with head drooped, the reindeer with the identical line of back and shoulder; these will serve till the end of the Upper Paleolithic.[22]

The drawings on pebbles provide a theoretical demonstration of the steps by which this illusionist device was achieved (Plate 38 and Figure 11). The stiff upstanding mane of a wild horse of Przewalski breed is defined, first, by a hard double groove, which is

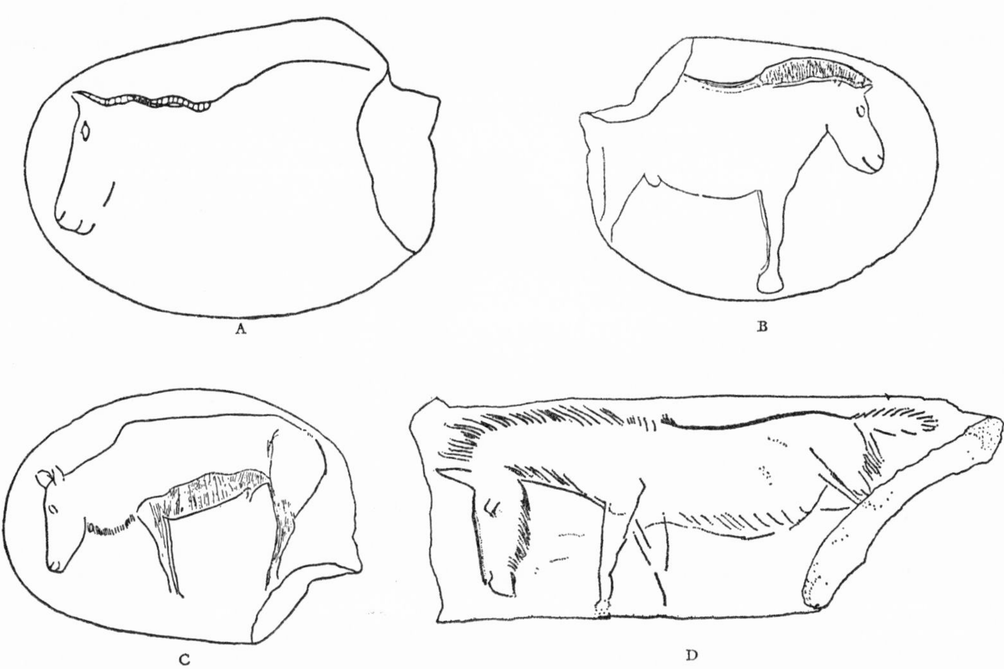

Figure 11. A, B, and C Three animal drawings superposed on a pebble from La Colombière, France (cf. Plate 38)
D Engraving on bone from Mas d'Azil, France

itself a continuation of the animal's back, and on the same pebble the long hair on a reindeer's neck is rendered impressionistically with a few detached strokes. There is no outline because the contour of the neck is hidden, and the same technique is used on the hairy monster (Plate 77) and the bone from Mas d'Azil (Figure 11D).

The artist who cut the single confident line of bear's or horse's back, and who can suggest with light strokes the long hair under the reindeer's throat, is no novice. These beasts are all carefully executed on durable material, and yet in spite of this, as art, they are ephemeral. The drawing of the different animals is hopelessly intermingled, and only great care and patience can disentangle the subjects. Quite unlike the carefully preserved small sculpture, which was sometimes carried into the grave, this is an art of action. The value must have rested in the act of scratching each consecutive subject, for there was no shortage of materials. The river that flowed just in front of the shelter of La Colombière carried any number of smooth pebbles. It was the individual pebble that, through the special treatment it had received, acquired essential value, like a medieval reliquary or images 'not made with human hands'. We do not need the darts protruding from the belly of the deer and the rhinoceros, or according to another interpretation the male and female 'signs', to tell us that these are *res sacra*, and not mere likenesses of animals.[23]

The La Colombière shelter was a summer camp, and this group of people who lit their fires under the rock, and left their engraved ikons in the hearth, were probably following the herds of migrating reindeer, ibex, and wild horses, all animals of the arctic tundra. For this landscape will have been very like that of Greenland today, with its strong winds in summer that cover the ground with fine dust, only grasses and

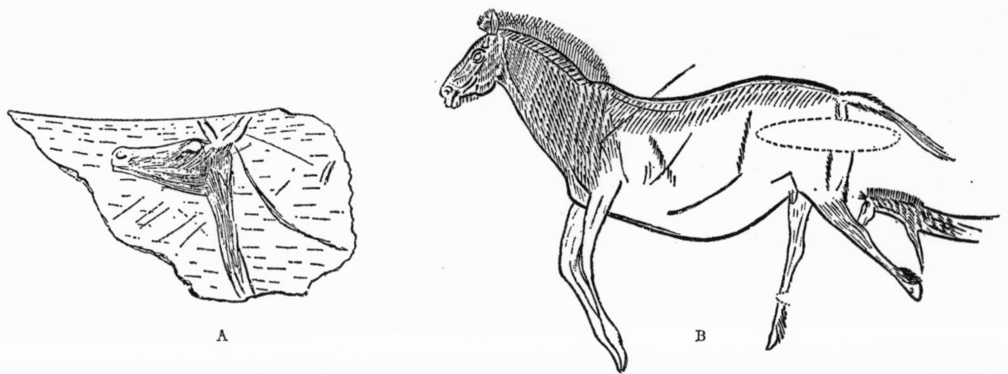

Figure 12. A Deer's head engraved on bone from Altamira, Spain
B Engraving on bone from La Mairie à Teyjat, France

sedges growing in sheltered valleys, and a few dwarf birch and willow. If the modern analogy holds, the great animal herds will have come up as near as they could get to the perpetual ice to escape the plague of summer insects. The reindeer of Figure 11C had shed its antlers in the late spring; so it was probably drawn then or at the very beginning of the summer.

A beautiful example of Magdalenian drawing is the horse from Schweizersbild (Plate 34). The contour of the body is suggested, but not defined, under the matted hair of mane and coat. Line and natural perspective are used to give the appearance of weight and volume, the illusion of reality. This engraving is one of the masterpieces of prehistoric art; but essentially the same technique is used for the horse's head engraved at Lascaux (Plate 35), another impressed in soft clay at Montespan (Ariège), and the head drawn in black paint at Niaux (Plate 36).

Shading as a first stage of chiaroscuro is a quite advanced artistic device in as much as it entails observation of the behaviour of light on opaque bodies. It is used boldly on the heads of deer at Castillo and Altamira (Figure 12A), and is more finicking on the stags and salmon of Lortet (Plate 39).

Impressionistic techniques and aims at illusion were the special achievement of the Magdalenian period (Plate 37), but whenever they weakened, pure pattern took charge again and was responsible for deviations like over-emphasis of the lower line of the horse's winter coat where the long hair of the back meets the shorter of the belly. In Plate 34 damage has removed the surface at this point, but the tips of the longer hairs can be seen running in a line across the flanks. The same line appears, more formalized, on a noble carving of a horse with its minutely engraved coat from Lourdes (Figure 13A), and this again is the source of a purely formal motif on a bone from that site and another from Isturitz (Figure 13, B and C). It appears again schematically on an engraving from Isturitz and on a horse painted in outline at Le Portel, and is disintegrating on a 'dagger' made from the lower jawbone of a horse found in Magdalenian levels at Pekarna (Plates 40 and 43). Here the duplicated line of coat may remind us of a much older engraving, also from Moravia, the Předmostí woman (Plate 23).

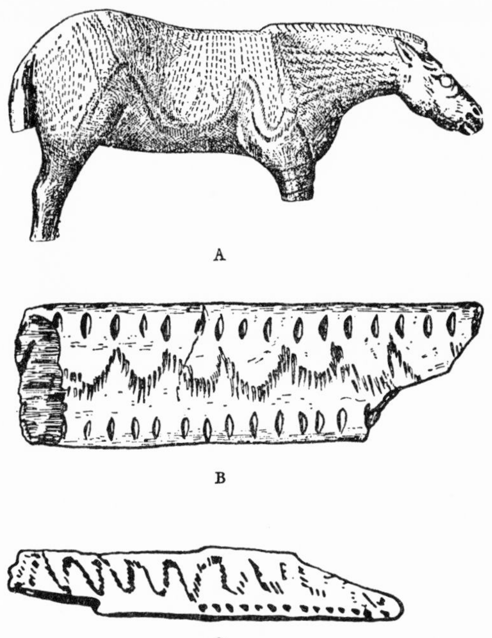

Figure 13. A Naturalistic horse from Lourdes, France, bone
B and C Engraved pattern of horse's coat: B from Lourdes, France, C from Isturitz, France

Many of the small engravings lack the vigour of the earlier work and have a miniaturist delicacy that tends to elaborate pattern at the expense of illusion. The stags (Plate 39) are characteristic of this delicate manner. The horse on a bone from La Mairie à Teyjat can be dated to a little after 13,000 (Magdalenian IV). Here a number of hair-fine lines represent the mane, but under them we are shown the hard outline of the neck, though actually invisible to the eye. In the same drawing the long hair of the tail and fetlock is given impressionistically (Figure 12B). The drawing of the invisible neck may be a rational addition which is quite different from purely decorative patterning. On a magnificent but mutilated carving of a bison from Mas d'Azil fine hatching of the coat follows and emphasizes the main contour of the limbs like a painter's high-light; while on a flat piece of bone from Isturitz there is a still more schematic engraving of a bison (Plate 26 and Figure 14). This is an early instance of that exploitation of animal anatomy and markings for decorative ends that was to have an immensely long history and was carried to extraordinary lengths by, for example, the Scyths. The end in view was the same that caused the pre-men of the Middle Paleolithic to shape their hand-axes in a particular way, the same compulsion of pattern that produced the Lespugue carving and the Předmostí engraving; and we find it pushed to extremes in the Mezin meanders and the spirals from Lespugue and Isturitz (Plate 42 and Figure 9). It can be experienced like the drag of gravity, so that the persistence of naturalism throughout most of the Upper Paleolithic argues for a *conscious* aim behind and directing it, a deliberate purpose towards naturalistic representation.

The Mezin meanders may have a skeuomorphic source in weaving fibres and basketry. On the other hand the Isturitz spirals seem to have evolved, like the pelt motif, from a natural detail. On one deeply carved bone rod the head of an animal, probably a horse, can be made out almost disappearing in the spiral labyrinth, while on

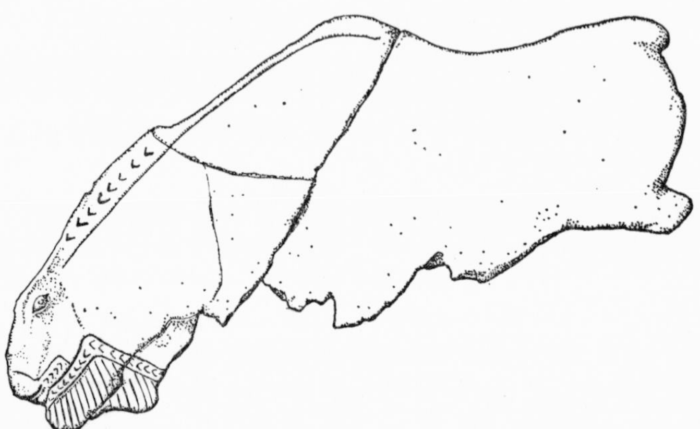

Figure 14. Bison carved and engraved on bone from Isturitz, France

another from Lespugue there are two motifs that may come from the human hand and an animal's head and will be echoed in the Bronze, and Celtic Iron Ages (Plates 197–8 and 254). Patterns like these, their origin probably forgotten, were often repeated and contrasted for purely decorative purposes and should be distinguished from the 'signs', so-called 'tectiforms', 'scudiforms', 'claviforms', sprinkled among and on top of the animals in many caves (Plates 41 and 44). These signs, usually painted in red, have been interpreted in various senses, in none of which the decorative element plays an important part, any more than in pictograms or other shorthand devices (see below).

Colour – Perspective – Illusion

Colour as decoration probably began with body-painting. Blood-coloured ochre, with its simulation of life, was spread under and on the bodies of dead Neanderthal men, and the rite which laps the dead in scarlet has been prolonged to the present day.[24] The geometric patterns engraved on the Předmostí woman may as well represent body-painting as tattooing (Plate 23). Carvings of the human figure in the round, and reliefs, were coloured red, giving them both life and likeness to life. Pencil-like pieces of ochre and manganese have been found in many caves and shelters, some with a point fine enough to rival a burin. The coloured outline and simple shading on the horse and deer from Niaux (Plate 36) only differ from engraving in the material used, not in its handling; but colour was also employed as an overall wash – or two or more contrasting colours show the markings of an animal, like the chestnut horses with black points opposite three cows at Lascaux – and to give volume and depth to solid bodies (Plates 53, 54, and 55).

The pigments used were natural minerals: ochre and haematite for the reds, yellows, and browns, and oxide of manganese for black and very dark brown, with some vegetable charcoal. The violet of Altamira and Lascaux probably came from a manganiferous mineral. No blue or green has survived, but we cannot be certain that they were never used, though it is unlikely. Colours may sometimes have been mixed, but this too is doubtful. It used to be taken for granted that after pounding the pigment to powder and thinning it with water, some kind of binding medium, animal fat or vegetable juices, was added in order to form a paste which would adhere to the rock. This could be applied with the fingers, or with a brush of feather or fur, or perhaps with chewed and shredded stick, or again it might have been dabbed on with pads of moss, lichen, or fur. The binding medium having completely vanished, it has been impossible to determine its nature, so experiments have been made using colour thinned with water and with no fatty medium whatsoever, with the surprising result that, whereas dry rock absorbed the liquid and left the colour liable to dry out to a powder on the surface, if the rock was damp and the paint not too wet, it was very well taken up and remained fast, while the presence of fat in the paint worked against this. The experiments were conducted in conditions that as nearly as possible reproduced those of a limestone cave, and after trying and rejecting animal grease, vegetable juice, blood, and honey, there was a partial success with a pastel-like application of pigment to damp rock.[25] The conclusion was drawn that mediumless paint applied to a damp surface would have the greatest chance of preservation, so long as humidity remained fairly constant. The technique may in fact have been closer to fresco than to oil or grease painting. A sidelight was the discovery that a liquid mediumless paint would run down the 'brush' when painting overhead, as for instance a cave ceiling, but that a pad of fur absorbed the excess moisture satisfactorily. The part played by moisture in the preservation of paintings helps to explain their long survival in damp limestone caves.

Brush-strokes of different thickness implying different brushes can sometimes be seen. Occasionally, and most strikingly at Lascaux, the colour was blown from a tube and sprayed over large surfaces, and colour-stained bone tubes have been found that held the powder. Lamps were of course necessary for working in the dark, and in fact hollowed stones stained with charcoal have been found. Sometimes hands were used as stencils pressed against the rock and the colour blown over them. This was done at Pech-Merle, where also colour was used decoratively or ritualistically for the spotted 'circus horses' (Plate 45). In the cave of Marsoulas (Haute-Garonne) the body of a black-faced bison is built up of dabs and splodges of black paint, perhaps as a painter's experiment like the draughtsman's experiments with line shading (Plate 46). Another bison close by is a more successful combination of strokes for the long hair and dabs for the 'wool' at the top of the head. The black and white bulls at Lascaux (Plates 47 and 55), among the earliest paintings in the cave, are a curious combination of subtle colour-shading and modelling at nose and cheek, along with a much flatter decorative treatment of the head and body, which are sprinkled with black dabs.

Perhaps we ought to remember that a continuous band of paint was not necessarily the most obvious way of making an outline, nor a colour wash of filling it. The 'outline' of the deer at Covalanas, Santander (Plate 48), is a string of small red dabs reminiscent of the technique of the relief-carver: hammering a number of hollows that almost connect and then breaking down the divisions (see Laussel, etc., above). The continuous painted line, on the other hand, would be more likely to occur to an artist used to engraving with a burin.

Figure 15. A Stone engraved with deer from Limeuil, France
B Stone engraved with young deer from Bout-de-Monde, France

We have seen perspective at its simplest in absolute profile, the line of sight at right angles to the subject and opposite its centre (Plate 17). Two limbs only are usually shown, but the off-side pair may be rendered schematically, as they appear on what may be the oldest drawing that we have, the stone from La Ferrassie (Plate 14). Though simple, this is highly artificial, for in reality wild animals are not often seen from exactly this position, nor do they wait with heads held obligingly in perfect profile. There is therefore an academic quality about many of the rather flat profile drawings. Although this pose was used throughout the entire Paleolithic, the aim at more natural perspective eventually led to a breakaway from a successful and therefore binding stereotype. It may have begun with the twisted perspective that showed antlers and horns as though viewed from the front, while the rest of the head is in profile (Plate 16). Further experiments led to the head being turned round and drawn in reverse profile, like the stags from Limeuil and Lortet (Figure 15A and Plate 39).[26] This device, with its concentration and economy, was often used in small-scale carving in the round (Plate 24). The startled deer of Covalanas give us three different essays. The centre animal seems to lift its head, but the position may only be an attempt to show it turning

A B

Figure 16. A Frontal view of stag engraved on reindeer antler from Gourdan, France
B Stone engraving of a cow from Limeuil, France

and looking round, which is what the animal on the right does, more successfully though at the expense of elongating the neck. The outside pair of legs give little difficulty and the pose is natural.[27] The last vestige of strain has gone from the leggy fawns at Le Bout-de-Monde in the Dordogne, and, smaller in scale and in spite of a little uncertainty and over-drawing of the legs, on the stone from Limeuil, also in the Dordogne (Figure 15). One of the deer on this last looks directly at us, the foreshortening appearing easy and natural. We get a completely frontal view of an antlered stag scratched on a bone pipe or tube from Gourdan (Haute-Garonne) (Figure 16A). This very rare pose is something of a *tour de force*, and might have been suggested by three-dimensional carving like the ibex of Plate 25.

The great bison outlined in black paint at Marcenac (Lot) is a superb materialization of the frontal view of a head set on a body seen from the side, but this time in natural, not twisted, perspective. It is as though the animal had just turned and lowered its head in menace or defence (Plate 49). This is the same as the bison on the Roc de Sers relief and was to become a conventional stereotype for this animal, for we see it painted at Lascaux and engraved at La Mouthe.[28]

The Marcenac bison introduces the empty 'screen' and the exploitation of the eye's creative activity, which must be left for the moment. Lascaux has many experiments in foreshortening such as the back-to-back bison of Plate 50, and there is a bull or cow engraved on stone at Limeuil that presents the top view of the head, which is less likely to be a natural pose than a more sophisticated version of the familiar twist[29] (Figure 16B). The scamping of feet and careless or inexpert drawing of legs that is often found may have a very natural explanation. The hunter-artist usually sees animals in movement; the aspect and features he knows best, and which remain longest distinct to his

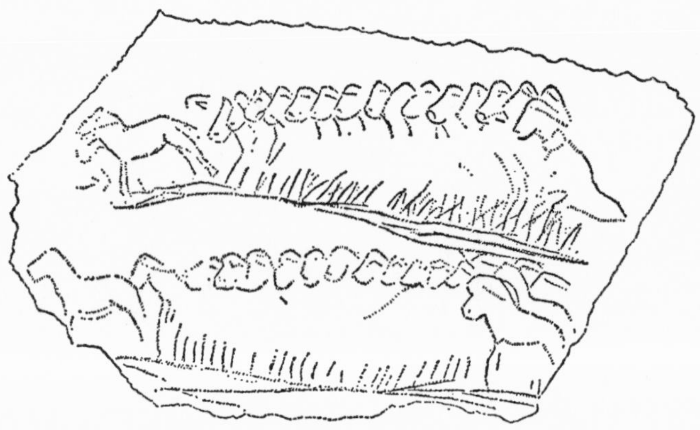

Figure 17. Bone engraving of horses from Le Chaffaud, France

inner eye, are those which he reproduces best, namely heads and backs, whereas feet are hidden in grass, undergrowth, or snow, which, added to the rapidity of their movement, means that they are least known, least observed, and so among the last features for which satisfactory *schemata* were evolved (see Plates 36 and 40, and Figures 15A and 17). The very peculiar drawing of the feet of most of the Lascaux cattle and bison is usually described as another instance of 'twisted perspective', and twisted it certainly is, but I do not think it is the same as that of horns and antlers, that is to say the front view of a cloven hoof attached to a leg in profile, but rather a combination of the things the hunter and tracker knows best: the *impression* of the cloven hoofs left in mud, earth, or snow, joined to an ordinary profile leg. The slots were so essential a part of the animal that they had to be added to any representation of it that was to be really complete (Plates 50 and 54). This explanation would not account for the tip-toe hoofs on which the Altamira and Trois Frères bison seem to float (Plates 51 and 74), but for them there is another explanation: the use of dead animals as models[30] (see below).

Of group perspective there is very little, but with two cows engraved on bone from Mas d'Azil someone had made the startling discovery that an object that is placed farther from the observer should be drawn smaller than one nearer (Plate 52). The lines do not run over each other and the nearer cow has depth and solidity; there is real weight in the flesh that hangs from the protruding hip-bone. This is another minor masterpiece like Schweizersbild, although the illusion of distance *may* be accidental and *is* very rare indeed. (Groups of animals will be considered when we come to the question of composition.)

The more interesting experiments in perspective are, rather oddly, confined to certain animals. Horses are almost always in full profile, heads and bodies. They stand, walk, and gallop but seldom browse or turn the head, and this holds good when a whole herd is sketched in movement (Figure 17). There are of course exceptions, like the horse turning its head at Angles-sur-l'Anglin. Deer on the other hand do all these things, and even on occasion meet us full face. Reindeer are only a little less versatile than deer, but bison are more stereotyped even than horses, usually appearing in full profile or with foreshortened shoulders and lowered head (Plate 49).[31] Rhinoceros and mammoth are always in full profile. Smaller, relatively insignificant animals like hares do not seem

Figure 18. A lion's head engraved on rock at Trois Frères, France

to have been stereotyped. The great predators – the lions, also bears – are usually in profile and walking away, or lying dead, but occasionally and alarmingly full-face (Figure 18). The constancy of the stereotypes and the persistence and power of these conventional images over wide distances from France to Czechoslovakia and perhaps even farther, to the Urals, and from Atlantic Spain to Sicily, are the strongest possible evidence for the unity of the tradition or family of traditions.

At the same time that the artists were making these experiments with outline, perspective, and pose, they were also concerned with volume and weight. In relief, with its natural range of light and shadow, the problem hardly exists; and if, as seems probable, the Paleolithic reliefs were coloured, the illusion of bodily presence must have been great. In some engravings, particularly those of the early deep group, relief is used for emphasis on parts of the body. A Combarelles horse has its head, neck, and shoulders carved in low relief, while the line of the back, legs, and mane are engraved.[32]

The illusion of volume has often been achieved in paintings and engravings with great skill and economy. Outstanding is the horse from Schweizersbild (Plate 34), where the perspective of the legs, the line from stifle to forearm, and from cheek to ear, and above all the movement, marvellously convey the animal's weight and mass. With even greater economy the artist of La Pasiega, Santander, has used a red line of varying width to suggest the volume and movement of a graceful animal that seems to start forward out of a walk. The salient points are picked out in broader colour, and there is a little shading on the neck. The method is that of chinese ink painting (Figure 19).

The drawing of the Lortet stag's feet not only gives them an appearance of weightlessness and reduces the credibility of the movement, but also affects the volume of the body, as can be seen by cutting off the feet, when both animals not only begin to walk, but gain in solidity and depth (Plate 39).[33] When shading is used mainly as decoration, volume again is lost. But it is in the earlier polychrome work at Lascaux that we

Figure 19. A and B Rock paintings at La Pasiega, Spain

see a painterly exploitation of colour to render volume and even sometimes texture. Reproduction in black and white can only hint at the vivacity of the original painting. A horse on the right wall of the axial (or painted) gallery is so oddly drawn, with tiny head and floppy feet, that uncoloured it is unbelievable; but bulk and texture come from the tawny shading of the body against the dense black of the nose and the powdery black of the mane, with contrasting paleness of the belly left as unpainted white calcite within its lower outline. In spite of its legs and head it is very much alive, and zoologists will say that here is a fair representation of a Przewalski wild horse (Plate 53).

The file of very dark ponies under the so-called 'leaping cow' in the same gallery (Plate 54) is treated quite differently, and they are probably of a different breed. The bodies are entirely filled in with a very dark brown paint, and with legs, mane, and outline black. This may be the winter coat, and the effect is of density and a rather clumsy solidity, and the movement is as though arrested in a rocking-horse canter. Some of the best modelling is on the cows painted in shades of red and ochreous brown. The three cows that balance each other across the roof of the axial gallery, and with which the horse already described makes the fourth quarter (Plate 53), are coloured a rich, warm red with some black on the head. The one directly facing the horse is darker where the shadow might fall on the chest and belly, and lighter on the neck and head. The hindquarters (not visible on Plate 53) are unpainted but outlined in red, and there is a lighter band between the outline of the back and the flanks. This may really be a stripe of paler hair, but the effect is of a glossy highlight. Whether accidental or not, it is a happy invention that reappears in other places. There is some very fine modelling on the large red cow just visible on the left of Plate 56. The black head and neck are disproportionately small, like the heads of some of the horses, and the long antennae-like horns seem to belong to a different animal (or perhaps a different stereotype was used), but in spite of this it is no less alive. The stippling of the great bulls in the 'Hall of Bulls' has not the sculptural quality of shading, as already remarked (Plate 55). The flatness may in part be due, like that of the Niaux bison of Plate 57, to the superpositions, which give a weightless and dreamlike quality to bodies even when competently drawn in natural perspective. Superpositions do not detract from the bulky solidity of the great black cow, whose outline has been incised upon a number of small horses, two heads of which can be seen immediately behind the cow's buttocks (Plates 44 and 58).

The polychrome paintings at Altamira, Santander, though the first to be recognized as Paleolithic, are certainly not the earliest executed.[34] Each of the rocky bosses of the main part of the ceiling in the great hall accommodates some animal; most are bison, but there are also deer, pig, horses, and numerous 'signs'. The finished effect of each animal is over-worked, but it is immensely competent. Colour is used both to pick out the natural points and as shading. The engraved line here and there has guided the colourist and is also used for emphasis of tail, eye, or horn. Thus the lighter patch under the belly of the deer has a 'shading' of fine lines which shows it to be a deliberate part of the modelling rendered in the complementary techniques of both draughtsman and painter (Plate 59 and Figure 20). The bison (Plate 51) has the texture of hair and mane, neck and shoulder all reproduced in painterly manner; yet, in spite of the subtlety of colouring, the black points of nose, beard, mane, and tail, the reds of shoulder, flank, and hindquarters, and the pale underbelly, and in spite of the glittering eye, this great animal has far less of the tension of life and the illusion of a heavy bodily presence than the much less 'correct' Lascaux bison of Plate 50. It is not simply absence of movement, or fading colour, for the very imperfect bison at Marcenac (Plate 49) creates a greater illusion, but it may very well have something to do with the use of dead animals as models. It is time to consider this possibility.

Figure 20. Engraved portion of painted and engraved deer at Altamira, Spain (cf. Plate 59)

Animals Dead and Alive

When it was first put forward, rather too much was claimed for the theory that Paleolithic artists made use of dead models.[35] But for much of the later art it seems very convincing. The peculiarities that suggest it are these: the sighting-point lower than the animal's body, sometimes even lower than the feet; the head seen from a lower point than the cheek so that it appears to be turned away; the off-pair of legs longer than the near; the underside of at least one foot turned up. In addition the tongue may hang out and the tail be raised. Most striking of all is the lack of muscular tension and of the compact fit of legs and body that belong to the standing beast. Even where bulk is ably rendered, the muscles and limbs look relaxed. The actual pose may be misleading, for photographs of dead animals often have an air of movement and life, but this is at odds with the other characteristics referred to.

These peculiarities fit almost all the paintings of the great hall at Altamira and many of the delicate engravings at Trois Frères (Plates 51 and 74), and also some of the delicate engraving at Lascaux, which is evidently later, perhaps much later, than the paintings. For example, a small horse engraved upon the flank of an earlier painted horse has the limp, relaxed body of the dead animal, and is a double, even to the same cross mark on the flank, of a horse engraved on bone at La Mairie à Teyjat (Plate 58 and Figure 12B). This must be a stereotype that has suffered the debilitating effects of constant repetition. If we compare these horses with Schweizersbild and La Pasiega (Plate 34 and Figure 19), it is not difficult to discern the living from the dead model. The Altamira bison that have been interpreted as 'charging', head down and feet bunched together, are dead and probably trussed for transport. The boar charging in a 'flying gallop' is stretched dead on the ground and ready for skinning. All these things only appear in a comparatively late phase of Magdalenian art: at Altamira, Trois Frères, Niaux, and on some Middle to Late Magdalenian small carvings.[36] The theory does not explain the twisted perspective of horns and antlers at Lascaux and other earlier sites, nor the twisted hoofs, which I believe to be slots, nor is it convincing for bears and lions (Figure 18). Within its limits, it is, I think, the best explanation for some characteristics of Paleolithic art, and must modify our ideas of the artist, who now is able to study his subject at leisure, and to sketch, correct, and verify, without the discomforts and difficulties of observing wild, shy, and often nocturnal creatures.

At least three kinds of horse are represented, descendants of which still exist, or did till recently: the Mongolian wild horse (*Equus Przewalski Pol.*), the steppe Tarpan (*Equus Gmelini Ant.*), and also the Icelandic and Shetland ponies of today, and a larger forest animal; but many differences in portrayal may be due to the existence of 'ecotypes' – varieties adapted to certain environments – rather than to distinct species.[37] Although horses are so often represented, their bones form a small proportion, between 15 per cent and 11 per cent, of the total found on inhabited sites.

There were evidently two kinds of bison, the small-horned European bison (*Bison Bonasus Linn.*), which survives in the Caucasus and on the Polish–Russian frontier, and a large-horned race with a larger hump for storing fat against the glacial winters (*Bison priscus Bojanus*). At Altamira the smaller forest bison, or an intermediate variety, is represented, but bones found in caves like Font-de-Gaume and Laugerie Basse belonged to a larger variety, and the huge humps of the Font-de-Gaume animals (Figure 21) may not be as mannered as they look, but rather due to a wish to emphasize a peculiarity of the larger breed. There may be other instances where what seems like a mannerism is really exaggeration of just that which identifies the sex or a particular breed.

European wild cattle (*Bos primigenius Bojanus*) survived till 1627, but the specimen of a bull in the well-known Augsburg painting was probably a weak, untypical survivor due for extinction, and the living aurochs standing 6 feet high with a deep, long body, short legs, and long tail was much closer to the Lascaux bulls of Plate 55.[38] In

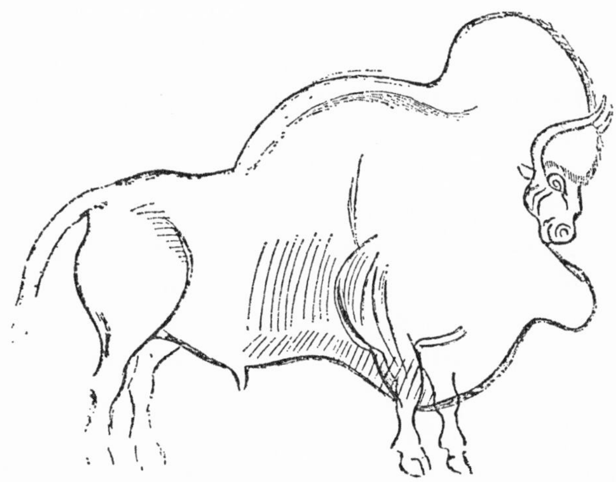

Figure 21. Engraved bison at Font-de-Gaume, France

a 'reconstituted' animal the winter coat was curly and there was a white stripe along the spine. This is carefully shown as a pale streak on some of the Lascaux cattle, although it has the appearance of a highlight. No doubt in life the animals were very variable, some black, some reddish brown. The white bulls of Lascaux, with their black legs, may be albinos like the albino bison that appear occasionally, and if so they were possibly chosen as subjects for the magical qualities of whiteness. The small heads of Lascaux cows, compared to the large heads of bulls, may have been picked on to mark the difference of sex, as with the arbitrary colouring in Egyptian wall-paintings. Whereas bulls are given their scrotum, a cow's udders are not represented. The milk of wild cattle was of no interest to the hunters, and in fact udders do not appear in art till cattle were domesticated (Plate 44).

The European mammoth (*Elephas primigenius Blumenbach*) was an enormous animal, larger than the African and Indian elephant, and larger than the refrigerated mammoth, found with flesh and hair preserved where they were trapped by the Siberian ice. The domed head, shoulder hump, the long hair and the curiously rigid tail are shown impressionistically in drawings and paintings from the Atlantic to the Urals (Plate 60).

This is what the eye saw and not the conformation of the body beneath, though this *was* once modelled by a Gravettian artist at Pavlov (see above p. 12). Strangely enough, the great tusks are not always shown.

The woolly rhinoceros (*Tichorinus Antiquitatis Blum.*) has also been preserved in a natural deep-freeze at Starunia in the Carpathians. It was just as depicted, with a fat-hump in front of the withers and hair growing in tufts and tangles. The artists seem to have been most impressed by the weight of the body, the pillar-like thickness of the legs, and the two horns in profile. The cave lion (*Felis leo spelaea*), which shared man's predatory activities, was larger than the African lion of today; it had whiskers like a tiger, and the chance of meeting this big cat unexpectedly in a dark place must have caused terror to cave artists, some of which is conveyed by a head-on view (Figure 18). The enormous cave bear (*Ursus spelaeus Ros.*), which could stand 10 feet tall, was extinct before the end of the Paleolithic. In representations it is distinguished from the much smaller brown bear (*Ursus arctos Linn.*), as in life, by its less concave profile and narrower face. These and the deer and reindeer are the animals most often depicted.

Red deer (*Cervus elaphus*) are forest animals, and where they are represented it is a good indication that the climate was not too severe. All deer are distinguished from reindeer in art, as in life, by the erect carriage of the head and by the absence of long hair under the neck, though buck do grow some longer hair in autumn and winter. Reindeer of both sexes carry antlers, but among deer only the buck, and they shed theirs in the spring, when the new ones begin to grow at once; thus portrayals of animals with or without antlers help to determine the seasons. A giant deer that carried its head low is occasionally shown; also the small Lapland reindeer (*Rangifer tarandus Linn.*) that thrives on tundra close to the ice, and the larger caribou (*Rangifer arcticus*), better adapted to the barrens and forest grazing. *Tarandus* was probably larger than the partly domesticated Lapland reindeer of today. Although there are more reindeer bones on sites than bones of any other animal (Kesslerloch 80 per cent, Schweizersbild 74 per cent), they are far from being the animal most often represented, which would hardly have been the case if the pursuit of food were the main purpose of this art.

All that we can learn of wild animals today tells us that, apart from those occasional exaggerations for which there is some good cause, and apart from the limitations of the hunter's view of the live and dead animal, the aim of this art was truth to nature and the illusion of a thing seen. Throughout this chapter I have been assuming that this was the case, and that the techniques of perspective, accurate drawing of limbs in motion, and chiaroscuro and polychromy to render volume and plasticity, were developed to this end. It may be an unwarrantable assumption, yet I hardly think that these experiments would have been carried so far, and just these results achieved, if the aim had not been greater illusion. The engraved outlines of the earlier art describe a flat area which the eye, in its creative capacity, fills out with the remembered depth and solidity of a living animal. The mechanics of this habit of our eyes has been often described. When given certain clues by the artist, we respond unconsciously and predictably. The mammoths, horses, and bison of Pech-Merle, outlined in black paint on a background of pale rock, are very much as they must have been when the cave went out of use.

The unfinished outlines above the horse of Plate 61 would have been unintelligible if we were not already familiar with the mammoth and bison *schemata*; but with this knowledge we can read them as symbols in a language so well understood that it had become unnecessary to repeat the whole image every time. The humped head of the mammoth and the back-line of the bison at the top of Plate 60 are echoes of the animals below and on the right (Figure 22). This sort of shorthand meets the explorer in many caves; occasionally the work may really be unfinished, but more often we are given more or less complete images in which the artist has counted deliberately upon the visual experience of the beholder to fill the empty places.

Figure 22. Painted outlines of bison and mammoth at Pech-Merle, France, rearranged (cf. Plate 61)

Paleolithic and Chinese painting are much alike in their deliberate use of emptiness. The Chinese dictum that a figure, though painted without eyes, must be made to look, was perfectly understood by the creator of the Marcenac bison (Plate 49).[39] Today, because of our different environment, we are often in doubt and fail to read the clues, but we still recognize the device. The artist in his craft is still surprisingly close to us, though in his imagination he is all of the fifteen thousand or so years of his true age before us.

Situation and Subject: Canvas and Composition

One cannot go far with later Paleolithic art without the strangeness of its situation demanding notice. The small sculpture of the Gravettians was usually found, as we have seen, inside houses or temporary shelters, and occasionally buried with the dead. The earliest drawings on pebble and rock walls were in easily accessible places, near, if not actually in, living sites. The large-scale reliefs were always in open places, or at any rate within reach of daylight. But now we meet something quite new: the deliberate use of darkness and of deep caves for the placing of paintings and large numbers of fine engravings.

Some idea of the labyrinthine wanderings, the cracks and chasms of the limestone caves may be had from looking at one simplified plan (Figure 23). Tuc d'Audoubert, which today communicates with Trois Frères, has to be approached by boat, rowing under the low entrance along 90 yards of the Volpe river, after which halls and galleries are crossed on foot, with paintings and engravings on the walls, and with many prints of the cave bear and a scatter of Magdalenian tackle (Magdalenian IV). The first explorers, in 1912, only reached the end of the great system, nearly 800 yards distant, by climbing a narrow chimney, and crossing another series of halls and galleries till they found themselves looking at two bison across a clay floor, in whose once soft surface there were impressions of many footprints (Plate 20).[40]

Figure 23. Plan of Tuc d'Audoubert, France

Lascaux is a small cave; the view out of the great 'Hall of Bulls' into the 'Axial' or 'Painted Gallery' (Plate 56) conveys something of the situation of the paintings. The widening of the passage above a sort of natural cornice marks the point where porous limestone meets non-porous. The smooth surface of the latter, with its skin of white calcite, provides the background against which colours show with velvet richness. This cornice, which occurs in some other caves as well, was used at Lascaux as a base-line for many of the figures: the larger cattle appear to stride along it, while for the deer of Plate 64 it becomes a river or lake out of which the swimming heads are lifted. The glimmering pallor of the calcite surface has been used with great effect in reserved areas like the light hair of a horse's belly left unpainted inside an outlined contour (Plate 53).

I have already referred to an ancient theory concerning the origin of visual art as arising through projection of an image on to natural objects which by their shape suggest the form of an animal or human being. Quite a number of these collaborations of man and nature can be found in the caves, where weird formations of rock and stalagmite looming in the semi-darkness easily suffer metamorphosis. A curiously ridged stalagmite in the Spanish cave of Castillo must have suggested the hind-leg and back of a bison struggling up a bank; only the horns and the colour of the body needed to be added (Plate 62). What is much more questionable is whether this sort of adaptation could have occurred had the *schema* for a bison not already existed. As far as our evidence goes, many of the animal *schemata* were already ancient when the first cave paintings were made. They had been evolved in simple outline on smooth surfaces (Plate 16 and Figure 5); once the eye had learnt this particular language, the artist could happily exploit whatever came to hand. A random group of natural hollows in a clay surface at Niaux were employed for the eye and 'wounds' of an engraved bison (Plate 63), while to take a much earlier example, one of the 'circus horses' of Pech-Merle owes the outline of its head to an abrupt edge of rock (Plate 45). Relief-carvers also made use of natural formations for heads and shoulders, even in the beautiful horse of Commarque; but it seems unlikely that prehistoric man *discovered* the shapes of animals in this way *for the first time*.

Today, even in the brutal electric light of the more famous caves, the background is never negligible. The images are volatile, altering from hour to hour, almost from minute to minute; they are the despair of the photographer and copyist. Partly this is because we can seldom view them twice from exactly the same position. The central right-angled view may be impossible because of the narrowness of the passage, or the position of the subject on the wall; and the slightest alteration in the line of sight changes emphasis and perspective in a way that does not happen with art inside buildings. We must forget the search for the most favourable angle of view, the correct lighting, the level floor, and tactfully placed chair or bench from which to admire a framed conspicuous masterpiece. Nothing could be less like the caves, where we crawl and crane, where everything alters, surfaces bend and are lit by a bending light. The only frame is the limit of illumination, and there is no distinct edge or end, but a growing indistinctness in which figures fade from shadow into darkness, or slide round corners, reappearing with a baffling change of scale, farther away, or quite close at hand. The absence of a frame also does away with one of the fundamental limitations of illusion: there is nothing to prevent the great Lascaux bulls stalking along the wall and away into the shadows.[41] The sense of movement is the hardest to catch in reproduction, but it is positive in the caves. The bear looms forward or moves off with head down, the larger cattle pace majestically away, deer swim in line or turn a nervous head ready to fly, horses canter and trot; but the mammoth, the rhinoceros, the bison stand rigid. This is a context well suited to the hunter's world and vision, in which things are seldom static, as they are for us who live in rectangular cubes and look at our pictures in rectangular frames.[42]

A first impression of the caves is likely to be of confusion, but the days are past when it could be said that Paleolithic art was altogether an art of isolated images. It is true that at Trois Frères, Pech-Merle, Niaux, we laboriously disentangle the profiles of individual animals. We find that the superpositions have much the same effect of alienation as the contradictory perspective in a Braque still-life; but there the similarity ends, for whereas the contemporary painter destroys the illusion but saves the composition, in the caves illusion survives the absence of composition. But if visual composition is absent or extremely rare, a sort of intellectual design certainly exists. The arrangements are far from haphazard, whether in small scale on bone and horn or on the grandest scale in the Great Hall at Lascaux, where bulls 16 feet long face each other like figures on a pediment (Plate 55).

Composition, of course, may mean several things. It is used by some writers on Paleolithic art for combinations of the same type of animal in different situations, and of the same animal with certain 'signs'.[43] The study of these repetitive groups is comparatively new; but juxtaposition, however often repeated, does not constitute visual composition. Apart from the superpositions, what distinguishes a scatter of independent animal portraits from a composition is agreement in scale between the figures (as in western naturalistic art), or the use of a relative scale dictated by a well defined hierarchical system, as in the sacred art of the ancient Near East and Egypt, and in Early Christian iconography. In the Upper Paleolithic we do in fact have a few instances of both (Plate 52 and Figure 24). Composition depends to a great extent upon frame. The surface of a bone scapula or a length of tine limits it on a small scale, while the limited available exposure of the rock face provides a frame of a sort for the relief carver on a larger scale; but in the winding galleries of the deep caves visibility is the only frame, and visibility alters with every movement. There is a sort of composition consisting in pairs of animals that face or follow one another, the pairs usually male and female, and there is repetition of the same animal figure. The carved frieze encircling a round building, the frescoes and mosaics that cover the domes and curved walls of Byzantine churches provide a rough parallel. The frieze is perhaps one of the simplest of compositions, and the figures of the Roc de Sers frieze are sufficiently alike in scale to appear deliberately composed. But the three female figures linked in a reciprocal movement at Angles-sur-l'Anglin are a composition in an altogether more sophisticated sense (Plate 33). Lines of heads: the chamois on a bone from Gourdan (Haute-Garonne), the 'swimming' stags of Lascaux (Plates 65 and 64) are related to the frieze. The black outlined bulls at Lascaux (Plate 55), in their pedimental grouping, are drawn to scale with each other, but the smaller red cattle and the deer and horses that surround them (usually taken to be somewhat later) are outside the composition, and there is no corresponding visual balance.

Pairs of almost identical animals that face each other, like the heraldic devices of later ages, are repeated so often that they must have had a special purpose (Plate 66). The bison with overlapping hindquarters at Lascaux are artificial in conception (Plate 50), but bison butting each other from Pekarna (Plate 67) are much more realistically posed. Different animals placed together on small objects of bone are often in proper scale – the deer and salmon from Lortet (Plate 39) and seals and salmon from Montgaudier – but how far such conventions were respected on the larger canvas of the caves it is difficult to judge, for it depends on knowing exactly which paintings are contemporary. This may be inferred for the male and female pairs, the 'heraldic' groups, and balancing dispositions like the three cows and small horse whose heads make a quadrilateral pattern in the Axial Gallery at Lascaux (Plate 53). The friezes of 'swimming' deer and ibex in line may really be simplified versions of herds on the move, but more impressionistic treatment of a herd does occur on the 'canvas' of small sections of bone. The lightly touched-in deer and ponies of Limeuil are confusedly alive, but overlapping lines break the illusion; this is not so with the galloping horses of Chaffaud (Figures 15A and 17). The first and last animals are complete profiles, two others are less complete, and the rest a haze of legs, manes, and noses. These little scenes are unusual in having the ground-line drawn so that there is the approach to an illusion of space around them. In Figure 17 the line divides the scene into two registers like the 'cornice' at

Lascaux. The sketchy, impressionistic treatment creates an illusion of perspective that is not there; for the 'nearest' and 'farthest' ponies are exactly the same size. However, in these scenes we feel ourselves in the presence of a kind of composition that has been the particular province of western naturalistic art. In Plate 68 and Figure 24 we have examples of that other species of composition which is formal and hierarchical and which came into its own with the seal-cutting artists of the Near East and Mediterranean not many centuries later. At Les Eyzies and again Raymonden (Dordogne), indeterminate human figures approach or surround a bison of majestic size. Two pairs of monstrous hands are scratched on one, and on the other the figures are gathered on either side of the huge backbone and dislocated legs. These scenes are formal, hieratic, cryptic. They could have arisen from arrangements like Roc de Sers, and they may be compared with the mysterious shaft scene at Lascaux.

Figure 24. Engraved bone from Raymonden, France

This last is one of the strangest and most discussed subjects in Paleolithic art. It occupies an otherwise bare wall in the shaft. Opposite it is a narrow ledge which gives a precarious footing from which it can be seen only after clambering down below the level of the 'apse', a domed chamber whose walls are covered with a tangle of engravings. At the foot of the shaft a great number of lamps were found, thrown down presumably after lighting the scene.[44] The pale rock of the background is so limited in area that it forms a sort of panel on which are painted, in very different styles, a rhinoceros, a wounded bison, a long spear, and two ambiguous bird-headed objects (Plate 69). I shall have more to say about this scene later.

Let us return now to that other sort of 'composition' that depends on comparison of the groupings of certain kinds of animal in a great number of caves, and between the different parts of a single cave. This was lately the subject of intensive study, the aim of which was to discover whether repetitions are frequent enough to be significant, whether the position of certain subjects near the entrance, in the middle, or the depths of the caves follows a consistent order, and to what extent representations are combined with 'signs'. A case for instance has been made out at Lascaux for a deliberate repetition of processions of horses in set relationship to cow, bison, ibex, and certain net-signs.[45]

It is possible already to make a few generalizations. In most caves deer, ibex, and various 'signs' and stencilled hands are found near the entrance; next follows an area of confused and incomplete animal figures, meanders, and fragments, and after these a central 'panel' on which are depicted one or other of the dominant beneficent animals – bison, cattle, mammoth, horse – along with some of the more complicated 'signs'. These are followed again by deer, and in the deep recesses, often difficult to reach, like the Lascaux shaft and the Hall of the Sorcerer at Trois Frères, we find the big cats, and man – not the natural, undisguised figure of the daylight art, but horned, masked, half animal, man himself, never woman.

As with other theories – dead animal subjects, re-enactments of the hunt, food magic, and fertility magic – too much has probably been claimed for universal rules of position and subject. Much more data are needed. The weakness of the theory is that it depends on completeness of study, and completeness, in spite of all the industry and care in the world, is virtually unobtainable. Subjects near the entrances or even to within a hundred yards of the entrance have disappeared, or the original entrance is no longer known. Nevertheless this very recent concentration on a cave in its entirety is wholly admirable and promises much for the future.

If the existence of a type of composition that is neither naturalistic nor decorative, but literary and intellectual, is accepted, then this is something peculiar to Paleolithic man. The subjects presented side by side but to different scale, or with overlapping outlines, not only destroy the illusion of reality by their contradictions, but offer no pattern in recompense, and this in spite of the delight in pattern that exists in the treatment of the individual subject. Comparison with our own contemporary art will not hold. However much the parts in a Picasso or a Braque overlap each other, however contradictory the perspective, the pattern holds the parts together; they are nothing if not compositions. When surrealist painters destroyed the logic of scale, they compensated for the loss of reality with *trompe-l'œil* effects and very solid modelling, and for the abstract painter the cohesion of pattern dominates. But these Paleolithic 'panels', without frame or pattern, or any of the other unifying devices, cannot I think be called compositions without the word losing all significance. A notional composition which depends on the interpretation of themes and subject is something so intellectual that it would belong to a history of thought, not to a prehistory of art.

In this chapter we have noticed, from time to time, evidence of a coherent tradition, or traditions: in the use of the same stereotypes for certain animals, the conventions ruling the portrayal of pose – loose for deer, strict for horse, bison, and mammoth; in the development, probably gradual (though this is guesswork), in techniques; and in the progressive mastery of problems of perspective, volume, and depth. A stylistic framework built on the surviving examples can only be relied upon if left extremely loose, with room for foldings, retrogressions, repetitions. Quite impressionistic animals were being engraved and painted in the later Magdalenian at the same time as more schematic representations, just as some of the latter are undoubtedly early. There is a distinction to be drawn between schematic exploitation of superficial characteristics, markings and patterns, for visual satisfaction, which is probably late; and the non-visual formalism for intellectual purposes which may be very early (Figures 13, 14, and Plates 13, 14). Even where the available *schemata* are so few, and the conventions so strict, the artist still has ample latitude in matters of style, taste, or what you will, which appear when comparing different sites. It would not be possible to mistake a bison from Lascaux for one from Niaux, Altamira, or Font-de-Gaume. Both Lascaux and Font-de-Gaume show that some very fine engraving came later than the painting, but superpositions do not always mean long intervals of time, and the differences cannot all be explained by chronology. If the Altamira polychrome paintings occasionally appear overblown and those at Font-de-Gaume sophisticated and fantasticated, these are a best subjective judgements.

'The Splendour of Forms Yet to Come'

And see how they run, the juxtaposed forms,
brighting the vaults of Lascaux; how the linear is wedded
to volume, how they do, within, in an unbloody manner,
under the forms of haematite and black manganese on
the graved lime-face, what is done, without,
far on the windy tundra
at the kill
that the kindred may have life.

David Jones

There is a vast literature concerned with the interpretation of Paleolithic art.[46] Theories going back to the first discoveries in the 1860s fall broadly into two groups, both of which we have met already: hunting magic and fertility magic (see above; Chaffaud was found as early as 1834, but its significance was not realized at the time). Some have favoured 'art for art's sake', and others made comparison with the art of children. Comparisons with the hunter's magic of contemporary primitives are out of fashion today, but that is because they have been worked too hard in the past. It is doubtless unwise, to say the least, to compare the artistic usages of aboriginal Australians or bushmen with those of Upper Paleolithic man in Europe, but they still can throw some light on the milieu in which he worked. There are subjects, like the wounded clay bear at Montespan and a horse outlined in clay and peppered with stabs, for which an explanation in some sort of hunting magic would have had to be invented if it did not already exist among living people.

Though the number of animals in the caves that are marked with darts or wounds is a small percentage of the whole,[47] yet nearly every cave has at least one. Some of the darts and dashes may not be weapons at all but male and female symbols already far removed from any attempt at representation. But where they are aimed at the heart or other vital organ, and where the animal shows its distress, we are almost certainly in the presence of hunters' rites, just as we were with the stabbed bears of the Pavlov hills and the panther of the Vogelherd (Plates 4 and 57). In the last chapter something was said of ritual re-enactments and their connexion with myth, with the hunt, and with the hearth and home. Now in the caves we find a setting for the re-enactment of the great hunting in the mythical beginning of time. It is this possibility of entering through ritual the timeless present of the beginning, and identifying today's or tomorrow's ephemeral event with that timeless event, rather than the crude magic of a mere rehearsal or propitiation, that may lie behind the 'wounded' animals, as it does behind the bison dances and crane dances of North American Indians and archaic Greeks.[48]

The second 'classic' interpretation of Paleolithic art, as predominantly fertility magic, has concentrated on the representations of pregnant animals and of male and female pairs, bulls and cows, does and stags (Plate 20), while lately an intense study of the 'signs' has brought reinforcement from a new quarter. In the past these signs were variously 'read' as tents, houses, traps, lodges for souls, but the new theory reduces almost all to simplified male and female symbols. 'Tectiforms', 'claviforms', 'scudiforms' disappear, and instead we have extreme abbreviations of the female silhouette and male and female sex organs (Plates 15, 28, 41, 53, 54, and 63 and Figure 8). The signs grouped as female are found usually in the middle region of the caves and the male signs nearer the entry and in the deepest parts. According to this theory, male and female signs are associated with individual animals in such a way as to explain the greater number of subjects along lines of a strict polarity of sex. Accordingly horse, ibex, and deer are, over and above their animal character, symbols of masculinity; and bison, cattle, and mammoth are the corresponding female symbols, even if this means that the female is represented by a bull and the male by a pregnant mare. It is possible to argue that the horses are not pregnant but that the convention of representation alone makes them look so; but in fact when the male sex of the animal *is* shown, as on the Niaux horse (Plate 37), the body, though deep, is neither so deep nor so swollen as the pregnant mares' (Plates 53 and 58). The bulls and male bison on the other hand have their full provision of male sex organs.

The interpretation of the signs as male and female is far more persuasive, but to carry this simplification over to the animals is a very big step indeed, the difficulties of which do not seem to have been sufficiently regarded. The conjunction of signs and animals can usually be interpreted in more ways than one: male sign and male or female animal *either* as complement *or* reinforcement. However interpreted, we are unlikely ever to read them all correctly; but they are certainly a step in the direction of that order of symbolism that would lead at a later time, and in more propitious circumstances, to the invention of pictographic scripts.[49] To some extent shorthand signs and symbols imply a deliberate resort to ambiguity and riddles, and, since artist and audience share the same tradition and environment, they are equally intelligible to each. That the drawing of gravid animals is not necessarily a form of fertility magic I hope to show below when putting forward another possible explanation, while it should be remembered of the male and female pairs that animals are at their most approachable during the rut, becoming comparatively careless of danger, so that a study of their appearance is less difficult at these seasons.

Even if symbols of sex were used in the caves, it does not follow that such symbolism can 'explain' the animals and human figures painted, engraved, and carved. We have no possible means of knowing what the reclining women of La Magdeleine or the three rock-imprisoned bodies of Angles-sur-l'Anglin, or the bearded man from the same site, signified to their creators; and to call them 'Venuses' or 'Matres' is as frivolous as any of those other arbitrary labels that artists and critics use – 'la source', 'terra genitrix', and so on. If we are tempted to recall that in Western Europe the Celts knew three linked goddesses, and that Greek mythology placed in the far west, by the Hesperides, three terrible beings with women's bodies, the gorgons, such fantasies are best forgotten. The other new theory, which claims to see in often-repeated groups and associations of animals the repetition of 'themes' – for instance horse and bovine (bison or aurochs), woman and bison – finds in this art illustrations of advanced mythology.[50]

I have already given some of the objections to the theory of compositions; the main one is the difficulty of distinguishing between a real association and mere juxtaposition. The existence of antithetical pairs and a few other conventional compositions adds to the improbability. We should be warned against a too intellectual appraisal. To take, for example, the large horse of Plate 53 from Lascaux. This is much more than a catalogue of its attributes: animal, species *equus*, good to eat, useful hide, or even Epona or Rhiannon, goddess or ancestral mare. Over and beyond this, it is the outcome of centuries of painstaking experiment and discovery in the art of representation. Moreover, the artist who brings so much skill to his portrayal of the natural animal is working in a different tradition from that which reduces the idea of male and female to a symbol as simplified as the symbols of a pictographic script. The painting of the 'signs', particularly of darts and arrows placed on animals, appears to be by the same hand, and this may be thought to favour the older interpretation as weapons and wounds. Whatever intellectual interpretation is read into them, there is one level at which appearance and meaning are the same; a grazing reindeer, a tired horse, a reclining woman, whatever else they are as well, are also just this. Later mythologies warn us against a too rigid division of functions among the gods, and the same is surely true of the animals, which can as little be limited to one particular: sex, fertility, or food.

Confronted with these animals, we are struck by their abundant personality. They are not neutral, as in later art, where human protagonists hold the centre and animals are prey or a sycophantic chorus. The dominating personality of the great striding bulls of Lascaux appals. Here is a world in which animals are never neutral; and of this we can be quite certain, the artists knew infinitely more about them than we, with all our zoological records, ever can; so the very little that we do know should be used.

The seasons of the hunter's calendar are regulated by the game on which he depends for life, and in a sub-arctic hunter's world the great animal migrations must have formed its regular pivots. What the inundation of the Nile was to the ancient Egyptians, what the twice-yearly migration of the caribou is to the barrens Eskimo of northern Canada, such were the regular movements of reindeer, horse, and mammoth in the life of Magdalenian hunters. They gave the year its fasts and festivals.

There are few places in the world today where you can still see a great migration, and those who have seen it admit to being overwhelmed by the experience. Vast herds of bison no longer move across the North American plains, but much farther north in the Canadian barrens, although far fewer than they were even within living memory, the caribou still provide an extraordinary spectacle. Since this is also a landscape as like to that of Europe in the last glaciation as any we can find today, it will, I think, be best to quote from a description of the migration when the animals come north at the end of the long winter:[51] 'From the distance they barely seemed to move and yet in a few minutes they had reached the centre of the bay and had begun to take on shape, the long skeins dissolved at once in endless rows of deer, each following upon the footsteps of the animals ahead. Here and there along the lines a yearling kept its place beside a mother who was swollen with the new fawn she carried. There were no bucks. All these animals were does, all pregnant, all driving inexorably towards the north and the flat plains where they would soon give birth, the surface of the bay for six miles east and west, had become one undulating mass of animals. The does gazed briefly and incuriously at us, and swung a few feet away and passed on to the north without altering their gait. Hours passed till the sun was on the horizon . . . below us on the undulating darkness of the barren plains a tide of life flowed out of the dim south and engulfed the world so that it sank beneath a living sea. There was a sound of breathing and of moving that was like a rising wind.' This was the feeling of the sophisticated watcher, but he had with him an Eskimo companion, of whom he writes, 'the man beside me was no longer there. In some way that I could not fathom he had gone from me and had flung himself into the living torrent. There was an ecstasy upon him then. The man was gone, his spirit had sought and found a union with the amorphous entity that had possessed the land. He spoke so quietly that it might have been that I heard the divided voices of the monstrous visitation I had witnessed. 'Tuktu-mie . . .' this is the host, the legion of the deer.'

I have quoted this description at some length for several reasons. It shows how fearless and how vulnerable the does are in the spring migration, and also that they are already pregnant, the bucks following in more ragged companies some time later. For the hunters, nearly starved at the end of the winter, the first migration of gravid does is the stuff of life itself, health and food for weeks to come, the end of the long winter fast and the beginning of the season of feast and plenty. Added to this there is the curious spiritual bond which the sophisticated observer could sense, though he did not understand it, because 'the man was gone'. Wherever there is complete dependence, there seems to be this bond between hunter and prey in which fear and greed play only a small part. In the normal way the human pursuer was hopelessly outpaced, so the walls of caves and hunters' tackle are covered with animals in that condition, and at that season, in which they could most easily be approached, mare in foal, buck or bull with doe or cow. The suckling doe or cow is an extremely rare subject, and will have been a sight rarely seen by men from close to, before animals were domesticated.[52] It is possible that in Plate 64 and Figure 17 we have an actual attempt to catch the impression of the great migration.

A concomitant of a great movement, like the one described, is the suddenness with which it is all over. The landscape, that a moment before was blotted out by the waves of moving heads and rumps, is suddenly quite empty, and there is nothing but the thousands of slots in soft ground, and the carcases of a few victims, to show that they were there and have gone. Their appearances and disappearances are as sudden and unexplained as the epiphanies of the gods, and it is no surprise to find in popular beliefs that certain animals and birds 'make' the season in which they appear. The cranes bring the spring and the swallow the summer. The use at certain times of dead models does not mean that the subject was to be represented as already dead. On the contrary, care was taken to give it the attitudes of life and movement which was only defeated by the artist's hard-won, and now perhaps involuntary, powers of truthful representation

If these volatile images owe something of their quality to the nature of the 'canvas' and the lighting of the caves, they also offer the really insoluble problem of what the artist and his 'audience' saw: not the image on the retina but the image in the mind. The limitations of our experience impose a barrier beyond any incidental differences of lighting and modes of approach. Our visual memories and everything that makes up our mental bias leave us incapable of seeing what they saw. Many stories are told of the plain incomprehension of a contemporary 'primitive' when shown a photograph for the first time. To him it is a smooth surface with superficial lines and shadings and that is all; there is no 'picture' there.[53] The reverse side of this is less well recognized, but should warn us of all that we miss, or misread, in Paleolithic art. In the galleries of Trois Frères and of Lascaux we are as much at a loss as an aboriginal today looking at his first photograph. It is very obvious, and also very easily forgotten. It limits all our attempts at interpretation. In spite of the skill of the artist and the modernity of many of his devices, we are simply not seeing the things he saw. Perhaps this is most damaging where emptiness is part of the design. A little of the way we can go. The bison (Plate 49), unfinished or not, is an empty screen inside a heavy outline which appears to fill as we watch it. Where the artist has left those calculated blanks at La Pasiega, Covalanas, or Lascaux, we can name horse, deer, bull, mammoth, and that done we have only memories of farmyard cattle, park deer, young or broken-in horses and ponies, circus elephants. But this is poor furniture compared with what the Lascaux artists could count on in their audience, when a few promptings were enough to bring to life the flickering ears, whisking tails, turning heads, light and shade on flanks and rump, steam rising from sweating bodies, the wet dog smell of bear, and the dry warning reek of lion; just as the sketchiest outline of a castle, a tug, a car will be quite as heavily loaded for us. We can only bring to these works our twentieth-century intellects and senses, poor substitutes for the emotional and sensual urgency, the religious and devout awe with which *their* contemporaries responded to *them*. Our emotions are not engaged, and we are cold before these images as a twentieth-century sceptic is cold before the heaven and hell of a Gothic altarpiece.

To summarize these points which the 'classical' interpretations tend to ignore: animals are only sufficiently approachable to study, remember, copy during the migration, the rut, or when they are dead. They are, of course, more approachable at night, and even at dusk, but that is little help to the artist. The special relationship between hunter and prey, that is not only physical, gives to Paleolithic animal art its peculiar power; the impression that the animals are not neutral. Without this relationship it is doubtful whether there could have been any such art at all. The representations which to us seem most successful are those where there is an equilibrium between the conservative power of the ancient stereotype and the free invention that comes from experience and observation, while what may be called the spiritual content has a counterpart and speaks in both. Communication was an essential of this art, and this brings us to the most equivocal of all its characters: man and monsters.

These two orders of beings lay outside the discipline of stereotype and the rhythm of *schema* and correction. Artistically the monsters, composite animals, half-human half-animal figures, are, with rare exceptions, of minor interest; but they have appealed to the imagination and curiosity of modern man ever since they were discovered. Transformations of one species into another are a different matter.[54] One of the Roc de Sers creatures looks like a deliberately outlandish combination of pig and bison, and this is still more true of the poor monster on the point of giving birth that stands at Lascaux at the entrance of the Hall of Bulls (Plate 70). It has an eager and appealing expression, the strong hindquarters of a horse, the bison's hump, incredible horns, and ring-markings of an animal that never was.[55] Perhaps its position in the cave is a clue to its interpretation, but we do not even know for certain that this *was* the original entrance, or whether it only *seems* to stand guardian to the whole paradise of animals.

Except for the few large reliefs of nude women we look in vain among Magdalenian representations of man for the beauty, sobriety, and truth that are present in the animals. We will not find them again for several millennia and then only on the southern limits of the old province of Paleolithic art. The semi-human figures seem to belong to a wholly different artistic idiom. A few on bone objects and in some caves share a family likeness – the fat women of La Marche and Pech-Merle; but there are no stereotypes for the human image as there are for animals, and as there were for the small Gravettian carvings of women. Often they look like rapid improvisations or creations of a particular occasion; as art they are discouraging. They come in a multitude of disguises: fish, lizard, and seal-headed beings at Los Casares, a bird's head and a bear's body at Altamira, the chamois men of the bone from La Mairie à Teyjat, and the bison men of Trois Frères, foetus-like figures, ithyphallic figures, monstrously fat women, more or less human bodies wearing horns or antlers or animal skulls, and the best known of all, the Trois Frères antlered 'god' and the bird-headed 'man' in the shaft at Lascaux (Plates 69 and 73).[56] They have been called everything from masked dancers to hunters in animal disguise, sorcerers and witch-doctors, ancestral spirits and gods.

There are two drawings which are interesting more for their subject than for any skill in representation. One is from La Colombière but found in an earlier excavation than the animals (Plate 71). It is another palimpsest, this time on bone. There is a horse's head, the antlers of a reindeer, perhaps the outline of a woman's body, and, much the clearest, a hairy, man-like creature with one arm stretched forward: man-like, but not like the sapient men of Cro-Magnon race who inhabited the rock-shelters and houses we have been considering (not, that is, as their skeletons show them to have been, nor even the de-humanized sketches which occasionally appear among other small engravings of rather later times). Either this is a caricature or it is a 'monster' like the giants of folk memory: huge, hirsute, slow-witted, uncanny. We may even question whether they were invention or memory. For generations sapient man had inhabited the same Europe as beings curiously like this figure. Folk-memory is certainly long, and in our imagination we often prefer repetition to invention, but whether men could still recall the earlier phases of this last glaciation it would be over-bold to speculate, let alone assert. So this remains a strange and unique image. The second representation is a scene scratched on a stone found at Péchialet. Two more or less human figures are occupied with a large bear (Plate 72). Further than that it is not possible to go, but the grouping of the figures suggests some sort of action, a narrative rather than a decorative or formal intention, although the outline of the left-hand 'human' figure echoes that of the bear.

The different interpretations of Lascaux and Trois Frères are typical of the problem. The scene of Plate 69 has been read as a hunting anecdote: a man killed by a bison which in turn is mortally wounded by a rhinoceros; or a scene of sacrifice, or black magic, or a shaman prostrate in ecstasy, the bird-head signifying his supernatural nature and the flight of the spirit. Some have compared the 'man' to other ithyphallic figures, and others have stressed the different idioms used for the solid rhinoceros, the more schematic disembowelled bison, and the very schematic 'man'.[57] The rod with a bird on top, sometimes called a totem, is more convincingly identified as a spear-thrower, like those Magdalenian ones that had the end carved as an animal or bird, or, once, a human head.[58] All that is obvious is that a gigantic spear has transfixed a bison. Even so long a spear could not probably pierce the hide of a rhinoceros, and that animal departs in good shape. The six marks below its tail probably belong to the scene.[59] There certainly seems to be a peculiar bond between the spear, the bird-spear-thrower, and the bird-headed 'man'. Is the latter perhaps an apotheosis of the spear-thrower, like the deified shields and axes of Minoan iconography? A great many javelins were certainly found on the floor of the pit below. It is better to say we do not know, but we do know that there was a special respect for bison. The bison menacing a man at Roc de Sers, the bison at La Mouthe, and another at Lascaux, are all in much the same pose. These may be acting out a secular scene, but the scenes engraved on bone from Les Eyzies and Raymonden (Plate 68 and Figure 24) have an air of ritual and perhaps convey a sacramental relationship. The rhinoceros on the other hand, an inedible and unfriendly animal, is associated neither with human beings, nor with other animals. It is appropriate that in the one composite scene in which it figures it should turn its back and walk away.

The rhinoceros and bison are familiar and much-used stereotypes. The 'bird'-man and spear-thrower are not, nor is the bison's wound. In that form they are unique to this scene, which may explain the different style of representation. Only some urgent need, some natural or supernatural crisis may have driven the artist, ill-equipped for the purpose, to make up a scene of these disparate elements.[60] The inaccessibility of the situation, reached originally, perhaps, by sliding down a rope, adds much to the strangeness, the atmosphere of something secret and deeply significant; while the scatter of lamps and javelins at the bottom of the pit tells us how often it was visited.

The aura of mystery and of remoteness is even greater at Trois Frères. As at Lascaux, the semi-human figures are found in the deepest ramifications of the system, though at a far greater distance in the so-called 'sanctuary'. Engraved on the walls are a tangle of animals and one painted figure, the 'sorcerer' or 'god', removed a little from the generality, like the Lascaux figure, but looking down from 13 feet above the ground, not hidden below in a pit. The immense labour of copying the complicated surfaces at Trois Frères is one of the most astonishing achievements of the Abbé Breuil; for the maze of lines and superpositions defeats the camera. All the visitor can make out, or the camera record, of the 'god' today are staring eyes and an indistinct shape, but the drawings show the figure in all its strangeness, reindeer antlers and ears, beard of a man or bison, the round unearthly eyes, paws perhaps of a bear, a horse's or wolf's tail, and human legs and male sex. The full face of man or animal is rare, but just at Trois Frères there are enormous full face heads of lions (Figure 18). At least two other figures, half bison half man, are engraved below among the animals (Plate 74). The smaller one (only 8 inches) is often reproduced along with the bison and reindeer immediately to the left of it, as though they formed a composition, or at least were linked together in the same action. But there seems no real justification for isolating these three figures. Nothing in the engraving holds them together more than the others, nor need the bow-shaped object, apparently suspended from the bison-man's nose, but actually superimposed on nose and forearm, belong to him.[61]

These powerful evocations of the animal and the supernatural are more carefully depicted than is usual with such figures. A peculiarity of this cave is the very high proportion of animals in the prostrate attitude of a lifeless carcase. It is by their energy and vivacity that the semi-human figures stand out from the welter of beasts, whereas elsewhere the contrary is more often the case. At Trois Frères the impression is forced upon one that the animal world has been in some curious way slighted. We miss the monumentality of the carved friezes, the nobility of Lascaux, the animal portraiture of Altamira, and the elusive, delicate movement of La Pasiega. It is as though here alone, the models being dead, the artist has not troubled, or wished, to bring them alive, but is content to surround his supernatural beings with a *battu* of carcases. This does not apply to all the work at Trois Frères, but it does to the great surcharged engravings in the 'sanctuary'. Compared with the animal-masked hunters of late Mesolithic and Bushman art, or the fourth-millennium animal musicians of the Ur harp and of Mesopotamian seals, we can see that they are something quite different, though superficially alike. This is a milieu in which the figures of myth are visibly materializing from the fluid outlines and vague contours of earlier Paleolithic thought.

Looking back now over the length of this art, we have seen how the artist had learnt to portray nature with truth and fidelity long before he went into the caves to find a canvas. The first slender body of carving and modelling with its domestic milieu was something very different. But there were also from the first hints of hunter's magic and perhaps the beginnings of shamanism. This first phase was dominated by the image of man, sometimes exaggerated or stylized, sometimes natural and harmonious. In the later phase it is the animal that dominates. If this should seem strange let us remember the caribou Eskimo on the Canadian barrens and the way in which the great migrations manifest themselves; the mysterious suddenness of their appearances and disappearances like the gods. The animals of the caves may be materializations of divinity in the form of those visitations, the animal epiphanies of Greek gods, and the animal metamorphoses and double natures of Celtic heroes (Chapters 8 and 9 below). Again there may be some link between the hunter's 'kill' and the animal sacrifices of more advanced societies. There is a sense in which the hunted animal gives its life for the hunter. These two aspects, the divine epiphany and the sacrificial slaughter, are perhaps united in the evolved iconography of the Raymonden scene.

The character of the shaman has been sketched already (p. 26): his power of returning to the primordial paradise in which men possessed immortality and were free to come and go between earth and heaven, and free too of the paradise to which the hunting rituals looked back; above all his special friendship with animals, speaking their language, enjoying the companionship of a familiar; something of this can, I believe, be discerned in the art of Paleolithic man. The attributes of the shaman did not vanish. We have latter-day echoes in the stories that surround the desert fathers and Celtic hermits with their familiar beasts, culminating perhaps in a St Francis endowed with greater spiritual powers than the greatest shaman. According to their poor capabilities, the wise men, or whatever they were, of the Upper Paleolithic mediated between man and that unknown world so great a part of which belonged to animal life.[62] The skill of the artist has given us some inkling of how this was done.

The contrast between the two cycles of art – the one in daylight, accessible, almost domestic; the other secret, inaccessible, remote from the mundane world – shows that there was room allotted for both, for the rites and rituals of everyday as well as those of the equivocal world of darkness, distance, and mystery. In spite of differences they overlap in time and geography, and though in techniques and in some of the subjects so different, the same stereotypes occur in both. The artist in the caves makes his animals no less beautiful than does the artist outside; friezes and heraldic pairs appear in both. The life portrayed in the caves mirrors everyday life in the world, but with a difference, as though slightly slanted.

The supernatural regions of Greek and Near Eastern gods were separated into a sacred mountain or firmament and an underworld, into Olympus and the House of Hades, approached by a cave or hole in the ground, while their social life reflects (to the point of scandal) the manners of men. The reindeer-herding Lapps, probably direct descendants of the reindeer hunters of the Upper Paleolithic (p. 74), believed among other things in spirits called *saivo* living under the earth, or in a sacred mountain, whose existence runs parallel to the life of men and with whom were linked beliefs in reincarnation and migration of souls.[63] The Celts in the far west described a world divided between two camps, the one of men, and 'the other camp' which belonged to supernatural powers, the people of the *sid* living beyond time under the earth. The two races, alike but distinct and inimical, maintained relations, and at special seasons the curtain was lifted and the two worlds communicated. Many myths are concerned with these occasions.

The underworld of Lapps, the other world of Celts, and to a less extent of Greeks, separate from, yet interlocking with, everyday things, mythical yet real, visited under special circumstances at certain seasons; is there not something in this of recollection, some memory distorted by distance and time of 'the other world' of the caves, as we see it in its art and supposed rituals? Lapps and Celts have little in common except that they now inhabit the outer perimeter of the world once lived in by Upper Paleolithic hunters; but if there ever was a common tradition and common memories alive throughout Europe they could have just survived into the historical period on those perimeters, as they seem to have done at the heart in remote valleys of the Pyrenees.[64] This is the more likely if the art of the caves and shelters was not the property of local tribes or clans alone, but, as I have suggested, something shared by mobile hunters free of great tracts of European plain and mountain. The caves were not abandoned all at once. There are Carbon 14 dates of around 10,000 at La Vache; Lascaux was visited as late as *c.* 6000 B.C.,[65] and there are other signs that in the Neolithic and even in the Bronze Age, men still occasionally frequented the same caves. When the tide of obliterating forest cut them off from the old easy intercourse of the hunting life, when the sacred places were no longer visited, the image of the caves may not have died, but have remained, no less obsessive for being no longer understood. As well as the physical barrier there arose a spiritual barrier, and the real journey to the cave sanctuary becomes the journey to Hades, the Land of No Return, the 'descent' of mystery religions, Annwn in Britain, and the Underworld journey of shamanic ecstasy.

In our approach to this world, and to its art as art, we are still very much at the beginning. It would be impossible and presumptuous from so few and defective monuments to judge the sum of an achievement in which sculpture, modelling, engraving, and painting encountered so many of the problems and forestalled the solutions of later western art. Spread over some twenty millennia, which is double the time that separates us from its last works, this is not a unit like Egyptian or Byzantine art, nor even the arts that we shall find in Neolithic and Iron Age Europe: it is multitudinous, unaccountable, and a fragment. Any pattern or progress it may appear to have is the result of selection and omission. Selection has in fact been employed in this chapter in order to concentrate attention upon the steps by which the artist as technician mastered his craft, and by which man explored and enlarged the region of the external world and of interior psychology which could be communicated by them. The method would be indefensible if the period were shorter, or the beginning other than a total blank. We see certain achievements, certain things done, and up to a point the order in which they were done, but the filling of the gaps and the arrangement of the details is arbitrary. The invention of 'natural' perspective or of the impressionistic depiction of soft or indistinct edges cannot be pinned down to one particular object – a bone from Schweizersbild or Pekarna – but still these inventions were made, and the lapse of time is so great that, if we suppose an area of probability around each imaginary fixed point, then our chosen examples should lie within its penumbra. It must have happened somehow so, but it would be rash to maintain that it had in fact happened exactly so. We are handling a perishable commodity and asking that it shall persist; a most elusive, equivocal language and demanding sense and syntax. The result is no more than a construction of a kind that, with a little luck, may serve as the temporary scaffolding run up around a building; it is not the building itself.

CHAPTER 3

MESOLITHIC ART: 8000–2000

Voces de muerte sonaron
cerca del Guadalquivir.
Voces antiguas . . .
F. Garcia Lorca

IN the early days of prehistoric studies Old Stone Age culture and society was thought to dwindle into a vacuum, the notorious 'hiatus' which preceded an age of polished stone implements, of potting and farming – virtually a fresh start. The 'hiatus' disappeared long ago from prehistory, its place taken by hunting, fishing, and fowling Mesolithic cultures. The lowering of Paleolithic and raising of Neolithic dates, based on Carbon 14 readings, has shortened drastically the period to be covered. In spite of this the 'hiatus' has remained in the history of art, and some explanation is required for what seems to be real decay from the masterpieces of a Paleolithic artist to the *graffiti* and repetitive patterns of Azilian, Maglemosian, and other Mesolithic hunters. After this lapse an entirely new beginning is supposed to have carried the development of art, by way of the ancient civilizations of the Near and Middle East, to Greece, Italy, and the modern world. In this chapter we will try to discover the reasons for change and decline, its real extent, and any signs of a new vision and of creative activities peculiar to the age.

This period runs from a little before 8000 to around 5000 B.C., and in some parts till considerably later. The first date marks the beginning of the phase of climate which we still experience, and from the seventh or sixth millennium groups of farmers were beginning to colonize Europe from the south-east, although the hunting way of life was not displaced till some time later. In the Near East life in settled, as opposed to temporary, villages and towns, with the beginnings of farming, goes back into the ninth millennium, so that in some places the existence of a purely hunting–fishing–fowling stage between true Paleolithic and Neolithic has been lost. The phase of climate and the pattern of the retreating ice have been carefully mapped in the northern half of Europe with the help of fossil pollens, clay sediments, and soils; and a chronological frame for the cultures and (though all too rarely) the art of the inhabitants has been worked out.[1] The peculiarities of this environment, compared with the Near East, explain to some extent the peculiarly European character of the civilizations that did eventually emerge.

Late glacial and post-glacial change was not all in one direction. From around 11,000 to 8000 light birch forest and parkland had alternated with sub-arctic steppe in the North European plain and in southern Scandinavia. Then, about 8000, a thicker cover of birch and willow forest followed by pine spread northwards and the temperature rose steadily till about 6000, when it was much the same as today, though a little more continental (see Table 1). Forest animals – red and roe deer, pig, beaver, and marten –

increased at the expense of arctic ones, and with fish and fowl provided the hunters' quarry. At the end of this time there was a massive invasion of hazel stretching from Ireland to Transylvania and from Estonia to the Pyrenees, where it was often five, twelve, and seventeen times more numerous than all other trees.[2] Uncoppiced hazel is a formidable barrier to communications, and it is not surprising to find settlements now scattered along streams, round lakes, and on shore-lines. A little later hazel gave way to deciduous forest, and the climate reached its continental optimum about 5000 B.C., after which it grew more oceanic with wetter, milder winters. Central and Eastern Europe were always more continental, with pine, spruce, and silver fir in place of the mixed oak forest, and in Russia the advance of forest over steppe was even slower.

As well as the changing climate there were great alterations in sea-level. Earlier coastal settlements were submerged by water released from the melting ice-cap and glaciers, though here too there were interruptions, and the old shore-lines are marked by the camping sites of Mesolithic strand-loopers. The present North Sea bed in early post-glacial times was above sea-level, and travelling hunters could pick their way among the dunes and meres from Yorkshire to Jutland. Vestiges of their hunting tackle are found there and as far as Pomerania and Estonia, all very much alike and all belonging to the 'Maglemosian' type of culture. As the sea-level rose the lakes became brackish, and the final separation of island and continent was complete by about 6000 B.C.[3] At the same time, close to the ice cap, land that had been depressed by its weight gradually rose, and the double movement tilted the whole Scandinavian land-mass and brought about extraordinary alterations in the Baltic.

The coast and hinterland of the Mediterranean had never suffered the extremes of glacial cold; so they provided a refuge for the tenderer trees and plants as well as for forest animals. The landscape of the first few thousand years after the end of the Paleolithic is so lost that today it is not easy to imagine. *Garrigue* and *maquis* were once deep, broad-leaved, evergreen woodland, with cool dark glades in which the still numerous forest game could be surprised and tracked. The great mounded tops of oak and elm spread up the mountains to where the pine-belt began, while on inland plateaux, like Central Iberia, there was grass steppe behind the forest. This was by no means a disagreeable habitat for man, particularly if he was armed with bow and arrow. At the same time the tideless sea was as tempting to small boats as the meres and lakes of Northern Europe and the great rivers of the East. The same Mediterranean climate and vegetation extended over North Africa, not only the coasts but the Maghreb, including the southern fringe of the Atlas massif, so that from the Nile valley to the Atlantic evergreen forest and grassland alternated, and game and the conditions for hunting it were much the same as in Iberia, and indeed all round the Mediterranean. There is some evidence for an abrupt alteration about 9000 B.C., with greater heat and drought driving the larger cattle north into the coastal belt.[4]

This was a very new environment, but to the men who experienced it the amount of change falling within a single lifetime would have appeared simply as the need to push a little farther north in a particularly hot summer and return to new winter camps not quite so far south, a very slight readjustment of life, where the stable element was provided by the favourite game animal. For the caribou Eskimo of Canada, referred to in the last chapter, hell is simply that place where there are no deer and never will be deer, and heaven one where deer can always be found.[5] This being so, the actual situation of camps becomes relatively unimportant, and the survival of social life with its memories, myths, and arts in the far north of Europe and Asia from the end of the Old Stone Age to the present day is easily understandable. There is evidence that this really happened in the skills of the northern Mesolithic cultures, which have so much in common with present-day reindeer Lapps of Finnmark and hunter-fishers of arctic Russia.

Migration was not the only solution to the problem of invading undergrowth, and many bands remained in the old camps and in great shelter caves like the Mas d'Azil (Ariège), discovering new ways of living, and of catching and killing the more elusive game. Mesolithic settlements are usually small. Star Carr in Yorkshire, a winter camp of Maglemosian hunters, is typical of them, with room on a brushwood platform for the tents or light huts of sixteen to a dozen people. This is very different from the large settlements, practically villages, of Moravian mammoth-hunters (see above, p. 11).[6] Three discoveries had made possible hunting by small parties or even a single hunter: these were the bow, the dog, and the boat.[7] Fishing and hunting from boats, stalking and lying in wait with bows and arrows, pursuing with dogs, bringing down birds on the wing, and netting fish, better armed and better clothed, Mesolithic man was a different creature from his Paleolithic forebears. More ominous for the future are signs of warfare between different bands which we see portrayed in the art of the Spanish Levant, or guess from the sombre evidence of a flint arrowhead in a human vertebra in Brittany.[8] Living in greater isolation and independence than before, it is possible that men developed a stronger feeling of ownership towards their hunting territory and hostility to other bands. On the Mediterranean coasts and hinterland the changes in climate were less striking, and the stimulus of new ideas came rather from outside, from North Africa and, especially towards the end of our period, from the eastern Mediterranean, when sea-communications gave rise to new sorts of settlement far transcending the strand-loopers' way of life with its easy harvests.

In this way the great environmental divisions of Europe were formed: the sub-arctic or circumpolar, the temperate forest, and the Mediterranean. In spite of invasions from east and south these divisions still stand, just perceptible under the blanketing of cities and internationalism of contemporary movements and styles.

Great as were the changes in climate and environment, they do not alone explain the disappearance of Paleolithic art. On the part played by isolation and lost mobility when forest, dense and deciduous, spread over parkland and steppe, I have already said something (p. 33). Both those who started the long, slow journey north and those who stayed within their territories in detached, hostile bands must have experienced a concrete rupture with the past, a shock to the elusive influence of place on art. The old sanctuaries could not attract and dominate as they once did, except, and to a much lesser extent, round the Mediterranean in southern Spain, Italy, and Sicily. Even more disconcerting than the cessation of large-scale art is the disappearance, about the same time, of small-scale artist's and craftsman's work. Compared with the delicate engraved and carved

Magdalenian spear-throwers and 'bâtons', the Mesolithic fish-spears, leister prongs, and so on, are almost without exception monotonous utilitarian objects. The inferiority of red-deer, compared with reindeer, antler and mammoth ivory does not explain the loss but supports a belief in the essential unity of drawing and engraving on small objects and on large surfaces as a single artistic tradition. Disruption of the one entailed the decay of the other.

Northern Europe

Mesolithic art in Northern Europe is almost limited to Scandinavia, though if we use Mesolithic in its wider sense the rock-carvings of northern Russia can be included. The rarity and poor quality of the more representational drawings on bone must be due to lack of interest; for geometric patterns on the same sorts of implement are often careful and intricate. An antler haft for a stone tool found at Ystad in Skåne, Sweden, has scratched on it two deer with shed antlers (Plate 75).[9] Before dismissing this poor little drawing, a few points are worth noticing: all four legs are shown, though reduced to sticks towards the bottom; both ears are given in a single plane pointing opposite ways; and there is hatching on head and neck. This is the same peculiar treatment of ears as was used by Magdalenian artists (Figure 12A). At Altamira the hatching on face and neck is in fact shading and gives three-dimensional depth; at Ystad it is merely a remembered trick. This is full decadence, the work perhaps of an inexpert doodler, but nevertheless a doodler with representational art in his bones. Somewhere he must have seen drawings of deer not unlike Figure 12A. The same antler haft has typical Maglemosian geometric engraving, a hatched net or honeycomb. Some tools with these patterns can be dated between 6800 and 5000.

The human figure is even rarer than animals, but it appears in a scene engraved on an aurochs' (long-horned wild cattle) bone club, found at Rymarksgård in Zeeland (Plate 76). The engraved line was filled with white, and the drawing seems to represent on the left a full face figure in movement with arms raised, and three more figures advancing towards the right, where a fifth person stands full face in front of an upright zigzag motif. This last represents water in the art and writing of Egypt and of the Orient; it was often used by Maglemosian artists, and it also occurs in just this form, though painted, in the hunter's art of Spain (Figure 35). Sometimes it seems to represent a snake.[10] The Rymarksgård date is probably early sixth millennium. Rudimentary as art, none the less in this little scene we probably have a portrayal of ceremonial or ritual. There is the same balance, the same type of composition, as in the scenes from Raymonden and Les Eyzies (Plate 68 and Figure 24), but now, as well as looking back, certain representations are foreshadowed which will only become fully explicit in the Bronze Age.[11] The triangular heads and conventionally hatched bodies are as serviceable to their medium as the blobs and lines of some Sumerian seal-impressions to theirs.

The likeness between geometric patterns on early painted pottery in Egypt and the Middle East and those cut on Mesolithic bone, including the zigzag, alternating triangles, and net pattern, are so close that they must be typical of a certain stage in the history of ornament; one perhaps that has been deeply influenced by basketry, net-making, and reed-matting. The meander patterns of Paleolithic Mezin are an earlier by-product of the same crafts (Figure 9).[12]

Most of the geometric patterns on antler ends compare poorly with those of Magdalenian craftsmen, but there are a few which are highly competent minuscule work, smaller than any Paleolithic drawing. There are, for instance, the repeated rather finicking animals on a slotted bone spearhead with flint insets from Kongemosen in Denmark.[13] The head, neck, and body are quite recognizable, though only about a tenth of an inch long (between three and four mm.). The tiny scale is reminiscent of Eskimo engravings, but the mathematical repetition suggests a symbolism closer to that of arithmetic than representation. This implement is important because it is dated by pollen analysis to the sixth millennium; and because it gives the key to another motif, a line of heads and necks that might have been taken for abstract notches (Bjernede, Plate 77). There are patterns that suggest stitching and leatherwork as well as nets and netting, so that decorative stitching and painting (like the painted Lapp drums of later days) may have relieved the drabness of Mesolithic gear. Tailored clothes were an early speciality of arctic people. But if we think of these patterns as taken from actual nets, reed screens, baskets, and stitched hide boats, something more than the mundane activity is implied. The net is a metaphor, so is the honeycomb; boats will carry gods and heroes; weaving of rushes as well as fibres is a fateful act of creation. Without trying to interpret the patterns too closely, or disentangle sacred from secular, the fact of their careful execution on durable material gives some warning of their role.

Pitted as well as incised ornament was used by Maglemosian artists, as it had been occasionally by Paleolithic. The pits in bone and amber are now so regular that it seems they must have been made by rotating a bow-drill. Some patterns are much the same as the incised ones, but there are also hints of human and animal symbolism. Pitted ornament has a vast Asiatic as well as European extension, for the pot-makers later used it too. Amber was often used in this way, and also carved and pierced. The strange properties of the fossil resin lumps which were found washed up after a storm on the Baltic and North Sea shores may have disturbed and certainly attracted the northern people. Native amber generates negative electricity when it is rubbed, and (like other resins) exerts forces of attraction which would certainly have appeared when it was drilled.

As far as we know amber is one of the first of the precious substances appropriated by man; not as early as red ochre, haematite, and coal, but preceding gold, silver, and gems. Its mysterious origin and the threads of plants and winged insects occasionally imprisoned in the lumps have given rise to many legends like the Greek ones of tears let fall by Phaeton's sisters when turned to poplars, and perhaps the golden apples of the Hesperides; for Tacitus records a belief that Baltic amber came from trees growing near the northern sun, their gums drawn out by its heat. He also records that when lit it burns like a torch with a thick scented flame and cools into sticky resin.[14] Much amber may have been consumed in this way, and its strange qualities are persistently connected with the sun. This fact may also have contributed to its use for small carvings in the round like the bear from Resen in Viborg, Denmark (Plate 78, bottom left), which is of a reddish golden amber with a fine netted decoration on the surface. Much simplified, it is very much a bear, with the same clean feel and smooth contours that Paleolithic carvers gave their animal and human figures; it also reminds us of the ancient veneration of the bear. The enormous cave bear whose dark encounters terrified Neanderthal and early *sapiens* man has become a warm golden bauble to caress in the palm of the hand.[15] The amber bird from Egesvang in Viborg (Plate 78, centre) has the same plastic qualities, and the animal in blackish amber with a long upper lip on the left of the Plate may represent an elk. The horse- or elk-head (bottom right) from Egemarke in Holbaek is a silhouette, almost flat, with on it a tremolo-like pattern of zigzags. Most of the dating is unfortunately more stylistic than exact.

This minor sculpture shows that the art of carving just survived during the post-Paleolithic centuries; it is rather better with rock engravings. The Maglemosians were lowlanders, but northwards the group of early settlements near Trondheim on the west coast of Norway and another in Finnmark on the Arctic Ocean, known as Fosna and Komsa cultures, beginning in the eighth millennium, may be connected with large-scale carvings of animals. There is another group in Jämtland in Central Sweden. Unfortunately there is no direct evidence for dating them, though attempts have been made to use alterations in the shore-line and sea-level.[16] The carvings are in wild, remote country and at a distance from sheltered settlements. They are often on vertical or very steep rock-faces directly above sea or lake, or near a stream of deep running water. This imposed even greater limits on the artist's freedom than the cramped darkness of caves. The reason is probably the age-old method of hunting which was still used in the eighteenth century: herds of animals being stampeded by beaters over cliffs and into rivers and the carcases collected by men in boats. Lapp legends have many stories of enemies lured to destruction in the same way. (On Plate 79 at Landsverk an elk is on the left; the second animal is said to be a bear.)

The engravings have suffered much from winter frost, snow, and rain, and painting is unlikely to have survived; nevertheless traces of red have been found inside the engraved lines.[17] The earliest works (Style A) are more or less life-size animals in strict profile. An outline, $\frac{2}{5}$ – $\frac{4}{5}$ inch (1–2 cm.) broad, was ground into hard *fjall* granite or, where occasionally a softer slate was available, an incised line with triangular section was used, and more rarely the old Paleolithic method of pecking. The favourite subjects are elk and reindeer. Unlike most of the deer family, the elk is not a graceful animal, and we cannot blame the artists for their failure to charm with these gaunt silhouettes, which are none the less faithful descriptions of the animal: forelegs slightly bent, drooping, despondent head, ears branching in opposite directions, the button tail and the long upper lip, much prized as a gourmet's delicacy in Siberia, and the 'bell' or bag of skin below the cheek, often believed to be the seat of the soul. The reindeer who shed their antlers in the spring are shown carrying them, but the elk who shed theirs in January do not. There are also occasionally bears and swimming birds, always with the same profile view at right angles to the line of sight with only two limbs shown, so that we seem to be back at the beginning of Paleolithic drawing, at La Grèze or Pair-non-Pair (Plates

16 and 17); but instead of making comparisons with the variety of Magdalenian fine engravings, we should look at the reliefs and deep engravings in the open, where we find the same monumental pose and two-limb profiles (Cap Blanc and La Chaire à Calvin, etc.; Plates 21 and 32). There is nothing particularly primitive in drawing two legs instead of four. Scythian artists of many centuries later sometimes used the convention, and it is almost invariable in Luristan bronzework.[18]

Naturalism here is an illusion – these are stereotypes in an iconography as conservative as that of the Egyptian pharaoh or Byzantine saints and fathers – and when change came it was not in the direction of greater freedom and realism, but towards a richer intellectual content and a sort of exact information. The angular elk body is caricatured,

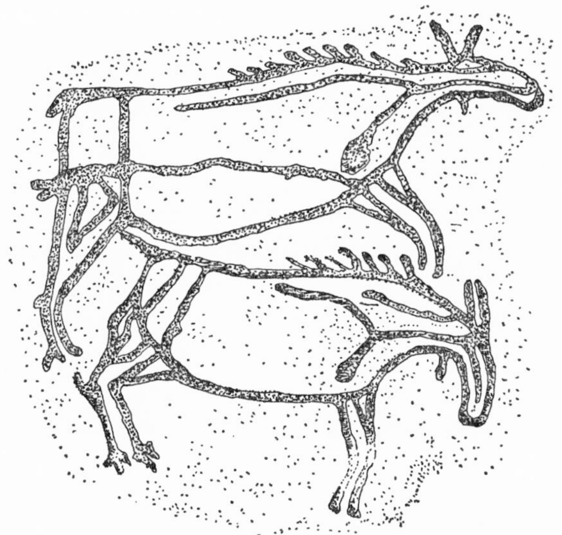

Figure 25. 'X-ray' engraving of elk on rock at Kløfterfoss, Buskerud, Norway

becoming almost square, but the power of the old stereotype survives in the bent foreleg and droop of head and neck (Plate 80; at the bottom is an elk-headed boat). Many later drawings are maps describing the animal's invisible organs and structure, not what the eye sees of a living presence. This anatomical or X-ray style is used today by many primitive people, including the Eskimo of Alaska, whose way of life is so like that of Mesolithic arctic hunters. In this 'B' style of Scandinavian rock art the profile line may still be naturalistic, but inside a 'life-line' leads to lungs and heart, or the whole animal is divided up into joints like a butcher's diagram (Figure 25). It would be wrong to think because of this that the animal had been reduced to a mere source of food; the beautiful carved stone and bone elk hammers, maces, and handles of the Neolithic and later centuries urge the contrary (Plate 156). As well as sustaining material existence, the elk is still a powerful symbol.

The later Norwegian drawings, both X-ray style and collections of quite small animals, sometimes with all four legs, lie lower down the cliffs than the big naturalistic ones, and appear to follow an old coastline of the warmer, wetter climate phase between 5000 and 2000 B.C. Some of the higher carvings may be contemporary with Maglemosians of around 5000, when the shore-line was sinking fairly rapidly. However, the old sharp division between 'hunter's art' and 'farmer's art' no longer holds; sometimes the styles are mixed, and the latest continue into the Bronze Age.[19]

Figure 26. Rock-engraving at Bessov-Noss, Lake Onega, Russia

There are no compositions, though pairs of animals and frieze-like groupings in single file do occur; more often the figures are scattered indiscriminately over the rock. This is particularly true of the small-scale and anatomical engravings. It is usually said that there is no connexion between this art and that of the Maglemosians, but in fact a tenuous link joins the Ystad deer (Plate 75) and small engravings at Vingen, Nordfjord; too little has survived, however, to provide any real basis for comparison.[20] One has to travel east through the great forest belt to find a real continuation of the Scandinavian arctic style. Near Lakes Onega and Ladoga in Karelia the same gaunt elk image was pecked out of the rock. Near the village of Pissannai in the region of Tomsk in Siberia, there are carvings that are in fact closest in style and technique to the Scandinavian. The animals occasionally overlap, but more often walk or trot in line ahead. They are without antlers, and the succulent upper lip is exaggerated. Sometimes there are lines across the neck, a detail not found in Scandinavia. Though elk predominate, there are also heron and fox, human figures and elk-headed boats. In places the surface has been polished and repecked as though a slate were wiped clean between sketches.[21] In Karelia too the animals are joined by man, now armed with bow and arrow and a chief actor. The artists were hunters and fishers like the Fosna and Komsa people, but from the rubbish of the settlements it appears that they were contemporaries of the Neolithic and bronze-using farmers living south of the forest in the third or even second millennium.

Very far north on a rock at Zalavruga near the White Sea elk are driven in line. The largest are life-size like those of Norway, and with only two legs drawn; most still carry their antlers, and a small human figure pecked in the same style pursues them on skis and aims an arrow. It is this appearance of man that makes the difference between the Russian and Norwegian carvings. Also at Zalavruga three skiers advance together carrying ski-sticks; like the two-legged elk, they are flat, with one leg and arm apiece. Unless the left-hand figure is a giant compared to the right-hand one, the positions are exactly the reverse of how we would arrange them in perspective; even so, and in spite of the rugged technique, they are grotesquely and comically real (Plate 81). A man with a wolf's head and tail appears several times round Lake Onega – perhaps a shaman in animal disguise – and a powerfully eerie effect is produced at Bessov-Noss by the conjunction of this figure with the crescent and disc that he holds or propels before him, following an elk (Figure 26). Both elk and long-necked water-bird sometimes carry the disc, which may or may not be the sun, while the crescent may be the moon. This surely is myth. In scale these scenes stand half-way between the monumental elk and reindeer of earlier Scandinavian art and the quite small figures engraved in the Bronze Age; they are also stylistically half-way between those flat but naturalistic profiles and the much formalized later figures (Plates 79 and 201). But the elk image lived on obsessively into much later times and will meet us again even at the end of the Bronze Age.

Southern Europe

Earlier probably than Maglemosian, certainly earlier than arctic Stone Age art, are the signs painted by Azilians; so named from the huge shelter in the Pyrenees, the Mas d'Azil, which was also frequented by Paleolithic men. It has been said of Azilian painted pebbles, as of some Upper Paleolithic subjects, that they could belong equally to the history of art or magic or writing.[22] The pigment is always red, either ochre or a mixture of the life-substance itself, blood; this and the choice of only smooth round pebbles for decoration prevents us from dismissing these simple signs as ephemeral doodles. Though probably derived ultimately from representational shorthand, they have gone a good deal farther than, for instance, the pictorial forerunner of cuneiform writing in which two semicircles can represent sun, day, or time. This was a stage immediately before the change to phonetic values, which is the final break with art, when the visual meaning of the symbol is disregarded, and it takes its place as a natural vehicle in the formation of the syllabary. But this ideal ladder from pictographs to syllables was not climbed once and for all; there were many false starts and rude set-backs. Paleolithic 'bâtons' with exact representations of ears or eyes, feet or antlers, had progressed some way up the ladder, and Mesolithic Europe does not seem to get much farther, probably because there was still no *need* for writing. The next step did not depend on development of the signs themselves but had to wait for a far more complicated economic and social situation. The cryptic symbols on Azilian pebbles are negligible in the history of art and a dead end in that of writing.

Though following directly Magdalenian culture, Azilian does not grow out of it but has its roots in the alternative Perigordian tradition of the Upper Paleolithic. The real continuation of Paleolithic art is not in the Pyrenees nor round the Baltic and the Arctic Ocean, but in that Mediterranean landscape where descendants of Paleolithic hunters lived on, in Calabria, in Sicily, and above all in Spain.

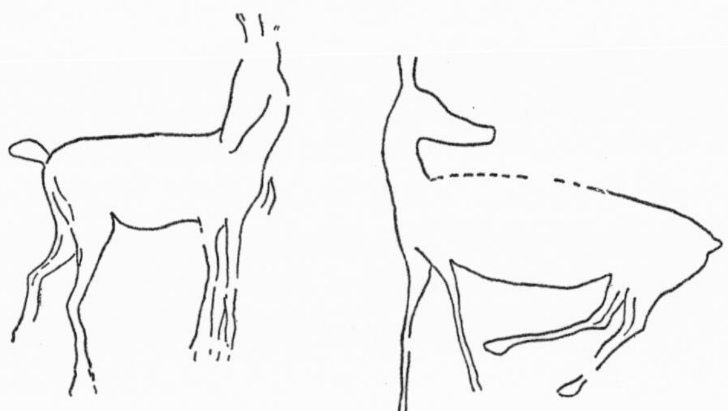

Figure 27. Rock-engravings in a cave on Levanzo, Italy

A rock shelter, Romito, in a wild mountainous part of Calabria, has a handsome engraving of a bull. It is a heavy, fleshy beast, very different from the lithe Lascaux bulls, but the feet are twisted to show the cloven hoof, and the animal stands on tip-toe as in that Late Magdalenian style that seemed to come from the use of dead animals. The engraving measures 3 feet 11 inches (1·20 m.), and all four legs are shown.[23] Romito is not much farther south than the Grotta Romanelli, where there are a number of very stylized engravings with Carbon 14 dates of 8690 and 7930. More interesting are animal engravings in a small, dark cave on the tiny island of Levanzo in the Egadi group off the west coast of Sicily which are dated about 8700.[24] The sea between Levanzo and Sicily is only 130 feet at its deepest and, as the shore-line has risen since the end of the Paleolithic, the islands were probably joined to Sicily when the cave was first used. The animals are still in the style of Late Paleolithic drawing that represented all four legs, and horns and antlers in natural perspective. One doe in particular is drawn with great freedom; the turn of the head reminds us of Covalanas, but without the unnatural elongation of the neck (Figure 27). Another deer turns and looks past the observer. Such freedom and command of pose would have appeared a sort of heresy in the far north. One of the Levanzo bulls has the same convex nose and thick neck as the Romito animal, and there is a bull following a smaller cow that is very like a subject in the Paleolithic cave of Teyjat (Dordogne) some three or four thousand years earlier.[25] There are too the same tip-toe stance and lolling tongue as we saw in the dead models of the

Late Paleolithic, all of which is quite alien to northern Mesolithic art. Levanzo also has a group of very stylized painted animal and human figures that are perhaps Neolithic in date and conform to the rubric of a widespread convention in male and female 'signs'.

It is not far from the Egadi Islands to Palermo on the north coast of Sicily, and here, on the lower slope of Monte Pellegrino, there are several caves and shelters. One, about five hundred yards from the present shore-line, overlooking the bay, is a vast shallow arch of the sort that often sheltered prehistoric living places. Very close to it is another, much smaller, called Addaura II, on the smooth wall of which, and in full daylight, there is a remarkable group of drawings (Plates 82–4). There are lightly engraved naturalistic animals in the Levanzo style, and scattered over some 6 feet of wall a number of human figures on a rather smaller scale of from 10 to 15 inches (25 to 38 cm.). They may be a little later than the animals; but there can be no great difference, for all were covered by the same skin of stalagmite, so that on the evidence of Levanzo a date not much after 8000 B.C. may be expected.[26]

There are thirteen human figures quite close together on the 'canvas', and in their way they are as surprising as the reliefs of La Magdeleine or the carving of Dolní Věstonice. The graceful naturalism, supple line, foreshortening, perspective, and movement are all quite new in drawings of man. It is as if the knowledge, slowly and painfully acquired by Paleolithic draughtsmen in the portrayal of animals, had been transferred at one stroke to the human being. It is not just a matter of technique but of a shift in vision and sensibility. The naked human body is viewed as possessing grace and strength in the same way that a deer or ibex is graceful and strong, it can be described by the same clean, simplified outline and is valued now, not only for its properties, but as a visual image. There are few obvious sanctions apart from the obliteration of features and neglect of extremities and perhaps the wearing of masks. The man on the right of Plate 84 with lifted arms is the only figure drawn with the ancient twist of body that we have followed from Laussel and can still follow into Egypt and Crete and the Near East. The serpentine line that runs from the right elbow to the left shin is something never seen in nature; it conveys a sort of spiral dynamism which is quite unlike the static convention of Egypt, though at home in the work of Cretan gem-cutters. The masked man in the centre is a fine piece of perspective drawing; as we look down on him, head, body, chest, and thighs appear to have substantial depth. Six very similar figures, all facing right and each with a great head of hair, stand or move diagonally across the canvas from bottom left to right, the pose slightly different in each, almost as in a slow-motion film (five are visible in part on Plate 84). All these figures are compact and energetic and the pose natural, but three others facing left are quite different. One carries a skin or some unknown bulky object and is unidealized, with a large stomach – it may be a woman (Plate 83). Another smaller was begun on the same lines, but never finished, and farther to the left still a man strides away carrying what may be branches on his shoulders (Plate 82). There is no ground-line nor any draughtsman's device for isolating or concentrating a scene; nevertheless the group at the top – two bound men and two masked with raised arms – is linked by the direction of movement and gesture into a single scene, a single moment of time.[27]

The interpretation of this group has been much discussed. Sometimes it is an execution, a self-immolation (strangulation), a dance with acrobats, or an initiation.[28] A point that has not, I think, been noticed is that the bound men could be falling through space rather than lying on the ground. This explanation would suit especially the man with arms free, while the 'executioners' could as well have lifted their arms after letting go a heavy weight, as in a threatening or rhetorical gesture. Before rejecting this explanation a custom may be recalled which survived into the time of the Roman Republic and later, though so ancient that its meaning was forgotten. According to this, *homines sacri*, usually monsters or parricides, were thrown alive into the sea or into a river, by which means they were handed over to the god for divine justice, having put themselves outside the competence of human sanctions. The execution was carried out with elaborate ritual which might include sewing the victim into a leather bag or animal skin and beating him with sticks from a lucky tree. The ordeal of the Tarpeian rock began in this way.[29] Addaura, lying just under a precipitious cliff, would not be at all a bad place in which to commemorate that 'older law' and, if we like, the figures with bag and branches could belong to the sewing-up and beating ritual. Nakedness adds to the probability of ritual, and it is noteworthy that no weapons are shown.

Whatever the meaning of this scene, and whether or not we interpret it in terms of ancient ritual, there is nothing at all like it in Egypt or (except on a few early seals) in the Near East. But in the Aegean after a few millennia we meet again just this union of natural gesture and slightly idealized forms. It is always possible that the art of North Africa may one day show us something like it. The vivacity and grace of some of the paintings already known encourages the hope. Physically the slender bodies, pointed beards, and mass of hair remind us of Libyans and people of the Delta as they appear on the Narmer Palette and in later Egyptian scenes of herding and warfare, as well as in Sahara paintings.[30] If there is an African element here, it is far less than the debt to European draughtsmen. Drawing of this quality, the accomplishment of these deceptively simple figures, is unthinkable without the centuries of trial and experiment that we have been following through two chapters. These are not examples of individual genius conceived *ab origine* in this place and at that time, but the fruits of history and tradition; another milestone and another pointer to the nature of European art.

In Spain there are more and closer connexions between Late Paleolithic and Mesolithic art. El Parpalló in the province of Valencia, and Los Casares and La Hoz in Guadalajara are Upper Paleolithic cave sites within a few miles of the centres of Mesolithic paintings. The first had a vast number of engraved and painted stone plaques, some very like the Levanzo animal style, though lying in good Paleolithic strata.[31] Three caves in the province of Málaga – La Pileta, Ardales, and Nerja – are on the high-road from North Africa and were still visited in the Neolithic and Bronze Age.[32] The situation near the sea-shore is again rather like Monte Pellegrino. The archaeology of the Iberian peninsula south of Cantabria and Asturias was distinctive even during the Paleolithic, and at some still unfixed time firm links with North Africa began to appear.

After 9000 B.C. a new culture that had emerged in North Africa spread northwards and eventually crossed the straits of Gibraltar, sweeping into Spain like the Arab invasion at the end of the seventh century A.D., so that after the arrival of these 'Lybico-Capsians', with their fine microlithic flint tools, the population of Iberia was made up partly of descendants of Upper Paleolithic hunters, and partly of people from Africa. Only the extreme north was unaffected by the change. The Azilian Mesolithic was entrenched on both sides of the Pyrenees, while the 'Levantine' paintings are clustered south-east of a diagonal running from Lérida to Cádiz (see map on pp. xxxvi–xxxvii).

The art is a mixture of the familiar and the new. Deep caves are no longer chosen for painting, but shallow overhanging shelters with smooth limestone wall surfaces. There is very little engraving at all, and none is very deep. Of many possible sites only a very few have paintings, and in these few there are many superpositions. They are usually on the sides of ravines and dried up water-courses in wild rocky valleys, a sort of country that did not attract the farmer, so that hunting and farming populations could exist side by side for a considerable time without disaster to either. The Cueva de los Caballos in the Valltorta gorge, Castellón, is typical of the sort of site preferred. It is a narrow platform, easy to defend, half-way up a cliff under a sheltering overhang. Near by are others like it. There are never accumulations of rubbish and hearths, so that dating is largely guesswork. A reasonable estimate places the beginning of this art around or sometime after 5000 and the end, if indeed there was a clear-cut end, about 2000.[33] At first figures are crowded into the limited space of the chosen 'canvas', and superpositions show a change from fairly large single naturalistic animals at the beginning to very small, very stylized groups and scenes near the end (Figures 28 and 33). This late work sometimes shows men leading horses. The cattle in the still fairly naturalistic style of Prado del Nevazo, Teruel, are probably domesticated.[34] Some sites were still respected and drew pilgrims in the first century B.C., for inscriptions in Latin as well as Iberian have been found.

At first the strongest impression given by this art is of something quite new, especially the small size of the figures, from 8 inches for the larger down to 1 inch (from 20 to 3 cm.). Nevertheless there are positive signs of indebtedness to Paleolithic traditions which will be noticed from time to time. The vivacity of the colour that can still be seen is due to two causes. A single coat of paint – natural haematite, limonite, manganese, or charcoal – is used, for example, at Remigia in the Gasulla gorge, Castellón (Plate 85), but so thinned as to be almost transparent, allowing the reddish or blue-grey colour of the rock to show through, so that the colour of pigment changes in quality and sometimes even approaches violet.[35] In other places two layers of paint were applied to the rock, a first coat usually of watery grey made from diluted manganese earth and perhaps ink from oak-apples, and an upper coat of very liquid reddish paint through which the other shines, imparting some of the light and life of a glaze. The outline may be no more than a few millimetres wide and must have been done with a different brush, perhaps of feathers. Instead of being drawn first, it was sometimes added after the two coats of wash; this means three stages of work apart from the preparation of paints and brushes. Techniques and tools are a good deal more complex than those with which Paleolithic artists got their grand effects; but in spite of this, colour is no longer employed to give depth or plasticity. The figures are quite flat, and only their animation tricks the eye into seeing, or seeming to see, a certain depth. Figures in black monochrome at Remigia and

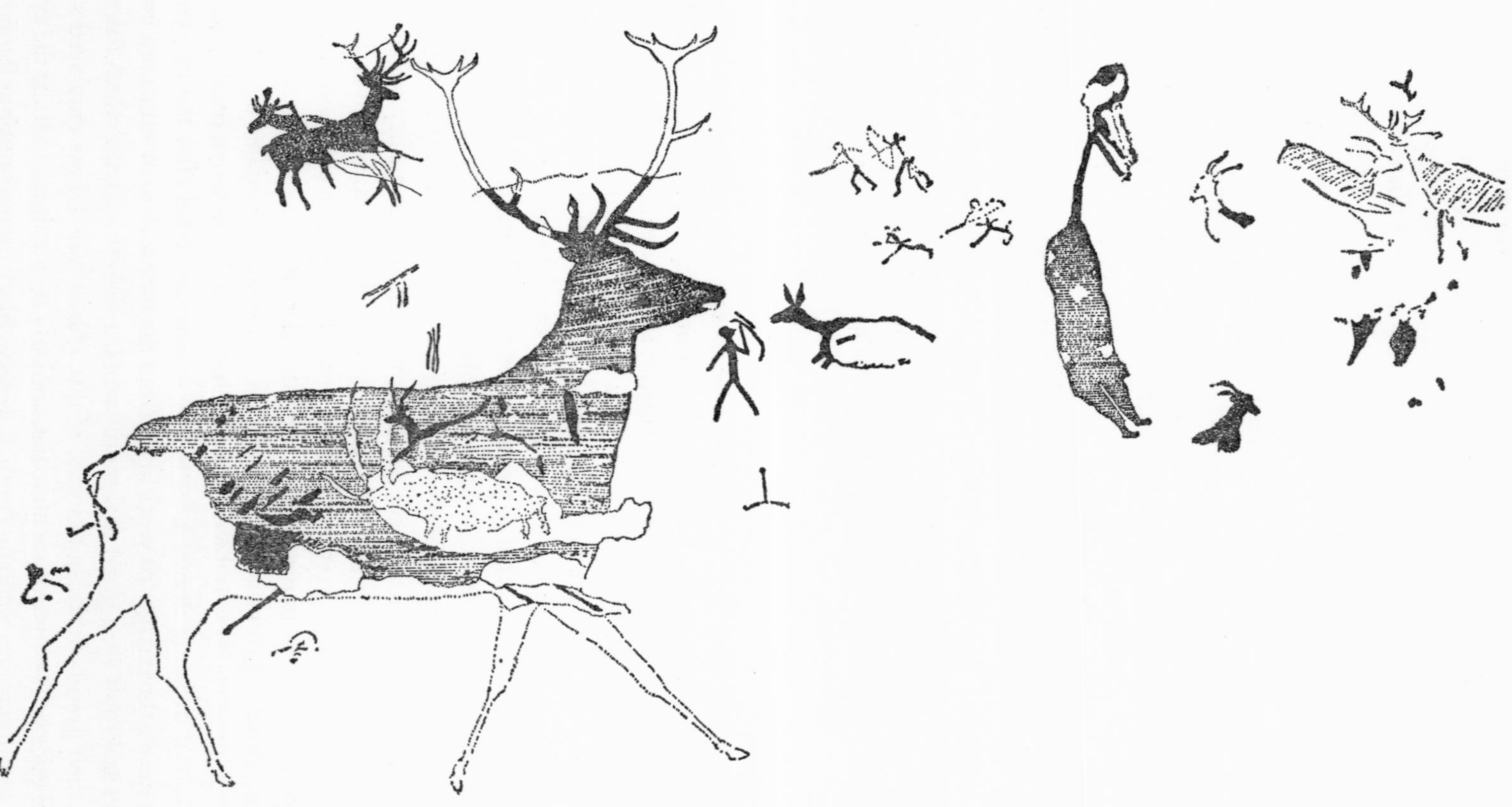

Figure 28. Painting of several periods in the rock shelter at Charco del Agua Amarga, Teruel, Spain

Cogul are among the flattest; but in some other places the space inside a black or grey outline is filled with red. If two colours are used, as at Cogul, where women have black legs and red skirts, or in the parti-coloured cattle of Prado del Nevazo, they are placed side by side, not overlapping as at Lascaux or Altamira. An odd technique is to fill a limb or body with parallel stripes or to zigzag down a figure in a number of short, almost horizontal strokes, which achieves at any rate economy in paint.

The medium for binding has been the subject of experiments using honey, fish-oil, blood, and also animal fat. The last did not give the transparency that can still be seen, but fairly satisfactory results were got from blood diluted with water and from honey. Good results have also been obtained by experimenting with a feather as brush and reddish ochre dissolved in water and white of egg.[36] The preservation of paintings in the dry air and exposed situation of the Spanish rocks is due to processes different from those which help to preserve Paleolithic paintings inside caves. Though normally almost invisible, they appear with great freshness when the rock is splashed with water, because they are covered by a layer of stalagmite a few millimetres thick, although this treatment in the end leads to deterioration. The action of rain-water on the limestone over a long period of time by saturating it with calcium bicarbonate left the layer of calcareous sinter when the moisture had evaporated. It is a natural process not unlike the artificially induced action of hydrate of lime in the plaster prepared for true fresco. It did not matter whether the rock was dry or wet at the time of painting; what did matter was the seepage of water through its clefts and cracks afterwards. As with Paleolithic painting in damp caves, the use of a fatty medium would have hindered more than helped preservation by delaying the formation of sinter or stalagmite.

There is much variety even within the 'naturalistic' phase of Spanish painting. The larger and earlier single animals are still very like Paleolithic subjects and are sometimes overpainted by figures in other styles (Figure 28). Some of the late figures are so reduced in scale that no real effect of depth could have been produced even if desired, but this is not yet the case at Remigia. The figures here are painted in flat silhouette, but with great vigour and life. One sort of illusion has been sacrificed to another; in place of plasticity and depth we are to have dramatic impact and action (Plate 85). The attitude of the goat at bay in the second cavity at Remigia is exactly that given by an Egyptian artist to his hunted ibex in the Eighteenth Dynasty tomb of Kenamun.[37] Another magnificent animal, the long-horned goat in the fourth cavity at Remigia, is in headlong flight, pierced in the belly by an arrow (Plate 86). Many animals are depicted in the same 'flying gallop'. This is nothing new: we saw it at Trois Frères and on the ceiling at Altamira, where it was combined with the greater length of the offside pair of legs, as they would be in the animal stretched dead on the ground (p. 56 above). But now we actually see the moment of death, the drama of the confrontation of quarry and hunter. In Plate 86 the goat has been flushed by trackers and driven at the gallop towards the waiting bowman. For this moment the old stereotype of the 'flying gallop' was ready to hand. Inherited from long before, it would become *the* convention for representing the illusion of speed, one which even the sophisticated eye willingly accepts in illustrations of top-hatted early-nineteenth-century jockeys, perfectly vertical on perfectly

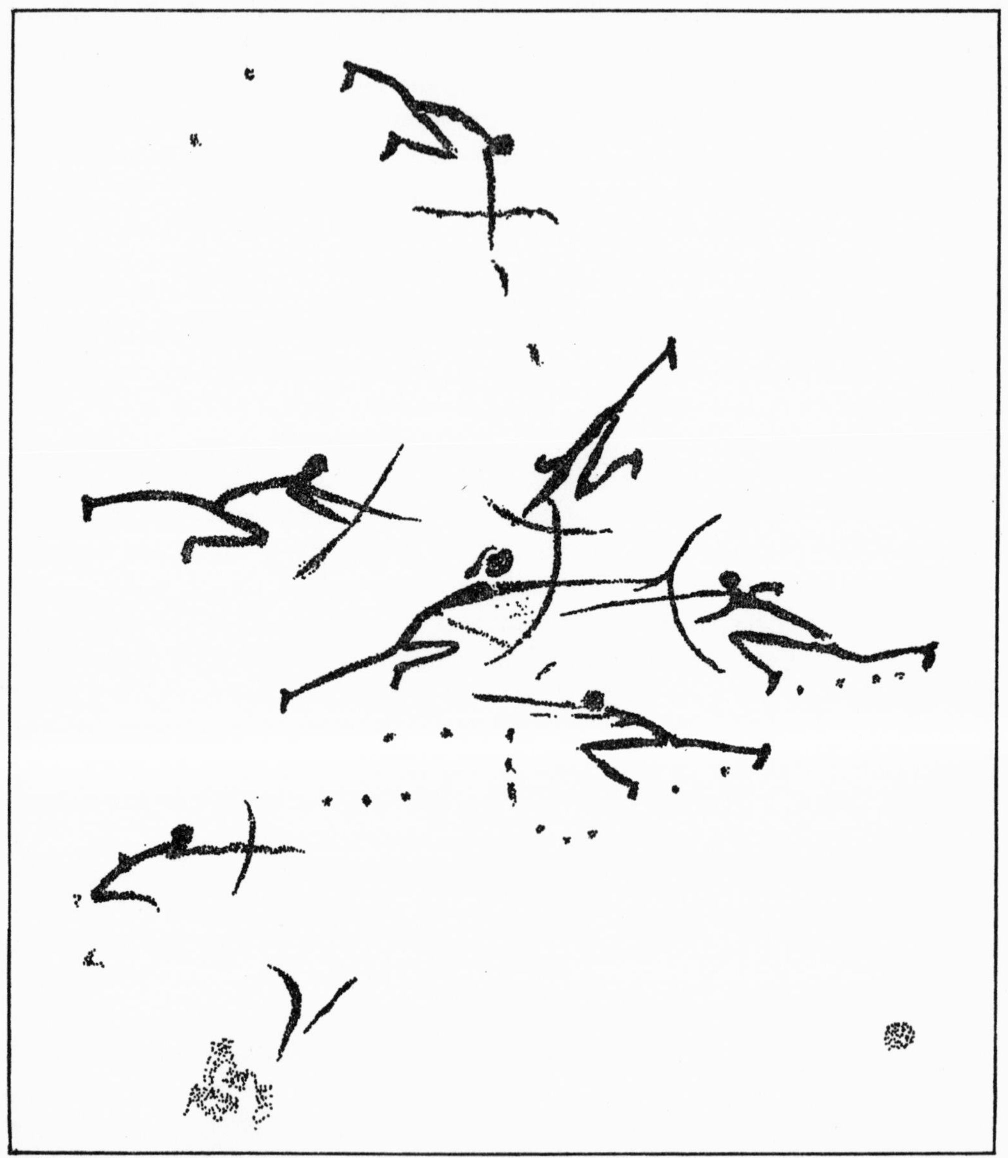

Figure 29. Rock painting at Morella la Vieja, Castellón, Spain

horizontal mounts, and, more to the point, old Egyptian wall-paintings or Cretan seals, all of which can very probably be traced back to the dead models at the fireside of an Old Stone Age 'studio'.[38]

The deliberate portrayal of dislocation and death is something new, though foreshadowed towards the end of the Paleolithic; but now we see hamstrung and newly slaughtered animals with dislocated legs (Plate 86), or carcases slung on a pole between hunters, and lines of wild pig and deer stretched dead on the ground.

It is rather surprising to find a return to the frontal view or twisted perspective in the treatment of horns and antlers, though in fact this had never been completely abandoned even by Magdalenian artists. Goats are usually shown in profile in natural perspective, but deer and cattle not so often. One peculiarity links the Late Paleolithic (Magdalenian II) art of Parpalló, Mesolithic Remigia and Cogul, and North African paintings of the 'bovidian' period, and that is the cattle with lyre-shaped horns that do not spring directly from the forehead but are joined at the base in a sort of stalk.[39]

A comparison of Plates 86 and 87 underlines differences in style. The dashing bowman from Remigia has little in common, apart from size and pose, with the stylized figures of Civil. The first is a nervously impressionistic transcription of arrested movement; a sketch, one would say, if it were not for the careful and complicated techniques already described, which rules out chance effects. The sketchiness is deliberate and final. Smaller and more schematized are the so-called execution groups of Remigia (Plate 89) and the duelling bowmen of Morella la Vieja, Castellón (Figure 29). The latter are mere pin-men, or rather a single pin-man in a single attitude is repeated and composed with great economy into a little scene full of drama. The running spearman from Garroso, Alacón (Plate 88), is one of many figures that look as if they were doing the splits. This strange position should probably be read, like the animal's 'flying gallop', as the sign of speed, streaming hair sometimes reinforcing the impression.[40] The upper body is always naked. Women wear skirts and men stringy garters or gaiters perhaps of grass and sometimes skirts or waist-bands (Figures 28 and 35); a few have animal skins round the waist with the tail hanging behind, or tail plumes and the Mediterranean circlet or coronet of feathers (Plate 86 and Figure 35). Animal disguises, masks, and horns were sometimes shown, and perhaps body painting; but monsters, headless or part-animal, are quite exceptional and quite distinct from the masked hunters.[41]

Most surprising is the new art of caricature; for what else can we call the long noses and ragged beards of the warriors stepping out so purposefully with bows over their head at Cingle de la Mola, Remigia? (Figure 30).[42] There is a beaky emaciated Papa Yokum type which can be seen any day round the Mediterranean or in Arabia. Another at Valltorta with a nose like the point of a pen and wild hair seems to be yelling as he picks out a spear or arrow; yet another scratches his head as he hurries along at El Mortero, Alacón (Figure 31). These are essentially the same as the Libyans and inhabitants of the Delta whom Egyptian artists from the earliest times represented as strangers and captives. They can be seen manning a boat on a fourth-millennium textile fragment from Gebelein, and as captives and slain enemies on the Narmer Palette, or herdsmen like the wild-haired emaciated character in the Middle Kingdom tomb of Meir.[43]

The small human and semi-human figures of the Paleolithic are, with a few exceptions, rather frightening. There is about them still a good deal of the ambivalence of the animal, something of the uncanny or the unfinished. But there is nothing in the least uncanny or incomplete about these self-important, preoccupied, or harassed little men, usually in a tearing hurry. If a good caricature should give the illusion of life without the illusion of reality, then the warriors of Figures 30 and 31 fulfil the requirements. They even look like relatives of the jolly crowd on the 'Harvester Vase' from Hagia Triadha in Crete. Exaggeration or caricaturing of features takes the place of the

Figure 30. Rock painting at Cingle de la Mola, Remigia, Castellón, Spain

play of expression, impossible to reproduce in flat silhouette, and perhaps this accounts for a similarity to the traditional characters of the old Greek *Karadjosis* shadow-play. But though a caricature is very far from being a replica of anything seen, we accept these grotesque profiles as clues to personality, just as we accept the 'flying gallop' as a symbol of speed, though our eyes may never have seen it. It may not be altogether chance that caricature and realistic and violent action should appear at the same time, since our apparent perception of movement has almost as much to do with character as the permanent physiognomy.[44]

At Civil, Valltorta, we have a new stylization which was to be used a great deal. Legs and hips are life-like, but the torso is drawn out to a thread, and the heads are without necks or with very short ones (Plate 87). These attenuated warriors who run, or pause to strain a bow and launch an arrow, combine in their own bodies the qualities of the weapon. Hollow backs and thread-like waists have become bows, while arms have

Figure 31. Two painted figures at El Mortero, Alacón, Spain

the slenderness and direction of well-aimed arrows. I suggested in the last chapter that the bird-headed figure of Lascaux might be an apotheosis or hierophany of the great offensive weapon of the times, the spear-thrower; and here perhaps in the Civil figures we see the new dynamic of the bow and bowstring. The tension of taut animal sinew is transferred to an idealized human body drawn out from the hips as the bow is bent for stringing. These taut, vibrant figures are at the opposite pole to the ponderous, earth-bound solidity of Upper Paleolithic sculpture and most Upper Paleolithic drawing. The difference in sensibility and purpose is as great as between a Romanesque and a Gothic building.

Composition, which proved so illusive in the Paleolithic, is now plain to see. The archers of Figure 29 from Morella la Vieja make an attractive design that is certainly composed; and in the Civil battle-piece, although the perspective is not that to which we are used, the pattern of curves and angles, the repetition of upright and slanting lines, above all the direction of movement, make a whole that is too satisfying not to be contrived.[45] Moreover, the space between the parties of combatants has been used dramatically as an element in the visual composition. This is something so new that it demands examination.[46] The simplest way of connecting two subjects is to place them close together and to give them a common interest or action like the plumed archer and charging goat of Plate 86; but a bowman is able to kill from much farther away. The more difficult problem was then how to unite the distant hunter and his quarry in the same action or scene. The Egyptian tomb-painter disregarded the interval and placed them close together, and this was usual in the Near East (see above, p. 89). But the artists of eastern Spain, with a canvas as large and uncircumscribed as the wall of a rock shelter, devised a method of showing the hunter and his prey by painting the animal's trail. In Plate 85 the elk slots come wandering out of the distance; at one end is the quarry, and somewhere along the trail there is the diminutive figure of the hunter, who leaves no print himself. But the trail is more than a device for linking distant subjects; to a trained eye it is as eloquent as a chapter of biography. If we follow the track of the goat from the bottom to the top, there comes a point where something has happened. The neat prints run up the rock face until they meet a number of indistinct blodges, which enlarged suggest the pads of a carnivore; while beside them are skid-marks, possibly those of a pursuer. Then comes a sudden change of direction, and the slots continue, but far less certainly, in the original direction, till near the top we come to the goat itself, halted by an arrow, shot from behind, fixed in its belly. It is about to receive the *coup de grâce* from a tiny figure in front. So much is clear, but no doubt a wise hunter could reconstruct a great deal more from the clues that the artist has set down. This practical tracker's device has some rather surprising consequences; for to visual composition it introduces the actuality of space, and on the conceptual plane it introduces linear and historical time. These statements call for some justification.

There is as little sense of space on the crowded walls of Trois Frères or Niaux as in Egyptian wall paintings in the Kenamun tomb with the hunt to which I have compared this scene and where the landscape is a mosaic of artifically joined independent fragments.[47] It is very different with the area separating the group of 'executioners' and the stricken 'victim' at Remigia (Plate 89). Here the empty space is necessary to a correct understanding of what has just happened, the distance is a bowshot, and it asserts the nature of the action as much as do the figures themselves. In the Civil battle (Plate 87) the difference in scale of the figures *may* stand for rank, as it would in Egypt or Mesopotamia, but the number of large figures seems too many for this explanation, unless they are heads of families? On the other hand it may represent distance from the observer. This of course conflicts with our ideas of spatial perspective, depending so much on ground-line and horizon united in a single plane understood as the earth's visible surface. The absence of surface plane makes the grouping appear artificial and decorative, but it does not do away with the dramatic importance of the space between the combatants. Lacking any reference for the interpretation of scale, there is the same ambiguity in the hunting and tracking scenes; we cannot tell whether the smaller archer drawing his bow on the goat in Plate 86 is less important or simply farther away than the figure above. This is not always so, and in some hunting scenes the distance on the canvas between hunter and quarry provides a context of wide world in which things happen. The trail as a substitute for ground-line and horizon acts as a medium both connecting individual protagonists and isolating groups within an envelope of space and time. When the artist painted the trail in Plates 85 and 86, this was one way of conveying distance; but he has gone further, and distance has become space.

Perhaps it is not merely chance that the exploration of space should coincide with the use of bow and arrow in war and hunting; for the new weapon, with its far greater range compared to the older ones (even including the throwing-spear), required a more delicate judgement of direction and accurate estimation of distance. The Paleolithic artists had used emptiness inside the contour of a body so that the eye should create depth, solidity, and volume, but the Mesolithic artist is using space between bodies with a knowledge and assurance that may well have arisen through the archer's special

Figure 32. Battle scene at Les Dogues, Ares del Maestre, Castellón, Spain

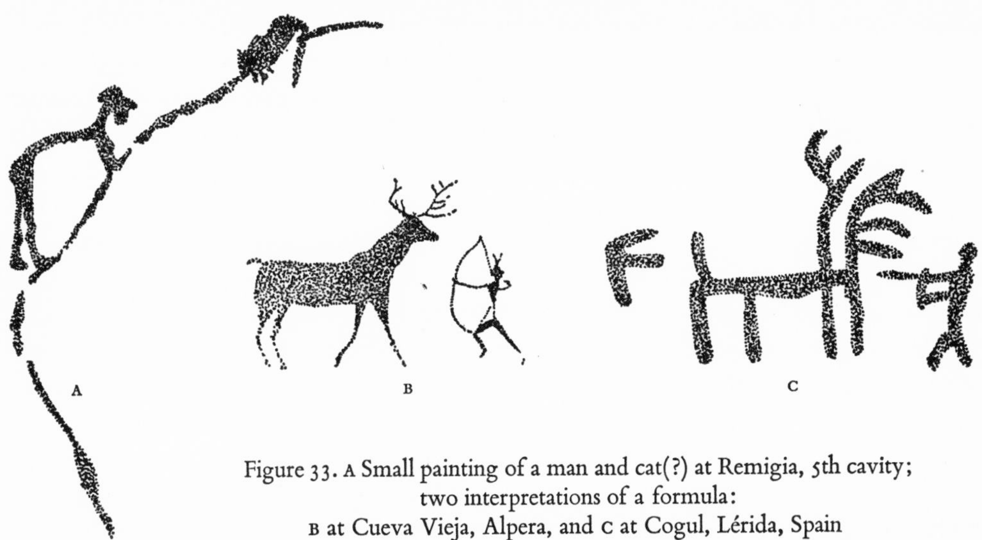

Figure 33. A Small painting of a man and cat(?) at Remigia, 5th cavity; two interpretations of a formula: B at Cueva Vieja, Alpera, and C at Cogul, Lérida, Spain

science. It will be a long time before space is converted into atmosphere, but at least another step has been taken in that direction.

Spanish Levantine art is often called narrative and anecdotal when compared with the static and monumental figures of Paleolithic art. The implications of this statement are not always made sufficiently plain; for they lead to a different concept of time. The horses of Cap Blanc and the bulls of Lascaux could be of the past, present, or future, it is immaterial which; they are timeless monuments, or rather they are stereotypes whose repetitions during millennia virtually unaltered are compatible with unhistorical concepts of time, whether cyclical, 'original', or metaphysical (see above, pp. 25 and 36). In narrative, however, the artist recreates something that happened in the past once for all, and which will be recalled by those who see it in time to come as a finished event, so that action, commemoration, and recognition rest in an irreversible order.

Most of the new subjects seem to be secular and incidental scenes of hunting and fighting. The battles look like real battles even when the figures are highly stylized, as at Civil. In other scenes the warriors are painted in an expressive shorthand, and the irritable, sketchy line conveys admirably the tension, speed, and incoherence of real fighting (Figure 32). There are also domestic scenes: gathering honey, climbing trees or creepers, a dead pig carried back to camp, an over-rash hunter chased by a bull or cow; and there is humorous observation. In Figure 33A a tiny, clambering man is brought face to face with what looks very like a pussy-cat. Caricatures remind us of the great comic characters of myth, and that this is the country of Don Quixote and Don Juan.

Whereas in the Paleolithic we were at a loss concerning the life and attitudes of the people, now there are so many genre scenes, domestic pursuits, and violent but unheroic actions, the observation of comic incident and character, in fact a new realization of the incidental and the transitory, that we are evidently approaching a historical sense. Some subjects, on the other hand, are often repeated and eventually reduced to a formula that comes nearer to the timeless stereotypes of the Paleolithic and the set pieces of Egypt and Mesopotamia. The archer confronting a stag at Cogul (Figure 33B and C) is a pictogram, but subject and arrangement are the same as the hunters of Cueva Vieja and Plate 85. The 'execution scene' is painted at least four times on one rock-face at Remigia, and again at Mortero, Alacón, and perhaps at Minateda (Plate 89).[48] In the clearest Remigia painting a party of archers stand close together waving their bows over their heads, while at a little distance the body of the victim lies pierced with arrows. The individual figures still stand in natural attitudes, though the bodies are fantastically elongated; but a few feet away the same group is mere sticks, and the bows are segments of concentric circles (Figure 34). It is again the old gravitation towards pattern and formalism. The pierced and stricken figure can probably be traced back to Paleolithic times: the small 'sorcerer' of Pech-Merle stuck with spears or darts, and others from Cougnac.[49] The constrained formality of these groups compared with the variety and confusion of hunting and fighting scenes encourages belief that this is a sacred ritual rather than a secular execution: perhaps the immolation of a chief or an initiation.[50] An awe-inspiring figure appears sometimes which may be a masked hunter, or more probably one dressed in the shamanic attributes of horns and hide. At Alpera a figure larger than the rest, and wearing a feather head-dress, certainly looks like a priest or shaman, but behind him is one of those mysterious triple zigzags like the Rymarksgård bone engraving (Plate 76 and Figure 35).[51]

The tiny size of these paintings is something of a shock after the Paleolithic. The Mesolithic artists had just as large a potential canvas as their predecessors in the caves, but they chose to compose small. The immediate impression is of something happening at a great distance, watched from a vantage-point which may be a little above the scene of the action. This weakens the viewer's sense of participation in what is going forward. There is something of paradox here, for in the graphic art of the Paleolithic, though man was seldom shown, he was the invisible participant in everything portrayed, while now that he has moved into the canvas and become a principal, there is a quite new detachment and objectivity about his portrayal. One result of the artist's detached observation is a decorative tendency; another is the almost opposite enjoyment in personal oddity and genial caricature. Here is man observed not *sub specie aeternitatis* but as he looked to his kin and clan, without illusions of grandeur. Even in success he is hardly heroic, and we are as far as can be from the royal hunt or battle piece of a pharaoh or Sumerian *patesi*.

Figure 34. Group of bowmen at Remigia, Castellón, Spain, 5th cavity

The quality that permeates this art more than others is the concentration on movement and on linear, not muscular, energy. It is an attempt to capture the look of speed itself, the bowstring tension of incredibly slender bodies, the flying gallop of animals and man. This is what distinguishes the scrawls of Figure 32 from the

Figure 35. Paintings at Alpera, Albacete, Spain

manikins of Paleolithic Castillo.[52] Moreover, the third dimension, apparently lost in the flatness of monochrome silhouette, is restored by the discovery of distance and space. The greatest achievement is in the understanding of movement and gesture, whether intuitive or scientific does not matter, and of transitory time; it is certainly the fruit of long experience, and we are at a far remove from primitive awe in the act of creation.

The people of Iberia went on painting, but the styles changed. In a hunt scene near Albocacer, Castellón, not far from Valltorta, the animals are wooden and the human figures extremely stylized. With the growing stylization there comes a blurring of categories, and the same sort of scratchy stag and sun symbols appear on natural rock and on the pots of Neolithic peasants. Male and female symbols like the 'Neolithic' paintings of Levanzo also appear, but they are common all round the Mediterranean (Figure 56D). These things hardly rank as art; more interesting is the odd fact that in the last centuries B.C., in much the same part of south-eastern Spain, an extremely lively if provincial style of vase-painting, with many small animated figures in flat paint, appeared among an Iberian population that owed something to Greeks and Phoenicians but included a native strain.

Beyond Europe

Until the end of the Paleolithic and for a little longer there was no call to look beyond Europe for sources and comparisons. During the four to five thousand years of the European Mesolithic, men's lives did not alter to any great extent. After the adoption of bow and boat and hunting dog nothing very revolutionary happened. Tools become more delicate and complicated, life perhaps a little more sedentary. Beyond Europe it is very different. In the Near East grain is being grown and harvested, animals domesticated, houses built with sun-dried bricks, plastered floors, and painted walls. Villages rise on the same site, one above another, and become towns. All this is the common history of the 'Neolithic Revolution', and the beginning of urban civilization. By the end of our period the representational art of the Near East is set in the mould from which it will not depart for centuries, and within which great masterpieces will appear. The finality and repose of seated pharaohs and scribes, the irreversible hierarchies and unaltering ritual of Mesopotamia, the monuments of architecture, these are outside the experience of Europe for a very long time to come.

There was, however, a moment when, it seems to me, even in Egypt, Asia Minor, Mesopotamia, and Iran something very different appeared, when it almost looks as if art might have taken a different road. The deer hunt and leopard dances of Catel Hüyük, a fourth-millennium Egyptian pot with an archer and hunting dogs on a white painted background, a textile with boats and boatmen from Gebelein, later still and in spite of inferior execution the paintings at Hierokonpolis, an archer on a pot from Sialk in Iran, a few cylinder seals from Uruk; all these have kept something of the hunter's world, the nomad's larger attitude to space, which are banished from the far more accomplished and sophisticated stone palettes, mace-heads, bone knife-handles, and carved stelai of Early Dynastic Egypt and Sumer.[53] At Catel Hüyük especially the atmosphere is wild, composition informal, and the style impressionistic; for this is a glimpse of a disappearing world painted when the plateau was still forested and hunting as important as agriculture. There are remarkably similar scenes painted on rocky outcrops of the desert in the once unexplored and almost empty Sahara and Maghreb. There are many styles, and a long period of time is covered; some are certainly as late or later than the East Spanish painting, with which they share much more than a similar way of life, hunting and pastoralism; the cattle with lyre-shaped horns on stalks have been referred to; they share many more traits in common.[54]

One remarkable object from the north-west Caucasus may perhaps be mentioned here: the silver bowl from Maikop in the Kuban-Terek region, on which is incised very probably the first landscape drawn according to natural perspective.[55] In the late third millennium something so far removed from the symbolic landscapes of the ancient world is unprecedented; but if there is a large gap between seventh- and sixth-millennium Catel Hüyük and fourth- and third-millennium Susa and Maikop, the geographical aspect must not be forgotten. At Maikop there is only one leg more needed to complete the circle which started in the far north. This last leg takes us by Karelia to the rock carvings of Onega and Ladoga, the earliest of which are probably contemporary with Susa I and the later with Maikop, while the life portrayed touches some (if not the most characteristic) aspects of Spanish paintings. The labour of pecking very hard rock compared to painting smooth rock accounts for more differences than there would otherwise be.

Wherever this art appears with its impressionistic naturalism, its small scale, its movement, and variety of scenes, it seems to stand on a borderline. The artists are somewhere between hunting and agriculture, between nomadic and settled living; their compositions between Paleolithic confusion, superpositions, and juxtapositions and the formal architectural designs of Neolithic and later civilizations. One may question whether this is not an extremely widespread phenomenon not unconnected with an attitude towards time, history, and man's place in the world. It is a breaking-down of some of the limitations which tradition and convention, backed by all the weight of primitive conservatism, had held so long immovable. To some extent they will be re-imposed; for it was premature, this new artistic licence. Reaction will undoubtedly follow, but it is a memorable episode all the same.

CHAPTER 4

NEOLITHIC ART IN EASTERN EUROPE: 5000–2000

The Background

She that loves place, time, demarcation, hearth, kin, enclosure, site, differentiated cult, though she is but one mother of us all: One earth brings us all forth, one womb receives us all, yet to each she is other, named of some name other . . .

David Jones, *The Tutelar of the Place*

THE surviving art of Neolithic Europe is above all a potter's art, and the farmers who colonized our continent in the sixth and fifth millennium were already accomplished practitioners. This art is often disparaged with slighting references to 'mother-goddess' figurines and the crude decoration of primitive pots, or pigeon-holed as a departure from naturalism towards geometric and abstract symbols, and a rejection of the visible world. If this is not so, we must start by establishing our credentials: the right to speak of Neolithic art in Europe at all.

A random selection might give the small clay head from Butmir in Bosnia in which are repose and classic proportions; for contrast another head from Predionica in Serbia, large, simplified, and forcefully three-dimensional (Plates 105 and 95), both broadly contemporary and not many miles apart; a small naturalistic basalt carving of a woman from Macomer in Sardinia; the more abstract purity of the marble 'Madre Mediterranea' from Senorbí on the same island (Plates 149 and 146); the bold invention of the Cernavoda man of Plate 111; and the tact with which formal and natural qualities are blended in a stone elk axe-head from Uppland in Sweden (Plate 156). I submit that in these examples, drawn from all over Europe, neither variety nor invention, aesthetic sensibility nor technical competence, are lacking.

Stone sculpture still flourished in Scandinavia and in the Mediterranean islands; elsewhere the sculptor's material is clay, and the painter's 'canvas' is the plaster of house-walls and the rounded surface of a pot. As a human activity potting is as new as the techniques and skills of husbandry, beside which it appears in Europe, and for the genesis of which we must look beyond Europe. Clay modelling on the other hand was one of the earliest of the arts of representation, as we have already seen. The small animal and human figures of the twenty-fifth and twenty-fourth millennia B.C. are already sculpture; some had even been baked in an oven of a sort (Chapter 1, p. 12). The advantages of preserving meat by the chemistry of heat and drying were known to Neanderthal man, perhaps before; and in the same way a cooked figurine of a bear lasts far longer and is more easily handled than an uncooked one. But the experiment was premature, and as far as we know these very early beginnings had no sequel, whereas the Neolithic potting and modelling that we find in the Middle East started a still unbroken tradition. The semi-nomadic hunter has no need of pots – in fact their fragility makes them highly impractical; and for this reason we shall find the pastoral herding inhabitants of a large part of Europe in the third and second millennia very poor potters. There is no lack of other materials for containers: baskets, leather bags, gourds, carved wood and bark. We know approximately when and where the earliest pots were made – in the Middle East in the seventh millennium – but very little of the circumstances, apart from one fact: they always come from houses in permanent or semi-permanent villages. This may well be the most important aspect of the whole business, for even the mammoth-hunters of Moravia were living in permanent huts when they modelled in clay. Houses and hearths, possibly ovens, are the essentials of early potting, and in South-East Europe at the bening of the Neolithic we find small rectangular houses with mud or clay walls and prominent hearths and ovens. These are like some very early houses in the Middle East, though unlike the more typical crowded continuous buildings of Hacilar and Catel Hüyük in Anatolia.[1]

All the earliest pottery was hand-made, and in Europe it remained so until around 400 B.C. The basic processes are still the same today: selecting the clay, basting, tempering, kneading, weathering. These operations are more laborious and more sophisticated than the preparation of pigment to paint a rock surface or knapping flint to make a burin to engrave a bone. The different tempering materials – chopped-up vegetable matter, sand, shell, mica, and 'grog' – were all accessible to primitive farmers, but each represents an experiment and a discovery, and so too for each stage in the work. Small vessels like figures were shaped with the fingers and palm, but larger ones were built up with strips or coils, or a combination of both. There is one moment and one only when the drying clay can be given its final shaping-up with a spatula and the walls burnished to reduce porosity; or perhaps a slip of finer clay is carefully prepared that will not crack and peel during firing. Finally comes decoration by burnishing, different sorts of impression, stamped dies; or painting with mineral pigments – haematite, manganese, and so on – for organic colouring burns out during firing.

One of the most disconcerting aspects of potting is the alteration in colour of the original earth and of the slips and pigments used. Iron compounds in the clay when fired at a fairly high temperature with a free supply of oxygen produce a red surface, but when the oxygen is reduced the result is a blackish pot or figure. Black can also be got by covering the pot, when still hot, with chaff or other vegetable matter. But local clays still react differently, and this difficulty of forecasting the colour must have been one of the first and most persistent problems of early potters. Some colours were certainly preferred and aimed at. In Neolithic Europe these were usually the reds or a bright black; greyish shades appear when the potter wanted to imitate a silver prototype. Sometimes the clay was painted after it had been fired to ensure the colour staying true, as we see on the third-millennium 'crusted wares' of Serbia and Moravia (Plates 104 and 129).

Pots and figures are generally fired in ovens, but they can simply be placed in an open hearth, the pots upside down, with brushwood heaped over them. This is what was done in Northern and Western Europe; but it is wasteful of fuel, and many pots are spoiled through cracking and distortion. Also the temperature cannot be raised above 750° C or an outside limit of 800° C. Baking ovens already in use in the Middle East were soon adapted to the potters' requirements; much greater temperatures can be got than in an open fire, and the ovens in the earliest houses of South-East Europe were probably used to bake the finer pots.

Pot-making is a complex and sophisticated craft requiring forethought and careful preparations compared to which an artist modelling clay into human or animal figures is still, as far as concerns technique, nearer to a Paleolithic wood- and bone-carver. But even a modeller of figures must prepare the earth and supervise the baking, though neither requires quite such rigour as in the making of pots. Both the potter and the modeller are more absolutely creators than the carver of stone and wood; for whereas the latter had the native rock in front of him when he set to work, with its roughness, its oddities of contour and wear and resistance, or the typical shapes and striation of bone, the pull of the fibres, the graining of wood, the modeller and potter had nothing but a figment in his mind. But he too must contend with the natural resistance of clay at different stages, and the extent to which it imposes its own limitations, so that the final object may look very different from the image in the artist's mind. For him too the imagination does not create *ex nihilo*; it can only beget upon a difficulty. But physically the potter and modeller has had to create the stuff of his medium in a more basic sense than any of the other artists we have met, and this remains true until we reach the higher sophistication of metallurgy. It is not surprising, therefore, to find the Creator of all things a potter, like the ram-headed Egyptian Khnum, or the Mesopotamian goddess Aruru who pinched off clay to create a primitive man, and the Hebrew prophet's 'we are the clay and thou our potter, and we are all the work of thy hand'.

Quite as drastic as the change in his medium is the change in the artist's subjects, even when they are still man and animal; for the domestication of animals went to the bottom of a primeval relationship, altering it at the roots. Man as farmer sees himself and his flocks and herds with different eyes from those with which the hunter watches the wild quarry in the forest. This alteration of the framework of the world must be, and is, reflected by the artist, just as the new physics or the microscopic world is reflected in the insubstantial or microscopic images of painters today. There may even be a parallel between the artist's responsibility for his medium, the earth which he has made for himself, and the new role of the husbandman who selects, enslaves, and breeds the once wild beasts. The ploughing ox team and the herded sheep are the creation of the farmer in a sense that the wild goats and cattle which a hunter shoots and traps are not. It is well to remember this when looking at the stiff, rather carelessly modelled animals of Jarmo and Catel Hüyük, Vinča and Hăbăşeşti, and comparing them with those of Gravettian Věstonice or Magdalenian Mas d'Azil (Plate 26 and Figure 42c).

The account of Mesolithic hunters and fishers in Europe given in the last chapter ran ahead of the more general cultural evolution, because Europe was no longer in the forefront, and while elk were hunted in Scandinavia, wild grasses were domesticated in the Near East. The magnificent scimitar-horned goat shot by Remigia hunters in Spain (Plate 86) has older, perhaps much older, *domesticated* relatives at Jericho and Jarmo and even in South-East Europe; and the nest of severed skulls lying on a bed of ochre at 'Mesolithic' Ofnet in Bavaria is not very much earlier than the nest of severed skulls with fine moulded plaster features and cowrie-shell eyes at Jericho. The first steps in farming in the Near East take us back almost to where the last chapter began. If the dog was the hunter's companion and scavenger, sheep come very early, then goats and cattle.[2] It appears that only animals themselves social in habit and used to living in herds have ever been successfully domesticated; for in the early stages of the relationship *both* sides must be able, and prepared, to enlarge the social group.[3] The pig, a scavenger, came early, but cattle probably not till grain was grown systematically, and then at first as robbers of the crop. In the early stages accident played some part no doubt, but, whatever the real order of events, they must have been closely linked: grain-growing, domestication of scavenging and crop-robbing animals, and life in permanent villages were all part of, and necessary to, the new economy.

The change is not simply from parasite preying on wild nature to lord of nature tamed. We have seen that the attitude of the hunter to his animal prey and sustainer was complex; that of the farmer to his animal slave and sustenance was even more equivocal. The old awe and religious mystery persist; the stages of domestication are spread over many centuries, and the spiritual change must have been as gradual, with the old attitudes exerting their strong drag. The early texts of Sumerians, Hittites, and Egyptians are full of the ambiguities of the human–animal relationship, and the same appears in their art. Sheep, goats, and oxen are pictured as domesticated slaves exploited with equanimity, while at the same time divine bulls and goats confront tiny cringing men and women bearing offerings. When farming spread into Europe the alteration was sufficiently recent for the relationship to be still insecure, but it is best to postpone exploration of the religious aspect till we have had a closer look at the objects themselves.

These great changes were taking place slowly between 9000 and 6000 B.C. If we are still looking for evidence of what used to be called a Neolithic 'revolution' or explosion, it is not so much in these early centuries but in the seventh and beginning of the sixth millennium that we shall find it. At that time men were moving down from the highlands to found the great valley civilizations, meeting and solving the problems of large-scale irrigation. This was the moment of advance, when specialization began to pay. At the same time they were moving outwards towards the savage world of forest and steppe, across the Caucasus into South Russia, over the Hellespont to the Balkans, mainland Greece, and island Crete. It may not have been immediately obvious which of these directions would prosper most. Elateia in Greece and Gornja Tuzla in Bosnia at the beginning may have looked as promising as Hassuna, Tell Halaf, and villages in the Fayum; but the same can no longer be said of, for example, fifth-millennium villages at Vinča in Serbia or Elsloo in Holland, and the rising civilizations of Anatolia and the Middle East at the same date (see Table 2).[4] The later history of Mesopotamia and the Nile Valley will only touch us occasionally and superficially, but events taking place on the Anatolian plateau, in the foothills and highlands of the Caucasus, and in the islands of the Aegean will need a constant watch, especially the first.

★

For the purposes of this study Neolithic Europe begins north of Rhodope and Pindus, in present-day Yugoslavia and Bulgaria, in the sixth and fifth millennia. Sites like Gornja Tuzla and Varoš in North Bosnia, Vršnik in Macedonia, Nosa and Starčevo in Serbia and Karanovo and Yassa Tépé in the Maritsa valley, and even Körös Gyálarét in Hungary, are the real beginning. The seventh-millennium explosion slowed down in the sixth, though it seems that the Varda–Morava watershed had been crossed and the Struma and Maritsa explored northward before 5000, with sites established on the rivers flowing to the Danube. During this thousand years between the founding of the early settlements and the exuberant proliferation of 'Middle' and 'Late' Neolithic cultures – Vinča, Boian, and their contemporaries – in the first half of the fourth millennium the whole of Europe to the Atlantic was crossed by parties of peasant farmers driving their small herds and carrying bags of seed-corn through the forests and along rivers, a quite extraordinary achievement.[5] As they went farther west and north, and as passing generations separated them from their Balkan beginnings, much was altered. There was contact too with still elusive native hunting tribes, which may account for some of the unsolved problems that surround the 'Danubian' or 'Linearbandkeramik' settlers, as well as for the signs of reversion to less strictly agricultural modes of life.[6]

South of Rhodope and Pindus settlements are very like the tells in Anatolia where one village rises on top of the crumbling walls of its predecessor, and the same is true of some, but not all, of the early settlements north of the mountains: Karanovo, Yassa Tépé, and Vinča, but not Starčevo. The mountain landscape of Anatolia and of the Balkans is like enough to provide few new problems. The seasons for sowing and harvest are approximately the same. Forests, though greater than today, were not dense, and the browsing herds would help to control their growth. Forest clearance was a problem that did not become serious till the Danube system was reached. The economy was advanced enough to allow permanent settlement, and models of houses exist as well as the plans: small rectangular one-family buildings with painted plaster walls, and plaster relief decoration. Farther north and west the houses change and ovens disappear.

The strong Anatolian flavour of this civilization cannot be entirely accounted for by a single seventh- or sixth-millennium emigration; there must have been other, later shifts during the fifth and fourth millennia, with men and animals moving more rapidly, since the worst physical obstacles had been overcome. There is little or no evidence for a southward movement from the Danube towards Greece at this time.[7] The new high dates of the European Neolithic, based on very consistent runs of Carbon 14 samples, linked with recent discoveries in Central Anatolia, explain the likeness between them, for Chalcolithic Hacilar is in fact contemporary with late Starčevo and early Vinča and Karanovo.[8] The brilliant and precocious potting and modelling of the Anatolian school, especially Hacilar Level VI, is linked with its European sequel and does much to explain the tremendous and explosive increase in the production of pottery and modelled figures on South-East European sites, which by the beginning of the fourth millennium had reached industrial intensity, without losing either vitality or originality, and which just survived the first appearance there of copper and gold.

A Modeller's Art: The Human Figure

After some rather tentative beginnings, from the middle of the fifth millennium for over a thousand years, Eastern Europe was the centre of an extraordinary development in the potter's art and in the modelling of free-standing figures; in this art Vinča in Serbia was pre-eminent. This site beside the Danube has given its name to one culture, but others, more or less contemporary with it, were only a little less prolific in potters and modellers. In one season's excavation at Vinča more than 437 figures were found, and the total from this site must be well over one and a half thousand.[9] At another site, not far distant, 80 per cent of all the finds were modelled figures.

The ambiance of this south-eastern potter's art stretches from the Maritsa northwards into most of Yugoslavia, but not to the Adriatic coasts, which come under different influences. In Hungary it covers the great plain (Alföld) and Trans-Danubia, in Rumania the Dobrogea, Muntenia, and Moldavia, in Czechoslovakia south-western Slovakia, southern Moravia, and then westward to Vienna. Farther north and west there are scattered figures, mostly of animals, and some anthropomorphic pots, but they are few and isolated, not an essential concomitant of traditional culture. The Dinaric and Julian Alps, the Tauern in Styria, the highland watershed between Moravia and Bohemia, and the Carpathians are the boundary beyond which other traditions and other customs prevailed. In the black-earth country north and west of the Black Sea, from Moldavia into the Ukraine, there was a vital extension. South of Rhodope and Pindus there is sculpture and modelling, but they belong to cultures that are not our concern (map on pp. xxxvi–xxxvii).

Vinča was not the beginning,[10] and one of the earliest pieces of clay modelling that have survived is a reminder of the sinister and mysterious which concerns the farmer no less than the hunter. It is a tiny head from Starčevo, slit-eyed and heavy-lidded; we are not to know whom it represents, nor even the more obvious 'what'. Are there two pairs of eyes or one? Is it human or animal (Plate 90)? This slit eye is not uncommon, and may have come from using shells for eyes like the cowries in the plastered skulls at Jericho and as at Catel Hüyük; but the closest ties are with Bulgaria, Macedonia, and Thessaly, especially Nea Nikomedeia.[11] The expression (if one may call it that) is nearer to the lizard gods and goddesses of Mesopotamia. The streaky hair provides a link with very rough little figures made by the Criş or Körös people, northern neighbours in Hungary and Transylvania who also made female figures (usually found headless), with huge posteriors that may be a clumsy attempt at rendering a sitting position. They are strangely reminiscent of some Paleolithic figures. The modelling and the potting of the Körös people were more brutal than those of Starčevo. Another standing female figure with a broad shelf-like posterior, perhaps as early, was at home in Bulgaria, whither it probably came from Anatolia (Figure 36, A and B).[12] Not only at the beginning but at intervals it seems that the art of modelling and of potting was revitalized from the same quarter.

As art these are fairly insignificant, but they show that their makers were already attracted by the malleability of clay, which could take the impression of an idea more

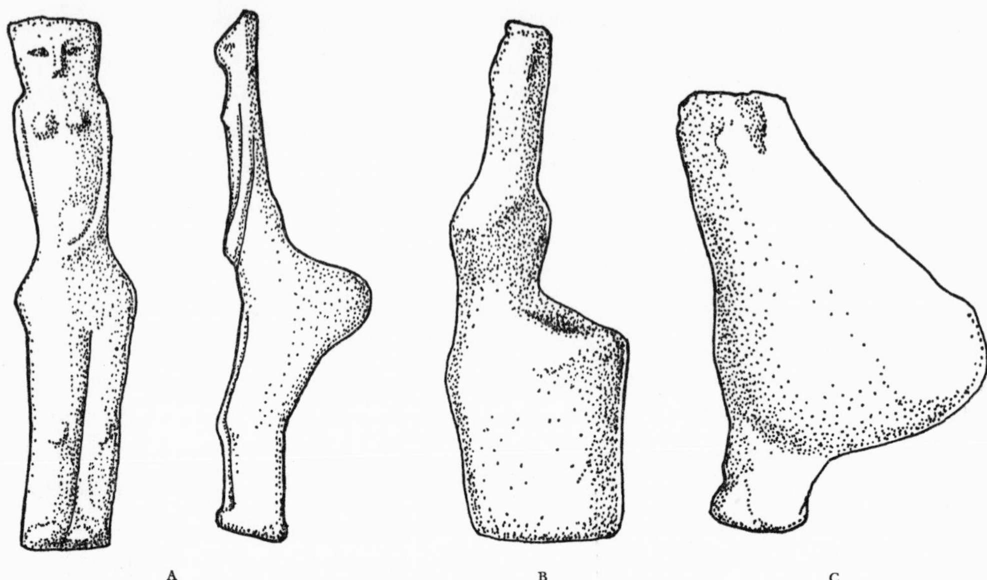

Figure 36. Early Neolithic clay figures: A from Karanovo I, B from Yassa Tépé, Bulgaria, C from Hódmezövásárhely, Hungary

obediently than wood, bone, and stone. Things did not stay at this tentative stage for long. The Vinča people were born modellers, and they copied in clay whatever interested them: animals, birds, snakes, shells, furniture. In strong contrast to the head from Starčevo we meet at Vinča a genial character in a pointed cap; this is a face you might expect to see grinning over a beer-mug at harvest-home (Plate 91). The cap is Anatolian, and the clay has been fired red. In Plate 92 we can speak of 'expression' without qualification; this farouche face *could* be a likeness.[13] The pierced ears are for attaching hair, headdress, or earrings, and are very common. If these persons belong to the other world and not the family circle (as seems more likely), they must suggest some remembered forebear, rustic guardian, or *genius loci*.

A different physiognomy, but also not far from nature, appears in the head from Predionica, Priština, a late Vinča village in the Morava valley (Plate 93).[14] It was covered with red paint after firing (crusted), and the eyes are pinched slits like those of the Starčevo head. Such naturalistic expressive faces are not common at this site. In contrast Plate 94 is non-committal, almost blank except for the melancholy just discernible in the washed-out features.

Predionica also has the most impressive of the highly stylized faces. Two are almost life-size ($6\frac{7}{10}$ and $6\frac{9}{10}$ inches; 17·5 cm. and 17 cm.), and the firing of the clay is a considerable technical achievement. The grey surface was well smoothed and left plain, not covered with red paint like the smaller heads and figures. In Plate 95 the impersonal and the awful have been invoked through a sort of solid geometry. The severe triangle, the apex of which is the chin, stretches to the hollow ear and is bisected by the nose. There is no softness in these curves and planes, but a dramatic concentration of light and shade. This is as three-dimensional as African Negro sculpture, and has about it an almost African strangeness. It is not only old, it is very alien. The second head is less alarming, perhaps owing to the modish chignon, for the incised and modelled pattern is practically the same and can once more be traced to Anatolia.[15] The ear has almost vanished, but the ear-hole is still there (Plate 96).

A third figure is on a much smaller scale ($7\frac{1}{10}$ inches; 18·5 cm.), but is complete (Plate 99). It sits on a four-legged stool, arms akimbo. The head is almost a replica of Plate 96, and from this we can deduce that if the life-size heads were originally attached to bodies the seated figures would have measured between 20 and 24 inches (50 and 60 cm.). Fragments of large-scale figures have been found in Rumania and Yugoslavia, so that we must reckon with the possibility of monumental clay sculpture in Neolithic Europe.[16] The whole figure was covered with red paint (crusted) after firing. The ears are pierced; there are four holes through the chignon and, since the back of the head and neck are rough and undecorated, it is likely that hair or a headdress were fastened on by their means. Holes through the arms are more difficult to explain: clothing, even wings have been suggested. Oddly enough, the limestone goddess with the leopard of Catel Hüyük also has holes in the arms.[17] There is no way of telling sex or identity, unless the amulet round the neck and the meander with a pronged motif on top that are incised on belly and buttock contain esoteric information. Moreover the fact that this and some other figures sit on stools and not on the ground may be significant.[18]

Another figure, undoubtedly a woman, and seated in the same attitude, could hardly be more different (Plate 97). It is from Čaršija, not far from Predionica, Priština, or from Vinča, and is probably of much the same date.[19] It is very damaged, the clay is fired nearly black, and the deep incisions and the little holes of the skirt or apron are filled with white. The heavy body is slumped on to a seat, and if this represents pregnancy it is in a very different fashion from the exuberant Asiatic goddesses of birth. The upper part of the figure is youthful, and the only real disproportion is the thickness of the legs, which might be due to potting problems; on the other hand painted Mesolithic hunters in Spain have equally thick legs (Plate 88). The necklet and speckled apron may remind us of the leopard-skin kerchief of one Catel Hüyük goddess and the armlets of another.[20] The Anatolian site is of course much earlier, so direct contacts are out of the question; but the popularity of these motifs at one time in the Balkans may have been due to the sacred character of the leopard and leopard-skin in Anatolia, as it was much later in Crete.

The god or goddess on a seat or stool comes at Vinča comparatively late. The earlier figures usually stand, but some squat on the ground, as generations of women must have done in front of hearth, oven, and grindstone. In Plate 98 from Vinča the hands rest conventionally on the belly. The modelling is naturalistic, and the artist has succeeded in suggesting the weight and mass of the body under the clothing, which appears to be a voluminous skirt with speckled stripes and some sort of shift above it. The date is later Vinča (Vinča-Pločnik) and probably much the same as Čaršija. Two standing figures are modelled in a manner designed to bring out the softness of the clay. The first from Vinča (Plate 102) is earlier than the seated figures (Vinča-Tordos). The body thrusts forward and has the jutting buttocks of convention, but the rounded contour from knee to shoulder is natural and not ungraceful, and the whole surface has been worked with a tool to give it a rippling, undulating texture, almost as though a clinging garment was drawn tightly round the body. This may be no more than a chance effect taken from the tooling of wood. The artists undoubtedly delighted in the rippling, for they used it on animals and on pots. It is never haphazard but takes account of the form of the object. A fragmentary figure from Gradac shows it at its most decorative (Plate 100). This is again late Vinča (Pločnik phase). In the rear view the ugly angular 'shelf' has gone, and spiral ripples underline the natural roundness. This idea appealed centuries later to Romanesque stone-carvers who, working in high relief, love to give us a three-quarter view of plastic spirals on angelic hams and haunches.[21] Light, shade, and texture were also the aim of the Neolithic potter.

One of the largest statuettes from Vinča, the foot-high (30 cm.) 'Vidovdanka', is a more stylized, one might say stylish, figure of the same type (Plate 101). There is little regard here for natural proportions, but as an independent piece of potting it has strength and coherence. The bland, smiling face is perfectly non-commital and, if you like, other-worldly. This 'Vinča face' was a gradual attainment; it is quite different from the 'Predionica face' or the 'Gumelniţa face'; it is still less like the naturalistic and expressionist faces. A side-view suggests a mask and the addition of a wig, but whether as mask or idealization this face, once achieved, remained for its creators, like the 'archaic smile', an entirely satisfactory stereotype; so much so that it could sit equally well on bird and animal (Plate 119 and Figure 43). Another figure, covered with a very light red or pinkish slip, owes its squat shape to the hollow walls, for it is in fact a pot with an open top (Plate 103). The last figure from Vinča proffers with the right hand the breast as though to a child and has, for surface decoration, a pattern of incised bands which were filled after firing with alternating red and black paint (Plate 104 and Figure 37). Like the rippling of Plates 100 and 102, this was a technical device used by potters as well as modellers. The effect, with the stylized Vinča face, is purely decorative, but the back has been modelled to show the hollow between the shoulders and the line of the spine. The opposing styles set up a curious tension.

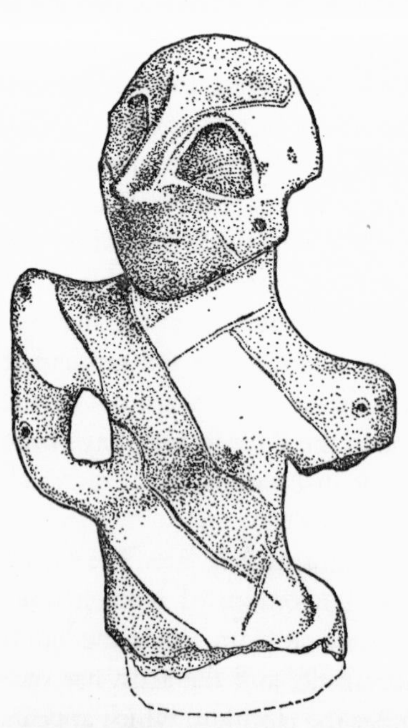

Figure 37. Clay figure from Vinča, Serbia, Yugoslavia, painted in two colours after firing (cf. Plate 104)

Not far away in Bosnia there was a rather different group named after Butmir, and here among many expert potters there was at least one fine modeller. Bodies are usually poorly worked, but among the heads one stands out by its unemphatic naturalism, presenting a norm against which the more expressive heads can be judged (Plate 105). The temptation to raise the voice, to over-emphasize, was always there; eyebrows are drawn up in a grimace of alarm or surprise (Plate 106), or the bulging eye is set where the cheekbone should be (Plate 107); but these are still 'likenesses' and belong to a different world or department of life from the faces of Plates 95 and 96. In the one case the natural physiognomy has been sacrificed to expression, in the other to pattern.

The Maritsa valley south of the Balkan range was geographically well-placed for closer ties with Anatolia and the Aegean, and 'tell' settlements, like those of Asia, abound. Modelled figures in the earlier Neolithic were often of the Anatolian type. But at the end of the Neolithic a new material, marble, was used, and a new culture, Gumelniţa, appeared (Plate 108 and Figure 39A). The skill required to work the marble brings us closer to the early civilization of the Cyclades, which still flourished during the third millennium. Whether it arose early enough to influence the later inhabitants of the great tell of Karanovo is doubtful, nor is there anything here of the severe and noble formality of the best Cycladic sculpture.[22] The Blagoevo lady is the least stylized and can be dated by the corresponding Karanovo figures. The rigid pose, left arm folded over right, is Cycladic, and so is the division of the abdomen, modelled above and flat below, which may be explained by the wearing of a skirt or 'Turkish' trousers (Figure 38A–B).[23] This toothy face is not at all like the long, narrow or blunted triangular 'Cycladic face'. One suspects that the artist would be happier working in clay. There is something of the undressed doll about these marble figures which is absent from Vinča. There are many more clay versions, and the Gumelniţa figure lasted a very long time in Eastern Europe. It was carried far north and subjected to extreme degradation, becoming no more than a flat triangle of bone or clay, or very occasionally sheet-gold, with small holes drilled in it. In this way the human figure becomes a token or trinket, and as such it reached East Prussia (Figure 39).[24]

North of the Balkan mountains, in the Dobrogea, at much the same time (*c.* 3500) something very different was happening among a distinctive group of people who had settled on the lower Danube and are known as the Hamangia culture. As well as making their own peculiar dark-faced impressed pottery, they modelled human and animal figures; but the man and woman of Plate 111 are outside their usual capacity.[25] Most Neolithic sculpture comes from houses, but these were buried with a single body in a grave of the cemetery at Cernavoda. The clay is blackish and very well burnished, with a surface that shines like coal. The style of the work, with its particular blend of natural and abstract shapes, is quite unlike any in the Vinča, Butmir, or Gumelniţa provinces. Symmetry has been carefully avoided, for though the woman's arms are alike, the legs are not. The man's legs are more or less alike, but arms and shoulders are slightly askew. It is not difficult to find elsewhere short, massive legs and elongated necks, but it is rare at this time to see the arms given a value essential to the equilibrium of the finished figure.

The woman, in form and pose, belongs to a well-known series of seated females that can be followed back to the beginning of Neolithic modelling in the Near East and from which she differs only in the unusual appearance of purpose in the manipulation of

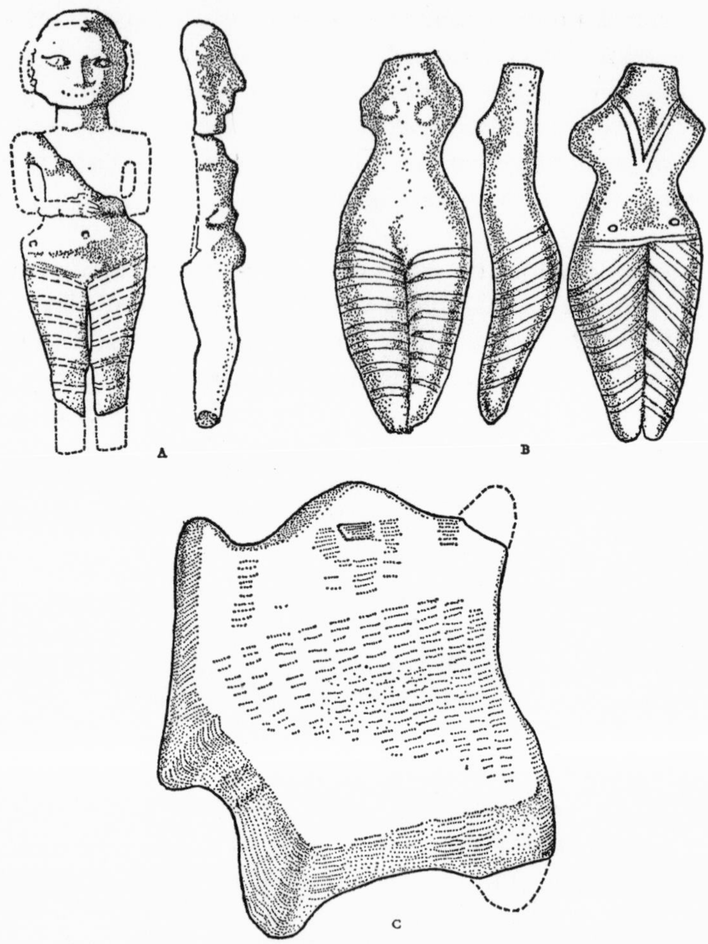

Figure 38. A Late Neolithic (Karanovo VI) marble figure from Blagoevo, Bulgaria, with 'trousers' added from clay example (cf. Plate 108)
B Clay figure from Yassa Tépé, Bulgaria
C Clay seat from Yassa Tépé

mass and proportion; but the companion-piece, the reflective man on the four-legged stool, is unlike anything else in prehistoric Europe, or indeed in the Near East. He is built up from a series of triangles and cubes, the unwanted material having been pared away with a sharp instrument. The pose is neither of authority nor of supplication. It is not found among representations of men or gods, except perhaps the dreamer god in a trance.[26] The Cycladic musicians, to whom he is sometimes compared, are all at work on their instruments. While working within the tradition of his people, this artist has accepted their idiom but transcended their limitations. It is impossible that one so much the master of his medium was not very well aware of what he was doing when he gave a particular expression to those fixed and anxious faces, and perhaps we come nearer here to the soul of Neolithic man than anywhere else.

Between the Hamangia and the Vinča settlements there was another group in the

Tisza valley that was again quite different. Following the Criş or Körös people, these were active hunters and fishers, as well as farmers. Their modelling is not distinguished, but they must have been accomplished textile workers, for their decoration, in whatever medium, leans to textile and matting designs (see below), while their religious ideas found expression in the decoration of pots rather than in free-standing figures. Many pots are in fact anthropomorphic. The seated man from a house at Szegvár-Tüzköves on the Tisza is built up more like a pot than a figure (Plate 110). There is little modelling. The stool, legs, arms, and head are solid and were fitted on to the hollow barrel-shaped body. The clay has been fired to blackish-grey.[27] The conception was rather more impressive than its execution. The back of the head is strongly modelled, but the face is sliced off and replaced by an insipid mask. The legs may have been strong, but the arms are poor spindles; nevertheless this is evidently intended for a figure of authority, and the unidentified sickle-shaped object on the shoulder looks like insignia of rank, as in the tradition of Asiatic and Egyptian priests and kings. Between this figure and the vessel with anthropomorphic decoration there is a gradation that can be followed within the Tisza culture (Figure 40). A and B from Kökénydomb probably once had face-shaped lids, but C from Szegvár-Tüzköves is simply a pot with a face scratched on it; the stool has become the foot and the chest of the figure the neck of the pot. The criss-cross incised pattern is ultimately textile but includes esoteric hieroglyphs, comb-patterns, and meanders, which either reinforce the identity of the person represented or express it in alternative terms.[28] It is not possible to say within the group which comes first, the pot or the sculpture, but there is certainly a relationship. The history of the anthropomorphic pot goes back at least into the fifth millennium in Anatolia. Nearer at hand Körös forerunners of these Tisza people had already had it.[29]

The same theme, but in a more sophisticated dress, is presented by a seated woman found at Bordjos near Novi Bečej, Serbia, and so probably under influence from the direction of Vinča, though claimed for Tisza on the strength of the incised decoration on the stool. She holds on her knees a great bowl as though proffering milk or water like the

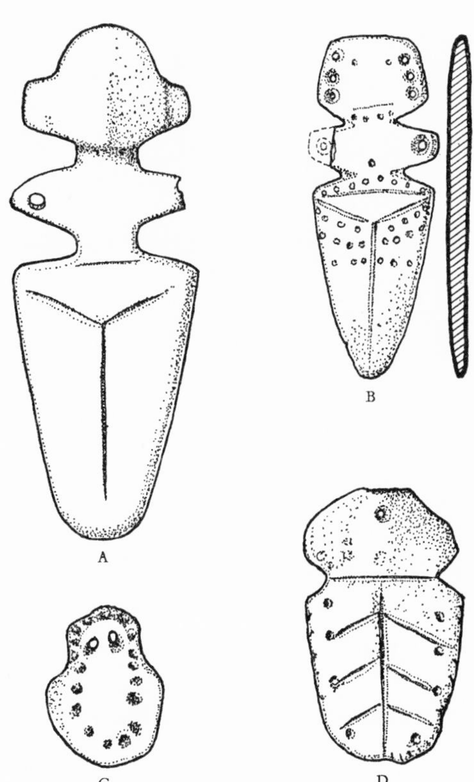

Figure 39. Progressive stylization: A figure from Karanovo VI, Bulgaria, marble, B Salcuţa, bone, C Hăbăşeşti, Rumania, clay, D Schwarzort, East Prussia, amber

Mesopotamian goddess with the flowing vase.[30] The light-coloured surface of the clay is badly worn, but enough remains to show a youthful, comparatively naturalistic figure, though the legs below the knee are as usual too short (Plate 109). The rectangular composition gives the impression of carving from a block of stone or wood more than building in soft clay. At Gaberevo in Bulgaria there is a headless male version of the anthropomorphic pot, perhaps an agricultural fertility spirit with its spout and the conventional phallic gesture like the colossal Egyptian figures of Min. Back in Rumania there is a female version found at Vidra among neighbours of the Hamangia people and contemporary with a late phase of their history. The body is covered with symbolic patterns and the head, now lost, formed the lid (Plate 112).[31] A face

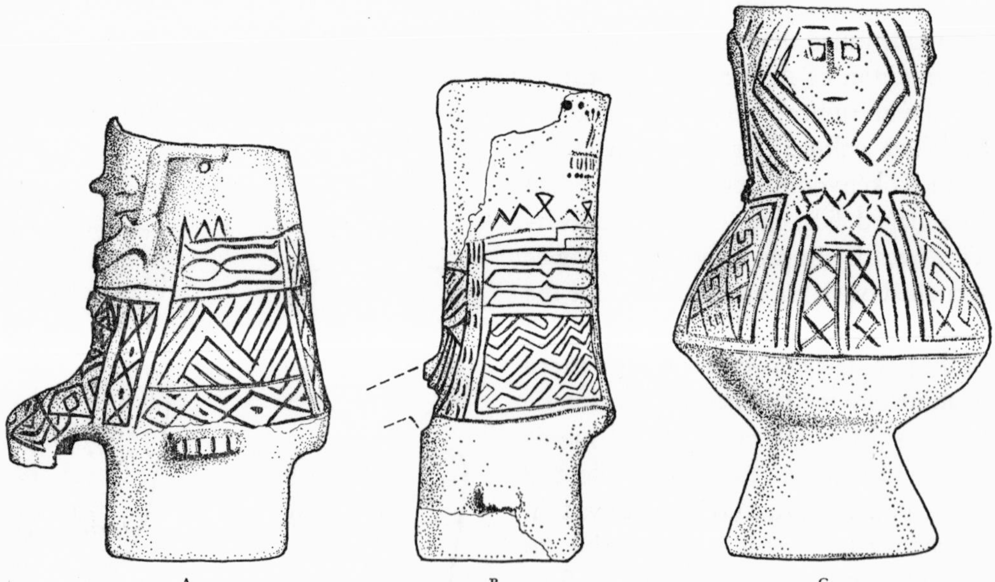

Figure 40. Gradations of pot and figure: A and B from Kökénydomb, C from Szegvár-Tüzköves, Hungary

drawn on a pot's surface, a jab for eyes and mouth and raised nose, is known in many Neolithic cultures, and once, in South Germany, we see it between modelled animal heads like a 'Mistress of Animals' flanked by her beasts.[32]

We ought to be able to trace sculpture in the round across Europe with the 'Danubian' farmers of the fifth and fourth millennium (Table 2).[33] They must have brought their gods with them, but the origin and history of these people is among the hardest to follow of any, and although the starting impetus and inspiration must have come from south-eastern settlements, they were in many ways very unlike the inhabitants of, for instance, Nea Nikomedeia, Yassa Tépé, Gornja Tuzla, Karanovo, and Vinča. Not only are the plans of the long houses very different, but also the solid fixtures. Clay ovens, impressive built hearths, indoor shrines are nowhere to be seen. In the forests of Western and Central Europe wood must have been the material, not only for walls but any furnishings as well, and all these of course have perished. Ornaments of spondylus shell from the Mediterranean show that men kept some loose contact with the south-east even at the limit of their explorations. Occasionally in Czechoslovakia, Germany, and Austria broken fragments of small figures are found among the pots;[34] poor relics, already too far from their Balkan and Anatolian source to survive in the new conditions. There is however one true contemporary continuation of the arts of Vinča and Butmir towards the end of their existence. This is in a farming community living in defended hill-top villages of south-western Slovakia and southern Moravia whose inhabitants made the so-called 'Crusted' or 'Moravian Painted Ware' (painted after firing) and also modelled free-standing figures.[35]

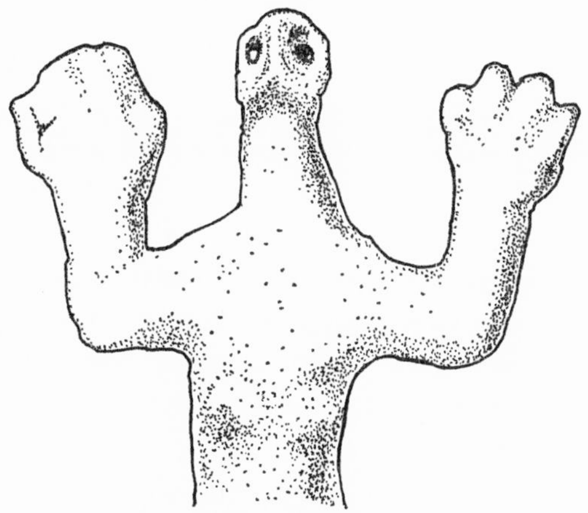

Figure 41. Clay figure from Štěpánovice, Czechoslovakia

Here there are again the sort of informal likenesses that we saw at Butmir and occasionally at Vinča (Plates 113 and 114). The head from Jaroměřice, near Roka (13 inches; 7·5 cm.), must have come from a fair-sized figure. The smaller head from Boskovštýn ($13\frac{1}{5}$ inches; 8·1 cm., with part of the body) is another portrait sketch. A complete figure of a naked woman from Hluboké-Mašůvky (14 inches; 36 cm.) is, on the other hand, formal and hieratic (Plate 115). The two halves of the figure look as though modelled to different scales; the lower massive, the upper slight, again like some of the figures in the Spanish shelter paintings. A necklace or kerchief is worn, the ears are pierced, the pose and the backward-tilted head is orthodox, so is the smile under the abrasions of the clay surface.[36] The arms may be stretched out in a ritual gesture, or they may have supported a vessel like the seated lady of Bordjos. Arms are so often broken that it is impossible to say when the 'vessel-bearer' appeared, but as soon as bronzesmiths returned to representational art she is there again. We know from other figures that these same people fell at times into Expressionist excesses (Figure 41), or oftener a lifeless symmetry. A standing woman of the symmetrical sort was found not along ago at Lang-Enzersdorf near Vienna, and another at Zauschwitz near Dresden, and that is virtually the western limit of the tradition of clay sculpture which we have been following till now.[37]

A great many of the smaller figures had holes for attachment to some extraneous object, a large vessel or household shrine; others were functional – containers, as well as representations of living things; and somewhere between them are the three-dimensional figures, and parts of figures, attached to pots, usually to the handle, but sometimes on rim or shoulders. Most are animal protoms (see below), but there are one or two which are in all other respects like the free-standing human figures. A group of mother and child is known at Vinča,[38] as well as twin-headed figures that share the same body. The most expressive treatment of the subject comes from Zengövarkony, Hungary, where it surmounts a pierced lug (Plate 116). The mother's arms enclose the child at her breast in an immemorial gesture of protection which has a touching humanity in spite of the crudity of the modelling. This is no 'death in life' like the Asiatic 'Great Mother'.

Only a very few from the thousands of Neolithic and Chalcolithic modelled clay figures have been touched on here; the greater part are quite standardized and poorly executed. The Cucuteni figure (Plate 117) is a rather better example chosen from a number, all of which have the same incised pattern, and the same proportions. This is true also of the Vinča and Gumelniţa provinces; nearly every excavation brings in its crop of repetitive small figures. The selection illustrated here may give an impression of greater originality and variety than really existed; every exceptional piece is simply the best of its class. The Cernavoda man (Plate 111) may really have been unique – we do not know – but the woman is only the most perfect of many; so are the Čaršija and Predionica figures. Yet there we seem to have an individual hand, an especially gifted artist, such a one as may at any time be thrown up from the commonplace crowd; and the crowd is necessary for his appearance. Among a score of almost identical pharaohs, one is an unforgettable individual; from hundreds of identical ikons there is one Lady of Vladimir. In their very much humbler way this is the case with our Butmir head and Cernavoda man.

In view of the anti-naturalism and decorative qualities of later prehistoric art in Europe it is well to bear in mind that from their first appearance, and for some one and a half thousand years thereafter, these communities of farmers were engaged in sculpture that could be extremely naturalistic, and that even when most stylized was still firmly rooted in a three-dimensional world of sight and touch. It is possible for us to meet these people face to face, as it were, in their own likeness, as never again until the arrival of Greek and Roman artists in the provinces. We are seeing them as they looked to each other, not disguised as archetypal 'Earth-Mothers' or emblems of virility, and this is true in a way in which it is seldom true of the exotic art of primitive peoples today; nor is it easy to find in the higher civilizations of the ancient world. The lack of polish and the technical shortcomings perhaps have added an informal humanity, almost intimacy, to some faces.

Alongside the naturalistic and homely there is always the hieratic and stylized, whether in Moravia, Serbia or the Dobrogea; and even if the body is natural, the face may be a formal diagram. The 'Vinča face' is exceptionally odd, especially when combined with a body like that on Plate 119. These abrupt changes of idiom may be due to the need to neutralize the disconcerting habit of our emotions to respond to 'expression'. Any roundish lump of clay that has been given a squeeze here and a jab there, a mere sketch of features, immediately becomes charged with expression in a language to which we respond whether we would or no, and which has nothing to do with the quality of execution. The Neolithic artists understood this, and they knew that one way of avoiding it is by rendering the face naturally but with a regularity that is perfectly non-committal, the 'classical' way of impersonal perfection (Plate 105); or else it can be done by means of a diagram. Then the parts of the face, though derived from natural features, are composed as pattern; ideal, abstract, decorative, unchanging, equally beyond the disturbing play of expression. This is the alternative mode, chosen long after by Celtic masters. Paleolithic sculptors had met the same problem and tried to resolve it by leaving the face blank, or covering it with featureless hair, and they also had used classical anonymity and pattern (Plates 8, 10, and 23). The reason then, as in the Neolithic, is more likely to have been avoidance of the particularity of life than of any danger in the quality of life itself. Deity must be shown as person transcending individual personality, and this is something that sophisticated art very seldom achieves. Byzantine artists could do it, or a Romanesque sculptor, but it is outside the normal range of western art. Given the difficulty of the task, the Neolithic artist did not do so badly (Plates 95 and 103).

A Modeller's Art: Other Subjects

Compared to the human face and figure, the animals are, with a few exceptions, poor, insignificant little objects, unidentifiable except as 'quadruped'. In Czechoslovakia and Rumania there are a few rather better representations but the majority may in fact be children's toys (Figure 42C). They are very like the little animals found at Jarmo and Catel Hüyük, and at the latter there is the same contrast in quality between representations of man and animal. In Late Neolithic or Chalcolithic Rumania there is a pointed, long-nosed animal, either dog, fox, or wolf, that lies curled up asleep (Figure 42B). It could be the same beast as was painted on pots in Moldavia and the Ukraine.[39] At Predionica a snake was modelled with its zigzag markings, but for the most part animals appear either as rhyta corresponding to the anthropomorphic pots, or as adjuncts of pots or furniture.

There is a bear rhyton from Abrahám in Slovakia, made by the same people as the lady with outstretched arms (Plates 118 and 115), which seems to show that the wild animal still receives more respectful treatment than the domestic 'slave'. However, to compare this representation with Plate 7 from Věstonice, a few miles and twenty thousand years apart, is one way of experiencing the different relationship to the animal world of Paleolithic hunter and Neolithic farmer. There are other bear rhyta, very like this, and some are painted;[40] but I know of no Neolithic representation of a horse, and deer, once so popular, only appear very occasionally in relief on the sides of large storage vessels (Figure 42A). There are, however, a few monsters. At Vinča and rather later in Bulgaria, animal and bird vessels breathe a spirit of fantasy or look like embodiments of myth. One of the strangest and oldest is the 'bird' from Vinča (Plate 119). This is one of

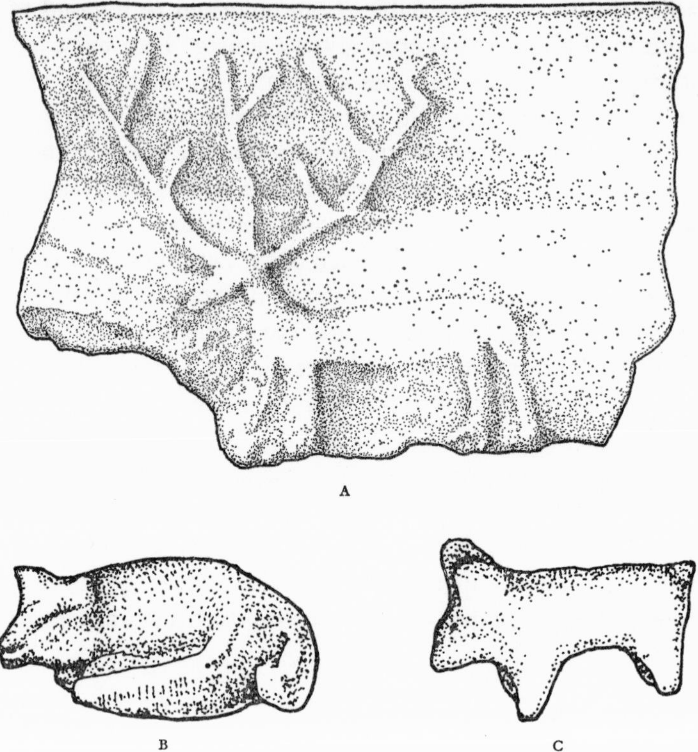

Figure 42. A Stag modelled in relief on the side of a pot from Csépa, Hungary
B Sleeping fox from Pietrele, Rumania, clay
C Bovine animal from Hăbăşeşti, Rumania, clay

a long series of bird-vases which were still being made in the Iron Age. In this original conception wings and tail are surmounted by the familiar, all-purpose 'Vinča-face', like an archaic siren or sphinx. A pair of knobbed horns or an elaborate headdress is worn, and the whole surface is rippled as on some human figures and ordinary pots. The spout is above the tail. This bird was seen as floating on the water, but the other animal pots stand on four, or sometimes three legs. In Figure 43 the Vinča-face has horns perhaps of a nanny-goat, and on Plate 120 three calves' heads decorate a miniature 'altar'. In Bulgaria goat and ram heads are attached to trough-like containers on legs, sometimes called lamps because of their likeness to similar objects in pre-Hittite Anatolia.[41] The beast from Kodjaderman in the Maritsa valley (Plate 121) certainly did not come from the farmyard; its top is closed, the beak a spout, and the date the same as Plate 108, that is to say the last phase of the tells (Karanovo VI).

The farmer-potters often attached calf- or cow-heads to ordinary pots. A gourd-shaped milk bowl of the Danubian group at Dukovany, Moravia, has four heads spaced round the top (Figure 44) in a way that already foreshadows the bronze cauldron with bull-protoms that became, in the hands of first-millennium bronzesmiths, an object of widespread admiration and high value (pp. 215, 241), while on a rather later (Chalco-

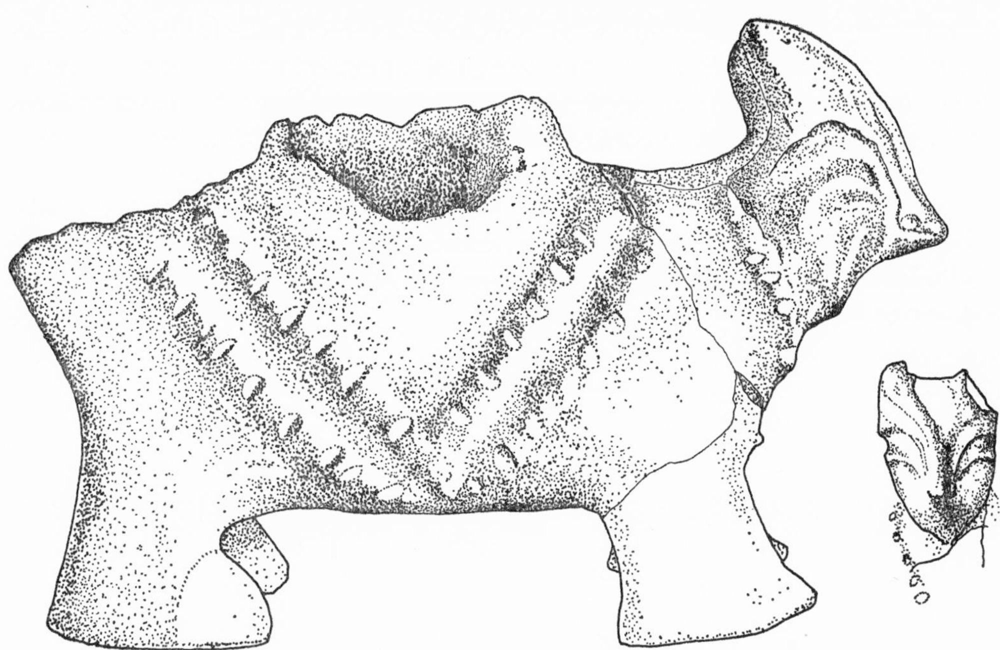

Figure 43. Animal pot from Vinča, Serbia, Yugoslavia

lithic) pot from Statenice-Černy the cow- or ox-head has a triangular forelock with dotted markings which again points to Anatolia.[42] The choice of milk-giving animals – goat, sheep, cow – cannot be due to chance. Although there *seems* to be a break between the two great series of animal pots, the one Neolithic and Chalcolithic, the other Late Bronze and Iron Age, this is not really so; for the horned animal, gradually degraded to a mere 'horned lug', survived right through the interval, just as the anthropomorphic pot survived as a pair of eyes or of breast-shaped bosses (Plate 166, Figures 67 and 84A, and p. 172 below). But there is never again anything quite like the outrageous experiments which we see in the Neolithic and Chalcolithic of Eastern and Central Europe, with that refusal to separate into different departments the pot as mere container and the animal- or man-shaped pot that is image as well as container.

Two examples will have to stand for many. A magnificent pot from Střelice, Moravia (Plate 122), not only has four horned animals standing round the mouth, as though approaching a pool to drink, but on the widest part are spaced out four hand-shaped lugs, and neatly pricked in the burnished surface of the clay there are four stylized human figures, three men and a woman in a wide skirt, with between them an identical ornamental motif. An unknown chapter of mythology may be hidden here. The second pot, from Svodín in Slovakia, has a painted surface and is an odd compromise with its upraised 'arms' and token breasts (Plate 123). A face-lid may have fitted over the neck, as in the Vidra pot of Plate 112. At Vinča there are a series of lids decorated with 'features' in the formal style of that culture. Plate 124 is one of several with the same pricked-up ears and slightly sinister pussy-cat look. There is a prototype in sixth-millennium Hacilar.[43]

At the same time there appears the peculiar boot- or leg-shaped pot which is so widespread and lasted so long that it must have had a place in cult or popular religion. A pair of joined feet from Hluboké-Mašůvky are used as pedestal for a nest or *kernos* of three small pots.[44] We can only guess at the significance of these bizarre vessels; whatever the motive of the makers, it is not likely to have been mere eccentricity. Somewhere in the background may be the idea of the vessel that moves itself, for later, when the wheel had come to symbolize movement, we get bronze and even clay vessels that trundled about on wheels. As usual, it is in Anatolia that the foot and boot vase enjoyed its full variety.

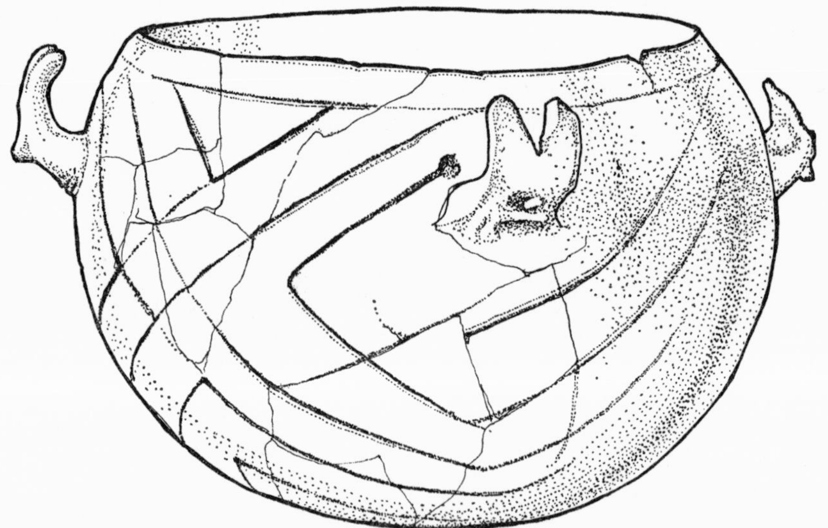

Figure 44. Pot from Dukovany, Moravia, Czechoslovakia

Small relief figures of deer, men, and women are placed round large storage jars by Körös, Cucuteni, and Tordos potters. But modelling was not confined to living things: houses, furniture, altars, kilns were reproduced in small (Figures 38C and 45B). There is often an animal head or ornamental finial on the real, as on the modelled, house, like the wishbone at Ariuşd (Figure 45A). House-models from the Maritsa valley have windows and wall decoration, and it is possible that Plate 121 is itself a house with an exceptionally large predatory bird as finial. One model has the lid off and shows the inside with its oven, storage pots on a shelf, cruciform hearth (or shrine), and grindstone with the housewife on her knees grinding by the entrance.[45]

This brings us to the decoration of the house itself. Fragments of painted plaster are often found in excavations, and sometimes there are large pieces with quite complicated designs; so we should probably think of the interiors as gay with red, black, and white paint (Figure 45C). Many of the subtle and beautiful curvilinear patterns painted on the pots of the eastern groups cry out for development over broad surfaces such as house-walls, and the wealth of weaving patterns transferred to pots and on the plaster-

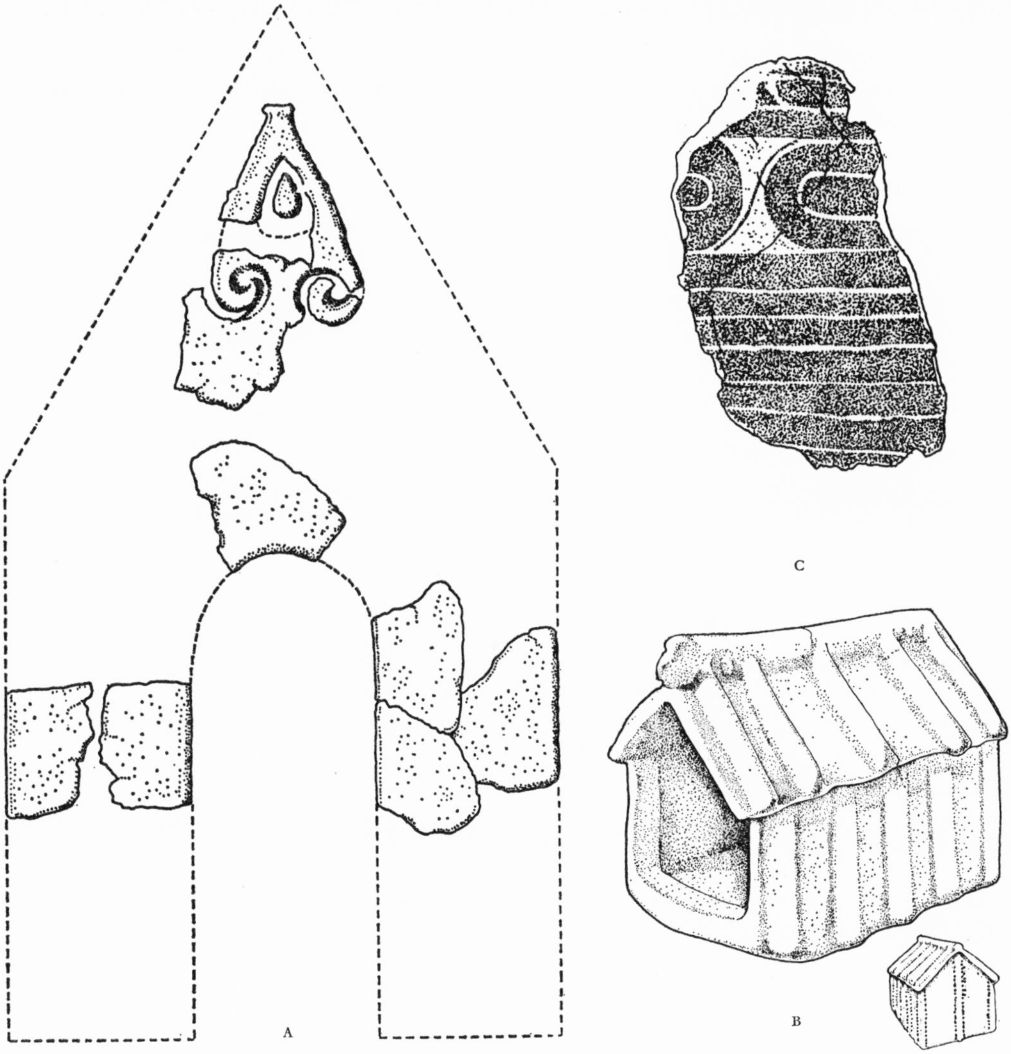

C

A

B

Figure 45. A Clay house finial and part of façade from Ariuşd, Rumania
B House model from Střelice, Moravia, Czechoslovakia, clay
C Painted wall-plaster from Karanovo VI, Bulgaria

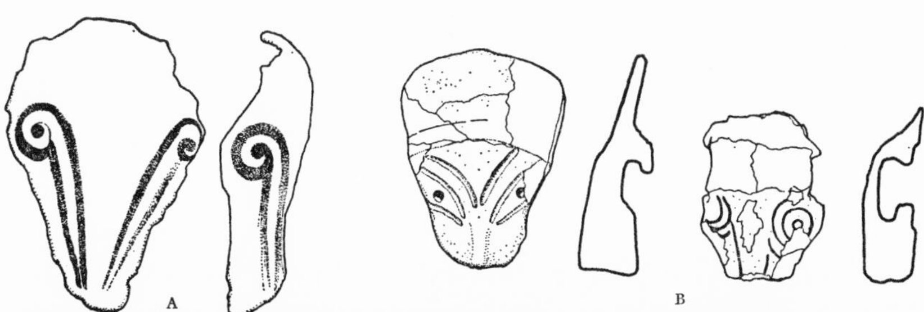

Figure 46 A and B Modelled clay bucrania from Vinča and Jakova, Serbia, Yugoslavia

work of houses in Hungary show that woven mats were used on floors and perhaps to cover walls as well (Plate 133 and Figure 40).[46] Houses also held shrines of different sorts. At Kormadin, Jakova, near Belgrade a large trough-shaped clay 'altar' with panelled decoration was connected with life-size bucrania, and at Truşeşti in Moldavia there is an elaborate screen over 3 feet high (Figure 47).[47] The three Kormadin bucrania came from two adjoining houses and stood on posts. No horn-cores were found, but the impression of the animal's forelock could be seen at the back of one. The faces have a conventional incised ornament, and there are others like them at Vinča (Figure 46, A–B). The likeness to the (much earlier) bull-shrines of Catel Hüyük is striking indeed. The two sentinel-like figures of the Truşeşti shrine have bowl-shaped concave heads; the ends of the screen recall the altar horns of Crete and Asia. Detached figures with the same peculiar head are found in other houses, always near the hearth. The type must have frozen, like the Gumelniţa and Vinča face, for we find versions at the back of a rather grand miniature chair or throne in another village of the same people.[48]

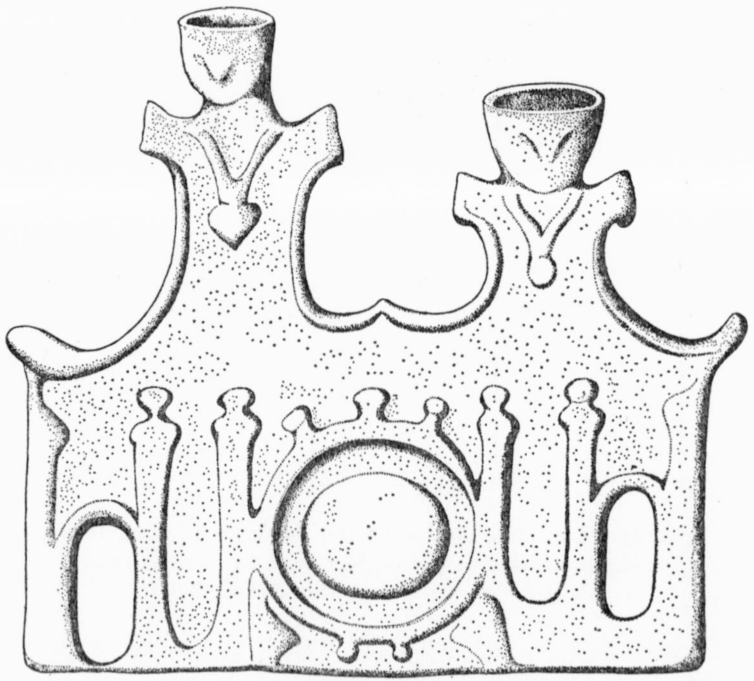

Figure 47. Clay shrine from Truşeşti, Moldavia, Rumania

The Potter's Art: Skeuomorph and Spiral

Although Neolithic (and Chalcolithic) modelling is often arresting and occasionally beautiful, the artistry and imagination of the new farming communities of Eastern Europe are probably seen at their happiest in the architecture and decoration of pots, especially the painted pots of the Rumanian and Ukrainian provinces. Here there is a variety and gaiety in the designs that is a delightful surprise. Farther west and north pottery of great technical excellence was produced, but the shapes and designs are monotonous, never escaping far from the limitations of the skeuomorph. This is something with which we today are equally familiar. The electric fire surmounted by imitation coals round which flickers an imitation flame, the plastic tea-tray that is stained like the grain of wood, or cement chopped up into 'crazy paving', these are commonplace superficial skeuomorphs designed to disguise the new material with a cosy familiarity. But there is another kind of skeuomorph that declares itself only in retrospect. Today the bodywork of the earliest motor-car reminds us much more of the horse-drawn carriage from which it developed, with all the appropriate knobs and flourishes of brass and wood, than of the streamlined fibre-glass sports car towards which it was (still unconsciously) directed. This sort of thing has been repeated in the history of almost every useful invention: in the art of potting as well as the internal combustion engine.

Forerunners of the clay pot – leather bags, ostrich eggs, gourds, baskets of reed, bark, or grass – can often be rediscovered at some moment in their transformation arrested and fixed in clay: smooth surfaces are criss-crossed by clay 'ropes' and 'cordons' or dotted with knobs that were once studs in wooden tubs (Figure 48B); the stitches that held together the parts of a leather vessel are copied by a stick pressed into the moist clay. Some shapes and ornaments had a very long life and were still more or less faithfully reproduced generations after the last original had been smashed, thrown away, and forgotten. This is true of ostrich eggs in Spain and gourds in Belgium.[49] Behind the persistence of skeuomorphic shapes the forces, sometimes contradictory, of use and tradition are always at work.

The reason why a skeuomorph appears in the first place is more likely to be change in material than in use, so there is a compromise: the clay cordon and the gourd pot. The new material may be easier to work or to find, but the innovation once made, the old conserving inertia, the quasi-religious penumbra that adheres even to mundane objects, must still be fought down all over again every time an 'improvement' is introduced. An object that is well adapted to what is required of it will not change; in our woodman's axe we are still satisfied with a three-thousand-year-old design. In a primitive society the repertoire of shapes and ornaments is usually small, the objects simple and durable, and the fight against alteration correspondingly tough. As time passes and ideas and inventions proliferate, the tempo of change quickens, and the hold on life of each subject, pot-shape or decoration, is correspondingly shorter. It also seems that, while the original material on which the skeuomorph is based is still in use, the pattern or shape will draw from it new life. Basketry patterns in pots remain vigorous and variable almost to the end. But when the original is forgotten, there is nothing to prevent the decoration lapsing into formality, and we get those nonsense patterns, corresponding perhaps to nonsense repetitions and rhyming games, the verbal acrobatics which illiterate peoples enjoy and are so good at.

The pots illustrated on Plates 125 and 129 and Figure 48A are agreeable, well-balanced objects. Sometimes the balance and harmony can be traced back to the original, the growing gourd or the basket held together by tension of plaiting and coiling. In this case choice of the model, or rather acceptance of the inherited model along with the resistance of the material and the limitations of the tools, are guarantees of a satisfactory shape. But not all the originals were harmonious and simple, and among pots too there are odd and repellent shapes. Gourd and ostrich egg may conceivably conform to some universal canon of harmony which is transmitted to the pottery imitation: a pineapple too is a beautiful object, but a pot built to imitate a pineapple is likely to turn out a monstrosity.

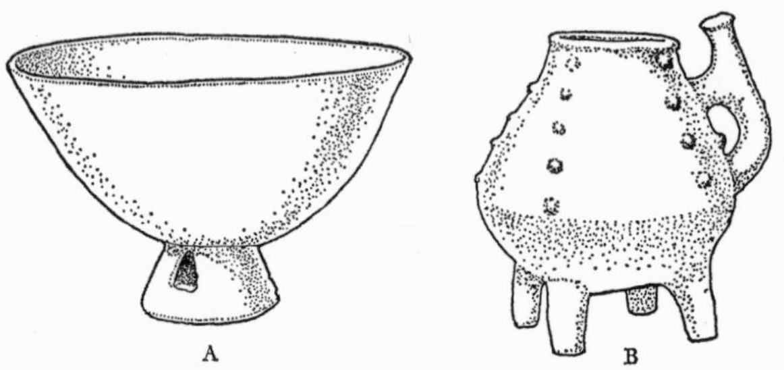

Figure 48. Pots from Karanovo, Bulgaria: A chalice from Level II, B mug from Level III (Georgiev)

Our Neolithic potters did not imitate pineapples, they had never seen them, but some of their productions are just as ugly (Figure 48B from Karanovo III, based on a wooden mug with knobs). If the ugly pot is at one extreme, the perfect oval of the ostrich egg, though beautiful, is not really very much better as a pot. Like other simple geometrical figures – circle, cone, square – its monotony soon becomes boring. If the ultimate pleasure of mathematics is, as we are told, aesthetic, an element of mathematics may well enter our enjoyment of shapes; but the most constantly pleasing pots are those which stand somewhere between the geometrical beauty of an egg and the rococo idiosyncrasies of a pineapple, in the balance between monotony and innovation, symmetry and too exact imitation of the accidents of nature.

Like the form, the decoration of a pot's surface can start from opposite poles, the one derived from use which, when the usefulness has ceased, becomes skeuomorph; and the other that treats the area of pot-surface as a canvas for the deployment of a design, either representational or abstract. Though in origin so different, in the course of time they may converge. When the meaning is lost, the visual symbol can also decline into ornament through the endless repetitions, due partly no doubt to laziness, but also to the residue of sacred content that still clings to a dead or dying symbol as to a dead and forgotten use.

Leather, chipped wood, and basketry originals may be divined in Plates 127, 128, and 129. The rectilinear ornament covers the whole surface. Sometimes the artistry or sheer technique of an individual potter transcends the rules: one such made the Danish pot (Plate 127) from Skarpsalling (Passage Grave Period). Memories of stitching can still be discerned, but decorative and architectural considerations are given more weight – even an undecorated zone has been permitted – and the result is one of the finest examples of prehistoric potting.[50] There is the same high standard of meticulous craftsmanship, though the technique is cruder, on two Late Neolithic squat bowls from near Stuttgart (Plate 128). These very few examples must stand for an enormous output of potting, because I believe that more is gained from following in rather more detail one distinct tradition that arose in South-East Europe. It is not obviously skeuomorphic, but is rich in decorative ideas and capable of a more self-conscious use of the pot surface as a canvas. It is long-lived and not dependent on place, situation, or people alone, but could at times jump frontiers and survive temporary disaster and all but obliteration.

This style, for so it may be called, seems to have arisen from interaction between several different although sometimes related groups. The first and most obvious difference between it and the pots we have been looking at is the preference for the curved line, although, like the rectilinear lattices, chequers, and triangles of a basket- or bag-pot, it too may have had 'natural' originals. Ever since we first became aware of the visible world nature has surrounded us with curves, semicircles, segments of circles, serpentines; these are organic and commonplace. It is the rejection of curvilinear and the choice of rectilinear patterns which is unnatural and which confronts us with man the maker. There has been a lot of controversy, over the years, on the subject of the ornamental spiral, which made its early appearance and had a lasting hold in Danubian lands, the Balkans, and South Russia, with subsequent journeyings around the ancient world. It is highly improbable, to say the least, that spiral ornament was invented once for all in the history of the earth. It is one of the 'basic scribbles' of a three-year-old child and may come even before the circle, and decidedly before rectangles and 'stars'.[51] Spirals occur in nature frequently from the microscopic foramnifera to the great spiral nebulae, or, more accessibly, in the shell of the common snail and whelk, and in a variety of vegetable growths. The loosening fronds of bracken and the serial imbrications of a pine-cone are two singularly beautiful examples among a host of others. Since the spiral is commoner in nature than the rectangle, the square, or the equilateral triangle (the cold geometric world of crystals is too remote from daily life), these only become current when man begins to hew and cut, to build and to weave on a loom.

Ornamental spirals are already used by Old Stone Age artists carving bone and ivory, where they seem to grow almost accidentally out of the two-dimensional projection of three-dimensional objects (Plate 42). Continuity could possibly be argued between this art, also much practised in South Russia, and the designs of Neolithic potters in South-East Europe, but the spirals of New Guinea or of the Maoris in New Zealand, or among Pueblo Indians and in Central Australia, cannot be accounted for in this way.[52] When it came to decorating Neolithic pots, the equable or Archimedes spiral was chosen, which is also the basket-maker's coil and the coil used in one method of building a pot. Painted white on a red background, it was already on pots in Serbia in the fifth millennium, and it was incised or painted at about the same date in the Maritsa valley.[53]

This is not quite the beginning of pottery in Europe even north of Rhodope, but sherds are extremely rare in the earliest settlements. What is found is often too fragmentary to give any idea as to the form of the whole pot, and the quality is that of homely kitchen ware poorly baked and ornamented, if at all, with impressions from a piece of bone, stick, or shell. But it may not be altogether chance that one of the favourite dies resembles two ears of corn. Rather finer ware is undecorated but usually covered with a slip and burnished. The shapes are not inelegant. Plate 125 from Starčevo is red-brown with a hollow foot. The bowl, also without the foot, is one of the earliest shapes south of Rhodope in Thessaly and Macedonia. Plain surfaces were soon followed by painted, and in the Maritsa valley the earliest settlements at the bottom of the tells already have pots with quite elaborate painted ornament. Plate 126 from Karanovo II is a clumsier form of chalice with hollow foot, but it has been burnished all over with a tool in such a way as to give a very lightly rippled surface (not visible in the photograph) over which the white paint was applied in a pattern still inspired by basketry or weaving.[54] Both these shapes, the bowl on a low foot and the 'chalice', had a long life, but many others were soon added to them including the 'ugly' pots of Vesilinovo (Karanovo III) (Figure 48B) which need not concern us. The bowl, *without* a foot, was used by Danubian colonists, who held to it with great tenacity. If they wanted to raise a pot off the ground, they gave it feet rather than a ring-base. The form is more closed than Plate 125, but otherwise much the same.[55] Whether the spiral and volute, which they incised on their bowls, came from the painted spirals of Starčevo (and Körös) is another matter; but from the beginning they had single spirals and double and interlocking volutes. The curvilinear patterns forming unbroken bands (hence Bandkeramik) are often effective, and there are also rectilinear patterns and meanders.

The Vinča potters did not paint their spirals but, as we have seen on the modelled figures, lightly grooved the surface, a technique that must be limited to very simple spirals if confusion is to be avoided. The Butmir neighbours of Vinča in Bosnia exploited with greater ingenuity quite complicated double-coils and rapport patterns of a deceptive simplicity. The coils start from adjacent poles and thereafter revolve about each other; the second coil probably began as a negative of the first. The design is so deeply incised that it gives an impression of relief. The aim was perfect regularity in the repetition of endless movement (Plate 130 and Figure 49). This ornament leaves little scope for development, and the mechanical accomplishment with which the patterns are executed may have been its undoing; at all events the style came to a sudden end. It is precocious in foreshadowing the patterns of painted ceilings and carved stone stelai of Late Helladic Greece, but though the grey colour of the ware is curiously stony, like an imitation of steatite, the monumental was never attempted, and it can hardly be related to the similar decoration of Maltese temples, though nearer to them in date (see below, Chapter 5). There are independent reasons for suspecting seaborne ventures from the Aegean to the Adriatic, through which a connexion with Early Cycladic spiral ornament is possible.[56]

Some very early curvilinear painted designs, possibly with spirals, appear in Rumania contemporary with Starčevo,[57] and these are followed by incised spirals ('Boian' style) which are much rougher than Butmir. The Danubian Bandkeramik influence was not so strong here as it was once thought to be, but there may have been influences from further north-east, where a group of farmers, settled on the Bug and Dniestr, have recently been identified.[58] They covered their pots with curvilinear designs in multiple line like the later Rumanian painted wares (Cucuteni, Ariuşd, and Tripolye styles). There was in fact something of real ferment, a melting-pot of peoples and arts interacting and overlapping, on the rich black-earth country, especially in Moldavia and the Ukraine, from a little before 3000, that is to say contemporary with the latest work at Vinča and Butmir (see Table 2 and map on pp. xxxvi–xxxvii).

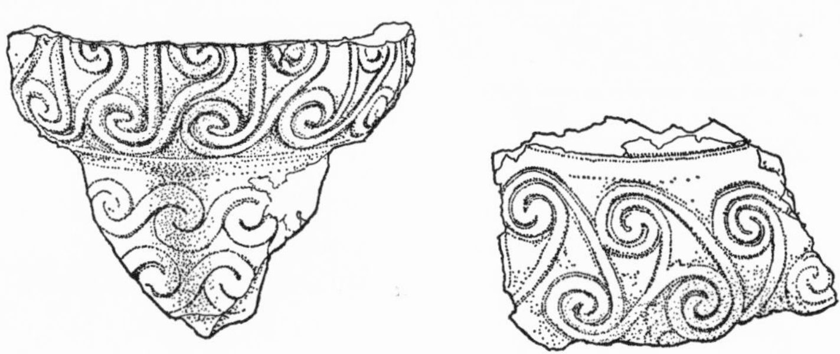

Figure 49. Spiral-ornamented sherds from Butmir, Bosnia, Yugoslavia

The best of the painted pottery from this region has no parallel elsewhere in third-millennium Europe. The biscuit is very hard and the clay well-levigated. The painters went far beyond the single and double coil. There are S-figures, loops, and coils full of movement and invention, as well as a richness of colour and considerable tact in applying it. There is also a feeling for the architecture of the pot, as in Plate 131, where the rectilinear meander covers the straight neck and spiral curves are wrapped round the body. The equiangular or logarithmic spiral is sometimes used now as well as the coil. It increases from a centre point or pole, or from a solid circle (the proto-conch), for one or two 'throws', after which it remains at the same width or, if linking a series of connected spirals, decreases in the same ratio (in spite of its textbook title this is the whorl of the common snail shell; Figure 52, next to bottom).

The interplay of techniques and motifs drawn from different sources makes rigid stylistic descriptions more than usually dangerous; however, a swirling multiple line in continuous movement round the pot is generally early (Plate 131, Cucuteni A), while later the movement is interrupted and the zones of decoration divided into metopes Figure 52, lower two; Cucuteni B), and at the same time the number of motifs increases: circles, circles with cross, lozenges, stars, and so on (Plate 136). Bands of colour may be edged with a finely drawn or painted outline, or the outline is incised. The matt colours are always applied before baking, so that the effect is quite unlike the contemporary 'crusted ware' of Serbia, Slovakia, and Moravia.[59] Colours are warm, rufous browns and blacks shading into dark maroon; when fresh they would have had an opulent glow. The texture is not unlike that of Middle Helladic painted wares. Plate 132 from Traian is comparatively early (Cucuteni AB) and combines red with black on white. Here almost the whole surface is painted, but in later pots (Cucuteni B) there

Figure 50. A Pot from Traian, Rumania, painted
B Pot from Truşeşti, Rumania, painted and incised

may be quite large areas of unpainted 'slip', especially on the lower part of the pot. The bottom of a bowl or flask or a lid is filled with trefoil patterns or various ingenious whorls and swirls (Figure 50A). Not all vases, naturally, are painted with the same disciplined logic, and in less skilled hands ornament lapses into a chaos of loops and squiggles (Figure 51B). It is the earlier, less elaborate, motifs that seem not only to survive longest, but to reappear centuries later in the plastic ornament of Bronze Age pots, and even on metal. Large spirals throw off little ones, and a filling motif repeats the coil of spiral or circle on Chalcolithic pot or Bronze Age sword and Celtic torc (Plates 171, 174, 254, and Figures 50B and 51A). These are in fact the controlling elements of the style, and are singled out because of their reappearances (Plate 295 and Figure 101B).

This ornament *qua* ornament is, I believe, on an equality with Middle Minoan and the finest of Early Mesopotamian wares. At its best it deserved to live, and so it did. On the other hand among later motifs some are frankly frivolous and seem to come from a sort of precocious Art Nouveau (Figure 52).[60]

Before leaving this pottery, there are a few examples of representation to notice. Nearly all are late (Cucuteni B and Tripolye B II). In the earlier phase we find, very occasionally, a diagrammatic human figure constructed from opposing triangles for chest and skirt according to a stereotype which is as appropriate to weaving as curves to modelling (Plate 133). Among the abstract and decorative designs of the later phase there appears an intruder: a singular animal, prick-eared, with fearsome claws and a plumed tail arched over its back (Plate 134 and Figures 52 and 53).[61] It is painted on pots, not once or twice, but many times, and in slightly different shapes, sometimes like a wolf, at others a fox, or a foxy or wolfish dog.[62] At Şipeniţ on the upper Prut it is usually small and marginal, like something strayed in from a different civilization, but at Valea Lupului identical beasts face each other heraldically on the neck of the pot in

Figure 51. Development of design on pots from Traian: A early three colours, B disintegrating

the central zone, with a peculiar sort of hedgehog between them, while snakes writhe on the shoulder (Plate 134). The stylization of the flat silhouettes is elegant and not quite serious. It may remind us of the liberties taken by those fine artists who worked at Susa and Sialk in the fourth millennium. The beast itself – we shall meet it again – has relatives in the Caucasus and descendants in Iron Age Europe (see below). The cattle on which these people depended for their livelihood were never painted. There are absolute sanctions that rule the choice of subjects.

In Moldavia, and still more in the Ukraine, we are on the edge of the great Central Asiatic province stretching from the Caspian to China, and south into Iran. The Caspian had itself been a focus for some of the earliest experiments in agriculture, and by the third millennium, when the Cucuteni and Tripolye cultures were flourishing, Anatolia was no longer the sole intermediary between Eastern Europe and the civilizations of the Middle East. From now on the Caspian, the Caucasus, and the South Russian steppe grew in importance; for we have reached the time when metals, and the countries that possessed the ores, were entering their long, troubled history of exploitation, trade, and brigandage. Small trinkets of gold and copper begin to appear in the middle and later Cucuteni, as they do on Vinča sites.[63]

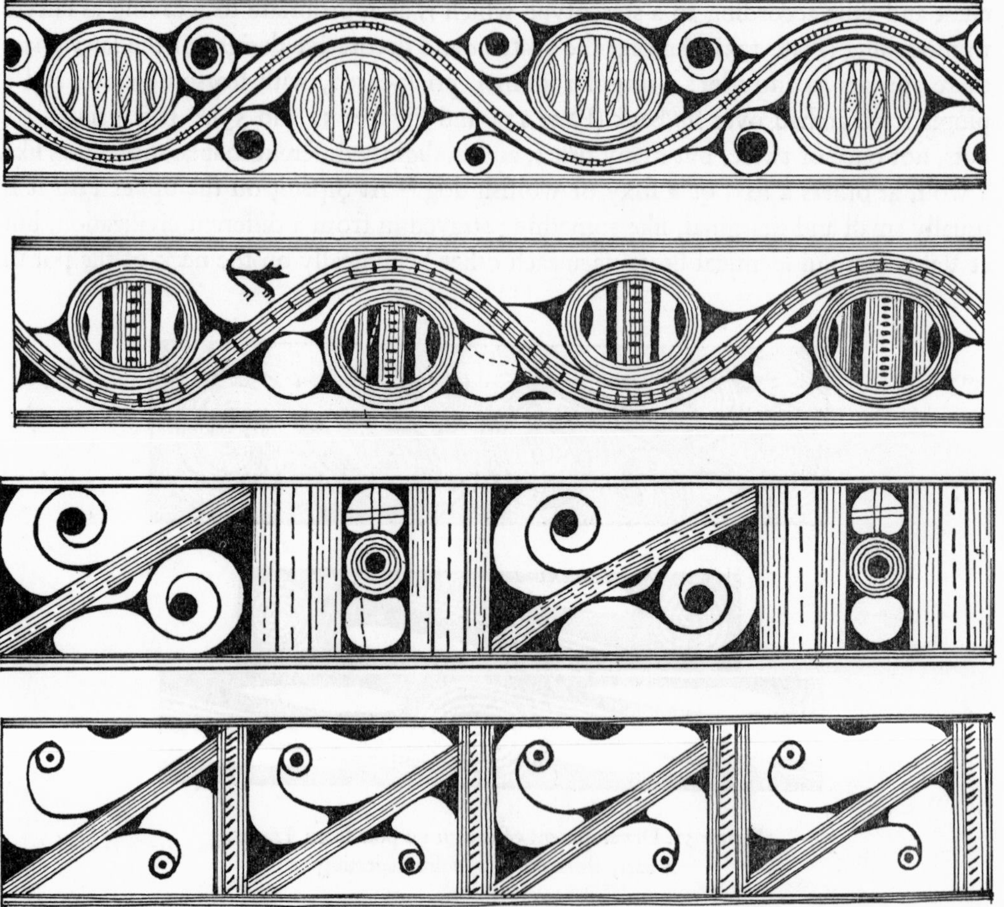

Figure 52. Motifs on painted pots from Şipeniţ, Ukraine, Russia

In the southern parts of Rumania and in Bulgaria pottery was painted in a different style, with larger and simpler designs. Very striking effects were obtained, and the finer pottery wares were given a beautiful metallic sheen by using graphite paint contrasting with bands of red and maroon. The spiral is here a broad S lying on its side, or there is a solid circle between diagonal lines, but the repertoire is limited (Plate 136).

Farther west the old Bandkeramik tradition was stronger, and the old shapes persisted, but ornament became richer and sometimes coarser. The surfaces of dark pots were scored over and filled with white or occasionally yellow paste, or larger areas were excised and filled with contrasting colour, or left boldly chipped (Plate 128) or incised. The colour is fugitive and easily lost by ordinary wear, so that it was probably limited to modelled figures, or pots not intended for profane uses like Plates 118 and 123. Crusted pottery spreads through Hungary into Slovakia and Moravia and as far as Lower Austria, where we have already met it. In Dalmatia, up the Adriatic coast to the Islands, there was another style of painting that is unconnected with the south-eastern tradition but may have links with South Italy and the Aegean.[64]

Figure 53. Motifs on painted pots from Şipeniţ, Ukraine, Russia

The spread of crusted wares is not simply that of a technique but of a whole culture, or nexus of cultures, with their gods, their houses, and also their Anatolian memories. Beyond Vienna a few of the favourite tricks of these people can be followed a little farther: the use of white paint in Silesia or animal protoms on handles in eastern Poland. In the western Alps dark-faced wares were enlivened by strips of light silvery birch-bark, cut out and glued on to prepared surfaces, with a pitch made from the burnt bark. The patterns – concentric semicircles and zigzags – could have been borrowed from farther east, and the overall effect is very like that of the paste-filled eastern ornament, or even some true painted wares.[65]

These are detached, not very significant borrowings or introductions. The tribes of Western Europe and the North European plain had already made their different compromises with the old hunters of the forests, mountains, and marshes.

The Potter

In spite of the intimacy of portraiture, we still do not know who the artists were, the modellers, potters, and painters of pots. We do know that much potting was done by women, for they have left their fingerprints in the clay, and it is fair to say that the housewife made her own, as she does wherever pottery is made by hand; but there is sometimes a difference between kitchen or household ware and the specially beautiful pot, or the pot for a special purpose, such as libations to gods or offerings to the dead. Then there were some very large storage jars, over three feet high, which must have posed considerable technical problems. None of the surviving ovens would have been large enough for firing them; most probably temporary kilns were built around them for the purpose and then destroyed, as is still done in Crete, where the men of certain families specialize in the making of the large wheel-turned pithoi. They travel from district to district building their temporary kilns wherever clay is suitable and there is plenty of wood for the fires. In Cyprus there are, or were till recently, families in which the women are by tradition master-potters, building by hand and firing huge eight-foot pithoi. This is a dying art, but it is said that hand-built pithoi are in some ways better than wheel-turned ones.[66] In Western and Northern Europe, kilns are not known, and all firing was probably done in the open.

Who the modellers of the clay figures were is another problem again. A modeller today can find his implements in the kitchen. The spatula, knife and palette-knife, roller and spoon, were all available in wood or bone to the Neolithic sculptor, though the knife-blade would have been flint or obsidian. Impressed surface decoration could be got with a hollow bone, the edge of a shell, or by cutting the clay and smoothing with a flint and bone tool; all homely things, easily acquired. The oven in which figures and smaller pots were fired was no doubt the same that baked the dinner. As far therefore as material and techniques go there is no reason why the housewife who made her own cooking pots should not also have modelled her household gods, ancestors, or whatever they may be. Doubts only arise on account of the industrial scale of the modelling; the huge number of figures from Vinča, the high percentage from Valac. So there is now the question of specialization. The inhabitants of a Neolithic village, practising subsistence farming with primitive tools, must have spent their entire lives at work in order to produce enough to maintain life. Each village, probably each household, was self-supporting and had to be. Cultivating the land, looking after the beasts, cooking, spinning, making pots and all the other gear and tackle of household and farm, consumed the hours and allowed neither man nor woman freedom to develop special gifts, nor was society organized for specialization in trades, and the opportunities of commerce and travel.[67]

But we must not overdraw the picture; there were no doubt idle winter hours round the fire, and even if its flames gave the only light, they would have been enough for arts requiring the cunning of the hand more than the sophistication of the eye. Part-time specialists did appear in answer to the need for flint-miners and stone-axe makers who would spend a season of the year away from their homes in mines and at the outcrops. The makers of the clay figures and the finer pots may have been part-time specialists of this sort. The point is not amenable to proof.

In many primitive societies the only full-time specialist is the priest or wise man, while in others he too must support himself, working alongside other men. Which of these patterns held in Neolithic Europe we have no way of telling, but the number of household shrines suggests that every householder performed some priestly offices. Usually, but not always, men take the larger share in house building, and it seems on the face of it more likely that men made the life-size animal and ornamental finials of Ariuşd, the bull-shrines at Kormadin, and perhaps also the monumental figures of Predionica and the architectural shrine at Truşeşti. All these were religious activities.

If potting was to a large extent a woman's art, weaving was entirely so; but the perishability of wool and vegetable fibres means that scarcely anything is known of its quality. A few fragments have survived from this time under unusual circumstances;[68] for the rest we can only reconstruct from the 'textile' patterns on pots and house-walls. Woven patterns like basketry are, and must be, geometric; transferred to pots and to walls they are still geometric, and to this extent we see in them what may be an enduring feminine, peasant contribution to art. The triangular version of the human figure painted or stamped into the clay of pots is characteristic (Plate 133). Hunting required the visual image in a way that agriculture does not; the hands here come to supplant the eye, and the making and decorating of utensils takes the place of representation, though not so much as is sometimes claimed.

CHAPTER 5

FROM THE MEDITERRANEAN TO THE BALTIC: 4000–2000

Thus she brought us to the deep-flowing River of Ocean and the frontiers of the world, where the fog-bound Cimmerians live in the City of Perpetual Mist.

The Odyssey, Book XI; translation E. V. Rieu

Malta, Sicily, Sardinia, and Iberia

THE arts of husbandry and potting were carried round the Mediterranean by the boat-load from island to island and peninsula to peninsula, as well as by that overland continental drive of men and animals that we followed in the last chapter. Compared with the slow but sure advance of land migration, and the gradual changes effected on neighbouring and alien tribes, sea migration is very rapid, but it is open to disaster, false beginnings, and annihilation. Not only men and women but breeding animals and seed-corn must be transported safe and dry, and wherever landfall is made the natives will certainly be unfriendly.

Some time before 6000 B.C. the first boatloads had reached Crete, probably from Asia Minor. From there, and from the Greek islands and mainland, others pushed gradually farther, and we pick them up point by point in Apulia, Sicily, Lipari, Malta, Sardinia, and the south of Spain, which last they had reached at latest by the fourth millennium. North Africa unfortunately is still very little known. There had been comings and goings across the straits of Gibraltar for a long time, but the North African population was very mixed and included a strong southern element. The Neolithic revolution took different forms there, and when in the Nile valley men adopted a sedentary sort of agriculture dependent on irrigation, westward of the Nile life was more pastoral than agricultural. The implications of the propinquity of North Africa are an unknown factor that must be remembered beside the more easily recognized voyages and explorations from the Levant and Aegean.

In spite of the discrepancy in time, the Odyssey has caught and held the climate of those early explorations; and a celebrated lecture which set out to describe ancient patterns and continuities in Mediterranean civilization begins with Odysseus drawing inshore to Cyclops-land and noting, 'prospector-like, both what it provides and what it does not *yet* offer, but might be made to yield'.[1] There are woods, springs, and wild goats on the one hand and deep soil for ploughing, herbage for grazing, and fine harbours on the other. This life of the coasts and islands was always in important ways different from that of Near Eastern 'tell-villages' (with which may also be counted the 'tell-villages' of South-Eastern Europe) and from the Europe of riverside and forest clearings, marsh, and moor-villages. Goats and sheep count for more than swine and oxen but less than hoe cultivation. Three crops – corn, wine, and oil – are the staple still, and have been for millennia. Land suitable for cultivation is limited, and as the population outgrows subsistence the farm is extended uphill by terracing and downhill by reclaiming fenland; even so over-population is a recurring danger. This is the background against which the city came into being: the Greek city-state, the cities of ancient and medieval Italy, and before them Cretan cities and Mycenaean citadels, and equally the walled hill-towns of fourth-millennium Sicily, Lipari, and Iberia.

None of these has the permanence of the great Mesopotamian and Egyptian emporia, and Myres calls them 'efflorescences emerging from time to time and relapsing when conditions become austere into ancient cultural roots'. The roots are the village with its society administered by a more or less formal council of heads of groups whose business it was to observe the farmer's year. The hinterland of mountains obstructs intercourse and concentrates life inward on local affairs, and only the herdsmen move with the flocks between summer and winter, upland and lowland pasture, 'wild seditious rambling like their charges' (and one may add like the hunters before them), encountering neighbours like themselves on the ridges, a frequent cause of disruption, for here agriculture spreads at the expense of pasturage.

Another cause of disruption and occasionally a stimulant was piracy. At first the distinction between piracy and commerce was blurred, and both were united in the ancient seaborne slave-trade. The sea-powers about whose enterprises we find grumblings in Egyptian and Syrian writings were piratical; and the siting of hill-towns overlooking, but away from, the immediate coast was an answer to the repetition of untoward incidents like that between Phoenician merchant-pirates and Argive women which, according to the history of Herodotus, began the quarrel of Europe and Asia. To just such incidents many other quarrels in other parts of the Mediterranean must have owed their beginning. Periods of danger and retreat to the hill-tops alternate with times of confidence when the demands of growing communities for essentials and for rarities – flint, obsidian, and later, and increasingly, metals – brought about the rise of market and bazaar towns conveniently placed in the coastal plains and harbours. The offshore island, small and undefended, was chosen time after time as a foothold and trading post by the men from overseas.[2]

Malta, at the very centre of the Mediterranean, lay well to the south of the coast-wise sea-lanes from the Aegean to Sicily and the west, and the Maltese pattern of life and culture is in many ways like a fragment of Asia hived-off and arrested: it is not easily assimilated to the prehistory of Europe. Yet it maintained intermittent relations with Sicily and had some influence on events farther west. We are not concerned with the earliest settlers but with those arriving, perhaps at the end of the fourth millennium, who were the first builders of stone temples. On Carbon 14 evidence there were, from about 2750 till 2000, some seven hundred years of intense building activity.[3] The builders were on the whole very conservative, content to repeat and elaborate the 'trefoil' plan of the earliest (Ggantija) temple phase. An additional pair of apsed chambers was added to the original three, and even, in the last (Tarxien) phase, two pairs, while at the same time the central apse almost disappears.[4] At first rough boulders were used, and smaller stones along with large upright slabs, for entrances and façades; but there are signs that the inside surfaces were covered with plaster and sometimes painted red. Then at a given moment the builders took to dressing the stone, aiming at a very smooth finish which the soft nature of the globigerina limestone made easy. In time they discovered that this stone was not suitable for outside walls, and for those a harder stone was used. Very large blocks were used for façades, trilithon entrances, and the lower courses; and where the walls are still standing to a considerable height, four or five courses of corbelling are preserved. In the latest period the 'step' between these courses was dressed back to give a smooth profile. Above the level of the corbelling the rooms were probably roofed with horizontal timber beams, since small models of flat-roofed shrines have been found. The slightly concave façades were truly monumental, and in front was a temenos sometimes entirely enclosed.

The facing slabs of the later temples were carved with great artistry. Exploration of the spiral and its organic possibilities was carried far: revolving about itself, forming a net, and throwing off tendrils and curlicues (Plate 137), sometimes against a pitted background. There is also cruder representational carving of animals in friezes. Inside the temples there were pillar stones and 'altars', sometimes carved, a great stone bowl, niches and small chambers in the thickness of the wall which may communicate through a hole with the temple itself. One of these holes is at ground level on the temple side and a little higher in the chamber behind, and it is tempting to deduce the rite of incubation, for in fact these temples are shaped around a liturgy. Everything in them bears marks of having had a liturgical purpose. This is also partly true of the extraordinary underground complex known as the Hal Safleini Hypogeum. This is on three levels, cut deep into the rock, and has many architectural features imitating beams, trilithons, pillars, and even corbelling. It is far more elaborate than the Sicilian and Sardinian tombs, which also imitate built structures; but like them, and unlike the temples, it was used for burial of the dead.

The entire seven-hundred-year span of building in Malta is homogeneous, insular, idiosyncratic. The only signs of outside influences are the sudden adoption of dressed stone in the third (Evans's D) building phase, and the spiral carvings. At this time the spiral motif was in full possession of the Aegean and the Balkans, but the recent revision of dates makes the Tarxien temples contemporary with Butmir (Plate 130) and between five hundred and a thousand years earlier than Mycenae and the Mycenaean grave-stelai. Even in Crete spirals only appear at the end of the third millennium, in Early Minoan III, so that a good deal remains obscure in this history. Curvilinear building in stone began in the Near East with the earliest village settlements, but it is essentially a Mediterranean style and, eventually, western also (below, p. 146), while the dressed stone and fine finish of the Maltese temples must have been learnt farther east.

At Tarxien in the western temple the base was found of a colossal statue perhaps more than six feet high. This is the only large carving found, but there are many small figures. Whoever modelled Plate 138 from Hağar Qim was a literal artist, seeing the human body unidealized, with almost scientific concern for truth, and complete mastery of his material. This unique figure (there is no other at all like it in quality) must have come from the same ambience that had produced the Hacilar clay figures, to some of which it is far closer than to any from the Aegean. But by far the greater number of Maltese figures are carved in stone and look closer to Syrian and Mesopotamian work. Some are very like the votive adorers of Tell Asmar in Mesopotamia.[5] The immensely fat reclining or seated women, so like the 'mountainous woman of ill-aspect' seen by Odysseus not far from these parts, were a native island invention. The pose of course had been used before, especially at Hacilar. These overgrown women with baby faces and tiny feet have about them something singularly repellent, like the horribly fat 'beauties' of the Canary Islands described by early Portuguese explorers, dropsical rather than erotic or maternal.

Some of the pottery with curvilinear decoration may have links with South Italy and the Adriatic, and there is a more intimate tie with Sicily, but on the whole Malta remained aloof, nursing its peculiar civilization, and when change came, sudden and dire, at the end of the second millennium, it declined to an inglorious stagnation, with a loss of faith that meant the abandonment of the temples; and so it remained, still practically without metals, until the arrival of the Phoenicians in the eighth or seventh century.

The prehistory of Sicily follows a characteristic island pattern. Lying between Crete and Cyprus and the more barbarous west, it experienced alternating spurts of activity following seaborne contact with the Aegean or the Levant, and periods of relapse to the 'normal' conditions that Myres has described. Stentinello villages are the earliest that we know, and they are already fortified, perhaps against native descendants of the Levanzo and Monte Pellegrino artists, but also no doubt from attack by sea, from the piracy and raiding that are almost as old as boats and boatmen.[6]

There is a very early simple impressed pottery dispersed all round the Mediterranean, and over much of the ancient world, but the Sicilian impressed wares are finer and more compactly decorated than any others in the fifth and early fourth millennium. The gourd prototype also is more convincing here than on the Danube (Plate 141). The impression made in the soft clay of a pot from Naxos near Messina and the shape of the pot have their closest counterparts in South Anatolia. The handles of Plate 139 (from Comiso) are also extremely Anatolian, but the impressed leaf decoration seems to be unique.[7] The impressions were usually made with the edge of a common clam or scallop shell (pecten and cardium), or with the hollow end of a small bone; as a result the surface has the broken texture of wool or fine weaving, especially when, as sometimes, the hollows are filled with white paste.[8] Patterns are abstract and geometric except for a double motif, either circles or lozenges with rays, which is evidently intended for eyes, like the face pots of the Danubians and northern people, while the furrows under the lower lid of Figure 54, A and C, recall the 'Udjat Eye' of the Egyptians.

Alongside the impressed wares in eastern Sicily there are painted pots like the shallow dish with a red star outlined in black on a buff ground from Megara Hyblaea (Plate 140). These flame patterns recall the early painted ware of the Greek mainland, but are also natural to textiles. They have nothing in common with the Bulgarian and Rumanian painted pottery, but are found in the Aeolian Islands, in Capri, and in South Italy, and possibly across the Adriatic in Dalmatia, if, as seems likely, the painted pots of Danilu and Hvar belong to this ambience and not to the east Balkans (see map on pp. xxxvi–xxxvii).[9]

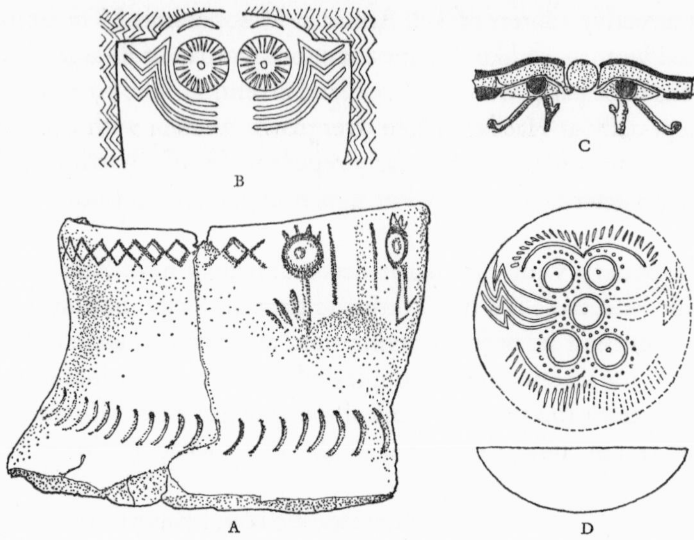

Figure 54. A Incised Stentinello pot from Trefontane, Sicily
B Development of design on stone image from Sierra de Morón, South Spain
C Egyptian 'Udjat Eye'
D Dish from Los Millares, Grave I, South Spain

Painted wares are followed by others on which the spiral appears incised on the walls or rolled into complicated plastic handles (Plate 143; Serra d'Alto style of Lipari, eastern Sicily, and Apulia). A little later again, in the Aeolian Islands and eastern Sicily, pots become much simpler, with smooth, clean lines. The fine well-fired red or buff Diana style monochrome ware may have a sober painted design like the brown line on Plate 142. Cylindrical or trumpet-mouthed handles probably owe their shape to ground stone vessels such as were made in Egypt and the Levant.[10]

Each of these Sicilian pottery styles is the result of an individual impact from outside, either casual landing or settlement. Some of those that took root continued to develop, others stagnated, and the local nature of each impact accounts for regionalism and conservatism. There is also a good deal of repetition, for the sources are the same: Anatolia and the Aegean, and occasionally Cyprus and Syria. Sporadic contacts with North Africa and Egypt can only be inferred now and then.

The same rather disjointed seesaw development lasted throughout the third millennium, the so-called Copper Age which, like the fourth-millennium Neolithic, has its painted, plain, and impressed ware (Plates 144 and 145).[11] There were two important innovations in the Copper Age: collective burial in rock-cut tombs, and the appearance of metal. Both came from the eastern end of the Mediterranean. The tombs are shafts, not very deep, from which one or two small chambers open off, or else interconnected chambers are cut in the soft rock like an imitation of a natural cave. The red monochrome cup (Plate 145) was found in one of these 'Malpasso' tombs. Like the earlier Diana ware, it has the look of a ground stone original. Metal is very scarce, and would be quite unimportant but for the eastern traffic which it proves. In continental Europe by the third millennium there were already heavy shaft-hole axes beside which the Sicilian copper trinkets look insignificant, but the comparison is hardly fair, for the axe-hoards were industrial and the centres where ore was found and worked not far off, while in Sicily ornaments and implements are consumer-goods.[12]

Great changes in Asia began now to agitate Eastern Europe and the Mediterranean, and because they ultimately reached a still Neolithic Atlantic they may be introduced here, although technologically they belong to the metal-using world with which we will be more concerned in the next chapter. From the middle of the third millennium till almost its end there was a time of troubles and unrest, like that at the end of the second millennium, only more profound and longer drawn out. There was an early wave that destroyed the first city at Troy, and brought to Greece its first metal-using civilization (Early Helladic); another destroyed Troy II and was followed by a third tide of destruction and upheaval at the beginning of the second millennium that swept Anatolia and ended with the rise of the Hittite civilization, the sixth city of Troy, Middle Helladic in Greece, and Middle Minoan in Crete. To the earlier of these events in the third millennium must be accounted the appearance of the Castelluccio culture in Sicily, which took root and lasted till the mid second millennium with new invaders also in Lipari, Sardinia, and Malta, where the temples were destroyed.[13] Not all these events were simultaneous, but all had their ultimate source in the unrest of the east. The Castelluccio dead were buried in artificial caves hollowed in the Sicilian limestone, which is soft and allowed some architectural features to be roughed out with little labour: recessed doorways, pilasters, and pillars in front of a prepared façade. Similarly in Sardinia in the Ozieri phase imitations of wooden buildings with beams and pillars were cut in the rock, and bull's head friezes of very eastern appearance sometimes added.[14] A few tombs at Castelluccio were closed with slabs smoothed and carved with relief spirals, and one of them is rather like the handle of a much older pot from Paternó, but more explicitly anthropomorphic (Plates 143 and 148). This is not ornament like the spiral-carved slabs in Maltese temples, but almost a pictogram which in some sort represents a union, the consummation of the grave, though whether the principals are goddess or god of death or resurrection or both we cannot tell. They are less important as art than as parts of a visual language of signs that also spread to the far west (Figure 56).

At the same time pottery has considerable charm. Shapes are varied, and the surface has simple matt-painted designs of multiple lines, all strictly rectilinear. Like the plain impressed wares of Lipari, this has some links with Early and more with Middle Helladic, as well as with the common Anatolian forerunners (Plate 144). A set of bizarre objects, usually called 'bossed bone plaques', have puzzled archaeologists for some time. The best-made come from Castelluccio tombs (Plate 147), but plainer ones have been found in Malta, Greece (Lerna), and Troy.[15] The Sicilian ones are carved on the long bones of an unidentified animal, perhaps sheep or goat. They are U- or V-shaped in section and taper from one end to the other. Great care was expended on the ornamentation, especially the reticulated background, and that is really all that can be said about them. One recent account sees in them representations of an 'eye-goddess', but this seems to strain the evidence. The various motifs – stars, dots, hooks – have appeared as ornament on bronzes or pots in many places and at different times.

Of sculpture there is next to nothing in Sicily. The contrast with Eastern Europe, the Aegean, and Malta is extreme. A few poorly made little clay figures from Neolithic Stentinello villages, the eye-pots, and some with hazily representational decoration are all we have, and the same austere iconoclasm rules until the arrival of Greek colonists in the eighth century.[16] This being so, it is all the more surprising that Sardinia, nearly two hundred miles farther north-west and well within the West Mediterranean basin, possesses sculpture in which there breathes the air of the East Mediterranean. The first explorers who discovered this pleasantly watered and wooded island are elusive; they may have arrived in the early part of the third or even during the fourth millennium, but effective settlement began only about the middle of the third.[17] These were the Ozieri people, and they brought with them pottery with incised curvilinear patterns, and also brought their gods: severe marble figures like the Cycladic marbles of the Aegean. Though none is exactly Aegean in appearance or material, the inspiration cannot be gainsaid.

Over twenty small carvings of women in local marble have already come to light. One of the largest comes from Senorbí in the south (Plate 146); it is also one of the most uncompromising in severity. A broken fragment from near Oristano is a good deal more plastic, with the line of collarbone shown, and another from Porto Ferro has a space cut out between the body and arms as in the Cyclades. Breasts and nose are the features given greatest prominence, or even the only features shown within the rectilinear outline. A number were found in tombs, but Senorbí stood in the open, the tapered base fixed into some sort of stand. Here is carving that is monumental in conception and in size. This cold, inviolate image, symmetrical and anonymous, hints to us, like other figures, of what men thought they saw when they peered across the stone threshold of the tomb. It is an image that persisted and that we will meet again later (Figure 60).

Another Sardinian stone carving of a woman could not be more different: in basalt, vulnerable, human, and broken, it was found in a rock shelter at S'Adde, Macomer, in central Sardinia (Plate 149). It is very difficult to find anything at all like this carving. The way in which the resistance and texture of rock, worn and weathered into natural hollows and bosses, has been exploited brings to mind much older Paleolithic figures, especially the reliefs of women from La Magdeleine and Angles-sur-l'Anglin. The nature of the basalt has given the same rhythmical asymmetry of body, but it is most unlikely that Upper Paleolithic men reached Sardinia.[18] In the broadest European terms such carving was perhaps predictable. The long, excessively narrow body, the heavy (but not pathologically steatopygous) figure we have met in Bulgaria and Yugoslavia. What is different is the material, for in Sardinia in the third millennium there were stonecutters who could work all sorts of local material. Basalt, obsidian, lava were cut, hammered, and chipped into axes, arrow-heads, and microlithic tools, and steatite ground to make pots. The clay pots too are often based on stone shapes, with a curious 'tunnel handle' which has two openings flush with the surface. Evidently these people found stone a sympathetic medium. Between the professionally brilliant carving of the Near East, Egypt, and Malta and the freer, more naturalistic *modelling* of Anatolia, Cyprus, and Eastern Europe stand these two figures, Senorbí and Macomer, announcing very conveniently permanent and divergent ideals of art.

In Chapter 3 we left Iberia, or rather eastern Spain, inhabited by bands of hunters who were also graphic artists working in a manner quite different from that of the Upper Paleolithic. Soon after 8000 the warm dry climate began to deteriorate. Impressed pottery of the common Mediterranean kind had probably reached Spain before 4000 B.C., that is to say about the same time or a little after farmers from the Danube system were spreading into Holland and Belgium. We do not know whether men came to Iberia by boat from the East Mediterranean, as they had come to Sicily and Sardinia, or whether they made the short crossing from North Africa, where cattle-herding was already established. The former is more likely, but some may have come from the other direction. In any case the earliest settled villages and cemeteries of round, stone-walled communal tombs are in the south-east, in Almeria, and ostrich eggs, presumably from Africa, were found in them as well as flat bone and stone idols which have an East Mediterranean look (Figure 56, A and B). Some of the pottery is pattern-burnished, which is again an East Mediterranean technique.[19]

These were followed in the same south-eastern province, and also in southern Portugal, by more advanced colonists, this time certainly seaborne from the East Mediterranean, and involving a real colonization by small adventurous bands sailing, not so much with seed-corn and cattle in their bottoms, as with mining and craftsmen's tools, metal axes and advanced ideas about building in stone and laying out defences. Their towns have walls and bastions, and they buried their dead in stone-built corbelled tombs of great magnificence (Figure 55). They are unlikely to have set out before the late fourth millennium, but their little towns were almost certainly still flourishing in the late third.[20] This Los Millares civilization, limited to half a dozen sites in Almeria, at the mouth of the Guadalquivir, in the Algarve, and on the Tagus, was something quite exceptional: the farthest west reached by the Mediterranean hill-town, the small defended citadel that overlooks a harbour or valley like so many that flourished in the Aegean. But whereas there the small towns might be sacked from time to time, or flattened by earthquakes, and new settlers would come from one or other of the neighbouring mainland civilizations, in Iberia they were too isolated, no more than 'brilliant efflorescences . . . relapsing back to ancient cultural roots', which means the small farming community: the village. Before this happened however the breath of change they brought with them was felt as far away as Orkney and Jutland.

They were also a powerful influence among their more primitive neighbours, the hunters of the interior, some of whom, as we have seen, may already have taken to herding cattle. Meanwhile something more than a natural process of debasement was happening to the hunter's art. The changes are almost impossible to date but very clear to see. Domestication of horses comes later than cattle, and schematic scenes with men leading horses, depicted in the rock shelters, should be contemporary with the first, or even with this second wave of settlers. It is sometimes possible to place a shelter

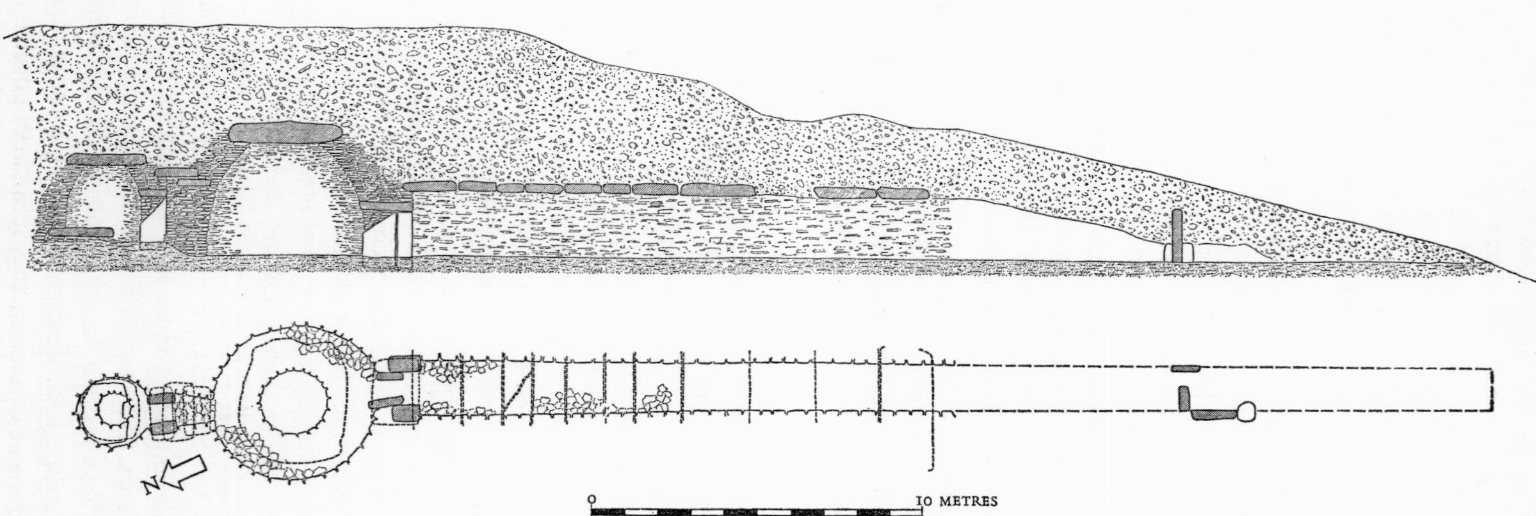

Figure 55. Plan and section of the corbelled tomb at Romeral, South Spain

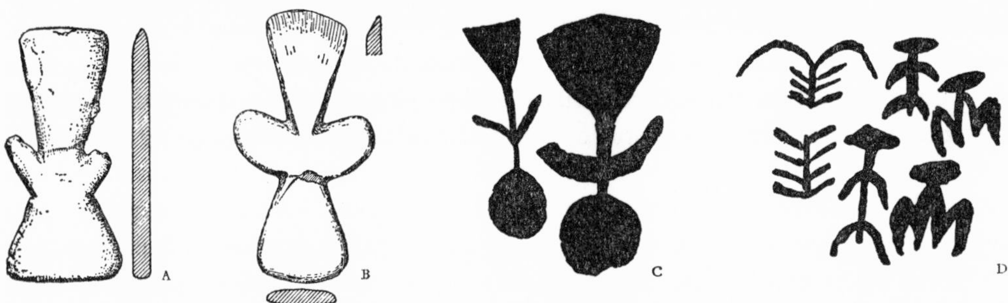

Figure 56. Small stone idols from A Loma de la Torre, Grave 2, Spain, and B La Pernera I; C and D Figures painted on the rock at the Cueva de la Siepe, Fuencaliente, Spain

painting beside a drawing on a pot and see the same pictorial shorthand representing stags, or place the painted human figure beside a stone idol (Figures 33C, 57A, and 56). Circles with rays appear in both milieus, and may be suns or eyes. When single they are probably suns, and once at least in a shelter the rays are represented as a halo of antlers reminding us of those myths in which the stag is the sun-bearer (Figure 57C).[21]

These events in Iberia are the exact opposite to the pattern in Eastern Europe. There the first arts of civilization, farming and settled life in villages, were introduced by a gifted people who, if they had to learn to adapt themselves to the new surroundings,

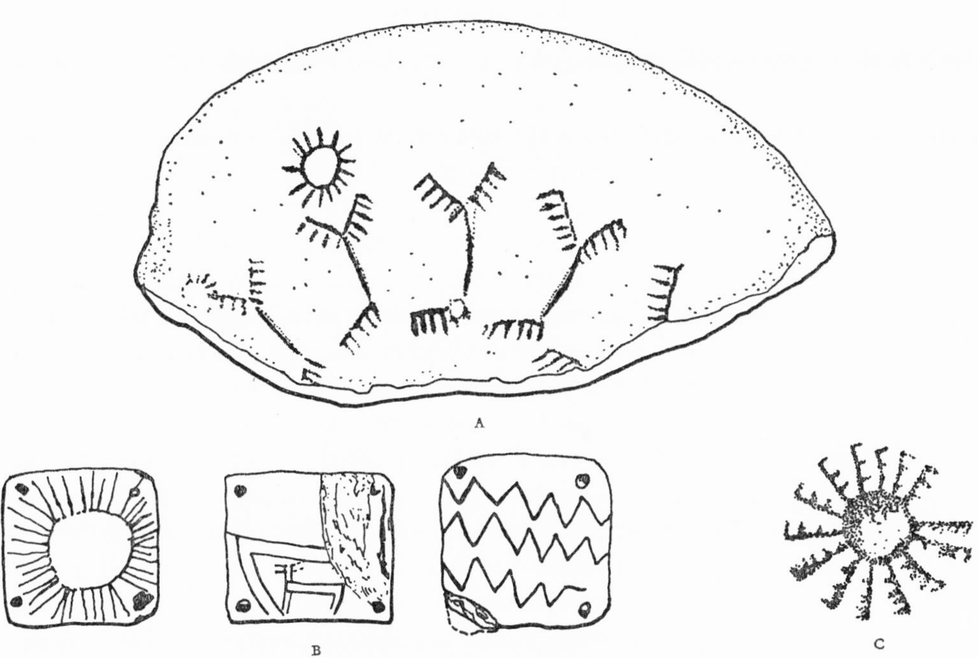

Figure 57. A Incised pot from Las Carolinas, Spain
B Stone plaques with incised motifs from Vila Nova de San Pedro, Portugal
C Painted symbol at Tajo de las Figuras, Spain, 'Antler Sun'

had very much more to teach their apparently quite uncreative neighbours. In Spain, on the other hand, it was the hunting tribes already in possession of the land who were the more gifted artists, but the spontaneity of their pictorial idiom withered on contact with the cultivators from the east and naturalistic painting was replaced by an intellectual symbolic art which is, at least theoretically, more advanced.[22] That at any rate is the usual view of Spanish Levantine art, but if the very late (second-millennium) dates suggested for some of the North African naturalistic paintings were to apply north of the straits, room must be left for a naturalistic, or at least impressionistic, hunter's and herder's art existing side by side with the formal language of the peasant villagers, the two interacting and overlapping.

There is another striking difference. In South-East Europe men lived in houses, not very substantial but reasonably well heated, with permanent hearths, closed ovens, and bright painted plaster walls. They did not, it seems, brood much on the hereafter, but buried their dead quickly, simply, and singly. In the west, fortification and the architecture of the tomb dominate the scene, not the comforts of domesticity. The use of stone in place of earth, wood, and wattle may be responsible for the sombre, granity aspect of the ancient Atlantic landscape. However that may be, it is by their building that we know these people, and in it recognize a preoccupation with size for its own sake, especially in funerary monuments, considerable technical ability in the manipulation of stone, and remarkable gifts for organization and perhaps coercion.

The Atlantic West

Iberia in the fourth and third millennia was, even more than Sicily, a frontier pitched between worlds: to the east and south civilization and cities, northward the Atlantic coasts and what is sometimes called the western megalithic province. Farming had reached these remote parts some time before the first megalithic tomb was built, and 'western' Neolithic was never a unity: it was made up of a few Mediterranean pioneers, who joined with indigenous hunters on the way north, and of easterners drawn from descendants of those early Danubian explorers who had reached Holland in the late fifth millennium, and who in turn mixed with hunting tribes on the North European plain. Cultivation may even have outstripped other domestic arts in a so-called pre-pottery Neolithic. However that may be, farmers possessing all the 'Neolithic' arts had reached Britain probably before the fourth millennium and France rather earlier.[23] These early farmers usually built in wood, and their pottery is soft and crumbling. We have now left behind the arts of sculpture in the round and of painted kiln-baked pots, but the economy was well adapted to climate and soil, and after a lapse of time the creative religious experience of these people was to find expression in building. This means above all the architecture of the grave, which varies from a simple stone box just large enough to hold the body of the dead person to huge monuments of several hundred tons' weight. They also planted stone circles and groves of standing stones which are as mysteriously impressive as they are difficult to date. Outlined on a grey sky or on the empty seashore, scoured, pitted, and denuded by the weather of many seasons, the megalithic tomb combines the grandeur of natural rock and the artistry of romantic ruin. A thirty-ton capstone shouldering the turf is a noble object; but much of this effect is accidental, like the lichen and the stonecrop in the crevices, and we must look behind the accidents to find the mason's craft. The stonework of Maes Howe, or of Midhowe in Orkney, where the courses of a retaining wall are set in a herringbone pattern, show an aesthetic intention, quite as much as the polished jadeite axe or the painted curves and scrolls on a pot (Figure 58). In the Cotswolds the natural fracture of oolite along narrow laminae was exploited then in very much the same way as until quite recently, and here again it is conscious artistry that we see.[24] We cannot reconstruct the tombs

Figure 58. Stone walling at A Midhowe, Orkney, and B Knowe of Yarso Cairn

as they once were, neat edges and glittering new-broken stone, but we can learn something about the means and method of their construction. There was, it seems, a standard measure, a 'megalithic yard' of just over 2·72 ft; and when a rectilinear monument such as a long barrow and some sorts of chambered tomb was to be laid out, the offsets from an axial base line were not arbitrarily chosen but were related to basic geometric ratios. For example, the outline plan of a chambered cairn in Gower appears to be based on an isosceles triangle with sides in the ratio of 4 : 1; a long barrow in Wiltshire has chamber and forecourt based on a triangle with a ratio of 2 : 1; and a barrow in Berkshire has its end and corners squared off at right angles.[25] Although this could have been achieved by trial and error, there is at least a strong possibility that the Pythagorean method of laying out a triangle with sides of 3 : 4 : 5 was already used. Mathematical and engineering principles like these are a more elusive cargo than a 'megalithic religion' or a boatload of oriental gauds.

Land- and seascape are as difficult to imagine as the tombs, but it is possible that the seaways were as busy during the centuries when chamber tombs were building as during the Viking raids or the *Landnahme*; and that islands and coasts were more populated than they are today. Here the evidence conflicts; for to have available the numbers necessary to manhandle the huge capstones, some of them weighing thirty and even fifty tons, would mean an adult population far greater than is usually represented in the burials, if the tombs were the charnel house of the whole community.[26]

Tombs are often grouped, two or three together, near to the best farm land. In Orkney they even correspond quite closely to the clusters of crofts, each with its church; farming methods had not changed much between the eighteenth centuries B.C. and A.D. Both depended on the same economic unit: mixed agriculture and fishing.[27]

The conclusion to be drawn is that chamber tombs were the private burial places of a noble or priestly class or family, or even the vaults of a powerful dynasty. Their distribution round the western coasts points to a movement from south to north, from the West Mediterranean to the Atlantic and North Sea; it took generations, perhaps centuries, to accomplish, and covers various self-contained enterprises. The style of building varies sharply from one region to another. The prototype, for example, of the round tomb with corbelled roof seems to lie in Iberia, and from there it reached Brittany, Ireland, and Scotland. This is again different from the colonization that brought an East Mediterranean type of settlement to Los Millares in the south of Spain and Lébous in the south of France. No doubt there were centuries of more intense building, just as there were in medieval Europe, but the megalithic age is a very long one. The earliest dated passage-grave off the west coast of Brittany commemorates a death in about 3280, and the great tomb at Maes Howe in Orkney may be a thousand years later, but both conform to a certain orthodoxy: a stone-built chamber with usually a corbelled roof, entered by a passage and covered by a cairn or mound. Moreover, megalithic tombs of a sort were still used on the eve of the Iron Age. There are three hundred and fifty stone-built tombs of different sorts in North-East Scotland and the islands alone, and in a few miles of Breton coast more than a hundred passage-graves.[28] Tombs may have drystone walling, vertical facing-slabs, or rough boulders. They vary in length of passage, number of side chambers, size and shape of main chamber. Sometimes there is devolution within a group from a relatively simple coherent plan to strange confused agglomerations, while sometimes later tombs show the finer work. To the eye of the expert excavator the plan of the tomb is more than a collection of walls and pavings; as much as church or temple, it is the vehicle of a ritual.[29]

Probably the finest of all the passage-graves are New Grange on the Boyne in Ireland, and Maes Howe in Orkney; unusually detailed descriptions exist of both.[30] New Grange has ornamental stones with the 'megalithic style' patterns and scribbles, but work there is still in progress, and since architecturally Maes Howe is perhaps the more impressive I shall describe the latter, and let it stand for its class *primus inter pares*.

The islands and skerries that make up the Orkneys are separated from the mainland by an eight-mile channel through which a dangerous current races at flood-tide. Only experienced seamen would settle here, but the soil is good, and the gulf-stream softens the northern climate. Maes Howe stands on a rocky knoll near the loch of Harray on Mainland, the largest of the islands. For its building the rock was levelled off and fresh clay packed in to form a platform some 250 by 200 feet. The mound has a diameter of 115 feet, is 25 feet high, and rises from within a ditched area. A partly walled passage, now about 53 feet long, leads to a chamber 15 feet square. The mound, built of mud clay and stones with a stone core, must have been raised together with the chamber and passage in a single operation. It has inner revetment walls and more careful stepped walling around the actual chamber. When the inner core had reached 2–3 feet, it could be used as a ramp to drag the large lintel stones into place, some of which are 18 feet long and weigh up to 3 tons.[31] In this way the rising mound was made to support the stone core round the chamber which would otherwise have stood up like an unsteady tower. The chamber itself has a vertical wall 4 feet 6 inches high, above which the slightly oblique fracture of the stone has been used to obtain a smooth face to the overhang, which reaches 11 inches at 8 feet 6 inches above ground level (Plate 150). Above this the courses project in steps to form a square vault. When complete they would have converged at about 15 feet, but now they only survive to 12 feet 6 inches. In each corner of the chamber is a square, upright buttress-slab supporting the masonry. The entrance on the south-west is lined by single slabs, and in each of the other walls there are almost square openings to cells of different sizes. Large blocking-stones lie in the chamber below the openings. The lintels and slabs facing them have been dressed with the chisel, and projecting edges of the corbelling are bevelled. The builders were of course helped by the natural fracture of the local flagstone, but some joints are so fine as 'not to admit the blade of a knife', and the uprights are accurately plumbed.

A scatter of bones and rubbish was all that was found inside when Maes Howe was excavated in 1861, but in the twelfth century Norsemen had entered through the roof, carved runes and beasts on the stones, and perhaps looted a great treasure, since one Hakon claimed that single-handed he 'bore treasure from this Howe' and carried it off in the course of three nights. Maes Howe has been compared to Stonehenge as a monument lifted out of its class into a unique position by the quality of its workmanship. Such skill is all the more unexpected because the local Late Neolithic population of this extreme north-west corner of Europe had few comforts and no pretensions. Their pottery was ill-baked and their ornaments and utensils of the simplest; but they were good stonemasons, and had to be, for there are few trees on the islands, and the houses at Skara Brae, a Neolithic village in Orkney, show how ingeniously wooden fittings and furnishings could be reproduced in stone. An exception can also be made in favour of the stone balls carved with spirals, knobs, and hatchings which evidently belonged to the same people and whose patterns lead back to the passage-graves of Brittany, Ireland, and Anglesey (Plate 151).[32]

The tombs are only half the picture; wherever they follow earlier settlement, their appearance does not, as far as we can see, affect the everyday life of the people. Farming methods, implements, and household pottery remain unchanged, and this is one of the reasons that have led archaeologists to describe the megalithic phenomenon as a religion brought by missionaries from the East Mediterranean: the tomb as nearer to a church than a castle, its noble occupants nearer to Celtic saints than to Norman barons.[33] Others have seen the builders as prospectors from far lands with an eye for country and mineral wealth. Certainly the spate of building in the Orkneys is very odd. Rousay, a rocky island of four by five miles, has fifteen large tombs, and Eday, which is seven by two miles, has ten. These are perhaps northern counterparts of sacred Delos, and the strip of land on which Maes Howe itself stands (along with a string of tombs, stone circles, and single stones) reminds us of Avebury or Stonehenge at the centre of a congregation of holy places.

There is no such thing as a single megalithic culture. Collective burial in caves and under stone-heaps and long barrows according to a certain ritual belonged to early coast-wise hunters and fishers and to the first farmers to reach the west. Also megalithic tomb building has a world-wide range and may occur at any period, so there need be no particular mystery about its advent. Men build with the material available: in the Mesopotamian plain with bricks, in the temperate forest with wood, round the rocky Mediterranean and Atlantic with stone. Whatever else megalithic building may be, it is essentially a technique. Faced with a megalithic structure – tomb, circle, or alignment – if we strip it and transpose the plan into wood, wattle, mud and daub, the chances are it will slip into place beside other far less impressive, because less durable, monuments: the fragile structures found inside earth barrows, wood circles, the single post-hole and the living tree. Even the direction of the spread of megaliths can be reversed.[34]

When Neolithic man designs a building in stone he has two obvious alternatives: the rectangle and the circle. Oval and trapeze-shaped buildings are known, but are less important variations. Today the rectangle seems a more economical choice, but it was not so formerly. The first pre-pottery Neolithic villages at Beidha and Jericho have round houses, and the same is true of Cyprus, where mud or brick domes rose on stone foundations and where the houses were also the tombs of the village fathers who lie buried under the floors. In Crete rather similar buildings were designed from the first as communal tombs, and in southern Spain a circle of stone walling enclosed the earliest Almerian tombs.[35] Much later in Iberia, in Britain, in Corsica, Sardinia, and Lipari, villages were built of round stone houses connected by wandering curvilinear walls. Sometimes roofs were corbelled, like the Irish clochan or beehive hut or the *trulli* of Apulia that still stand today.

There is no need to look for a single source for all these buildings. Moreover, since architecture, like the other arts, must always be either growing or declining, once started in a certain direction and where competence and the ambition to build well exist, the results will be much the same in the Argolid or Almeria. The excellence of a corbelled roof will not be very different, subject to the nature of the local stone, on the Boyne, in Brittany, Tuscany, or anywhere else. There is no need to look for a temporal connexion, as has sometimes been done, between all the different builders.

In the whole of Western Europe there is very little, during these centuries, that can be called art, especially graphic art. The walls of some tombs and single stones are covered with a sort of monumental scribbling. It is strange to remember the laboriousness of the technique, pecking hard rock with stone hammers, that went to produce these particular results, which seem more appropriate to the pencil of a doodler. It would be wrong to blame the inadequacy of the tools, for the same technique produced the Laussel man and the lady of Plates 18 and 19. Sometimes a rough-out of the design was incised first, then deepened with hammering, and occasionally the grooves were polished.[36] There are several styles of decoration and Brittany has more than Britain or Iberia; but although the spiral was used in Ireland, it is very rare there.

Since Breton chamber tombs were in use for some two thousand years, it is not surprising if the symbols change and the handwriting grows slack or incoherent. Gavr'inis or Goat Island, Larmor-Baden, is a tomb with a long passage and small chamber both lined with twenty-nine great stone slabs of which twenty-three are completely covered with a carpet of scribbles. Among these are a few simple representations of the local slender greenstone axe, and a figure which has been interpreted as a pair of snakes flanking a rod or 'caduceus' (Plate 152). Architecturally the tomb cannot be compared to Maes Howe or Romeral, but like Maes Howe it stands in one of those intensely frequented centres of religious pilgrimage or settlement where tombs, single stones, circles, and alignments are crowded into the landscape as though ground was precious and as though there were not hundreds of miles of exploitable seashore and farming hinterland. On the strength of its carvings, deeply pecked in the granite, Gavr'inis has been called the finest of the Breton tombs. The dominant motif is an arc or semicircle of multiple lines which surround and grow out of each other and bring to mind the

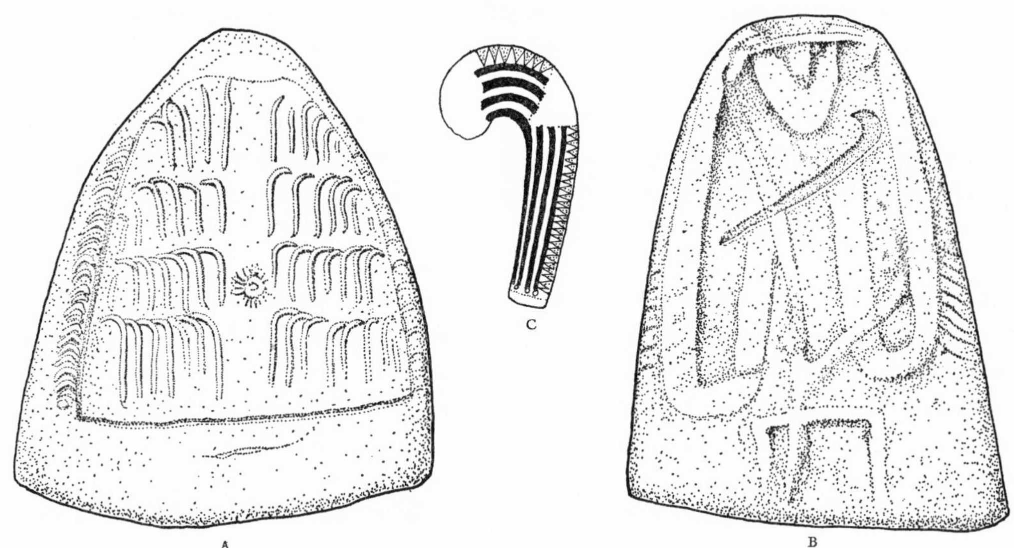

Figure 59. A Pecked design on endstone of chamber-tomb at Locmariaquer, Brittany, France
B Carved stone stele from Castelnau-Valence, France
C Stone emblem from Casa de Moura, Portugal

trailing five-finger patterns of the Paleolithic period. They are supposed to have had an anthropomorphic source, but interpretations are more than usually risky here, for the same patterns appear on metal in the Near East, or even on the tympana and capitals of Romanesque churches.[37] No more than spiral and circle do they come from any single source, nor are they likely to have signified the same ideas at such very different times.

Formal composition is rare, but the endstone of a chamber tomb known as the Tables des Marchands, Locmariaquer, is itself symmetrically pointed and carries in relief a symmetrical arrangement of crozier-shaped objects in four rows (Figure 59A). The thing represented – crook, sickle, plume, or whatever it may be – was evidently important. We see it single on many other stones, and it is carved on the body of anthropomorphic stelai in Gard and Aveyron. Small stone models of the same shape engraved with geometric designs and found in Portuguese tombs may have the same significance as the strange insignia on the man's shoulder in Hungary (Plate 110 and Figure 59, B and C), but like the 'boats', 'heads of cattle', 'yokes', and so on, these are uncertain subjective readings. Even the axe may mean one of many things: weapon, tool, sign of god or goddess.

When we recall that hollows or cup-marks were battered into rock at La Ferrassie by Neanderthal men whose minds are entirely beyond anything we can imagine, it seems better not to try to interpret. This is perhaps even more so where signs are identical with some Egyptian or East Mediterranean symbol. A zigzag which is the Egyptian and oriental water sign, though it looks the same, need not mean the same on the Atlantic as on the Nile or Euphrates.[38] In the Aegean on the other hand the sea was at one time represented by a network of spirals. On the baked clay 'standards' from the Cyclades it surrounds, within a zigzag border, those same boats in which, no doubt, the early explorers set out for the western Mediterranean. This same stylization was used by the Assyrians on their reliefs two thousand years later, and it reappears in the Adriatic around 700 B.C.[39] Although linked spirals look the same, it does not follow that they have the same meaning on Butmir or Cucuteni pots, Mycenaean stelai, Irish passage-graves, or enigmatic stone balls in Scotland.

Reasonable scepticism about interpretation of the language does not mean denial that a language is there for the reading. That it remained intelligible for a very long time is confirmed by Early Christian art, where the spiral is still a symbol of great power. It is used alongside, and distinct from, the newer language of animal interlace and Roman or Hellenistic naturalism. There is a bronze crucifixion from St John's Athlone on which the latter tradition demanded portrayal of a physical body, but, superimposed upon it like a buckler, is a pattern of spirals in the native idiom, which no doubt, for those able to read, made an equally lucid and possibly an identical statement. Here in fact is a key, like the Rosetta Stone or the Behistun inscription, but none alas was provided at Gavr'inis or New Grange. A good case can be made for seeing degraded versions of the stylized ornamentation of small Iberian idols of bone and stone in many megalithic scribbles, but any attempt to analyse all the lozenges, chequers, wavy lines, and relate them to this or that Spanish or Portuguese idol would turn this chapter into a technical review of dates and contacts out of place in a general account of prehistoric art.

Signs scratched on small clay plaques with holes in the corners found at Vila Nova de San Pedro in Portugal are in a rather different class. Whether they were worn as amulets or fetishes or offered as votive gifts, each one is a coherent picture – sun, quadruped, zigzag, triangle – that halts on the brink of communication. The signs are single and definite, but they were never systematized, for society in the west had still to live through another two thousand years of illiteracy. Nevertheless the invention of the pictographic scripts of the Near East is most understandable against a background of many such abortive beginnings. We have suspected them already in the Paleolithic and Mesolithic milieus (Figure 57B).[40]

In the French midi stelai have been found on which rudimentary human attributes are hammered in relief, or occasionally pecked and hollowed out, along with adornments or insignia such as axe, girdle-knot, cross-straps. One from Mas Capelier is just as like another from Saint-Sernin, both in Aveyron, as one nineteenth-century icon is like another (Plate 153): a triangular face with roughed-in nose and eyes, the horizontal lines on the cheek that may be tattooing, token breasts, hands, and feet; the latter are quite standardized, and though they look more like tassels, they always have the five toes or fingers. The object below the chin could be a strap joining the girdle, or a long pendant, or a hone or knife on a string. Some figures have a cross-strap with a ring buckle, and sometimes we find the plume or sceptre-shaped object we have seen in Brittany and another that could be a hafted axe, or even a knot like the sacred knot of Minoan and Mesopotamian iconography. Figures like that on Plate 153 with breasts must represent the woman, but others with sceptre and axe could as well be male (Figure 59B).[41] None show any evidence of artistic vigour. They look like dutiful reproductions of the divine

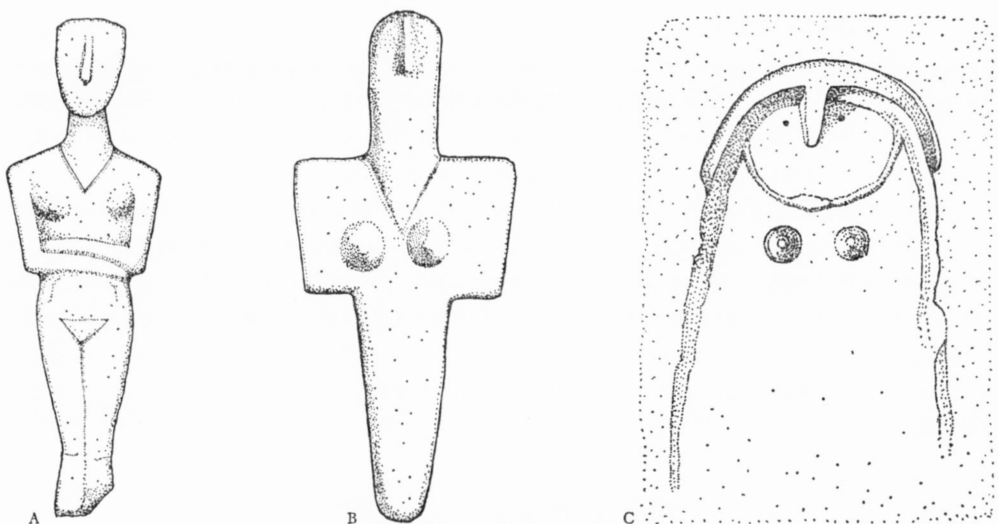

Figure 60. A Marble figure from the Cyclades, third millennium
B Marble from Senorbí, Sardinia (cf. Plate 146)
C Carving in chalk-cut tomb at Coizard, Marne, France

attributes done as best he could by an unsophisticated worker bereft of efficient tools and (much more important) the living tradition of craftsmanship. It is in fact a sort of provincialism that may exist in any dark age anywhere.[42] Somewhere in the distance is the figure of the goddess with the flowing vase, well known in a comparatively late and very beautiful version at Mari where she wears the usual cross straps and girdle; also a whole platoon of small stone worshippers with libation vases from Tell Asmar have feet and legs summarily rendered in a way that could well be the source of the 'tassels' on the western stelai; or again the stone colossi of the Egyptian agricultural fertility god Min may stand as distant prototype of the male figure.[43] This is not direct inspiration, just as these are not primitive carvings in the sense of original creations of a young culture, but copies of copies that have drifted too far from the original to be more than barely intelligible. They lack that individual style which the Senorbí marble, and even the more nearly abstract Iberian idols, have so richly. They are, I believe, groping imitations of a higher culture that was never directly experienced, but without which they would never have been produced.

The stelai stand single, though occasionally they were re-used in tombs with the image hidden, rather as a shaft of a Saxon cross is built into a Norman chancel; but farther north in long gallery-like stone-built tombs in the Paris basin a female presence was carved on wall-slabs under the form of breasts and necklace alone;[44] and in tombs excavated in the chalk scarp overlooking the Marne valley the image is a round-topped niche cut in the wall of the antechamber to the tomb itself. At Courjeonnet it is on the left side of the entrance: a wedge-shaped nose in relief, a single-strand necklace, and an axe. At Razet, Coizard, nose, necklace, and breasts are alone permitted. Sometimes a little colouring survives, black for eyes and yellow for the gold, or probably amber, of the necklace.[45] If these are the tokens of the underworld queen, she is a northern offspring of the Mediterranean marble goddess whom we have followed from the Aegean. To compare Senorbí and Razet is to see the same restraint, the plane surfaces and the few features in high relief (Figure 60). Axe and breasts do not as a rule appear on the same image, so that axe-images may really be male gods.

In spite of some points in common, this whole tradition seems rather different from that which produced the stelai of the midi and the Iberian idols like Figures 54B and 56, A and B.[46] There is no more a single tradition of western Neolithic art than there is a single tradition of tomb-building, and if one party left Iberia for Ireland, another could have set off from the Aegean or Levant, ventured round Sicily up the Tyrrhenian Sea to Sardinia and Provence, and ultimately to the chalk country of the Marne.

From the Caucasus to the Baltic

There were other megalith builders on the Black Sea and in the West and North Caucasus who were quite independent of Western Europe. Massive stone-built graves imitate the houses of the living. Their stone walls are decorated with patterns that, like the wall-plaster of houses on the Tisza, seem to copy woven hangings and sometimes skins; and all this reappears far to the north-west on the Saale.[47] In Central Germany the burial chamber was usually built for a single body, and the great stone slabs that wall it are punched or hammered with herringbone and other textile patterns that have little in common with the western megalithic ornament. One slab from Leuna-Göhlitzsch, Merseburg, near Halle, shows the dead man's bow slung from wall or rafters and the quiver with six fletched arrows, as well as the wall-hangings of his house, once coloured red, black, and white, which when fresh must have added to the illusion of a furnished living-room (Plate 154).

The earliest farmers had brought with them to the north the intensive Danubian economy with grain cultivation as the staple, and the few cattle, stalled during the winter, and fed on leaves harvested in late summer. A change came around 2500, and animals were allowed to browse the open forest, which in time they destroyed, creating the typical northern landscape of heath and moor, pastoralism this time increasing at the expense of cultivation. The owner of the Leuna-Göhlitzsch house-grave, coming later, would have been a herdsman and occasional hunter.[48]

Among the earlier colonists of the German plain were people who had the same general south-eastern background, and some but not all of whom built graves in stone.[49] Their pots are crude and simple, but the sharply incised patterns which they printed into the clay are often effective, and the priests or shamans of one group used pottery drums on which ornament is sparsely employed against an empty background in a way that runs counter to any supposed primitive *horror vacui*. Polished stone axe-shaped objects made by the same people are no more utilitarian implements or tools than the exquisitely polished slender jadeite axes of the western world. The patterns were dictated by traditional iconographic conventions, and even as ornament are effective (Figure 61B).

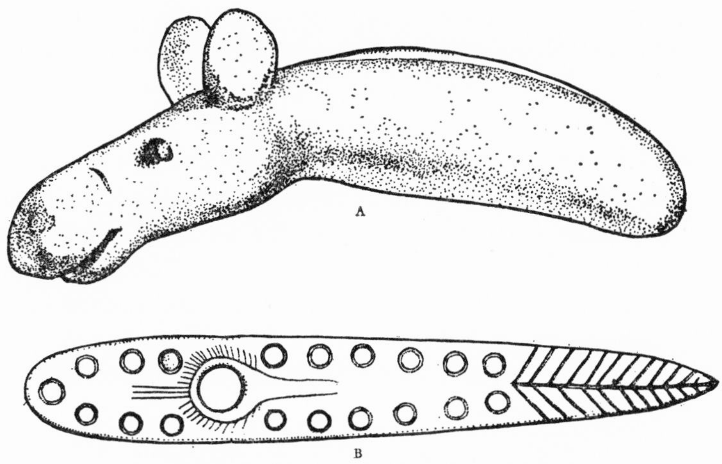

Figure 61. A Stone axe from Alunda, Sweden (cf. Plate 156)
B Ceremonial stone axe from Radewell, Saxony, Germany

The level of technical craftsmanship throughout Neolithic Europe was very high, whether polishing stone tools or knapping flint, decorating some exceptional pot or weaving coloured stuffs. Pride in good work is a language we can understand when the intangible material of fear, hope, awe, and worship escape us. It was a fine craftsman who made the superb pot from Skarpsalling that was found inside a passage-grave, and another the face-pot from Svinø (Plates 127 and 155). We have seen these and other faces on the Danube and in Sicily, and there were many more in Iberia. It is an idea that goes back to the Near East and the roots of Neolithic civilization.

In Denmark and South Sweden the eastern and western megalithic traditions mingle and interact. In dolmens and passage-graves the western addiction to size for its own sake has full play. Huge boulders were used to roof chambers and passages. The rock is not laminated like Cotswold oolite and Orkney flagstone, so the fine parallel fractures were impossible here even if desired, and the building is coarse, like the work of giants at play with boulders; but a closer scrutiny reveals here too the careful craftsman.

In the evergreen forests of Scandinavia, Finland, and around the North Russian lakes life had hardly changed since the retreat of the ice. The country belonged still to the hunter and fisherman, and he, as we have seen, was an artist who carved the rock faces with representations of men or gods, spirits, and animals. He also carved stone, slate, wood, bone, and amber with small animal figures in the round, or worked his tools into shapes with heads of elk or swan. One of these is a polished stone axe with the butt carved as an elk's head (Plate 156 and Figure 61A). It was found at Alunda in Uppland (Sweden), but probably made in Karelia, for these precious objects were carried great distances like the small art of the Upper Paleolithic. A wooden spoon with an animal-head handle, though found in a bog at Puntala in Finland, is made of pine from the Urals,[50] and there are many from Russia itself. The spoon or *kvosh* with swan- or goose-head handle is very graceful and survived in Russia until the Middle Ages; and in Siberia strange wooden markers in the same tradition with a flying swan or goose were raised on posts over burials till quite recently. There are a few human figures, but they generally owe more to influences from inside the Carpathian ring and even from the Balkans (Figure 39D).

To compare these small-scale carvings with those of the Upper Paleolithic is to see a fundamental difference. In the former the suppression of detail and of all illusionist devices so that only the essential character remains has made them more completely three-dimensional, like the Mesolithic bear from Resen (Plate 78), and like some of the older Eskimo art.

From Karelia to the Urals and from the Saale to the Caucasus the circle that began in the Near East is again complete. The house-graves, in particular, bring us back to the early metallurgy of the Caucasus and Anatolia that was already spreading its revolutionary influences over the Balkans, the Mediterranean, and the Ukraine.

Gods and Emblems

At the beginning of the last chapter I expressed dissatisfaction with the 'mother-goddess' label for describing the clay and stone representations of Neolithic Europe; but can we, I wonder, in all honesty go any farther? The favourite subjects of artists in South-East Europe were, as we have seen, a female person or persons; standing, sitting, occasionally reclining on the ground or on a seat, clothed or naked, usually alone but sometimes with a child, and sometimes supporting or proffering a vase. She can be modelled with some realism or else stylized to the limits of what is recognizable. Though fewer, there are also male figures, the most impressive seated on stools; and there are a number of detached heads that look almost like character sketches from the life. Animals are nearly always domestic and poorly executed, but the few wild beasts – bear, wolf, snake – are more life-like. Finally there are human- and animal-shaped vases where the idea of the vessel for life-giving or life-restoring liquids is personified. In the west, pattern and emblem, though at a far greater remove from nature, were executed with the same devotion.

In Anatolia the monuments spoke plainly enough of a dichotomy. Their peculiar value is that they go back far beyond the earliest written text to the time when the change from hunting to farming was actually taking place; and there for the first time, at Hacilar and Catel Hüyük, we catch sight of the *dramatis personae* of the new religions. There is the goddess who gives birth, sometimes with her son or linked with an ox and the husbanded grain.[51] But there is also at both sites the *potnia theron* standing beside leopards or seated on them and nursing their young, while stag and vulture were painted on the walls of shrines.

It was inevitable that so profound an alteration should have been accompanied by commotion and left visible scars. With the earliest recorded mythology and ritual of Mesopotamia, Egypt, and Syria we are already in the aftermath, and the agricultural gods are settled in their seats. The records take for granted that at the centre or 'in the beginning' is the receptive earth, who is wife and mother, made fertile by a sky husband and father – An and Ki, Ge and Ouranos are schematized exemplars of this situation – but as late as the first millennium A.D. in Ireland there are many stories that spring from the same set of ideas. In all a newly arrived or arisen chieftain must propitiate or marry the goddess, the 'Tutelar of the Place', in order to make good his sovereignty and legitimize his position, over against those in possession. In later Celtic legend and ritual the goddess has become the sovereignty personified. This allegory satisfies so well that we hardly stop to question it. It is as primordial as the rain from heaven that makes the fallow fertile when the seed is sown.[52] But until the practice of husbandry there was no particular reason to think of the earth as either male or female. Fertility to a hunter was the appearance, at need, of large numbers of edible animals. The waxing and waning seasons were important, but for different reasons than the farmer's. The times of plenty were not the same, nor the calendar of festivals.[53] In that context the allegory falls to the ground. The hunter's god is one who comes, the farmer's one who rises. Nature spirits could be indiscriminately male or female. If trees are usually female, in Greece and Anatolia rivers are gods, but in Ireland they too are female.

When the mistress of animals and the hunter-god were displaced in the new religions they did not vanish completely and forever. Some of their attributes were inherited by younger gods, just as farmers were still sometimes hunters. Under other names men sacrificed to Artemis and Britomartis as well as to Demeter and Dione. The fruitful earth is therefore, with perfect propriety, represented as a young goddess, a newcomer, rather than a matriarchal mountain; and this youthful figure is the one we see oftenest in Neolithic Europe (Plates 109 and 115).

If, as seems possible, the Hattian goddess and the spring- and river-god with bull attributes are present already in the bull-shrines of Catel Hüyük and the clay figures of Hacilar, it may be supposed that these also were among the gods that the first farmers carried over into the Balkans, along with most of their material culture.[54] Here is the likeliest explanation of the bull shrine at Kormadin and the seated goddess with a bowl, or as herself the vessel (Plates 109 and 112 and Figure 46). Her companion is the god either on a throne or modelled on the side of large storage jars. If he can also be identified, on the Anatolian analogy, with the ox or bull protoms perched on rims and handles of pots, he grows in importance. The position is appropriate to a god of streams and underground waters.

The greatest differences between Neolithic and earlier art are in the animal figures. The forest and its wild life only became frightening and hostile when men began to clear it with fire and axe, a 'crime' that changed wild nature from ally into enemy. When certain animal species were domesticated, the wild relatives also became enemies who trampled and robbed the sown land and so were driven away from field and homestead.

In Europe the relationship between hunter and farmer was probably much closer than in the great urban centres of Mesopotamia and Egypt, separated by extensive farmland or desert from the hunters in the mountains. In Europe small settlements in forest clearings and riverside tells were from the first subject to pressure from hunter bands who appeared and disappeared, very like the wild animals, on the fringes of their lives. We know that the purer agriculture of the pioneers gave way to a mixed farming and hunting better suited to the terrain, and probably as a result of actual contacts between tribes.[55] The hunter's religion was still alive in Celtic myths and legends of the first millennium A.D. The modified pastoralism of the Bronze Age may even have added power to the older gods, and Late Bronze Age artists often took subjects from the hunt. Whatever the reason, Neolithic representations of animals are poor, and it is possible that the medium, clay, is one of the causes. The raw clay is a piece of mother earth, and the artist who refines it and then urges it into shape is domesticating and copying nature in her mode of operation, not in her appearances only. If we possessed wood-carving from this time it might illustrate different subjects, and in fact the amber and stone of Scandinavia and the northern forest do just this: elk, bear, and water-bird are portrayed in sober naturalism, man seldom and in a different idiom. At the end of the Neolithic the farming, stock-raising people of Moldavia and the Ukraine were still making small crude clay figures of cattle, but cattle were never painted on their pots; instead there was a wolf-like animal (Plate 134 and Figures 42C, 52, and 53). It is essential to bear in mind the fact that the material dictated to a great (though still unknown) extent the *kind* of subject portrayed.

Stone-carving in the far west is often taken as evidence of a 'megalithic religion' along with evocations of a great goddess of the earth as tomb and as source of all life. The stony presence – breasts, necklace, girdle – in built graves and chalk-cut tombs of northern France may be a sister to Persephone, but the rock-tombs are almost indestructible, and for this reason we may have got the balance wrong. Neither the axe nor the eyes are necessarily always female. Some stelai have a male representation, and nearly all known groups of Neolithic cultivators had the phallus fetish and symbol of male virility. Later around the Mediterranean the standing stone – Herm, Terminus, Janus – is a god. Certainly the later western religions knew a goddess of death and battle, the Morrígan, who was also love and fertile earth; but equal honour was given to a god of abundance with club and cauldron of life. If Celtic goddesses are, as it seems, primordial and native, and if Celtic chieftains accepted them in spite of this, then there is no *a priori* reason to exclude the 'good god' from the Neolithic farmsteads. In an illiterate society, though art may contain the main evidence for religion, it only lifts the curtain on a tiny portion of the whole religious and spiritual capacities of the people. There is so much that is accidental about its survival, and the visual arts themselves are so partial, that it would be quite wrong, for instance, on the strength of western megalithic art and of a selection of clay figurines, to see Neolithic Europe exclusively devoted to a goddess of death and fertility, and the Bronze Age rejecting this devotion and substituting something quite different.

It is almost unbelievable that the builders of the island sanctuaries of Orkney, and of other tombs round the Atlantic, were not in some way devoted to the sea. Seamen are very conservative when it comes to the dangers of their lives. The *oculi* still painted on boats are only one of many reminders. A model of a boat, lapped in gold leaf and found at Caergwrle in Wales, though probably of the tenth or ninth century, seems in its decoration to carry on the tradition of megalithic art.[56] But the art shows us no sea-god or goddess. Probably many lesser gods and 'culture heroes' began their beneficent activities teaching useful arts as long ago as the Neolithic (some had begun earlier, as we have seen). Spinning and weaving are creative occupations as much as pot-making, and this is recognized in the persons of the fates. The three sisters who spin, draw the thread, and cut it, or time past, present, and to come, the link with birth and prophecy, are all probably Neolithic. Binding the dead, the sacred knot in the art of Crete and Mesopotamia, and later, among the Celts, the war-goddess weaving the blood-stained web of battle, all show how far away we are from a merely profane activity. Every housewife spinning and potting, every farmer choosing wood and carving his tools, exercised a part of the creative activity of the gods.

When the subject modelled is an article of furniture, we are not to think of it as the profane material thing it appears to be to us. The chair probably began as a throne. Some of the model seats, sofas, and stools from Bulgaria, Rumania, and Serbia may represent birth-stools and life's beginning, but some may rather be seats of authority (Plate 110 and Figure 38c). To sit while others stand is a sign of social superiority, and the use of separate seats may have arisen from the place where the superior person, divine or mortal, usually sat to advise or judge. In Egypt Isis *was* the throne, and at Catel Hüyük and Hacilar goddess and god sit on animal thrones: the young god on a leopard and the old on a bull, and the great goddess between a pair of leopards (or lions) with her arms resting on the heads of the animal supports.[57] The complicated iconography of the chair begins in seventh-millennium Anatolia, and passes through a long line of Asiatic lion and bull seats, royal and imperial thrones, till it reaches the modern world. The clawed foot of an Empire sofa was once a god. The cold and damp of Europe may even have brought about an earlier secularization of chairs, since boggy sites were often chosen for the defence of houses, but wooden furniture leaves no trace.

In the course of time all these religious occupations become secular. Perhaps this happens with woodwork and potting when wood and clay are supplanted by the superior strength and endurance of metals. The prestige of the smith, from the first a specialist living apart, grows at the expense of the housewife. But although her creative capacities are reduced, she remains a field-worker, a Demeter, and the distaff side retains one supernatural activity. Even Zeus must bow to the Moirai, and the old women who gather to dress and keen over a corpse do so in the role of fates and 'strong binders'.[58] So in peasant arts, whether decorating pots or other household gear, the textile original of the design is seldom far away, and where we see it, we see the influence, oblique or direct, of the women.

With the material of the last two chapters before us, we are in a position to ask whether there is anything strikingly different in the Neolithic art of Europe compared to the art of Asia at a corresponding stage. I think that there is; for as well as the awe-inspiring Predionica idols, the monumental simplification of Senorbí, the printed eyes and stony breasts, there is a new quality. In some of the faces, in the Macomer woman and the Zengövarkony mother and child, there is a human quality, diffident, intimate, and awkward, for which you look in vain among the great and beautiful monuments of Asia and Egypt. Homely finds from excavations – querns and loom-weights, little heaps of carbonized wheat, beans, and crab-apples – may tempt us to see these people as not unlike the peasants of some very remote mountain valley in Europe or the Middle East today, but there was still a strangeness and wildness in them that can, and should, shock. Cannibalism and human sacrifice are known; and though some would see in both a sort of innocence, an immature sacramentalism, they do really measure a great distance.

CHAPTER 6

BRONZE AGE ART: 2000–1200

Hayin has gone up to the bellows
The tongs are in the hands of Khasis
. . . he may smelt ore
beaten work for a god.

Baal (fourteenth century B.C.)

Nine years with them I wrought much cunning work
of bronze brooches and spiral arm-bands and cups and
necklaces in the hollow cave . . .

Iliad

Weland knew sorrows in his Wermland days.

Song of Deor, *c.* A.D. 700

Metals

IN a history of art, only one of the prehistorians' 'age' labels comes near the facts. In the Bronze Age most works of art are bronze; it is necessary therefore to say something by way of introduction about the early technology of metals. In Europe in the third and second millennia those paths that were to separate into 'design', 'industry', 'science', and 'alchemy' were still one whole, one craft, one closely linked series of operations housed under one roof. The artist of this age needed the sinews of the smith as well as the hand of the draughtsman and the faith and imagination of the religious. That the ancient world set a high value on dexterity is shown by names like Daidalos, Kathir wa Khasis, and Weland.[1] The smithing gods Hephaistos and Vulcan are uncouth characters, but credited with the most sensitive workmanship.

The earliest stages in the discovery and exploitation of metals are, as usual, out of reach, and a good deal of guesswork goes to their reconstruction; but it seems likely that the beginning was closely bound together with the firing of pots in kilns, and that no very great length of time separates both discoveries.[2] Use of free or 'native' metals does not alone constitute metallurgy. The brightness of gold and dusky red of copper were noticed first of all because they looked pretty. Deep blue azurite and sea-green malachite were picked out of the rock or from the beds of streams, and hammered or ground into small ornaments, like any other bright stone. Only slivers could be prised from the rock with stone tools, but metals washed out and lying in the beds of streams would catch the eye where water brightened the colours. Native silver is fairly common but comes in quantities too small to work, but more can be got as a by-product of the smelting of lead ores. The people of the Caucasus and Anatolia were particularly fond of silver, and were probably producing moderate quantities from the beginning of the third millennium. In prehistoric Europe, apart from Spain, it was little used until quite late in the first millennium.

Free copper is not very common, but there was probably a good deal in surface outcrops that have been worked out since.[3] Copper ores, oxides and sulphides, occur in large deposits. The oxides are found at no great depth and were the first used, for they could be won from open-cast mines. The sulphides lie deeper and must be mined with pit, shaft, and gallery. Nevertheless sulphide ores were worked in Central Germany in the Early Bronze Age.[4] Tin, which combined with copper makes the most dependable bronze, was eagerly sought and was certainly mined in the third millennium.[5] Cornwall owes its early importance to its tin deposits, and there were other sources in Brittany, Central France, the Erzgebirge, Bohemia, Tuscany, Spain, and Portugal.

The next step from cold-hammering of native metal was the discovery that gold and copper could be softened by heating and then hammered into different shapes, and that when cooled after this 'annealing' the metal was harder than in its first state. The change is less radical than between the unfired clay and the hard-baked pot; but the third stage of heating at much higher temperatures until the metal fuses and can be run off into a mould is on a technological level with the most advanced potting (and cooking) operations, and it is still only the beginning of metallurgy.

Experiment has shown that metallic copper could not have been accidentally fused in an ordinary fire. A good wood fire is only 600°–700° C, but 1,085° C is necessary to melt the metal, and such temperatures were in fact produced in Egyptian and Mesopotamian pot kilns; which means that copper could have been melted before the end of the fifth millennium and probably had been by 4300.[6] If metallic copper alone had been available, it is not likely that metallurgy would have progressed very far. It was the discovery that a fairly pure metal could be got from compounds by heating them with charcoal in a reducing atmosphere that led to the next great advances: reduction of the oxides by smelting, and then roasting and smelting the sulphides. Carbonate ores of copper will reduce at 700°–800° C; although this is still more than the heat of an ordinary fire, it was easily exceeded in a potter's kiln, and in fact the two-tier kiln in use in the Near East provided a good reducing atmosphere.

The usual method of reducing *oxides* was a charcoal furnace with a forced draught. If kilns were being used already to *melt* native copper, accident could have led to smelting, for the mineral impurities attached to the copper, in process of melting, would reduce in the oven, and the smith would find that he had more metal at the end than he started with. Alternatively small pieces of an ore used in colouring painted pots, malachite or azurite, could have been accidentally reduced in the baking chamber of a two-tier oven. Theoretically smelting could have preceded melting, but this is not nowadays thought very likely. Before the grey *sulphide* ores can be used, they must first of all be oxidized by roasting in the open.

Smelting was quickly followed by the use of standard alloys, especially the tin-copper alloy which gives bronze. Here once more accident could have opened the way. If in the course of reducing copper ore some cassiterite (tin-stone) was accidentally smelted with it, the smith would soon notice that instead of the soft red copper he had a much harder yellow metal that gave out a different sound when hammered. Weapons and implements made from the alloy were stronger too; so, though 'pure' copper did not go out of use, bronze became the universal commodity of the 'Bronze Age' till it was gradually superseded by iron. Ordinary 'gun-metal' contains 10 per cent tin, and this also became the standard in antiquity.[7] Arsenic, though it hardens the metal, makes it brittle, so is less satisfactory, though both make easier the processes of casting. The one drawback is the rarity of cassiterite or tin-stone, which may have to be carried great distances. The impurities in native metal make it possible up to a point to discover by analysis where they come from.[8]

Native gold is seldom pure, and the impurities cause differences in colour. Transylvanian gold is pale because of its high silver content and so is Irish, but in Ireland from the Middle Bronze Age (late second millennium B.C.) a copper alloy was added, perhaps to make that 'red gold' which Celtic poets distinguish from the yellow. Different qualities of metal were selected for different ornaments, undoubtedly on aesthetic grounds. The Irish lunula on Plate 170 is of yellow beaten gold. Since copper alloy makes the metal easier to cast and harder in use, the red gold of Ireland may have been deemed altogether superior.[9]

Once invented, these techniques spread rapidly from early centres, probably in North-West Persia, to Anatolia and the Central Caucasus, and so west into Europe, where the potter's kiln had preceded them. The rise and scope of metallurgical schools is more dependent on the source and availability of metals than on the tribal pattern: geological more than political. Yet as industry grew, so did its dependence on the carrying business, the journeys of merchants and the hazards which they encountered, which, with the state of water and land transport, set limits to the influence of one or other centre. Great political upheavals sometimes led, even in prehistoric Europe, to a scattering of craftsmen, a diaspora of a sort more often experienced in the older civilizations of the Near East. The presence of this body of highly skilled specialists in itself made significant changes in the pattern of society.

Like the history of explosives, the history of metals begins in the aesthetic instinct, the pretty eye-catching thing, the gold or copper bead and bright paint; but there was never a Golden Age in Europe, or anywhere else. It is not obvious, in spite of our habits of thought, why gold should have stood highest in the hierarchy of metals – in Egypt at one time silver was more highly valued. In small quantities it is commoner than native copper. It is not more beautiful than azurite, malachite, calcedonite, torbonite, and other brilliant ores, and though it can be melted and cast as well as hammered, gold is too soft for use as weapons or tools. Yet from the first it possessed its symbolic 'aura', its incomparable prestige, and this was probably because of its incorruptibility. The plunderer breaking into a grave finds everything decayed, flesh and fibre in disorder, the once bright copper become a green mould pitted and disfigured with warts, silver dulled and distorted; only the gold still looks as bright as when it came from the bench. Blow the dust off and you have the treasure, perfect in its pristine contours. To lay beside a dead chieftain a golden replica of his dagger or his cup, or to invest him with his golden collar and bracelet, was to ensure him their use for ever. To cover his face with a golden mask was to cheat corruption as completely as by the embalmer's art.

Although gold is the only metal that remains entirely uncorroded, others can survive in good condition through the phenomenon known as 'cathodic protection'. When metals touch in the presence of a conducting solution of salt, as they often do when buried underground, the 'nobler' survives at the expense of the baser, so that they can be arranged in a hierarchy from gold through silver, copper, lead, tin, and finally at the base end, iron. In every case if they are in electrical contact the baser metal is sacrificed to the nobler. This accounts for the preservation of bright inlays of copper in heavily corroded iron weapons. Moreover, alloyed metals corrode more than unalloyed, base silver than pure silver.[10]

The smith had to be a man of many crafts. The complicated techniques of casting call for the dexterity of the stone- and wood-carver as well as a rule-of-thumb knowledge of the chemistry of metals. Casting in an open mould, usually stone, was most practical for making the early flat-axes, knives, chisels, and so on, but was limited in its uses, so that closed bivalve stone moulds came into use for making spears, socketed axes, and other more complicated castings. It is less difficult to get a good casting with a bronze or earthenware mould. For a thin sword-blade like Plate 171 the mould, probably of clay, would have had to be heated to dull redness at the moment when the molten metal was poured in. Stone moulds too must be pre-heated to avoid cracking. To make a clay mould, a 'pattern' was carved in wood and pressed into the block of clay, another clay block was moulded over it, the pattern was removed and the clay baked. If the implement was socketed, a core was also moulded in clay, and much care was needed to keep a true register between the two blocks and between the core and the blocks, while passages had to be left for pouring in the molten metal and vents for the escape of air and gases. The best positions for these were only found as the result of long experience. The sense of design, of balance and utility, were called for from the moment that the mould was cut from the stone with a negative replica of dagger or pin; or the 'pattern' of sword or bracelet carved in wood. Quite as much skill and artistry were needed to carve some of the complex and beautiful moulds as for the positive carving of an elk-head or marble goddess. Once the metal was melted, it must not be left to stand; and so the timing of operations was very important.[11]

A method of great theoretical elegance and simplicity, but requiring much skill in its application, is casting by *cire perdue* or lost wax. A model of the object is made in beeswax, coated on the outside with clay or a clay mixture, and embedded in sand for support. The whole is then heated till the wax has either burnt away or run out through the holes provided to receive the molten metal. The mould having become hard, the metal is poured in and allowed to cool, after which it is broken and the object given the necessary finishing touches. This gives a solid casting; but if a hollow casting is required, for instance for the Scandinavian 'belt-boxes' or 'hanging bowls' (Plate 197), where the metal is often not more than 1 mm. thick, or if metal is scarce and economy necessary, the wax could be modelled on to a clay core. This is how the Býčí-Skála bull and the Trundholm horse were made (Plates 185 and 219). With the latter the method can be followed very closely.[12] The core was built up in layers only 2–3 mm. thick so as to be less likely to crack or deform when heated. When the earless, eyeless model with stumps for legs had dried, a more exact model was moulded over it in wax 1–2 mm. thick. The tail stump with a hollow socket, the feet, hocks, and ears were entirely wax. Two pins were passed through the body and five little bronze plates were fixed under the belly to hold the core in place; details of eye and nostril were traced in the wax, which then was covered with clay 8–12 inches (20–30 mm.) thick and probably built up like the core in layers, the one nearest the wax being particularly fine. The whole would then have been baked for several hours. In the course of baking the rather large amount of organic stuff which was mixed with the clay would have burnt away, leaving it sufficiently porous to take up air and gases from the hot metal; when the melted wax had run out or burnt away, the molten metal (in this case about 90 per cent copper) was poured in, and finally the mould broken. Two small faults were found in the casting, which were made good by casting-on with a fresh mould and fresh metal.[13] Finally the ornament on neck and head was worked with punches, and the eye picked out with pitch. Three possible methods of casting 'belt-boxes', all by *cire perdue*, are shown in Figure 62. A large, solid core 'C' would be slow in cooling, but the hollow cores 'A'

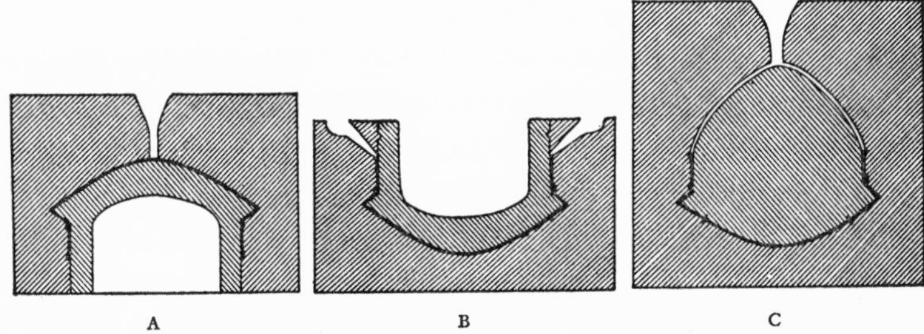

Figure 62. Three types of mould for casting 'belt-boxes' by *cire perdue*

and 'B' would give a more regular casting with less danger of distortion, because cooling would be much quicker. A great advantage of the wax method was the possibility it gave of applying quite fine decoration to the mould itself, but undoubtedly most of the finer work, like Plates 172 and 173, was done on the cold metal with a tracer or a punch after planishing (an all-over hammering of the surface).

Casting and the use of moulds did not mean that forging was abandoned. Gold lunulae like that of Plate 170 were beaten 'to the thickness of a visiting card' before decoration by the Early Bronze Age smiths in Ireland; and much later cold forging combined with annealing, that is applying continuous and slowly diminishing heat, also heating and quenching in water, were probably used on gold and bronze bowls and vessels like those on Plate 192. Very careful examination is often necessary to distinguish between forged and cast work. Before tongs and anvils had been much developed, cold forging was simpler than hot, and though bronze with a tin-content of more than 6 per cent becomes brittle and difficult to work when cold, if hammered red-hot it may shatter. Hammering and annealing from a fairly thick casting was the only way to produce sheet metal, and it took great skill to forge sheets of the thinness used in vessels like those of Plate 192. This technique remained unchanged into the Middle Ages.

Larger bowls, buckets, and cauldrons, and even occasionally animals, were built up from several plates riveted together. From Spjuterum, Öland, there is a bizarre attempt to rival cast bronze (*cire perdue*) animals like those of Plates 185 and 219, building the body up from quite small sheets riveted together. This barbarous technique has produced a frightening and ferocious wild bull (Plate 215). Hand-forging of rivets called for considerable skill, and the rivet-pattern was used as decoration as well as serving its true function; it was sometimes even imitated by hammering the metal into bosses (Plate 207). Bowls and cups of gold and thin bronze that came from Central European workshops at the turn of the second and first millennia were made by 'sinking' and 'raising'. Sinking gives a rather shallow bowl which can be beaten very thin. A suitable ingot was chosen and cast between slabs of baked clay; this gave a disc-shaped ingot that was beaten into a hollow vessel on the work bench, or else by continual hammering on the inner face with a convex-faced tool, starting near the centre of the ingot or disc, and directing the blows in a long spiral round and round. The metal, from being slightly convex, would at the end have become a saucer-shaped bowl. The Irish lunulae got their characteristic curve in this way (not visible on Plate 170).[14] During the process frequent annealing would be necessary to keep the metal pliant.

Raising gives a much deeper vessel, like the cup on Plate 192. The blows are directed on to the *outside* of the ingot with a raising-hammer, while it is held tilted against a special two-armed anvil (the stake) and slowly rotated so that the hammer-blows spiral round it. The height of the vase depends on the kind of hammer used. Periodic annealing and quenching will again be necessary. Hollow or narrow vertical necks and rims can be got by raising, and the vessel will take naturally an angular 'metallic' shape, whereas sinking gives a more rounded shape. Finally there comes the 'trueing' and 'planishing' over stakes shaped to support the part to be finished. This is the way that fluting was produced on bowls and jugs. In the Late Bronze Age bowls were being made in at least one Central European shop by the advanced technique of spinning, for which a rigid lathe with considerable power is needed.[15] Large bosses on amphorae (Plate 192) were hammered up from behind, the metal sheet lying in a bed of yielding pitch, clay, or soft wood. Very fine repoussé designs could be got by using various punches (Plates 184 and 190). Ribs and bosses could be sharpened by a wooden punch used on the top surface. The silver belt from Mramorac (Plate 231) is probably chased, the metal being laid on a bed of pitch, or block of wood, and worked from the front and the background beaten down with a punch so that the design stands out in relief.

Most Early and Middle Bronze Age decoration was drawn on the surface of the metal with a tracer. Later this technique was largely superseded by repoussé work till it almost died out, except in the west; but it re-emerged, and in the last centuries B.C. the two techniques are combined with some striking results (Plate 287). The tracer is a small chisel which is held so that the top slopes back and away from the direction in which the point is meant to travel. Each blow of the hammer drives the tool a little way into the metal and a short distance forward. The heel of the tool may leave a slight mark or 'stitch' at the bottom of the groove at each blow, but in really careful work this is hardly seen, though it may be exaggerated for decorative purposes (Plate 175).[16] As the metal is compressed, little ridges appear on either side of the groove, or if it is very thin and lying in a bed of pitch, a ridge might appear on the underside which wear and polishing remove. A bronze tracer will make a groove in gold, silver, copper, or bronze, and the work varies from comparatively coarse to extremely fine. Curved as well as straight lines can be drawn, but to trace a sharply curving line the backward slope of the tool must be greater (Plates 171 and 172).

The difference between tracing and engraving is that in the latter the tool, graver or burin, actually *cuts* the metal, ploughing through it. Experiment has shown that you cannot engrave gold or copper, let alone bronze, with anything less hard than steel, so that engraving does not appear till a steely iron was in use, which in Europe means from the eighth century B.C.[17] The anvil could be a block of any hard, close-grained stone, but there were also bronze anvils, and by the Middle Bronze Age some of those used by goldsmiths were themselves ornamental objects.[18] There were special hammers for raising and sinking, tracers (some very fine, for the cutting edge of the tracer used on Plate 170 may have been no more than 1 mm.), steel gravers (a square rod with a diamond-shaped face to the point), ordinary carpenter's chisels, and various sizes of punch. The use of a compass for composing designs raises points of much interest and will be considered below (p. 180). It has been suggested that the clay cores used in casting Scandinavian 'belt-boxes' or 'hanging bowls' were framed on the lathe because of the regularity of the curve and diameter. If this is so, then by a curious reversal of the usual order of events, the lathe will have come to Europe ahead of the potter's wheel. An elementary lathe was used in England early in the second millennium to turn shale and amber cups.[19]

Making a hole in bronze is a special problem. A bronze punch can pierce semi-hard sheet metal of thicknesses up to 0·75 mm. Paleolithic man had already discovered some uses of rotary power, probably using a bow-drill to make holes in stone and to make fire. Neolithic polished stone axes had holes drilled with a hollow bone or reed fed with sand and water as abrasive, but these were all useless on bronze, and metal drills were not used till steel was available in the Early Iron Age. Before this the holes in heavy metal must be obtained in the casting. Bronze files, flat and round, were in use before the end of the European Bronze Age.

This brief résumé of techniques and tools has shown that casting and ornamenting with a tracer on the one hand, and forging with bossed repoussé decoration on the other, require a different tool-kit, though sharing some of the same basic processes. It is easy to understand therefore how workshops could grow up in different parts of Europe, and at different times, specializing in one or other process. The traced line is to the bronze artist what the brush-stroke or groove of a flint burin on bone antler or soft stone was to his Paleolithic forerunner. The control and freedom with which he uses it, almost from the beginning, is the measure of his maturity as a craftsman. At the same time the smith's tools take us a long way from the Neolithic kitchen-workshop or the hunter's simple pack.

If, as suggested in Chapter 4, the potter and modeller is more materially a creator than the painter and carver, then the case is even stronger for the metal-worker. More than the potter, much more than the carver, his medium is his own creation. The discovery of ores, roasting and smelting, pattern-making, carving moulds for casting, modelling wax, melting in crucibles, and the casting itself and planishing, all this must be accomplished before the draughtsman has in his hands the 'canvas' on which he will incise his design, and this again requires greater manual control than decoration of a pot or piece of bone. Equally the raising and sinking of cups and bowls, with bossing-up of repoussé decoration, call for quite as much delicacy in the use of hammer and punch as that of the carver of a statue at work on native rock with hammer and chisel. These men should interest us quite as much as the painters of Lascaux and the potters of Vinča and Cucuteni. Their operations required above all forethought, and forethought of a sort that is not so very unlike the farmer's when he hoes or digs in the cold months, plants seed weeks before the spring shoots will appear, and who finally must gather, winnow, parch, or roast the grain before he can eat. All this takes place in his mind when he turns the first autumn sod. In the same way the smith when he selects the lumps of formless ore for smelting sees already the sword-blade or bracelet polished and incised with spiral, scroll, and tendril. All through these strange transformations he, as much as the farmer, depends on the cooperation of his gods. The mysteries performed by charcoal and in the crucible are the counterpart of the winter mystery of the dormant seed and its spring resurrection, for the same earth who is mother of seeds and young animals mothers the ores, which the primitive smith thinks of as a sort of embryos. By his rites, spells, and songs, as well as in his practical experience and skill, he can accelerate or cause the 'birth' of the metal.[20]

Forged metal is no longer simply a stone; it is a 'charged' stone, and dangerous as well as valuable. Wherever there is smithing there is a special ritual, and there are rules and superstitions many of which were preserved in the medieval guilds. The emotions aroused today by talk of radio-active isotopes, and the precautions required in handling them, provide a rough analogy. Some danger remained in the finished object – tool, weapon, or ornament – when it had left the smith's hands, especially in his own tools. Worship of the hammer shows this, but weapons too were thought of as having personality. The latter-day Celts mourned the time when swords would cry out at the banquet. Runes and many poems name and praise famous weapons, old heirlooms, with the list of their battle honours. A few names – Hrunting, Durandal, Excalibur – have survived by chance. I have no doubt at all that the noble weapons illustrated on Plates 171 and 178 had their names and were sung by the minstrels of the time.

It is possible that there was from the start, as there certainly was later, a difference in the status of the metal-worker in Europe and in the Near East. In all primitive societies today, and some not so primitive, the smiths are men apart, either despised as pariahs and outcasts, or esteemed as magicians on a level with chiefs and priests. Both extremes exist in Africa, and in that continent at least it seems that the degradation of the smith goes with pastoral and nomadic life, and his elevation with a sedentary life and land cultivation.[21] In a society where prestige is based on ownership of cattle or horses, it is easy to see how the smith, tied to the earth that holds his ores, and to labour with his hands, is little esteemed, though he may be feared; but in the settled communities of peasant-farmers the smithy has something about it of the temple, the smith the priest, and the anvil the altar. We know nothing at all of the status of the first smiths among their village compatriots in the hills above the Tigris and Euphrates – perhaps they were still 'wise men', shamans, or adepts at kiln-baking; but later, in the complex civilizations of Egypt and Mesopotamia, it appears that they were of little account, mere cogs in the great administrative machine whose apex was the temple or the palace. If not actually a slave, the metal-worker was a tied labourer who worked to order with the minerals issued to him by the priests or the king.[22]

Matters were very different in fifth-century Greece, when a few workshops were producing unparalleled castings like the Delphi charioteer and the Zeus from Artemision. The artist, whether citizen or metic, had a decent standing and worked himself in the studio-foundry, watching, guiding, and performing many of the most intricate operations.[23] This decent status had existed from the Homeric age, but later in Greece and Rome smiths were degraded to factory hands, usually slaves, and with loss of status many of the special ceremonials and taboos of the profession also lapsed, and technological or mechanical invention was hindered. The Dark Ages restored the craftsman-smith to something of his old position, giving back to his work an impetus which lasted right through the Renaissance, and only collapsed with the Industrial Revolution. In barbarian Europe in the second millennium B.C., as in the world described by Homer, the smith probably worked directly for the men who themselves were to use axe or dagger, and whose interest in experiment and improvement was urgent and informed.[24] The Celts valued their craftsmen along with poets and warriors, and the complete hero had to be something of a smith as well as a singer and fighter.[25]

There may be a connexion in the old civilizations between literacy and the devaluation of craftsmanship. With bureaucratic growth a host of scribes and priests imposed themselves between the craftsman making weapons and the clients who would use them, the fighting-men and captains, while the peasantry was too poor and discouraged to invest in new and superior tools. So there was an extreme conservatism in tools and weapons, many of which remained virtually unchanged for two thousand years, from 3000 to 1000, after they were perfected, and Egyptian smiths of 400 B.C. were still using the same inefficient tools that are depicted in tombs two thousand years before, for 'clerks wielding pens would not be interested in saws or sickles'. This state of things was to lead eventually to that separation of theoretical science, linked to philosophy, as an occupation for gentlemen, and the practical sciences and crafts passed on by precept and example and confined to illiterate craftsmen. Only the goldsmiths maintained a better position.[26]

The urban civilizations of the Nile, the Indus, and Mesopotamia were necessary to the *early* advances of metallurgy, since they commanded the resources needed to search out in distant lands the ores and alloys, collect them into one place with the workers, and assure the latter time and security to become full-time specialists. Such wealth was of course envied by the chiefs and tribesmen in the hills and along the coasts of the Levant, who got what they could by raiding and trading, and set themselves up to ape their great neighbours. Ras Shamra in Syria, Mycenae, and Troy belong to this category. Away in the north the barbarian tribes of Europe were at once safe from attack and conquest, and too poor to fall a prey to the dangers of bureaucracy and centralization. At the same time they were near enough occasionally to reach the rich markets, exchange goods, or welcome travelling merchants and craftsmen. They could in Childe's words 'benefit from the Urban Revolution, but postpone the class division it entailed till the new professional craftsmen had won for themselves a status they never acquired in the Ancient East'. The survival of native Iron Age craftsmanship beyond the Roman *limes* made possible the Dark Age revival with its barbarous but wonderfully vigorous arts, which seem so strangely to echo the past across almost a thousand years of history.

The Background

In the last two chapters we have seen Europe gradually diverging from the countries of the Near East; its farming economy, at first based on crops, going over more and more to animal husbandry, the rise of its distinctive styles of pottery, its rough but not unskilled building in stone, and the exploration of lands and islands to west and north. All this is very different from the concentration and complexity of city life in the Near East, already a forcing-ground of civilization. These separating paths will not begin to converge again until the barbarians have the power to menace as well as emulate their more civilized neighbours. The urban civilizations will hardly concern us in this chapter except as a distant source of commodities and inventions, but Anatolia and the Aegean exert an increasing influence, especially in the spread of metallurgy.

Merchants and pedlars must have preceded smiths into Europe – the finished products of the craft travelled ahead of craft-practice; and this is one of the reasons why the earliest metal objects to appear, the copper awls and blades, gold rings and pins found from time to time in 'Neolithic' graves and houses, made no appreciable difference in the conditions of the life of the men who owned them. When heavy serviceable tools of copper first appear in Eastern Europe – flat axes, pickaxes, and axe-adzes with shaft-hole for the handle – they are not found in houses but heaped together in hoards along the routes to and from the deposits of ores, and on old salt-ways. In villages there is hardly ever a sign of metal-working, neither crucibles nor smithing tools. This work must have been carried on close to the outcrops and far from the eyes of uninitiated men.[27] The ores chiefly exploited during the third millennium were those within the Carpathian ring, in Transylvania and in the Balkans, but very little farther west.[28] It is curious that these heavy implements of serviceable design, well suited to forest clearance, hardly ever show signs of wear and are often unfinished. It has been suggested that they were objects of prestige, like the magnificent weapons of the second millennium, or even units of exchange, but such questions must remain unanswered. In addition small roundels of copper and gold were worn sewn on to the clothes in which the dead were buried, or were hung from the neck. They are often decorated with tiny bosses produced by hammering and pouncing on sheet metal.[29]

Throughout Europe, west as well as east, the effective use of metals only comes with the exploitation of ores, including the sulphides, and with the use of alloys. The men who lived at the turn of the third millennium were exercising a deliberate choice when they accepted from older civilizations the art of smelting, but rejected for another thousand years the potter's wheel, for both were by this time in use all over the Near East.[30]

The face of Europe was changing in more ways than one, and before turning to the achievements of second-millennium bronzesmiths, some at least of the changes must be sketched in. The heavily forested landscape of the beginning of the third millennium had at its end been thinned into heath and moor which pastured the large herds of sheep and cattle that now roamed the same plains that were the feeding ground of bison and reindeer before the forest enveloped them.[31]

In the middle of the third millennium, when the changes were far advanced, new people appeared from the east who are known to archaeologists under various names taken from a typical possession or rite: ochre-grave, battle-axe, corded-ware, single-grave, boat-axe, and so on. They were more warlike than the earlier farmers and sat more loosely to the land, but they were not necessarily nomads in our contemporary sense. The nomadic herding life that we recognize today seems to have grown up only rather late and on the fringes of a more balanced agriculture and stock-breeding. These men evidently practised mixed ranch-farming, and the extent to which their lives and thoughts were involved with their animals is shown by the rites of burial which they occasionally conferred on their cattle.[32] But there is no animal art to betray this pre-occupation, only beautifully shaped and polished stone axes based on metal prototypes but quite unlike the axes and adzes of the earlier East European hoards. They were poor potters and unskilled in metallurgy, acquiring their small trinkets from Caucasian and Carpathian workshops. But as soon as they had wealth enough they spent it ostentatiously, and their practice of burying chieftains under imposing barrows with their richest possessions and heirlooms piled on and around the body has provided us with our best source for the recovery of works of art and value. This is particularly true of the second millennium and the so-called 'Tumulus People' who were in part their inheritors. It took a very short time for the new sort of life to spread across Europe.[33] But branches of these people found their way over the greater part of Central and Northern Europe from Rumania to Sweden, and eventually some crossed the North Sea to Britain (Table 2).

It used to be possible to explain these events as due to the arrival of nomad warriors from the Russian steppe, migrating like the Mongols, with their cattle, covered wagons, and battle-axes; but it was not as simple as that. In the North Pontic region and the Ukraine, unlike the rest of Europe, village life was becoming more rather than less agricultural. Perhaps those elements in the population that were least attracted to the routine of regular cultivation took themselves off, with some encouragement and re-inforcement from the hunter tribes who were always present on their northern flank, and travelling west were joined by other still unconverted hunters. The lasting and profound nature of these events can be felt through the entire Bronze Age, and it would be as wrong to explain them as due simply to the arrival of nomads as to explain the rise of sheep-farming in fourteenth-century England and the disappearance of villages as due to an invasion of nomad shepherds from the continent. But some change in population there certainly was, and it is this that is generally held responsible for the introduction of Indo-European speech. Nor were these events confined to Europe.

In an earlier chapter I referred to the unrest that swept Western Asia at the end of the third millennium and which led to new landings in Sicily, Malta, and Sardinia. The unrest in Anatolia at the end of the Early Bronze Age and the royal burials at Alaca Hüyük were due to warlike tribes perhaps from the Caucasus and highlands of eastern Anatolia raiding and warring on the frontiers of civilization. More or less contemporary with the changes north of the Black Sea, south of it another great circling movement of men was crossing Anatolia, a part of whom pushed north again to

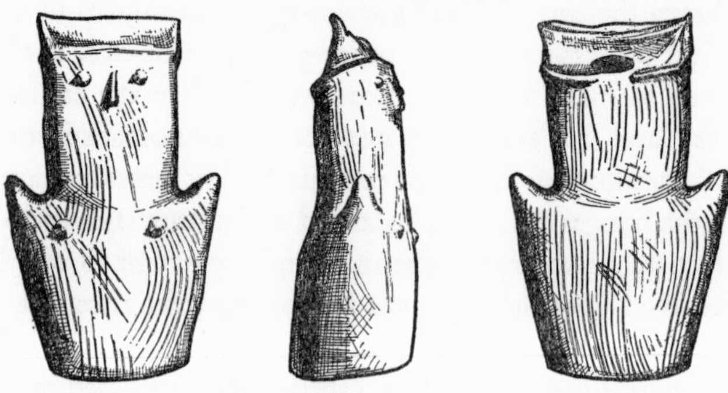

Figure 63. 'Baden' cremation urn from Center, Hungary

cross the Hellespont or Dardanelles into the Balkans and even to reach the Danube some time before 2000. This seems the best explanation for the appearance of the 'Baden' people, who were certainly not nomads, but who drove ox-wagons and sometimes buried the ox-team with careful ceremony. These Baden people had neither distinctive houses nor burials, but they did occasionally cremate the bodies of the dead, and on at least one occasion placed the ashes in clay urns shaped like a human figure, a sort of miniature mummy-case. The ashes were put in through a hole behind the headdress, or through the open top. The faces have the same self-satisfied smirk as some from Vinča and are in fact very little later (Figure 63).[34] The Baden people were not much better metallurgists than their ochre-grave and battle-axe contemporaries, but unlike them they were accomplished potters, especially in the earlier phase. They made quite new styles of vessel with a smooth dark surface and metallic shapes (Plate 158). Their 'winged' handles and the fluting of the surfaces were carried up to the Carpathians and the Bakony. The potter's art of Europe was profoundly affected by this new influence, and the shapes of vessels never altogether lost a certain professionalism, a tolerance of plain surfaces and of deliberately restrained or marginal ornament. The little flask from Mokrin in the Banat (Plate 157) is several centuries later than Plate 158 from Ruma, and another (Plate 161) from Omoljica is a little later again, but all in their different ways have felt this influence.[35]

During the third millennium 'tell-villages' from the Maritsa valley to near the confluence of Tisza and Danube come to an end, while not long after others begin to rise on the Hungarian plain and as far west as the Bakony. Tószeg, west of the middle Tisza, is one of the largest, lasting through much of the second millennium. Like the mounds of Anatolia and tell-settlement in general, it depended on permanent occupation and on building with impermanent and bulky material, chiefly mud. This looks like a real shift of population, or at any rate a north-westward drift of the more lasting sort of settlement with its proof of greater security. Other sites were settled in the hilly country round the great plain and defended with ditch and palisade, in the foothills of the Carpathians from Monteoru in Muntenia to Věteřov in Moravia and Barca in Slovakia, till a network of small townships covered the land.[36]

Changes were also taking place in Western Europe towards the end of the third millennium. The fine, hard-textured red ware with neat impressed ornament known as 'bell-beaker' is extraordinarily consistent from Spain to Britain and from the North Sea to Czechoslovakia. Again new people are suspected, but burial rites were not at first affected nor did the 'Neolithic' population give up their megalithic tomb-building, but simply accommodated the new arrivals, who seem to have introduced metal-working to the west on a quite small scale at first. This body of metallurgical skills spread up from Iberia to Brittany, Britain, Ireland, and Denmark, and met others coming from Italy (by way of eastern France) and from the Balkans and the Carpathian ring (by way of Moravia and Germany). It is not possible to say exactly what was the role of the 'Beaker People', and the beakers themselves lose definition and become contaminated with other inferior potting traditions.

At this point we have assembled before us the *dramatis personae* of the Bronze Age, a long period in the course of which barbarian Europe matured so that by its end it confronted the eastern and Mediterranean states, no longer as a mere source of slaves, furs, timber, and ores ripe for exploitation, but as a threat to their stability, a menacing hinterland. There were still untouched hunting tribes in the northern forest, and the farming tribes themselves had intermingled with hunters and with each other.

In a few areas – the Saale is one and southern England another – there were concentrations of wealth even in the early second millennium, but only in the Carpathian ring, on the Hungarian plain, and in a few favoured sites round the Mediterranean did men live in security behind walls or surrounded by a *cordon sanitaire* of deforested and cultivated land in a milieu in which skills and arts could flourish and develop their own character. In time the many individual cultural groups of the Early Bronze Age cohere into two major groupings more or less opposed in their characteristics. The one probably contains more of the eastern and pastoral element, and because of its burials under round barrows (inherited from the same quarter) is known as 'Tumulus'; and the other, because it buried the dead in large cremation cemeteries or urnfields, is known as 'Urnfield' and inherited more from the settled inhabitants of the tell-villages and towns of the Danubian and Carpathian lands. But it is a mistake to project back into an earlier, less homogeneous age the Tumulus–Urnfield dichotomy of the Later Bronze and Early Iron Age. In general population was increasing, warfare was endemic, the cart or chariot was adopted, the art of fortification much advanced, and the solitary and still rather uncouth figure of the shaman had, by the end, become a member of a priesthood. Purely European shifts and changes brought this bright period to an end, but while it lasted it produced some brilliant potting as well as metal-working. The prehistory of the second millennium is extremely complicated, and it would be impossible as well as unnecessary to follow its ramifications here. Our purpose will be served better by confining ourselves to the more important schools of decoration, especially in metal-work, and the workshops that produced them, and also to the potter's craft where it deserves attention.

Bronze Age Potters of Eastern Europe

The rather dismal pottery of the beginning of the second millennium is followed by a wonderful renaissance. Although the best of the 'western' bell-beakers are fine products of the potter's craft, they are monotonous and limited. The dark-faced 'metallic' wares that followed Baden in Yugoslavia, Hungary (the Banat), and Czechoslovakia are more inventive and ambitious (Plates 157 and 159). Just as there was a period of special brilliance in the fourth millennium with the painted wares of Rumania, Bulgaria, and the Ukraine, so in the second millennium there was another, and one gets the impression that south of the Erzgebirge and inside the Carpathian ring everything happened at once. This is partly because the chronology and relationships of the different 'cultures' are not yet worked out satisfactorily.

Coarse dark pots with encrusted white ornament from Sarvaš are contemporary with the elegant little flask from Mokrin (Plates 157 and 160), but here one senses wood-carving in the background. Turning from this to Plate 159 from Patince is like going from the farm kitchen, where blankets, saddle-cloths, and bodices are worked with bold designs and wood is carved, to a villa at Pompeii, all painted friezes and elegant arcading. The effect *is* elegant, but thin. Patince was a large cremation cemetery, and this kind of vase was only made for the grave where up to thirty or forty of different shapes stood together with the urn.[37] At another large cemetery at Cîrna below the Iron Gates in Oltenia a rather spidery but ornate ornament was used with great confidence (Plates 162 and 163 and Figure 64). There are the same stamped circles and arcading, but employed with less restraint; a notched bone or toothed wheel made the impression in the clay. About three-quarters of the five hundred pots found in a hundred and sixteen graves at Cîrna are decorated in what could be called the 'embroidered style'; and here the rite was strict, with ashes always inurned. One or two rather complicated motifs, though never absolutely identical, are repeated so often that they should rank perhaps as emblems like the 'Cappadocian symbol' or Hittite 'Royal Sign', or the patterns based on octopods that cover Late Mycenaean pots and that are scarcely recognizable as such unless one knows what has gone before. The same motifs are used at Cîrna on the dress of small clay figures which will be described later.[38] Another Rumanian group (Wietenberg) built up its ornament from geometric spirals. In one case the pattern on the inside of a shallow dish, an elaboration of the swastika, is identical with second-millennium seals from Alişar and Beycesultan in Anatolia (Figure 65, B–E). This repeats a very ancient dependence, for around 4000 B.C. Criş-Körös and Tisza Neolithic settlers stamped their bodies and perhaps textiles and pots with clay stamps the patterns of which are virtually identical with stamps from Catel Hüyük in Anatolia.[39] The use of similar motifs in Rumania, on Pannonian crusted ware in Hungary, and in Hittite Anatolia looks like contact; and though no single Hittite seal has been found north of Rhodope, these

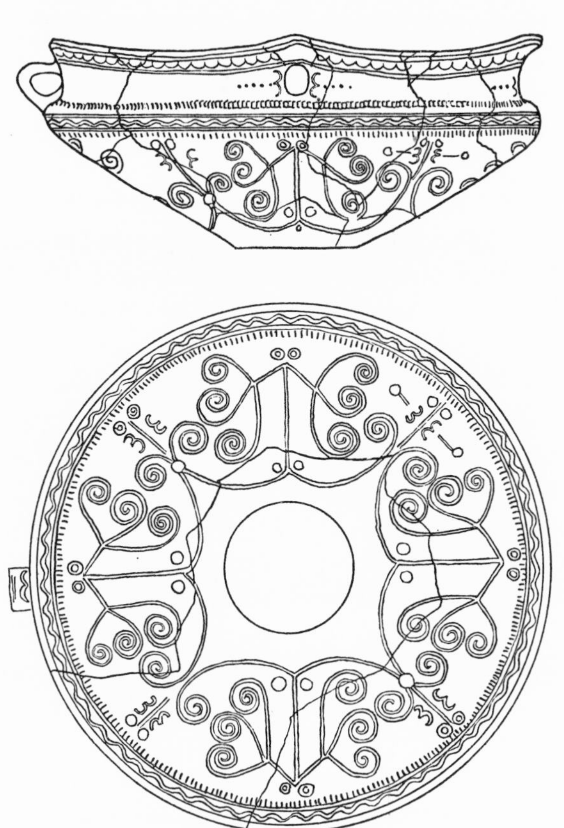

Figure 64. Handled bowl from Cîrna cremation cemetery, Rumania

small durable objects used as property marks might conveniently be carried on merchant ventures and so lost when things went wrong. Geometric spirals used by 'Wietenberg' potters in Rumania are too common to be tied to any one source, but a large and handsome clay hearth with spiral patterns is very much in the later Mycenaean style.[40]

Very different again is the bold and simple three-dimensional ornament of Otomani potters (Plate 165). In Slovakia and the Hungarian plain and parts of western Rumania this style had great influence and a long life. Linked three-dimensional spirals surround the body of the jug or bowl, foot-ring bases and horizontal fluting remind us of metal vessels; but there is also a curious harking back (it cannot be direct inheritance) to the

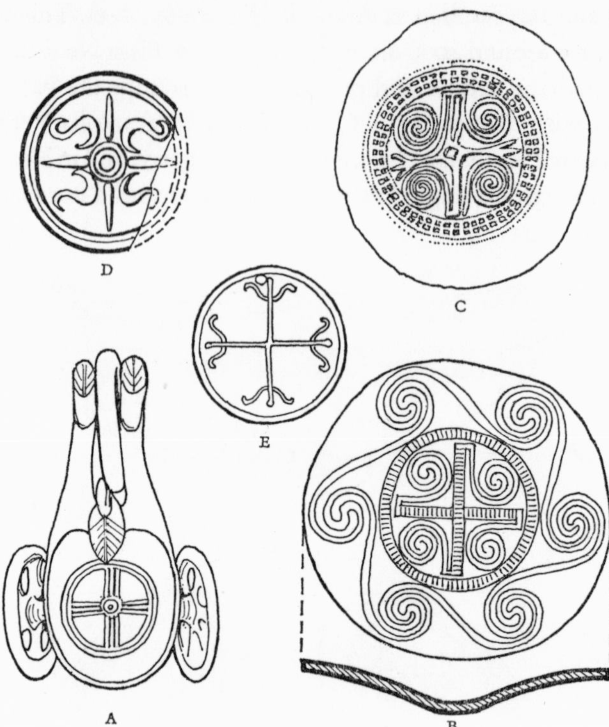

Figure 65. A Clay tricycle with water birds from Dupljaja, Yugoslavia, seen from above (cf. Plate 168)
B Motif incised on a plate from Wietenberg, Rumania
C The same motif on a twelfth-century ivory seal from Beycesultan, Turkey
D Hittite 'Royal Sign', impressed medallion on pot from Kültepe-Kaniş, Turkey
E 'Pannonian' motif from Kölesd, Nagyhangos, Hungary

painted patterns of Cucuteni or Tripolye pots from Moldavia and the Ukraine (Plate 164 and Figures 50B and 53 top). The multiple painted line has become parallel ridges, and the centre of the spiral which once contained a cross-in-circle or solid roundel now holds a boss (Plate 136). Sometimes the ornament is almost too Baroque, and Plate 166 from Barca in Slovakia comes perilously close to the 'pineapple pot' invented for Chapter 4 (p. 122 above). These pots belong to cult not secular uses, and the solid bosses may be reminders of the goddess (Plate 146). The nearly contemporary and overlapping styles of potting, from Muntenia and Oltenia in the east to Moravia and the Banat in the west, are loosely linked by the lower and middle Danube in that area of more settled and probably more secure agricultural societies that was described above as characteristic of the new Europe of the second millennium.

With the return of fine potting it is no surprise to find the human figure once more modelled in clay, but this Bronze Age modelling is very different from the Neolithic. Form is no longer important; attention is transferred to the surface, which is covered with a sort of handwriting that is both decorative and communicates information through particular designs and through the repetition of motifs like those on the pots and on some metal-work. Most of the figures are solid above and hollow below with bell-shaped skirts (Plates 167 and 169 and Figure 66). They are enough alike to allow our treating them together. Most belong to the Cîrna–Žuto Brdo group of the archaeologists, and to what I have called the 'embroidered style'. They have been found in twenty-two different sites just above and below the Iron Gates, and within the group there are two outstanding figures: Kličevac and Dupljaja.[41]

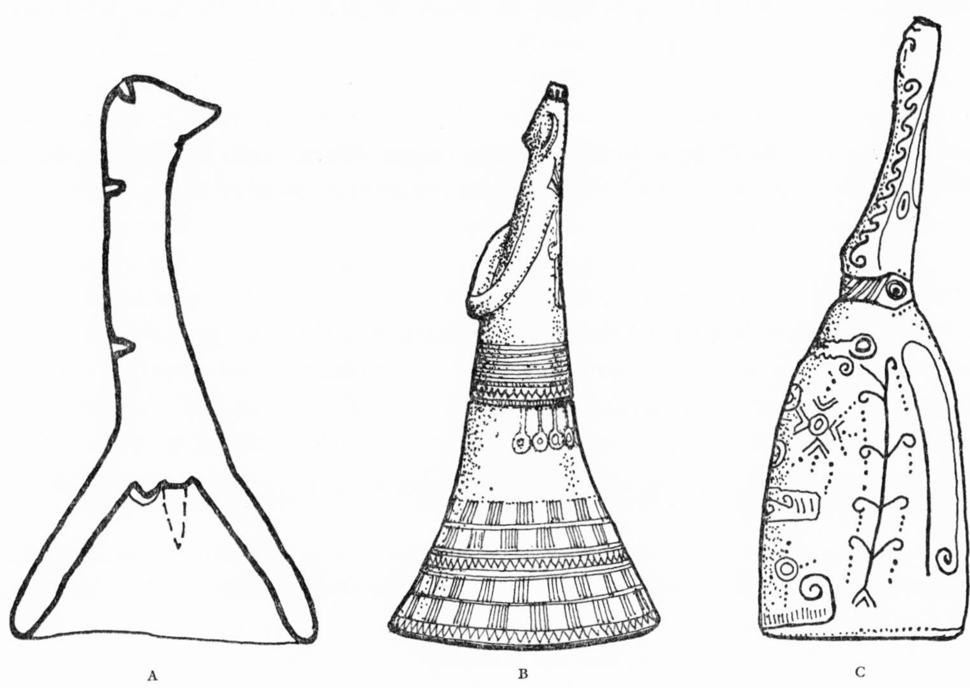

Figure 66. A Side view in section of standing clay figure from Dupljaja, Yugoslavia
B Side view of Kličevac clay figure, Yugoslavia
C Side view of figure from Cîrna, Rumania

Kličevac was another Middle Bronze Age cemetery like Cîrna, and this figure was the largest and most impressive of them all (Plate 167 and Figure 66B). Its destruction therefore in the First World War is a great loss. Fortunately photographs and drawings exist of different views.[42] It is 12·6–13·4 inches (32–34 cm.) high against a usual size of well below 12 inches. It is hollow below and solid above; the spiral-ended choker, representing gold or bronze, is typical, and so is the pendant. The hair at the back is braided and hung with rings and pendants that recall a Neolithic motif found on Tisza figures,[43] and round pendants dangle from the belt, showing incidentally a use for the small gold roundels which are found at this time. The most striking features are the many-rayed circle that appears three times, on the throat and below each shoulder, and the portrayal of the face, and to these I shall return. Stamped concentric circles are used on many figures, and over the presumably later ones they are scattered rather aimlessly.[44]

Dupljaja is a defended site only a few miles and the width of the Danube from the Kličevac urnfield. Two figures standing on wheeled vehicles were found, unfortunately without context, and the better is illustrated on Plate 168.[45] This figure, about 4 inches (just under 10 cm.) high, is of the usual bell shape. The head and upper body are solid clay, but the hollow skirt covers male genitals, so what we have here is a god of sorts. Like other figures he wears a spiral-ended choker, and a spiral pendant hangs from his neck. Concentric circles dangle from the belt and delineate the eyes, and a larger circle is placed on the middle of the chest above the hands. He stands on a three-wheeled carriage and immediately in front is a water-bird, perhaps a swan, and two larger birds of the same family but wearing collars form the forward ends or shafts of the carriage. In the floor is cut a cross-in-circle or four-spoked wheel on which the figure must stand, and the group is completed by a puzzling conical object shown in the Plate under the car (Plate 168 and Figures 65A and 66A), but sometimes reconstructed into a parasol supported over the figure, or else as a buckler, neither of which explanation is very convincing. It is ornamented like the god's own dress. There are other puzzles beside this. Prehistoric and ancient Near Eastern carts and chariots, two- and four-wheeled, do not have shafts, but a pole between the pairs of animals to which they are yoked, horses as well as oxen; but here the order is reversed: two poles and one wheel. In the Late Bronze Age iconography of Danubian lands the sun is often shown as a wheel travelling in a bird-ended boat, and it is reasonable to assume that the assimilation of sun, wheel, bird, and god had been completed by the probable date of Dupljaja, towards the end of the second millennium.

It is unlikely that the sun would have been visualized as a wheel by men who had never seen a cart with spoked wheels. The solid-wheeled ox-wagon is a shabby conveyance for so swift and far-seeing a god. If not on wheels, he goes in a boat or on wings or on his own legs, two or four, like the 'sun-stags' and 'antlered suns' of Iberia (Figure 57, A and C). I believe that what we have at Dupljaja is not so much a god on a tricycle as a small cult scene of the god and his bird – familiar or epiphany, perhaps in a boat, or on a 'float' which has been given wheels for pushing and pulling it about during the action of the ritual. The purpose of the lid could have been to cover the symbol on the floor, which it does very well, on those occasions and at those seasons when the god himself was removed from the carriage. The face, though it has ears and mouth, with a beak like the birds, fails to impress as the really terrifying Kličevac image does. If there is a mystery here, it may well have been hidden in the symbol, the cross-in-circle, which the god impersonates.

At this point the imagination of sober prehistorians is apt to take off on a wild goose (or swan) chase. The Hyperborean Apollo borne by swans down from Thrace, and Dionysos his complement and antithesis, become old Balkan gods; nor is this basically unlikely, for we are not far from the home of Salmoxus and the adventures of Aristaeas. But without going so far as identification of person and name, we may agree that, where wheel, water-bird, and god are joined together, the conception of the sun is probably not far distant. More important, this scene implies already a more elaborated ritual and ceremonial than any of the Neolithic figures, although they, as art, are far more interesting. Dupljaja carries us forward to a new stage and prepares us for what we shall find in Central and Northern Europe in the Late Bronze and Early Iron Age at Trundholm and Strettweg and Gemeinlebarn.

The second Dupljaja figure is moulded in one piece with the car, which has a single pole broken off to a stump, so there is no way of knowing whether there were birds or animals attached; but swastikas are prominent on the top of the head, over the genitals, and on the breast. If we turn back to Kličevac (Plate 167) with all this in mind, the three star-like symbols, the immense nostrils and ringed staring eyes may seem to convey a brilliance of dazzling heat as powerful in its barbaric manner as the face of Helios on a coin of Rhodes.[46]

A long robe does not mean female sex, as we have seen, but the figures found at Cîrna in Oltenia, in the same large urnfield from which came the pots of Plates 162 and 163 and Figure 64, must be feminine. The dress is indeed the same as is still worn by women in parts of Europe, especially in the Banat: a long blouse tucked into a broad belt of stuff or metal with a clasp at the back, embroidered aprons or panels back and front, sometimes fringed, and a sort of bolero with a low open front.[47] There are over a dozen figures between 10 and 5 inches high (Plate 169 and Figure 66c). They were often broken before they were buried and then placed on the shoulder of a large vessel; the stamped decoration is produced in the same way as on the pots, and some of the motifs are identical. There are borders of linked spirals, Greek fret or key pattern, circles with dots and rays round them; a plant meanders up a skirt and spirals hang from the belt. The features have degenerated still further from the Kličevac formula to a lyre, which as a pattern was used on pots as well (Figure 67). But the most constant and

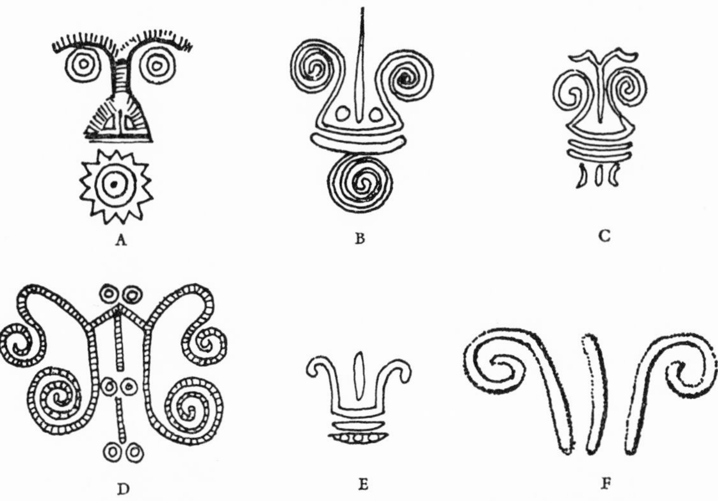

Figure 67. The face motif on figures and pots: A Kličevac, B Orsova, C Kovin, Yugoslavia, D 'M' motif on a pot; face motif simplified, E on figure, and F on a pot from Cîrna, Rumania

elusive motif both on figures and on pots is that called the 'M' (though sometimes it is a 'W') with spirals suspended (Plate 162 and Figures 64 and 67D). On the pots it is central, and on the figures too it is often placed on the stomach. It is not confined to Cîrna but appears occasionally in Yugoslavia.[48] Whatever its meaning, it must have stood for some great power: or it could be that the very contrary is the case, and that we are now in a milieu of such sophistication that the symbols are stripped of ancient powers and can be safely exploited for decorative ends. This is an irreversible devaluation, not the same as the force which works on every representation to turn it into pattern; for the pattern may be as numinous as was the representation.

Oxen were the animals most often represented by Neolithic modellers; now it is birds. Occasionally, as at Dupljaja, they appear with men; at Cîrna they perch on the lid of a pot, and from this time onwards flocks of little birds and water-birds invade European art. It has been suggested that on the Danube they act the role of the modelled wheels farther north and east, coming together momentarily at Dupljaja, and again in the early first millennium.[49] Temporarily the ox has almost disappeared. A third-millennium head from Moravia was mentioned earlier (p. 117), and there is another larger and a little later from Jevisovice which has, as well as eyes surrounded by rays, the same triangular forelock.[50] These are almost the last; we do not meet oxen again till the turn of the millennium, when they are usually cast in bronze, by which time something curious has happened: they have been merged with the bird, or more accurately, the ox's horns have been inherited by the ubiquitous birds.

It is possible to track down different characteristics of the embroidered-style figures in much older Neolithic work. An early-third-millennium figure from Salcuţa in Rumania has the bell skirt and stomach-spiral of many Cîrna figures; the braiding of the hair of Kličevac can be carried back through an Early Bronze Age pot from Tószeg to the Kökénydomb pot-figures and the Tisza Neolithic. The flat-topped Kličevac headdress is not unlike the Baden urns from Center (Plate 167 and Figures 63 and 66, B–C). Nevertheless these are great distances of time. If this gap is to be bridged at all, it is by looking west into Croatia and Slovenia, where the Neolithic tradition of modelling included birds, boots, and altar horns and survived very much longer than farther east.[51]

At the other extreme from these roughly made clay figures are those metropolitan works of art, the Cretan faience 'snake-goddesses' and priestesses and their demotic counterparts in clay, and the contemporary ivory and faience figures found on Mycenaean sites, which are often called in to provide prototypes, without always taking account of what this may mean. First of all Crete must be excluded, for after the middle of the fifteenth century Minoan civilization was everywhere in retreat. The painted clay figures of the fourteenth to thirteenth centuries (Late Helladic III), mainland equivalents of the simpler sort of Late Minoan figures, are inferior to Kličevac, quite unlike in dress, and, except possibly for the earliest 'phi' type, unlike in gesture. In fact it is easier to compare the latter with Neolithic modelling of fifteen hundred years and more earlier (Cucuteni style).

Metallurgical Schools

There is good reason to think that metallurgy was introduced independently to Eastern and to Western Europe; and a likelihood that in Eastern Europe it was introduced more than once. The workshops from which came the fine ornamented swords and axes of the second millennium were not descended from those that had produced heavy copper shaft-hole axes in the fourth and third millennium. Some weapons, for instance axes, have a distant likeness to those of the Caucasian Bronze Age and second-millennium Anatolia, especially when they are compared with the flat axes that the rest of Europe was using, but there is far more that is different and new. The manner of introduction and the organization of the industry are virtually unknown to us, but since hoards of weapons and tools are found together, and sometimes the objects are unfinished, there may have been travelling smiths able to add decoration to please a particular patron.[52] Stone moulds for casting are found in settlements now, which shows that smiths were working within the community that had, as it were, caught up with them. Particular styles of metal-work range farther than pottery styles. The Transylvanian–Hungarian–Slovak province was served by a group of closely connected workshops sharing a common tradition. Their work is richly decorated and easily recognized, and some of it even reached Scandinavia.

Except for a handful of very grand treasures and the furnishing of royal graves, the weapons and implements of the ancient Near East are plain, unadorned objects of use. Even in the Aegean in the second millennium there are more plain weapons than decorated. The contemporary Bronze Age of Eastern and Central Europe and Scandinavia is really exceptional in the very high percentage of the whole metal production that carries ornament. This is new, and it is European, just as the shapes of castings break more and more away from earlier prototypes. The reason may well lie in the status of the smith and his relationship to his clients, which was hinted at earlier in this chapter.

At a time and in a region where pottery was so richly ornamented, the rarer and more costly products of the smithy-studio were perhaps naturally given a still finer decoration, and the forging of gold and silver into handsome but entirely useless swords, spears, and daggers introduces the prestige article.[53] Such things are the ornaments of an heroic society, but they had a real value beyond simple glorification; for it has been said that in such a society all that for us passes as foreign relations and diplomacy, was conducted by gift-exchange. The need for metals deprived both the heroic 'great house' and the barbarian village of self-sufficiency; 'the circulation of treasure was as essential a part of heroic life as its acquisition . . . display was a concrete expression of honour and friendship'.[54] The secular gesture, as well as the service of the gods, is now a pretext for the possession of expensive works of art. The articles given were often of gold, so that ostentation, prestige, and the reserves of wealth were bound together: wealth as wealth and wealth as symbol. Heroes boasted of the gifts they had received and given, but these were ceremonial acts, and for this reason the objects themselves had genealogies.[55] If this is true of a Greece just emerging from the dark age into the eighth century, the society described was far closer to the barbarians of second-millennium Europe than it was to the wealthy bureaucratic institutions of second-millennium Crete and Late Mycenaean Greece. Very little treasure and few objects of high value or beauty have survived from the dark age in Greece, particularly in metal-work. There is nothing really comparable to the swords of Apa and Hajdusámson or the gold bracelet from Bellye (Plates 171 and 175 and Figure 68A).

The earliest essays at ornament in Eastern Europe had been made by hammering small bosses in sheet gold, and this continued to some extent in gold-work, even repeating the curvilinear patterns, spirals, and concentric circles produced by the tracer (Figure 68D).[56] The heavier ornament of axes was obtained by casting from a carefully worked mould, but by far the greater part of Early and Middle Bronze Age ornament is traced. It is a draughtsman's art of great delicacy. The hair-fine hatched triangles and zigzags of a gold lunula from Ireland (Plate 170) are typical of the geometric rectilinear patterns which were for centuries the main repertoire of western ornament, and at first also in Central and Northern Europe (Plate 179). You see it on triangular daggers, flat axes, pins, and all sorts of bijouterie. It might be a continuation of the plaited and basketry patterns that were used so successfully to carpet the surface of Neolithic pots. The curvilinear decoration put out from workshops within the Carpathian ring (and to a much lesser extent from Northern Italy and Austria) is more inventive and more original, but its source is still mysterious. It is really no more Mycenaean than the clay figures from Cîrna and Kličevac are Mycenaean; but in the same region originality and inventiveness were also what distinguished *Neolithic* modelling and potting.

With very few exceptions, this is a non-representational decoration based on the spiral and semicircle. This in itself is by no means original. The non-representational Bronze Age art of the Aegean uses both, and even when it represents nautilus, octopus, and flower-head, it still delights to play at spirals. In the Danubian province the spirals, though divorced from representation, are used not so much geometrically as organically. They do not simply flow from measured point to point but grow like tendrils, and in this respect they foreshadow the Celtic artist's manner of working (Plates 173 and 174 and Figure 68, A and B). The command of balance and rhythm in the filling of space, well adapted to the odd shapes of blade and butt, would be less surprising if these men could have inherited the gifts of the fourth-millennium potters.[57] The sword and axe found in a hoard at Hajdusámson in Hungary are probably among the earliest works decorated in this style, though estimates of the real date vary greatly.[58] Curved lines are of course more difficult to draw freehand with a tracer than straight ones. There is no sign here of drills or compasses; the draughtsman worked from a series of points used as anchorage in setting out his design, and in spite of astonishing regularity the hesitation of the hand can be seen (Plate 173). Swords and axes in a hoard found at Apa in Rumania are a little later but in the same workshop tradition (Plate 172 and Figure 68, A and B). The spirals on the butt of the axe have sprouted very characteristically prolongations marked out only as dots that curl away in the opposite direction from the main volute (three can be seen on Plate 172). The ground between the spirals is powdered with triple dots, and the design makes an attractive whole.[59]

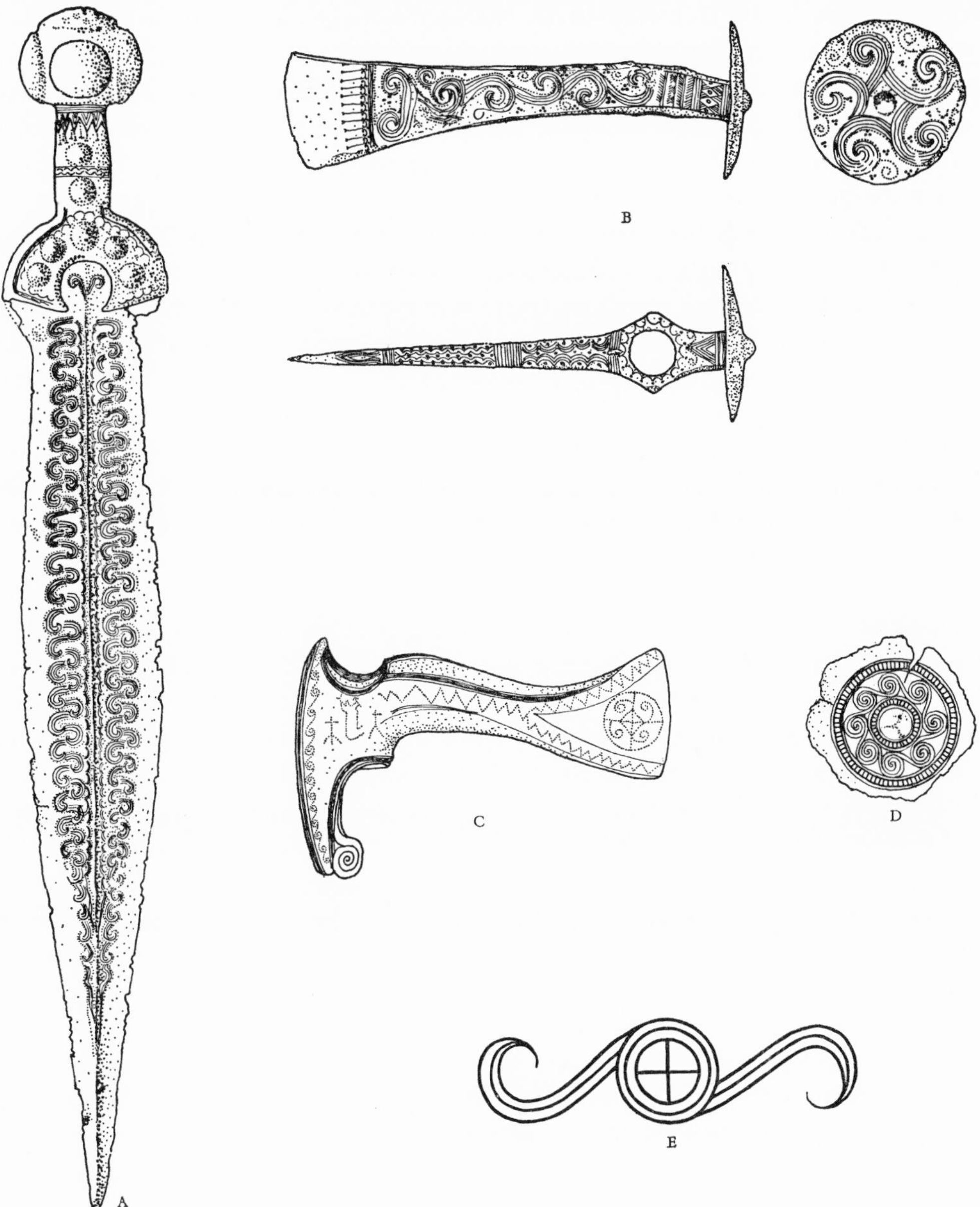

Figure 68. Incised ornament on bronze and gold from Transylvanian–Hungarian workshops: A bronze sword and B shaft-hole axe from the Apa hoard, Rumania, C axe and D gold repoussé disc from the Tufalău (Cófalva) hoard, Rumania, E motif on a bronze axe from Megyaszó, Hungary

A gold bracelet found alone at Bellye in Hungary is a magnificent casting and carries decoration in the Hajdusámson-Apa tradition (Plate 175). The three ribs of the 'body' have been incorporated in the scheme of decoration in the same way as the mid-rib of the Hajdusámson sword. The 'anchor dots' can be seen plainly, some of the lines have been deepened with the punch, and a border outlining the broad curved terminals has been filled by a line of tiny toothmarks probably produced by a punch of a different kind.[60] The tapped *pointillé* ornament reappears on much simpler bronzes in Denmark, and these will concern us shortly (Plate 179).

Axes, and apparently only axes, sometimes have a recognizable emblem, an eight-pointed star, a cross-in-circle between volutes (a remarkable reminder of Cucuteni and Tripolye pots), and once, between illegible signs, something intended for an animal (Figure 68, C and E).[61] With the cross-in-circle we meet again a problem in interpretation which first arose with the decoration of pots, and with the Dupljaja figure. It is hardly likely to have represented a spoked wheel in the fourth to third millennium, when it was painted on Cucuteni pots, any more than in Middle Helladic Greece; for the earliest known really operational four-spoked wheel is early-sixteenth-century and was attached to a silver model of a boat in an Egyptian funeral treasure. The spoked wheel and the horse, between them, made possible the invention of a light chariot and a revolution in warfare. The wheel is a symbol *and* a machine, and it is probably in the former role that small clay model-wheels begin to appear in settlements in Czechoslovakia. Quite possibly they were all once attached to model carts or cult-scenes like Dupljaja. When some centuries later we see a cross-in-circle or four-spoked wheel heraldically flanked by birds, serpents, or volutes, it is undoubtedly the sun, a fiery wheel spinning across the heavens (Plate 192, left). There is little or no evidence that it had this meaning in the Near East, where the flaming disc is represented in other ways. The only possible exceptions are among the Mitanni and the Hittites, both – be it noted – horse-driving Indo-Europeans.[62] In Europe the little wheels are very often found with bone tubular harness, cheeks and flat discs, both carrying a geometrical ornament based on the circle. The small tubes and the disc of Plate 176 come from Nitriansky-Hrádok, an important settlement in Slovakia on the edge of the plain, and are good examples of the style.[63] This tight geometric ornament is distinct from the Hajdusámson–Apa tradition, and its mechanical exactitude shows that it was produced by compasses or some other rotary device. An unfinished ornament on a marble lid from Surčin, Croatia, puts this beyond doubt (Plate 177). Spaced dots are used in setting out as in the Hajdusámson–Apa style, but though the patterns may seem to coil spiral-like, they are in fact built upon the concentric circle with a minimum of free-hand drawing. Bone and antler show the mechanics of the ornament best, especially the so-called pulley-pattern, but it was used also to decorate gold cups and bracelets, though in their case it was less austerely geometric, and so less unlike the Hajdusámson–Apa style.[64]

The closeness of this ornament to patterns stamped in gold and cut in ivory and bone and found in the shaft-graves at Mycenae in the sixteenth century has been used to date the middle phase of the Hungarian and Czechoslovak Bronze Age. But given the instrument, probably compasses, the pattern itself is of such simplicity that it cannot be limited to any place or time. In bone it comes from the acropolis at Mycenae long after the date of the shaft-graves, and it appears in the Middle Bronze Age of Anatolia and sporadically in Syria from the sixteenth to the twelfth century. However, the connexion between the cheekpiece on Plate 176 and bone cheekpieces from as far away as Alaca Hüyük and Beycesultan in Central Anatolia (there are none in Greece) does throw interesting light on the spread of horse-driving, which, taken with the spoked wheel, now means the light cart and probably the technique and skills of chariotry. The war chariot is heroic furniture *par excellence* and could not have reached Central Europe till after 1450.[65] The close ties established between harness (the bone cheeks), spoked wheels, and compass-drawn patterns in Central Europe suggest not unimportant changes in society at about or rather after this date.

These two ornamental styles could be roughly distinguished as 'flowing' and 'growing', or as symmetric and asymmetric; they are very rarely found in the same sites, but it is far from clear whether this is because of a difference in date (which would not anyhow be very great) or because of tribal or economic and workshop differences. In any case we can say that from around the middle of the second millennium and for the next one or two centuries, at a time when the ornament of Western Europe was rigorously geometric and rectilinear, there were in Central and Eastern Europe two or possibly three distinct and vigorous styles: the first asymmetric, organic, non-representational, partly new and partly an indigenous Neolithic legacy; the second curvilinear, geometric, mechanical, symmetric, and loosely bound up with rotary techniques (compasses and wheel), and undoubtedly foreign; and the last an emblematic curvilinear style frequently used on pots and clay figures (Cîrna, Žuto Brdo, Kličevac) and occasionally on bronze or gold discs and pendants, some of which may have come from Anatolia. Traces of these differences can still be seen as differing nuances within the more uniform styles of Late Bronze Age workshops.[66]

After this the centre of gravity moves away to the north. The coordinated patterns of Hajdusámson–Apa progressively disintegrate into isolated geometric motifs: concentric circle and half-circle, like the breakdown of the flowing, plastic, curvilinear Otomani pottery into the disconnected blobs and bosses of a later style.[67] Of the second style little survives beyond the concentric circle and perhaps an occasional use of compasses, and only a very few of the second-millennium 'emblems' turn up in the first millennium in different techniques. It is much harder to find an explanation for the reappearance, in Scandinavia some centuries later, of something very like the first style, than it is to understand its disappearance from the middle Danube. The tendrils or branches of spirals, the multiple line with dotted fringe, the minutely fine tracing are all so like that an explanation must be attempted (cf. Plate 198 and Figures 72 and 73).[68]

The pattern of teaching and learning, imitating and rejecting is a very complicated one, and the first moves may have been made long before this Central and East European style came to life again on the Baltic. The transference, if such it was, certainly did not happen all at once; there was no single trek of craftsmen or setting off of convoys down the Oder and its tributaries. Demand arose and was fostered (as today) through the introduction of samples either by capture, gift, or barter. Some of these samples, swords and ornaments from southern workshops, have been found (Plate 178). The flat wide blade with an abrupt narrow mid-rib is the same at Stensgård and Torupgårde in Denmark as on Plate 171 from Hajdusámson and on one of the Apa swords, but the spiral is absent; it probably had not acquired any significance for these new patrons. That the Oder was more used than the Elbe is borne out by the distribution of the imports.[69] This easterly route had brought the scant metal of the third millennium up from the south-east, but the eclipse of metallurgy there and the new conditions of the second millennium made a fresh start necessary in the north as well as in South-East Europe. Flat axes for use, neckrings for prestige, and small knives came from Bohemia, southern Germany, and the western Alps, and even the precocious but essentially conservative British workshops sent lunulae of Irish gold and their own flat axes; but none of this led to a native northern metallurgy. Without raw supplies of their own and still without the proper organization for exchange and trade, northern flint-knappers made copies of bronze weapons that are in their way *tours de force*. A dagger from Hindsgavl is one of the finest flint objects ever worked (Plate 181). By a reversal of the usual operation of the skeuomorph, the now almost superseded flint imitates the natural splay of a bronze haft, and polished stone axes have the dorsal casting-seam of a metal prototype.

The first northern workshops were established probably by craftsmen from south of the Erzgebirge soon after the importation of those magnificent 'samples', the swords from Torupgårde and Stensgård, perhaps in the early fourteenth century. Among their first products were the heavy cast axes called after Fårdrup (Plate 179), which are in fact simplified copies of Hungarian and Transylvanian axes like those on Plate 174 and Figure 68B. But here too the curvilinear decoration has been replaced by simple rectilinear motifs; however, the source of inspiration is not in doubt, and the punched line on the axe on Plate 179 is like that of the Bellye bracelet (Plate 175). A bronze 'scimitar' from Rørby in Denmark also probably came from one of the earliest northern workshops, even if it owes something ultimately to Asia, for on one side of the blade a representation of a typical northern double-ended boat with a ram has been drawn with the tracer.[70] The rest of the decoration is geometric rectilinear (Plate 180).

When the northern workshops did adopt the spiral it was in a tight geometric form that limited the designs, but technically the execution was brilliant and could only come from an extremely disciplined and professional workshop. The bronze ornament from Langstrup (Plate 182) was worn by a woman on the front of the belt, and the spirals were drawn freehand with the tracer. The artist who designed the axe from Brondsted (Plate 183) with the buoyant expanding blade had less need to rely on the tracer – the carving of the mould ensured a beautiful casting – but this is a later development.[71]

The Riches of the North

The immense treasure accumulated in the north in the course of a comparatively short time from the mid fourteenth century to about 1200 needs explaining. It owes much, but not everything, to two factors controlling survival: the rite of single burial under a barrow and the practice of a religion in which offerings were exposed in wild and boggy land, to the gods of lakes and meres. The lines of round barrows, steeper and higher than we are used to in England, that stand humped along the skyline in Jutland and Seeland cover hollowed tree-trunk coffins or stone cists, where, in place of the disorder of a freshly opened passage-grave with human bones and broken pots higgledy-piggledy, all is found composed and seemly. The body is stretched out as it was buried, wearing cloak and kilt, or if a woman a shift, with weapons or bangles. The warrior's gear and the heavy ornaments of the women are ideally typical of the heroic world, where wealth is worn on the body, and surrendered with the body to the grave. The rite inherited from those 'battle-axe' and 'single-grave' invaders referred to earlier is a plainer counterpart of the royal tombs of Asiatic dynasts.

The other repository of extraordinary wealth is the peat bogs, that from time to time give up, singly and in heaps, weapons, drinking-vessels of gold and bronze, and idols of bronze and wood. From peat bogs come the two most precious prehistoric treasures that Denmark owns, the Trundholm 'sun-car' and the Gundestrup great silver bowl or cauldron. This was also how the Langstrup disc was found and the Torupgårde and Stensgård swords (Plate 178), which last were certainly not plain weapons for slicing heads and arms but a part of ceremonial. Many of the swords that have been found singly in peat were thrown into the water singly, perhaps like the most famous of them all to be caught by 'an arm and a hand' that shook, brandished, and then vanished under the water. It is the continuation of an observance begun by Upper Paleolithic hunters when they flung the weighted bodies of reindeer into the water and stood the heads up on posts. The dedicated wealth, accessible, exposed, and notorious, was never touched by the living, but it made of certain wild places 'Ferne halwes', a goal of pilgrimage and 'Domschatz' combined.

Engravings on rocks, which were still part of the northern traditional arts, corroborate the evidence of graves and bogs that axe, spear, boat, and wheel were reverenced, also probably horse and serpent. Of these only the last has earth roots; otherwise there is little to show the tie of locality which was so strong in the house-shrines of Neolithic cultivators in South-East Europe and in the temple-tombs of western stone builders. Boats, wheels, and sun-discs are made to travel, yet fetters of locality held man to the inland waters. Where now we see sour peat and heath there were then meres, inlets, and pools, some of which must have been regarded as outposts of the other world inhabited by spirits who demanded tribute and gifts. The uncanny atmosphere of this landscape lived on long enough in the imagination of the people to enter the lays and epics of the Early Middle Ages. When Beowulf fought the 'Merewif' at the bottom of the dark pool, there were ancient swords, 'the work of giants' (that is of unknown or foreign manufacture), and an awful light glimmering; and from the sinister waters of Tarn Wathelyne, now a Lancashire field, rose the grisly ghost of a dead queen to rebuke the pride and glory of the world.

The bogs are wonderful preservers, saving the fibre of skirts, woven tunics, and cloaks – even the flesh and flaxen hair of a young girl or the unspoiled features of an old man; but before pollen analysis had become a science by means of which changes in climate could be given values in centuries, votive finds were hard to date. Unfortunately the horse with 'sun-disc' found in 1902 at Trundholm near Nykøbing comes from that time (Plates 185 and 186). I have already described briefly the *cire perdue* method by which the horse was cast (p. 160 above). No comparable casting is known till much later, and even then they are rare (Plate 219 is one of the few), but the *cire perdue* technique itself was used more, and perhaps earlier, in Scandinavia than in Central Europe.[72] Discs alone, without horses, are not so rare in Scandinavia and even in Britain, but there is only one other find of horses.

Bronze discs, two cast separately round a clay core, form the centre of the Trundholm 'sun'. A bronze ring was placed like a hoop round them and cast on, the pattern was traced on the bronze, and finally a thin sheet of gold pressed into one side, taking the impression. This pattern is not the same on both sides. The gold face has an extra outer zone which perhaps represents rays; and where on the bronze face the middle zone has pairs of true spirals within a series of loops, the golden has pairs of concentric circles that are both linked and held apart by loops which, instead of flowing in one direction, progress like the steps of a dance, twice forward and once back. The loops probably come from the pulley-pattern, and, if the fixed circles are removed, we get a motif that was often used in the Late Bronze Age (Plate 197 and Figure 69B). It is a subtle and harmonious design, and it may not be due to chance that terms belonging to music and the dance come to mind; circling and spiralling movements were more natural to people used to the ring-dances which we see portrayed on earthenware and bronze than they are to us, who are forgetful of the formal continuities of dance and ritual.[73]

Reins once ran from the horse's throat to a point on the disc higher than the tail stump (the position of the loop in the photograph is wrong). The four-spoked wheel must have come from Czechoslovakia or the middle Danube, where so many clay ones were found. The arrangement, two under the disc and four under the horse, tells us nothing about carts except that the theory of a wheel revolving on an axle was understood. We know from slightly later representations on rocks and on small metal gear that in the north the sun does not travel across the heavens in a cart or chariot, but as a disc or single wheel drawn by an animal or bird, or else both travel in a boat or run by themselves. Like the wheels of the Dupljaja scene, the purpose of these was to move horse and sun through their appointed places in the performance of the ritual. Examination has proved that only one face of the disc was ever gold; the other always showed the duller metal. It is supposed therefore that people and priest (we can now reasonably use that term rather than shaman or wise man) stood facing south for the sun's ceremonial. Facing the meridian they would see the small gold image moving in glory from east to west like the real sun; but if at sunset the carriage was turned about, the journey back was made by the bronze face, darker, duller, and so representing the invisible sun at night.[74] If this reading is correct, we have an insight into ancient observances and the use of images where human hands moved the symbols of the great powers enacting the drama of day and night.

I have called the disc the sun from the start, for so it is usually described, and this is surely right; but the horse too is no ordinary animal, as can be seen very well from the patterns worked on the surface of the neck and head (Figure 69A). It is a simplified, three-dimensional animal and a symbol of something other than the individual slave or servant of man. The punched and incised pattern is of Danubian origin (though adopted in the north), as a comparison of Figure 69A and Plate 167 shows. The very limited vocabulary is the same on the horse and on the Kličevac god: concentric circles,

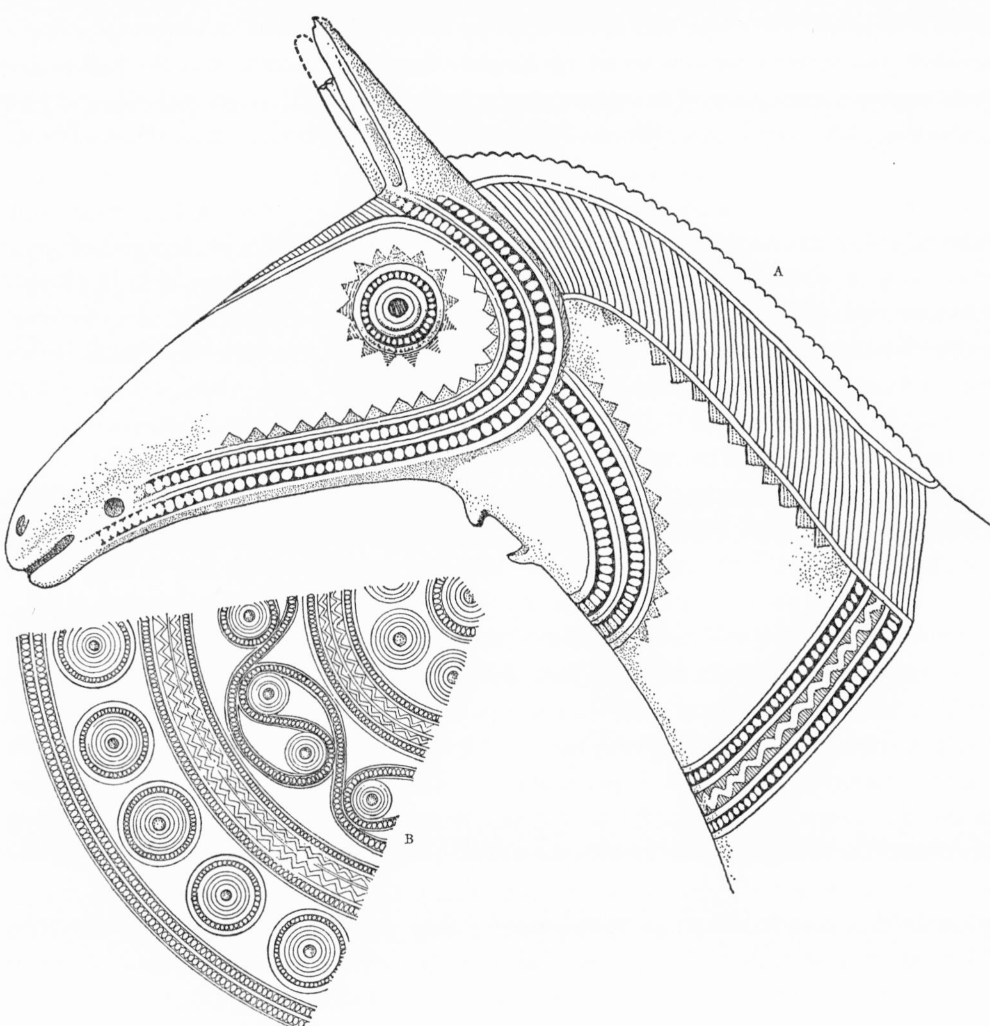

Figure 69. A Head of the Trundholm horse, Denmark, from an old drawing showing incised ornament and punched zigzag band
B The Trundholm disc, gold face without the outermost 'rays'

hatching, zigzags, and a border of triangles. The Tageborg horses in Skåne had inset amber eyes, and the Trundholm eyes are represented as stars or suns like the suns on the throat and shoulder of the god, for which reason the other patterns are unlikely to represent mere harness. As far as the difference in material allows, the same language is spoken by both. Without going so far as to claim that the Trundholm scene was made not far from the Danube, I believe that the workmen who made it had learnt their craft in one of the Central European workshops. According to the latest study of Trundholm, it comes from the end of the thirteenth century, which may also be the date of Dupljaja and Kličevac, though they could be rather earlier.

Before leaving Scandinavia for a time, the great tomb at Kivik, Bredarör, in Skåne must be described. This is a megalithic long cist under a mound on the wall slabs of which there are drawings that have nothing at all to do with western megalithic scribbles, but which are a mixture of Bronze Age sophistication and the indigenous northern rock engraving. The subject matter, within the limits of its execution, is very interesting. The site is on a little rise looking east over Hanö bay, close to a small harbour. The surviving mound has a diameter of 250 feet (75 m.) and the reconstructed chamber, 13 feet by 3 (4 m. by 1 m.), had eight stones, six of which still have carvings. The original order of the stones is not known and one is lost.[75] The old method of pecking was used, and the work is very shallow. The subjects are arranged in horizontal registers with a predilection for symmetry. The 'lost' stone, according to a drawing, had antithetical hafted axes with wide flamboyant blades as on Plate 183. On the other stones there are doube-ended northern boats, antithetical horses, zigzags, four-spoked wheels, more axes (unhafted), and wheels. But it is with the last two stones on the left, numbers 8 and 8a, that the human climax is reached (Plates 187 and 188).

At the top of 8 is a chariot and a charioteer who stands upright holding the reins and wears a sword; in front of him and moving in the same direction are four men with swords. Below are antithetical animals, horses or possibly boars, and to their left a spiny, fish-tailed creature and another quadruped. In the bottom register there is a procession of eight long-robed figures, women or priests, their arms held in the same constrained gesture, down and away from the body. They follow a single man with arms raised. The last carved stone is much restored. At the top and half obliterated is an emblem which the early drawing shows to have been not unlike the winged disc of Hittite monuments. Below is a procession of four men, the two in the rear blowing horns, no doubt the northern lurer. In front are a man with an axe and the leader with arms raised as though clapping. All approach an irregular enclosure in which stand two men on either side of a post or stem from which hang a pair of large round objects, possibly drums or fruits of the sacred tree (as they would be interpreted in the Near East). Eight long-robed figures appear again in the middle register, grouped on either side of a large anvil or horned altar, tub, or possibly coffin. In the lowest register two omega-shaped enclosures are approached by four men, one of whom blows a horn.

Compared with contemporary gold- and bronze-work, the artistic level is not very high, but neither is it naïve or tentative. These roughly rectangular stones are the nearest we have yet come to a panel picture, but the space within the frame is divided horizontally as in Egyptian and Near Eastern mural art, and on bronze situlae: the great symbols of the gods on one hand and the ceremonial on the other (see below, p. 224). This is very different from the seemingly haphazard Scandinavian rock-carvings, even though surrounded like a palisade by ancient and invisible boundaries dividing the sacred from the profane surface.

Kivik is probably the earliest representation of a chariot north of the Alps, and it is the best. Various conventions were used on the Swedish rocks, the animals rendered diagrammatically back to back or facing either side of the pole (Figure 74B), whereas here they simply conform to that rule which dictates that one object should not screen another. The reins may not pass in front of the horses' bodies but sail over their heads, and for the same reason horses and wheels are set one above the other. There is no communication through physiognomy or expression such as the Spanish painters and East European modellers had mastered. The language used is that of expressive gesture alone, and it says all that is needed. It is a language we have almost lost, and the inhibited movements of everyday life are reflected in our arts today. In order that the gesture should have unimpeded play, 'mimes' wear masks or conventional make-up to obliterate expression and formalize physiognomy. Kivik has preserved for us traditional gestures which, arising from sacred dance and chorus, had grown into something more stately and hieratic.

The usual interpretation, and probably the correct one, is that these scenes and objects belong to the solemn interment of the dead like the scenes painted round a Dipylon memorial vase. The charioteer may be the dead man himself, the long-robed hooded figures mourners and officiants; the men are the dancers and musicians whose part is so important in ceremonial. The omega-shaped enclosures and the circle may be the sacred enclosure of the god, or perhaps of the tomb itself before it was covered by the barrow, and there is the boat of the dead or the war canoe of the living chieftain. Most of this is already familiar in the ceremonial of the ancient pagan world without limitation of time or place; but in almost parallel detail it is depicted on the Hagia Triadha sarcophagus, where scenes painted round the outside show the funeral rites of a dead Cretan of the fourteenth century, or perhaps the dues rendered to his deified spirit. Processions, players, dancers, axes, boats, two-wheeled chariots are all there and, strangely alike, the priestess with arms held stiffly towards the altar.[76] Even if these are bare coincidences, this kind of portrayal and these subjects have taken us clean out of the world of village wise man or tribal shaman into that of professional priest and craftsman at a time when ceremonials may have been valid across many frontiers.

The dead man buried here was a great chieftain or sea-captain. There is nothing else like Kivik, but Kivik is a little later than Trundholm and belongs already to the time of raids and wars that brought the Bronze Age civilizations of the Eastern Mediterranean to an end in the twelfth century. There is ample evidence of contact between the Baltic and the Mediterranean in the centuries before 1200.[77] It needed only a little of the Viking spirit to launch the war canoes and carry them down the great rivers to the Black Sea, or through the Balkans, where adventurous younger sons or exiled chiefs could join one of the war bands of raiders who were swarming over the Aegean and Asia Minor. Some returned (see Chapter 7 below), though whether so far as the Baltic must remain an alluring possibility. If admitted, the imitation of southern ways and southern grandeur is easy to understand.

Stonehenge and Irish Gold

While metallurgical arts were experimented with and the foundation of great workshops established in Central, Eastern, and (rather later) Northern Europe, metallurgy in the west remained for most of the second millennium technically conservative with a very limited repertoire of patterns, and the same is true of the West Mediterranean. In Ireland the horizon of the native goldsmith was confined to hammering and to punched and traced decoration, howbeit of consummate delicacy (Plate 170). Bronzesmiths were far less adept with moulds and complex castings than their contemporaries on the Continent. But they were not left indefinitely to their own devices. Even if the gold came from near-by Wicklow, the craftsmen who made the Gleninsheen 'gorget' worked in a foreign workshop tradition. But though Plate 184 is very like a cast Danish bronze gorget (apart from the terminals), it was beaten from an ingot, and so technically it is closer to the gold bowls of a different tradition (see p. 193 below); it is also far later. Some time after 800 compasses were adopted, it is not certain from where, and used on paper-thin gold sheet.[78]

Western metallurgy was conservative, and potting, with the exception of the bell-beaker, poor in quality, heavy, and over-decorated in a coarse style; but it is quite otherwise with masons' work. The megalithic tradition of tomb building continued in pockets,[79] but there are signs that temple and tomb are separating and that the former may now stand in its own right, an architectural monument for living men. A number of wood and stone circles were raised by Late Neolithic and 'Beaker' people, among them the largest of all, Avebury, and the most famous, Stonehenge, in its earlier (second or Prescelly) phase. These are hardly architecture any more than the stone avenues of Brittany, Wessex, and other Atlantic provinces.

The sarsen circle and horseshoe at Stonehenge are quite another matter; and just as Maes Howe is unique among tombs, this is unique among circles (Plate 189 and Figure 70). The date is probably early to middle second millennium, and the authors were undoubtedly the chieftains of the Wessex culture whose round barrows, scattered over Salisbury Plain, remind one of the tall barrows of Jutland. Long before this third phase there was a Neolithic bank and ditch, post-holes for a wooden structure in the entrance, a circle of pits and a cremation cemetery, and perhaps three standing stones (Stonehenge I).[80] In the second phase stones of spotted dolerite were brought from the Prescelly mountains in Pembroke and erected in a double circle within the older bank and ditch. The latter was partly filled in, the wooden structures dismantled, and the avenue, a long ditched and banked processional way leading to the river Avon, was constructed. To bring the bluestones from South Wales was an extraordinary feat, but apart from this none of the earlier work is unique in the British Neolithic. There are other avenues, including the much more impressive one at Avebury, and other stone circles. It is with the third phase that the difference comes. The bluestone circle was dismantled and the sarsens brought twenty-four miles from the Marlborough Downs, dressed, and set up in the middle of the Neolithic circle, though not with exactly the same centre. Later the bluestones were dressed and set up, dismantled and re-erected in the present circle and horseshoe to echo in small the plan of the sarsens.

Just as the smiths of Eastern Europe, as time passed, refined their techniques, so the masons of Stonehenge made use of refinements unthought of by the older megalithic tomb-builders: dressing the stones over their whole surface, polishing much larger surfaces than had been done anywhere in Western Europe before, fixing the lintels with mortice and tenon, and causing the uprights to taper towards the top with a slight convexity, and the sides of lintels to incline inwards towards the bottom for purely visual ends. The lintels of the trilithons are up to six inches wider at the top than at the bottom, making them appear vertical to the eye, and in addition all the lintels are curved on both sides, the curvature of the outer being the more pronounced.

The prehistorians most closely concerned with recent work at Stonehenge boldly claim for Stonehenge III the benefit of superior skills and techniques drawn directly from the Aegean, that is to say from Mycenae. The case is persuasively argued, but for

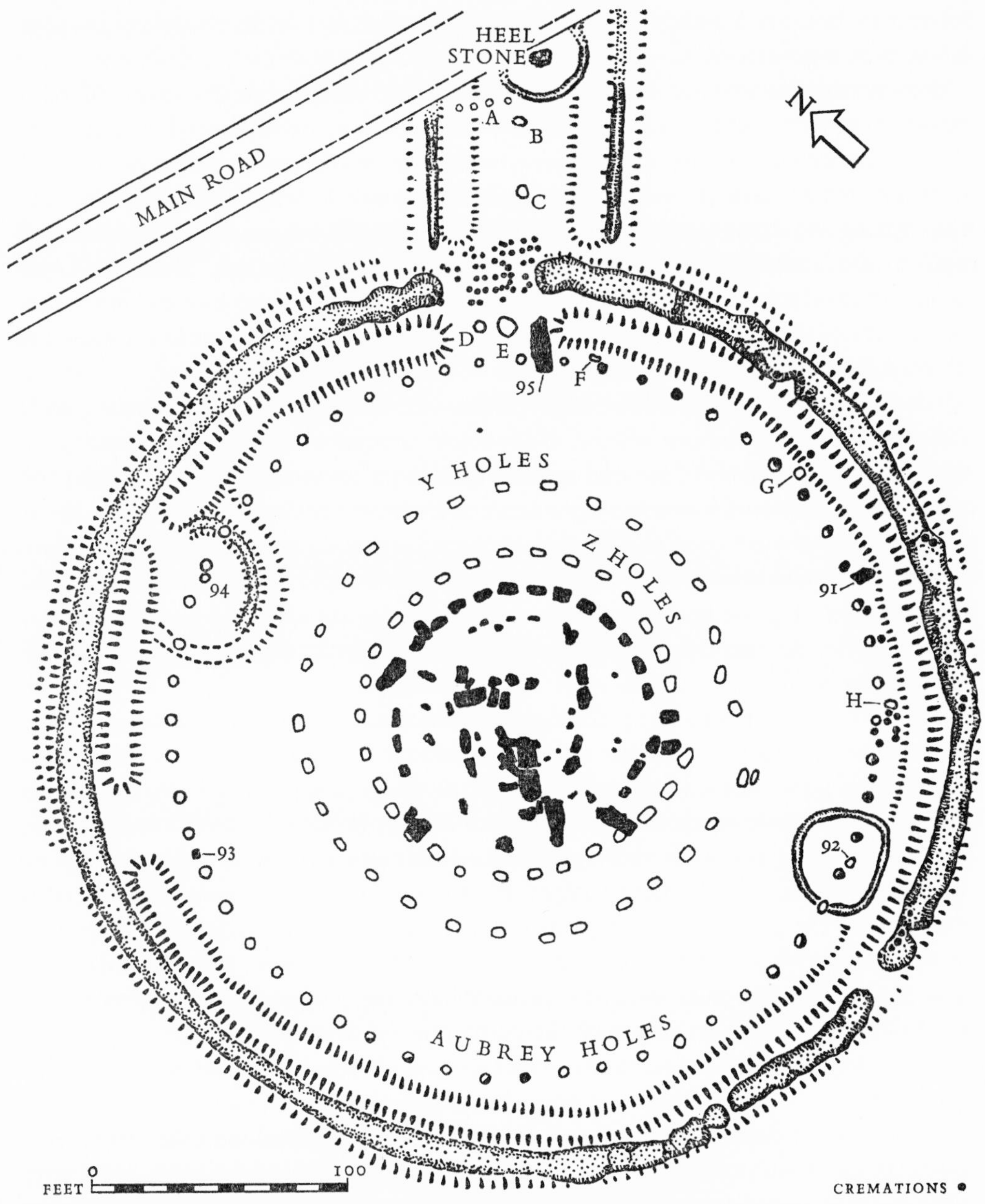

Figure 70. Plan of Stonehenge, Wiltshire

a moment I would like to suppose that this was not so and to ask how much we could claim as native West European. Tenon and mortice and the beam-like lintels of circle and trilithon are borrowed from carpentry, and the long history of wooden buildings in Neolithic and 'Beaker' Britain, the cemeteries of the Lower Rhine, the unroofed wooden circles like Arminghall in Norfolk, and Woodhenge (which may in fact have had a roof and therefore lintels) provide a respectable ancestry on one side. On the other side undoubtedly lay the dream of grandeur in which weight and size were ends in themselves, the ability to organize immense gangs of workers and the techniques of manipulating very large stones, all of which belonged to the megalithic tomb-builders. The obsession with size that had driven two hundred able-bodied men to move a fifty-ton capstone on to the support of a Neolithic burial chamber, or a hundred men to work three years on the Avebury ditch, were gratified by new but not absolutely dissimilar feats. The largest stone at Stonehenge weighs fifty tons, no more than the capstone of a chamber tomb; but it is estimated that it would tave taken 1,100 men five and a half years to move all the sarsens, one at a time, from the Marlborough Downs to Stonehenge, while fifty masons working ten hours a day, seven days a week would have taken two and three quarter years to remove three million cubic inches of stone in the process of dressing, and there was also construction of special engines for raising the stones and handling them throughout all the stages of this extraordinary work. Even so, it is still a difference in degree and not in kind. If Neolithic engineers could lay out a triangle on the Pythagorean principle, the builders of Stonehenge had only advanced another step when they set out and bisected a right angle in order to obtain the centre of the circle. The levelling of the tops of the lintels is so accurate that some instrument, water-level or plumb-line and square,was evidently used, and such could have been already among the carpenter's regular tools. Far more difficult to account for is the understanding of entasis. This is the point that more than all others led archaeologists to fall back on the Mycenaean builder.

The men of Wessex in the mid second millennium, it is argued, could not unaided have accomplished all this. They were, by western standards, rich, but they had no resources of their own, no ores and apparently little agriculture. They enjoyed pastoral independence, cattle-ranching and sometimes acting profitably as middlemen between the ore-producing regions farther west and the Continent. Even so they do not make any very great showing beside their Central European and Nordic contemporaries. What they did have was a sacred site of great antiquity and powerful associations. Stonehenge must have been holy for over a thousand years when the sarsens were erected; it was holy long before the bluestones were brought expressly to *this* place from what was no doubt a sacred mountain and seat of the gods in the far west.[81] The first bluestone circle was set up on solar principles, so that when the axis of symmetry of the sarsen structure was aligned on the midsummer sunrise this was in accordance with ancient inherited wisdom: the wisdom of an agricultural people; for it is the men who sow who need a calendar and whose curiosity is led to number the days of the solar year. Stonehenge with its midsummer axis is a magnificent instrument for this purpose, but a couple of stout stakes driven into the earth in open country would serve equally well and leave no trace behind, besides which the Wessex culture was more pastoral than agricultural. Very ambitious claims have been made recently for the astronomical competence of the Neolithic designers of Stonehenge and for its use to predict winter and summer solstices and eclipses through a three-hundred-year cycle. These subtleties, though mathematically plausible, are historically quite implausible, especially when account is taken of the fact that the Greeks were not able to calculate the summer solstice correctly to within a day until 432 B.C.[82]

The calendar means more to a primitive society than observance of the correct days for reaping and sowing. It embodies the principle of stability and order, the support of cosmos in the face of chaos; and so it it was treated in the great civilizations of Sumer and Egypt, where the sun is the law-giver who sees everything. Even if the men of Wessex were less occupied with cultivation than their precedessors, the very fact to which Stonehenge is the chief witness, the immense capacity for organizing men to act together, shows the value set on those qualities. Stonehenge is certainly the fruit of mixed traditions: the refined skill of the carpenter building with large timbers, and the tenacity and *folie de grandeur* of the megalithic mason; whether yet a third and more sophisticated mind from one of the old civilized centres was also needed is I think an open question.[83] The absence from the British Isles of any curvilinear ornament on metal-work, apart from the circle, argues against direct contact with the Aegean, where curvilinear styles were paramount.[84] The next development in western ornament was an adaptation of the Continental boss-style, first used by gold- and later by bronze-smiths. Curvilinear ornament only reached Britain, with the shock of revelation, with Celtic art in the later first millennium. The fact remains that, whether a wanderer from the Aegean or a Wessex man, there was someone on Salisbury Plain around 1500 B.C. whose aesthetic faculties were so developed that he required that an upright should *look* straight rather than *be* straight and knew how to make it so.

CHAPTER 7

FERMENT AND NEW BEGINNINGS: 1200–500

One with the plough's blade or the keel of the ship,
we were searching to find the first seed
that the ancient drama might begin again.

When we awoke we journeyed towards the north, strangers
plunged into mists by the spotless wings of swans that wounded us.
On winter nights the strong wind from the east maddened us,
In the summers we were lost in the agony of the day which could not die.

G. Seferis; translation Keeley-Sherrard

A NEW and more convincing picture of the East Mediterranean at the moment of collapse of the Hittite and Mycenaean worlds is beginning to emerge.[1] During the later thirteenth century the men of mainland Greece and the islands were bound into a very loose 'empire' under the ruler who lived at Mycenae; but they were already quarrelling among themselves, and, like Romans, Byzantines, and Turks after them, they employed northern mercenaries in their little wars. Some of these adventurers introduced a new weapon, a terrible long slashing sword, strictly utilitarian now and very different from the rich ornamental weapons that an earlier generation had carried in life and worn in death. They seem to have taken advantage of their position to spy out the wealth and weakness of the princes who employed them, and to have carried home reports of the technical wonders of southern workshops along with some of the actual products: a corselet of beaten bronze, and a cup won from an enemy or given by a friend. This was remembered, and a generation or so later (perhaps less) they returned, not as poor men looking for employment but as well-armed enemies to plunder and destroy.

One brief terrifying raid would have been enough to devastate the Mycenaean order, already weakened and menaced from within and from the Asiatic side;[2] for our northern raiders were only one of many bands who at this time were overrunning Western Asia. They were part of a much larger movement with eastern prongs that need not concern us, though one of them destroyed the Hittite power in Anatolia. There is some evidence also of crop failures and famine in the eastern Mediterranean. This is the story as it is usually told; what is new is the recognition of depopulation in central and mainland Greece implying an overland attack that hardly touched the islands nor even the east and west seaboards. Men came down from the mountains plundering and destroying, but they went no farther, they left no gear – only a depopulated land from which the inhabitants had fled in their boats. Some went to the near-by islands, but others to Cyprus, Palestine, and Egypt, where a firm date for these events is given by the defeat of the great land and sea raids by Rameses III in 1191, described in inscriptions and pictured on the walls of Medinet Habu. Some may even have reached Sicily and Sardinia (see below). But the raiders returned north with their loot and their prisoners, among whom were bronze- and goldsmiths and probably wheelwrights. Back on the Danube and in the Carpathians they set them to work forging and hammering, while the bulky loot which they had carried off provided many and better patterns. In this way a new metallurgy was born or transplanted, the boss or beaten style, which was to have, for many centuries, a dominating position in Central Europe and far beyond, while the old, slow, delicate work of casting and drawing with tracer and punch went out of fashion. Bossed and hammered sheet-work had been produced by goldsmiths for centuries. Perhaps they found it more economical of their costly material than heavy castings; but it is a long step from such simple objects as the Cófalva and Ostravul Mare discs (Figure 68D) to the advanced forging of the twelfth and following centuries (Plate 192). Sudden and devastating raids and the carrying off of craftsmen were common in Western Asia, though comparatively new to Europe, but this interpretation seems best to meet the existing evidence.

There were many causes of change: social, climatic, religious, as well as the sharp stimulus of emulation following that brief sweet taste of an outgoing Aegean civilization. There was shifting of tribes, discovery of new sources of mineral wealth and improved methods of exploiting them, and most of all perhaps the speeding up and widening of contacts through improved communications. So the introduction of iron-working was one among many causes of change, a late-comer and not the most important.[3] In these centuries between 1200 and 500 Europe begins to take on a more familiar conformation. The tribal groups later known as Illyrians, Celts, and Germans were already there, and by the end of this time were occupying respectively those south-eastern, central, and northern regions from which they make their first historical appearance. Population was certainly growing, and the bulk of the people were agricultural and to some extent tied to the land. They buried their dead in huge cemeteries using the cremation rite, but concentrations of richer burials, often under barrows, in Bohemia, Württemberg, and Bavaria begin to look very like tribal capitals. Already in the twelfth century there were a few exceptionally grand graves in which a chief lay surrounded by parts of the funeral cortège – the harness and the wagon, or fine bronze cups and bowls from the last feast. This still seems to reflect southern ideas of grandeur rather than an invasion from the east, for even wagon burial had reached the Aegean before the end of the Mycenaean civilization. The shift westward of groups of very grand burials possibly reflects a shift in more advanced tribal organization as well as in the intenser exploitation of land. It is even possible that the grape was introduced.[4] The appetite of Central European chieftains for weapons and table-ware (including wine-strainers), chariots and bangles like those of the southern nobility certainly gave a great push to the mining and prospecting industry.

The circumstances that had led to the grand burials of the twelfth to eleventh centuries did not persist – there are few in the centuries immediately following – but the size of urnfields continued to grow; then came a partial return to small barrows, and in the sixth century to inhumation as well, with some of the largest and richest of all the chieftains' graves in which we may see the culmination of the heroic society whose beginning it was possible to detect a thousand years before on the Hungarian plain and in the foothills of the Carpathians.

The Northern Arts

Although the northern tribes round the Baltic were always ready to import and use the fine products of Central European workshops, they were also evolving their own highly individual sequel to the Hungaro-Transylvanian linear style of some centuries earlier. The older Central European craftsmen were brilliant masters of casting and tracer-work, but, when the new fashion of sheet-working, hammering, and riveting with bossed ornament was established, their occupation was gone. Brutal as were the new techniques compared to the refinements of draughtsmanship and modelling, the new range of goods – cups, bowls, and buckets – and the technique of raising and sinking, to which was added in due course spinning (see p. 162 above), demanded a highly specialized knowledge and the same long craftsman's memory within his tradition. Moreover, this sort of ornament gave variations of texture and colour impossible to obtain by the alternative techniques (Plates 190–2). These arts are no more likely to have evolved independently in Central Europe than casting or smelting many centuries before. The use of bronze table- and kitchen-ware was customary in the palaces of Minoan, Mycenaean, and Asiatic princes, and to them and to the break-up of their world we owe the rise of the new European industry.

What happened then to the Transylvanian and Carpathian workshop style and its masters? I believe that they were not exterminated, nor converted (though a few may have been), but that they migrated, following earlier generations who had found employment on the Baltic among the wealthy and warlike tribes whose swords and other military gear made a dazzling display in the thirteenth century (Second Northern Period or IIbc). This migration probably took place in the first half of the twelfth century, but it is still another two hundred years before a free curvilinear style comes to ripeness in the later Period IV and in V (between 1000 and 700).[5] At the same time in the twelfth century other craftsmen may have moved west into Switzerland and beyond, where heavily incised bronze-work had a short vogue, but compared to the northern work it was poor, with the usual marks of a disintegrating style: meaningless repetitions, fragmentation, and dislocated designs. Only in parts of Yugoslavia, especially on the Glasinac plateau, a fine linear style with the whole spiraliform repertoire remained valid and vital and, unlike the north, abstract (Plate 193).[6]

There were other innovations in the north as well as those in metallurgy. Large cemeteries of flat cremation graves look like an extension of the same rite that had spread through Danubian lands, from Pannonia to Transylvania, during the middle centuries of the second millennium. There are important finds of objects on the southern frontiers of the old 'Nordic Province', where northmen met the inhabitants of the great plain, and a series of fortified settlements that can almost be called towns were in process of building and are better evidence for advances in civilization than the showy but unproductive grandeur of Nordic graves and bog sanctuaries.[7] From just this region of interaction something very important arises in the sixth and succeeding centuries (see below, p. 232). A few brooches, implying a change to the South German dress-style with shoulder-pins, had appeared before 1200, but now there are many more; also bronze razors in place of tweezers and ornamental 'belt-boxes' in place of the earlier disc ornaments. Danish archaeologists deny any change in population, but there may be some doubt on this score.[8] Without looking for a substantial invasion, it is possible that small groups of newcomers were sufficient to introduce a new religious atmosphere as well as new techniques in the specialized calling of smiths and armourers. Standards of competence and the press of competition in a fixed market naturally limit the number of centres at work on the production of luxury goods at any one time. If Mecklenburg flourishes, Seeland languishes.

For a short time at the end of Period II and in III (twelfth century), even in the Nordic Province a heavier sort of ornament with openwork patterns intended for coloured resins and other inlays was preferred; it gave relief and variety to the surfaces. The temporary disappearance of the linked spiral in favour of geometric concentric circles may be due less to the centrifugal tendency of the design than to the attraction and precision of a new machine: compasses. Any immigrants from the south that there may have been only added strength to the northern mastery of casting and casting-on, which can be seen perhaps at its finest in the lurs or trumpets. They are always found in pairs, each tuned to more or less the same pitch, and each pair is identical except that the sinuous twist goes in opposite directions. These facts show how they have been developed from the natural horn of large cattle, probably *bos primigenius*, where the great horns also curve upwards and inwards in three dimensions. They were cast in segments and then joined, using *cire perdue*, with core and chaplets (Plate 194). There are earlier and simpler horns from at least the tenth century, but the very long twisted ones from Tellerup and Husby are ninth–eighth century (Period V).[9]

For the ceremonial use of lurs we have the evidence of rocks and grave-slabs (Plate 187 and Figure 78). The eclipse of the spiral was temporary, and in the early first millennium (Periods IV and V) it returns. But when this happens, it is already very different from the abstract decoration of Plates 173, 172, and 175. The spirals of Apa and Hajdusámson had, as we have seen, a freedom of growth that was organic rather than geometric. It is the same on the blade-space of razors in the north (Plate 196 and Figure 73); but something has happened to free them from the prohibition on representation, in Central Europe almost complete, so that now they sprout horse-heads, bird-boats, and human figures with axes or trumpets (Figures 72 and 81A). The northern smiths were rubbing shoulders with men used to a contrary and very ancient tradition which, though it had become stilted in its later days, had long ago given the powerful outline of the great elk at Landsverk (Plate 79). The rocks in Norway and Sweden were still carved, still numinous, still 'charged', but the subjects had changed from those that absorbed Mesolithic and Neolithic hunters. The designs traced on bronze knife- and razor-blades, diadems, and belt-boxes in the studio-smithy: the boats, armed men, dancers, and leaping figures have a rhythmic vitality very different from the stiff little figures of the Kivik slabs. The dynamic of the spiral has taken possession; whereas on the rocks the figures are still scattered haphazard, on the bronzes they are composed into scenes within, and dependent upon, a frame that limits both space and time (Plate 196 and Figures 71, A and C, and 72).

Another branch of northern art that appears first probably in the eighth century is that of cast bronze figures of animals and human or divine persons. They owe their existence to southern invention and a tradition of animal art that is quite different from the Geometric Hallstatt school, and leads back through the 'East Hallstatt' province to the Caucasus, eastern Anatolia, and Iran. But different as are the traditions behind them, the rock carvings, the incised and the cast bronzes, all to some extent speak the same iconographic language.

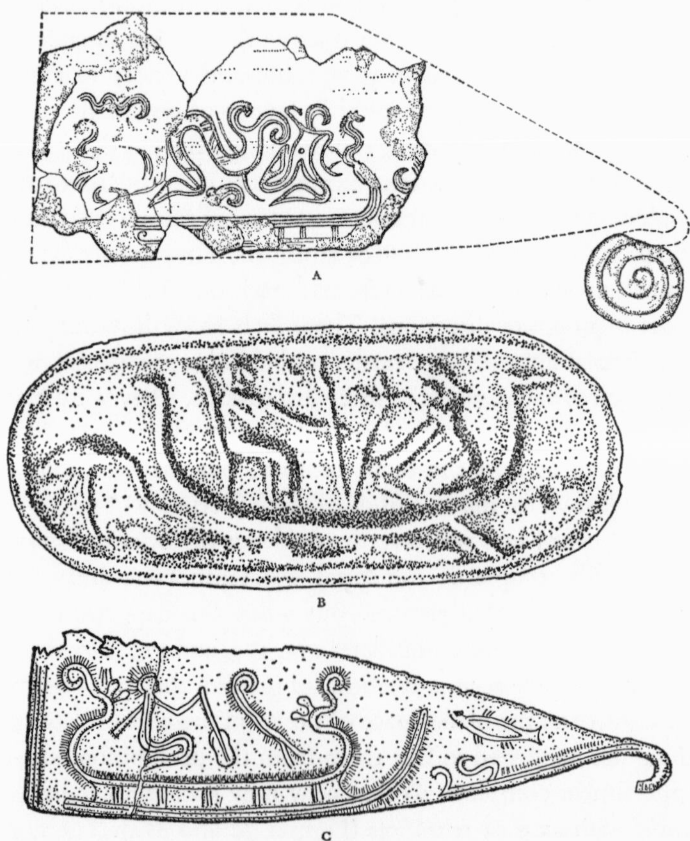

Figure 71. The 'Tableau on the Boat': A bronze razor from Borgdorf, Schleswig-Holstein, Germany
B Phoenician *hippos* on jewellery from Aliseda, Spain,
C bronze razor from near Bremen, Germany, all eighth to seventh century

'Razor Style' and the Tableau in the Boat

Of the three northern schools, that of the 'razor art' has the richest content and portrays a number of conventional scenes. The earlier razors (late twelfth or early eleventh century, Period III) are plain with an animal head, usually horse, for handle. The razor is itself boat-shaped, and the head stands for the animal prow of the contemporary northern war-canoe. These small blades were not mere charms, like the dangling jangling pendants worn by Etruscan and Hallstatt Iron Age Europeans, nor were they purely utilitarian. In primitive societies shaving and cutting of hair are acts involved in solemnity, and the role of the razors was perhaps closer to that of christening mugs, and their decoration to the small painted 'shrines' carried about on their persons by Early

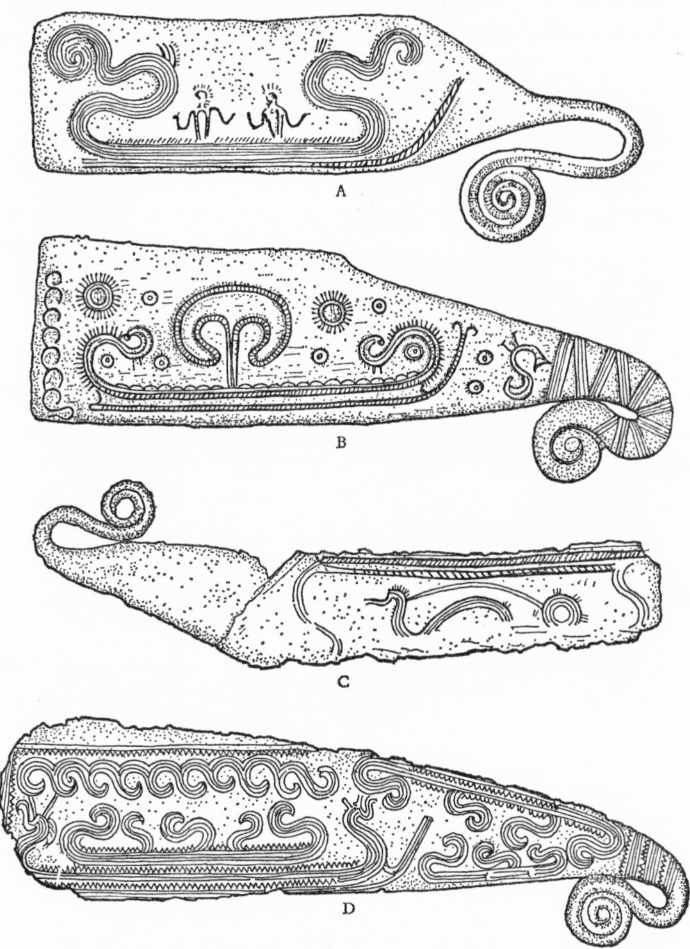

Figure 72. Figured razors: A from Voele, B from Honum, C from P. Ketting, Laaland, Denmark
D from Aurich, East Friesland, Holland, all Period V

Christians in the east: one man might have a Calvary and another a simple cross, and so the owner of Figure 71C carried with him a representation of the *dramatis personae* of a sacred scene, while another had a simple spiral or triskele. The plain razor with a horse-head handle from Darup (Plate 195, centre) is one of the earliest, and, though simplified, the modelling would be hard to better on so small a scale. It is less stylized than Trundholm (Plate 185), but later razor handles have lost the momentary touch of nature in favour of an elegant swan's-neck loop or a simple spiral or occasionally a wheel and, still natural, a human head (Plates 195, top, and 196).

The sacred tableaux are staged *on* a boat, or above it, or between two boats, and boats are the subject most often represented. Sometimes the incised picture-boat follows the outline and uses the three-dimensional prow of the razor-as-boat, or boat contains boat like a chinese puzzle (Figure 72D).[10] The boat itself before it writhes into fantasy looks workmanlike and seaworthy and is probably taken from the war-canoes with ram that would carry a leader and as many as possible of his band. The type goes back perhaps

Figure 73. Patterns based on spirals: A fourth-millennium painted Cucuteni pot from Traian, Rumania, B mid-second-millennium bronze axe from Apa, Rumania, C bronze 'belt-box', Denmark, D razor from Tolagården, Denmark, E from P. Vester Törslev, Randers, Denmark, C–E eighth–seventh century

three or four hundred years in the north, for it is the same that was incised on the Rørby scimitar (Plates 180 and 203). Sea and lake were potent in northern religious thought, as we know from the treasure in the bogs, but the sacred tableau in the boat had a place in most of the old religions. In Mesopotamia it stood for journeying gods and their gifts carried from one river city to another, and sometimes for the boat of the dead. In Egypt too it is the boat of the dead, but it also carried shrines, or it is the sun's boat. On Cretan gems of the second millennium the goddess and her bowery shrine float in an animal-prowed boat; practically the same scene is brought much nearer to Northern Europe on a Phoenician jewel found at Aliseda in Spain, where the boat is a 'hippos' with horse-heads at each end (Figure 71B), and in Greece it is Dionysos who brings the vine with flutes, serpents, ivy, and animal metamorphoses.[11] While the northern artists were incising these timeless tableaux, artists in Boeotia were engraving rather similar scenes on the catch-plates of safety-pins, and in their case we know that the subjects were taken from the great epics current or being composed at the time.[12]

Even when the horse- or bird-head of the northern boat has become a simple coil, ears or a crest betray its source (Plate 196 and Figure 74A). The animal-prowed boat was probably in the beginning thought of as self-propelling, itself a god, as in Mesopotamia. In the boat the sun must often be represented, and sometimes it is drawn behind its animal, as in the Trundholm group (Figure 72C). Horse, orb, and worm, fish and bird are all recognizable, with other signs not easy to interpret. The trinity – sun, bird, and pelta (palmette tree or axe, the third member is open to various interpretations) – come together more than once (Figure 72B).[13] A line of crested spirals may represent waves of the sea; but apart from a few direct representations, the meaning of the scenes and symbols is beyond our reach. Nevertheless in as far as they belong to a familiar genre, the guess will not be far wrong that sees them as cosmological transcriptions showing forth the great acts of gods and heroes.

Not all the decoration has even the tenuous link with representation that we see here; some contemporary northern artists were working in a strictly abstract idiom. The running spirals on the 'belt-box' from Stevneskov, Svendborg, Denmark (Plate 197) describe the same dancing figure that decorated the gold face of the Trundholm disc, but without the pivotal concentric circles (Figure 69B and p. 184 above). Elsewhere the human and the animal struggle to withstand the centripetal tug of the spiral. The animal that began as a quadruped with horse's head becomes by repetition a series of tumbling coils, a head at one end with ears and mane and somewhere below vestigial legs, as though the abstract attacks from the tail upwards, leaving the head longest to nature, like Daphne melting into the laurel (Plates 196 (Skivum) and 198). Or the figure is dislocated like the Scythian beasts, or the horse-head boat and sun-disc becomes a scrolled pattern while still keeping the functional 'ram' of the boat (Figures 72D and 73E). The daring with which motifs are manipulated, the liberties taken with nature, and the wiry strength and logic of the underlying pattern are a foretaste of Celtic and Dark Age ornament; and in this almost accidental way the northern dragon appears upon the scene independent alike of east and south (Plate 196 and Figure 71A).

The Carved Rocks

There are many Bronze Age rock-carvings in Sweden, some in Norway and Denmark, and on Bornholm. One important group in Skåne is in rich agricultural country close to the sea. Here at Simris and Järrestad the carvings overlook the shore from a hundred yards or so, and none are more than four miles from it. Smooth, flat, highly-polished rocks almost flush with the ground and tilted towards the sea were chosen. The carving is very shallow pecked into the surface. Boats are again the favourite subject, but there are also two-wheeled carts, axes, serpents, footprints (possibly later than the rest), and two larger figures, one ithyphallic supporting an immense hafted axe, the other horned and gesticulating. He appears to wear an animal's skin, and has much about him of the

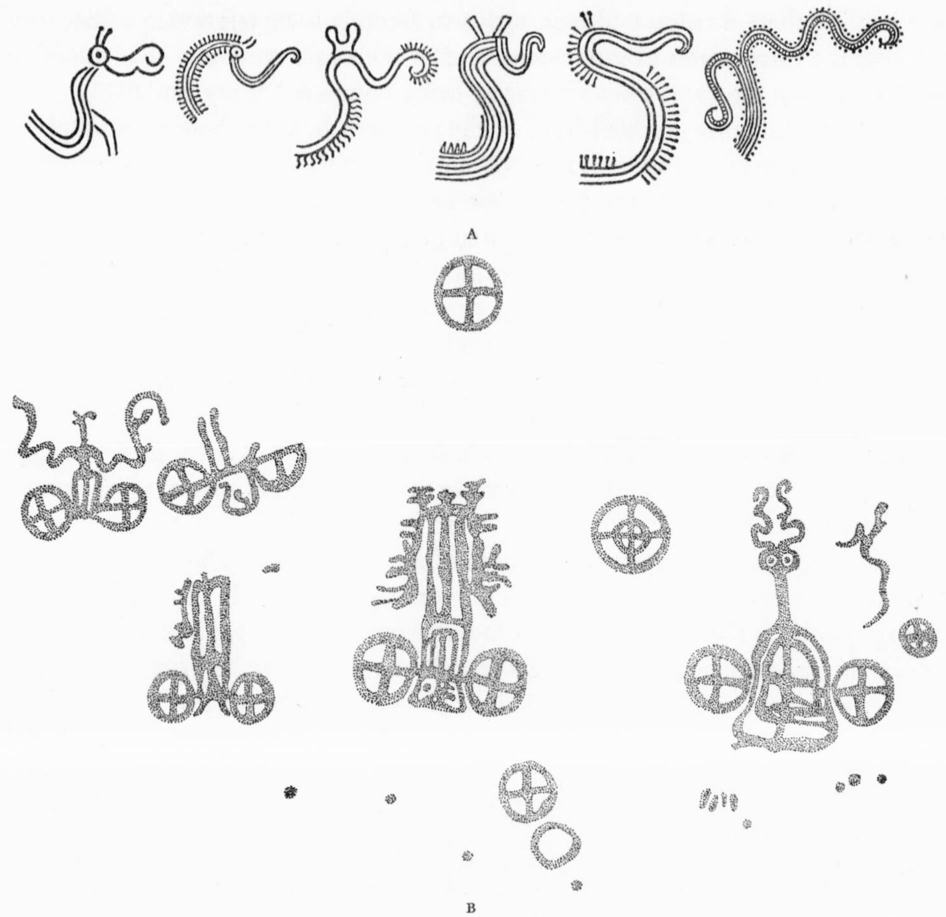

Figure 74. A Northern noses from elk and horse to dragon and spiral: bronzes from Vestrup, Denmark, Billeberga, Sweden, Bremen, Germany, Aurich, Holland, 'Denmark', and Maasbüll, Germany

B Carts or chariots pecked in the rock at Frännarp, South Sweden

shaman of older days (Plates 199 and 200 and Figure 74B).[14] The axe of Plate 199 has the same outline as that on Plate 183 from Brondsted.

Another group near Norrköping in Östergotland, on the east coast, has boats, weapons including (but only here) swords, and small animals in a style less schematic than elsewhere: goat, deer, pig, and strange long-necked cattle with yokes, or humps like the Asiatic zebu, and some antithetical pairs (Figure 75). Among the more schematized human figures some are grouped, and there is a procession with a captive giant. Other figures, alone or in pairs, support enormous weapons or spiral symbols. Ships too are ornamented with the ubiquitous spiral, as they probably were in reality.[15]

On the west coast in Bohuslän, between Göteborg and Oslo, there is a very large group, this time in poor forest country among barren rock and small cultivated clearings. The carvings are on rounded hummocky outcrops of granite, the surfaces often quite steep, so that site and landscape are entirely different from the other two groups. Settlements are unknown, but each group of carvings overlooks a little agricultural valley, and cairns found scattered along the coast are thought to be the burial-places of the farming and fishing communities who practised this art. The sea level has fallen even within the last thousand years, and the cairns must once have stood on offshore islands of the dead. Except for cup-marks, which account for 80 per cent of the whole, the favourite subject is again boats, but here they are more often manned by standing or

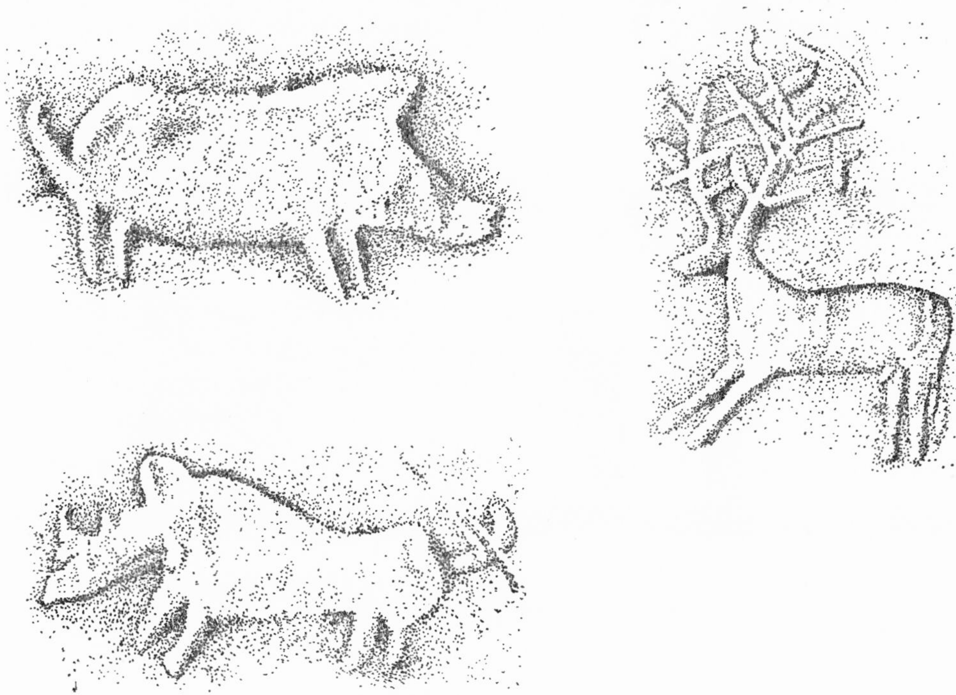

Figure 75. Rock-carvings at Norrköping, East Sweden

kneeling or horn-blowing figures much as we saw them on the razors (Plate 203 and Figure 80, B and D, and Figure 76B, near the boat). There are also oxen, more naturalistic elk and hunting scenes, and one of a man with a bow and arrow and pack of dogs. The figures vary much in size, and there is at least one very large man with a spear (Plate 204).

The Bohuslän style is different from the others, and there are subjects not found elsewhere. A general view of a rock at Fossum (Plate 201) shows the usual haphazard scatter of scenes: a man with a long spear stabs an animal, perhaps a doe, there is a disc surrounded by crab-like figures, men with axes and men blowing lurs, two more men drawing bows; there are also the usual boats and there are feet. Just outside the photograph on the left there is a long-haired woman (Figure 76A, cf. Figure 97A), and three crouching or dancing men can be made out to the right of centre (Figure 77A). The artist shows a single leg in the same absolute profile as earlier carvers used for elk, but the attitude and profile look very much like the wooden masked Tungus shaman with a carved dancing-stick who can be seen in ethnographic reconstructions.[16] The horned ithyphallic men with tails appear several times blowing lurs at Kalleby or standing in a 'chariot' at Vitlycke (Figure 78 and Plate 202). The atmosphere here is one of magic, and subjects and portrayal alike are closest to the rock art of Ladoga, the White Sea

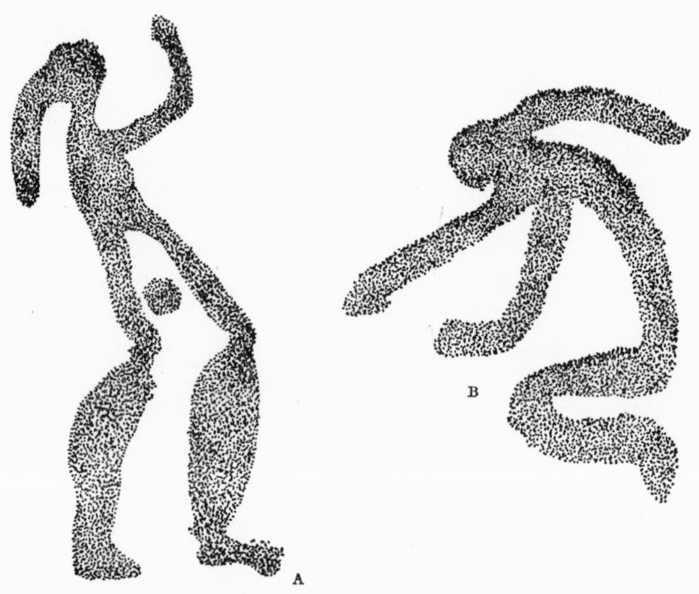

Figure 76. Rock-carvings in Bohuslän, West Sweden: A at Fossum, B at Vitlycke

regions of North Russia, and the Urals (see above, Chapter 3 and Plate 81 and Figure 26). At Vitlycke there is a copulation, perhaps a hierogamy; there are ploughing scenes, and an animal suckling its young (Figure 77B). The disguises belong to the old order, but the plough, the cart, and mounted combat came from the south. On the whole it is these domestic subjects that were carved on rocks in the Val Camonica in the Italian Alps at much the same time. All this group is more bucolic as well as magical, and there is an interest in fertility and generation that is absent from the repertoire of the bronze-smiths. Among the man-like protagonists we may, if we please, see adumbrations of the gods of later ages: Odin with the spear, Thor with the axe or hammer, Uller the bowman who could cross the fjords in boat-shaped shoes, the worm that encircles the world. But it would be rash to give names and fixed attributes to these persons, even if something of their future glory were already vaguely formulated.

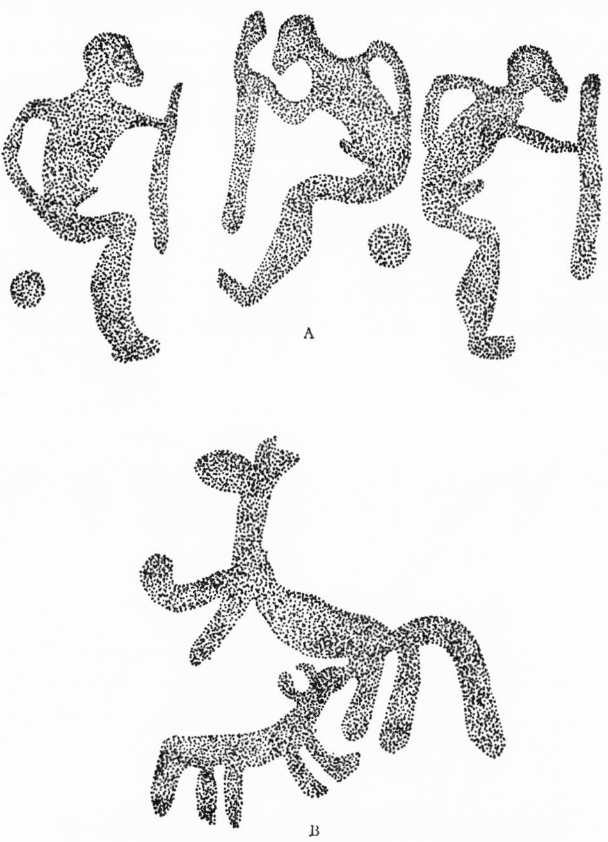

Figure 77. Rock-carvings in Bohuslän: A at Fossum, Tanum (cf. Plate 201), B at Bacha, Sweden

Figure 78. Rock-carving at Kalleby, Tanum, Bohuslän, Sweden

Cast Bronze Figures

The third branch of northern art, figures cast in the round, in one respect throws light on a peculiarity of razor art, while razor and rock art help in the interpretation of single figures. The 'goddess' of Plate 206 is eighth century (Period V), and so are most of the other bronzes of this sort. The technique is new, for unlike the *cire perdue* Trundholm horse, they were cast in multiple moulds with the help of 'casting-on' of parts.[17] The immediate source was probably in Eastern Europe, but behind this, technique and inspiration lie in the Caucasus, in eastern Anatolia, and in western Iran. But if some of the subjects are new, others are not. The vase-bearer on a knife handle from Itzehoe,

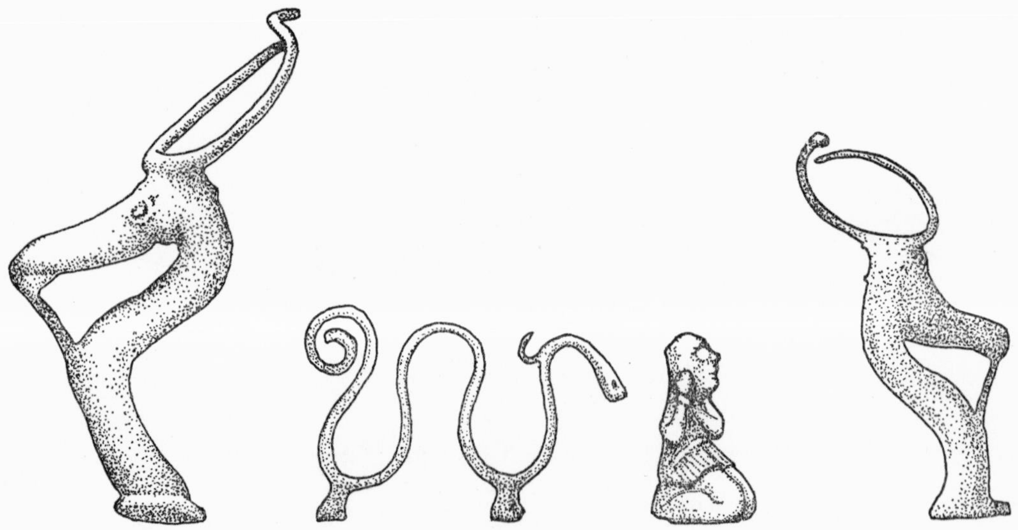

Figure 79. Cast bronze figures from Fårdal, Denmark, arranged as a tableau

Denmark, is a poorer relative of the great goddess bearing a bowl at Strettweg (Plates 205 and 218), and there are many others in Central and Eastern Europe, in Italy, and in Sicily. Nor is this surprising if behind her is the Asiatic goddess with the flowing vase and all those Neolithic clay pots that were modelled as women or with women's breasts; while looking forward is it just possible to surprise the mysterious grail-bearer who was both a hideous hag and a beautiful young woman?[18] The kneeling goddess from Fårdal with inset gold eyes once held an object in her right hand. She was found together with a bronze crested serpent and two long-horned animals. Each has at the base a tongue-like projection with holes for rivets, and so, using the Borgdorf razor as exemplar, a tableau has been reconstructed of the goddess holding the serpent with a cord and kneeling in a round boat with animal stern and prow (Plate 206 and Figures 71A and 79). A warrior in a horned helmet found at Grevensvaenge can, with the help of sketches made soon after he was discovered, be set up as one of a pair kneeling in a boat and holding up great Nordic axes, as in the scene on the Vestrup razor and the rock at Vitlycke (Figure 80).

A pair of horned helmets have actually been found at Viksø in Denmark, though they were probably made in Central European workshops or even in Italy (Plate 207), for they are beaten out of sheet metal and enriched with embossed ornament. The largest bosses are terrifying eyes, and very small ones reproduce the antithetical birds of the southern workshops. Once there were crests ending in a hooked bronze beak and

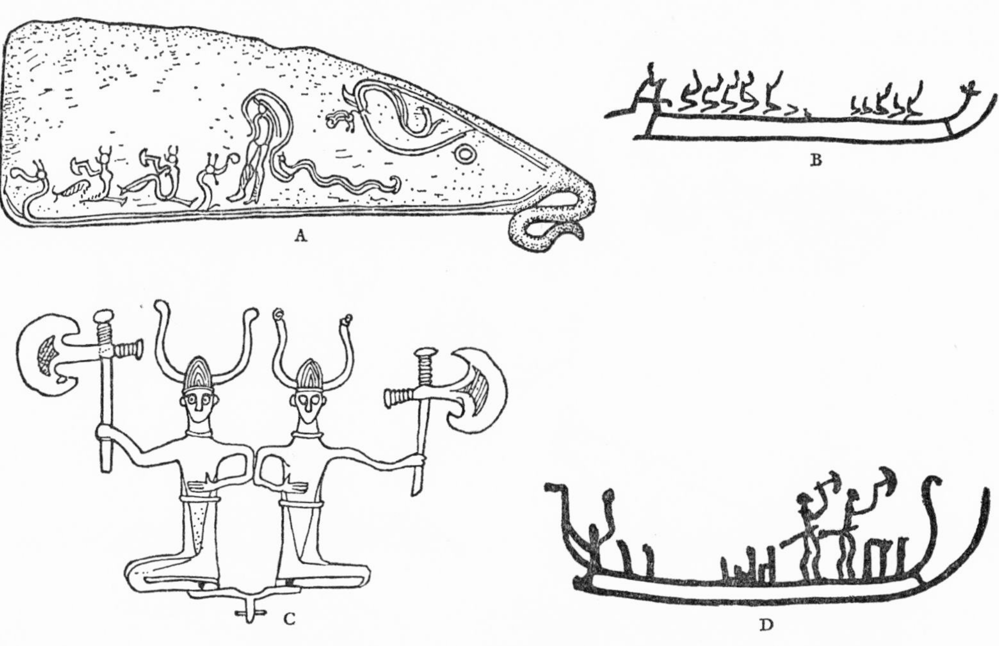

Figure 80. A Bronze razor from Vestrup, Denmark
B Rock-carving at Vitlycke, Tanum, Bohuslän, Sweden
C Drawing of horned and helmeted figures from Grevensvaenge, Denmark, as found
D Rock-carving at Vitlycke, Bohuslän

perhaps animal badges such as we see worn on the Gundestrup silver bowl, for there are sockets on the top to hold them. With the help of razor and rock and the Grevensvaenge tableau we may plausibly interpret these tremendous helmets as used by protagonists in a ritual drama, and this is more likely than that they were ever worn in battle. The bronze figures themselves are evidently the *disjecta membra* of composite scenes of which there is one complete example in existence, the Strettweg carriage or 'float' (Plate 218), which is also made up of separately cast figures, staged between animal protoms. The extraordinary bull from Spjuterum, Skåne, is a northern curiosity. Hammered out and riveted together like a cauldron, it still manages to be far more frightening than the technically accomplished cast bronze bull from Býčí-Skála (Plates 215 and 219).

In northern workshops the horse is the favourite animal, and horse-heads decorate a sceptre or ceremonial ornament found at Svartarp in Västergotland, Sweden (Plate 209). This intelligent-looking pair explain the identity of another head found at Alvena in Gotland. No horse, however roman-nosed, ever had a profile like this (Figure 81C), nor is this particular exaggeration found anywhere else, not on Caucasian horses nor the bugle-nosed Geometric horses of Greece, nor in Italy. Its source lies no farther away than the forests that surrounded the Scandinavian farmsteads where three-dimensional animal carvings had existed for some five or six thousand years, where the elk

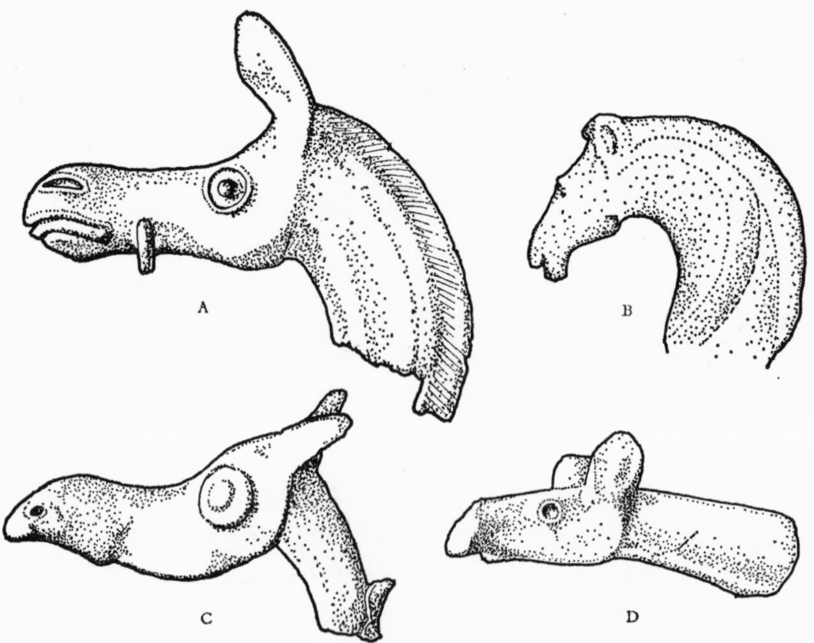

Figure 81. A Bronze horse-head from Svartarp, Sweden (cf. Plate 209)
B Part of ceremonial bronze axe from Sárvíz-Kanal, Hungary
C Bronze elk-head from Alvena, Gotland, Sweden
D Stone elk-head from Säkivärvi, Finland

was pre-eminent as food and as a sacred animal, and where it still lives wild today. In Finnmark especially, and across the northern forests to the Urals and beyond, stone carvers were shaping the butts of axes and wood-carvers the handles of spoons and ladles into bird- and elk-heads, very much as the bronzesmiths were beginning to furnish knives, razors, and precious vases with bird- and animal-head handles (Figure 81D).

The Darup artist felt no doubt that he was representing a horse. His naturalism, a little simplified, is very much the same as that of peasant carvers, but it did not stay for long. Ears were lengthened and bound round with gold ribbon and so were faces, turning a portrait into a trinket; and this trick was seized on by tenth-century (Period IV) goldsmiths when they added handles to imported bowls already ornamented with hammered star, ring, and boss[19] (Plates 195 and 210). It may be chance that gives these high-handled cups or dippers a distinct look of the northern ship with its external strut. The exaggeration of the horse's roman nose and lip was more obsessive, but as we know the north already had the elk stereotype, and this particular image with the long upper lip and round ears was transferred with the characteristic economy of the artist, regardless of its unsuitability, to the horse (Figure 81). The Svartarp and still more Alvena artists exaggerated the lip far more than did the carver of the Alunda elk (Plate 156).

At about the same time the razor draughtsmen lengthened the noses of *their* horses till they became another decorative spiral, especially when employed as prows of boats, though the round elk ear is recognizable when all the rest has been abandoned to arabesque (Plate 196 and Figures 71, A and C, and 74A).[20] This trick endured long enough to penetrate subtly into Celtic arts and to become, long after, a strand in the prehistory of animal interlace.

The casting smiths were now, through the mediation of Central European workshops, in touch with a tradition that is neither Nordic nor Mediterranean but eastern, looking back to the Caucasus and north-western Iran. It was from this region that iron-working probably came, and this particular style may have spread with the same impetus (see p. 211).[21] A pinhead from Rovalls, Vänge, in Gotland combines a human and a goat's head in a style that is more Iranian than European, and a handle of a knife with a hook-nosed man standing perhaps on a bird, found at Simris in Skåne, points in the same direction (Plates 208 and 211). Although the Svartarp 'sceptre' has an indigenous incised pattern on the tube, knowledge underlies it of the so called 'Thraco-Cimmerian' horse-sceptres of Eastern Europe, which are themselves a late development of the oriental prestige battle-axe or hammer (Figure 81B).[22]

These bronze castings are Northern Period V or later, that is eighth and seventh century. Only comparison with razor art, which can be dated reasonably well, and the rather rare carvings of recognizable weapons can date the rock carvings. A battle on horseback with oblong shields at Tegneby, Bohuslän, could not have occurred before the local Iron Age. The figure on the Bremen razor is in reality probably in the kneeling position of the Fårdal goddess, and on the rocks this figure becomes a single flowing line (Plate 206 and Figures 71C and 76B) which in turn suggests two (much later) Gundestrup figures, one leaping or dancing and another holding the sacred wheel (Figure 96, A and D). A boatload of men with lurs or axes at Vitlycke suggest the Vestrup razor once more (Figure 80). The circle with surrounding rays visible at the top left of Plate 201 also appears elsewhere, and at Tegneby it has a long-haired attendant who stands in the position and with the gesture of the ministering priestess on the Gundestrup bowl (Figure 97, A and C).[23]

The differences between carved rocks and incised razors with the same subjects are a matter of style and may owe not a little to the bronzes having been the work of professionals and the rock carvings not. The professionalism of the artist-bronzesmith (and goldsmith), the inheritor of craft 'mysteries' and custom, vetoes improvisation and experiment outside the received style. This ensures the survival of the art and of a certain standard of execution; but if it is abruptly confronted with something alien and vigorous, the style does not evaporate, it moves elsewhere. The abstract tendency of the later Period V and VI decoration in the north is a reassertion of an older, stronger professionalism (Plate 197 and Figure 74A).

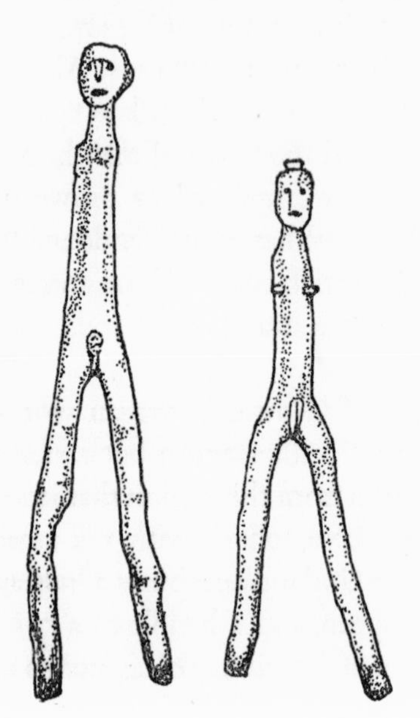

Figure 82. Wooden figures from Aukamper Moor, Schleswig-Holstein, Germany

The men who carved the rocks probably came from a different order of society. Their spiritual ancestors are the shamanic masters of the White Sea and Urals and of the 'arctic' art of Scandinavia. As such they were *amateur* artists closer to the hunter; while the pictures on the rocks are the imprint of a ritual action that in its performance was as dedicated and holy as the dance and sacred drama. When they turned from hunting scenes and wild animals to ships, wheels, carts, and warriors they were doing something adventurous and difficult but still within their traditional competence. For the professional bronzesmith on the other hand the act of casting or of tracing, for all its delicacy, concentration, and seriousness, was subordinate to the finished article which, when it had left his hand, he might never see again.

How much wood-carving was done in Northern Europe it is not possible to say because of the perishable nature of wood; but from Ireland to the Urals there are scattered a handful of gaunt figures preserved in acid bog that are evidence of a cult of male virility.[24] The warriors with round shields who stood gazing blankly out of pebble eyes in an animal-ended boat at Roos Carr in Yorkshire, though probably at least as late as the sixth century, are three-dimensional materializations of the boat scenes of Scandinavian rocks and razors (Plates 203, 214, and 216). Some may have been ceremonially dressed and undressed like the goddess Nerthus whom Tacitus described in a famous passage. At Aukamper Moor near Eutin, in Schleswig-Holstein, not far from the home of Nerthus, two tall and very rudimentary figures were found. The female is in fact just an eight-foot nobbly branch that would need a great deal of dressing-up and visonary enthusiasm to turn it into an 'earth-mother' such as Nerthus must have been (Figure 82).

Iron and Orientalizing

A comparison between the spread of bronze technology and of iron shows how much closer-knit now were Europe and Asia, Black Sea and Baltic, Mediterranean and Atlantic, region to region and sea to sea. In Western Asia iron had been known and occasionally used from the third millennium; the Hurrians in Anatolia were probably the first to work it efficiently. The Hittites used it in the second millennium but without exercising a monopoly. It was, however, only towards the end of the millennium that it spread west into Syria and Cyprus, and east to Iran and Mesopotamia. People in the Aegean had a few iron knives and other oddments by the twelfth century, and rare objects had even reached Central and Northern Europe in the eleventh. From the eleventh century it was also known in the Koban. Throughout the Caucasus its use was increasing in the ninth but only became common in the eighth century. The same is true of Greece, with Italy following rather later. Both drew on the same Syrian and Cypriot sources, though it is not impossible that others in eastern Anatolia were also known.[25] In Europe north of the Alps from the later eighth century iron was becoming really viable, and this not more than some four centuries after the beginning of its spread outwards from Anatolia and north-western Iran, whereas bronze technology had taken several millennia to cover the same ground.

Iron was at first rather gingerly employed as a jewel or mark of prestige, but its potentialities as tool and weapon, and the abundance of iron ores compared to copper and tin, led to the setting up of bloomeries in many parts and the production of the great 'Hallstatt' iron sword, and eventually of agricultural implements. It also gave quite small communities their chance of economic freedom, setting up their own foundries, each village with its smithy, though this was hardly accomplished before the end of the 'Hallstatt Iron Age' in the fifth century.

Wrought irons were obtained by the direct process. The ores were heated by charcoal in a hole in the ground, or better a furnace, where the impurities forming a fluid could drip away and the ore be reduced to a spongy, pasty mass, the blooms. After cooling, the blooms were heated in another furnace and hammered into a compact mass, so driving out scoriaceous matter. This is neither easy nor economical, and many heatings and hammerings were necessary, much metal being lost by the way. The reduction temperatures were less than 600°–700° C., and the result is a very pure wrought iron. Iron was not cast, but steel was sometimes produced unintentionally, since repeated heatings of the iron between hammerings would impart sufficient carbon to produce a carburized wrought iron or steel.[26] To overcome the brittleness of the steel, quenching, tempering, and annealing were carried out, but without the benefit of special furnaces the success of the result depended entirely on the skill and judgement of the individual smith, since every ore with its different impurities would react differently. Superior ores such as the spathic of Noricum were especially sought by the masters.

Iron stands lowest in the table of 'nobility', most corruptible of the useful metals, and it is impossible to estimate at all what has been lost through corrosion; but we have from Celtic La Tène blacksmiths a few magnificent wrought-iron objects which certainly required centuries of workshop tradition at the back of them. One by-product of iron-working put into the hands of the bronzesmith the steel graver, opening the way to a new range of decoration, tremolo patterns or 'rocked-tracer', first used by Greeks in the eighth century and north of the Alps not more than two centuries later.[27]

In the eighth century two events occurred which may seem remote, but which were to have incalculable repercussions in Europe. In 745 Tiglath Pilesar III drove the Urartians, who had come originally from a small state in eastern Anatolia, out of Syria and back to their native mountains. This gave Assyria a Mediterranean shore, at the same time upsetting Greek colonists and Phoenician merchants. Then, towards the end of the century, we hear for the first time of the elusive people whom the Greeks called Cimmerians, the Assyrians Gimmirai, and the Hebrews Gomer. They overran Urartu, and some passed on to the south of Lake Urmia while others sacked Gordion. Farther east around 680 we hear of Scythians pressing on the Medes in Azerbaijan and the Zagros, and for nearly a hundred years tribes with these names (or who were given variations on these names by their neighbours) were marching and countermarching across Anatolia and north-western Iran, sometimes plundering and destroying on their own, sometimes allied to one or other Asiatic state, and giving their name to a 'Cimmerian Land' in eastern Cappadocia.

Herodotus, writing in the mid fifth century, tells a story of nomadic Scyths living in Asia hard-pressed by the Massegetae, a tribe later found in Chorasmia, and forced across the Araxes into 'Cimmeria', where there was a battle in which the Cimmerians were worsted and many killed. He thereupon concludes that the Cimmerians must have entered Asia to escape the Scyths, who, pursuing them, 'took the wrong route by mistake', keeping the Caucasus on their right, and found themselves in Media. There is also an account of the sack of Sardis by the Cimmerians and their flight from Asia Minor at the end of the seventh century. Archaeologists often identify the Cimmerians with a people settled in the south of Russia in the later second millennium, called after the pits entered from the side in which they buried their dead, 'catacomb'; and the Scyths they identify with the 'timber-grave' group living to the east on the Don and Volga, and named from their timber-lined burial chambers under large barrows.[28] It is not easy to reconcile Herodotus's Massegetae and Scyths in Chorasmia with his 'Cimmerians' north of the Black Sea: the geography is far from clear, and we probably have in these passages a hundred years of Cimmerian activity condensed into one action. Confused accounts of far-off Asiatic battles have been grafted on to intelligent deduction based on the presence of Cimmerian place-names in the Crimea, which in the fifth century was a part of Scythia. It is therefore, I believe, perilous to use Herodotus in support of a Cimmerian invasion of Europe driven forward by Scyths in the eighth century, as is often done. There is no *literary* evidence at all for nomads entering from the east before the end of the seventh century. The archaeological evidence is another matter.[29] But if too much has been made of one passage, perhaps not enough notice has been taken of that other which describes the final exit of the Cimmerians from Anatolia. Strabo, Callimachus, and other Greek writers describe the devastation of Ionia by Cimmerians and Treres, the latter a tribe from Thrace, after which some of the barbarians moved south but others north into the Troad. Then at the end of the seventh, or more probably the beginning of the sixth century, the Lydian king Alyattes 'drove them out of Asia', which can only mean north into the Balkans. By this time the Scyths also were finished as a threat in Western Asia. They had by now become thoroughly 'medianized' and were streaming north through the Caucasus to join their relatives in the classic Scythian homeland on the South Russian plain, leaving a series of great barrow burials in the Kuban and on the Dniepre.[30]

The mistake has lain, I suggest, in making a unity of certain disunited events and calling them all 'Thraco-Cimmerian'. First of all, in the course of the eighth century a great deal of utilitarian horse harness of a special brand appeared in Europe. This is an archaeological fact, like the increased use of iron. The same simple tackle is found over much of Europe from Macedonia to the Netherlands, often in otherwise 'normal' burials and merchants' hoards. The interpretation is less simple. It is possible that nomad bands trekking west into Europe brought with them smiths and iron tinkers who could travel as light as the gypsies who went with Tatar armies in Central Asia. Old Djartchi' oudar, the personal blacksmith of Ghenghiz Khan, carried his few tools on his back; but other explanations are possible. Bits with horse-head ends found in Europe are simpler versions of Urartian horse-bits.[31] In the first half of the eighth century the Urartians were campaigning against the Kulhai or Colchians, who were in tradition famous bronze- and iron-workers living on the eastern coasts of the Black Sea. For a time after 750 it seems that Urartu had access to the Black Sea as well as controlling the trade route from western Iran to Trebizond, and Greek ships were active in these waters from the eighth century, even though the first colonies were not settled for nearly another two hundred years. Traditionally and plausibly they were there after metals: the raw iron and bronze and the finished articles.[32] Nor are Greek boats likely to have been the only ones trading on those shores. By these means there were quicker and more profitable opportunities of bringing iron and arts from Anatolia and the Caucasus than in the saddle-bags of nomad horsemen.

The bronze-work that now includes animals in a new style is not peculiarly 'Cimmerian' or (before the sixth century) Scythian: it is an offshoot of the art and technology of the Caucasus, the Elburz, the Zagros, and Central Anatolia from the end of the second millennium, each following different regional fashions. So there are three distinct questions: that of the horsemen, of iron, and of 'animal' style bronzes. Sometimes they coincided, but the history of each is separate and different. Horsemen from Russia there may have been, but their name is uncertain, and the time of their arrival cannot be calculated from Herodotus's Cimmerian battle. Equally important for Europe were the politics of Colchis and Trebizond, Urartu and Phrygia, Greek exploration, and above all the free movement of the metal-worker and artist, especially at times of tribal and interstate warfare.

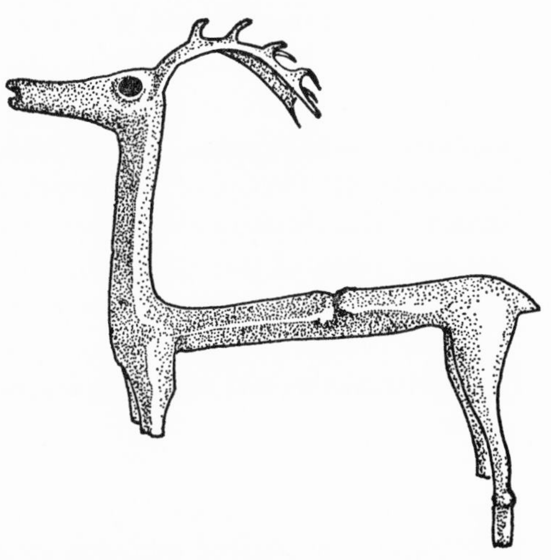

Figure 83. Bronze stag from Sevlievsko, Bulgaria

The goat from Sisak and the stag from Surdak in Yugoslavia are conceived in the new spirit, and so is the strange animal regarding its tail from Prozor (Plates 212 and 213). Compared to the run of

'Geometric' Hallstatt bronzes the contours are soft, lines ripple and flow. The stags in the Strettweg tableau look stiff beside a damaged but still elegant animal from Sevlievsko in Bulgaria, with its modelled hindquarters and backward curve of antler (Plate 218 and Figure 83).[33] This orientalizing style comes from Iran and the Caucasus, but it also contributed something to La Tène metallurgy. It was even felt on the Baltic, and it was this that made the Simris and Rovalls bronzes different from the other northern castings (Plate 208). Nor was it only perceptible in metallurgy. Four animal rhyta from Dalj, a site in Yugoslavia on the Danube, are difficult to match anywhere, but the two larger suggest Anatolia, and there are crane vases of a different kind at Marlik in northern Iran (Plate 217).[34] There can have been no direct relations between such distant regions, but all are in some degree indebted to a common heritage. Dalj existed

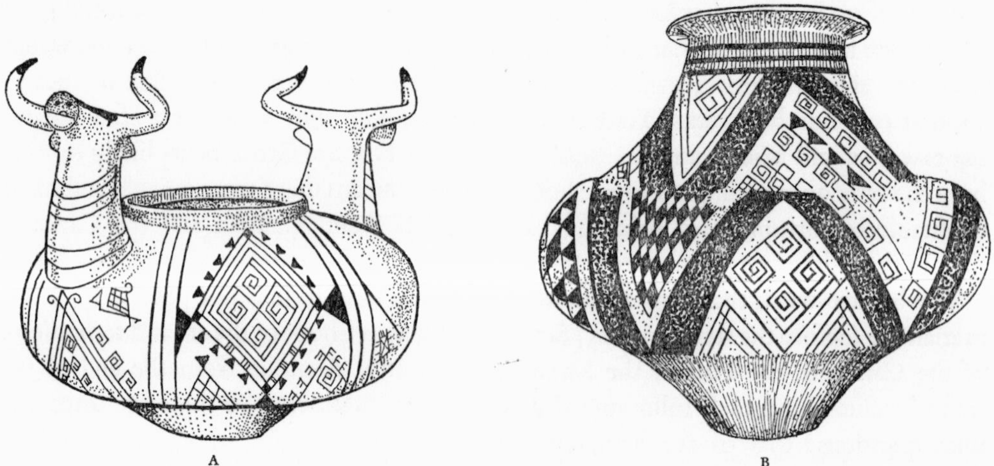

Figure 84. A and B Painted pots from Gemeinlebarn, Austria, found in a seventh-century (Hallstatt C) tumulus

from the seventh century to the fourth (Hallstatt C to La Tène), and these four vases probably come from early in its history. The surface is covered with a highly-burnished red slip on which chequerboard and rectilinear meander patterns are painted in graphite. This is now very worn and cannot be seen at all on Plate 217. The pots from Gemeinlebarn in Austria (Figure 84) give an idea of the sort of patterns used. When it is well-preserved the surface glows with metallic sheen. The rectilinear patterns have no local ancestry; they are often and rather uncertainly compared to Greek Geometric, but are really closer to Phrygian painted wares, though the use of graphite paint may be a return to the south-eastern Gumelniţa tradition. A large clay hearth from Donja Dolina in Bosnia has a giant version of the Phrygian spool handle and a very Phrygian meander below it (Figure 85). Fluted bronze bowls (phiales) found in graves on the Glasinac plateau near Sarajevo may be Greek, but they started in Phrygian Central Anatolia, and the large bronze bowls that are sometimes called by archaeologists

'Thraco-Cimmerian' owe their T-shaped handle attachments to an Urartian or Phrygian source – probably the latter; for the plain T was used as an everyday version of the 'siren handles' of their grander vessels, vast numbers of which have been found stacked in graves in the eighth–seventh-century Phrygian royal cemetery at Gordion. In Anatolia and Urartu the T often carries a bull's protom, and this too was accepted in Europe, though it may have come independently (see below, p. 241).[35]

The number of Anatolian objects or objects with an Anatolian air found spread over the Balkans in the first half of the last millennium has not yet been satisfactorily accounted for. It could be linked to the spread of iron-working or to the trading enterprise of the first Greek colonies, founded in the seventh century in Thrace, acting as middlemen, yet this does not quite meet the facts of the problem. It does not account for Macedonian and Bosnian pins at Phrygian Boghaz Köy,[36] nor for bronze ornamental fittings with a broad axe-shaped tongue and heads of bull, ram, and goat that have been found in Bulgaria, and whose ancestors are axes with animal-headed spikes common in Luristan and the Caucasus. Perhaps the upheaval caused by the departure of the *historical* Cimmerians out of Anatolia at the end of the seventh century played some part in it. Some of these orientalizing objects may be presents, some may have come from travelling merchants and itinerant craftsmen, but others must be flotsam from the once enormous riches of the spoilers of Western Asia by whatever name we call them: Cimmerians or Thracians, Treres or Scyths.

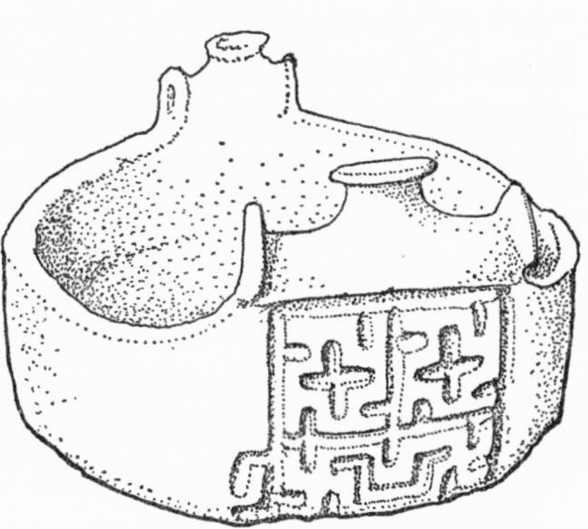

Figure 85. Large ornamental clay hearth from Donja Dolina, Yugoslavia, seventh–sixth century

The gold hoards of Michalkov in western Ukraine and of Fokoru in Hungary, with diadems, bracelets, and safety-pins, belong to the same orientalizing milieu but with more of the true Scythian style, which did indeed reach Rumania and the Hungarian plain along with the Median 'akinakes', but probably not till the end of the sixth century.[37] It is tempting to think that the gold treasure from Valcitran in Bulgaria with cups and krater, dippers and servers, all the furniture of the symposium, might belong to the spoils of Phrygia. The discs with raised rings and high central bosses are worked like Phrygian bowls, and the silver and niello inlay on the largest disc is in the idiom of the inlaid furniture in the King's Tomb at Gordion. Nothing like Valcitran is known, but then virtually nothing is known of Phrygian gold.[38]

Hallstatt Geometric

In Central and Western Europe the centuries between 1200 and 600 B.C. were not conspicuous for achievements in the arts, in spite of rising population and greater prosperity. After 600 the picture improves, but compared to the free, fluid, but rather blurred forms of orientalizing Hallstatt bronzes the 'Geometric' style is stiff and unimaginative, though at its best it has cleanness and definition. The iconography is very limited: there are small bronze pendants, charms to be hung from belt or bracelet that are cast in the form of a wheel or a shield, an axe or lance, a leaf, a bird, a horse. Among this crowd of not very important amulets and personal fetishes there are a few of an altogether superior order. The most famous is probably the 'cult-wagon' or 'ritual car' that was found in a barrow, perhaps of the seventh century, at Strettweg near Graz in Austria (Plate 218). In the grave were also a bronze urn with twisted wire supports in which the ashes lay, and iron horse-bits.[39] Though far more imposing, the Strettweg tableau is related to such things as the vase-bearer from Itzehoe and the Dupljaja god in his bird-drawn carriage (Plates 168 and 205), and to wheeled bowls with attendant birds found at Milaveč in Bohemia, Skallerup in Denmark, and Peccatel in Mecklenburg. It may have been re-staged. The tall figure in the middle supports on her head a bronze bowl, perhaps incomplete. She is the goddess with the vase, but here for the first time in Europe she carries her vessel on her head. For this purpose she has the same little protective cushion that women wear today when carrying heavy vessels in this way on their heads. What is odd is the symmetry of the staging of the tableau. Before and behind the goddess are two mounted warriors with pointed helmets, oval shields, and raised javelin or thunderbolt; between them stand an ithyphallic man with an axe and a woman; in front again is a great stag with powerful antlers between two sexless persons or perhaps young girls. All are naked except the goddess, who wears a broad belt and earrings, and the horsemen, who wear helmets. The goddess stands on a wheel of eleven spokes set in the openwork floor to which the individual figures are attached; the four corners end in does' heads.

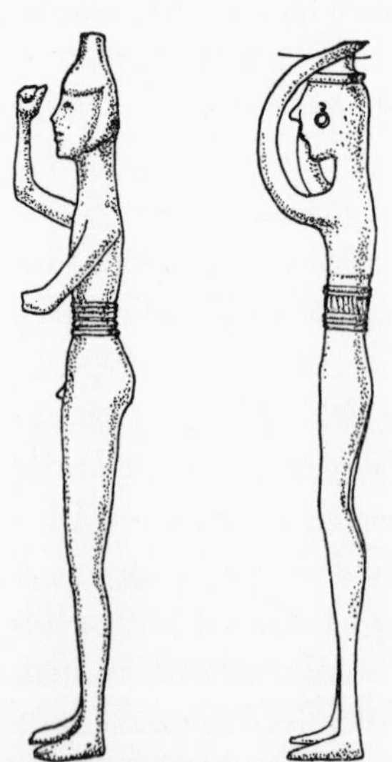

Figure 86. A Bronze figure from Olympia, Greece, seventh century
B Strettweg 'goddess', Austria (cf. Plate 218)

The Strettweg goddess is unthinkable apart from Greek Geometric bronzes; there is in particular an early-seventh-century warrior from Olympia with the same slender proportions, the exaggerated leg that measures slightly longer than the rest of the body to the top of the head, the same tight ribbed belt. The warrior raises one arm, where the goddess raises both, and he probably held a spear or a thunderbolt like the Strettweg horsemen (Figure 86).[40] The stance of the horses pulling back is what we see in horses that stand on the handles of the Greek tripod-lebes.[41]

This scene has been described as a procession to the sacrifice, with the stags the victims; but this I much doubt. One writer sees a Celtic pantheon, and not far from here some centuries later Celtic tribes revered a 'god of the mallet', and a goddess called Aeracura who had a 'horn of plenty' or basket of fruit.[42] But the name is not important. This goddess is a young athlete who balances her vase with a precision and a calculation which is in a manner Greek. The Greeks had no colony on the Adriatic till Durazzo was established in 627, but they had been exploring for some decades previously and I believe that at least in this one figure at Strettweg we either have a Greek craftsman working to native orders or a native craftsman who had been to school in a Greek workshop.

Somewhere behind this stiff but haunting scene may lie an Artemis and Actaeon at an earlier level of the myth. Or if these are magical stags, then they have a very ancient place in European and Asiatic cult. The Huns brought the story, no doubt already very old, that the stag descended from the clouds with the sun on its forehead and on its flanks the moon and the stars. On earth it hid near lakes and rivers and, when a hunter approached, it turned and told him that it was not lawful game but a celestial creature.[43] That something of this sort was known in Europe appears from the widespread christianized version, the confrontation of St Eustace or St Hubert with the stag bearing a crucifix between its antlers.

The stocky bull from the cave of Býčí-Skála in Moravia is in a wholly different style (Plate 219). The cave had been used probably in the sixth century for the burial of a chief with his cart, his bangles and brooches, his table-ware, and forty-odd immolated companions, most of them women. Among the relics of a strange and terrible rite were a human hand and parts of a detached human skull that are said to have been found strewn over with corn. Europe has now caught up with third-millennium Ur. The bull was cast by *cire perdue* and had an iron band hammered into the back and iron triangles in the shoulders and forehead. The eye-inset is lost. This is not Greek nor Etruscan, Scythian nor even Caucasian in style, nor like bulls from the eponymous Hallstatt cemetery, which are slender and stringy.[44]

Potting in these centuries is for the most part dull but competent, often imitating metal in shape and decoration with fluting and graphite paint which tells us something of what we have lost in fine bronze, gold, and silver table-ware. In a tomb at Gemeinlebarn in Austria some rather peculiar pots were found. The tomb was a rectangular chamber lined with oak beams and covered with a great barrow. It held an iron sword of about 3 feet in length, parts of iron chains, a knife, pins, amber rings, and pots. This was a considerable personage and the pots are not mere utensils. Several have heads of long-necked bulls on either side of the opening and rectilinear meanders and quirks in graphite paint (Figure 84). There were also larger vessels, probably three in all, which carried figures modelled in the round standing on the shoulder, and with little bronze birds set into holes around the rim (Plate 220).[45] The *dramatis personae* are very much the same as at Strettweg, though no single figure is elevated above the rest; but here is the woman or goddess who carries on her head a bowl, and another with a tub or basket, here are horsemen with shield and spear, standing figures of men and women, and a proud stag. In spite of this, it is no more a hunting scene than is Strettweg. The date is approximately the same. The same *dramatis personae* are also depicted in a different technique and style on the sides of embossed bronze pails (see below), and we are probably here on the fringes of a developed mythology. It is not necessary to look beyond Europe for the ancestry of the bull-headed pots or of the many that are shaped like birds, for they were made first in the distant Neolithic era and they were also still being made here and there throughout the duration of the Bronze Age.

The well-known group of large vessels from Sopron (Ödenburg), Hungary, with scenes scratched and stamped on them are also native inventions. The impressed circles we have seen on figures of Kličevac type, and these figures are based on the old textile-derived triangle. They are chiefly interesting for their subject matter. One in particular shows a carriage with a muffled upright object that is perhaps the image of a god on a sacred journey, veiled from the eyes of the profane. Farther west pottery was decorated with impressed circles, and a very fine cut-out or *Kerbschnitt* technique, with the purpose of covering the whole surface with a carpet of decoration. The dish from Sternberg near Gomadingen in South Germany (Plate 221) has a greater sense of overall design than many of these ornate and extravagant chattels. The date is seventh century and so is much the same as Plates 217 and 220.

Sea-Roads West

In Eastern Europe a lot is unexplained and doubts abound, but fortunately matters appear more straightforward, at least in their grand outline, in the central and western Mediterranean.

In the unquiet years after 1200 there had been in Sicily, as in Crete, a move away from the coasts to more defensible places on the heights. Raiding parties, repulsed from their attacks on Egypt, had discovered Sicily, Sardinia, and probably Italy too. At the same time the immense size of cemeteries of well-furnished rock-cut tombs at Pantalica and on other East Sicilian sites speaks against the poverty and recession that we connect with a dark age. The age may have been violent and dangerous to live in, with sudden shifts of population from one side of a sea or a strait to another, but it was not notably depressed and fragmented. There was activity in the minor arts, in smithing of weapons and bangles and, especially at Pantalica, the production of a new and superb red monochrome ceramic with a glossy surface which (now in the twelfth century, for the first time on native-produced wares) has been thrown on the wheel.[46] The bowl on a tall stand (Plate 222) is over 3 feet high. The colour and quality of the ware, the shape of handle and the metallic line, all point to an earlier Anatolia before the collapse of the Hittite Empire, while high stands look forward to metal vessels of rather later and hint at a second-millennium metal repertoire that had nothing to do with the Aegean. But this was only a prelude to the greater changes that followed.

The years around 745 were again crucial, for that was when Assyria gained its Mediterranean footing (see above, p. 209). From 700 onwards the Phoenicians were exploring the central and western Mediterranean. They may have reached North Africa even earlier. In 666 they experienced a crisis when Tyre was taken by Assurbanipal the Assyrian. One consequence was a great scattering of skills and artists, with free craftsmen looking for markets and patrons over the sea. In detail the degrees and manner of oriental and Greek participation are debatable, and debate depends as often as not on the works of art themselves. Much may hang on a griffin's second side-lock or the musculature of a lion's haunch. We need not explore all these niceties that belong to the province of classical and Etruscan art, but we do need to understand the context, the limits of possibility within which our European artists must operate, and these undoubtedly include the presence of craftsmen and artists trained in Urartian and Assyrian centres working in Greece, especially Ionia and Samos, in Crete, and in Italy in the eighth and seventh centuries.[47]

Fortunately Etruscan origins do not concern us but only regions north and westwards. The first Greek colonies in Italy and Sicily were planted by Euboeans, evidently with a view to exploiting the natives as far as they could and trading with them when exploitation would not do. Pithekoussai or Ischia in the early eighth century was designed for the Etruscan trade. Cumae south of Naples followed in the middle of the century, and Naxos in Sicily in 734, all Euboean foundations. But it was the Euboeans also who, through the success of their trading station at Al Mina on the North Syrian coast, did business, first with Urartu, and after 745 directly with Assyria. It is significant that in the eighth and seventh centuries the same Greeks were in touch with Cypriots and Egyptians (even if only in the role of mercenaries) who were also competing with Phoenicians on the coasts and islands of the Mediterranean.

The Cretans and Dorians were not much later than the Euboeans (Syracuse and Gela), and through the Ionian Greeks there were possibilities of indirect relations with Phrygia and Lydia. By these means, and by direct Phoenician enterprise, oriental arts and fashions began all at once to exert their fascination on the inhabitants of Italy, Sardinia, Spain, southern France, and even to some extent up into Central Europe. Distances were shrinking fast, and the region of hearsay and fable was pushed still farther out. Men from Tyre and Sidon circumnavigated Africa in 609 and were trading through the Pillars of Melkaart (which the Greeks translated Heracles) and northward up the Atlantic shores of Spain to 'Tartessos' and perhaps farther (p. 198 above). Those same Phoenicians coasted round Sardinia looking for metals and had settled there perhaps as early as the eighth century, certainly by the beginning of the sixth; so that when Athene and Zeus were worshipped by the Greeks of Syracuse, Moloch and Astarte had their temples at Capo Sant'Elia and Sulcis in Sardinia.[48] If the Phoenician trader brought only perishable cargo he would leave nothing for the archaeologist. A point to remember is that the merchants who went in search of metal must themselves have known something of metallurgy, and for the long voyages that were undertaken from time to time it was necessary to have a smith on board. From such men as these the natives might pick up new tricks and skills.

The voyages and settlements of the eighth and seventh centuries were not at all like those earlier explorations that had carried tomb- and temple-builders to Malta in the fourth millennium, planted small townships in South Spain in the third, or trafficked in obsidian in the Aeolian Islands in the second; the Cretan and Mycenaean settlements at Taranto or on Lipari come nearer to what was now happening. Those early adventures remained something exotic; they fretted for a time and then disappeared leaving a tumble of stones or a few sherds. The exploits of the early first millennium belong to our own world, and we still live the consequences. In the former times there may have been too great a gulf between natives and strangers, but now the strangers were better fitted to build for permanence and the natives to learn and profit. So behind the Phoenician colonies in Sardinia a native civilization appeared that was able to produce very original works of art, and rather later another appeared in Spain.

A new 'frontier-spirit' was abroad, which Myres compares to the aggressive, independent, and austere individualism of nineteenth-century California. Greeks and Phoenicians both possessed it; both chose at first a small offshore island or defensible promontory for their settlements. Some were never much more than temporary trading posts, but others were founded deliberately with the end in view of creating a new home, a political unit that might one day equal the parent. This could be done now without fear of losing those precious contacts with the homeland, or rupturing the life-line to the great centres of civilization farther east; something which earlier settlers risked. It is no chance that now the boat appears everywhere: painted on pots, carved on graves, and cast in ornamental bronze as lamps, dishes, and furniture of the gods. The Mediterranean was criss-crossed as never before by the cautious fleets of colonizers, the thrusting boats of merchants on their regular runs, and the predatory roving pirate. The characters of merchant and pirate were often not very different: both carried slaves, and both occasionally traded *and* raided, and through one or other enterprise magnificent objects of oriental art found their way into the heart of Europe. It is this that concerns us.

The more enterprising of the natives certainly came out half-way to meet them. The Sardinians, like the Etruscans, had a reputation for piracy; the Adriatic too was an ideal field of operations. Everything in these centuries is tending to accelerate the growth of cultures and societies. On the great continental plains the horse, and on the seas skilled navigators, brought men from distant places, who formerly could have known nothing of each other, into disconcertingly sudden confrontation, and this was very fruitful. Between them Urartu, Phoenicia, Cyprus, and an orientalizing Greece are responsible for such novelties as bronze sculpture in the round from Sardinia and the 'situla art' of North Italy and the eastern Alps, as well as for the wealth of Etruria.

The second millennium was a time of great building activity in the central and western Mediterranean, and towards its end and in the early first millennium the impetus moved away from monumental tomb-building to secular work: towers, castles, villages, and even little towns. The flower of all this activity was in Sardinia. At Su Nuraxi near Barumini in the south-west (Plate 223) and at hundreds of other sites play was given to a curvilinear style which at one time was extraordinarily widespread in Western Europe and which, had it not been for the conquests of Greece and Rome, might have held the ascendant for many more centuries. As it is, we see it in Iron Age townships of Iberia, in Iron and Dark Age Ireland, Scotland, and Wales, in Bronze Age Dartmoor and Cornwall, in Corsica too and in the Balearics, and in the second millennium in the Aeolian Islands. It is based on dry-stone walling, sometimes rough, but often of superlative quality; but in Sardinia mortar was used at Barumini and in other nuraghi. The typical unit is a round structure, a single room or room with radial partitions (Scottish wheel-houses) or a tower (Sardinian nuraghi, Corsican towers, Scottish brochs). False vaulting is customary, giving beehive corbelled construction over rooms;

and if large stones are used to vault straight passages a very similar result can be produced at Mycenaean Tiryns, at Hittite Boghaz Köy (under the rampart), and at the nuraghi of Sant'Antine in Sardinia.[49] Staircases and passages are contrived in the thickness of walls and the units are linked by double curvilinear walls either as covered passages or open streets. These conservative principles and technical limitations sometimes lead to an extraordinary likeness between buildings of different times and far-away places, between a Scottish broch of the first and nuraghi of the eighth century B.C., and small round buildings anywhere from Spain to the Orkneys. Against this tradition the classical and oriental courtyard house and rectangular temple, as well as the Northern and Eastern European long house, come in collision. There can be no compromise between them and, except in the architecture of defence, the curvilinear goes under.

There are in Sardinia about 6,500 nuraghi, some mere towers, some complicated village sites with a central castle keep. The earliest go back to around 1400, but at Barumini most of the building was done between the mid eighth and late sixth century. On internal architectural evidence and with the help of a few imports and Carbon 14 dates the nuragic civilization has been divided into three periods: early nuragic from some time in the second half of the second millennium down to about 950, full or middle nuragic from 950 to 560, followed by decadence with the Carthaginian domination of the island.[50]

Springs of medicinal water and wells were enclosed in buildings from about the eighth century. The earliest, Sant'Anastasia, is comparatively simple, and only the lower part of the cupola survives (Figure 87, partly reconstructed); but later ones are more

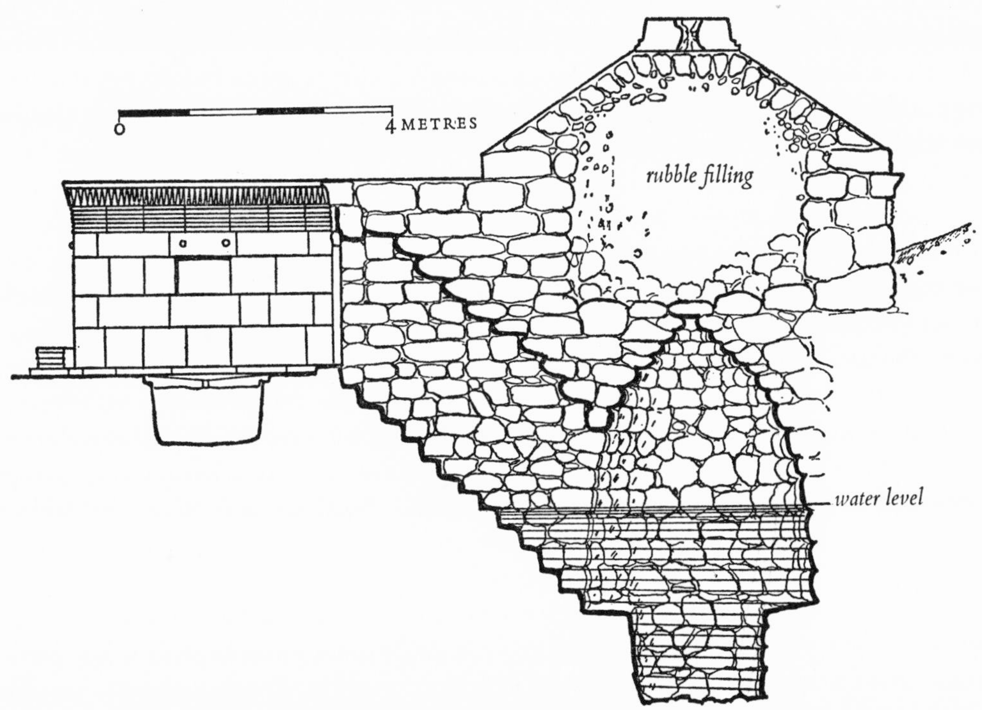

Figure 87. Sant'Anastasia, Sardinia, a well with partially reconstructed buildings

sophisticated with ashlar walling and owe something to Etruscan or Phoenician experience. The addition of paved forecourts, sometimes with benches, and the number of bronze and other votive offerings found in and around wells shows them to have been, as it were, inverted temples whose towers plunge downwards into the earth, like the underground workings and sacred pools of Palestinian Gibeon. Carved stone bulls' heads on the early sites and bronze bulls in later ones suggest some connexion with Anatolian cults of the goddess, the spring in the cave, and the young god in his bull persona (see Chapter 5 above).

Out of some 400 known Sardinian bronze figures, only one has come from a datable excavation. A few found their way into Etruria in the seventh century, but the majority come from hoards of votive gifts, from foundries and from rifled tombs and houses. The date of most is probably eighth to sixth century.[51] They vary from $\frac{3}{4}$ inch to 16 inches (2 to 40 cm.) in height, and many were fitted to weapons or utensils or fixed to stands. They do not appear to have been worn as amulets or grouped into tableaux, but to have stood in the cult places built round tombs, springs, or wells. Stone stands or footings have been found in which swords were fixed with animal or human figures poised on the tips like the ancient Cretan sword and double-axe cults in sacred caves (but without the figures). *Cire perdue* was probably used in casting, and the metal-worker who could produce by this method the two wrestlers of Plate 224 from Monte Arcosu was no tyro. Since division by date is impossible, these statuettes have been divided into two stylistic groups, one called (not very happily) 'Geometric', the other 'Mediterreanized Barbaric'. I prefer, and will use, the shorter 'formal' and 'informal'; Plate 225 (from Teti, Abini) is of the first group and Plate 226 (of unknown provenance) the second. Compared to the strict conventions that governed the enormous quantity of small bronze sculpture that had appeared almost everywhere in the first half of the first millennium, it is surprising to find so much freedom and such a very nonconformist outlook in Sardinian workshops.

The formal groups to some extent follow conventional stereotypes: the standing warrior, a hero, chief, or god, always armed, wearing a cloak and carrying a staff, or the archer with his bow at the ready; these become familiar by repetition. But it is only necessary to compare them with the innumerable bronze 'Reshefs' and 'Baals' from Syria, Palestine, and Cyprus, or seated cult figures, male and female, which vary only with the competence of the artist and smith from the nineteenth to the sixth century, to recognize the originality of the Sardinians. From the 'informal' group Plate 226 introduces not a god, hero, or chief but a 'character', talking, gesticulating, the perennial under-privileged frequenter of quays whom you may meet today in any large Mediterranean port. It almost looks as though a Sardinian artist were poking fun at the ubiquitous Levantine trader in the person of one of his gods.[52] The archer from a large votive hoard found at Teti, Abini (Plate 225) is very different. The physiognomy is no less striking: long straight nose, narrow face, level eyebrows. Impassive, aristocratic, and in control of the situation, this could be the image that any Sardinian would like to have of himself. Clothes and weapons, the visible signs of dignity and rank, are given careful treatment. Some few statuettes are endowed with a double complement of eyes and arms and must represent gods, but the horns of the Teti warrior are ambiguous and justify a short digression.

Let us say, as we must, that there is a point at which the literal appearance of an object ceases to coincide with the received meaning, when the appearance has become a symbol for something other than itself; but this being so, where to locate that point is the nicest of problems.[53] The horned animal was revered by Paleolithic hunters in their art. At some time after this, in Western Asia certainly, and perhaps elsewhere, the sacred numinous content was thought to be concentrated in the horns, which were an outcrop of the life-substance, so the gods are depicted as men endowed with horns. In Mesopotamia and Anatolia a tiara with many horns was worn by great gods, few horns by lesser. From there we pass, particularly in the twelfth century in the eastern Mediterranean, to a helmet with a single pair of horns attached to it. A twelfth-century bronze god at Enkomi in Cyprus wears his bull's horns very much as 'El', the great god of Ugarit, is addressed as 'Bull'; but horned helmets on the Warrior Vase at Mycenae are worn by the ordinary soldiery. What then of the horned Sardinian helmets? Are they attributes of gods and demi-gods, or are they, like the horned helmets found at Viksø, mundane headgear, and are the Viksø helmets themselves numinous and dramatic (Plate 207 and p. 205 above)? The problem is and must be insoluble, and it is well to remember the extent of our ignorance.

Statuettes of women are also 'formal' and 'informal'. Those who carry baskets or pitchers on their heads are usually the latter, and cloaked standing women such as Plate 227 from Coni or Santu Millanu Nùoro, are the former. The long face, the eyebrows that meet in a straight line, the absence of expression are the same as in the heroes and chieftains. The gesture of the arms extending the cloak like a Virgin of the Misericord enveloping mankind is another of those foreshadowings of quite other times and arts that we have met so often. This lady stands midway between a fifteenth-century French or Italian painting and the third-millennium carving of Plate 146. She still has the long neck, the prominent nose, the flat body, and the distance of the Senorbí goddess; she is by descent Mediterranean daughter of Mediterranean mother. The same face appears on Etruscan clay urn-covers of the seventh and sixth centuries, and if this is due to anything more than chance it might mean that all the bronze 'priestesses' are really mourners, even the goddess of the tomb who broods over Razet near Coizard (Figure 60c). This is the face of the mother in many seated groups of mother and son, but not in all. The artist who modelled the wax for casting Plate 230 from Santa Vittoria near Serri may have intended a goddess, but when he went into the foundry he did not shut his mind and memory to life in the village outside. Sometimes the 'child' is a fully-armed young warrior, and these groups have been interpreted as a mother mourning her son killed in battle; but elsewhere both seem to be engaged in emphatic conversation, and here at Santa Vittoria the supercilious infant on its mother's knee is certainly not dead.

The wrestlers from Monte Arcosu near Uta (Plate 224), as well as being a most skilful casting, show that wrestling was to the Sardinians what boxing was to the people of Italy. There is also a 'good shepherd' with the sheep on his shoulder, and musicians who play the double pipe or 'launa' still heard at village festivals. Among the animals a few have real life: a crouching monkey in the middle of a bronze dish and a tense fox. Others are only heads that form the end of a little votive boat or lamp which may also have birds on posts and a procession of animals along the rim. Monsters are rare but not unknown, and there are models of chests on wheels and of a nuragic castle with its central and corner towers.

This is, on the whole, a language of heads and gestures. There is no interest in the body as having weight or mass or contour – it has line and a silhouette, but that is all; but such expressive treatment of the face as in the 'informal' group has hardly been seen since the Butmir and Moravian heads of Chapter 4 and the Spanish shelter paintings (Figures 31 and 32 and Plates 106 and 115). This art is as evanescent as a pencil sketch and as far as possible from the conceptual style of Egypt or of Greek Geometric, and yet its chief parent is a very formal art indeed, that of the Syro-Phoenician tradition. This has dictated the kind of figures used: the large head, the long neck, stick limbs, and flat, straplike body. When the artist made his model for Plates 224, 226, or 230, he did not please himself in the matter of proportion and scale as a modern sculptor could, for both were 'received': what he did was to direct attention to gesticulating and admonishing hands, expressive faces, elegant linear patterns, all of which is quite unlike contemporary Etruscan art. But then Sardinia had no knowledge of Greek work. Sardinian artists were as ignorant of its three-dimensional qualities and monumentality as of its technical brilliance; and as a result Sardinian sculpture remained small in scale, a minor art. At the same time it enjoyed more freedom in the portrayal of the evanescent moment and of those 'fleeting appearances' so abhorred by Plato, than the classical world enjoyed before Hellenistic times.[54] It is as anti-classical as it is anti-oriental. Here and there an artist seems at this very moment to have broken free from the strict sanctions of a cult and to be celebrating his freedom. In the 'informal' style in particular the broken surfaces and blurred contours that belong to clay modelling stimulate the imagination and convey atmosphere in a way that the wholly realized perfection of an archaic or classical bronze does not do, nor was meant to do.

It is very hard for us to estimate the level of the Sardinian bronzesmith's art. For one thing today we are in danger of an exaggerated admiration because of our taste for the imperfect and the unfinished. Where the artist's intention is unknown it is impossible to judge how far he succeeded, and whether lack of finish is willed or due to faulty technique. Almost as much as in the Old Stone Age we may be sure our eyes do not see the same object that he saw. We can only number and compare and, according to our contemporary lights, enjoy. Without pitching the claims too high, we may recognize here, tentative and jejune perhaps, the flicker of something singularly European.

Where we might have looked for another shoot of this artistic activity, in Sicily, there is none. Across the narrow strait of Bonifacio in Corsica large stone stelai were set up, with features and weapons carved on them in light relief, but these are something again different, remembering on the one hand Neolithic stelai in the midi and on the other rock carvings of weapons in Liguria and the north of Italy, along with the more sophisticated subjects of the end of the second millennium and the early first.[55] Only out to the west, when the Carthaginians reached Spain, very inferior but not dissimilar bronze figures were produced in native workshops. But Iberian artists were happiest painting pots with their gay, strenuous, crowded patterns, some flowery, some with birds and animals or with combats between spindly warriors; and in fabricating luxurious jewellery.

On the fringes of the Etruscan world another art appeared that concerns us. Among pieces of hammered bronze table-ware, produced in workshops of the twelfth century and later, in Central Europe, there is a pail with a round shoulder and short everted neck. Like the bowls, helmets, and shields, it is often decorated in repoussé boss-work with the proud symbol of the sun-boat: a cross-in-circle flanked by water-birds or sailing in a bird-ended boat (Plate 192). Later pails are usually plain, have a sharper shoulder, and are built up from several sheets riveted together.[56] Then, around 600, there appear the first of the small, comparatively fragile pails provided with lids that are decorated in a representational style in repoussé, or else are embossed all over.

The twelfth-century prototype may have been made by craftsmen trained in the Aegean, but the useful pail is none the less a European invention and not, like most of the bronze table-ware, oriental or Mediterranean; and this is also true of the rich but simple boss decoration. The representational work is on the other hand unthinkable apart from that orientalizing spirit which we have seen radiating out from Syria, Cyprus, and Anatolia in the eighth and seventh centuries. At its first appearance the pail is usually one of a set with smaller cups, bowls, and sometimes a strainer too. If these belong to wine-drinking, then the pail takes the place of the crater or of the stamnos.[57]

Figured pails (we had better now conform to custom and call them situlae) fall into two groups, one around 600, and a much larger group that may begin as early as the end of the sixth but which is mostly fifth, lasting into the fourth century. Dating depends on Greek imported vases and copies of them. They are found and may have been produced in three different centres: on the upper Save and Drave in Slovenia and Carinthia, in the Alpine foothills and the Alto Adige, and north and south of the Po around Bologna and Este respectively. Except for the Po valley, these were mining areas exploited since the twelfth century; and the Save and Drave, where population had increased rapidly since the end of the second millennium, were centres of intense iron-working. Here several trade-routes met, and the Scyths were in nodding distance eastward over the Hungarian plain. The heights were fortified for settlement, cemeteries of flat and tumulus graves and urnfields were large, and the population was by now probably Illyrian. The southern situlae come from among even more advanced native societies in closer touch with provincial Etruscan interests.[58]

Situlae and bronze belts decorated in the same style are found in the richest of the men's tombs. Some situlae held cremated ashes and were among the most valued possessions of chiefs, priests, and perhaps merchants. We can take the Vače cemetery near Ljubljana, and the finer of its two figured situlae, as examples from the Sloveno-Illyrian centre. Most of the graves were under round barrows, but this appeared to be flat, and charcoal, perhaps from a cremation, was scattered round the pail, together with a bracelet and some sherds. The situla is $9\frac{1}{3}$ inches (23·8 cm.) high and $8\frac{3}{4}$–9 inches

(22–23 cm.) in diameter and is made from two trapeze-shaped bronze sheets on which the design must have been drawn in colour, for there are no signs of incising or pricking out. They were then laid on a bed of pitch or some other yielding substance, and the inner surface was hammered with punches of different sizes. After this the other surface was worked with hammer and chisel, and the shading and details of features and clothes added with the burin. Finally the sheets were riveted together, the base folded and hammered on, the rim beaten round a lead ring for greater strength, and staples riveted through for the twisted bronze rod handles. The date arrived at on stylistic and general grounds is fifth century, a hundred years later than the Benvenuti situla found in a grave at Este, which may be as early as 600.[59]

Situla art, whether on pails, bowls, or belts, has a common repertoire drawn from a common Mediterranean and Near Eastern stock: the line of animals, natural and monstrous, musicians seated and walking in procession, boxers in front of a trophy, foot-soldiers and horsemen, hunting and ploughing, the symposium and connubium or, according to whether the occasion was profane or sacred, communion and hierogamy. Some are so alike as to declare the work of an individual artist – Vače for instance, and Magdalenska Gora, both in Slovenia – but there are also great differences. In the early group either there are only animals or the animals dominate, and there are winged lions, man-headed sphinxes, and other monsters. The later group varies more in quality. If the Certosa di Bologna is the best, it is also the most Mediterranean, and for this reason I have preferred to illustrate Vače; for the style is both individual and characteristic (Plates 228 and 229) – characteristic in the hairlessness of the men (on all except the Benvenuti situla), the funny hats, dumpy bodies and big heads, and individual in the vitality and enjoyment that are its most engaging qualities. The subjects in their order, limitations, and repetitions are always solemn and hieratic and do not on the whole suggest ordinary secular pursuits. Even the scenes of ploughing and hunting the hare are from high antiquity appropriate to a great man's obsequies, like musical and boxing contests; still more the meal and the serving-women, the procession of horses and armed men. A horse was buried with the situla in one of the Magdalenska Gora graves (V, 6–7). Even the connubium has a polite counterpart in the wedded couples moulded in the round for the lids of fourth-century sarcophagi at Vulci. A tripartite division of zones between war, peace, and mythology has been suspected at least once.[60] Only the Benvenuti situla stands apart and seems to record some heroic or mythological action, like the songs with which a minstrel celebrated the passing of the chieftain.

The arrangement of the scenes on the situlae, one above another in zones, is oriental, but it had also been adopted by second-millennium Aegean artists, no doubt under oriental influence, and again by geometric and orientalizing Greek vase-painters. We have seen it in the north at Kivik; it was scarcely ever used by the Celts. The lines of pacing and grazing animals on the earlier works are very close to Corinthian models, but the winged lion, the type of wing, and the mane along the back are oriental, while the beast with a limb in its mouth, very rare outside Italy, is peculiarly Etruscan. Lions are a special problem. The immigrant craftsmen who created the earliest Etruscan orientalizing style knew what flesh-and-blood lions looked like, but their North

Italian and Alpine imitators knew them only by hearsay. They were familiar with wolves and bears and other ravening beasts, and the Vače lion under Plate 229 is surely drawn from a ferocious shepherd dog like those of the Greek and Balkan shepherds today. One peculiarity that is not so likely to have come from oriental work is the sprig of vegetation that hangs down from above as well as rising from below by the feet. It has shrunk from the palmette that it still is on Benvenuti, and the convention, I think, was the same as was used by Minoan and Mycenaean artists when they hung their rocks from the sky on a Vapheio gold cup or Shaft-Grave niello dagger. It is there to show the other side, the world beyond and behind the picture.

Representations of a solemn meal or drink party are again more oriental than Aegean, and the vessels on bulbous bases that stand as high as a man's armpit, or his chin if he is seated, must represent the bronze Urartian ones introduced from North Syria or the Black Sea.[61] Scenes like this would not have meant very much in the high Alpine valleys if they depicted only the strange rites and peculiar practices of foreigners down on the Po or Adriatic, and had not already had a place in their own society. For their own rituals we should perhaps substitute the wheeled cauldrons and pots with birds and modelled figures like Skallerup, Strettweg, and Gemeinlebarn. The large birds that perch and brood over vessels remind us of these as well as of the Krannon and Tiryns birds. Others perch on the backs of animals, like the vulture on a lion's back on an oriental shield from Crete.[62] Whether they are divine birds or birds of divination, rain or thunder charms, they, with bird-bowls, bird-boats, bird-headed stands, birds on beds, sceptres, chariots, all combine to give a powerful impression of the bird epiphany of gods in Europe, an idea to which the chancy memories of folklore add substance.

Given the situation in the Mediterranean in the first half of the last millennium B.C., it is not surprising that so many different styles and sources can be detected in the art of the situla. I cannot agree with the very high claim sometimes made for its quality as specifically European or 'Illyrian' art in the sense of non-Greek and non-Etruscan. On the contrary, I believe that it is in essence not of Europe. There is a gaucherie that betrays the artist working in a way that is uncongenial, too much at variance with the temper of the craftsman and the craft, so that the result is neither civilized *nor* barbarian but provincial, like the work done in Gaul and Britain under Rome. This provincialism is present in much of Hallstatt art, for it is a period when Europe was absorbing the Mediterranean before rejecting it, and the best situlae are the most Mediterranean. But compared to the assurance of boss-style bronze-work, or of the mature northern 'razor style' and its Central European forerunners, situla art is weak and sometimes quaint, and that is not a word one would apply to the others. The craftsman is no bungler, he has tools and material at will; what is lacking is the humanistic spirit behind natural representation. That was a thing for which he still had little use. If we find these northern imitations of oriental themes themselves so much more oriental than the Greek, or even the Etruscan, intermediaries, this is not really surprising; for an art that came like a revealing flash to the Greek world was fearfully strange to other Europeans, and after struggling with it for a little while they gave up. The last of the situlae are debased, incompetent, inept; truly not a beginning but an end.[63]

CHAPTER 8

CONTINENTAL ART IN THE LAST CENTURIES B.C.

If only the brown leaf were gold
The wood sheds when the year is old,
Or if the waves had silver spray
These too would Fionn have given away.
Old Irish, trans. F. O'Connor

THE Celtic La Tène art of the last four centuries B.C. that is illustrated on Plates 236 to 285 is perhaps one of the oddest and most unlikely things to have come out of a barbarous continent. Its peculiar refinement, delicacy, and equilibrium are not altogether what one would expect of men who, though courageous and not without honour even in the records of their enemies, were also savage, cruel, and often disgusting; for the archaeological refuse, as well as the report of classical antiquity, agree in this verdict. In spite of this La Tène art is a style, in its way as distinct as Egyptian, classical Greek, Romanesque, or Mayan. Not all art in barbarian Europe in these centuries was La Tène art, and about the others there will be something to say; but no other approaches the significance of La Tène, which is more professional, surer of itself, appearing to accomplish time after time what it set out to do; and yet so unpredictable and idiosyncratic, so exactly poised and consistent, telling much and concealing much, anti-classical yet as disciplined as the best classical art. It is too limited perhaps to be really great, yet it has an extraordinary toughness and persistence, so that it lives on through the Middle Ages, where it lies concealed, a source of tension, an invisible pole, even when apparently obsolete and forgotten.

The beginning of the Celtic La Tène style is a watershed, but only in art. Celtic languages are older than La Tène art and so are Celtic societies, though when and where to start looking for them are still open questions. It is usually agreed that Hallstatt tribes in South Germany, Bohemia, and eastern France were in the full sense Celts in the sixth century, and some of them probably from a good deal earlier. Celtic names were introduced into Spain by Hallstatt invaders, and the presence there of Celtic tribes is attested by Greek and Roman authors, but there is little true La Tène art in the peninsula; while in Britain a most extreme form of La Tène appeared quite a long time after the first Celtic landings.[1] If the La Tène Celts with their great tribal capitals behind walls and ramparts, and the immense burial mounds of the chieftains are typical of the heroic society, ramparts and mounds are much older too.

It is now time to recall a sentence quoted at the beginning of this study, that 'Celtic art has no genesis' but 'flashes up' all at once mature and perfect. There is a sense in which this dramatic statement is still true; but since we have gone over the ground in the centuries before, we may now feel that it does not really reflect the state of a Europe in which diverse traditions were already straining against and colliding with each other, building up a situation that was indeed explosive politically as well as in the arts, and that only *appears* to lack antecedents if we turn our back on a large part of the evidence. Jacobsthal admitted a problem and only partially resolved it when he said that Celtic art had three roots: the classical art of the Mediterranean, an eastern art meaning principally Scythia but in some ill-defined way Persia as well, and 'native' meaning Hallstatt geometric art.

Of the classical root of this (characteristically Celtic) triad he has given an unsurpassed exposition. With the account of the eastern root he was himself dissatisfied, for the points of contact are elusive, while the European root fails through limitation to one among a number of different traditions. On the classical side I shall have nothing new to add; on the eastern side I believe that more account could be taken of the impact of Persian Anatolia, especially in view of the old habit of contact between Eastern Europe and an earlier Anatolia, and of the Achaemenian penetration of Europe. But more important is the broadening of the European basis to include, beside Hallstatt geometric, an already orientalizing Hallstatt, and the wholly European curvilinear non-representational, or only ambivalently representational, style that had its beginning in Eastern Europe, found its way to the Baltic, and so turned south again, reinforced, to places and to men made newly receptive through their contacts with Mediterranean civilizations: the same men who had rejected it in the ninth and eighth centuries. It is among these many protagonists and extraordinary complexities that we must look for the sensitive point of emergence, the actual beginnings of La Tène art in the course of the fifth century.

The Roots

During the foregoing sixth century legitimate trade and the exchange of gifts brought some of the finest contemporary Mediterranean work in bronze and gold up into Gaul and over the Alps. Greeks and Etruscans had by this time outgrown the heroic society with its complicated grades of giving and returning gifts: all such ostentatious gifts were now directed into the treasuries of the great sanctuaries of the gods and to the cities themselves. But the European tribes were still ruled by old, though not petrified customs, and would so remain for centuries to come. The tombs of great chiefs were packed, like southern sanctuaries, with rare objects of value, sometimes useless or scarcely understood but very grand. An exaggeration has been noticed, an almost lunatic ostentation. When at the Heuneburg on the upper Danube a Celtic chief employed southern engineers to surround his tribal citadel with a wall and rectangular bastions of mud brick on a stone footing, according to Mediterranean principles, he set them not as a defence against enemies on the vulnerable west face (there he preferred the known and proved rubble and wood), but to the north-west, opposite a friendly settlement, where they would most impress subjects and neighbours. He thus turned even the art of fortification into a luxury article, like the overlarge imported black-figure crater found in fragments on the site.[2]

This accords with the bronze crater, probably Spartan or Corinthian, found in a princess's tomb at Vix near Châtillon-sur-Seine that is notoriously the largest and heaviest of its kind, something to astound the barbarians.[3] The bronze hydria from Grächwil, with a 'Mistress of Animals' and her supporters on the neck, is again an exceptional object; and a bronze cauldron with griffins' heads lifting over the rim found in a rather later tomb at Sainte-Colombe (Côte d'Or) is only a little less grand. The superlative Greek workmanship seen on the gold diadem worn by the princess at Vix, and of the bronze vases, crater, and cauldrons from Grächwil, Vilsingen, and Kappel am Rhein had an electrifying effect upon Celtic bronze- and gold-work. Apart from the technique of granulation, which was still unknown to them, they were hardly at all inferior technicians to Mediterranean craftsmen, and well able to value and judge the stuff that came into their hands. From what follows, it appears that they found more to learn from the southern goldsmiths than from bronzesmiths.

At the beginning of the sixth century the Alpine passes *and* the Rhône valley were used by traffic from the south while, to judge by later history, skins, beasts, slaves, and hides would have been sent south for barter.[4] Then, from about the mid sixth century, through the enterprise of Phocaean colonists settled at Massilia and of other Greek settlements in the south of France, the Rhône became paramount in importance. By this route wine and oil could travel north to Mont Lassois and Vix on the Seine, and to the Heuneburg on the Danube. After 500 B.C. this route lapsed, and there was a shift eastwards and a return to the Alpine passes perhaps due in part to Italian politics and the enterprise of the Etruscans (now well settled in the Po valley) and the Greeks at Spina on the Adriatic.[5] The bronze flagons that came north in the early fifth century are all Etruscan, but vases from the hands of named Greek painters were also imported and found their way into the burial chambers of a later generation. These tombs were bigger than ever before, as much as 40 feet (12 m.) high and over 200 feet (65 m.) across. Sometimes they cover light two-wheeled chariots in place of the earlier heavy four-wheeled carts or hearses. The graves are now clustered near together, and one such cluster between the Moselle and the Saar may belong to a 'Royal Dynasty'. Another cluster in northern France, though not under barrows, is almost as rich and as early.[6]

These are the people archaeologists call La Tène A, Ia, or simply Early La Tène. The Rhineland group were not a first generation of conquerors: they are only greater than their fathers, whom they follow on the same land, more pushing, more flamboyant, more confident, but essentially the same Celtic aristocracy who loved strong drink in an exotic cup. Their artists knew well what they were about when they sifted the foreign gauds, accepting some and refusing some. There was no one yet to *impose* acceptance, as happened so disastrously when Roman conquered Celt. Classical stereotypes – palmette, lotus, lyre, tendril – were taken, naturalistic figures rejected, elements of composition were taken, narrative rejected, and so on. When Gaulish tribes came down into Italy there were more and closer opportunities to learn and borrow. From scraps of recently collected evidence it seems that the great raid that culminated in the attack on Rome in 379 B.C. was far from being their first appearance in Italy, but that from as early as the mid fifth century some Gauls were fighting, dying, and being buried south of the Alps.[7]

*

If Greek and Etruscan had been the only exotic influences at work north of the Alps, the history of La Tène art might have been very different; but there were lights too from the east bright enough to take some of the dazzle out of the new Mediterranean discoveries. We do not have to wait for Celtic tribes to make their plunge into Thrace, to reach Delphi and catch their first sight of the Bosphorus, since at any time during the fifth century Asiatic fashions and ideas could have seeped up as far as the Danube. How this should be needs some explanation.

When in 513–512 the great Persian king Darius crossed into Europe, he overwhelmed and enslaved the Getae who lived south of the Danube but made little impression on 'Scythian' tribes north of the river; these still sat loose to the land. Who the Getae were we do not know; the name may be Iranian, and, according to Herodotus, they differed from the Thracians in their customs, being more warlike and more disciplined. Herodotus also knew of 'medianized Scyths' under the name Syginnae who lived north of the Danube, dressed like the Medes (which probably means they wore trousers), and had small rough-coated horses that they drove in chariots. Their border almost reached the Eneti on the Adriatic. He continues rather testily 'They call themselves colonists of the Medes, but how they can be . . . I for my part cannot imagine; still, nothing is impossible in the lapse of ages'. Today it is easier to accept the Syginnae's account of themselves, and even to see one of the ways by which those peculiarly Celtic-sounding shaggy ponies and trousers could have come from farther east into Central Europe. Mention of the Eneti lends point to the discovery of 'Scythian-style' ornaments at Villach and Magdalenska Gora in Slovenia.[8] They include ox-heads and animal whirligigs that are poorer versions of the great silver treasure, either Scythian, Dacian, or a mixture of both, found at Craiova in Wallachia and others in Bulgaria which are probably fifth-century. Native Europeans and eastern 'nomads' probably had a good deal more in common and lived in closer touch with each other than is usually allowed, borrowing at times specific ornamental motifs;[9] still more the Celtic artists were to employ the same subjection of anatomy and of the animal contour to pattern, the broken-backed beast and the treatment of joints; all of which had a profound influence on their art without ever being exactly imitated.

After the failure of Darius's campaign his general Megabazus was left in Europe with orders to conquer Thrace. This, as far at least as the coastal strip, he succeeded in doing, and, following the usual Asiatic practice, a part of the native Paeonian population was transported and resettled in Asia. We hear of an embassy to the Macedonian king and of the murder of the ambassadors with the loss of servants, luggage, and carriages.[10] There is news of gold and silver mines and of the tribes that worked them, some of whom lived on 'piles' in a lake; stories too of a Garden of Midas where many-petalled roses grew wild, as they grow now, though cultivated, in Bulgaria, and where Silenus was captured, and other legends with tantalizing but unreliable hints that link Phrygia and the Balkans. From this time until the Persian and Greek wars the Persians kept a footing in Europe, so that when the great army of Xerxes crossed the Hellespont in 480 to revenge the defeat of Marathon the whole Thracian coastland was pacified and for the moment friendly. Thracians and Paeonians were pressed into the Persian expeditionary forces as auxiliary infantry, and held as hostages, though the wilder tribes like the Satrae, living in the mountains, with their gold and silver mines, remained aloof.

Amazing stories were told for years afterwards of the immense treasure with which the army travelled: tents full of gold and silver furniture, goblets, bowls, anklets, swords, chains, and embroidered clothing. Much of this treasure fell into Greek hands, like the tent of Mardonius after Plataea, but it is more than likely that a part reached the Balkan tribes with returning Thracian and Paeonian auxiliaries. Xerxes himself abandoned much with the sick and wounded on his way back. There was the 'sacred chariot of Zeus' left at Siris which the Thracians sent north up the Strymon, we do not know how far. However much we discount the details and look askance at accounts based on Greek knowledge of their barbarian neighbours, it is none the less important to remember that for thirty-odd years, between 512 and 479, and especially around the last date, there were opportunities for Achaemenian works of art, passing from hand to hand as gifts or plunder, to reach inland tribes independently of Greek trade and enterprise. One of these works, a beautiful silver amphora with handles in the form of the Achaemenian horned and winged lion, was buried in a native grave at Duvanli near Plovdiv and not far from Mezek, where, some time later, a Celtic intruder was to be buried with parts of his chariot. But it is not with the 'Plastic Style' of that time (early third century) that Achaemenian work like the Duvanli amphora is to be linked, but with the more nearly contemporary fifth-century beginnings of the 'Early Style'.

Many great barrow burials in the South Balkans held fine Greek vases and jewellery. One of the graves at Trebenište on Lake Ochrid had a great bronze crater only less imposing than Vix, and the faces of the dead chieftains were covered with gold masks that are a strange reminder of Mycenae, as though time had stood still in the Balkans, or rather the tardy northerners had just reached a stage corresponding to that of Peloponnesian chiefs a thousand years before.

Illyrian and other tribes in Yugoslavia and in the East Balkans had themselves very good craftsmen. We know from their graves, and hoards of lost valuables, that they wore wide silver and gold belts like Plate 231 from Mramorac near Smederevo, with very closely hammered decoration that gives the metal a nap or bloom. A belt like this was found at Novi Pazar in West Serbia with a Greek black-figure vase of about 500 B.C. Sometimes amber beads are found carved into human heads, and there are chains of the sixth–fifth century with pendants that hang from brooches like the silver ones of Štrpci and Čurug (Plate 233). The latter is a large collection of jewellery including also silver earrings with granulation (Plate 232) and heavy silver bangles with snake's-head ends. Some of these, especially the knobby brooches, may have had some influence on the 'Plastic Style' of La Tène ornament, but it was for the most part an unimaginative, restricted, and repetitive repertoire. There is a relaxed luxury about these bangles that may be oriental or Hellenistic; for instance the elaborate ornament from Bukjovci in Bulgaria with chains that hang in loops from four brooches like Plate 233 has pendants, one of them a many-petalled flower, and a human head, perhaps a reminder of the roses of Kazanlak. Another brooch from Bulgaria is of a different type but has a human head rather like Bukjovci above a dog's or lion's head that looks out from between two birds (Plate 234). Here the links are with the northern shores of the Black Sea.[11]

Gold helmets that have come to light in Rumania are decidedly oriental in fashion. One reputedly found in the Danube near the Iron Gates has quite sophisticated relief ornament. But the helmet, or better tiara, from Poiana-Coţofeneşti is uncompromisingly barbaric (Plate 235). Silver beakers were found with it and with a silver helmet in a barrow at Hagighiol; these too have a very oriental look both in shape and decoration, like inexpert versions of the Marlik beakers in northern Iran; and it almost seems as if the maker of the Poiana-Coţofeneşti tiara had once seen the seventh-century gold pectoral found at Ziwiye in north-western Iran, or the tower-shaped tiara of the Great King himself, or, more prosaically, he may simply have copied the conical shape and tight curls of an astrakhan hat. The sacrifice of the ram on the cheek-guard is performed in the Mithraic position. Hagighiol gives a date probably around 400 B.C. for this group.[12]

Who the authors of this art were – Getae, Dacians, Illyrians – is hard to say, but they were certainly very mixed. Into this world the Celts exploded, probably rather after their first appearance in Italy, though the great expansion, whatever its immediate cause, kept up a fairly continuous pressure from the end of the fifth century. There were Celtic mercenaries in the Peloponnese in 369–8. In 335 a Celtic embassy met Alexander the Great on the Danube, and in 310 they were harassing the Illyrians. Not long after, in 298, they were repulsed in Bulgaria, but in 281 there was another attack, and in 279 they raided down into Greece and sacked Delphi. Some reached Chersonese and crossed into Anatolia, where they were to remain as Galatians into our era, still speaking their own dialect. As mercenaries they even reached Egypt. It is possible that Celtic warriors are shown in the wall paintings of a corbelled fifth–fourth-century tomb recently discovered at Kazanlak in Bulgaria.[13] In a frieze depicting warfare, two combatants carry long oval shields with blunt ends that look Celtic, and they wear a different cap or helmet to the rest. There were Celts at one time in the Dobrogea and the delta of the Danube. From the fourth century, but chiefly in the second, they were over the Carpathians between the Vistula and the Oder. Those that had stayed in the Balkans at the beginning of the second century were driven back towards Central Europe, where they mingled with the older populations. The great size of the cemeteries there and the growth of *oppida* show a concentration of people and great social development in the years between 125 and 50 B.C.

The native background to Celtic art and to the Celtic expansion is equally important and even more difficult to isolate. The Hallstatt geometric workshops continued in business; their tradition was strong and can still be recognized long after the rise of the new style, especially in harness, in late situlae, and in the goldsmiths' embossing and stamping (especially belt strips and diadems) and trade tricks of wheelwrights and cartmakers, all of which show continuity. But this was certainly not all. There is no difficulty in finding likenesses between La Tène and northern Bronze Age decoration – many instances will be referred to in this chapter – but here the problem is the point of actual contact, the physical possibility of direct influence.

The 'razor' and other northern arts that we followed in the last chapter spread gradually south, first into Mecklenburg and then farther. Geographically and politically frontiers were ill-defined and fluctuating, but one, marked by great fortifications (Burgwälle) and hoards, for some considerable time ran through Thuringia to where the Hunsrück-Eifel meet the Rhine. Northern Germanic cultures, like that known to archaeologists as Jastorf, in the neighbourhood of this line, met, in the west Hallstatt South German cultures, and in the east 'Lausitz'. By the eighth century West Mecklenburg and North-West Brandenburg were already a part of the Nordic Province, but also they were in touch with the metallurgy of the Swiss Alpine region and the urnfields of Central Western Europe, and like them experienced an irruption of horse-harness of the so-called 'Thraco-Cimmerian' kind. In the sixth century there was depopulation in South Sweden coinciding with a change from barrow-graves to urnfields, while south of the Thuringian forest there were again barrow burials at first over cremation graves but later over inhumations (Hallstatt D 2 and Early La Tène); farther north on the Saale, ashes of the cremated dead were placed in clay urns shaped like miniature houses. These sometimes discrepant archaeological factors are not easy to interpret, but the overall picture agrees with extensive north–south contacts, both hostile and peaceful.[14]

The Rhineland was solidly Celtic, and German tribes are not recognized there till Caesar writes of them. Even then, however, they are not archaeologically attested, and in fact Caesar's reporting may be suspect on some points.[15]

These then are the most important of the contrary factors that converged and jostled in an auspicious moment in that part of Europe that lies between the Rhine, the Alps, the Böhmerwald, and the Hungarian plain. Greek, Etruscan, Achaemenian, Scythian, Dacian, Illyrian, Nordic influences were all there in greater or lesser degree, stimulants and irritants that gave rise to a political, spiritual, and aesthetic entity strong enough to survive for several hundred years.

A new factor was the massive adoption of iron for common tools and weapons. The elaborate network of trade and communications which the rarity of some ores had imposed on Europe must still have been maintained, but the much greater availability of iron ores made changes here also (see above, p. 208). The prestige of the Celtic smith that was remembered in the epic tales of the Irish tradition may well be older than them, and is now corroborated by archaeological discoveries such as the elaborate burial of craftsmen. According to texts written down in the eighth century A.D. but referring to much older times, there were in the tribe below the king, first a class of nobles; below them the *aes dana* or men of art – that is to say lawyers, leeches, jewellers, poets – men who had the right to move freely from tribe to tribe; and below them again, the common freemen.[16]

A peculiarity of Celtic tribes was that when something set them in motion they split apart in different directions, so that the name of the Boii is heard of in Italy as well as in Bohemia and later in Gaul, and that of the Volcae in Central Europe, southern Gaul, and Asia Minor.[17] In this way workshop teams may have split and scattered, accounting for the extraordinarily rapid spread and homogeneity of, for example, the

La Tène 'Plastic Style' in Bohemia and France or the 'Sword Style' in Hungary, Switzerland, and northern Gaul.

It was not till the second and first centuries B.C. that the large Celtic *oppida* enjoyed a short independent prosperity. Something approaching town life in the Mediterranean sense was lived inside the ramparts, in close accord with the farming economy of the countryside around. Many large centres existed such as Manching in Bavaria, Bettingen in Baden, and Bibracte near Autun in Gaul.[18] They had their organization for obtaining metals, their resident workshops; there were precincts and holy places, and occasionally built temples. Yet when all this has been said and mapped, it remains true that life was still lived to a great extent on the frontiers. The wilderness was still on the doorstep, the world divided between men and 'the other camp' of supernatural powers against whom 'man situated in the midst of the supernatural, and himself possessed by it, defends with difficulty by force or by magic his small domain, which is always surrounded by invisible tribes and subject on certain ritual days to direct invasions'.[19] The primordial battle between chaos and cosmos was still joined on all fronts, and Celtic art was itself a part of the protective armament in this supernatural warfare.

In a history of art we may be forgiven for leaving to one side the finer chronology and detailed vicissitudes of the different sections of the Celtic world, especially since these are still open to quite fundamental rearrangement. Our concern is not with these but with the genesis, growth, and decay of La Tène art. For this the landmarks set up by Professor Jacobsthal still stand. They begin with an 'Early Style' that is more symmetric and representational than what followed, more classical *and* more oriental, and much less peculiar. It appeared during the first half of the fifth century, and a little over a century later it gave rise to the 'Waldalgesheim Style'. The dates depend on Greek and Italian wares found in Celtic graves north of the Alps and in Gaul, and to some extent on Celtic objects found in Italy.[20] At its most characteristic this is non-representational, flowing, sinuous, asymmetric, almost the opposite of the Early Style. Then there is a 'Plastic Style', appearing probably at the beginning of the third century, that is boldly three-dimensional, as the name implies. It is at first linked to Waldalgesheim but also directly to the Early Style, and it is very widely dispersed.[21] There is a 'Sword Style' that also combines elements of the Early and of the Waldalgesheim Styles, but in a quite different manner. It can be more rigorously asymmetric and is much more limited in its regional extension, with two concentrations, in Central Switzerland and in Hungary. It probably did not arise till the end of the third century. Then with the gradual advance of Rome a heavy, monumental, rather spiritless classicism engulfs the Continent.

These are the landmarks, but the styles do not follow each other in any orderly fashion: one is absent from a whole region, and another lasts too long, and a tangle of links and connexions binds them together. In the British Isles the insular La Tène, though it has points of equivalence with the continent, is on the whole so different, and had so different an aftermath, that it is best treated apart.

La Tène Art: The Early Style

It is probably true that the paradox of the Early Style, that it is so much closer than the later styles to classical *and* to oriental models, is a sign of the immaturity of the Celtic artist. But not for one moment was he content merely to copy, nor the patron to applaud secondhand work. A selection drawn from the chieftains' graves in Germany and France brings forward at once many lasting La Tène themes: the face, the fantastic beast, the man-devouring beast, uses of inlay and openwork, metamorphoses, mythology, types of beauty, and even, though less certainly, the individual workshop (Plates 236 to 242). It is comparatively easy to find the springboard for this Early Style, but much more difficult to account for the direction of the spring, which comes from deep psychological roots. We can pick out the classical models, sometimes rather tight and dry, for the palmette and lotus bud, tendrils, S's and lyres, but transferred to a La Tène bracelet or brooch they look entirely different.

The cast gold ring with a moustached face from a later-fifth-century grave at Rodenbach, Rhineland (Plate 236), is inspired by Greek and Etruscan goldsmiths' work.[22] The beaded line on the bracelet is a substitute for granulation, but as a contour, sweeping from the animal's head over flank and haunch, it is used in a manner probably learnt from the Scythian school, although something of the sort existed even in the Paleolithic (Plate 26 and Figure 14). The animals seem to be griffins, for the pose is leonine. The backward look and heraldic grouping are perhaps more oriental than Mediterranean, but the physiognomy of the faces on both ring and bracelet is Celtic and is as loosely linked to a classical Silenus as to an Iranian 'Zurvan'.[23] The 'egg-cups', locks, and spirals have been soldered on to the gold bar of the bracelet with much skill. Heads like these are often called 'masks', but this is a term that I propose to consider in the next chapter.

Jewellery of equal grandeur was made, perhaps in rivalry, for the Rheinheim dynasty a little to the west in the Saarland.[24] The richest tomb held, like Vix, a princess, and with her body were bronze table-ware, a mirror, beads, brooches, gold necklets, bracelets, and other gauds (Plates 237–9). One bracelet and a necklet have two busts each of a winged goddess with a bird on her head. She owes something to the 'Mistress of Animals' on the Grächwil hydria (p. 228 above), but the wings are folded tightly back, and in place of the standing eagle of Grächwil, on the goddess's head there is a predatory beak sunk into its wings; a pair of owls under the 'balusters' takes the place of the sitting lions, and the three balls under her chin are powerful signs in Celtic iconography. There is therefore no need to go south of the Alps for the immediate inspiration for this figure, and if something more *were* required, it might be found northward, where the Fårdal goddess (Plate 206), though wingless and birdless, is not dissimilar, and her coral inset eyes have the same beady stare. The realistic bronze cock on a brooch (Plate 239) is also from Rheinheim. It has red coral inlay, and the only La Tène peculiarity is the 'comma' or 'tear-drop' pattern on the wing, which is the same as was engraved on the haunches of horses on the bronze scabbard from Grave 994 at Hallstatt (Figure 93).[25] The oriental cock and hen came to Greece in the late eighth century, and it had taken them three hundred years to make the further journey to the middle Rhine. I believe this plain fowl had a long and extraordinary progeny and will be met again on the backs of mirrors in England.

A much more Iranian taste appears in the bronze and coral belt-buckle from another aristocratic grave, at Weisskirchen in the Saar (Plate 240). The supernumerary horns of the royal lions of Susa, Persepolis, Duvanli, and the Oxus treasure are remembered in the curled spiral crests that here look more like a frivolous decoration. The group might almost belong to the mythology of Luristan;[26] yet in spite of the incongruous boots and awkward stance of the inner pair of man-monsters, even this piece makes a harmonious whole that bears the imprint of a 'style' without those discordances of barbaric work such as appear on Plates 228 and 235. Strongly Iranian also are four gold neckrings found with bracelets at Erstfeld, Canton Uri, Switzerland. The bracelets are typical of Early Style jewellery and particularly close to those of Rodenbach, Rheinheim, and other Rhenish tombs; but the neckrings, with half-bird, half-human figures, and the prominent ibex are eastern. That similarity to Iranian bronzes that is latent in much Celtic work is here explicit.[27] Openwork lends itself to evocations of the forest and looks forward to such things as the Gloucester candlestick and the Souillac pillar, where, as here, half-animal creatures grip and peck each other, enmeshed among branches and tendrils woven of their own limbs.

A bronze flagon in the Rheinheim tomb was native Celtic work; the chieftains of this generation no longer needed to send for such luxuries over the Alps to Italy, for their own artists had begun to produce flagons that, though they look very different, owe their ultimate inspiration to the old southern models. Such are Klein Aspergle, Dürrnberg, Borsch, and Basse-Yutz. The great lady buried around 450 B.C. at Klein Aspergle in Württemberg, though in a subsidiary grave (the main grave had been plundered), had a very fair copy of an Etruscan flagon to which native imagination had attached two animal and two ambiguous faces (Plates 241 and 242 and Figure 88A).[28] The ambiguity is entirely Celtic, for though the two smaller heads of Plate 241 are unquestionably animal and the others not, it is far from obvious where the difference lies; probably it is that hallmark of sapient man, his chin. The goggle-eyed stare and the plasticity, especially of the centre head of three, gives a cross-link with rather later plastic work such as the Brå cauldron and its owls (Plate 256).

Little remains of the original bronze of the flagon from a cremation under a tumulus at Borsch, Bad Salzungen, in Thuringia except the handle, but this is magnificent (Plate 243). It is the only La Tène flagon handle made entirely from the body of a gripping or drinking animal, head, back-legs, and all. Notwithstanding the withered fore-legs and a finicking incised pattern on the body, there is a fierceness here which sets the lions of a classical hydria (like that found recently at Paestum) in the polite Landseer company. The basketry pattern on the animal's neck is not common on the Continent, but became very popular in the British Isles.[29]

Dürrnberg, near Salzburg, dated about 425, is the most southerly of the early La Tène chariot graves. It too held a flagon, and here we are close to Etruscan and Greek goldsmiths' work and especially to the workshops of Spina on the Adriatic (Plates 244

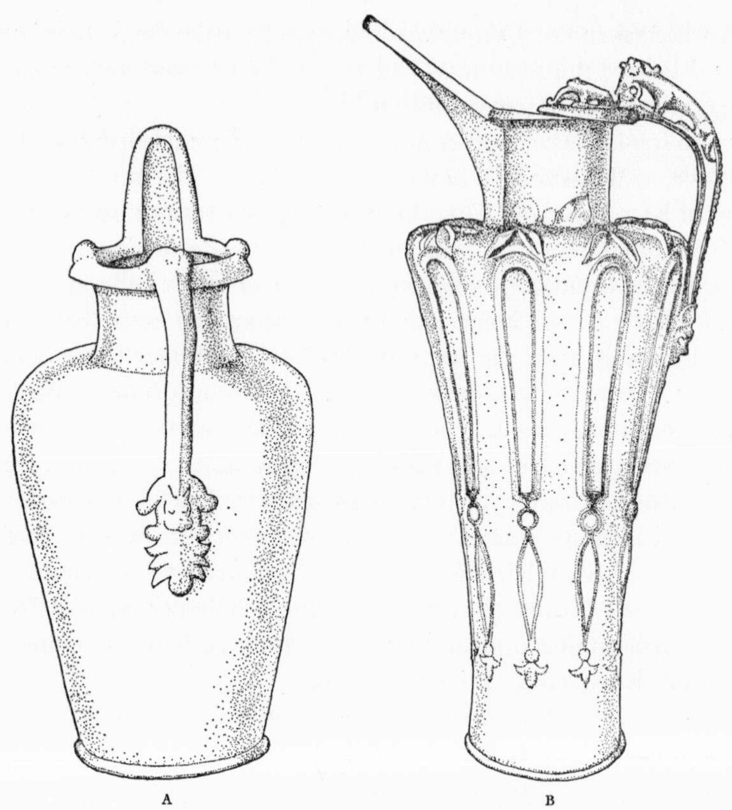

Figure 88. Bronze flagons: A from Klein Aspergle, Württemberg, Germany
B from Dürrnberg, Austria (cf. Plates 241–2 and 244–5)

and 245 and Figure 88B). The animal does not form the whole handle but crouches upon it, resting its chin on a delicate human head, naturalistic apart from the size of the eye, that is held between its paws. Two smaller animals that flank the handle-beast are cast in one piece with it. They belong to the same predatory race and bite on to the tails of some creature whose body they have just wolfed. Below the handle appears the same beaded line that we saw at Rodenbach and Rheinheim simulating Etruscan granulation. The face at the bottom of the handle is a different type from that on the rim, and whereas a Greek or Etruscan goldsmith would have placed his palmette above the head, we see it here below, at the base of a double chain of S's (Plate 244).[30] The sunk repoussé panels on the body of the flagon are a rare feature of 'Early Style' work that reappears much later in Britain (see below, p. 259). There were a number of graves at Dürrnberg, and the bronze spout from Grave 46 in the 'Plastic Style' is presumably much later (Plate 257; below, p. 241).

All these native flagons have much in common, but another pair found at Basse-Yutz in Lorraine are very different and were probably made appreciably later, in the first half of the fourth century, though the shape – tall, slender, and sharp-shouldered – is like Dürrnberg (Plate 246).[31] The use of coral and red enamel round the base and spout is novel on a flagon, though common on brooches and other trinkets. The engraving is coarser than usual. The animals too are very different, and can only be compared to the small sitting animals on the Parsberg brooch (see below and Plate 248). Spiral ears and joints are met in the Altai oftener than in Western Europe, and the parallel planes and deep-cut lines belong to the wood- and bone-carver rather than the metal-worker. The hatching of the fell is unmetallic too.[32] These creatures, apart from the swimming duck at the tip of the spout, are among the few orientalizing animals that really look more Scythian (i.e. from Russia) than Iranian. The engraving of the rectilinear geometric patterns of the spout and the 'sprung palmette' and leaf-curls between the corals of the throat-guard and foot is again rather coarse. The layout, with the three animals and the human head at the base of the handle, as well as the shape of the flagon, link it to the earlier La Tène group, so that all in all this is an eclectic piece, masterly in the combination of its elements, and subtly not quite a truly La Tène masterpiece.

A brooch with two heads from Oberwittighausen in Baden is entirely characteristic of La Tène art in the physiognomy and in the peculiar ambiguity of the heads that stand in the same relationship to one another as do the Klein Aspergle heads (Plates 247 and 241, and see p. 281 below). Another brooch, from Parsberg in the Oberpfalz, has surface decoration in the style of the Borsch and Dürrnberg flagons, and heads at either end of the bow that are slightly out-of-focus versions of one another (Plate 248).

Bronze openwork in a sober, disciplined, and brilliantly decorative style was sometimes produced, especially in northern France (Plates 249 and 252), and here we meet dragons generally in pairs. An openwork ornament from a chariot grave at Dürkheim in the Rheinpfalz has lost most of its tracery; only the solider part with the confronted beasts has survived (Figure 89A). It may have come from one of the rolls of a swingletree. The tomb had an Etruscan bronze stamnos and tripod that date it to the mid fifth century.[33] The parentage of these animals and of the harness dragons from another early chariot grave, this time at Cuperly on the Marne (Plate 249), is usually looked for among swastika whirligigs with animal heads found in South-East Europe. Jacobsthal did not hesitate to call them Scythian or Scythian–Iranian, and most writers have followed him.[34] The zoological problem is complicated by an invasion of lyres and palmettes from south of the Alps which originally had nothing to do with dragons, but which got caught up with them. Something certainly came from the eastern direction, and we have already seen how this could have come about in the early fifth century at the time of the Greco-Persian wars; but something also I believe came from Northern Europe, which already possessed in its own peculiar 'razor art' an animal with a long curly snout (p. 207 above). Originally this was an ordinary elk and later a horse. In Plates 249 and 251 the horse's ear is recognizable, but in Figure 89 it is a griffin's crest. When it stood at either end of a northern boat it was ready to be turned into a lyre by bringing the heads together. A wooden stand or platter from Høstad in Norway illustrates this very well (Plate 250).[35] The same creatures are scratched on a pot from La Cheppe (Marne) (Plate 251), and they are often seen on scabbards and on buckets. Sometimes they have legs like Figure 89A, often they end in graceful S-spirals or simply subserve the convention of the lyre.[36] The engraved ribbon patterns and stippling on the Dürkheim, Cuperly, and

La Bouvanderie bronzes are exact forerunners of the early medieval manuscript treatment of the great capital letters.[37]

Perhaps the most beautiful of all Early La Tène tracery is that on two bronze discs found in a tomb at Saint Jean-sur-Tourbe (Marne) (Plate 252). These in their fashion are counterparts of Figure 69B and Plate 197. They share the same flowing, dancing rhythm, and the skill with which the pattern of the outer openwork zone changes from single to double loop, from profile (as it were) to full-face, is something for which the Bronze Age masters had prepared the way; moreover it is possible still to sense the compass half-circle and dot of the old pulley-pattern somewhere in the background as it is on Plate 263 and Figure 92B (see below, Chapter 9).

These few examples must serve to represent the first phase of Celtic La Tène art. This was the style that antedated the great Celtic expansion, the style that was carried down into Italy and eastwards from Bohemia to the Tisza. Though greatly changed, it continued to mould and influence long after the rise of a new style in the old La Tène heartland on the middle Rhine. It was still current in the late fourth century, when it appears in Italian graves at Canosa, but the new style was then close on its heels. In Gaul too it lived on, and eventually crossed the channel to Britain.

The Waldalgesheim Style

During the middle years of the fourth century a new tendency appeared within the Early La Tène style; it is at its most characteristic in a rich grave at Waldalgesheim, one of the last of the great Rhenish princely burials and situated rather to the north of them in the Hunsrück. It was a double grave of a man and woman buried with chariot fittings, gold, jewellery,and bronze table-ware which included a late-fourth-century Campanian bucket. On jewellery, chariot-fittings, and above all on two sheets of bronze with repoussé busts, the new style is displayed. The busts are alike and are both very damaged (Plate 253). They show a figure wearing a 'Hathor' or 'Astarte' wig foreign to Greek and Etruscan representations. A La Tène goldsmith had used it conventionally in a fifth-century tomb with Early Style objects at Schwarzenbach, but it is misunderstood and soon changed into a 'leaf-crown'.[38] The holes in the chest have been 'turned' and probably held corals, so this, like a gorgon, was a female person; the pose too is like that of the gorgoneia, frontal and hieratic. The serpentine pattern on the shirt or breast-plate has come as far from southern wreaths and tendrils as the patterns of the Hajdusámson axes and sword (Plates 173 and 171). It may have begun as an ivy-leaf tendril, but now it is entirely different, odd, and very typical of La Tène. This is also true of the gold necklet and bracelets from the same grave (Plate 254 and Figure 89B), though the development shows that the pattern is in fact symmetrical. Faces emerge from among the coils, and on the necklet a rayed petalled flower nestles at the centre of the spirals, very like an old Middle Minoan vase-painter's motif.[39] The illusion of asymmetry is enhanced in the development by the plastic coil of the bracelet, which achieves a true interlace. A flat bronze ring has a central swastika with oblique wings giving an overall symmetry which yet simulates asymmetry with extraordinary ingenuity.[40] These are

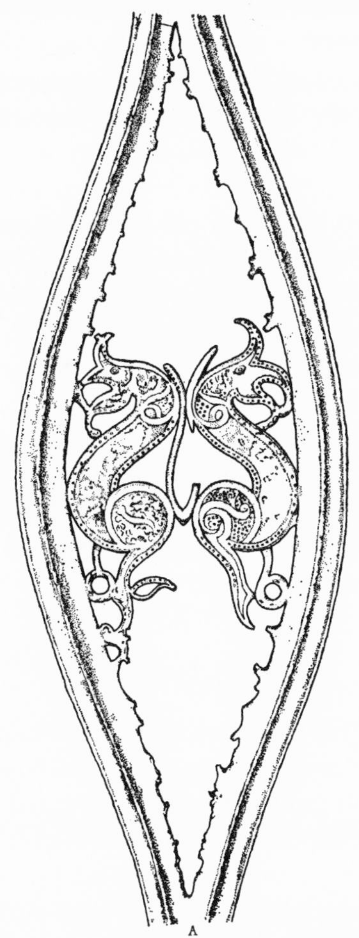

A

B

Figure 89. A Bronze openwork tracery from a chariot grave at Dürkheim, Rhineland, Germany
B Development of relief design on gold bracelet from Waldalgesheim, Kreuznach, Germany

patterns that seem to run counter to basic human conventions; but we shall return to the whole question of asymmetry in La Tène art in Chapter 9. Since this is a true style, it cannot be understood by taking to pieces the parts and turning them back into tendrils and palmettes, any more than a voice can be described by measuring decibels; yet the ear will recognize what it knows, and the eye instantly recognizes the 'Waldalgesheim tone', whether here in bronze and gold or in monumental stone (Plate 268) or in an otherwise alien milieu (Plate 255, on the handle attachment).

The Waldalgesheim style had not yet emerged when the Celts descended on Italy, but it is seen on swords in late-fourth-century graves in the tombs of the Celtic Senones at Ancona, and also perhaps in Picenum between 325 and 300. The style was carried east, and is at its most wayward on the neckguard of a helmet found at Silivaş in Transylvania.[41] It also just appears on a few of the scabbards in the great votive deposits of La Tène itself. None of these are likely to have been much earlier than 200 B.C. There is some evidence for a migration of tribes from the Neckarland in the second half of the third century, and it has been suggested that these may have been the Helvetii, who we know were settled in Switzerland in the first century B.C.[42] If this should be so, it might provide the occasion for those few examples of Waldalgesheim style in the huge underwater deposits, and so have been a factor influencing the emergence of the so-called 'Sword Style' (see below). There is a cryptic quality in Waldalgesheim which seems to require that its appearance should be under cover of some other style, and in this covert manner it survived for a long time, and just reached Britain.

The Plastic Style

A delight in heavy bangles and bold designs is in no way new or surprising, but two factors make the La Tène Plastic Style both original and consistent: a wayward attitude towards symmetry inherited from Waldalgesheim, and, more important, a peculiar decorative treatment of animal and human forms. Oriental animals, Urartian, Assyrian, Achaemenian, are more or less naturalistic, although monumental and simplified. They are patterned with spirals, flames, and wing, mane, and joint motifs, but they wear these ornaments like a very grand dress-uniform that can be taken off and still leave the animal complete. This is to some extent true even of Early La Tène animals, but in the Plastic Style the mass and contour of body and limbs *are* the pattern. No superficial stripping of locks or brows is possible without destruction of the composition (Plates 256 and 257). Scythian artists did the same, but in a different way. This changed attitude to living forms becomes the very essence of a style that is balanced between nature and solid geometry. These swirling shapes are either simplified and formalized renderings of natural contour or, with unabashed enjoyment, they plunge into abstract whorl, spiral, and helix. We see them on linch-pins, terrets, bracelets, rings, and all sorts of mounts and fittings. Much of this work has been found in Eastern Europe, and it is a curious fact that this is where comparable plastic whorls had been used in potting for hundreds of years (Plates 164–6). But it was equally accepted in the west, where there was no such Bronze Age tradition of plastic ornament.

The roots of the La Tène Plastic Style go back into the fifth century. An ancestor of the owl on the rim of the cauldron found at Brå in Jutland is, as we have seen, the little monster on the flagon rim from Klein Aspergle (Plates 256 and 241).[43] The inward-looking bird has the beaky fierceness of the griffins on early Greek and oriental cauldrons, very different to the mild, ingenuous, outward-looking oxen on either side of the handle (Plate 255). There is a long history behind bronze cauldrons with bulls' heads or with harpies or sirens round the rim that leads back into Western Asia in the early first millennium. The Brå oxen are closest to the Phrygian version.[44]

This great bowl, measuring over three feet (1 m.) across at the mouth, would have held 600 litres or 28 gallons. It was found in a bog and had been deliberately smashed, so that it makes one more in the long tale of open-air or underwater offerings. The rim is of solid bronze over an iron hoop, and the body, most of which is lost, was of thin bronze sheet. The shape was much the same as the eastern prototype. The animal heads are cast solid with the handle and bolted on to the rim. On the ring fitting immediately behind the owl's head is a relief tendril in pure Waldalgesheim style (cf. Plates 255 and 256). The ring for the chain from which the cauldron hung is iron with a thin bronze covering. The dating, on style alone, is reasonably given as third-century, when Waldalgesheim was still in use and even Early Style not too far off. The bowl was not made in Denmark, but was one of the first purely La Tène works to reach the north. The workshops may have been in Bohemia or in Moravia, where it has stylistic affinities and where bulls had been represented since the Neolithic, whereas in Scandinavia they are rare at any time.[45]

A spout with two characteristically divergent back-to-back heads was found at Dürrnberg near Hallein in Austria in a later grave than the flagon from that site (Plate 257). Stylistically it is more advanced than Brå, though it has a link there, and with France as well as Moravia.[46] A group of bronze ornamental fittings found in 1941 at Brno-Maloměřice shows the plastic animal style at its best (Plates 258–9). This was a stray find, but Celtic graves have since come to light near by. There are some dozen-odd pieces of bronze openwork and a few plaques and rings. At first they were thought to have covered a wooden flagon or other vessel, or to have embellished an elaborate driving yoke, but neither interpretation is altogether convincing.[47]

Nothing here is quite what it seems; two strikingly naturalistic human heads with contrasting expressions could stand for genial and sardonic 'humours' (Plate 260). The largest single piece has a boldly modelled animal's head that is usually called a bull, but could be an ibex if the upper curved extension is allowed to be horns. They have the characteristic notching and the same curve as an Achaemenian ibex ornament. At the back of this head there is a pair of eyes under beetling brows, apparently isolated, but the object can be inclined so that a face appears that is as subtly human as the other is animal (Plate 258 and Figure 90, left). Viewed from below, even the large head looks human. We could apply here words written about another La Tène object, the 'pony cap' from Torrs in Scotland: 'Good as the design is it does not wholly please when viewed on the flat . . . the craftsman always had in mind the appearance of the piece *in use* . . . sufficient interest must be concentrated for the owner's pleasure, the design of

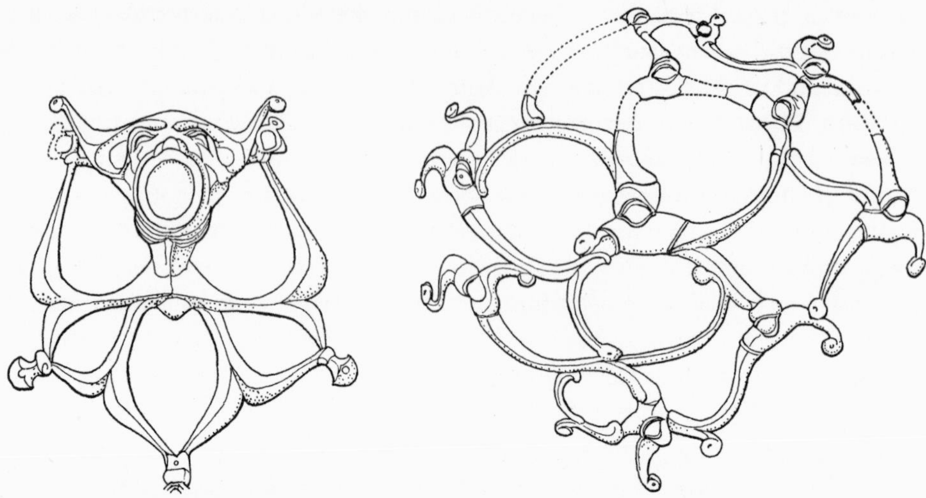

Figure 90. Part of bronze openwork ornament from Brno-Maloměřice, Moravia, Czechoslovakia

the front sloping down and away from him will be foreshortened to *his* eyes and look as "tight" as the back.'[48]

Eyes appear obsessively in the knots or joints of an openwork bronze 'net' where limbs, beaks, or horns divide and sprout (Figure 90, right). There may be behind this the conception of joints as foci of strength, to be underlined like the spiral heart- and flame-shaped insets and mouldings of Scythian and Asiatic animals. Even in quite unrelated arts, for example those of the Indians of the Charlotte Islands, joints are marked with an 'eye' motif which may be a cross-section through the joint.[49] Yet another face seems to be in flight between shrunken limbs, and the last considerable piece is a bird

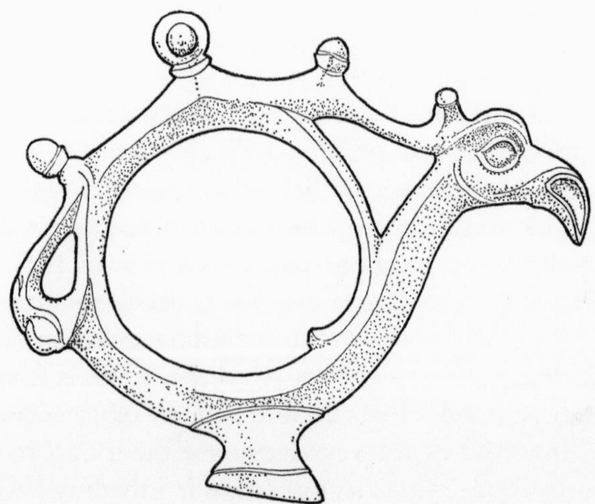

Figure 91. Bronze bird from Brno-Maloměřice, Moravia, Czechoslovakia

with a hooked beak. Unlike the others it is cast in the round; the head and neck are three-dimensional, yet the body is no more than an arabesque outlining a void (Figure 91). Strange and disconcerting though they certainly are, these objects, like certain bronzes from 'Luristan' and the creatures of medieval manuscripts, almost persuade us, against reason, that such things really could be.

A group of rings and tubular fittings from a doubtful source, probably in northern France and sometimes given as 'Champagne' or 'Paris', are in much the same style as Brno-Malomĕřice and the Dürrnberg spout, though coarser in workmanship and conception.[50] The head of a linch-pin and a section of tube are both broken off from the

Figure 92. A Iron and bronze tube from France (cf. Plate 262)
B Bronze bracelet from Tarn, France (cf. Plate 263)

tackle of harness or cart. They are of iron plated with bronze, and the face of Plate 261 is a logical development from Plate 236 (bracelet). The three heads on the other piece (Plate 262) suggest Brno-Malomĕřice and Brå by the treatment of hair and eyes. They are in high relief, and each fills the involution of a running spiral, or rather a plastic whorl, as wheel, cross, or flower filled the spirals of a Cucuteni or Otomani pot (Plates 136 and 166). They have been so caught into the whirling rotation of the pattern as not only to follow each other round, but to look different ways (Figure 92A).[51] But this is not all. The face is in three-quarter profile and the two sides do not match: on one side is a large open eye and a mole or wart, on the other a 'beatle fringe' and a tiny closed-up eye. This could be the very picture of the Irish hero Cú Chulainn (or some predecessor) in the crisis of his contortions when the fury was on him, and he would 'draw in one of his eyes so that a crane could not reach it in his head, and would thrust out the other so that it was as great as a cauldron in which a calf is cooked'. Nor was a mole considered a blemish, for the same hero claimed four as marks of great beauty.

Some broken harness, including a linch-pin in a style very close indeed to the objects just described, give a hint (it is no more) at a date, or rather a *terminus ante quem*, for they were found in a great tomb at Mezek on the slopes of Rhodope in Bulgaria. Here certain Celts broke down the bronze doors of the family vault of Hellenizing Thracians of the fourth and third century to make room for their own barbaric obsequies, which meant walling up the warrior's own chariot. This event is supposed to be linked with a Celtic defeat by Antigonas Gonatas in 276, for after this date the impetus of the long thrust south was broken.[52]

The examples of the Plastic Style at which we have been looking have some relationship, though tenuous, with representation, but there is also a body of entirely unrepresentational work. Fittings and bangles with heavy three-dimensional plastic ornament are found right across Europe, from Hungary and Czechoslovakia into France. A heavy bracelet, probably from Tarn, is unexpectedly tidy and symmetrical (Plate 263). Care has been taken to give it 'colour', with the contrast of stippled and plain background and bosses that imitate the form of coral studs. A projection of the design reveals something else: an affinity with the old second-millennium pulley-pattern based on interlinked circles (Plate 176 and Figures 92B and 103A).[53] The Aurillac gold bracelet (Plates 264 and 265), also from Tarn, is rightly considered one of the most perfect La Tène works. It weighs 6¾ ounces (192 gm.) and is 3 inches (7·8 cm.) across. The oval hoop (not visible in the photograph) is rusticated to look like a pair of natural twigs. Catch and hoop have been skilfully masked by what at first sight appears to be an irregular confusion of curls and whorls that blister and bubble; but in fact the repertoire of shapes is severely limited, and there is order and discipline in the arrangement and repetitions. The beaded line common to much Early Celtic art can be glimpsed threading in and out. We have a simple interlacing band in the Waldalgesheim bracelet (Plate 254 and Figure 89B), but here is a sort of interlacing that is exuberantly three-dimensional. By a form of *legerdemain* the artist has hoodwinked us into believing we see a nature that is not there. The impression of acorns, buds, leaves, and the other conventional concomitants of a classical wreath turns out on analysis to be nothing of the sort; it has nothing at all to do with organic forms. There will be more to say about this later on.

Jacobsthal thought that Hungary was the most likely centre for this style, but in fact the sources are uncertain, and if the baroque silver jewellery that was made and worn in the Balkans in the fifth and fourth centuries may have been one (see p. 230 above and Plate 233), another could as well be in Carthaginian and Etruscan gold-work, certainly for the Tarn province.[54]

The Sword Style

While the Plastic Style allowed free rein to three-dimensional tendencies, an exactly opposite tendency towards flat, linear designs showed itself in what Jacobsthal called 'the Hungarian Sword Style', because so much of it was lavished on the scabbards of

Figure 93. Parts of bronze scabbard from Grave 994 at Hallstatt, Austria, early fifth century

iron swords found in Hungary (Figure 94A). But an even greater number of swords, many of them with ornamented scabbards, have in fact been found in Switzerland, so that this work is best simply called 'Sword Style'. The Swiss sites, with La Tène itself at the head, were in and on lakes and rivers. Huge numbers of bronze and iron weapons and other objects have been drawn up from the mud and peat that were once deep water; they must have been offerings to the rivers and lakes and the spirits living in them. These numbers do not therefore reflect the real distribution of swords in use; ones and twos have come from all over Europe, from the Carpathians to Ireland. Those from the British Isles are rather different and will be described later. Richly ornamented scabbards go back to the very beginning of the La Tène period. On the sword from Hallstatt that has already been referred to several times (Figure 93) there are engraved in the Italian manner men on horseback and on foot; but the horses have on the haunch a motif that is pure La Tène, and so is the flourish that fills the tip, while cast in the round on the chape is the two-headed monster that La Tène art made its own, though it had not invented it. The Rhenish chieftain buried at Weisskirchen had a very handsome scabbard embellished with fine gold-work, and engraved in 'Early Style'; but it was undoubtedly Waldalgesheim that acted most strongly on the new art of the swords, probably between 250 and 200 B.C. As already suggested, this was in some way linked to the population changes that took place at the end of La Tène I ('A' and 'B'): the emptying of the Neckarland and new arrivals who may be the Helvetii in Switzerland.

The addiction to asymmetric patterns is at its most extreme on a spear from Neuchâtel (Figure 94B).[55] The basis of these designs, both symmetric and asymmetric, with a few exceptions such as bird-headed triskeles and triads of deer, is the classical floral repertoire – palmette, lotus, and the rest – selected long before by the artists of the 'Early Style', and now infused with the wandering and wayward spirit of Waldalgesheim.

Figure 94. A Design on sword from Bölcske, Hungary
B Asymmetric design on iron spear from Neuchâtel, Switzerland

Monumental La Tène Art

Until now we have been in the La Tène smithy-studio with gold- and bronzesmiths' work, but La Tène religion sometimes demanded the monumental, so that wood-carver and stone-cutter also worked for the tribe and its gods. There is less cause for surprise at the scale of these monuments, sometimes over life-size, since the discovery of a life-size stone statue of an armed man that once stood on top of a Late Hallstatt barrow at Hirschlanden near Stuttgart. In one respect this last is the exact opposite to most La Tène figures; for the legs are naturalistically modelled, and it is the upper half of the body that is formalized in gesture and style of representation.[56]

It is more than three centuries now since a four-sided tapering stone pillar was found at Pfalzfeld, not far from Early La Tène chieftains' graves in the Hunsrück (Plate 267). Probably, like Hirschlanden, it once stood on a barrow, and the top supported a head or heads; the present height is 4 feet 10 inches (1·48 m.). Drawings made soon after it was found show a good deal more decoration than it is possible to see today.[57] This, like other monuments soon to be mentioned, shows the stone-carver deeply influenced by, and working in the same tradition as, the gold- and bronzesmith. Nor is this surprising, for the 'patterns' used by both, whether oriental or Mediterranean, came in the form of gold jewellery and bronze table-ware. The ornament, as was usual in the Early La Tène period, is symmetrical, and the S-scrolls of the border have the same double parentage – classical palmette and Bronze Age dot and circle – as the Dürrnberg flagon handle and the openwork discs from Saint Jean-sur-Tourbe (Plates 244 and 252). Each side carries a human face under a large 'leaf-crown', as it is sometimes called, though very little like a crown or leaves. It probably started as the 'Astarte' or 'Hathor' hair style.[58] In La Tène iconography it came to stand as a symbol for the supernatural and divine like the conventional horned headdress of Asiatic gods. Sometimes it looks more like horns, especially on Janus heads, and sometimes like the wings of the Rheinheim torc and bracelet (Plates 237 and 238). But there is also that strange emanation the 'Hero's Moon' that rose from the forehead of Cú Chulainn in his battle fury 'as thick as a whetstone', and the 'Hero's Light', perhaps the same, that appeared on his forehead when after the last battle he bound himself to the pillar stone in order to die standing upright, and that remained visible as long as his soul was in him.[59] On the brows of each Pfalzfeld head is another mysterious sign, possibly the same trefoil that the artist of the Rodenbach gold ring set between the brows and under the chin of his goddess. It is a triple figure that, in characteristic La Tène fashion, can be read in two ways: either as vestigial palmette (or lotus), or as the triple cord that we see round the neck of another Rheinheim 'goddess' (Plates 236, 237, and 238).

We may get some idea of what the top of the Pfalzfeld pillar was like from a reddish sandstone head, 12 inches (30 cm.) high, found at Heidelberg (Plate 266). The trefoil sign on this forehead is more distinct and is placed like a Hindu caste mark. Here again two languages overlap – those of symbolic pattern and of representation – so that when occasionally the trefoil appears in isolation we may suspect the sacred presence, just as the spirals of the Athlone crucifixion may have represented the crucified Christ (p. 148 above). Or, in another idiom, the classical palmette has been stripped to an essential trefoil in the same way that Late Assyrian artists stripped and formalized earlier and more naturalistic trees to evolve their 'tree of life'. The Heidelberg head, unlike most of these monuments, is not a Janus, for on the back there is a purely abstract pattern, not very accurately cut, but still suggesting some acquaintance with compass geometry (Figure 95B).[60]

Another 'bilingual' monument was found at Waldenbuch in Württemberg. It is a pillar of the local sandstone, very damaged, and now standing only 4 feet (1·25 m.) high. The decoration in shallow relief connects this as surely with Waldalgesheim as that of Pfalzfeld connects it with the Early Style.[61] The clumsy naturalistic arm stretching across the body contrasts with the abstract decoration below (Plate 268 and Figure 95A). Not far from Waldenbuch, at Holzgerlingen, another figure was found, this time a slender sandstone pillar 7 feet 6 inches (2·3 m.) high. The head is complete with frowning face, and in fact there are two heads, for this *is* a Janus, and only the horned or moon-shaped crown is broken (Plate 269 and Figure 95c). When complete it may well have stood, even more convincingly than the Pfalzfeld or Heidelberg horns, for some sort of Hero's Moon. The arm with raised thumb (seen best on Plate 268) suggests the gesture of the Hirschlanden figure and of certain sixth-century Etruscan grave stelai and of the Capestrano warrior.[62] At Hirschlanden and probably in some La Tène images we have monuments to the divinized or heroic dead, but the bleak

Figure 95. A Carved stone pillar from Waldenbuch, Württemberg, Germany (cf. Plate 268, another face)
B Back view of stone head from Heidelberg, Germany (cf. Plate 266)
C Head of stone figure from Holzgerlingen, Germany, restored (cf. Plate 269)

countenance of the usual Janus seems better suited to that custodian of the universe, the opener and fastener who knew the past and foresaw the future. The Janus of the Aeneid was carved of cedar-wood, and probably a wooden carving was the forerunner of this beam-like block.[63]

In the Celtic shrine at Roquepertuse in Provence Janus heads stood over a doorway or gate. The stone is broken where it would have joined the architrave, but it is plain from the carving that the faces were never meant to be seen from the side, for there the modelling ceases (Plate 270). They were once painted, and they are not identical, but like the Brno-Maloměřice pair one is less severe than the other. The eye is typical bronze- or goldsmith's work.[64] There is the stump of a crown, moon, or horns between the heads, there were niches for human skulls below, and originally a large, lumpish bird looking over its shoulder stood on the architrave. As soon as the light had faded from the forehead of the dead Cú Chulainn the disgusting Morrígan and her sisters, Celtic battle-goddesses, came as crows and perched on the pillar-stone to which he had bound himself; and perhaps some similar thought lurks behind the eschatology of Roquepertuse. The lapse of time between the text and the monuments may seem too great, but this too must be considered later (p. 281 and Chapter 9, Note 5).

The Janus heads are thought to have reached the Celts from Italy by way of the Rhône, but at present the earliest Celtic Januses appear to be in Central Europe or on the Rhine, at Rodenbach or at Brno-Maloměřice. The sanctuary at Roquepertuse cannot be dated nearer than between the sixth and second century. The carvings are not likely to be earlier than fourth-century and may be later. They certainly owed something to their Greek and Italian neighbours, and a crudely carved frieze of horses' heads is a poor reminder of classical friezes, either carved on buildings or, like the horses of the Vix crater, decorating some imported *objet d'art*.

Inside the sanctuary there were originally five over-life-size stone figures, two of them seated between acroteria and therefore undoubtedly inspired by classical or Phoenician models (Plate 271). Like the heads they were painted, and an old drawing shows engraved and painted meanders and crosses filling chequers on the chest, and probably on the back of one, where there is an unexplained excrescence that might be a shield or tabard; but its purpose is probably to provide a field for the sacred device. The pattern within a square and the pose are almost exactly those of two small bronze figures attached to handles, found in Viking graves in Norway, but stemming from Ireland.[65] The strong modelling of the legs has been taken for classical schooling, but it is already there on the 'native' work of Capestrano and Hirschlanden, both of which are a long way from classical models. The cross-legged pose need owe nothing to India – it is in fact very widely used – but the quite extraordinary likeness to a half-life-size clay figure of the first century B.C. that sat on a square clay ossuary in the fortress of Koi-Krylgan-Kala in the Kizil Kum or Chorasmian desert is one of the enigmas of prehistory.[66] Some iron object was held in the left hand of the Plate 271 figure which has stained the stone.

If we turn back from this comparatively civilized figure to the barbaric stone pillar at Waldenbuch (Plate 268 and Figure 95A), a fresh attempt can be made to 'read' the 'bilingual' monument. The arm again holds some indeterminate object. The sunk crosses and step patterns on three faces correspond to the painted chequers of Roquepertuse, and the pleats of the skirt on the latter to the vertical lines below the arm on the former. This is the same dress as the horseman wears in Figure 93. Below again, where there should be the legs, crossed or not, we are back with the La Tène vernacular and a version of asymmetric Waldalgesheim spiral. It is possible that these are joint symbols, like the flourishes on the horses of the Hallstatt scabbard.

A much smaller stone carving, and probably one of the latest independent works, was found at Euffigneix (Haute-Marne) (Plate 272). Though carved in sandstone, it is only

$10\frac{1}{4}$ inches (26 cm.) high, and so might have been designed for household or personal rather than tribal and public cult. The heavy features are quite unlike the narrow sardonic heads of Roquepertuse, Holzgerlingen, and Brno-Maloměřice, but closer to the colossal heads of earth giants that supported pillars carved by Roman artists when they had tangled with barbarians.[67] The eye and ear are now in natural perspective; nevertheless this is still true Celtic work. The technique owes a great deal to the wood-carver, and we have here a link with the *xoanon* described by classical authors; not the 'informia truncis' of Lucan, but work of fine craftsmanship. The carving of the large eye on one side of the block (Plate 273) is virtually identical with that of a stag's head resting in the jaws of a griffin that was found in Barrow 2 at Pazyryk in southern Siberia.[68] There is also the same mixture of scales between subjects in relief – birds at Pazyryk and a boar at Euffigneix – and in the round: the griffin, stag, and man. A jumble of images and scales like this is in fact more Scythian than Celtic, but the boar on the front face is entirely La Tène, and Celtic it must be.

Two more late works must complete our survey of stone carving in Europe before it succumbed to Rome. They come from opposite ends of the Celtic world. At Mšecké-Žehrovice in Bohemia a large ragstone head (Plate 274) $9\frac{1}{2}$ inches (24 cm.) high was found on a site that was evidently both iron-foundry and sanctuary. The features are as decorative and diagrammatic as at Heidelberg, but far more like the little bronze creature of the fifth-century Klein Aspergle flagon (Plate 242) – so like that I wonder the second-century date usually given is not too low. In spite of these qualities, the features have such personality that they have been taken for a caricature of a contemporary figure. In addition, precisely the same sort of stylized physiognomy was used with similar results by twelfth-century church carvers.[69] The other carving, that of the toothy sandstone monster from the Bouches-du-Rhône, 3 feet 8 inches (1·12 m.) tall, and known as the 'Tarasque de Noves', is certainly late (Plate 275). It has a mane, and so is probably intended for a lion. The heads under the paws have the grim, yet almost humorous, detachment of death. The physiognomy is that of the Roquepertuse Janus, but with beards added. Just such faces look at us out of the Book of Kells. Although it ends *below* its chin, the beast may be devouring an arm, like Etruscan monsters, or perhaps it has dropped its portion to snarl at the intruders. Whatever the interpretation, the thing was meant to terrify, and it still does. It is a forerunner of the dreadful lion that chews an arm while trodden down by the feet of a saint, not far away, on the west portal of Saint Gilles-du-Gard.

Stone carving on a monumental scale was done in the Celtic parts of Spain and Portugal, though there is little of the La Tène style in the over-life-size bulls, boars, and warriors of Guisando (Ávila) and Mortalegre in Portugal, but rather a plain imitation of classical or Phoenician models. There is something of the Late Syro-Hittite style in these blockish animals. A collection of deeply engraved stone stelai in the Buelna valley in Galicia have wheel and whirligig emblems and a scene with men and a horse, and these are a little more Celtic.[70]

Only very rarely was a monumental effect attempted by the bronzesmith. Smith and carpenter must have worked together in the wheelwright's shop, and may have done so occasionally in the service of cult. Many fine metal torcs or neck-rings and bracelets are thought to have adorned images of the gods rather than mortal men, and the bronze mask found at Tarbes in the Pyrenees was probably fastened to a life-size wooden image. With its formalized spiral hair-motif and angular nose it seems to carry us back to a far older Mediterranean tradition, almost to the marble goddesses and patterned stonework of the third millennium (Plate 276; cf. Plates 137 and 146).

The bronze god from Bouray (Seine-et-Oise) was made by a specialist in sheet-bronze working, probably a cauldron-maker. The face and head were cast, and the eyes, one of which survives, were inset with white and blue glass (see front cover). The features are carried out in the style of the heads on cauldrons and buckets from Rynkeby in Denmark and Marlborough in Wiltshire (see below, p. 270 and Plates 281 and 297), and on a much smaller bronze head found at Garancières-en-Beauce (Eure-et-Loir); the outlining of the eye is typical of the bronze-worker.[71] The curious stunted legs have been thought to end in a deer's hoof rather than a foot; whether or not this is so, the position of the legs is not that of the Roquepertuse figures.

The great bronze boar, 4 feet 2 inches (1·26 m.) long and 2 feet 3 inches (0·68 m.) tall, from Neuvy-en-Sullias (Loiret) is the finest of all those boars that are known to have been used as standards, and is a superlative work (Plate 277). This site on the Loire lay opposite the Celtic sanctuary at Fleury-Floriac and close to the later Christian sanctuary of St Benoît. The great treasure that has been found here was probably not buried till after the Roman conquest of Gaul, perhaps by the native priests, for it comprises the wealth and gods of a Celtic people. Some of the smaller bronze figures have the heaviness of provincial work, but the boar is entirely La Tène, and is I fancy an emblem from before the conquest, one of those supernatural animals like the Welsh Trwyth. Lithe, tense and aloof, this is the spirit of 'boar' created by an artist who understood the points and power of the living animal. A small bronze cock found at Piedmont near Bussy-le-Château (Marne), where it sat on the lid of a bronze vessel (Plate 278),[72] is as proper a bird in the bronzesmith's idiom as the horse of Plate 4 is in the Paleolithic bone-worker's. Another cock (Plate 279), this time of wrought iron and of unknown provenance, but probably from France, is a bird of a very different feather; for featheriness is what it embodies to a startling extent. Ruffled, angular, with its knowing eye and scrawny body, this is a long way from the elegant, arbitrary outline of Plate 278.

From the same treasure at Neuvy-en-Sullias that held the boar, but this time probably dating from after the loss of native freedom and patronage and so from the lowest limit of our period, comes the bronze figure of a dancing woman (Plate 280). Though she owes much to a Venus with hands to her hair, there is a quality in this figure that distinguishes it from the clumsier provincial imitations of Greco-Roman work; the proportions of the limbs are natural, but the body is stylized and attenuated, as though in this way and by this attenuation it could be made to transcend its own weight and to embody the movement of the dance as she steps forward on her toes. Pre-conquest Celtic sculpture in the round is static, and this attempt to portray movement is new and hints at what the artist might have achieved if there had been more of mutual respect in the fusion of styles. One has the impression that this is a 'fashionable' anatomy giving the body, though far more extreme, the proportions of an Eve of Van Eyck or Van der Goes.

The Rynkeby and Gundestrup Cauldrons

The North German and South Scandinavian 'Nordic Area' and the British Isles, equally distant from the La Tène heartland, responded very differently to the impact of La Tène art. In the north certain fine works of La Tène craftsmanship – a cauldron like that from Brå already referred to, a ceremonial cart, and a few cast bronze figures – were received into a strongly consolidated Germanic province. A few Celtic artists may have been employed from time to time, but without setting up and nourishing a native school. Westwards, on the other hand, an actual migration of artists and of their patrons introduced the continental La Tène style at the level of small and unimportant ornaments and objects of purest utility. This never happened in the north, though the Dejbjerg cart and the Rynkeby cauldron are two of the finest La Tène works.

Rynkeby on Funen is another bog votive.[73] The inner and outer sheets are riveted together and to the lower part, and the cast bronze bull protoms then riveted on. It was probably smaller than Brå, with a diameter of 2 feet 4 inches (70 cm.). The human face and stiff little bulls of Plate 281 are in such contrast to the repoussé animals of the surviving inner panel (Plate 285) that one would judge them from a different shop or hand. The pair of confronted animals is entirely La Tène. On the left there is a boar, on the right a wolf-like creature. They are long-legged with spare bodies, and are rendered according to the same convention as that used by the Magdalenian artist who, even in naturalistic work, allowed the farther pair of legs to appear longer than the nearer, a draughtsman's trick probably adopted here, as in the Upper Paleolithic, from the use of dead models (p. 56 above). In other respects the animals are well-observed. The boar's snout is not more exaggerated than by the artist of the Calydonian boar on the François Vase. The tusk and curled tail are also typical of the animal (cf. Figure 75).

The creature on the other side is not unlike the dead hound of the François Vase, though it may be a wolf. Boar facing wolf is possible as personal or tribal insignia, or boar facing hound as the climax of the hunt. Celtic legend in Britain also had a supernatural boar-hunting. I am inclined to agree with the opinion that the ribbed object above the second animal's head, which at first sight appears to be attached to it, is only a larger version of the 'horns' shown beneath.[74] The teeth are perhaps too much of a good thing, though hardly more exaggerated than the hog's snout, which they balance. Both beasts are species well known to the artist: the boar so often hunted and carried on standards (Plate 277) and the wolf or savage guard dog and hunting hound. They are shown among conventional foliage and with the numinous triple sign familiar in La Tène work. A sixfold rosette formed in the same way appears on the Aylesford bucket, and the blank, lifeless face of Plate 281 is very like one on the vat from Marlborough (Plate 297). In fact these three vessels from Rynkeby, Aylesford, and Marlborough are evidently related to each other (see below, p. 269). Dating is by style and uncertain, but the first century B.C. is often proposed, and is required by one of the British vessels.

There is no such guide to help in dating the most famous and teasing of the northern cauldrons, the noble silver vessel found in 1891 at Gundestrup near Børemose in Jutland, yet another offering to the northern gods and wildernesses (Plates 282–4). Study of the soil has shown that it was not drowned, but stood plain to see on dry land for some long time. It had been dismantled and the ornamental silver panels laid inside the bowl-shaped base, so that the great 'cauldron' that we see today has been reconstructed with the help of small portions of bronze rim and iron hoop. Between this and the base the sheets have been fitted back to back. At the centre of the base is a medallion decorated in high relief. The seven outer panels, of from 9¾ by 8–8¼ inches (25 by 20–21 cm.), and five inner, from 15¾–17 by 8–8¼ inches (40–43 by 20–21 cm.), were originally soldered together to make a vessel about 16½ inches (42 cm.) high and 27 inches (69 cm.) across. The decoration was hammered up from underneath, and chased and finished on top. The large busts of the outer panels and the medallion of the base (Plates 283 and 282) were once covered with very thin gold foil pressed on to the silver, and some of the busts still have red and blue glass in their eyes. Even allowing for an extra panel on the outside, it must have been clumsy, and with its high relief decoration would have served ill as a container of liquids. Its first purpose will rather have been didactic and liturgical, like a painted shrine or reliquary.

Much has been written about this strange object: it has been brought up from the Black Sea and from Gaul, and the dates proposed run from the second century B.C. to the fifth or even sixth A.D.[75] Unlike Brå and Rynkeby it is not, I believe, specifically La Tène, or even Celtic in the wider sense, but is thoroughly eclectic, in spite of some similarities, mostly iconographic, to other Celtic works. The differences are not due simply to a later date, since a very pure Celtic style could survive in the extreme west for a thousand years. We are not now so much in the milieu of a native style as of hopefully provincial imitations of alien arts, in the same way that the situlae of some centuries earlier were imitations.

A Celtic element possibly appears in the squatting antlered god of one panel who may be the 'horned one' Cernunnos seen on Gallo-Roman altars and named in an inscription on the altar that stood under the present choir of Notre-Dame-de-Paris.[76] But the wearing of antlers is not confined to the Celtic world; it belonged to the northern shaman, as to Mesolithic societies in Europe. Moreover, human skulls and antlers pierced to be worn as masks and found in an eighth–seventh-century cave in Slovakia, are presumably pre-Celtic, witnesses of grisly religious rites, while we have already seen that neither to squat nor to wear trousers is any more peculiarly Celtic. A better case can be made out for the narrow shields carried by spearmen on Plate 283; relatives of these can be seen in the Kazanlak painted tomb and carried by 'Illyrians' on reliefs from Durazzo.[77] The war trumpets with animal mouth-pieces of the same panel are unequivocally Celtic. These had taken the place of simpler lurs and trumpets by at least the second century B.C. and were in use till the first A.D. Classical writers called them 'carnyx', and described the Galatians using them in the second century B.C. to terrify their enemies when their hoarse battle calls reverberated out of the animal's jaws.[78] The horsemen of Plate 283 have animal-crested and horned helmets, and on another inside panel a wheel-turning figure wears a helmet with knobbed ox-horns (Figure 96A). To mount bronze horns on a helmet, to give it eyes, a crest, and sometimes a curving beak was at least as old as the eighth century (Plate 207), but it is not confined to Europe: the Pisidian infantry that came over in Xerxes' army had crested helmets with ox-horns and ears as well, while the Persian cavalry wore helmets with hammered bronze animal devices, probably in repoussé but possibly in the round like later Germanic gods and heroes. Some of the small cast bronze boars, horses, and stags and detached horn-shaped objects from La Tène workshops may once have been fitted in this way to helmets.[79] From all these considerations it seems that the really Celtic La Tène elements are very much less strong than is often claimed.

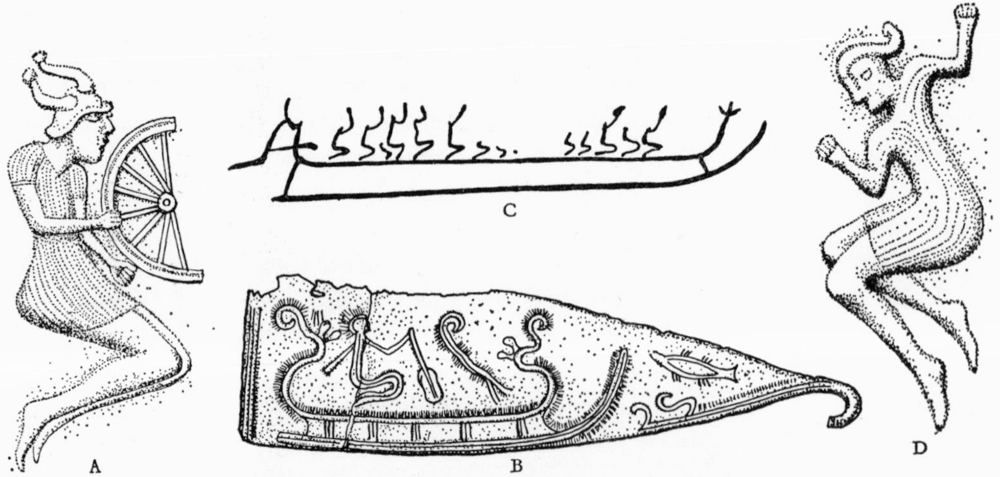

Figure 96. A Wheel-turning figure on the bowl from Gundestrup, Denmark
B Bronze razor from near Bremen (cf. Figure 71C)
C Rock-carving at Vitlycke, Bohuslän, Sweden (cf. Figure 80)
D 'Dancing' figure on the Gundestrup bowl

The classical element is difficult to localize because of the high degree of standardization and wide dispersal of Hellenistic and Roman works, but something of general layout may be owed to late free-style red-figure Attic vase painting, a florid product designed for the colonial world, much of which found its way to Black Sea ports (Kerch Style). In the west on large Italiote craters you see just this interlocking of scenes at different levels which yet retain their individual identity, and which is the opposite of the tidy zonal arrangements of the Asiatic descriptive style, and equally, as we have seen, of situla art.

Perhaps the most teasing element in the whole gallimaufry (if indeed it is not a chimaera) is the Nordic. A dancing, leaping figure appears three times at Gundestrup. It is neither classical nor Near Eastern, but I believe we have already met it on eighth-century northern razors, and on contemporary rocks (Figures 76B and 96); and the woman, priestess or votary, who with a bird fluttering over her head dresses the hair of the grim goddess of Plate 284, has a simpler counterpart in an otherwise incomprehensible symbol on the rocks at Tegneby, Tanum (Figure 97A, and see above, p. 207).

There are besides other subjects quite exotic and disturbing: elephants and griffins, horned serpents, hippocamps, spotted leopards, a winged horse, and a man riding a marine creature. Some of these have an oriental source, some classical, some, like the man wrestling with a lion, could be either, for though he is usually named 'Hercules', oriental kings and heroes had been wrestling with lions for thousands of years, and the

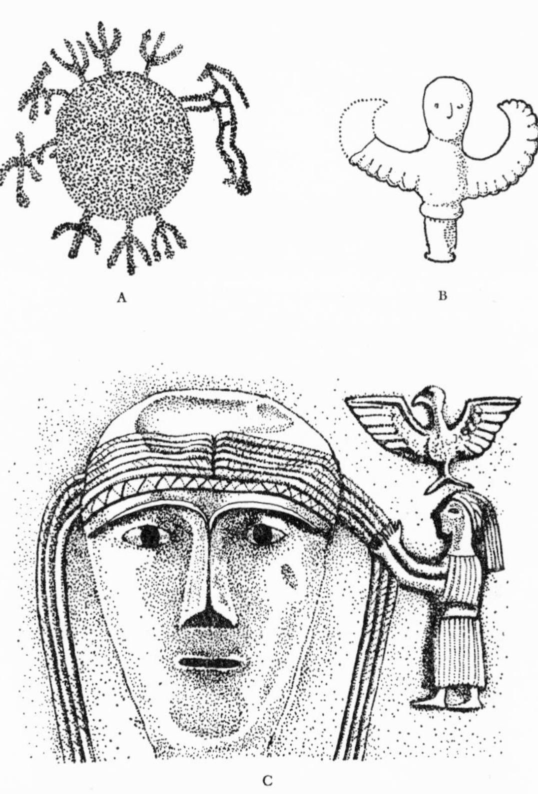

Figure 97. A Rock-engraving at Tanum, Bohuslän, Sweden
B Helmet crest from Vače, Yugoslavia
C Simplified drawing from a panel of the Gundestrup silver bowl, Denmark (cf. Plate 285)

group only *becomes* Hercules and the Nemean lion when the Greek or Roman context is past doubt. Here on the periphery of both worlds we cannot be certain.[80] The crouching or bounding dog or jackal of some panels has a forerunner on the gold tiara from Poiana-Coţofeneşti (Plate 235) and the silver beakers from Hagighiol, and the beaker shape leads again back to 'Amlash' and Marlik.[81]

The surface has been chased to convey different textures – hatching for smooth-coated animals, a curved punch for rough hair, and a moderate-sized round one for the leopard's spots and the belts worn by men and women. These are the stock-in-trade of Asiatic goldsmiths from ninth-century Hasanlu and earlier. In this form they are not as characteristic of Achaemenian Persia, Luristan, or Greece as of those intermediate and surrounding regions which still lack a proper name and study. The Gundestrup base with its portrayal of an animal's body in outline, or very low relief, while the head is in the round is thoroughly oriental (Plate 282).[82]

At least three hands have been detected on different panels. They were very differently gifted, for whoever worked the round plate at the bottom was a more sophisticated artist than the others. The busts of gods, four male and three female, on the outside panels are noble, with simple severity. The bust in the centre of Plate 283 is certainly intended as an ideal type, but one may doubt the benevolence of the lady on his right, who seems to spurn a falling man and hound, while her two female attendants are no more reassuring (Plate 284). The short, curling hair of the god is made an excuse for elegant pattern, but on the head just visible on an inside panel on Plate 283 the curls have become the statutory horns of an Asiatic deity. The small, pursed mouth (a few blows of the hammer) is shared by all, and can be seen on a gold head in the Oxus treasure, and on a silver vase from Mastjugino, near Voronesh.[83] In the outside panels the composition is formal, antithetical, heraldic. We are confronting religious concepts and the outward visible counterparts of a creed. There is no movement, only existences. Men, dragons, animals are literally in the hands of the gods. On some of the inner panels on the other hand there *is* movement, mostly circular, and action if only in the sense of Eliade's re-enactment of exemplary events. The procession of warriors around a tree in one panel is probably a circle only interrupted by the man thrust into a tub.[84]

The great bull of the base medallion is the masterpiece. It once had horns of another, probably precious, material. Though the pose may owe something to Near Eastern ivories or classical coins where a bull stands, or advances with lowered menacing head, the impression given, and I believe intended, is of a vast animal just roused and lifting itself for action.[85]

Problems of date and provenance remain, but the margin of error has narrowed. If spurs and carnyx deny a date before the end of the third century B.C., the comparison of animal representation, especially Asiatic, and the crumbs of history which can be accepted, make the second century, if anything, more likely than the first. Comparisons with La Tène III objects are less compelling than once appeared. First-century B.C. coins, barbarian and Greek, throw light on iconography and on some tricks of style; but coiners were seldom iconographic inventors, and on the whole I believe a date around the turn of the second and first centuries B.C., though earlier than often given, may not be too early.

When looking for the country of origin of this, and indeed of the Brå and Rynkeby cauldrons also, we are not looking for a workshop that turned out a special line in great liturgical vessels. The artists who hammered and chased the ornamental sheet roundels and phalerae were not necessarily the same men who tinkered and coopered-up the vessel into its ultimate shape: cauldron, bucket, or tub. This may have depended on local taste and requirements. The fine studio work could have been done in distinct and distant workshops. One such which produced the Rynkeby panel was evidently within the La Tène world and probably in western continental Europe; but another, from which came Gundestrup and perhaps some of the silver-gilt phalerae, must have been in South-East Europe not far from the Black Sea,[86] where the oriental and Hellenistic worlds overlapped, where there was a local and well-established tradition of silver-working, and where Celtic tribes had settled or were moving into and across the land.

Such is the likely milieu, the time and place, for the creation of this odd and eclectic masterpiece. Only the northern element (if such there is) remains obstinately inexplicable. The fact of the bowl having been dug up where it was in Denmark suggests the possibility that the potentate who offered this sumptuous object to his gods might have carried north craftsmen from South-East Europe, or have demanded of them some local themes; for these artists could turn their hands as well to elephants, griffins, and dragons as to leaping and dancing Northmen, the Celtic carnyx, the strange helmets, and the presences of the gods.

Pots

We shall not find the best of La Tène art in its pots, in spite of the adoption in the fifth century of the fast wheel: that is to say as early as the first appearance of metal-work in the new style and some two thousand years after its invention in Western Asia. The fast wheel meant an entirely professional product, even if the housewife still moulded her own cooking pots. For the great feasts that were as much occasions of glory and display among Celtic tribes as among Homer's Greeks, there were wheel-turned pots of high finish to supplement the bronze vessels. There was a special liking for high pedestal feet that often seem too heavy for the body. Much of the pottery is plain, much incised with patterns adopted from 'Early Style' metal-work, but some of the most attractive vases were painted. They come from the same region in northern France, and are as early as the great chariot burials. Graphite paint had been used on Hallstatt pots for typical Hallstatt geometric patterns: the variations on squares and chequers. Greek wares imported to north-eastern France and the Upper Danube from the Mediterranean coast were often imitated, but none of these Late Hallstatt vessels approach the elegance of the pots from Prunay (Marne), though the colours are the same. In Plate 295 the pattern is in red on a silvery, almost purple graphite background, and sometimes light buff was used on red.[87] The motif of opposed horse- or dragon-headed S-spirals was shared by potter and metal-worker (Plate 251 and Figure 89A). From the last century B.C. we know that professional potters, goldsmiths, and perhaps furniture makers worked in close enough concord to share patterns. Pots from the Glastonbury Lake village, a gold 'torc' from Broighter in Ireland, and bone slips, insets, and weaving-combs from Lough Crew all display the same compass-derived patterns (below, p. 265), and indeed it is now time to turn to insular La Tène art.

CHAPTER 9

INSULAR LA TÈNE AND THE PROBLEM OF LA TÈNE ART

Knife has gone into meat, and drink into horn and a thronging in Arthur's hall. Save the son of a king of a rightful dominion, or a craftsman who brings his craft, none may enter.

Culhwch and Olwen, trans. G. and T. Jones

IN the first half of the last millennium B.C. these islands were still drowsing on, unaware of the new civilizations of the Mediterranean and by their position safe from the pressure of eastern invaders. But from time to time they were fretted by exotic imports, for they lay at the end of a long and devious supply route by which large bronze buckets and cauldrons travelled from Central Europe and from the Mediterranean across France to be imitated by craftsmen in England and Ireland. The bronze shields and lurer of Northern Europe on the other hand had here plainer versions, strictly for parade purposes (they were too brittle for use), which like the cauldrons had a simple ornament of large rivets.[1]

Into this conservative world the first invaders of Celtic speech penetrated, perhaps by the eighth century, or soon after. The evidence, chiefly linguistic, is obscure and open to different interpretations. They may have brought the knowledge of iron-working or a new type of Hallstatt sword, and they certainly came before the emergence of the La Tène style on the Continent. In this respect Britain was like Iberia.[2] The native population was not at first much altered; throughout the country as a whole people still lived in isolated farmsteads of round houses unaffected by the Continental style of building with settlement in village or town.[3] But from some time after 400 B.C. bands of Celts who possessed more or less of true La Tène culture were beginning to arrive in the British Isles. These adventurers, whatever set them moving, must have known enough of what lay ahead not to be misled by the glamour of exotic wealth that had led one Brennus (tribal god or chieftain) to Rome, and another to Delphi. They came in search of a solider and more prosaic commodity: cattle, and land for cattle-raising, for these were a chief source of wealth and status and provided the standard currency; and they brought more of luxury than they found.

One group, known as the 'Arras culture', settled in Yorkshire, where burials with horse-gear have been found in which there seems a memory of earlier cart-burials on the Rhine or in northern France. Another group chose the south-west, where the great hill-forts with multiple ramparts that still dominate the landscape are relics of their wars. Others reached Northern Ireland and parts of Wales, and in the first century B.C. a more compact settlement carried certain well-organized 'Belgic' tribes: forceful, bellicose, and no longer anonymous, into South-East England. These last struck their own coinage, possessed the fast wheel for potting, and maintained ties across the Channel, first with a free, and later with a Roman Gaul.[4]

At the beginning of these changes the population was still broadly that of the second millennium, agricultural and, especially in the north, pastoral. But the bands of adventurers with their Hallstatt or La Tène culture and arts possessed a sort of superiority that in the end coloured the whole society, masking its earlier strata. This very mixed society had an unexpected stability, for it survived the years of Roman occupation, in Ireland as a continuity, in Britain discontinuous because of that occupation, but emerging after the Roman withdrawal in a form that can be recognized in the Irish heroic stories, although these were not written down till many centuries later. The legal texts are a further source of information, and describe among other matters the status of the craftsman.[5]

Native goldsmiths still worked with the old techniques almost to the end of the millennium. In the centuries following that which had seen the smithing of the Gleninsheen gorget (Plate 184), Irish smiths developed exquisite skill and sureness of touch so that they were able, with the use of compasses, to decorate a small gold conical hair ornament with concentric repoussé rings $\frac{1}{120}$ of an inch apart and five to the millimetre, the line not continuous but formed of compass impressions $\frac{1}{100}$ of an inch apart. This is work technically more delicate than any discovered in Western Europe, and it gives 'a kind of bloom on the surface of the gold like Etruscan granulation which it may have been imitating'.[6] Craftsmanship like this was the schooling of the artists who were to produce the masterpieces of Celtic Hibernian work. But La Tène art in Britain is heralded, like Greek and Etruscan imports of the sixth century on the Continent, by single curiosities that tell virtually nothing of the people who brought, or more probably received, them.

Perhaps the first of these isolated objects is a much-damaged bronze hanging-bowl found at Cerrig-y-Drudion in Denbighshire (Figure 98). The incised ornament, the palmettes and 'fans', have been seen as coming from continental Waldalgesheim work, but in fact the tight, crimped drawing has less in common with the flowing sinuosities of typical Waldalgesheim than with an advanced Early Style. The antecedents of this ornament lie in northern and eastern Gaul, in the decoration of helmets like those of Berru and Canosa, flagons like Besançon, the Sausses Champenoises bowl, and even the Weisskirchen scabbard.[7] The Canosa helmet, though found in Italy, is Gaulish work and may be late-fourth-century, and so may the bowl from Cerrig-y-Drudion. I believe that any relationship to Breton potting is collateral, not direct. The hatched carpet or 'basketry' background of the design was to be idiosyncratic of much British La Tène work. Continental artists preferred scattered dots and pouncing for their backgrounds, though alternate hatching was sometimes used in the Early Style. The choice of British artists may be partly due to alternate hatching being already in the repertoire of native goldsmiths.[8]

The masterpieces of *à jour* work in northern Gaul probably inspired a graceful openwork sheath from the Thames at Hammersmith. Work in the true Waldalgesheim Style is very rare in Britain, but a sword sheath found farther up the Thames at Standlake near Oxford combines it with background hatching done with a rocked tracer, the same that had been used by many Continental Hallstatt and La Tène artists, but to draw the pattern and not, as here, to fill in its background. The plate at the tip of the sheath has a wandering tendril that reminds us more of mixed work like the handle of the Brå cauldron or the Waldenbuch stone pillar (Plates 255 and 268) than of the finer goldsmith's work of the Waldalgesheim grave itself. There is a bracelet with a thin, wiry version of Waldalgesheim ornament from a chariot burial and a horn-cap from another chariot, and there are a pair of spoons and a brooch or two.[9] Other pieces reflect the Plastic Style, but (with the exception of a bracelet from Clonmacnoise in

Figure 98. Bronze bowl from Cerrig-y-Drudion, Wales

Ireland) with a very insular slant. A few of these objects may have been brought by fresh Celtic bands from the Continent, but apart from the cluster of swords and daggers in and around the Thames (some of which may have been introduced by traders, though most are native work), they are too scattered and isolated for use in identifying their owners.

The bronze pony-cap and the horns found at Torrs in Kirkcudbright, and most of the other metal-work to be described, bring us into a truly native La Tène milieu. When *they* were produced, and it is impossible to be exact about the date, it was in well-settled workshops, able to develop their own tradition, and in close touch with a local market. The Torrs cap owes more, I believe, to Plastic than to Waldalgesheim inspiration, in as far as the Continent has any part in this very insular work (Plate 286 and Figures 99 and 100). The two horns are shown for convenience on the plate in the old, incorrect reconstruction: in fact they have nothing to do with the 'cap'.[10] They are ornamented in a different style, and probably formed the lower end of a pair of drinking-horns. The repoussé pattern of the cap is a 'net' like the Brno-Maloměřice openwork net, but here based, not on the eye as joint, but on a bird motif, with only the

Figure 99. 'Pony-cap' from Torrs, Scotland, the bronze repoussé pattern projected (cf. Plate 286)

heads remaining at the ends of the labyrinth. The bronze sheath of an Early La Tène sword from La Tène has an engraved 'net' that comes closest to this repoussé design.[11] The drinking horns ended in drooping birds' heads of some elegance and sufficient character to identify the surviving one as probably a shoveller (cf. Figure 90).

Two shield bosses from the Thames at Wandsworth are equally bird-obsessed. On the long boss (Plate 288) two birds, reduced to head, beak, and leg, are given in profile between lugubrious human faces. It is easier to see how this dislocation could have happened to them on the round boss (Plate 289), where the two repoussé birds are themselves the ground for engraved motifs, one of which is a dislocated bird of the same family. Shoulder, wing, and leg are all represented, but drawn out end to end, or actually detached and floating, as though all that was required was a serial catalogue of parts, a notation in which each has its own equal decorative value. Scythian artists went a long way in the same direction with their dislocated fighting animals, but, griffins apart, they had no birds, and the dislocation was never so extreme. Where a complicated design must be fitted to a limited field, especially a round or oval, as on Minoan seals, the same dislocation may take place, but not for the same reason. Scythian and Minoan artists were obeying formal requirements imposed by a piece of bone to carve, an area of the human body to tattoo, or the surface of a gem; the Celtic artist used the same methods in order to express himself in two languages at once.

These obsessive birds were hatched from a Hallstatt egg in the central La Tène province. We have seen how water-birds of all sorts were common there in the Bronze Age, and were carried farther north, while the exotic cock may have been seen at Este, in situla art, before it reached Rheinheim (p. 234 above). Birds sit on Early Style fibulae; they were unknown to Waldalgesheim, but were carried over into the Plastic and Sword Styles, from which they probably reached Britain. From the very natural bird of Rheinheim (Plate 239) to the Brno-Maloměřice emblem, the bird triskele on a scabbard from Obermenzing, and the bird 'net' on one from La Tène, or to the mixed Waldalgesheim scabbard from Cernon-sur-Coole in Champagne, was a long journey in a short space of time (see p. 281 below).[12]

The Torrs drinking-horns and the round Wandsworth boss are engraved in a way which links them with some of the bronze scabbards. The rather coarse line is what we have seen on the Basse-Yutz flagons and on the Cerrig-y-Drudion bowl, and will see again on a shield and scabbard from the river Witham. The motifs spring in the first place from the classical repertoire of acanthus and palmette, but modified to fan and leaf spiral. On the flagons and bowl the design was symmetrical, but on the later bronzes it is boldly asymmetric. We have seen some beginnings of asymmetry on the Continent (Figures 94 and 95A and Plate 253). This incipient asymmetry may well have gained strength from the concentration in Britain on zoomorphic subjects seen in profile. A peculiarity of the engraved design on the Torrs horns is the bar or 'stop' in the pattern (Figure 100, and the middle of the horn on Plate 286). An explanation has been put forward according to which the design itself is taken from a scabbard and this bar is a relic of the functional binding bands. Alternatively it is possible that the bar represents not just a break but a hiatus in the pattern. If so, then two Continental designs show us by analogy what is left out: a bracelet from Waldalgesheim and a spear from Lake Neuchâtel have a curvilinear motif very like Torrs, flanking in the form of asymmetric wings an elaborate rectilinear swastika.[13] Such swastikas had been popular in the Hallstatt Iron Age, and there is one chased on the silver belt from Mramorac (Plate 231 and Figure 94B). They could have been personal, tribal, or divine blazons.

A gilt bronze scabbard mount found in the river Witham near Lincoln (Plate 287) has perhaps the most successful marriage of techniques. The asymmetry is bold but not forced. Relief and engraving are a unity: the one underlines and completes the other instead of repeating it as an independent, and possibly superfluous, statement. With the help of the Wandsworth round boss we can interpret the upper repoussé member as the wing and the lower as the leg of a bird, dislocated, serialized, and now so abstract that its use seems more instinctive than conscious; but since this is another bilingual design, it can also be read as a dissected palmette.

The shield found in the river Witham may well be the supreme work of a British La Tène armourer. A nineteenth-century drawing shows best the original shield, with its ghostly blazon beneath later repoussé work (Plate 291). When its first owner had it, it was slightly larger than it is now. The sole ornament of this first shield was the

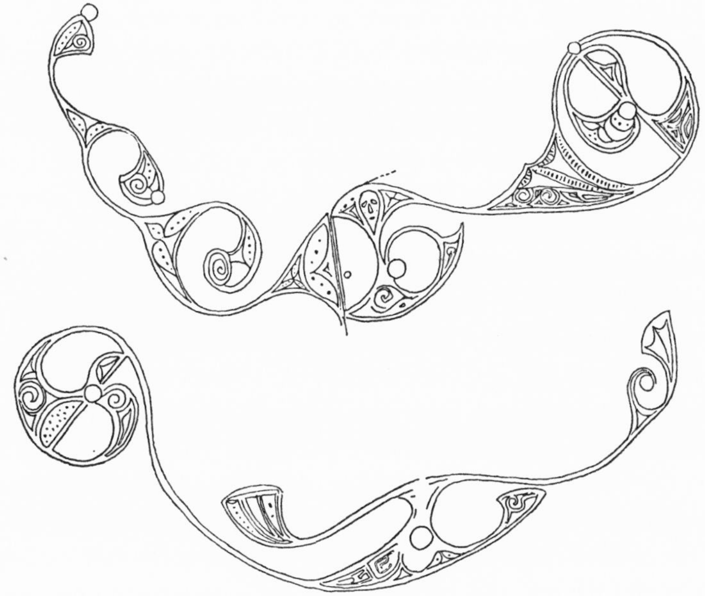

Figure 100. The engraved design on the Torrs drinking horns (cf. Plate 286)

blazon of the boar in thin bronze sheet nailed to the background. Though this is lost now, the stained outline and small rivet holes can be seen. The thin metal was probably of an alloy that would make it stand out in colour from its background. Nothing quite like it is known from anywhere else, but *small* animal cut-outs, usually part of some larger subject, are known in France and Germany and have recently come to light in Wales (Figure 89A). The outline of the boar caricatures the tough slenderness of the wild animal's body and the jutting snout. It is as brazenly stylized as the Satan of the Temptation in the Book of Kells, whose long, limp legs, after a thousand years, exactly repeat the legs of our boar.[14] Some time later a new owner ripped off the boar and caused *his* smith to substitute a very beautiful and sophisticated design which is worked up from beneath in repoussé with spaces for inserting red enamel. The middle boss of three is symmetrical about an imaginary diagonal, and this links it with the simpler long boss from the Thames (Plates 288, 290, and frontispiece). The end roundels have engraved within the repoussé ring dry, crisp wing and fan patterns and whorls and 'leaves' that are like Cerrig-y-Drudion on the one hand and the Witham scabbard on the other; freer than the first, less happily fused with the relief than the latter. Below the roundels are staring animal heads, full-face like the gorgons of classical tradition. This piece is a synthesis in which plastic modelling and heads of animals (corresponding to the Continental Plastic Style), a hard engraved line (as in the advanced Early Style), and the asymmetric freedom and precarious balance of the Sword Style are united in an entirely successful and entirely insular work of art.

The blazons on the shields of Celtic fighting-men greatly impressed their Greek and Roman antagonists and are shown among the trophies on the arch at Orange, along with swords, trousers, and the carnyx. A little more about shields can be learnt from the old Irish literary tradition. According to one manuscript, there was a law in Ulster by which every hero must carry a different device on his shield; and the story tells that, when the greatest of the heroes Cú Chulainn ordered his shield from Mac Enge the smith, the latter confessed that he had exhausted his powers of invention, at which Cú Chulainn threatened to kill him, notwithstanding that as a smith he was under the special protection of the king of Ulster. While he sat perplexed in his hut a stranger appeared who listened to his troubles. Then: 'Clear the floor of thy workshop,' said the stranger 'and let it be sprinkled with ash to the depth of a man's foot.' This was done. Then the stranger produced a 'fork' the name of which was *luath-rindi*, 'ash-graver'. One prong of the fork he placed in the ash, and with the other he described the device to be graven on the shield. Then he departed, and the armourer saw him no more.[15] This story shows how necessary it was for the new owner of the Witham boar shield to replace the old blazon with his own, and it shows the rough and ready way of making a blueprint for a large design; but though compasses suggest geometry, the finished shield of Cú Chulainn was probably no more *obviously* geometric than the disc from the river Bann with its bird-headed triskele, or the Battersea shield, or pages of animal and abstract interlace in the Lindisfarne Gospels.[16] It cannot be taken literally as a tale of the introduction of compasses to Irish workshops; such would have been an anachronism, since very fine compass-work can be seen in the gold of some centuries earlier.[17]

In spite of the beauty and brilliance of its composition, the shield found in the Thames at Battersea is, compared to Witham, rather chilling. It is constructed from four pieces of metal and must have been a dazzling object, with its original mercury gilding and red glass in true cloisons setting off the hatched metal swastikas. The technique is superb and the relief crisp and confident. The sharpness of the planes that appear to cross over in mid-sweep compares with the best Continental Plastic work (Plate 292).[18] In iconography the bird with its asymmetry has been suppressed, but a bull- or ox-head with great curving horns appears twice *en face*, and the whole design is frontal and symmetric. In this respect the Battersea shield is developing in a contrary direction to asymmetric works like the Waterloo helmet, the Llyn Cerrig Bach, Anglesey, plaque, and some of the mirrors (see below).

The bronze helmet from the Thames at Waterloo Bridge (Plate 293) speaks the same language as the Torrs, Witham, and Wandsworth bronzes, though it is evidently later than these and there are signs of strain. The horns with their ornamental rivets remind us of insular round shields and cauldrons of the Latest Bronze Age; the repoussé style on the other hand, with its sunk areas within a rounded contour giving light and shade, was incipient on the Torrs pony-cap and overt on the round Wandsworth disc. In place of an engraved 'echo' of the repoussé design there are coloured studs and enclosed areas of 'basketry'. We can, if we choose, still find the dislocated bird on the lower strip in front of the helmet (probably added a little later), but the deliberate use of the voids to give a new lightness is the most striking feature. It is an adventurous design and has been much praised, but it holds the beginnings of decadence. The creative vitality is there, but a little self-conscious, a little jejune; and if it looks back to the armourers of Torrs and Wandsworth, it has a closer link with the goldsmiths' work to be seen at its best on a torc in the East Anglian hoards from Snettisham, on a similar fragment from Cairnmuir, and on harness bronzes from Ringstead in Norfolk and Ulceby in Lincolnshire.[19]

Gold- and bronzesmiths shared up to a point the same repertoire and the same 'pattern books' (in whatever form these came – bone slips, wood, or metal; only the first are *known* to exist). But goldsmiths' art has its own ramifications on the Continent and in Ireland. There is a connexion, though I believe only collateral, between gold torcs with animal motifs from Frasnes-lez-Buissenal in Belgium, the torc from Broighter in Northern Ireland, and the gold alloy (electrum) torc from Hoard E on Ken Hill near Snettisham. There were five hoards here in all, and some included coins, among them a gold stater of the Gaulish Atrebates. Concealed at the time of manufacture inside the terminal of the torc (Plate 296) was a quarter stater not minted before 50–25 B.C. This gives a *terminus post quem* within the last third of the last century, when Belgic princes of the Trinovantes and Catuvellauni were striking coins and making a stir in South-East England. The bangles are not all of the same date, and a hollow torc from Hoard A may well have been made earlier. The Hoard E torc with its 38·3 ounces of silver is the 'white gold' of the poets. The relief ornament was cast and the detail chased. It is this detail of the 'basketry' background and the crinkly line (also used on the Witham shield, frontispiece detail), produced by tapping along a fine ridge, instead of beading or filigree, which is peculiarly British. The fine gold torc from Broighter has a tubular ring in place of twisted wire, 'pinhead ornament' instead of crinkly line, and in place of basketry the smooth areas are covered by intersecting compass-drawn circles. The 'pinheads' are Continental and occur on the Frasnes-lez-Buissenal torcs, but the compass-work was tried out on slips of bone, some of which have been found at Lough Crew and which may have served as patterns. Compass-work on pots at Glastonbury has already been mentioned (above, p. 257). Ultimately all these buffer- and ring-ended necklets and bracelets hark back to Asiatic ceremonial rings – Assyrian, Phrygian, and Achaemenian – while the Frasnes-lez-Buissenal animals are remarkably Scythian.[20]

All the work so far described is interrelated, but the web of relationship is so complicated, at once so pervasive and so elusive, that I find it impossible to recognize regional workshops. Tricks of style occur on widely dispersed objects, and probably the products of workshops travelled as far. Until better chronological landmarks have been established than yet exist, differences of date may be mistaken for differences in locality, and at all events it is the overriding consistency and harmony of the insular tradition that strikes the observer. The rareness of really characteristic work of any of the Continental styles in the British Isles limits the usefulness of those, all too few, dates which have been recognized across the Channel. The Waldalgesheim work on the Standlake scabbard does not help with dating island work like Torrs and the various finds from the rivers Witham and Thames. If, as appeared in the last chapter, a developed 'Early Style' was still current till the end of the fourth century, overlapping with Waldalgesheim, which had emerged in the middle of that century and which in turn lasted until it melted into the Sword Style in the second half of the third century or even the beginning of the second; and if the Plastic Style began at, or soon after, the opening of the third century, then it is a reasonable guess that the years from 350 to 200 were the crucial time when the new spirit of La Tène came to bear on Britain, with the turn of the third century probably the most important of all. The Plastic and Waldalgesheim Styles and the newly emerging Sword Style were all active then, and it may not be due to chance alone that we have had to refer several times to the late Plastic Style of Brå and Brno-Maloměřice and to the Early and Early Middle La Tène swords of La Tène itself, all of which lie probably around the turn of the third century.[21] With this as a point of departure, we may provisionally see the series from the Torrs pony-cap to the Waterloo Bridge helmet as running between the late third and the first centuries B.C.

The most curious and arresting aspect of insular La Tène is how from the first it strikes out and away from Continental models. It does not lose touch, but it follows its own self-sufficient line of growth. In a way it is more 'Celtic'; it exaggerates the new qualities, and to this fact I shall return. One of the many differences between the British and Continental Celts was that while the latter went to the blacksmith for the ornament of a fine scabbard, the former still called on the bronzesmith, who gave him workmanship that is as unlike Continental 'Sword Style' as insular Plastic is unlike Continental Plastic.

The finest scabbards came from Northern Ireland, three from Lisnacroghera (Co. Antrim) and one from the river Bann at Toome. The only English scabbard as rich as these is from Bugthorpe in Yorkshire (Figure 101). Contrary to opinions formerly prevailing, there is no more than a collateral relationship between the Irish and English groups.[22] That much fine bronze war-harness has come out of the Thames probably means no more than the use of the river as a highway for travel and commerce, but the Lisnacroghera scabbards, like Llyn Cerrig and like many rich collections of La Tène bronzes on the Continent, and above all La Tène in Lake Neuchâtel itself with over 2,500 different drowned objects, ranks as a place dedicated to the waters and those watery cults which we have already met in the north and elsewhere. Of the Irish scabbards, Lisnacroghera I with its wavy line and Toome are nearest to Continental fashions. An iron scabbard from La Tène is almost an unfinished sketch for the former,

Figure 101. Bronze scabbards: A from Lisnacroghera (no. 2), B from Toome, Northern Ireland, C from Bugthorpe, Yorkshire

and there is a hint of Lisnacroghera 2 in another from Italy.[23] Lisnacroghera 2 is unadventurous, relying heavily on compasses, but number 3, though less harmoniously laid out because the mid-rib contradicts the movement of the design, looks forward to manuscript paintings of the next millennium (Plate 294). The frothy lightness of the hand-drawn spirals is something new; they cry out for colour. The basketry background may be a link with British work, but the birds and animals have been dropped and the pattern is quite abstract.[24]

This sudden prominence of Northern Ireland is probably due to one of those bands of immigrants, chiefs and their retinue, arriving at a moment when the continental Sword Style had fully emerged, perhaps in the late third, but more probably in the early second century B.C. The dangers of the new style can be seen in a scabbard from the river Trent, in some late mirrors, and even to some extent in the Waterloo Bridge helmet. When tension is relaxed we are on the edge of Art Nouveau. These scabbards and the swords which they held are quite distinct from swords and scabbards with moulded ornament, and from the short antennae daggers with the handgrip in the form of a human figure which Britain shares with the Continent. A very recent discovery of bronze plaques, including parts of shields, from Tal-y-Llyn in Merioneth, if placed beside the great Llyn Cerrig Bach hoard with which they have much in common, and a certain number of other objects found in Wales, show that this highland region also was no backwater. Some rather early Continental connexions have been claimed for the Tal-y-Llyn bronzes, but where likeness comes from a given motif alone it is unsafe to use it as a criterion of date.[25]

British bronze mirrors were as much emblems of rank and objects of glorification as were swords, scabbards, and shields. They are remote offspring of Greek and Etruscan mirrors, and along with the traditional shape the idea was accepted of using the mirror's back as canvas for a finely engraved design. The British mirrors have been subjected to searching analysis, and they may reveal more of the peculiarities of insular Celtic art than any other set of objects.[26] The dates probably run from the late first century to a climax around A.D. 30. I illustrate the Mayer Mirror, without provenance, but considered one of the earliest (Plate 303). The three roundels are symmetrically balanced. The design inside is still linked to such first-century B.C. work as the Llyn Cerrig bird plaque. It is a typical profile drawn with a firm, clear line. The draughtsman occasionally faltered when setting out a design like this, but not the master of the Mayer Mirror. This has been called 'hardly credible virtuosity', but in fact the steadiness and control had been learnt long before in the Bronze Age goldsmith's shop, and can now proclaim itself with the confident restraint of Giotto offering his *tondo*. The basketry areas, produced with a rocked tracer, are almost as insistent as the outlined circles and ellipses of the main pattern and stand in lieu of colour, as on some of the scabbards.

From this we pass on to the almost mechanical perfection of the well-known Desborough and Birdlip mirrors, with their sophisticated symmetrical designs, and from them to the frighteningly mad disintegration of Old Warden and the late, loose Billericay (Essex) mirror (Figure 102). This whole series of engravings springs from a fertilization of the motif of three linked circles, in an old European Bronze Age tradition, with the classical lyre-palmette (Figure 103). Where the tension between these poles is taut we get Mayer and Birdlip: a perfect balance of ballooning patterns poised like performing seals. When tension slackens, on the late mirrors and scabbards, there is merely flatulence and a gangling Art Nouveau.

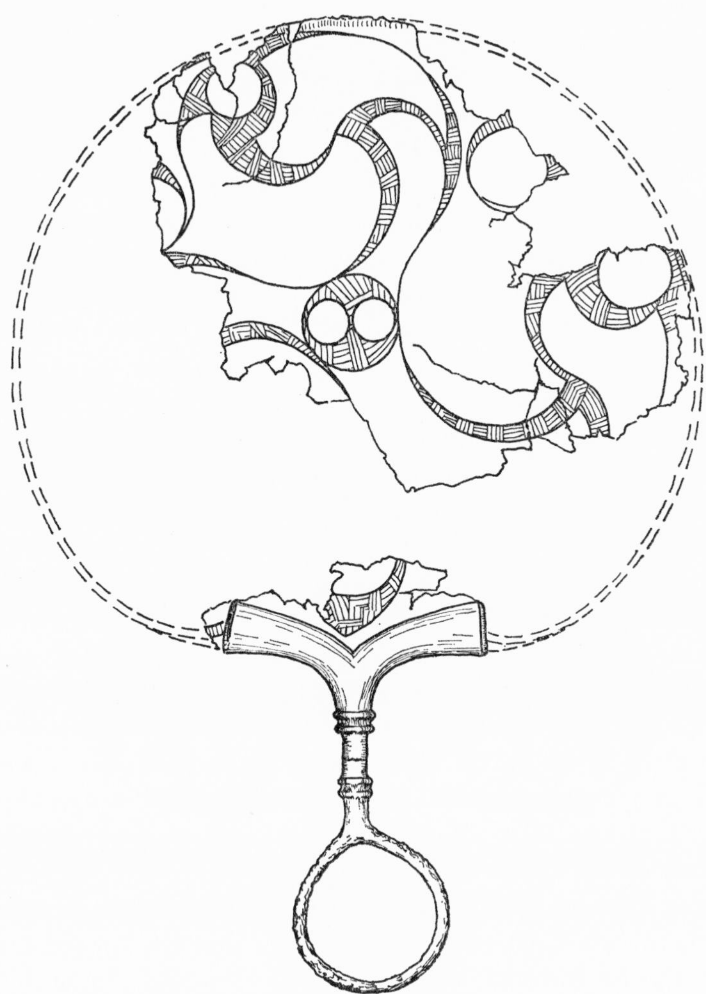

Figure 102. Bronze mirror from Billericay, Essex

In the last chapter I ventured a guess – it was no more – that the repoussé panels of the Rynkeby cauldron came from the same quarter, perhaps the same workshop, as the repoussé panels of the tub found at Marlborough and the bucket from a late-first-century B.C. grave at Aylesford in Kent. Some Continental workshop was, I believe, the source of these decorative pieces as of the scabbard horses from Kelheim;[27] lightly transportable, they could be adapted to whatever use suited the local magnate.

Wherever this workshop was, it was well to the west of that which put out the Gundestrup panels; on the other hand the work is far more representational than suited the taste of the insular Celts, the relief is softer, and the contours flow into each other without sharp planes, appealing to a very different sensibility from that expressed in the Battersea shield, the Deskford boar's head, and the rest of the Late Plastic bronze-work.

Figure 103. A Bone cheek-piece from Veselé, Slovakia, Czechoslovakia, second millennium
B Classical palmette
C Restored pattern on the back of the bronze mirror from Colchester, Essex

The Rynkeby animals flank a threefold whirligig which is evidently the sacred symbol (Plate 285), and a sixfold whirligig between birds' heads and beside a pair of opposed horses is the main subject of the Aylesford bucket (Plate 301). At Marlborough, however, the central role is taken by frontal visages which remind us of Rynkeby's outside panel and the Bouray god (Plates 297, 281, and front cover). Perhaps the heads under huge crests at Aylesford are similar guardians, but their long-faced, thin-jawed physiognomy is related to that of the Brno-Maloměřice pair. These heads have come a long way from Phrygian and Urartian harpies and sirens, but the debt must be acknowledged, though the debtor knew nothing of it. Much later the Irish were to tell fabulous stories of their ancestors living and fighting in Greece, Scythia, and Egypt; the truth behind the history of their arts is much stranger than these fables. The iconography of this bucket and tub is dominated by horses, natural and fantasticated. Opposed horses had figured on the Kivik grave slabs, and we have seen a great number of horse-headed boats and serpents in northern razor art (Plates 196 and 198): this must be remembered before setting off to ransack Scythia and the east for their ancestors. The Marlborough horse with lowered head, in particular, belongs to the same family as the pair on the Kelheim scabbard (Plate 297). The Kelheim horses were once lyres, or are on the way to becoming lyres, and the S-spiral of their bodies helps to explain the curiously doubled-up bodies of one Marlborough pair whose long tongues sketch yet another lyre. Still more is this true of the Aylesford horses (Plates 300 and 301). A rationalizing artist has given them legs and put them face to face, or rather neck to neck; but if they are up-ended like the Kelheim or Dürkheim 'dragons' (Figure 89A), they describe the same flourish, while the legs appear as the afterthought they are, and belong to pantomime. In this way dragon and hobby-horse meet. The crests of the Aylesford horses and the tongues of one Marlborough pair were already in the repertoire of northern razor art, and there is no need to call in griffins from Russia.

The profile faces interspersed, sometimes in pairs, among the horses and heads *en face* of the Marlborough tub are appropriately compared to the heads on Celtic coins. We can see the same wild locks, the moustaches, the prominent nose and heavy mouth (Plates 298 and 299). The S-spiral lock, a profile rendering of the Astarte hair-style that we have seen full face on Waldalgesheim gold-work and elsewhere in Celtic art, is less easy to find on coins, but a woman-headed horse, perhaps Epona the horse-goddess, seems to wear it.[28] There are horses of every kind on the Celtic coinage of the first centuries B.C. and A.D. Not a few are from the same stable as the Marlborough horses. These were the received schemata, and it would be unwise to use them for close dating. Some are quite naturalistic and the work of Mediterranean die-cutters, and others not much more than illogical flourishes with sticks and blobs for limbs, like soldier ants. Somewhere half-way in this progress is the long-backed, dazzling white beast that steps delicately across the Berkshire Downs above the Vale of White Horse to which it has given its name.[29]

At the end of the last century B.C., or not till the beginning of our era, there was a return in Britain to three-dimensional work which at first sight is oddly like the continental Plastic Style of two and a half centuries before. It may be in part due to Mediterranean contacts through the Romanized Belgae, but it is still entirely Celtic. Once more the contours of the animal describe ornamental patterns, as in the Plastic Style, but the planes tend to sharpen and the relief to form crisp lozenges. There are ox-head attachments for cauldrons or buckets, brooches with dragon heads, birds, and a very fine handle for a spun bronze bowl from Keshcarrigan in Northern Ireland. To these may be added a bowl found as far away as Poland which may also be British work. It has an animal's head as spout that has the parted mane of Anglo-Saxon and Romanesque finial dragons.[30] There is also now more use of coloured enamel.

In their coinages we see the destructive side of the Celtic aesthetic as well as its ingenuity; its tendency to anarchy and loss of nerve when confronted with inimical classical models as well as its skill in altering them to its own ends where possible (Figure 104). In this case the models were particularly intractable, hard and stereotyped, but there are some very pleasing as well as characteristic designs. The gold stater of the Parisii (Plate 302, top) is based on the Macedonian gold stater. It has the head of the young god or chieftain in idealized profile on the obverse, and on the reverse a playful horse, crested and surrounded by dots and flourishes all of which were no doubt as legible to the tribe as the lettering of the Greek original to literate peoples. Above it is a canopy which may have begun as the Macedonian chariot but is now something quite different. On a gold stater of the Andecavi, a tribe north of the Loire, the charioteer is present but crowded on to the rump of the man-headed horse, while an 'earth-giant' supports them. These are windswept and very vigorous figures. Finally a gold stater of the Virudini has the now familiar elk-nosed horse, with an equal-armed cross below the head and a lyre under the body (Plate 302, bottom, cf. Figure 74A).

The La Tène ironsmith was almost as much an artist as the bronzesmith, but his work has been the victim of corrosion and seldom survives in quantity or in a form that does justice to his art. For the most part he worked in wrought iron, but he had also experimented with steel, the result usually of accident but leading him towards the beautiful pattern-welding of sword-blades. Though iron was not used in Britain, as on the Continent, for the finer decoration of scabbards, our smiths wrought superb fire-dogs with ox- or horse-head tops, like the severe but subtle Lord's Barton set from Cambridgeshire (Plate 304) or the whimsical horses from Capel Gormon in North Wales. Much fine work in bronze and iron that carried on the La Tène tradition lies too late in

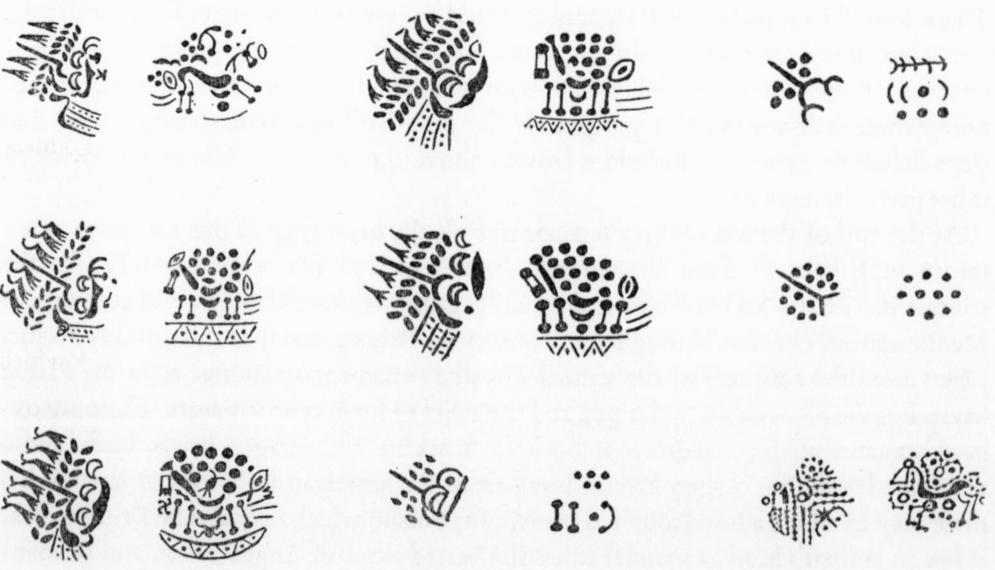

Figure 104. Gallo-British coinage, broken-up versions of the gold stater of Philip II of Macedon, the head of Apollo on the obverse and the chariot on the reverse

time for our study, for Rome was moving in, and the native arts prepared to go underground.[31]

A case is sometimes put forward according to which La Tène art was already in full decline *before* the Roman impact, so that in fact when Rome took over native arts it was to breathe new life into them. But this view does not allow for the reappearance of barbarian Celtic art in full vigour with the old qualities, transmuted certainly, but quite as anti-classical as formerly, the moment that the Roman umbrella shut up, or for the fact that just beyond the frontiers they had survived unbroken an incredibly long time and without benefit of Rome.[32]

A Footnote to Insular La Tène Art and Invasions

After this short exploration of insular La Tène art it is worth while pausing to consider a little longer one or two conclusions. Here, unlike the Continent, it is *only* with La Tène civilization that we meet a true art, or indeed much sign of a visual awareness of beauty at all. Craftsmanship there had been of high quality, but of art little indeed. Yet almost from the start insular Celtic plunges away from the parent, not in the direction of its own Geometric past, but in a positive exaggeration of what is new and strange. Common motifs were subtly modified, like the 'trumpet spirals' into which triskele and plain spiral were drawn out. There is admittedly a reinforcement of some rather old-fashioned techniques like alternate hatching or basketry, and tremolo or rocked tracer work and eventually a combination of the two on the mirrors. But the greatest achievements of insular La Tène were two: its peculiar brand of asymmetry, and the exploitation of the negative pattern, meaning emptiness, the value of the voids. In place of the Waldalgesheim, Plastic, and Sword Styles there was an insular version, different and more extreme, yet corresponding to each. At this point style becomes a matter of historical as well as art-historical importance.

There is a disconcerting division of opinion on the extent of social and tribal change, the weight of invasion or its lack that lies behind these developments in the arts. It has been suggested that La Tène art came to Britain, like the Vix crater to France or the Grächwil hydria to Switzerland, as an exotic rarity, implying nothing more than occasional commercial enterprises and the heroic conventions of gift-exchange, while at the same time inspiring the native craftsmen to prodigies of invention. Or it is said that it came on the bright blades of a few chieftains and their bands of personal followers. In either case the bulk of the population would have been left undisturbed. A third possibility is that there *was* a substantial change of population, with fresh immigrants from the Continent settling over most of the country. The first two alternatives may apply to the very beginning of La Tène art in Britain. Men will adopt a superior weapon or a piece of beautiful jewellery without altering any of their habits or admitting new blood into their society; but it is another matter entirely with the appearance of the mature La Tène style in Britain, because this is something fundamentally different, it is above all a new language.

On the Continent the style arose fast certainly, but not incredibly fast. Stages can be seen and mapped; the underlying classical, eastern, and northern bases have been laid bare. But in Britain, apart from a few early imports like the Cerrig-y-Drudion bowl, and outside the pioneering work of one or two swordsmiths, the new art comes at one blow; the shields, bracelets, scabbards, horsebits are entirely committed, entirely uncompromising in their rejection of the past. There is a practical problem here of transmission, of what *that* man taught or showed *this* man. All development must come back to this humdrum work. On the one hand there is craft tradition based on materials and their use, workshop practice, the right treatment of specific subjects; and on the other hand style, an intangible element but also communicated by example and spreading from individual to individual. Even Roman workshops were family or dynastic affairs.[33] Where both craft *and* stylistic tradition are new, we are surely in the presence of new men. But this is not all. It is most unlikely that a language so new, and yet so perfectly adapted to its content, was open to the esoteric understanding of the artist and closed to his patrons the chieftains, the great house, the military aristocracy. They too must have been masters of the language; the designs and abstractions that seem strange to us were natural to them. They did indeed *see* in that way and analyse the visible world thus and thus; but such a revolution is inconceivable without substantial numbers of new men, men whose fathers had lived through the formative years of La Tène art on the Continent. Wherever we see single works of art, a pony-cap in Kirkcudbright or a bronze sheath in Antrim, this does not simply mean that someone has acquired a rich and strange treasure, like the owner of the Vix crater with its foreign mythology; it means that there was a full-blooded La Tène Celt who spoke the same spiritual language as the artist, with the same accent.

I suggested earlier in this chapter that the later third century was the crucial period when all the elements that find a place in insular La Tène had either just emerged, or not yet vanished. Historically this was when the Galatians were settled on the Halys, when the Romans began to press on the Celts in North Italy, and when there was a good deal of movement inside the Celtic heartland, including perhaps an exodus from the Neckar valley. This is also a time when on archaeological grounds many prehistorians believe that Britain was invaded from the Continent, with substantial settlements in Yorkshire and in South-West England, and perhaps independently in Ireland and Wales.[34]

With all its fantasy, the *Book of Conquests* still presents a credible scenario, a paradigm of how the invasion could have taken place or, equally important, how it seemed to have taken place to the descendants of the conquerors. 'As for the sons of Mil, they sailed in a great expedition on the sea to Ireland, and did not pause in the course until they saw at a distance the island from the sea. And when they saw Ireland their warriors made contention of rowing and sailing to their utmost in their eagerness and anxiety to reach it; so that Ir son of Mil advanced a wave before every other ship by reason of his strength and valour.'[35]

Triskele
The Three Legs of the Problem: Tension, Ambiguity, the Ideal

The gyres! the gyres! Old Rocky Face look forth;
Things thought too long can be no longer thought,
For beauty dies of beauty, worth of worth,
And ancient lineaments are blotted out.

W. B. Yeats

Now that we have passed in review a number of the finest La Tène works of art, let us return to some of the problems left untouched here and in the last chapter. What *was* this art that appeared so suddenly, and why did it take this of all possible turns? Enough has been said of the forerunners – Mediterranean, Eastern, and European; but when we have analysed patterns into their parts and traced the pedigree of motifs we are left with this enigma. What is the La Tène style?

For a style to stay true to itself for over a thousand years it requires more than the artist's usual conservatism and the tenacity of the *schemata*. These would not have held if they were not expressions of a mind, a way of looking at the world and of feeling about it; of a world of thought as well as the visual world. We are as it were listening to a tone of voice which could survive the brutal imposition of alien accents and come up at the end with almost the same intonation. It is not any single characteristic such as reliance on formal pattern – *that* is as old as the mammoth-hunters of Předmostí – nor is it simply in the motifs used, for very little was invented new. It is something else that has been added: a certain kind of tension, a certain ambiguity, an altered ideal leading to altered constructions, along with some intimations of lineage and continuity.

First the tension: tension entails a tug of opposites, and an equilibrium, often kept at risk. These opposites are on the one hand the old European curvilinear repertoire, the carpet spirals, compass-based 'pulley-patterns' that were used long before in the second millennium by Hungarian and northern metal-workers and bone-carvers, and even by third-millennium potters of Butmir and Cucuteni; and on the other hand the conventional flora of classical ornament: palmette, lotus, tendril, bud. The European repertoire had not died with the Bronze Age. We have seen it alive in Bosnia and in the north in the eighth and seventh centuries (Plate 193 and Figures 73 and 103).[36]

The classical motifs are the interlopers, but they provide the needed pole, the contrary tug. When looking at the openwork border of the discs from Saint Jean-sur-Tourbe or the Cuperly dragons (Plates 252 and 249), it will not do to identify classical lyres and leave it at that, without also remembering the pattern of the Trundholm sun-disc, the bone from Nitriansky-Hrádok, and the 'belt-box' from Stevneskov (Figure 69B and Plates 176 and 197). The same is true of the Battersea shield and many other typically 'Celtic' works. Palmette and lyre have been absorbed, but so have running spirals and 'pulleys'. The design owes its strength to its tension, balanced exactly between these poles. When the attraction of one becomes too strong, the art suffers. The flood of Greco-Roman art loosed into Western Europe from the first century B.C. upset this equilibrium and, except in Ireland, where it hardly reached, the result was either a spiritless repetition of provincial copies, or else the desperate and illogical disintegration and flatulence that were the peculiar vice of bad La Tène.

Sometimes it seems that we are not so much looking at an acrobat on the tightrope of tension as at a conjuror. He holds in one hand a coil made up of the geometric and sprouting spirals of the old Bronze Age repertoire, and in the other a garland of classical leaves and flowers. He moves first one arm, then the other, and crosses them backwards and forwards until our eyes lose track of the movement and both become fused into a single growing thing that is both organic and abstract. It is very tempting to say that the first steps on this path were taken in Transylvanian and Hungarian workshops when the bronze-workers of the mid second millennium made their running spirals not only *flow* but *grow* (above, p. 181 and Plates 171–5).

We have seen how compasses altered the style of Bronze Age decoration, and in the dichotomy of Celtic art compasses gave strength to the European side. The setting-out points on the Lough Crew bone slips, Glastonbury weaving-combs and bridle cheeks, or the Minster Ditch scabbard are very like the setting-out points of Bronze Age compass-decorated bridle cheeks and bone roundels, and the pricks and rulings on the backs of decorated pages of the Lindisfarne Gospels, but the finished designs are quite unlike; each is of its own age. In Ireland the Tuatha Dé Danaan, the older semi-divine race which the historical tribes had supplanted, considered their artists to be gods. I have already quoted the Irish story of the stranger with the compasses who instructed in their uses the smith designing Cú Chulainn's shield. This stranger was a god, and medieval Christianity also knew God with the compasses, the *elegans architectus* who builds the cosmos. For Boethius the compass was symbolic of the art that comprehends the whole, and it is possible that another Irish shield described as having five wheels was itself a model of the universe.[37] Bronze shields were in any case for display, like hatchments, being much too brittle for use.

The Waldalgesheim Style achieved the most critical, because precarious, balance and a strange species of ambiguity: a blurring of definition, not between man and animal but between man, animal, and plant, and with it the wilful avoidance of symmetry. This is perhaps the most elusive art style of any we have met, and the most difficult to analyse. The coiling of the tendril at the bottom of the Standlake scabbard or on the handle of the Brå cauldron is in itself no more eccentric than the linked spirals growing on the Apa or Hajdusámson swords, or for that matter on the bones from Isturitz (Plates 42 and 171 and Figure 68A). In all a sinuous line is arranged to fill a long, narrow space, but something more is needed to explain the patterns on the Waldalgesheim busts and bracelets (Plates 253 and 254). Here is a departure from old standards of symmetry. Our eyes look for the return of the pattern and are disconcerted by its loss. This is also true of the Sword Style and of a great deal of insular La Tène. Sometimes, as we have already observed, the asymmetry is not real but simulated, and this is very revealing, for the purpose is a characteristically Celtic sort of illusionism, a visual *legerdemain* that suggests plant forms without actually representing them. The essence of the living creeper has been captured, but none of the particulars. The moment we see the symmetrical development of one of these designs (Figure 89B), the vegetable interpretation disappears. It is sometimes the same with the Plastic Style; we have the illusion of organic form without the reality (Plates 264 and 265). This is what Jacobsthal called 'the Cheshire style'; it can never be pinned down to *this* thing, *this* place, *this* time. Nothing is quite what it seems; even geometry is simulated, not real.

Compasses were sometimes used directly, as for instance on the Eygenbilsen flagons, but there are many more *freehand* designs based on compass constructions, where only close analysis shows everything to be just a little out of true.[38] The rigid geometry is masked by the dynamic of the chosen pattern that runs counter to, yet depends upon it. A description of the hexameter as a regular trellis which supports the irregular twistings of the vine is not inapt. The poetry is the vine, not the trellis, but the trellis must be there. The poetry of Celtic design is the organic pattern, not the geometry that holds it up; but without the geometry it droops to incoherence. The metrical analogy could be pushed farther; for, like feet of different length, these patterns are composed of motifs with their conventional shape and names – 'trumpet-spiral', 'fish-bladder', leaf, fan, tear-drop – and these conventional statements, if combined into compositions, have a great deal more to say than a simple adding-up of the parts.

Creeper-like meanderings are not the whole of La Tène asymmetry, especially in the British Isles. Perhaps the way to approach the designs on scabbards and the backs of mirrors (Plates 287 and 303) is to ask not 'why asymmetry?' but 'why symmetry?' All representational art is asymmetric; the very idea of the opposite is naïve. The antithetical heraldic group is the nearest approach to absolute symmetry possible in a composition; it is also as nearly static as a face viewed from the front. The Předmostí engraved figure (Plate 23) is probably the earliest strictly symmetrical pattern we have, and inevitably it is a frontal diagram of the human figure. If we accept without question the asymmetry of any profile and any narrative, why should we feel uneasy about the asymmetry of the Bugthorpe scabbard or the Mayer Mirror? The lineage of the mirror patterns has in it a profile of a bird like the Rheinheim cock. The artist has transformed the essential asymmetry of the profile into an idealized asymmetric geometry. This sort of pattern is (pace Jacobsthal) less static than a symmetric pattern. There need be no beginning and no end, and the movement is perpetual. Perhaps the special magic of the three-limbed figures, triskele and triquetra, is that as nearly as possible they have the best of both worlds, symmetric and asymmetric; the movement is endless, yet the pattern is rounded and completed. The reconciliation of three or more independent entities involves discovery of the point at which they coincide, the centre of the triskele, 'like three independent deeds meeting in one deed. An effect should have a cause, but in the tales the effect is produced by several causes which result in turning a commonplace into an enigma.'[39] The discovery of points where unrelated things coincide is one of the great arts of seers and magicians. Coincidence is like punning, itself an ancient art bound up with theological and cosmological concepts.

In this art no dislocation, however savage, is barred so long as the composition achieves harmony. It is invertebrate not in a pejorative sense, but quite literally; for the liberties that are taken with the bony structure deny natural law, like Cú Chulainn in his distortions when 'he made a dreadful wonderful bow of himself like a rainbow in a shower of rain'. The eye is still recognizable when everything else is resolved, or dissolved into geometric circles and ellipses (Plate 303 and Figures 90 and 99). The comma sign is another constant; it is the joint-sign of Scythian art and possibly a symbol of strength (p. 234 above), and perhaps in Britain it should sometimes be read as tear-drop, since the fairy woman who loved Cú Chulainn was called Fann because 'there is nothing in the world except a tear to which her beauty could be likened'.[40] It is in these patterns that the way is prepared for the carved stones, crosses, and pages of manuscripts on which animal and vegetable life is indistinguishable, where the joints sprout foliage or heads or unexpected limbs and tails. Nothing is whole or in isolation, but everything interlinked, protean. That which starts as a man may end as a vine or a greyhound. It is a quality also possessed by some 'Celtic' writing that seems to lack a permanent centre, when the new idea sprouts from the knee-joints of the old to form a momentary focus which as quickly dissolves.

As well as the ambiguity between classical floral and European geometric motifs, there is a peculiarly insular ambivalence between the positive and negative readings of the pattern. To give such formal weight to the voids is something alien to the classical Mediterranean mind. Most ambiguous are the animal and human transformations. These too are the visual equivalents of puns and riddles. They juggle with the normally accepted categories of thought in a way that we know again in 'Celtic' writing, from early narrative and legend – where one explanation will never do if two are possible, or better three: the threefold births and deaths of heroes, tall stories and marvellous coincidence, shape-shifting, man and animal, human and monster, classical and barbarian – down to the poetry of Dylan Thomas and the prose of James Joyce.[41]

Ambiguity is nowhere more baffling than in the La Tène face. Jacobsthal wrote of it as 'a construction', but this in itself is nothing new. We have seen one fearful example of the face as construction in the Kličevac image, and before that there was Predionica (Plates 167 and 95). But the La Tène face is quite different. It is there from the beginning of the Early Style, at Weisskirchen and Rodenbach. The beady, bulging eye may owe something to the use of shell or glass set into figures of bronze and wood. The line of the nose runs into the eyebrows, which themselves curve away in an arabesque on the head (Plates 240 and 247). When they formed the features, it appears that La Tène artists looked analytically at such Greek and Etruscan representations as the goddess of the Grächwil hydria and the gorgon of the Vix crater and made *these* their models, not the faces of living men and women. They saw that lips, eyebrows, and nostrils were composed of curls, commas, and spirals. In *their* language spirals, commas, and curls were 'received' eloquent symbols of great antiquity, so they arranged them into a design that would stand up by itself stripped of any attempt to imitate appearances.

The insistent symmetry of the starkly frontal view was of course a help in pattern-making. The faces of Plates 236 and 274 can be 'read' in two ways and speak the two languages, as do the evangelists of St Gall and Kells. The full face has its terrors, perhaps due to the eye that paralyses, whether on a butterfly's wing or in the mirror held up to the gorgon or basilisk. The Egyptians hardly ever represented it on their reliefs, nor did the archaic Greeks; but man also learnt to *exploit* this terror, inventing fabulous creatures 'with the sole object of wringing from them this paralysing power'. When painted in the form of eyes, circles, and masks it made his ships and houses and shields invincible, for 'the ocellus is equivalent to the Gorgon's death-dealing look'.[42]

Nearly all writers on La Tène art refer to faces like those of Plates 244 and 260 as 'masks', calling to mind the gold sheet placed on the face of a dead prince at Mycenae, Hallstatt, or Trebenište, or the wooden masks worn by northern shamans, or even the tragic and comic masks of the late classical theatre. But this is a mere label, and misleading. The reality is, I believe, far more complicated. In classical Mediterranean art we expect to recognize certain stereotyped characters by their physiognomy – satyr and silenus, Ethiopian, Gorgon, the Egyptian Bes, and even the Iranian Zurvan – and it should perhaps be asked whether La Tène artists do not also show us stereotyped physiognomies. There is for instance one long-jawed, long-nosed, clean-shaven type (Plates 260 and 270). In old age it has the severe and not ignoble features of Tolund man, preserved for us in an alkaline bog in Denmark from the first century B.C. or A.D. In youth it is like Lug Lamfada at the second battle of Mag Tured, 'as bright as the sun on a dry summer's day', but he is also the implacable vengeful Lug of the 'Fate of the Children of Tuireann'; not a genial father and provider, but a brooding ancestor or doomed and dedicated hero (Plates 269 and 301). There is also a dignified bearded face that could stand for Sylvanus, Sucellus, the Good God, the Dagda; and a very young unmarked one with short hair, another version perhaps of the tribal hero or young god (Plate 245 and front cover). Later Irish mythology presented two realizations of the heroic type in which heroism as a social function opposed heroism as a natural force.[43] But we cannot name any of them, and the labels derived from the *interpretatio romana* or from Romano-Celtic inscriptions, or from later mythological writings, are all irrelevant, although the categories and qualities may be permanent and true.

It is rather odd how very different all these types are from the blunt features and unruly elf-locks of 'the Gaul' of Roman art; but until the conquest, Roman sculptors only saw him 'in chains' or 'dying'. A moustached, almost Mongolian face with wild hair sometimes appears on early jewellery, again in profile on coins, and perhaps on the Marlborough tub (Plates 236 and 299). Authentic Mongols are not likely to have been seen, and this probably belongs to the Silenus, Bes, and Zurvan stereotype.

While these artists show us types which may correspond to figures of mythology or formal categories of thought, it seems as though they are also struggling to portray some ideal of beauty that is not ours. The barriers between are so opaque that any clue should be grasped thankfully, and this is my excuse for turning once more to the Ulster Epic Cycle. When the poet sets out to describe Cú Chulainn, the hero *par excellence*, he is said to surpass every man in his gifts and physical attributes, quantitatively as well as qualitatively. He had not five but seven fingers to each hand and seven toes to each foot, seven pupils to each eye which 'glittered with seven gem-like sparkles'. Nor is this all, for he had four moles – one blue, one crimson, one green, and one yellow – and 'between one ear and the other he had fifty clear yellow long tresses that were as yellow as wax of bees or like a brooch of white gold as it glints in the sun'. As an anatomy of beauty this sounds oddly, because it is in fact a description not of nature but of a pattern, not an appearance but an intellectual, almost mathematical conception. The perfection of the hero who is 'master of all the talents' is conveyed better by geometry than by particulars of natural physiognomy. This is the poetic counterpart of the ideal pattern faces of Plates 266, 274, 290, and 292. The colours too are quite formal; the colours of the four moles and the hair are beautiful in themselves but imitate nature no more than in a Byzantine mosaic or manuscript painting. In the description of Conchober in the 'Intoxication of the Ulstermen' we have another equivalent to the carved and painted 'pattern faces'. When he arrives before Tara Luachra his face is 'comparable to a moon in its great fifteenth . . . his red beard was fair, forked and pointed, his bushy reddish yellow hair was looped to the slope of his hood'. We must probably allow also for that widespread number-mysticism, something of which the Celts almost certainly understood, along with possessing a gift for turning even narrative into ideal formulae.[44]

Before leaving the representation of man something must be said about the so-called 'Têtes Coupées' in La Tène iconography, for they are as much an accepted classification as the 'masks'. Classical authors describing Celtic manners write of enemy heads fastened to the harness of the returning warriors, and nailed up as trophies on houses; or of the skull of an especially redoubtable enemy embalmed with oil of cedar and carefully preserved. This straightforward trophy-hunting has been given a more sinister extension by stories of human sacrifice in sacred groves (one existed near Marseilles), to which the discovery of a sanctuary like Roquepertuse, with its niches for human skulls, gives more substance. But one classical author repeats another, sometimes with rhetorical and doubtful embellishments, so that, while a dubious shadow lies over the character of the Celts, there is little of fact to take hold of.[45] Apart from these stories, the art does bear out an obsessional preoccupation with heads.

Many carvings have survived of a sombre head under murderous paws (often broken), but a claw on the forehead is enough to identify the subject. Or else faces stare with the impassivity of Homer's 'strengthless heads of the dead' out of the jaws of a devouring beast (Plates 275 and 245). These are of a different order from the limbs slobbered from the jaws of Etruscan devourers. It is the same subject that was used in the early Middle Ages to portray the power of the dog over the souls of unrighteous men, but there is little in surviving Celtic mythology from which to construct a beheading death-demon. On the other hand decapitations were performed harmlessly by uncanny, but not always hostile, supernatural persons, while severed magic heads converse sententiously and are consulted as oracles.[46] In occupied Gaul and the Rhineland colossal heads were carved, sometimes with a hollow for libations. The head as seat of the soul is not an idea peculiar to the Celts, nor is its representation *pars pro toto*.

An attempt has been made to distinguish heads without neck or body as gods, and with neck as victims, but this too seems doubtful. Two-fold or 'Janus' heads in the Rhône and Rhine valleys, and three-fold or tricephalic ones in North-East France, Belgium, or Ireland, have been connected with the 'Mercury figures' referred to by Caesar, but the intellectual concepts that lie behind such representations are only confused by giving them such irrelevant and arbitrary titles. The idea of The Three which is in one sense I, Thou, and the Third Person is very deeply rooted in many religions.[47] A shift of emphasis towards the head does perhaps mark a different conception of man in Northern European art in general. In Southern Europe the head is usually no more emphasized than any other member and may even be very small, whereas north of the Alps, even when not disproportionately large as in some German and Flemish paintings, it gathers to itself more and more of the 'life', especially in Expressionist painting of a few decades back.

But we have not yet done with ambiguity; it is nowhere more baffling than in the transformations. Human heads are often paired with an animal or bird which may be the *alter ego* of god or hero, for the Celts change skins easily from mare to lady and from hero to hound and back again.[48] The brooch from Oberwittighausen (Plate 247) showed us the ambivalent relationship of the two heads that are so alike, and yet only one has an animal's ears. This is matched by another brooch from the same site where again the lower head is a bearded man but the upper is this time pure animal, and leads on to a brooch from Ostheim where the animal is lost in abstract pattern.[49] These are friendly-looking beasts, but not all were so mild. There can be no doubt of the threatening and baleful character of the 'Tarasque de Noves' (Plate 275), and in some roundabout way this horror must be related to Greek and Asiatic lions. Some lions still hid in the Thracian forest east of the Strymon, and Galatians may have hunted them in Anatolia, but no western La Tène artist is likely ever to have seen one, any more than the situla artists of North Italy and Illyria (above, p. 225). They were in no position to distinguish a real lion from any fabulous destroyer. For them all were fabulous, all fair subjects for the imagination and for ornamental fantasy. So here among the descendants of Achaemenian royal lions and their Greek offspring we meet the mastiff-lion, the wolf-lion, and the peculiarly Celtic pug-faced lion of the flagons that was to live on into the milieu of manuscript illumination, where we see it again and again with its jaws insatiably and futilely gnawing the air or its own alienated limbs. It has also that peculiarly Celtic persuasiveness that makes the incredible credible: this little monster has in fact recently come to life in the Boston Terrier and the *Bouledogue Français*.[50]

Lion-griffins and eagle-griffins made little headway in Central and Western Europe, yet, as we have seen, birds were everywhere at the beginning of the last millennium B.C. Usually the bills are turned up, so they are not predators but water-birds, beneficent squawking and honking spirits of the lakes and rivers. Then something happened. Birds on situlae have sickle-sharp beaks and begin to look like predators. They perch on heads and pick out eyes; nor is the round-eyed stare of the Rheinheim and Brå owls reassuring. Hecate has made over her cock to Irish Brigit, and the mantic swans and Aphrodite's doves change plumage with the scald crow, the sinister Badh. When the Morrígan met Cú Chulainn in the enchanted place in a chariot harnessed to a chestnut horse with one leg and a pole through its body, she transformed herself into a black bird in order to utter a gloomy prophecy, by which it is understood that this is none other than the black crow who fed on the slain after battle. She also boasted that she could turn herself into an eel or a grey wolf or a white cow with red ears.[51]

The sea-god Mannanan foretells the life and death of his son Mongán: 'He will be in the shape of every beast . . . a wolf . . . a stag . . . a spotted salmon in a full pool . . . a seal . . . a swan.' Transformations like these, sung of and portrayed on brooches and flagons, were probably the grounds on which classical writers credited 'the druids' with Pythagorean beliefs in metempsychosis along with much occult cosmic wisdom. But behind such speculations there may be nothing more than that primitive metaphysic which does in fact rest in the hinterground of Pythagorean teaching as Apollo inherits the mantic power of the shaman, for:

> Empedocles has thrown all things about;
> Hector is dead and there's a light in Troy;[52]

Jacobsthal wrote: 'In this world the borderline between pregnant and faded form, between pure significant myth and ornamental play, is blurred'; and it is precisely in *this* milieu that we find adumbrations of the heroes and monsters of medieval romance. Though monsters were singularly lacking from Bronze Age Europe, they have now appeared and were to persist in the visual arts as long as almost any other order of beings. We have seen how their image grew out of abstract spiral patterns when these came into contact with the representational traditions of northern forest art (p. 199 above), and how they were at first independent of Etruscan and oriental monsters and dragons, though reinforced later from both directions, and especially from the east. They certainly inhabited the west long before Christian missionaries arrived and turned them into devils. At first these 'devils', contorted and shaggy with huge heads, are very far from the later medieval variety and curiously like the 'Earth Giants' of Celtic coins and Gallo-Roman sculpture, huge figures ending in snaky coils that support a cavalier on a prancing horse (see Plate 302, left, bottom).[53]

The primitive supernatural world began with the wilderness almost at the gates of the village or homestead, and its inhabitants, constantly driven back to the limits of the world controlled by the civilizing races, were always about to invade it and devour their produce.[54] In hot countries the desert beyond the sown is the home of chaos, but in Northern and Western Europe it is the dreary moss and infertile heath, the Wasteland, Whinny Muir, King Pellam's Launde and the desolate mere, 'water-demon places . . . where forest trees leant over the white rocks – that joyless wood. Below lay the water bloody and boiling'.[55] This was the setting, but when the history of the conflict came to be written down, the monsters are found to have pedigrees as long as the kings'. They are made, perhaps in deference to some prehistoric memory, the children not of Satan but of Cain. Belonging to an older world than the children of Abel, they are the first-fruits of the Fall and so a sort of elder cousins to mankind.[56] Like the Titans or Centaurs, they are the powers of chaos confronting the small known cosmos of each tribe or community. The idea of this conflict, whether of Tuatha Dé Danaan and Fomorians or of Chthonioi and Ouranioi, is probably as old as man. We have taken note of it in all the stages of this history. *Mutatis mutandis*, the two sides of the Doom on the church tympanum and the centaurs and lapiths of the temple pediment set out the same confrontation.

The bird and animal transformations of Celtic heroes and gods placed them too, for the Christian artist and poet, on the side of the adversary; nevertheless consanguinity was acknowledged, perhaps subconsciously, and assured them finding their way into churches, cathedrals, and cloisters up and down Christian Europe, as well as into illuminated manuscripts and balladry. There is no reason to think that visual memory was less strong than oral. We have surmised that the features of Neanderthal man were depicted by a *sapiens* artist, and the 'Green Man' peering through hawthorn leaves in the Norwich cloisters and at Southwell is the true descendant of the Brno-Malomĕřice heads (Plate 260). It is not surprising that La Tène heads have been found in museums mistakenly among medieval antiquities, for often they are indistinguishable. Even the extraordinary Mšecké-Žehrovice face has its close counterpart in St Mary, Bedford, and La Tène 'lyre' dragons and firedrakes after centuries of migrations and turmoil turn up again coiled around Romanesque arches.[57]

These then are the key words, the legs of the triskele, at the point where things unrelated coincide: tension, ambiguity, ideal construction. I think I have said enough about ambiguity, the 'mercurial, shape-shifting, enigmatic magic'. The Celtic hero is partly a magician and lives 'in a world saturated with magic', and so do the *aes dana* or men of art who rank immediately below the nobles.[58]

The ideal constructions belong to a way of thinking, a preoccupation with geometry or pseudo-geometry and the fascination of numbers. We have seen this in its literary expression, in the ideal and abstract features of a material face and in narrative.[59] 'It is not the properties of the world which determine their construction, it is their construction which determines the properties of an artificial world of concepts implicitly defined by the natural laws they have chosen.'[60] Selecting the properties they required and discarding the rest, Celtic artists sometimes achieved an intellectual beauty of a far more sophisticated order than that which produced the Predionica clay figures or the Senorbí marble; for it is now more self-conscious and it is overlaid with intricacy. It is well expressed by a contemporary poet, himself a Welshman, reviewing an article on Celtic Christian art. It has, he says, 'an elusive hardness, a bent towards the intricate and towards the abstract, there is also a certain punctiliousness with regard to received formulae, at least some of the characteristics are . . . observable from La Tène to Finnegan's Wake'.[61]

The idea of divinity is so stupendous that it can be expressed by objects of the greatest simplicity – a stone, a log, a sign; but as doubts increase, so does elaboration of the image. The swagger, the braggadocio of the Celtic story-teller is a sort of compensation for the loss of divinity in the heroes whose exploits he records. He divined that he *ought* to be describing the stupendous; but since they had shrunk to mortal heroes, language and description was exaggerated to restore the grandeur of dethroned gods. These descriptions, each one more fantastic than the last, are not meant to represent fact: they are the embroidery of fact, coruscations of hyperbole that dance over a simple tale like the decoration of the gold bracelet from Aurillac that almost smothers a functional rod, or the floral shirt of the Waldalgesheim 'bust'.

Tension is perhaps the most important leg of the triskele: tension between the old

European tradition that we have traced from Neolithic potting through Bronze Age smithing into the La Tène workshops, and the Mediterranean sort of literal and monumental representation. In Celtic La Tène art this tension reaches a crisis and is resolved in a wonderful synthesis; for in a real sense it is the fulfilment of everything that went before, taking its occasional realism from the Mediterranean, inheriting plastic metamorphosis of linear design from second-millennium potters of Eastern Europe, the manual dexterity and professionalism of the bronzesmiths and their flowing curvilinear designs; but rejecting the narrative style that had appeared briefly in Mesolithic painting and that continued outside Europe. The easiest way to test this suggestion is by comparing a number of plates: for instance the heads from Predionica and Brno-Maloměřice, from Senorbí and Holzgerlingen, Brassempouy, Butmir and Bouray, figures from Macomer and Angles-sur-l'Anglin, even perhaps Sireuil and Vinča, Laussel and Strettweg, Lespugue and Heidelberg (Plates 96 and 258, 146 and 269, 10, 105 and the front cover, 149 and 33, 11 and 101, 18 and 218 (with Figure 86), 13 and 266).

CHAPTER 10

POSTSCRIPT

I DO not hope in this all too short review to have presented the prehistoric art of Europe as it really was (which is beyond discovery), but only as it appears to one interested inquirer. Its beginnings are invisible and incomprehensible, its end is visible but still largely incomprehensible. If we label certain bones *homo neandertalensis* and others *homo sapiens*, and classify hand-axes and harpoons, having given these things a name and made our definitions, we are apt to think we have 'explained' them, added something to real knowledge, and this of course is our error. Definition is not explanation, but unfortunately it is often our only possible approach. The search for origins is a part of defining and of naming; it seldom explains much, never explains all.

We began this story with small groups of not yet sapient but already man-like creatures. Mankind 'seated round a fire' was already a creator, already engaged in gratuitous action, already a strangely complex, unpredictable being. Much later and for a short time (reckoning as a prehistorian) Europe was in the van in the invention, practice, and multiplication of all sorts of art; and then again it lost that place. Viewed from the European side, the rise of civilizations and arts in Mesopotamia, Egypt, and the Indus valley has an explosive suddenness. In fact there was a steady, not over-fast, development from the seventh and sixth millennium until a specific moment around 3000, when a certain maturity was reached with the temple and tomb buildings at Warka, Eridu, Saqqara, with the Second-Dynasty slate carving of Kha-Sekhem and the splendid stone heads of Warka and Khafaje. If this progress is compared to what happened in Europe after the arrival of the first farmers at the end of the seventh millennium, we find that, aesthetically and iconographically speaking, not till the end of the Hallstatt Iron Age around 500 B.C. have we arrived at about this same point. Northern rock engravings of 1100 to 600 may be comparable to the Hierokonpolis wall paintings of the late fourth millennium; sixth- and fifth-century figured bronze situlae of Italy and the eastern Alps are not much more sophisticated than the First-Dynasty Narmer Palette; and predynastic Egyptian pots have 'signs' like Hallstatt Iron Age ones. But these sorts of comparison will not get us very far. Europe does not provide a slow-motion copy of what had already happened long before in Egypt and Western Asia because at all stages, from the beginnings of agriculture on, it was open to, or could be subjected to, upsetting cross-currents and fertilization from more advanced people. Its story lacks the linear simplicity of those grand innovating civilizations of Mesopotamia, the Nile, and the Indus valleys. As well as its acceptances, Europe was continually rejecting much of what was offered; acceptance of smelting and rejection of the potter's wheel early in the second millennium was noticed. The weakness of evolutionary systems of art history is that they give the impression of inevitable progress, or at any rate of direction; but this is seldom true to the known facts.

In technology Europe went ahead, and European smiths were often more advanced and inventive than those of Egypt or Western Asia. Something here may be due to the status of the smith in a warlike barbarian tribal society. With the rise of La Tène our art, however, does bear comparison with the enormous advances in Old Kingdom Egypt and in Mesopotamia after 3000 B.C. This flowering, though long delayed, was not, as we have seen, so inexplicable as it appeared at first glance. Celtic Europe produced an art that was wholly original and which had an extraordinary power to survive, as is shown in its reappearance in manuscript painting and ecclesiastical stone-carving a thousand years after the beginnings. It is not a long span compared with the conservative traditions of Egypt, or even Byzantium, but the stresses to which it was subjected were very great, and the contrary and alien forces so much more seductive. Persistence and conservatism in art are often disparaged, but they often were, and are, a source of strength feeding the bloodstream.

I have on the whole presented the case *against* a single evolutionary logic of art history. Some changes have lain more or less in linear order – the change from hunting to farming, the secularization of wealth in the Bronze Age heroic society – and these had their effects on the arts of the time; but they are not really irreversible. Only a complete revolution in the environment might have reversed the processes. On the other hand it does seem that there is a 'right' moment for the great advances, and that before that moment comes there are false starts and many setbacks. This is certainly true of writing. First steps towards the invention of a script were taken, but not pursued, with Paleolithic 'signs' (whether or not they can all be pigeon-holed as male or female symbols), and later among Mesolithic hunters with Azilian painted pebbles and the notched bones of the Maglemosians, or again in the sign paintings from Neolithic Sicily to Iberia and the stereotyped plaques of Vila Nova de San Pedro in Portugal: in all these we see premature fumblings. It is the same with modelling in clay. The first essays around 25,000 B.C. at Dolní Věstonice in Moravia had no sequel until nearly 8000 B.C., which was the real beginning, but in Western Asia, not Europe. A 'right' moment that was missed came at the point of impact between Roman art in Western Europe and the art of the Celts in the first century B.C. The Neuvy-en-Sullias 'Venus', stepping lightly forward on dancing feet, shows how the static figures of La Tène carving and bronze-work might have been set a-moving, but the opportunity was let slip, something of mutual confidence and respect was missing, and instead we get an international or provincial style on the one hand, and the loosening and weakening of native Celtic work on late mirrors and coinage on the other.

Sometimes similar conditions automatically produce similar results at widely separated times and in distant places. The perfectly utilitarian mat- and textile-working leads to a range of similar and recurring patterns – human figures with triangular bodies, cross-hatching and rectilinear meanders – which also survive in peasant arts today; and since weaving is usually woman's work, this is possibly a female contribution to the arts.

The first subject of the artist was the isolated figure, man or animal; but later in dark caves, on rock walls in the daylight, and on small possessions of bone and antler, figures were combined with others in various ways. Animals then outnumber man, yet man, though seldom portrayed, participates in whatever is shown, either in disguise or abbreviated to a sign, or simply an unseen but sensed spectator; whereas in the much later Mesolithic art, especially in eastern Spain, though man is portrayed at the centre of the action, he is viewed, as it were, from a distance with far more detachment and objectivity.

It is a perfectly fair assumption that Paleolithic artists achieved what they set out to do. Stages of learning are generally passed through astonishingly fast, and inexpert fumblings belong to a period of decline, or when the attempt is made to imitate another art too remote or alien. This is what happened with the stone stele carvers of the midi at the turn of the second millennium and in other examples of provincialism, even on the sixth- to fifth-century bronze situlae. An Aurignacian carver of hand-axes and a Magdalenian painter at Lascaux or Font-de-Gaume did what he wanted to do; when the need changed, so did the kind of skill. 'Mesolithic' painters in Spain, no longer interested in volume, weight, and the appearance and texture of three-dimensional surfaces, concentrated upon, and were altogether more concerned with, gesture, narrative, distance, space, the transitory and the incidental.

At this point a generalization seemed justified: that these particular aims and qualities usually appeared in a society that was undergoing transformation from hunting to husbandry, so that we find them in very different places and at different times: on house-walls in seventh- to sixth-millennium Anatolia, in North Africa, and two or three thousand years later on rocks near the White Sea and, as inferior fragments, on pots in Early Dynastic Egypt, in Iran and Mesopotamia. Wherever it occurs, this is a comparatively brief episode and one that may have something to do with a new awareness of linear time and history as well as with strictly technical problems of representation.

The altered relationship to the animal world of man as hunter and man as farmer was inevitable and seems to account for differences between the commanding bulls and bison of Lascaux and Tuc d'Audoubert, and the tiny, toy-like horned animals found on Neolithic sites such as Hăbăşeşti, or the heads attached to Neolithic and Bronze Age pots. Sometimes, in the Vinča 'bird' of Plate 119, or the bird-headed Dupljaja god of Plate 168, a human personality seems to be entangled with the animal, until the latter is reduced to a metaphor: a pair of horns signifying strength or divinity, or a horned helmet on the head of a hero or warrior.

The rise of the heroic society in Europe in the mid second millennium, and in settings as different as Translyvania and Wessex, again changed the subjects and techniques of art and ornament. This sort of society, in many ways so like the Dark Age of Greece before the rise of classical civilization, or that other European Dark Age at the time of the great migrations, culminated in the Late Hallstatt and in the La Tène Iron Age before the second century B.C. The conventions of giving and receiving gifts between heads of households and of clans, and the prestige that this gave, no doubt encouraged the design and display of gorgeous, though useless, weapons and of the warrior's whole panoply as well as the furniture of the feast, cups and bowls of gold, silver, and bronze.

But this was secular wealth, though it might sometimes be dedicated to the gods in watery sanctuaries or in tombs.

The same 'heroic' centuries probably saw the rise of an organized priesthood in place of the village or tribal wise man. From very early indeed we have the portrayal of stereotyped situations and rituals. In Paleolithic art there were the scenes scratched on bone found at Raymonden and Les Eyzies, and these were followed by the Maglemosian Rymarksgård scene (Plates 68 and 76 and Figure 24). There are the 'execution rituals' painted on the rock face at Remigia in Spain and (less certainly) engraved at Addaura in Sicily (Plates 84 and 89).

The building of megalithic and dry-stone tombs by men in the west and north of Europe, no less than Maltese temples, or Stonehenge and Avebury in Wessex, obeyed the needs and followed the shape of their ritual and liturgies. The engraved stones of the great tomb at Kivik in Skåne, the simple machinery of the Trundholm 'sun car' or the Strettweg tableau, as much as the elaborate and repetitive scenes of the bronze embossed situlae, are evidences of ceremonial observance already highly evolved. Today religious ritual still preserves something of that total activity in which speech, chant, movement, gesture, poetry, and rhetoric all combine. At some time in its remote prehistory the visual arts may have grown away from such a total activity, but the representations themselves come to us comparatively late, as hived-off fragments of a once whole and single ceremonial, with dance and song, mysterious progresses, robings and withdrawals. Art as a tool of religion is alive in the Paleolithic cave paintings, in Neolithic modelled figures, and in Iron Age Hallstatt charms and amulets jingling on a chain.

We can increase by a little our inadequate understanding of the prehistoric past by tracing backwards movements, the latter end of which are recorded in the *historic* past. Progressive secularization of the material world is one such movement. The difference between two intersecting lines and a crucifix, between a wineglass and a chalice, a water lily in a pond and the sacred lotus, or any pair of tools and the hammer and sickle emblem should help us to appreciate what we have lost and cannot recover in the Gundestrup cauldron, the axe from Radewell, the vase-bearer of Bordjos, and the curious pot from Svodín. In the days when swords cried out and challenged their owners, every weapon had a personality and a pedigree. The cooking-pot, tool or weapon 'charged' with the rites and processes of its construction, the signings and recitations that belong to the smithy as well as the open hearth and deepest cave, lead backwards in a widening circle that may once have comprised all animals and all objects impinging on man. If this impression of the holy and numinous is (as seems likely) one of our basic attitudes, then it has been gradually pared away from more and more of the environment until today many people can say quite literally that for them 'nothing is sacred'.

This is an inevitable barrier between us and all the works of prehistoric man. It is more obvious standing in front of the procession of animals in the great Hall of Bulls at Lascaux than before a case of rather drab Neolithic pots in a museum gallery. The paintings are easily recognized as husks of old enchantments, just-surviving fossils of a once palpitating magic. As with the ammonite, the husk remains, the contents of living cell and organism, of life and direction, are lost. But even here there is the curious fact that this art was created by men like ourselves, and that just as biologically we are their heirs, there resides in all subsequent art an inherited portion of their world.

Beside art as religion there grew up art as decoration, and beside the processes of secularization we have the skeuomorph, and the irreversible devaluation of symbols, one example of which was the Kličevac–Cîrna face that became mere embroidery on a pot surface (Figure 67). It is a process that works on the content as much as on the forms, and it is quite different from the gravitational drag towards abstract pattern.

Occasionally there have been intimations of two or more idioms current at the same time, and even on the same monuments. These I have called 'bilingual', and a good example was the Waldenbuch pillar with its partly representational, partly conventional carving. An Early Christian crucifixion was quoted on one hand and the scribbled rocks at Gavr'inis on another, with the Heidelberg head and the Roquepertuse seated figure (pp. 148 and 247).

I do not think it is wholly chance that throughout this story some themes recur. We have seen art in the celebration of life, and art as mediator and propitiator of death and the other world. The two cannot be wholly separated, but the first has given the goddess with the child and at the hearth, the goddess with the vase and as the vase, the mistress of animals and the life-giving or life-bringing animal. On the other hand there is the soul's journey to the other world and its inhabitants, the masked and disguised men, the animal or bird as psychopompus, to which is linked in some curious way the art of the caves; and there are as well the boats and chariots, especially the boats. At the same time some subjects common in the art of other regions are curiously few or absent: the animal combat and combats between man and animal. Monsters, hierogamies, and the tree of life are also rare, at least until late in the last millennium B.C., when they can generally be traced to some recent borrowing from beyond Europe.

Less tangible, more abstract subjects also recur, for example the threefold figures, the triune god of La Tène iconography, like the three river goddesses of Ireland, and the three bosses on pots in Central and Eastern Europe and on third- and second-millennium gold- and bronze-work. The unity that emerges from itself, becomes another, and is ultimately reunited with itself – this is not an idea invented by sophisticated classical and Renaissance thinkers but is foreshadowed by the three figures in the rock at Angles-sur-l'Anglin of 12,000 B.C., as well as by the romanized *matres*. The 'I', 'thou' or 'you', and the third person, all the triskele and triquetra patterns of La Tène art, seem to share a common, and probably very ancient, process of thought. Most persistent of all is the recurrence of the old enmity between chaos and cosmos, order and confusion.

Almost from where we began we have found startling anticipations of the finest work of the recent classical and Renaissance past and of its great 'discoveries', but in a milieu where continuity and a common tradition are inconceivable. The proportions and pose of the tiny Ostrava Petřkovice nude were the same as those of the Hellenistic Graces. Ten millennia or more later, and still Paleolithic, the reclining nudes of La Magdeleine were already disposed like river gods of antiquity, while oblique glances at the great figures of the Parthenon and the Cappella Medici are not entirely ridiculous.

A fawn carved in reindeer antler looks back over its shoulder and tucks up its legs exactly as fawns and other young animals have been carved thousands of times since the Upper Paleolithic; or the natural and very beautiful curve of an ibex's or wild goat's horns is made to embrace a rod of bone just as the Achaemenian carver or gold-worker made them embrace a stone bowl and a gold rhyton, or the La Tène bronzesmith of Brno-Maloměřice who gave the same sweet curve to the bronze 'horns' above the animal's head of Plate 258.

The so-called 'flying gallop', a convention for representing speed in racehorses, and apparently used for the same reasons in the art of Egypt and Crete, could, not implausibly, be carried back to the dead models stretched on the ground for study by a Magdalenian artist at the camp-fire or under the sheltering cliff. The profile convention by which only two legs are shown of a quadruped and two limbs of a man, though apparently primitive and early, appeared at different times and places with the elk and their human or spirit hunters on Mesolithic rocks, and with Scythian, Dacian, and Luristan beasts and monsters.

Beside so much that is strange and unapproachable we may now and then be surprised by something so familiar that it seems a commonplace. The concentration on the head *pars pro toto*, whether a horse's head on a Magdalenian spear-thrower or the human heads on La Tène flagons and brooches, is really no more than our own sort of shorthand when we put a head on a coin or a stamp, or like the portrait heads which we do not find odd when they hang on our walls or stand on plinths in public places. The style of the Addaura engraving that is, up to a point, natural and graceful, but still idealized, is to us a familiar convention; and, in a different material, the tender carving of the basalt nude from Macomer and the humble Zengövarkony pot whose handle is rubbed and pinched into the likeness of a mother protecting her baby with encircling arms, are very accessible, very much a part of our humanity. Again among Sardinian bronze figures of the seventh and sixth centuries and among Neolithic heads of the fourth and third millennium there are some that make us start with a shock of recognition. The idiom is our own. Our own too is the occasional 'classical' type, with its careful avoidance of expression, as well as those faces that are all expression, and that lean over into caricature. Coming from the same milieu as the 'Vinča smile' and the mysterious Predionica idol, they could not be much more different from them. It is the same with the animal sculpture of the first and of later Paleolithic peaks, and the very direct, but far from naïve, carving of the Alunda elk. Whatever sympathy may lie between these, lies also between us and them, and comes from a quality in ourselves. It is the psychology of *homo sapiens* that has changed so little in thirty thousand years.

Certain high points of achievement have stood out in this history: carving in the round of between 30,000 and 20,000 B.C., painting and engraving around 15,000, clay modelling in the fourth and third millennia, the odd and unique art and architecture of Malta in the third millennium, the delicate craftsmanship of the metallurgist in the second millennium, the complexities without a future of nuragic building in Sardinia, and the lively variety of bronze statuettes from the same island; a few quite exceptional stone-built tombs scattered round the Atlantic coasts that, by reason either of their scale or of the quality of the building, stand apart from the generality; and above all Stonehenge, a unique and still inexplicable structure, an abstract and distillation, as it were, of the whole western curvilinear building style. These emerge the more clearly for their background of mediocrity, repetition, sloth, and incompetence.

Apart from those discontinuous effects that seem to owe their recurrence either to parallel circumstances or to some permanent slant in human psychology, there are some which are continuous, where we can see a single style or mutually connected styles spreading, developing, and changing. That eastern curvilinear ornament that appeared in the Balkans and East Central Europe in the Neolithic is one example. We have seen it in the beautiful and astonishingly diverse patterns of Cucuteni and Tripolye potters, and on the plaster-work of Neolithic houses. At the end of the third millennium it may have been interrupted for a time, but in the second the same qualities appear in the superb plastic spirals of Otomani pots and in the patterns incised on Transylvanian and Hungarian gold and bronzes where it is linear, abstract but free, seeming to grow unhampered by the discipline of geometric design. We followed it to Scandinavia, where, meeting an old and still basically representational style, it was modified in the course of the eighth and seventh centuries with reluctant concessions towards representation. Again we saw it return in an auspicious moment to Central and Western Europe in time to play a not insignificant part in the shaping of the La Tène style, which inherited many of those qualities that had been its hallmark; the tendril-like growth of spirals, loops and lyres that hesitate between abstract and organic representation. It could even, much altered, be pursued into the migration period, and further into the Middle Ages.

Another sort of continuity, this time of a single feature, lay behind the curious history of the elk profile which was faithfully and soberly traced by Mesolithic artists on northern rocks; later it was carved in the round on a stone axe or bone spoon, and later still adopted by the bronze workshops. There it was transferred to the now far more important horse, which appears with this peculiar, long-lipped profile, incised on eighth- and seventh-century razors, or cast in the round on a handle or as an amulet to make a pleasant jingle. Eventually, taken up by Celtic craftsmen, it appears on La Tène lyre animals and with an ordinary horse's body on coins (Plates 251 and 302, bottom right).

We have seen that the cave paintings are one comparatively short episode in the history even of Paleolithic art. Life was ordinarily lived round the hearth in the entrance to a cave or under a sheltering rock, but the penetration of really deep caves hundreds of yards from the light of day was a single extraordinary phenomenon. In an attempt to probe the reasons for this peculiar deviation from normal human habits the possibility was broached that it had something to do with the known habit of some sick and dying animals, among which are the larger apes, of entering a dark cave, from which the fortunate may sometimes return to the world cured, but where others vanish for ever. If there were already some connexion between caves, death, healing, and the unknown in the background of man's thought, then when he turned from the daylight sanctuaries and their art, and the homely hearth, in order to explore the unknown and the other world, these memories would have been ready to hand. Enlarging the range of subjects both of his art and his mythology he founded new sanctuaries in which a new sort of art came into being.

The loss of these sanctuaries during the climatic and social upheavals that followed the last retreat of the ice brought a rupture in the traditions of art, but it seems possible, though the ground here is more than usually treacherous, that the dichotomy that existed within Paleolithic art itself was dimly remembered in the myths and folk tales of many parts of Europe, for the life portrayed in the caves mirrors everyday life in the world but with a difference as though slightly slanted (p. 73). Among Lapps, as among Celts, the other world, underground, inside the hills, or under the mountain runs in a way parallel with the everyday world, of men. The entrance to this other world, even when it takes on the more sombre aspect of Hades, is very like the entrance to Tuc d'Audoubert or Trois Frères; and though there are other plausible sources and interpretations for the other-world journeys of gods and heroes, the visible landscape, as it is described to us, may owe something to a faint memory of actual journeys in real surroundings.

If there is any one overriding problem concerning the forms of prehistoric art it is the problem of naturalistic representation. There is no such problem about the abstract, about pattern, symmetry, formality; these are part of our make-up, and they are present at a very deep level, not only in man but apparently in all forms of life from the most primitive, and in inanimate matter. The constructions of birds and insects, the honeycombs and nests possess it, and, more surprisingly, so do those animals and birds that, when given a choice, show preference for *regular* patterns and rhythmical movement over the random and muddled; for repetitions and symmetrical arrangements over confusion. Because of this, the regularity of the hand-axe, the symmetry of the Předmostí diagram, the pattern-faces of Bronze Age Kličevac and La Tène Mšecké-Žehrovice have an almost inevitable and instinctive propriety. No, the problem is elsewhere, it is in some way tied up with the will to achieve a likeness and to reproduce an illusion of the visible world; that is to say with natural representation or whatever we call it.

That this was deliberately willed we cannot doubt when we have watched the Paleolithic artists and seen the painful stages by which, for example, the hard, unnatural line surrounding a soft object like a mane or forelock gave way to natural softness and the haze of fur or hair round a sensed but unseen contour. Or the degrees by which natural perspective of bodies gradually took the place of various conventional perspectives, so that it could eventually lead to that type of composition in which perspective and scale are harmonized and which was adopted by the main line of western art.

In painting, engraving, and relief this schooling could be followed at least a part of the way, but with sculpture in the round either we lack those earlier essays or else the story was quite different, and skill, knowledge, and the will to use them came at one blow. This I think is unlikely. Quite near the beginning we even found intriguing but unverifiable signs of a deliberate attempt at portraiture: not simply the wish to represent natural man as he looks to the eye, but to represent an individual man or woman with his or her peculiar physiognomy and bodily structure. At the time of the Brno II man or Dolní Věstonice woman this cannot be more than the barest possibility, something to be reckoned among the many surprises and oddities of our human past, for if it *were* so it would be a matter of considerable importance. We may feel more confident about some of the modelled Neolithic clay heads that are neither idealized nor caricatures, and again in the less formal group of Sardinian bronzes (Plates 92 and 230).

It is from such fleeting likenesses that caricature and expressionist faces may arise. These we had in the East Spanish shelter paintings, though not much more than silhouettes, as well as among Butmir and Moravian modelled heads. They come from the sort of instantaneous observation that is hardly found again till the Hellenistic period. But after these, and the seated and squatting figures from Vinča and Čaršija – which, though rather clumsy, convey the natural weight of a body, which is not easy to do on so small a scale – why did not the modellers continue with greater naturalism? For they did not; instead, after an interval, we get Cîrna and Dupljaja, where the significance lies in the ornamentation of the surface and in interpreting a decorative handwriting. The reason is of course the existence of that other force dragging towards the formal and abstract, to the pattern that is desirable in itself and for itself; so that the impetus of natural representation seems either to move in waves from crest to trough and up again, or in jerks as though struggling with the forces that want to overmaster it. It is a conflict that sometimes brings disaster, but it has also brought our greatest works of art.

In the last chapter I used the metaphor of the tightrope and of two poles. The poles are permanent. Sometimes they stand for natural observation and ideal construction, or for that European abstract curvilinear style and the representational style that grew up in the Mediterranean world. I have tried to show that when these meet, the result is very much more complicated than a simple sapping of the one by the other; it is not a history of degeneration. Equal, or nearly equal in strength, there is between them a permanent tension which I believe the student of European art of any period ignores at his peril. Because of it, the conventional flora and fauna of twelfth-century illuminated manuscripts – celery-stick trees and leaves like scallop-shells – show not only a vision of the natural world distorted by stereotype and the 'gravitational pull towards the distinctive conceptual image that dominated representation' (p. 6 above), but also the ideal forms struggling to rid themselves of the tyranny, the bit and curb of representation. It will not do to think of Mediterranean classical art as surrounded by a barbarian patchwork, contact with which leads to disintegration; on the contrary, it has more often faced a strong, independent, and integrated art. Collision between the two *may* lead to the disintegration that we see on some coins and mirror-backs, but it may lead to the Brno-Maloměřice animals and the Witham shield and scabbard.

Sometimes the tension is more acute, sometimes less, sometimes one side will dominate, sometimes the other, and it is this that shapes the 'style' of that particular moment. These styles have no beginning and no end; they are always there, because the ingredients existed before and will exist after. Only the particular blend is not likely to occur again. So the Cucuteni pot, the Hajdusámson axe, and the La Tène torc (Plates 131, 174, and 254) are like and yet unlike. It is this fact rather than any temporal continuity that explains resemblances between La Tène sculpture of the first century B.C. and Romanesque sculpture of twelve hundred years later; while on the other hand the likeness between Celtic art in the west before the Roman conquest and in the sixth to eighth centuries A.D. *does* depend on a demonstrable continuity.

I have endeavoured in these pages to identify the source of the tensions. The poles are not simply geographical; there was a moment when the representational force was operating from the edge of the northern forests (pp. 152 and 206), but oftener it stems from Western Asia or Greece, Italy or the Islands. Nor can we afford to forget that open back door into Europe through which the animal art of Central Asia, inhabiting a great open-ended arc from China to the Baltic and the Danube, presses in in one or other of its periodic manifestations. That art runs parallel with European art, having made its own different synthesis. It is far less influential in Europe than the native and the Mediterranean poles.

To some extent the sources of tension are permanent features of the psychological landscape. The role of 'the other world' is taken today by the unconscious or the subconscious. It is the same realm of chaos, the irrational twilight opposed to the rational world of everyday. When *we* try to portray our subconscious images, we are doing what the prehistoric image-maker did when he portrayed 'the other world' of myth and magic. It may be true that an individual artist today can feel the same tug of the poles, and it is just possible that this causes those essentially fortuitous resemblances (which have often been pointed out and are very striking) between an individual 'modern' artist and some ancient work;[1] I say fortuitous because in the ancient work, whether it is a Paleolithic painting, a Neolithic pot-design, or a Byzantine Theotokos, originality is never sought. The lines have been laid down by rigid tradition, and there is only the least possible 'play' to be taken up by individual invention. If we do find originality, it is less *willed* than due to some obstinacy in the medium which led to emergence of a new thing that is still a version of the old. With very few exceptions it is useless to look for an individual hand even in La Tène art – the workshop is still the nearest we can get; but we should remember, at the same time, that the workshop is very often a single family with its store of inherited knowledge.

I have left to the last, because I have no satisfactory answer, the question of whether or not there is in prehistoric European art anything that is outstandingly different when compared to art in the rest of the world. There is at times perhaps more than elsewhere a way of leaving the work unfinished, or with an unfinished appearance, a sort of sensitive roughness, if such a description may be used. It is this that gives to Macomer, Santa Vittoria, Zengövarkony (Plates 149, 230, and 116) human vulnerability and a something more that arouses a response, a generous and spontaneous sympathy in the beholder. The scale, too, is human rather than ideal and formal. The world is looked at and meets us at eye-level, not level with the knees of towering gods, as in Egypt and Babylon. Experiments are not disguised but shown naked for what they are. Even the attempts at largeness and grandeur, building tombs of unmanageable rock, are disarmingly gauche and optimistic.

Of course this is only partially true, and much evidence could be brought to show the opposite qualities; but the point I would like to make is that those opposite qualities are shared by the art of many other civilizations, while the former things are rather rare outside Europe, and even in Europe their occurrences are intermittent and capricious. They are not even at all strong in the most original of all the European styles, that of La Tène; and perhaps this is why, in spite of its great beauty and professionalism, La Tène art is often uncomfortably foreign. Here, we are made to feel interlopers, and that things are going on about which we know very little. But in those other objects, those most 'European', it is as though an eye is caught among strangers, or a voice recognized in a crowded room and we are in some peculiar way, in spite of thousands of years and incompatible circumstances, among friends.

LIST OF THE PRINCIPAL ABBREVIATIONS

A.A. Hung.	*Acta Archaeologica Academiae Scientiarum Hungaricae* (Budapest)
A.S.	*Anatolian Studies* (London)
C.I.S.P.P.	*Congrès international des sciences préhistoriques et protohistoriques* (Rome)
I.L.N.	*Illustrated London News* (London)
I.P.E.K.	*Jahrbuch für prähistorische und ethnographische Kunst* (Cologne)
P.P.S.	*Proceedings of the Prehistoric Society* (London)
R.I.A.	*Les Rapports et les informations des archéologues de l'U.R.S.S.* (*VI Congrès international des sciences préhistoriques et protohistoriques*) (Moscow)
S.L.E.M.	*The Social Life of Early Man* (Wenner-Gren Foundation for Anthropological Research, 1961)
V.I.K. Hamburg	*V. Internationaler Kongress für Vor- und Frühgeschichte Hamburg* (1958) (Berlin, 1961)

NOTES

CHAPTER I

1 1. Described by P. Teilhard de Chardin as 'Suppression of the Peduncles', in *Le Phénomène humain* (Paris, 1955), translated as *The Phenomenon of Man* (London, 1959), *passim.*

2. P. Jacobsthal, *Early Celtic Art* (Oxford, 1944); D. Diringer, *The Alphabet* (London, 1947), 20.

3 3. J. R. Napier and J. S. Weiner, *Antiquity*, XXXVI (1962), 41; L. Leakey, *Antiquity*, XXXVI (1962), 119; K. Oakley, *Frameworks for Dating Fossil Man* (London, 1964), 291–3 and tables 295, 172–3.

4. P. Teilhard de Chardin, *op. cit.* (1959), 165: 'The power of a consciousness to turn in upon itself, to take possession of itself as an object endowed with its own particular consistence and value.' In E. Cassirer, *The Philosophy of Symbolic Form* (Yale and O.U.P., 1953–7), this is virtually the theme of the three volumes: art as a step in the awareness of self, and the emergence of self-consciousness at higher levels of awareness, and most of all self-awareness.

4 5. C. Coon, *The History of Man*, 2nd ed. (London, 1962), 63; K. Oakley, in S. Washburn, *S.L.E.M.* (1961), 191.

6. K. Oakley, *P.P.S.*, N.S. XXI (1955), 36, and *idem*, *op. cit.* (Note 3), table on p. 295, i.e., during the Mindel-Riss Interglacial. Some scholars doubt whether flesh was cooked before the last (Würm) glaciation, thinking that fire was used solely for protection, but there seems to be sufficient evidence to the contrary. Cf. K. Oakley, in S. Washburn, *S.L.E.M.* (1961), 181 etc., with refs.

7. C. Sherrington, *Man on His Nature*, Pelican ed. (London, 1955), 225; R. Brain, *Some Reflections on Genius* (London, 1960), 177.

8. R. Brain, *op. cit.*, 176, suggests that this stage could not have been reached until a sound could be communicated divested of its emotional content. The problem facing primitive man was how to make a noise that would convey 'lion' without causing panic or fury as though in the presence of a lion. In order to rob the voice of most of its emotional overtones the nervous system must have developed a method of filtering them off, as has been done on a special telephone. Biologists now refer to animal rituals as symbolic.

9. E. Cassirer, *op. cit.* (Note 4), I, 181–2. In some p. 5
languages verbs of saying derive from verbs of showing.

10. D. Morris, *The Biology of Art* (London, 1962), p. 6
144. Chimpanzees also make tools of a sort, peeling a stick to catch ants, but as far as I know this is only for instant use.

11. D. Morris, *op. cit.*, 159–60. Two sorts of monkey, a crow, and a jackdaw, were presented with eight sets of cards in pairs, one of each pair having a regular pattern and the other an irregular; *all* chose the regular more often, and the capucin monkey every time. Professor Rensch, the experimenter, commented that steadiness in the course of a line, radial or bilateral symmetry, and the repetition of equal components in a pattern were decisive.

12. R. Ardrey, *African Genesis* (London, 1961), 117 f., 147, 174, although uncritical and exuberant, is at present the best and most accessible account of a 'revolution in the natural sciences' and deserves to be read and pondered by anyone concerned with the human past. See now also *The Natural History of Aggression*, Institute of Biology Symposium, ed. J. Carthy and F. Ebling (1965).

13. R. Caillois, *The Mask of Medusa*, English ed. (London, 1964), 125 f., reminds us that men and insects have in common that they are kinds of beings that live in societies, but where the societies of insects show 'every worthwhile adaptation, every modification which has value over thousands of centuries incorporated and preserved in the organism . . . antennae . . . feelers . . . compound eyes, quite apart from the somnambulistic infallibility of its instincts, man, on the other hand, had the ability to create tools . . . weapons . . . clothing which is not part of his body . . . this faculty is capable of unlimited development'. Man's freedom implies an imprecise, ambiguous language, not an exact system of unequivocal signals. Caillois maintains convincingly that insect morphology and built-in behaviour correspond to something similar in man, some obsession, some irrational but compelling belief or course of action.

14. J. Napier, *Antiquity*, XXXVI (1962), 41; K. p. 7
Oakley, *op. cit.* (Note 3), 151 f.

p. 7 15. D. Brothwell, *P.P.S.*, XXVII (1961), 155; J. Piveteau, *Quaternaria*, II (1955), 69.

16. D. Jones, *Epoch and Artist* (London, 1959), 156: 'For here with the barest minimum of skill and without any, or much shining out of *splendor formae*, we would appear to be in the domain of sign (sacrament)'.

17. The Würm I, II, III of a few years back will no longer do; a complex Early Würm was followed by the Göttweig Interstadial, followed by another advance called either Würm II or Middle Würm, etc.; see H. L. Movius, *Current Anthropology*, I (Sept.–Nov. 1960), 354; K. Oakley, *op. cit.* (Note 3), 166. Dating by the radio carbon method, that is by the fixed rate of decay of the radio-active isotope of carbon (C^{14}) in certain organic materials such as charcoal, and carbonized grains, can be used for the last thirty or forty thousand years, but only becomes really effective when many samples are available giving runs of dates. In Europe this is not till the sixth millennium.

p. 8 18. J. Jelinek, *V.I.K. Hamburg 1958* (1961), 436; found in Francouzský Street and known as the Brno II burial.

p. 9 19. Göttweig Interstadial and beginning of Würm II advance. Most recently the uncertainty of date (W2–W2/3–W3) is stressed, but it still seems likely to be earlier than Dolní Věstonice (W2/3; see below). Czech prehistorians now refer to 'Brno Man', not Combe Capelle; E. Vlček, *Investigations archéologiques en Tchécoslovaquie* (Prague, 1966), 42.

20. At Willendorf an Aurignacian of the wet oceanic phase of the Würm II or Early Middle Würm glaciation is followed by Eastern Gravettian in the cold continental phase that ended about 26,000 or 25,000; see Note 17 and F. Felgenhauer, *V.I.K. Hamburg 1958* (1961), 258, with C^{14} dates, not very consistent so near their limit of usefulness but centring on 30,000 B.C. The statuette, an old find, belongs presumably to the Gravettian facies, but see Note 19.

21. In view of the early date of the Brno II carving and the C^{14} dates for 'Gravettian' at Willendorf, there is no need to 'explain away' the Vogelherd stratigraphy (G. Riek, *I.P.E.K.*, VIII (1932–3), 1).

22. The same finer breed may be portrayed occasionally, drawn on bone, and painted in the caves; P. Graziosi, *L'Arte della antica età della pietra* (Florence, 1956), trans. (London, 1960), plates 17c, 218b (all references here are to the Italian edition; the numbering of the plates varies between editions).

23. C. Coon, *op. cit.* (Note 5).

24. A number of C^{14} dates are available for the p.
warmer phase, Paudorf Interstadial within Würm III; or Paudorf Oscillation in Middle Würm Early/Main Phase (see Table 1).

25. C. McBurney, *Antiquity*, XXXV (1961), 107.

26. See Notes 18 and 19.

27. B. Klíma, *Antiquity*, XXVIII (1954), 4.

28. B. Klíma, *Dolní Věstonice* (Prague, 1963), p.
German summary, 237, and Note 33 below.

29. B. Klíma, *Antiquity*, XXX (1956), 98.

30. K. Clark, *The Nude* (London, 1956), 70–86. p.

31. According to B. Klíma, *loc. cit.* (1954), the area of the hearth was 4 feet 3 inches by 1 foot 4 inches (1·30 m. by 40 cm.). Cf. B. Klíma, *op. cit.* (1963), 270; *idem*, *Antiquity*, XXXII (1958), 8.

32. B. Klíma, *loc. cit.* (1958), figures 3–4.

33. B. Klíma, *Pamatky*, LII, 2 (1961), 311.

34. Described by Klíma, *loc. cit.* (1954), as the p.
most highly developed Pleistocene skeleton from Czechoslovakia; for average expectancy of life see H. Vallois in *S.L.E.M.* (1961), 222.

35. Phalanges and part of the pelvis of the fox were found. Cf. later 'shamanic' burials (described by S. Piggott, *Antiquity*, XXXVI (1962), 110), with heads, hoofs, and skins. The marks on the mammoth bone are not now thought due to its use as a bench for leather-work (Klíma, *op. cit.* (1963), 261 f.).

36. B. Klíma, *op. cit.* (Note 33), develops the idea of a true attempt at portraiture, the model being either a living person or an ancestor. A curiously similar distortion occurs occasionally in Egypt, e.g. Fourth Dynasty reserve head of an official (W. Smith, *A History of Egyptian Sculpture and Painting in the Old Kingdom* (Boston, 1946), plate 7e). See also Celtic heads; T. Powell, *Prehistoric Art* (London, 1966), ill. 232.

37. *Pace* E. Gombrich, *Art and Illusion* (London, p.
1960), 93, 116.

38. A. Mongait, *Archaeology in the U.S.S.R.* (London, 1961), 94, with two views of the Kostienki woman, figure 8,2.

39. A. Mongait, *op. cit.*, 95, figure 8,5.

40. Kostienki site I goes with Willendorf II/4 and Kostienki IV with Ságvár, Hungary; Borsevo

II, and Mezin; V. Gordon Childe, *Institute of Archaeology (University of London), Annual Report and Bulletin* (1956), 8, B. Klíma, *op. cit.* (1963; Note 28), 274, and M. Góbori, *Archaeologia Austriaca* (1960), 57.

41. See Note 44 below.

15 42. P. Graziosi, *op. cit.* (Note 22), 53–4 and plates I and 2a; see now M. Chollot, *Collection Piette*, Musée des Antiquités Nationales (Paris, 1964), 223 f.

43. E.g. the photographs in Jens Bjesrre, *Kalahari* (London, 1960), facing pp. 105 and 128; for the pose cf. the sixth-millennium Hacilar 'birth-giving goddess' (J. Mellaart, *A.S.*, XI (1961), 59, figure 20, and perhaps plate xb).

44. P. Graziosi, *op. cit.*, 58–62, and *Atti VI C.I.S.P.P.*, Rome, *Relazione Generale* (1962), 315 ('no Italian Venus figure is dated except Chiozza, which came from an alluvial deposit...'); but for figures of the Trasimeno type see now H. Delporte, *Bulletin de la société préhistorique française*, LIX (1962), 812, on the Tursac 'Venus' found beneath Solutrian levels. The Final Perigordian of western archaeology is Gravettian in East Europe; see Table I. For the androgynous interpretation see S. Giedion, *The Beginnings of Art* (London, 1962), 233 f.

45. R. de Saint Périer, *L'Anthropologie*, XXXII (1922), 361, 379; *ibid.*, XXXIV (1924), I, gives the arguments for date.

16 46. D. Peyrony, *Préhistoire*, III (1934), I f.; A. Leroi-Gourhan, *Préhistoire de l'art occidental* (Paris, 1965), 242. These are all Leroi-Gourhan's Style I: Abri Cellier, Aurignacian I, Castanet Aurignacian II; La Ferrassie has Aurignacian II, III, IV. Style I lasts from 23,000 to 17,000, cutting across the conventional 'periods'; see Table I and note in Bibliography.

17 47. A. Leroi-Gourhan, *op. cit.*, 244, 249.

48. E.g. the horses incised on a block from Labatut, the rhinoceros on a pebble from Le Trilobite, and the mammoth from Laugerie Haute (P. Graziosi, *op. cit.* (Note 22), plates 18–19).

49. P. Graziosi, *op. cit.*, plate 165b; S. Giedion, *op. cit.*, 329 and 333. The Pair-non-Pair engravings are deep and according to Daleau, who discovered them, date from the end of the Solutrian, and Breuil's Aurignacio-Perigordian. There are some reliefs as well.

50. A number of red outlined paintings in the Rhône valley are now thought to be Solutrian. P. Graziosi, *op. cit.*, plate 17c. Dr B. Rosselló in a lecture in London in 1967 has given evidence for a possible Solutrian date for this group.

51. A. Leroi-Gourhan, *op. cit.* (Note 46), 244, p. 18
figures 29, 257.

52. A. Leroi-Gourhan, *op. cit.*, 249–50; the figures in the 'diverticule' in V, d, e, f, figures 294–303. The argument is necessarily stylistic, but the Gargas style is in any case quite unlike the other Style II caves, Los Hornos and Pair-non-Pair; the paintings are also in a deeper and darker position than is usual with Style II (see p. 44).

53. K. Absolon, *I.L.N.* (7 November 1925), 898; B. Klíma, *Archaeologia Austriaca* (1959), 39.

54. P. Graziosi, *op. cit.*, 143–6; A. Laming-Emperaire, *La Signification de l'art rupestre paléolithique* (Paris, 1962).

55. Laming-Emperaire, *op. cit.*, 192–3, table IX, p. 19
308.

56. G. Lalanne, *L'Anthropologie*, XXII (1911), 256; *ibid.*, XXIII (1912), 129; *ibid.*, L (1941–6), 18; and very good photographs in S. Giedion, *op. cit.* (Note 44), figures 316–21, colour plate XX. One relief is described as fallen and lying on its face in the lower of two Solutrian levels, while the standing relief was in an area from which the Solutrian had disappeared. It is therefore not very logically dated, by the finders, 'Aurignacian'.

57. The right side of the figure is more complicated, for, if this theory works, the body faces forwards, the legs to the right, and the arms and the face to the left; but even this is not very different from the usual Egyptian profile convention, nor from the twisted perspective applied to animals by Paleolithic artists (see Note 59 below). The theory explains the left foot, which is blurred in some photographs. See also the Eve of the Expulsion on the Hildesheim door, in K. Clark, *op. cit.* (Note 30), figure 251.

58. K. Clark, *op. cit.* (Note 30), 119, figure 95. p. 20

59. The First Dynasty Narmer Palette and fourth- p. 21
century reliefs, e.g. the portrait of Nectanebo I in the British Museum.

60. S. Giedon, *op. cit.* (Note 44), figure 332.

61. H. Martin, *Préhistoire*, I (1932), 1–8; *idem*, *I.P.E.K.* (1927), 113. The semicircular arrangement proposed by Martin has been disproved by a subsequent find of two blocks in position. A. Laming-Emperaire, *op. cit.* (Note 54), 222–4, 350–2, also confirms the Solutrian date.

p. 21 62. P. Graziosi, *op. cit.* (Note 22), plate 151a.

p. 22 63. A. Laming-Emperaire, *op. cit.*, chapters IX–XI, where this dichotomy is developed; also pp. 40 and 73 below.

64. E. Gombrich, *op. cit.* (Note 37), 93 f. and 116 f.

p. 23 65. W. Dampier, *A History of Science*, 4th ed. (Cambridge, 1948), xxvii; M. Eliade, *Myths, Dreams and Mysteries* (London, 1960), 162, on shamanism and the return to the primordial paradise.

66. K. Popper, *The Logic of Scientific Discovery* (London, 1959), 280.

67. E. Cassirer, *op. cit.* (Note 4), II, 200 f.

68. M. Bowra, *Primitive Song* (London, 1962), chapter 6, 174 f.; E. Cassirer, *op. cit.*, II, 181–2: 'Things united by "sympathy" coalesce mythologically into the unity of one genus.' This is not quite animism or totemism.

p. 24 69. E. Evans Prichard, *Nuer Religion* (Oxford, 1956), 141.

70. M. Eliade, *op. cit.* (Note 65), chapter on 'The Cares of the Cannibal'.

p. 25 71. 'Misfortunes' in Eliade's terminology, 'terror' or 'anguish' in Teilhard de Chardin's.

p. 26 72. Å. Hultkrantz, *Journal of the Royal Anthropological Institute of Great Britain and Ireland*, LXXXIV (1955), 81; G. Gjessing, *The Circumpolar Ice Age* (*Acta Arctica*, II) (Copenhagen, 1944), *passim*; M. Eliade, *Shamanism*, trans. (London, 1964), *passim*.

73. F. Cornford, *Principia Sapientiae* (Cambridge, 1952), 123 f.: 'The Tatar shaman, the Brahman seer, the mantic Odin claimed the power of transforming themselves into birds, beasts and even inanimate things ... but the difference between metamorphosis and metempsychosis is, after all, not great ... the unity of all life, the kinship of all living things is the fundamental principle.'

p. 27 74. F. Cornford, *op. cit.*, chapter VII, *passim*. Cf. the artist and craftsman in Celtic and Ugaritic mythology, etc.

75. E.g. Alberti's famous theory quoted by E. Gombrich, *op. cit.* (Note 37), 105.

76. E. Gombrich, *op. cit.*, 139, and the chapter called 'Pygmalion's Power', into which, chronologically speaking, all our prehistoric art would fit.

p. 28 77. E. Cassirer, *op. cit.* (Note 4), I, 183, and II, 26 etc.: 'although myth, language, and art interpenetrate one another in their concrete historical manifestations, the relation between them reveals a definite systematic graduation ... towards a point where the spirit not only is and lives in its own creations, its self-created symbols, but also knows them for what they are'.

78. Å. Hultkrantz, *loc. cit.* (Note 72), 89, quoting Daunias.

79. F. Hančar, *Praehistorische Zeitschrift* (1939), 86. p. 2
Such simple ejaculatory prayers are very primitive and probably ancient. According to C. M. Bowra they belong to the level of composition preceding song (*op. cit.* (Note 68), 30).

80. They were first cousins once removed. See also M. O. Baba, *Journal of the Royal Anthropological Institute of Great Britain and Ireland*, LXXIX (1949), 27.

81. M. Nilsson, *The Minoan Mycenaean Religion*, p. 3
trans. (Lund etc., 1927), 448, for the Pre-Greek origins of Eileithyia. See also the 'Neolithic' *potnia theron* of Anatolia (J. Mellaart, *loc. cit.* (Note 43), plate IXa, and *A.S.*, XIII (1963), plate XXIV). In Anatolia the 'Lord of Animals' was apparently as old (*A.S.*, XIV (1964), 76, figure 29).

82. R. Onions, *The Origins of European Thought* (Cambridge, 1951), 236–45 and 241 note 1.

83. A. Bridge, *Images of God* (London, 1960), 24.

84. P. Alexander, *The Patriarch Nicephorus* p. 3
(Oxford, 1958), 27, 29.

CHAPTER 2

1. P. Woldstedt, *Eiszeit und Gegenwart*, IX (1958), p. 3
151, *ibid.*, XI (1960); summary in *V.I.K. Hamburg* (1958), 864; H. Movius, *Current Anthropology*, I (1960), 166; K. Oakley, *Frameworks for Dating Fossil Man* (London, 1964), *passim*. There is a Carbon 14 date of 14,150 for the 'shaft of the dead man' at Lascaux (*Radio Carbon*, VI (1964), 247).

2. A. Laming-Emperaire, *La Signification de l'art rupestre paléolithique* (Paris, 1962), table II and 176; C. McBurney, *Antiquity*, XXXV (1961), 107; A. Leroi-Gourhan, *V.I.K. Hamburg* (1958), 498; *idem*, *Préhistoire de l'art occidental* (Paris, 1965) (see note to Bibliography). In the latter work the author includes the so-called Solutrian reliefs of Le Roc etc. in his Style III along with the Magdalenian paintings of Lascaux. Style III therefore includes 'Solutrian' and Early Magdalenian, and Style IV Middle and Late Magdalenian.

3 3. E.g. Altamira and Castillo; see P. Graziosi, *L'Arte dell'antica età della pietra* (Florence, 1956), plate 31, c and d; A. Laming, *Lascaux* (London, 1959), 41, 111.

4 4. P. Graziosi, *op. cit.*, maps I and II and references.

5. O. Bader, *R.I.A.*, *VI C.I.S.P.P.* (Rome–Moscow, 1962), 1, figure 1 (red mammoth).

6. P. Graziosi, *op. cit.*, 126c (Los Casares).

5 7. See *The Times* (26 April 1965), 11.

6 8. A. Schultz, in *S.L.E.M.*, ed. S. Washburn (1961), 83, gives present-day examples and mentions teeth of Pleistocene orangs found in deep clefts.

9. An important exception is Graziosi's magisterial work, which is fundamental for all studies of the subject; see also S. Giedion, *The Beginnings of Art* (New York and London, 1962), with provocative comparisons with contemporary artists that do not perhaps allow enough for the tight traditionalism of the prehistoric artist hemmed in by sanctions. See also H. Kühn, *Die Felsbilder Europas* (Zürich and Vienna, 1952).

10. A. Laming-Emperaire, *op. cit.* (Note 2), 257, suggests 1,000 years, but if we accept the very persuasive arguments which precede this estimate it seems unnecessarily long.

7 11. See the heap of identical ibex-head pendants at Labastide; P. Graziosi, *op. cit.* (Note 3), plate 53a.

8 12. D. Garrod, *P.P.S.*, N.S. XXI (1955), 21 (general discussion of ornamental spear-throwers; most are horses (26), ibex (7), birds and fish (5)).

9 13. Magdalenian VI at La Vache (10,740 B.C.), and fine engraving at La Mairie à Teyjat (see Table 1).

0 14. P. Graziosi, *op. cit.*, plate 82h (from Mauern); the Mezin ones are sometimes called birds because of the long neck and tail 'tuft', but more probably are schematic versions of the human figure.

1 15. The full publication has not yet appeared; see the reports by S. de St Mathurin and D. Garrod, *Comptes-rendues, Académie des inscriptions et belles-lettres* (1949), 138; (1950), 86; (1951), 52. Also *L'Anthropologie*, LV (1951), 413 (Magdalenian III; there is a Carbon 14 date of 12,210).

16. Illustrated in colour in *I.L.N.* (15 March 1952) and P. Graziosi, *op. cit.* (Note 3), plate 156.

17. This is the opinion of the excavators, D. Garrod and S. de St Mathurin, *I.L.N.* (15 March 1952), 454. For the theory of 'associations' see p. 66 and Note 43 below.

18. Most authorities accept them as about the same date or a little later than Angles-sur-l'Anglin (A. Laming-Emperaire, *op. cit.* (Note 2), 355 and table VIII; P. Graziosi, *op. cit.* (Note 3), 163; A. Leroi-Gourhan, *Bulletin de la société préhistorique française*, LV (1958), 391–2; *ibid.*, II (1954), 125). This site is not to be confused with La Madeleine (Dordogne). p. 42

19. It is, of course, a perfectly natural attitude; see figures in the round at Hacilar, Anatolia (*A.S.*, XI (1961), 39, figures 19, 21, and plate X). p. 43

20. S. Giedion, *op. cit.* (Note 9), 386, plate 250. p. 44

21. H. Movius, *Archaeology*, II (1949), 22–30, describes the American excavations and refers to the earlier work of Mayet and Pissot in 1914–15; there is an analysis of the drawings too (see also H. Movius, *Ampurias*, XIV (1952)). J. Allain, in *Bulletin de la société préhistorique française*, LV (1958), 544, has doubts as to the pre-Solutrian date, based on certain similarities to Magdalenian industry and bone-working. In view of the long persistence of Gravettian industries not far away in the western Alps and Italy, it is possible that La Colombière is not so much precocious as old-fashioned. See also A. Leroi-Gourhan, *loc. cit.* (1965; Note 2), also arguing for the later date.

22. Plates 37 and 69, below and P. Graziosi, *op. cit.* (Note 3), plates 20–1, 211. p. 45

23. P. Alexander, *The Patriarch Nicephorus* (Oxford, 1958), 4–5, on the fourth-century Christian concept of *res sacra* and 'images not made by human hands'; see also p. 65 below. p. 46

24. A. Blanc in *S.L.E.M.*, ed. S. Washburn (1961), 123. p. 48

25. K. Herberts, *The Complete Book of Artists' Techniques* (London, 1958), 297, 308–23, 329. Animal fats and wax could only be used on dry surfaces and must be kept warm during use. Blood penetrated well but darkened too much, vegetable juices were deemed too difficult to abstract, though this may be doubted. p. 49

26. P. Graziosi, *op. cit.* (Note 3), plate 76a. p. 51

27. H. Breuil, *Four Hundred Centuries of Cave Art*, trans. (Montignac, 1952), 345, considered these 'Perigordian' and so early, but P. Graziosi, *op. cit.*, 186, compares them convincingly with La Pasiega.

28. A. Laming, *op. cit.* (Note 3), plate 16; H. Breuil, *op. cit.*, figure 339. p. 52

29. Also the same on some of the sacrificial oxen of the Parthenon frieze.

30. P. Graziosi, *op. cit.* (Note 3), plate 248 etc.

p. 53 31. The crouched and trussed bison of the Altamira ceiling are each circumscribed by the area of a single roof-boss. See Note 35 and p. 56 below.

32. H. Breuil, *op. cit.*, figure 53.

p. 54 33. On the round stem of the original bone the feet are not in view with the body; the position of the legs is in fact correct for a walking deer.

p. 55 34. See the well-known account retold by H. Breuil, *op. cit.* (Note 27), 51, and description of the technique of the painting, 53. For the general lay-out, see Graziosi, *op. cit.* (Note 3), plate 233.

p. 56 35. P. Leason, *P.P.S.*, N.S. V (1939), 51, an illuminating study by an Australian artist. See also C. McBurney, *loc. cit.* (Note 2), 113.

36. According to C. McBurney, *loc. cit.*, at least 75 per cent of all subjects.

37. F. Zeuner, *A History of Domesticated Animals* (London, 1963), 303, 310, etc.; F. Hančar, *Das Pferd* (Vienna, 1956), chapter 1.

p. 57 38. F. Zeuner, *op. cit.*, 205 ('reconstituted' aurochs in Berlin Zoo, figure 8,3); A. Laming, *op. cit.* (Note 3), plate 48b (at Augsburg).

p. 59 39. E. Gombrich, *Art and Illusion* (London, 1960), 208–9. Compare his figure 170 and our Plate 49 and Figure 19.

p. 60 40. The Comte de Begouën and his three sons were the discoverers, and the story has been well told by H. Breuil, *op. cit.* (Note 27), 230. According to Leroi-Gourhan (1965; Note 2), the art of his Style II is still found within reach of daylight, and only with Style III are the deeper, darker situations sought out. Gargas would seem to make an exception to this if the engravings in the 'diverticule' are really Style II; see Chapter 1, Note 52.

p. 61 41. On the function of the frame see Quatremère de Quincy quoted by E. Gombrich, *op. cit.*, 278.

42. It is recorded of some African children that, when given crayons and pieces of paper, they scribbled over the whole page and seemed surprised when they came to the edge 'as if they expected the blank space to stretch infinitely in all directions', and this was explained as due to the different concept of space experienced by children 'growing up in round huts without furniture, or living in a public courtyard and under trees, as compared with the western artist whose first impressions of space would come from exploring rectangular rooms with rigid boundaries and filled with objects arranged in order' (M. Fortes, *Institutions of Primitive Society* (Oxford, 1954), 86).

43. A. Laming-Emperaire, *op. cit.* (Note 2), 271–87; A. Leroi-Gourhan, *Bulletin de la société préhistorique française*, LV (1958), 307–21, 384–95, 515–28; *idem*, *op. cit.* (1965; Note 2), 433–63.

44. H. Breuil, *op. cit.* (Note 27), 113; A. Laming, p.
op. cit. (Note 3), 93.

45. See Note 43. Professor Leroi-Gourhan's work (1958 and 1965) is based on study of 62 caves and a statistical record of 2,151 'subjects' including about 233 'signs'; see also A. Laming, *op. cit.* (Note 3), 178 f.

46. See full descriptive bibliography in A. p.
Laming-Emperaire, *op. cit.* (Note 2), 260–372, to which add M. Eliade, *Myths, Dreams and Mysteries* (London, 1960), 62 f.

47. 10–20 per cent according to Laming-Emperaire, *op. cit.*, 135; Leroi-Gourhan puts it even lower.

48. P. 24 above. A subject explored in Professor p.
Mircea Eliade's many works.

49. A. Leroi-Gourhan, *loc. cit.* (1958; Note 2), 389, figure 3; 500, 2, and the judgement that 'les signes revèlent une remarquable conventionalisation des symboles et un comportement figuratif qu'on pourrait presque qualifier de préideographique'. Also *idem*, *op. cit.* (1965; Note 2), where the theory of signs and animal polarity is worked out in tables and charts.

50. A. Laming-Emperaire, *op. cit.* (Note 2), p.
283 f., and A. Laming, *op. cit.* (Note 3), 199.

51. Farley Mowat, *The People of the Deer* p.
(London, 1952), 9–10, 65. The quotations from this book are made by kind permission of the author and of the publisher, Messrs Michael Joseph Ltd.

52. A doe suckling her fawn appears once scratched on stone in the East Spanish cave of Parpallò (P. Graziosi, *op. cit.* (Note 3), plate 102 f).

53. M. Vernon, *The Psychology of Perception* p.
(London, 1962), 62.

54. E.g. horse and bison at Roc de Sers, horse p
and ibex at Pair-non-Pair, etc.

55. See however R. Caillois, *The Mask of Medusa* (London, 1964), 101, on eyes, circles, masks, and the exploitation of their power to paralyse, from moths to Medusas.

56. For something approaching a corpus of these, see E. Saccasyn della Santa, *Les Figures humaines du Paléolithique superieur eurasiatique* (Antwerp, 1947). The 'ghosts' of Los Casares are surely fish-headed

men; others have dog's skulls for heads (E. Ripoll Perelló, *Ampurias*, XIX–XX (1957–8), 178, figures 8, 2 and 11).

71 57. H. Kirchner, *Anthropos*, XLVII (1952), 271; G. Bataille, *Lascaux* (Lausanne, 1955), 117.

58. D. Garrod, *loc. cit.* (Note 12).

59. According to Leroi-Gourhan's theory these signs are masculine; see *loc. cit.* (1958; Note 43), 389, figure 3.

60. E. Gombrich, *op. cit.* (Note 39), 63, 77 (limitations of the artist's choice).

72 61. H. Breuil, *op. cit.* (Note 27), 167 f., gives a detailed account of this work, and, figure 129, an enlarged drawing.

73 62. M. Eliade, *Shamanism*, trans. (London, 1964), *passim*.

63. Å. Hultkrantz, *Journal of the Royal Anthropological Institute of Great Britain and Ireland*, LXXXIV (1955), 1, 89.

74 64. See Chapter 9 below; many songs and legends were probably carried west from their ancient home in the heart of continental Europe.

65. There are two Carbon 14 dates from Lascaux which have no connexion with the paintings, 6110 and 6320; see also Chapter 3, Note 32.

CHAPTER 3

75 1. J. Clark, *Prehistoric Europe: The Economic Basis* (London, 1952), table on p. 12, and H. Movius, *Current Anthropology*, I (1960), 373. Also S. Jørgensen, *V.I.K. Hamburg* (1958), 440; K. Oakley, *Frameworks for Dating Fossil Man* (London, 1964), 69–80.

76 2. J. Clark, *op. cit.*, 14.

3. For the rapid rise in sea-level until about 6500 see F. Willis, *V.I.K. Hamburg* (1958), 864.

4. C. McBurney, *The Stone Age of North Africa* (London, 1960), *passim*; E. Higgs, *P.P.S.*, N.S. XXVII (1961), 144.

77 5. F. Mowat, *The People of the Deer* (London, 1952), 265.

6. J. Clark, *Star Carr* (Cambridge, 1954), 4–9, 220–40.

7. Bow and boat may already have existed at the end of the Upper Paleolithic, but evidence is defective. The earliest known bows are from Denmark in the sixth millennium (Holmgård and Åmose), and a paddle found at Star Carr dated mid eighth millennium is evidence of boats by that date. Also found were bones of domestic dog, still very wolfish (M. Degerbol, *P.P.S.*, N.S. XXVII (1961), 35).

8. M. and S. Péquart, *Téviec* (Paris, 1937), 52–3.

9. J. Clark, *The Mesolithic Settlement of Northern* p. 78
Europe (Cambridge, 1936), 172; for the relations with Upper Paleolithic art, 177–80.

10. E. Baumgärtel, *The Cultures of Prehistoric Egypt*, rev. ed. (London, 1955), 59–64 (discussion of upright and horizontal zigzag and its relationship to Egyptian hieroglyphs and Mesopotamian pictographs).

11. Chapters 6 and 7 below: the Kivik tomb and northern 'razor art'.

12. Baskets and mats are among the earliest finds p. 79
from pre-pottery Jericho, Catel Hüyük, and the Fayum.

13. S. Jørgensen, *V.I.K. Hamburg* (1958), 440, plate 48, 3, 4.

14. *The Germania*, 45; Apollonius of Rhodes, *The Argo*, bk IV; preferable I think to Wicklow gold, proposed by C. Hawkes for the apples of the Hesperides, *Folklore*, LXXII (1961), 443.

15. See also the 'Neolithic' bear from Samus, p. 80
Siberia (*Antiquity*, XXXVII (1963), frontispiece, and XXXVI (1962), 244, editorial).

16. J. Clark, *op. cit.* (Note 9), 66–78; H. Shetelig and H. Falk, *Scandinavian Archaeology* (Oxford, 1937), 16 f.; R. Indreko, *V.I.K. Hamburg* (1958), 422.

17. At Leiknes, Tysfjord (H. Shetelig and H. Falk, *op. cit.*, 105).

18. Adaptation of the outline of one animal to p. 81
make another is a trick reminiscent of the Paleolithic, e.g. Fykanvatn (H. Shetelig and H. Falk, *op. cit.*, 104), also superpositions; at Forselv is an engraved grid like the painted grids at Lascaux. See H. Kühn, *Die Felsbilder Europas* (Zürich–Vienna, 1952), 93, also p. 84, figure 64, for a rare example of an animal looking back (at Leiknes).

19. At Ausevik on the west coast of Norway. p. 82
But the hunter's subjects, elk and reindeer, are more schematized than the earliest outlines. Professor Hagen of Bergen has worked out an interesting progression from the animal with pattern inside the outline, through patterned hide to pure diagram; described in a lecture in London in 1964.

p. 82 20. H. Shetelig and H. Falk, *op. cit.* (Note 16), figure 7.

p. 83 21. A. Okladnikov, *R.I.A., VI C.I.S.P.P.* (Rome–Moscow, 1962), 5; W. Raudonikas, *Les Gravures rupestres des bords du Lac Onega*, I (Leningrad, 1936); *ibid.*, II (1938); A Mongait, *Archaeology in the U.S.S.R.*, trans. Thompson (London, 1961), 113.

22. D. Diringer, *The Alphabet* (London, 1947), 21–2 (reissued 1962).

p. 84 23. *I.L.N.* (7 October 1961), 579.

24. *Radio Carbon*, III (1961), 99; 9694 ± 110 B.P.; P. Graziosi, *Rivista di scienze preistoriche*, V (1950), 1 f., and VIII (1953), 123 f.

25. Cf. P. Graziosi, *loc. cit.* (1950), figure 26, and *idem*, *L'Arte della antica età della pietra* (Florence, 1956), plate 66b.

p. 85 26. J. Bovio Marconi, *Bollettino di paletnologia italiana*, N.S. VIII (1952), 5; *idem*, in *Quaternaria*, II (1955), 201; A. Blanc, *Quaternaria*, I (1954), 176; P. Graziosi, *Bollettino di paletnologia italiana*, N.S. X (1956), 285.

27. The man on the left of Plate 84 in profile may belong to the group, but, as well as overlapping with the figure above (which does not much matter), he belongs in appearance and gesture to the series just described as moving from left to right across the 'canvas'.

p. 86 28. See Note 26. Graziosi's criticisms seem well founded and convincing.

29. H. Rose, *Primitive Culture in Italy* (London, 1926), 183 f.

30. See tomb of Ramose (N. de G. Davies, *Tomb of the Vizier Ramose* (London, 1941), plate 37); for later characteristics of Libyans see G. Wainwright, *Journal of Egyptian Archaeology*, XLVIII (1962), 89.

31. L. Pericot Garcia, *La Cueva de El Parpalló* (Madrid, 1942); for the sequence 'Solutrian', Epigravettian, Magdalenian, *idem*, *V.I.K. Hamburg* (1958), 662.

32. Nerja, a recent discovery, had naturalistic outline paintings of animals in an upper gallery. The lower gallery was frequented in both the Neolithic and Bronze Age (*I.L.N.* (5 August 1961), 216).

p. 87 33. M. Almagro, *Atti VI C.I.S.P.P.* (Rome, 1962), 319; J. Camón Aznar, *Las Artes y los pueblos de la España primitiva* (Madrid, 1954), 317, suggests 5000–3000. See also E. Higgs, *loc. cit.* (Note 4), 144, for important climatic changes in North Africa.

34. Camón Aznar, *op. cit.*, 422, 379, etc.; F. Zeuner, *A History of Domesticated Animals* (London, 1963), 67.

35. H. Obermaier, *Quartär* (1938), and K. Herberts, *The Complete Book of Artists' Techniques* (London, 1958), 330–43.

36. J.-B. Porcar, *Excavaciones en la Cueva Remigia (Castellón)* (Madrid, 1935), 66, and see Note 35. p.

37. H. G. Frankfort, *Arrest and Movement* (London, 1951), 95, plate 37, describes the tension of a tragic situation and a subtlety of posture that suggests imminent collapse, which we also see here.

38. The only moment when this position is reached in life is when clearing an obstacle on the downward jump just before landing. The goat of Plate 86 *might* have been driven over a precipice, but the offside pair of legs are still too long. p.

39. And at La Pileta and on the (probably domestic) cattle of Prado del Nevazo and Las Olivanos; Camón Aznar, *op. cit.* (Note 33), figure 142, 303; M. Almagro, *Ars Hispaniae*, I (Madrid, 1947), figure 8; for Remigia, Camón Aznar, *op. cit.*, figure 336; for Jabbaren, N. Africa, H. Lhote, *The Search for the Tasili Frescoes*, trans. (London, 1959), figure 28; J. Lajoux, *The Rock Paintings of Tasili*, trans. (London, 1963), 105, 120. p.

40. Camón Aznar, *op. cit.*, figure 339.

41. Camón Aznar, *op. cit.*, figure 332.

42. Warriors, not hunters, for they advance towards a battle-scene (Camón Aznar, *op. cit.*, figures 308, 320; see also figures 344, 388).

43. C. Aldred, in S. Piggott (ed.), *The Dawn of Civilisation* (London, 1961), plate 4, and p. 126, plates 13–14; H. G. Frankfort, *op. cit.* (Note 37), plate XXVA.

44. E. Gombrich, *Art and Illusion* (London, 1962), 292: 'Expression in life and physiognomic impression rest on movement no less than on static symptoms, and art has to compensate for the loss of the time dimension by concentrating all required information into one arrested image.' Also p. 284 for the curious statement that sophisticated caricature does not appear till the sixteenth century. p.

45. There are other confused and chaotic battle-scenes of which this cannot be said, e.g. La Mola, Gasulla (Camón Aznar, *op. cit.* (Note 33), figure 320). p.

46. This *portrayal* of space is a quite different matter to the *concept* of space, without which visual

art is hardly possible and on which see the chapter, 'The Space Conception of Prehistory', in S. Giedion, *The Beginnings of Art* (New York–London, 1962); also pp. 61 f. above.

47. Note 37; nevertheless this is claimed to be the nearest approach to topographical cohesion in pre-Amarna Egypt.

6 48. For Remigia cavity 5, J.-B. Porcar, *I.L.N.* (6 February 1960), 210, figure 5; Camón Aznar, *op. cit.* (Note 33), figure 390 (but perhaps part of the battle).

49. S. Giedion, *op. cit.* (Note 46), figures 308–11.

50. Perhaps something akin to the Thracian rite described by Herodotus in Book iv, where a messenger is sent to the other world by being thrown up and caught on the points of spears. The shooting of arrows during thunderstorms seems to have been connected with rain-making. Another 'execution' at Vieja, Alpera (Camón Aznar, *op. cit.*, figure 327, enlargement from our Figure 35) (archers on right, victims invisible).

51. In the often quoted Cogul 'dance' scene the figures were probably painted at different times, so that the woman may have nothing to do with the male figure in the centre.

7 52. E. Ripoll Perelló, *Ampurias*, xix–xx (1957–8), 167.

53. J. Mellaart, *A.S.*, xii (1962), plates xiv–xviii; Catel Hüyük level III shrine, deer hunt and dances, *A.S.*, xiv (1964), plates ix, xii, xiv, and figure 20, mostly level VII; E. Baumgärtel, *op. cit.* (Note 10), 64, figure 13; *ibid.*, ii (1960), plates 8–10; D. Wiseman, *Cylinder Seals of Western Asia* (London, 1959), plates 1–2. For naturalistic seals of the Uruk period, see B. Goff, *Symbols of Prehistoric Mesopotamia* (New Haven–London, 1963), figures 242–73; R. Ghirshman, *Iran*, trans. (London, 1954), 40, figure 13b.

9 54. H. Lhote, *op. cit.* (Note 39). The likenesses to Spanish paintings were first pointed out by Obermaier, but there are also parallels with Catel Hüyük: men wearing leopard-skins etc. The links with Spain are chiefly in the 'round-heads' and naturalistic or 'Bovidian' styles, the same ham-strung and slaughtered animals and the same archers and honey-gatherers; these were Neolithic pastoralists, and it is possible that this art came *from* Spain, but not of course the negroid traits very strong at some periods and more marked in the photographs in J. Lajoux, *op. cit.* (Note 39), 146–50 and 167, than in the water-colour copies.

55. H. Frankfort, *The Art and Architecture of the Ancient Orient* (Pelican History of Art) (London, 1954), 115, figure 46 and plate 124a, b.

CHAPTER 4

1. S. Piggott, *Ancient Europe* (Edinburgh, 1965), p. 101
44, figures 13, 14, 16; for Hacilar and Catel Hüyük, J. Mellaart, *A.S.*, viii–xiv (1958–64). There are some more continuous buildings at Yassa Tépé, Plovdiv; see P. Detev, *Annuaire du musée national archéologique, Plovdiv*, iii (1959), 3 f., especially plan ii.

2. F. Zeuner, *A History of Domesticated Animals* p. 103
(London, 1963), *passim*, and the review by E. S. Higgs, *Antiquity*, xxxviii (March 1964), 80, for sheep at Zawi Chemi, Shanidar 8900 B.C., domestic goats and wild cattle at Catel Hüyük level XX, domestic cattle first in level VI, and domestic goats and sheep in seventh-millennium Jarmo and Jericho. For animal bones at Nea Nikomedeia, Macedonia, see R. Rodden etc., *P.P.S.*, N.S. xxviii (1962), 271.

3. F. Zeuner, *op. cit.*, 36.

4. For Carbon 14 dates ascertained up to October 1964, G. Clark, *Antiquity*, xxxix (March 1965), 45. Compare Tell Halaf 5620, Hassuna 5090, Fayum A 4440, Hacilar VII 5820 with pots, and in Europe, Nea Nikomedeia, Macedonia, with pots 6230, Körös Gyálarét 5140, Gornja Tuzla VI 4690, Vršnik 4915 *late* Starčevo. So early Starčevo, like Körös, must be fifth-millennium; *idem*, *P.P.S.*, N.S. xxxi (1965), 58; and now R. Ehrich, *Chronologies in Old World Archaeology* (Chicago, 1965), *passim*. See *Radio Carbon*, v (1963), 176, vii (1965), 187, and viii (1966), 27 etc.; *Ausgrabungen und Funde*, viii (1963), 281; *ibid.*, x (1965), 1; and see Table 2.

5. They had reached the Low Countries soon p. 104
after the middle of the fifth millennium: Elsloo and Geleen 4320.

6. D. Garašanin, *V.I.K. Hamburg* (1958), 303; Benać, *ibid.*, 75. 'Pre-pottery Neolithic' in Europe, if there was such a phase, is quite different to the a-ceramic stages in the Middle East and will probably resolve itself into the adoption of some of the advantages of the new economy, by hunting tribes in contact with farmers (G. Clark, *P.P.S.*, N.S. xxiv (1958), 24).

7. M. Garašanin, *Bericht der Römisch-Germanischen Kommission*, xxxix (1958), 25.

p. 104 8. See Note 4 and Table 2. The discovery of 'tablets' with scratched signs very like, in form, the Mesopotamian Jemdet Nasr script (*c.* 3000 B.C.) in Neolithic levels at Tărtăria in Rumania, with all its possible implications, is still too controversial to be considered here; N. Vlassa, *Dacia*, N.S. VII (1963), 485; V. Milojčić, *Germania*, XLIII (1965), 2, 261.

p. 105 9. The Faculty of Archaeology of Belgrade University alone possesses 1,300 figures, or parts of figures, and many more are scattered among the museums of Europe.

10. M. Garašanin, *loc. cit., passim*; V. Dumitrescu, *Dacia*, N.S. II (1958), 35; D. Berciu, *Contribuţii la problemele Neoliticului in Rominia* (Bucharest, 1961) – all useful surveys; see Note 4 and Table 2. Lepenski Vir is a new and perhaps earlier site.

11. R. Rodden, *loc. cit.* (Note 2), plate XII; *idem, I.L.N.* (18 April 1964), figures 1, 2, 7, etc. Still nearer to shells Otzaki Magula, Thessaly; V. Milojčić, *Neue deutsche Ausgrabungen im Mittelmeergebiet* ... (1959), 225, figure 1e; P. Detev, *loc. cit.* (Note 1), 32–4. Large cowries were used for eyes at Catel Hüyük.

12. P. Detev, *loc. cit.*, 36–7; G. Georgiev in *L'Europe à la fin de l'âge de la pierre*, Symposium 1959 (Prague, 1961), 64, figure 3, 1.

p. 106 13. Mid-Vinča (Tordos/Pločnik borderline), see M. Garašanin, *loc. cit.* (Note 7); the man in the cap is earlier (Tordos phase).

14. Vinča-Pločnik phase. This is a recently excavated site in the Kosova-Metohije district (R. Galović, *Predionica* (Priština, 1959)). Wattle and daub huts, Vinča-style pottery, and many figures were found. The 'spectacle vases' provide a link with Rumania (Cucuteni).

p. 107 15. For Hacilar, J. Mellaart, *loc. cit.* (1961; Note 1), plates VIII–XII, figure 27, 3.

16. R. Vulpe, *Izvoare* (Bucharest, 1957), 229, figures 230–1, and now Lepenski Vir.

17. J. Mellaart, *loc. cit.* (1963), 88, figure 24, where they are equally difficult to explain, unless as a vestige of detachable limbs, like G. Georgiev, *loc. cit.* (Note 12), 70, figure 4, 1.

18. J. Banner, *Praehistorische Zeitschrift*, XXXVI (1958), 244, where similar signs are collected and discussed; see also below, Note 28. A figure at Vinča sits on an altar (M. Vasić, *Prehistoriska Vinča* (Belgrade, 1936), III, 123, no. 555).

19. It is not itself dated, but there are sufficiently similar figures from Vinča at recorded levels, though these only provide a very rough relative scale. See M. Vasić, *op. cit.*, plate 113, no. 524, also p. 54, nos 299–300; for a reassessment of Vasić's stratigraphy, B. Jovanovič, *Starinar*, II (1960), 19. In spite of the realism of the body, the face was probably stylized.

20. J. Mellaart, *loc. cit.* (1963; Note 1), 87–9.

21. Good examples at Autun, Vézelay, etc. p

22. For early figures see Notes 1 (Detev) and 12 p (Georgiev); also V. Mikov, *Archaeology*, XII (Summer 1959), 88. The key site, Karanovo, a 19-foot 'tell', is numbered I–IV by Mikov, and I–VI by Georgiev, who has been followed here. Cycladic marble sculpture was carried to Crete towards the end of the third millennium (Early Minoan III). This sculpture must cover a long period, and there is more variety in the smaller figures than in the better known large series; see now the site on Saliago, Antiparos.

23. Left arm over right is not invariable in the Cyclades but is more usual. The skirt or trousers come from Yassa Tépé; P. Detev, *loc. cit.* (Note 1), 53–5.

24. R. Indreko, *Suomen Muinaismuistoyhdistyksen Aikakauskirja Finska Fornminnesföreningens Tidskrift* (*Helsinki*), LVIII (1957), 61, see figure 1, 1. Closer than the Upper Paleolithic 'idols' cited from Mezin it is Late Neolithic Gumelniţa, while they join hands in the other direction with the Baltic Mesolithic; cf. Chapter 3.

25. D. Berciu, *op. cit.* (Note 10), 510; *idem*, *Antiquity*, XXXIV (December 1960), 283. Most Hamangia figures are headless, with long, rod-like necks; *idem*, *Cultura Hamangia* (Bucharest, 1966).

26. J. Makkay, *A.A. Hung.*, XVI (1964), 61. A p. second similar figure is now reported from Rumania.

27. J. Csalog, *A.A. Hung.*, XI (1959), 7 ff., p. figures 7–10; J. Makkay, *loc. cit.*, 1 ff.

28. J. Csalog, *loc. cit.*, figures 1–3; J. Banner, *Germania*, XXXVII (1959), 14; see also Note 18.

29. J. Mellaart, *loc. cit.* (1960; Note 1), plate XV; R. Rodden, *I.L.N.* (18 April 1964), figure 13 (the gourd-shaped original?); G. Gazdapusztai, *Archaeologiai Értesitö*, LXXXIV (1957), 3, plate 1 ('Gorzsai Venus').

30. M. Grbić, *Archaeologia Iugoslavica*, I (1954), 15, p. argues for 'Egyptian influence', but the likeness is more probably due to an original carving from a block.

31. The arms are largely reconstructed.

32. H. Quitta, *Praehistorische Zeitschrift* (1960), 176, figure 13, from Cannstadt.

33. H. Quitta, *loc. cit.*, 1 f., 153 f.

113 34. E. Hoffmann, *Kultur der Bandkeramiker in Sachsen*, 1 (Berlin, 1963), plates 62 etc.; J. Poulík and B. Forman, *Prehistoric Art* (London, 1956), plate 27.

35. J. and E. Neustupny, *Czechoslovakia* (London, 1961); *idem, L'Europe à la fin de l'âge de la pierre* (Note 12), 289, with further references. Lengyel, a related group in Trans-Danubia, had very similar pottery but lacked the figures and paint.

36. See detail in J. Poulík and B. Forman, *op. cit.*, plate 52.

37. H. Ladenbauer-Orel, *I.P.E.K.*, XIX–XX (1954–63), 7, cf. J. Poulík and B. Forman, *op. cit.*, plate 46; W. Coblenz, *Ausgrabungen und Funde*, X (1965), 67.

114 38. M. Vasić, *op. cit.* (Note 18), III, 119, nos. 552, 554; Vasić thought Plate 104 was from a mother and child group.

115 39. D. Berciu, *op. cit.* (Note 10), figure 279 (Gumelniţa culture). There is also a bitch from Ruginoasa; for painted animals see below, Note 61.

40. Another from Abrahám in B. Novotný, *Počiatky Vytvarného Prejavu na Slovensku* (Nitra, 1958), plate 26; and over the Carpathians at Şipeniţ, West Ukraine, in O. Kandyba, *Schipenitz* (Vienna, 1937), photo. 5. There are probably others, cf. J. Mellaart, *loc. cit.* (1961; Note 1), figure 27, plate XIV reconstructed. This type of pot has a long history in Anatolia.

116 41. G. Georgiev, *loc. cit.* (Note 12), plate XX (from Yassa Tépé and Kapitan Dimetrijevo); cf. T. Özgüc, *Kültepe Kaniş* (Ankara, 1959), plate XLIV, 4; F. Zeuner, *op. cit.* (Note 2), 195, figures 7, 23 (from Assyria).

117 42. J. Poulík and B. Forman, *op. cit.* (Note 34) plates 33 'stroke-ornamented ware' and 73 'globular amphora'. Animal protoms crossed the Carpathians into Poland, see sheep's heads on a pot handle from Cmielów (Trichterbecher; Late Neolithic) and oxen, possibly yoked, from Kreżnica; W. Hensel, A. Gieysztor, *Archäologische Forschungen in Polen* (Warsaw, 1958), figures 11, 12.

43. J. Mellaart, *loc. cit.* (1961; Note 1), 68, figure 27, 3; this removes the chronological difficulty in attaching them to the better-known series from Troy.

44. J. Poulík and B. Forman, *op. cit.*, plate 36; p. 118
cf. plate 103, which is Late Bronze Age.

45. S. Piggott, *op. cit.* (Note 1), figure 24 (Ariuşd), and from Popudinia, Ukraine; see V. Childe, *The Dawn of European Civilisation*, 6th ed. (London, 1957), figure 73; for another view, M. Gimbutas, *The Prehistory of Eastern Europe* (Cambridge, Mass., 1956), figure 56. The models are all of the small, one- or two-roomed houses of South-East Europe. None have been found of the long houses (up to 150 feet) of the Danubian groups farther west and north, which must have housed units larger than the natural family, or housed the family and beasts.

46. For Hungary see J. Banner, *Kiadványai*, II p. 120
(1942), plate VI, 5 (Kökénydomb), and J. Csalog, *A.A. Hung.*, IX (1950), 95 (Szegvár-Tüzköves); also B. Jovanović, *Starinar*, XI (1960), 140, figures 38–40.

47. B. Jovanović, *loc. cit.*; and for Truşeşti, S. Piggott, *op. cit.* (Note 1), figure 25 (restored); M. Petrescu-Dîmboviţa, *Analele Ştiinţifice Universităţii . . . din Iaşi*, III (1957), plate IV (Cucuteni A, so contemporary with late Vinča); *idem, Praehistorische Zeitschrift*, XLI (1963), 172.

48. At Ambrojevici Lipcani; see *Dacia*, O.S. III (1927), 39–45, figure 8.

49. Gourds do not grow north of the Bakony p. 121
Mountains; as prototype of Danubian pots they may have been overworked, but H. Quitta, *loc. cit.* (Note 32), 185, probably goes too far in denying it altogether. The flat bases of his figures 1 a–d etc. are the result of putting a pot down on a flat surface when the clay is still soft; to avoid flattening it must be stood on its rim.

50. An Etruscan gold bowl from Praeneste, p. 123
M. Pallottino etc., *Etruskische Kunst* (Zürich, 1955), plate 27, shows how a good design will recur where there is no possible connexion.

51. For Kellogg's scribbles, see D. Morris, *The Biology of Art* (London, 1962), 116 f.

52. A very early 'Neolithic' spiral is engraved on a stamp at Jarmo (*I.L.N.* (15 December 1951), 994, figure 9), and also at Catel Hüyük (Mellaart, *loc. cit.* (1964; Note 1), figure 41, 9).

53. Starčevo IIa; see M. Garašanin, *loc. cit.* (Note 7), 7–8, note 34; G. Georgiev, *loc. cit.* (Note 12), plate VI, 3. See also D. Garašanin, *Starčevačka Kultura* (Ljubljana, 1954), plate 17 (rapport spirals in red on white); E. Zaharia,

Dacia, N.S. VI (1962), 5 f. (with light on dark curvilinear patterns that appear to include a spiral at Leţ, a Criş-Körös site).

p. 124 54. M. Garašanin, *loc. cit.*, plate 2, 3–4; D. Garašanin, *op. cit.* (Note 53), plates 15 etc.; V. Mikov, *loc. cit.* (Note 22), 91.

55. V. Milojčić, *Hauptergebnisse der deutschen Ausgrabungen in Thessalien 1953–8* (Bonn, 1960), figure 7 (Proto-Sesklo at Otzaki Magula); cf. P. Detev, *loc. cit.* (Note 1), figures 44 etc. (these approximate to the 'gourd shape').

56. J. Korošec, *Neolitska Naseobina u Danilu Bitinju* (Zagreb, 1958); A. Benać, *Glasnik Sarajevo*, N.S. XI (1956), 167 ff. (Kakanj, Butmir, etc.); G. Novak, *Prehistorijska Hvar* (Zagreb, 1955), *passim.*

57. See Note 53.

p. 125 58. T. Passek, *R.I.A.*, *U.R.S.S.* (Rome–Moscow, 1962), figures 1–3.

59. V. Dumitrescu, *Habaşeşti* (Bucharest, 1954), and *Pamatky*, XLIX (1958), 265; for Traian, V. Dumitrescu, *Materiale*, VI (1959), 157, *Dacia*, O.S. IX–X (1941–4), 10; H. Schmidt, *Cucuteni* (Berlin–Leipzig, 1932); R. Vulpe, *Izvoare* (Bucharest, 1957); see also C. Matasa, *Archeologia Moldovei*, II–III (1964), 11.

p. 126 60. Especially from Şipeniţ; O. Kandyba, *op. cit.* (Note 40), figures 12, 43, 51, etc.

p. 127 61. O. Kandyba, *op. cit.*, figures 72, 75, 80; D. Dinu, *Materiale*, III (1957), 161 (at Valea Lupului).

62. At this date the dog would not yet have lost its pricked ears and high tail; F. Zeuner, *op. cit.* (Note 2), figures 4: 12, 13, 22, 23.

63. At Hăbăşeşti, Valea Lupului, Izvoare, etc., first half of the fourth millennium, corresponding to Late Ubaid and Uruk in Mesopotamia. See also Note 8.

p. 128 64. See Note 56, Hvar etc.

p. 130 65. The pots from St Aubin and Egolzwil II are usually compared to incised or channelled pots of Brittany and the Atlantic west, but I am not convinced by this: cf. E. Vogt, *P.P.S.*, N.S. XV (1949), 50, plates VI–VII, and H. Ladenbauer-Orel, *loc. cit.* (Note 37), C 1–10 etc.

66. R. Hampe and A. Winter, *Bei Töpfer und Töpferinnen in Kreta, Messenien und Zypern* (Mainz, 1962), *passim.*

p. 131 67. V. Gordon Childe, *What Happened in History* (London, 1942), 55 ff., the classic description of this milieu.

68. E. Vogt, *Geflechte und Gewebe der Steinzeit* (Basel, 1937); M. Hald, *Olddanske Tekstiler* (Copenhagen, 1950); A. Henshall, *P.P.S.*, N.S. XVI (1950), 130.

CHAPTER 5

1. J. L. Myres, *Mediterranean Culture*, Frazer Lecture (Cambridge, 1943), *passim.* p. 1

2. The Neolithic inhabitants of the Aeolian Islands, dependent on the exploitation and marketing of obsidian, planted villages close to the sea (the Castello, Lipari) and on the coastal plain (Diana), while in the late third millennium in Sicily, and at the end of the second millennium in Sicily and in Crete, there was a retreat to the hills. p. 1

3. J. D. Evans, *P.P.S.*, N.S. XIX (1953), 41, and *Malta* (London, 1959), 84; for new higher dates D. Trump, *Antiquity*, XXXVII (December 1963), 302; amended sequence *I.L.N.* (11 August 1962), 210 *ibid.* (14 September 1963), etc.

4. J. Evans, *op. cit.* (1959), figures 13, 17.

5. Hağar Qim is Evans's Phase D; cf. J. Mellaart, *A.S.*, XI (1961), plates VII, IXa, etc., from sixth-millennium Hacilar. A standing figure from Lerna in the Peloponnese could be a link but is far more austere. See also Sesklo, in C. Zervos, *Naissance de la civilisation en Grèce* (Paris, 1963), I, plate 130; cf. J. Evans, *op. cit.* (1959), plate 60, and L. Woolley, *Mesopotamia and the Middle East* (London, 1961), plate on p. 59, left-hand figure. p. 1

6. B. Brea, *Sicily* (London, 1957), 36 (Sperlunga rock shelter with Mesolithic traditions contemporary with Stentinello pottery).

7. J. Mellaart, *loc. cit.* (Note 5), 159, figures 2: 15, and 22; for the Naxos pot, B. Brea, *op. cit.*, plate 6, and cf. Mellaart, *loc. cit.*, figures 4: 14–17 (from Mersin, fifth-millennium or earlier).

8. See especially a Stentinello pot illustrated in B. Brea, *op. cit.*, plate 8.

9. E.g. Sesklo painted pottery in Greece (and see Chapter 4, Note 56, for Dalmatia).

10. Compared to the east, western Sicily was backward, though in the Late Paleolithic and Mesolithic it was there that sites were concentrated (compare the two maps in B. Brea, *op. cit.*, 27, 39); however, lack of exploration may be partly responsible. What *is* there is quite different from the eastern styles, having more in common with p. 1

Western Europe (Moarda, Villafrati, Conca d'Oro, etc.).

11. Serraferlichio and Sant'Ippolito painted, Piano Quartara (Lipari) plain, San Cono and Piano Notaro sometimes plain, Malpasso always. It is even partly true of the second millennium with plain or ribbed Pantalica and painted Agrigento wares.

37 12. Their counterpart in Eastern Europe is among Baden and Late Vinča people with their small metal trinkets; not with the axe-hoards of Tisza-Polgár and Bodrogkeresztúr that preceded them.

13. Castelluccio in Sicily, Capo Graziano in Lipari, Ozieri in Sardinia; J. D. Evans, *P.P.S.*, N.S. XXII (1956), 98; B. Brea, *Antiquity*, XXXIV (1960), 132; and Tarxien cemetery, Malta.

14. B. Brea, *op. cit.* (Note 6), plates 34–7, and M. Guido, *Sardinia* (London, 1963), plates 11, 14, 17–18, figures 9–10.

15. J. D. Evans, *Antiquity*, XXX (June 1956), 80. The best dated (Lerna) is Middle Helladic, that from Troy II or III rather earlier; a central date around 2000 is likely. Evans believes in a Sicilian source.

38 16. Mycenaean trade and settlement made little impact on local styles but remained exotic; however, it is very useful in providing dates for the later phases of the local Bronze Age.

17. M. Guido, *op. cit.* (Note 14), 36, for relative dates. The absolute dates require raising since the publication of Carbon 14 dates for Malta; see Trump (Note 3).

18. M. Guido, *op. cit.*, 47–8, for a balanced discussion of the problem. The shelter had served as a camp site, and microlithic tools were found as well as fragments of other figures and some pottery which suggests the Ozieri phase; it could however be a little earlier. Among Paleolithic carvings a very damaged figure from Brassempouy is very like it, see *Collection Piette* (Paris, Musée des Antiquités Nationales, 1964), 47334, p. 416. See also the Li Muri stone vase, unless this is an import. It is certainly earlier than Ozieri (M. Guido, *op. cit.*, figure 4).

39 19. G. and V. Leisner, *Die Megalithgräber der Iberischen Halbinsel*, I. *Süden* (Berlin, 1943), 5, 404, etc.; B. Blance, *Antiquity*, XXXV (September 1961), 200, compares the pottery to Tigani and Troy I; the date should now be approximately 3500–3000 (see Table 2).

20. B. Blance, *loc. cit.*, 192. The Carbon 14 date for Los Millares, 2345, is too isolated to be relied on too much; compare possible beginnings of Troy, Thermi, etc., *c.* 3500, agreeing with S. Weinberg, *Chronologies in Old World Archaeology*, ed. W. Ehrich (Chicago, 1965), 304. See also J. Arnal and Martin-Granel, *Germania*, XLI, 2 (1963), 229; and see map on pp. xxxvi–xxxvii.

21. Stag on Los Millares pot, G. and V. Leisner, p. 141
op. cit., plate 96, 1. The small stone idols from Almerian sites, contemporary with the beginning of Los Millares and some even earlier, are a more convincing link with the paintings on rock because less universal as a type; cf. Figure 56. See also however Levanzo, in P. Graziosi, *Rivista di scienze preistoriche*, V (1950), figures 6–11.

22. H. Kühn, *op. cit.*, 96 f. p. 142

23. So far there is no 'western' Neolithic date as early as the 4320 of Danubian Elsloo, but a house in Brittany at 3390 and a passage-grave at 3280 show that we may expect them from any time in the mid fourth millennium (see Table 2). Under the label 'western' it is usual to include Cortaillod, Chassey, and Windmill Hill, but in fact the 'eastern' element may be strong in all of them.

24. V. Gordon Childe, *Institute of Archaeology* p. 143
(University of London) Annual Report and Bulletin, II (1939), 29. See also O. G. S. Crawford, *The Long Barrows of the Cotswolds* (Gloucester, 1925), especially Belas Knap, plate opposite p. 89.

25. R. Atkinson, *Antiquity*, XXXV (December 1961), 292; A. Thom, *Antiquity*, XL (June 1966), 121.

26. Atkinson, *loc. cit.*, estimates two hundred able-bodied men as necessary to move the Tinkinswood capstone, implying a further population of around three hundred, but there were only fifty burials, and even this is rather high for the British Isles.

27. V. Gordon Childe calculated a probable population of around four hundred in eighteenth-century Rousay, which also is about what the soil could have supported at the time the tombs were built (*The Prehistory of European Society* (London, 1958), 127).

28. A. Henshall, *The Chambered Tombs of Scot-* p. 144
land, I (Edinburgh, 1963), 57, 121, 219; P.-R. Giot, *Brittany* (London, 1960), 42.

29. T. Powell, *Antiquity*, XXXVII (March 1963), 24; S. Piggott, *The West Kennet Long Barrow* (London, 1962).

p. 144 30. A. Henshall, *op. cit.*, on which the following description is based; see also S. O'Ríordáin and G. Daniel, *New Grange and the Bend of the Boyne* (London, 1964).

31. At Quoyness just such a ramp edged by a retaining wall has in fact been found (A. Henshall, *op. cit.*, 127).

p. 145 32. S. Piggott and G. Daniel, *Ancient British Art* (Cambridge, 1951), plate 18. There are six different patterns, none well dated, but one was found at Skara Brae; see V. Gordon Childe, *Prehistoric Communities of the British Isles*, 2nd ed. (London, 1947), plate 4, 2.

33. V. Gordon Childe, *op. cit.* (Note 27), 124.

p. 146 34. Circular structures such as Woodhenge in Wiltshire, and the Sanctuary at Overton; for long barrows, e.g. Nutbane, Hants, and 'mortuary enclosures' on Normanton Down, etc., see F. de M. Vatcher, *P.P.S.*, N.S. XXVII (1961), 160. Also S. Piggott, in *La Fin de l'âge de la pierre*, Symposium 1959 (Prague, 1961), 557.

35. Jericho pre-pottery A, Kirokitia in Cyprus, Messará tombs in Crete, Leisner's Almerian I, and Miss Kirkbride's recent work at Beidha.

36. A good example of this more elaborate technique is the New Grange entrance slab; S. O'Ríordáin and G. Daniel, *op. cit.* (Note 30). See also T. Powell and G. Daniel, *Barclodiad y Gawres* (Liverpool, 1956), 41; for pecking, O. Crawford, *P.P.S.*, N.S. XXI (1955), 156 (incised rough-out at Four Knocks).

p. 147 37. A. Varagnac, *L'Art gaulois* (La Pierre-qui-vire, 1956), Capacités Chrétiennes, figures 11 and 26; M. Gimbutas, *The Prehistory of Eastern Europe*, I (Cambridge, Mass., 1956), plate 10 (Maikop). See also Alaca Hüyük: silver jug.

p. 148 38. For widespread Mesolithic use of the sign see Plate 76 and Figure 35 and Chapter 3, Note 10.

39. Compare any typical 'baking-plate' with the Khorsabad eighth-century waterscape with floating timber (A. Parrot, *Nineveh and Babylon* (London, 1961), plate 48), and the Novilara stele with a sea battle on one side and running spirals on the other (C.-A. Althin, *Studien zu den bronzezeitlichen Felszeichnungen von Skåne* (Lund, 1945), I, 54–6, figures 20–1). The Cycladic standards are themselves diagrams of a female body, perhaps a goddess of the sea, Greek Thetis or Ugaritic Asherah.

40. Pp. 66 and 83 above.

41. For the newly found stele from Castelnau- p.
Valence, see C. Hugues, *Bulletin de la société préhistorique française*, LX (1963), 365 (Rosseironne). Some *drawings* of stelai are very misleading.

42. See the remarkably similar stone figure recently found in Thessaly at Soufli Magoula, in *Archäologischer Anzeiger* (1959), 58, figures 1–2, and others at Troy, Alalakh, Tiritace, etc.

43. H. Frankfort, *The Art and Architecture of the Ancient Orient* (*Pelican History of Art*) (London, 1954), plate 62; S. Lloyd, *The Art of the Ancient Near East* (London, 1961), ill. 63; S. Giedion, *The Eternal Present*, I (London, 1962), plates 137, 140. Note the symbolism of the figures on the girdle-flap, the plume like the 'crozier-shaped' objects of Portugal and Brittany.

44. Aveny and Epône are among the best; G. p.
Goury, *L'Homme des cités lacustres*, II (Paris, 1932), plate XXIX.

45. G. Goury, *op cit.*, plates XXXIV–XXXV, and J. de Baye, *Matériaux*, XVI (1881), 295–6, figures 141–2; also photograph in S. Piggott, *Ancient Europe* (Edinburgh, 1965), plate VI.

46. J. Arnal and C. Burnez, *Bericht der Römisch-Germanischen Kommission*, XXXVII–XXXVIII (1956–7), 58, however, believe that there *is* a direct connexion. Iberian idols and midi stelai share facial tattooing or painting.

47. T. Powell, *Antiquity*, XXXV (September 1960). Also H. Behrens, *Neue Ausgrabungen in Deutschland* (Berlin, 1958), 93 etc., on one of the more richly decorated graves, which has been re-erected in the Landesmuseum für Vorgeschichte at Halle; see also M. Gimbutas, *op. cit.* (Note 37), figure 27 (West Caucasus).

48. J. Troels-Smith, *V.I.K. Hamburg* (1958), 825. p.

49. For TRB, Baalberger groups, etc., see *Ausgrabungen und Funde*, III (1958), 185 f., and *L'Europe à la fin de l'âge de la pierre*, Symposium 1959 (Prague, 1961).

50. H. Shetelig and H. Falk, *Scandinavian Archaeo-* p.
logy (Oxford, 1937), 118, plate 12b, from Finland and Russia; see M. Gimbutas, *op. cit.* (Note 37), plate 43, and Figure 81D, p. 206 below.

51. J. Mellaart, *A.S.*, XIII (1963), 94–5. p.

52. Nevertheless in Egypt the roles were reversed, with the sky goddess supported over a male earth.

53. The New Year is an agricultural festival. Hunters had not the means to determine it accurately (see p. 67).

54. J. Macqueen, *A.S.*, IX (1959), 171, throws very interesting light on Hattian mythology, earth-goddesses, and river gods. The latter, in his human as against animal (bull) form, is the hero of the fight with the dragon, which emerges in a rather new light.

154 55. Bones of *wild* animals increasing in later middens compared to domestic, change of winter stalling and feeding of beasts to pasturage in the forest, appearance of fortifications in the Late Neolithic settlements.

155 56. S. Piggott and G. Daniel, *op. cit.* (Note 32), plates 28–9; J. Corcoran, *V.I.K. Hamburg* (1958), 200.

57. J. Mellaart, *A.S.*, XI (1961), figures 22–3; *ibid.*, XIII (1963), plates 20c, 24, figure 21.

156 58. R. Onians, *The Origins of European Thought* (Cambridge, 1951), 356. The sympathetic function of acting out what is to be accomplished or was once performed 'in the beginning' is taken over by the web of the fates.

CHAPTER 6

157 1. The name of the Syrian craftsman god, like Daidalos the cunning worker, means dexterity and intelligence. Weland probably comes from old Norse vél, contrivance.

2. Copper 'slag' as well as beads and tubes of native copper hammered 'perhaps with the aid of heat' are reported from Catel Hüyük Level VI (sixth millennium), and go back to Level IX (late seventh millennium); J. Mellaart, *A.S.*, XIV (1964), 111, and XVI (1966), 183. General works are R. Forbes, *Metallurgy in Antiquity* (Leiden, 1956–64), I–IX, especially vol. IX; L. Aitchison, *A History of Metals* (London, 1960), vol. I; H. Coghlan, *Notes on the Prehistoric Metallurgy of Copper and Bronze in the Old World* (Oxford, 1951); and R. Tylecote, *Metallurgy in Archaeology* (London, 1962).

158 3. There are European sources of native copper in Cornwall, Ireland (Wicklow), France, Italy with Elba, Spain, Norway, the Faroes, Germany, Hungary, Slovakia, Rumania (Carpathians), and south of the Danube and in the Urals.

4. H. Coghlan and H. Case, *P.P.S.*, N.S. XXIII (1957), 91; H. Otto and W. Witter, *Handbuch der ältesten vorgeschichtlichen Metallurgie in Mitteleuropa* (Leipzig, 1952; S. Junghans and others, *Bericht der Römisch-Germanischen Kommission*, XXXIV (1951–3), 77 f., and S. Junghans and E. Sangmeister, *Germania*, XXXV (1957), 11. See also H. Kaufmann, *V.I.K. Hamburg* (1958), 453, who argues from the archaeological distributions that this source was only used from the Middle (Tumulus) Bronze Age. There are other European sources in Transylvania and the eastern Alps that became very important. A recent important appraisal is J. Butler and J. van der Waals, *Helinium*, IV (1964), 1, 7 and V (1965), 3, 227.

5. Tin bangle at Thermi Town IV on Lesbos (H. Coghlan, *op. cit.* (Note 2), 16, 24, 130). Not all the sources commonly quoted in the literature are reliably authenticated, nor were all available at the same time.

6. Kilns have been found at Susa and Tepe Gawra and in Predynastic Egypt, able to fire pots to a maximum of 1,100–1,200° C.

7. True bronze, distinguished from accidental p. 159
due to impurities, must have a tin content of 3 per cent or more.

8. When this line of inquiry has been carried further, much will be learnt on the organization of the metal industry and the scope of the different workshops. H. Coghlan, *loc. cit* (Note 4), 102–3, and J. Butler and J. van der Waals, *loc. cit.* (Note 4).

9. C. Hawkes in I. Foster and L. Alcock, *Culture and Environment* (London, 1963), 204–10; Group I in Ireland with 18–23 per cent silver, mostly Late Bronze Age; Group II with 10–12 per cent, Early Bronze Age. The artificial alloy of gold and silver 'electrum' is only suspected with gold below 60 per cent.

10. H. Plenderleith, *The Conservation of Anti-* p. 160
quities and Works of Art (Oxford, 1956), 189–90.

11. H. Coghlan, *op. cit.* (Note 2), 48 f., 56, for a detailed description of founding operations. The fourth- to third-millennium shaft-hole axes and axe-adzes of Transylvania and Hungary, being very nearly pure copper, required strict observance of a very complicated procedure, and at all stages the modern experimenter has expressed himself amazed by the skill of the ancient craftsman.

12. H. Drescher, *Acta Archaeologica* (Copenhagen), XXXIII (1962), 39–62.

13. Itself a complicated technique; see H. p. 161
Drescher, *Der Überfangguss* (Mainz, 1958).

14. H. Maryon, *American Journal of Archaeology*, p. 162
LIII (1949), 94 f., and *Proceedings of the Royal Irish Academy*, XLIX (1938), 181.

p. 162 15. S. Piggott, *Antiquity*, xxxiii (June 1959), 122–3.

16. H. Maryon, *loc. cit.* (1949), 115.

p. 163 17. Circumstantial evidence comes from the patterns worked in Greece first, but soon after in 'Hallstatt' Europe; see tremolo or rocker patterns of Boeotian fibulae and Hallstatt plaques, etc. (P. Jacobsthal, *Greek Pins* (Oxford, 1956), 209; H. Maryon, *loc. cit.*, 117).

18. In the hoard of Porcieu-Amblagnieu (J. Déchelette, *Manuel d'Archéologie*, ii, part 1, figure 49, 4), and there are others.

19. H. Coghlan, *op. cit.* (Note 2), 61, 93, and see Note 15.

p. 164 20. R. Forbes, *op. cit.* (Note 2), vii (1963), 104 f.; M. Eliade, *The Crucible and the Forge* (London, 1962), for the growth, transformations, and generation of ores as a basis of alchemist theory.

21. Compare the Masai cattle-breeders and other pastoralists of East Africa with the smiths of the agricultural Congo and West Africa.

p. 165 22. R. Forbes, *op. cit.*, viii (1964), 94–7.

23. See the scenes on the Berlin 'Foundry Kylix', where parts of a statue are being cast separately, probably by *cire perdue*, and the artist in his 'Hephaestean hat' is at work with his assistants.

24. This applies to the Iron Age and Bronze Age; but see below, pp. 192 and 232.

25. Chapters 8 and 9 below.

26. V. Gordon Childe, *The Prehistory of European Society* (London, 1958), 93–8; B. Farrington, *Greek Science* (Penguin ed.) (London, 1953), 141 ff.

p. 166 27. I. Nestor, *X Congrès des sciences historiques* (Rome, 1955), *Académie de la République Populaire Roumaine*; P. Patay, *Slovenská Archeológia* (Bratislava), vi, 2 (1958), 301; M. Roska, *Közlemények*, ii, 1 (1942), 15. Professor Piggott has recently queried the priority of the Middle East in copper and bronze metallurgy (private communication).

28. The archaeological cultures concerned are primarily Tisza-Polgár followed by Bodrogkeresztúr in Hungary, Cucuteni, Vidra, and Gumelniţa in Rumania, and the latter in Bulgaria, and Jordansmühl, a northern extension over the Carpathians.

29. P. Patay, *Archaeologiai Értesitö* (1958), 1, 37; V. Dumitrescu, *Hăbăşeşti* (Bucharest, 1954), 435; E. Lomborg, *Acta Archaeologica* (Copenhagen), xxxiii, 1 (1962), 1, tracing the northward traffic by the Oder.

30. The fast potter's wheel was in third-millen- p. 1
nium Troy (IIb), and even in Crete (which was very late in adopting it) by 2000.

31. G. Clark, *Prehistoric Europe* (London, 1952), chapter v, *passim*; K.-H. Otto, *Ausgrabungen und Funde*, iii (1958), 202. The ecological change was a long, slow process begun in the Middle Neolithic; see Chapter 5, Note 48. The forest disappeared after two regenerations. Grazing cattle were far more damaging than farmers with choppers.

32. B. Piotrovsky, *R.I.A.*, *U.R.S.S.* (Rome–Moscow, 1962), discussing nomadism in connexion with third-millennium Transcaucasia, explains transhumance as due to the exhaustion of pasture, so that stock-breeding has lost its connexion with cultivation by the end of the third millennium. See S. Piggott, *Antiquity*, xxxvi (1962), 110, on the burial of animals and for references.

33. Carbon 14 date for an 'ochre grave' at Hamangia in the Dobrogea 2580 and 'Corded-Ware' in Saxony from *c.* 2500.

34. J. Banner, *A.A. Hung.*, xxxv (1956), 136 f.; p. 1
N. Kalicz, *Die Péceler (Baden) Kultur und Anatolien* (Budapest, 1963), and *idem*, *Inventaria Archaeologica Ungarn* (1962).

35. The same metallic qualities distinguish third-millennium (Early Helladic II–III) pottery in Greece, and Anatolia is full of it, including the Alaca Hüyük royal graves. The Early Bronze Age Unětice and Věteřov cultures carry it north from Moravia and Bohemia.

36. S. Piggott, *Antiquity*, xxxiv (December p. 1
1960), 285. For house and site-plans in general see now S. Piggott, *Ancient Europe* (Edinburgh, 1965), *passim*.

37. S. Dimitrijević, *Opuscula Archaeologica* p. 1
(Zagreb), 1 (1956), 5, on the Vučedol culture; M. Dušek, *Gräberfelder aus der älteren Bronzezeit* (Bratislava, 1960), 219, for Patince 'North Pannonian Ware'. These are two extremes; between lie many related cultures: Nagyrev, Kisapostag, etc. Vučedol begins around or before 2000; see Table 2.

38. V. Dumitrescu, *Necropola de la ... Cîrna* (Bucharest, 1961); this is the Girla-Mare Cîrna group of Rumania related to Dubovac-Žuto Brdo of the Banat and Serbia.

39. I. Boná, *A.A. Hung.*, ix (1958), 225, figure 6, p. 1
for Pannonian patterns very like Middle Bronze

Age Anatolian, and also *Archeologia Moldovei*, i (1962), 76, figure 8 (Monteoru culture with medallion), and pots in T. Özgüc, *Kültepe-Kaniş* (Ankara, 1959), plate xxxii, 1, which must however be considerably earlier; V. Dumitrescu, *op. cit.*, plate lxxx, no. 273, for a similar use of medallions on pots; D. Popescu, *Die frühe und mittlere Bronzezeit in Siebenbürgen* (Bucharest, 1944), plate xi, 11, for the Wietenberg pattern, and for a twelfth-century ivory seal from Beycesultan see S. Lloyd, *A.S.*, vi (1956), plate xiic. The Tǎrtǎria Neolithic impressions may be an analogous case, see Chapter 4, Note 8.

40. K. Horedt, *Nouvelles Études d'histoire* (Bucharest, 1960), figure 5, p. 40.

73 41. See map in G. Kossack, *Studien zum Symbolgut Urnenfelder- und Hallstattzeit Mitteleuropas* (Berlin, 1954), with additions; for Nova Selo, Balta Verde, etc., see V. Dumitrescu, *op. cit.* (Note 38).

42. M. Hoernes, *Urgeschichte der bildenden Kunst* (Vienna, 1898), plate 4 and pp. 220–4; M. Vasić, *Revue archéologique*, xl (1902), 187; N. Vulić, *Kseiga Pamiatkowa ... Prof. Wlod. Demetrykiwicza* (Poznan, 1930), 120, plate xi, shows profile view, and Vasić the other objects – clay throne, etc.

43. More likely this than a comb; see Babska figure and Chapter 4, Notes 18, 28.

74 44. E.g. back view of Dalj figure, a derivative from Kličevac. They were later used very generally to decorate Hallstatt pots.

45. F. Millekar, *Starinar*, ser. iii, v (1928–30), 20, *ibid.*, n.s. ii (1951), 270; G. Kossack, *op. cit.* (Note 41); D. Boskovic, *Archaeologia Iugoslavica*, iii (1959), plate 24, 12; E. Sprockhoff, *Jahrbuch der römisch-germanischen Zentralmuseum, Mainz*, i (1954), 67.

75 46. See the silver coins minted *c.* 408 with a rose on the reverse. The sex of Kličevac is not indicated, for the two star-like symbols that might be breasts are actually outside the body, as can be seen from comparison with other figures.

47. V. Dumitrescu, *op. cit.* (Note 38), dates Cîrna between 1500 and 1200 and Kličevac at the end of this period, but there seems no compelling reason for making Kličevac so late within the series.

76 48. On a bird from Dubovac near Kovin, M. Garašanin, *Bericht der Römisch-Germanischen Kommission*, xxxix (1958), plate 17, 5; cf. V. Dumitrescu, *op. cit.*, plate cliv, a, etc.; note also 'tree of life' (Plate 169).

49. I. Boná, *A.A. Hung.*, xii (1960), 109–10.

50. See Chapter 4, Note 42, and J. Poulík, *Prehistoric Art* (London, 1956), plate 73: 'Globular Amphora' culture contemporary with 'Corded Ware'. The triangle is both Hittite and Phrygian, not Aegean.

51. Vučedol, with several phases bridging the Late Neolithic to well into the Bronze Age, and the related Laibacher Moor or Mostiščarska of Slovenia, especially the site of Ig near Ljubljana, whence comes a hollow figure like the Bronze Age ones; see also Mondsee pottery in Austria.

52. Cf. a decorated dagger from Barca I Slo- p. 177
vakia, Otomani culture, and an undecorated and perhaps unfinished dagger in a hoard from Kelebia, Hungary; L. Hájek, *Kommission für das Äneolithikum und die ältere Bronzezeit* (Nitra, 1958), 59, figure 12, and A. Mozsolics, *Antiquitas Hungarica*, iii (1949), 17.

53. Gold daggers from Perşinari-Ploeşti and Mačin in Rumania, and silver spears from Borodino, Bessarabia; S. Piggott, *op. cit.* (1965; Note 36), plate xvia; M. Gimbutas, *P.P.S.*, n.s. xxii (1956), 143.

54. M. Finley, *The World of Odysseus* (Penguin ed.) (London, 1962), 70, 136.

55. *Ibid.*, 113.

56. The Cófalva, Şmig, Ostravul Mare style; p. 178
A. Mozsolics, *Antiquitas Hungarica*, iii (1949), 14; D. Popescu, *Studii şi cercetǎri de istorie veche*, vi (1955), 865; *idem*, *Cercetǎri Archeologice in Transilvania* (Bucharest, 1956), 158.

57. Continuity is lacking, but even the unambitious pots of the beginning of the second millennium carry rough versions of the same motifs, rows of semicircles filled with dots and so on; see Schneckenberg and Glina III pots (G. Bichir, *Dacia*, n.s. vi (1962), 87, figures 9, 1–2, and 6).

58. A. Mozsolics, *A.A. Hung.*, viii (1957), 119, Early B III period; see now *idem*, *Mitteilungen der anthropologischen Gesellschaft in Wien*, xciii/xciv (1964), 104 (the 'depôt horizon' from the end of the sixteenth into the fifteenth century).

59. D. Popescu, *Dacia*, o.s. vii–viii (1937–40), plates i and iii; for the typology of the axes see I. Nestor, *Marburger Studien*, 178 f., also E. Lomborg, *Acta Archaeologica* (Copenhagen), xxx (1959), 69 f., and A. Mozsolics, *loc. cit.* (Note 58, 1964). Three dots or bosses on bronzes, and bosses or hollows on

pots appear so often that they must have had a special meaning; according to A. Mozsolics they are confined to the Hajdusámson-Apa horizon.

p. 180 60. A. Mozsolics, *A.A. Hung.*, I (1951), 81; *idem, loc. cit.* (1964).

61. E.g. the axe in the Kelebia hoard, and at Apa; and for Megyaszó, see E. Sprockhoff, *P.P.S.*, N.S. XXI (1955), 262, figure 4. They could be property marks like stamp seals, or else symbols of deity. See also M. Novotná, *Pamatky*, L (1959), 1.

62. E. Porada, *Corpus of Near Eastern Seals* (Washington, 1948), plate 157, no. 1028E, plate 160, nos. 1047 (five spokes) and 1048; see Note 65.

63. A. Mozsolics, *A.A. Hung.*, XII (1960), 125 (antler and bone cheeks with their Anatolian links); see also A. Točik, *Studijné Zvesti Aúsav*, III (Nitra, 1959), 42, plates II and III, *idem, ibid.*, XII (1964), Veselé, figures 27 and 29, clay wheels and bonework; K. Tihelka, *Kommission für das Äneolithikum und die ältere Bronzezeit, Nitra 1958* (Bratislava, 1961), 77, also V. Spurný, *ibid.*, 134, clay wheel models from Czechoslovakia; R. Hachmann, *Die frühe Bronzezeit im westlichen Ostseegebiet ...* (Hamburg, 1957), 70.

64. A. Mozsolics, *loc. cit.* (1964; Note 58) (gold cups from Kom. Bihar and Pipe and Kárász bracelets).

p. 181 65. T. Powell, in L. Foster (ed.), *Culture and Environment* (London, 1963), 153 f.

66. For instance see J. Hampel, *A bronzkor emlékei Magyarhonban* (Budapest, 1886–96), I, plate 25, 2 and 4.

67. The way runs from Otomani and Füzesabony (Tószeg C) to Pilinyi and Egyek, but the Felsöszöcs type of decoration shows the moment of collapse and provides a very curious parallel with what had happened over a thousand years before to the latest Cucuteni painted pots; A. Mozsolics, *A.A. Hung.*, XII (1960), 113, cf. plate LXXI, 1 and 5, and O. Kandyba, *Schipenitz* (Vienna, 1937), *passim*.

68. See below, pp. 195, 199.

p. 182 69. E. Lomborg, *Acta Archaeologica*, XXXIII (1962), 1, and XXX (1959), figure 7. Period I saw the earliest imports from south of the Carpathians and the establishment of northern workshops (Fårdrup and Rørby work), Kersten's Bronze Period I and IIa; to be developed in the massive production of bronze and gold of Lomborg's II (IIbc), see *ibid.*, 52.

70. The lines above the gunwale may not represent paddles but oars raised before dipping for the pull, both sides being shown, like the two wheels of chariots, one above the other. This would give a boat about 80 ft long with sixteen rowers, as suggested by Mr T. Lethbridge in a letter; the object is frequently illustrated, see S. Piggott, *op. cit.* (1965; Note 36), figure 78.

71. These axes are generally found in pairs and were evidently for ceremonial use; see below, Chapter 7, Figure 80C.

72. H. Drescher, *loc. cit.* (Notes 12 and 13); H. p
Thrane, *Kuml* (1962), 80.

73. On the Roga circlet from Schwerin, and on Late Bronze Age pots from France, etc.

74. H. Drescher, *loc. cit.* (Note 12), for this ingenious and – I find – convincing explanation.

75. The chamber has been reconstructed and the p.
numbering of the stones is that of C.-A. Althin, *Studien zu den Bronzezeitlichen Felszeichnungen von Skåne* (Lund, 1945).

76. M. Nilsson, *The Mycenaean–Minoan Religion*, p.
2nd ed. (Lund, 1950), 426 f., gives Egyptian and other parallels for representations of a widespread cult of the dead.

77. Campstool based on Egyptian or Cretan model found at Guldhøf, Vandrup, Denmark, and a sword not of Mediterranean manufacture but inspired thence buried in a grave at Dollerup, among other examples, and 'Teshub' or 'Reshef' from Šernai in Lithuania.

78. G. Eogan, *P.P.S.*, N.S. XXX (1964), 268; the p.
gorgets and Lattoon gold disc belong to the 'Dowris Phase' with its new influences and revival of gold working; the gorgets themselves may be as late as 600 (Dowris B). The prototype seems more likely to have been the northern Period III collars than the openwork Period V ones referred to by Eogan, p. 306. See also J. J. Butler, *Bronze Age Connexions ... Paleohistoria IX* (Groningen, 1963), 167 f. The gold 'cape' from Mold with its Period III connexions would belong to an earlier generation working in the same tradition (T. Powell, *P.P.S.*, N.S. XIX (1953), 161). There is further evidence of compass-work on the Caergwrle boat-bowl; see J. Corcoran, *V.I.K. Hamburg* (1958), 200.

79. In France, the Scillies, Northern Ireland; S. Piggott, *Neolithic Cultures ...* (Cambridge, 1954), 219. In the western Mediterranean domestic building in stone continued and increased; see Chapter 7.

80. Heel Stone and D and A. All Stonehenge data are taken from the exhaustive and masterly account

in R. Atkinson, *Stonehenge* (Penguin ed.) (London, 1960), without following Professor Atkinson all the way in his speculations concerning foreign participation.

190 81. R. Atkinson, *op. cit.*, 176.

191 82. Recently speculations have appeared about the possible use of Stonehenge as an astronomical observatory for the prediction of eclipses of sun and moon. They have come from two astronomers: first Professor G. Hawkins of Boston, and then Professor F. Hoyle of Cambridge: G. Hawkins, *Stonehenge Decoded* (London, 1966), *Nature*, CC (1963), 306, *ibid.*, CCII (1964), 1258, and F. Hoyle, *Antiquity*, XL (December 1966), 262. Hawkins has been answered by R. Atkinson, *Antiquity*, XL (September 1966), 212, and the controversy promises to continue. No more can be done here than draw attention to it, but the paraphernalia seems excessive for a purely solar purpose and the rising and setting alignments of the moon would require generations of observation to obtain results, which seems unlikely in view of the Greek evidence referred to. See G. Huxley, *Interaction of Greek and Babylonian Astronomy* (Belfast, 1964). The real question is not whether these speculations are astronomically and mathematically sound, but whether they are probable in terms of the total context of third- and early-second-millennium man in southern England vis à vis the rest of the world. See also A. Thom, *Antiquity*, XL (June 1966), 121.

83. Since Stonehenge I is not exotic or out of place in the native Neolithic, and if Phases I–III are a religious continuity, then what is new is limited to technology and aesthetics. Whoever the gifted stranger was, he must have subjected his own religion to that of the natives, and this may seem odd in an organizer of thousands.

84. Neither faience nor drilled amber beads prove direct contact, in spite of claims made to the contrary from time to time. They are as delusive as the bone cheek-pieces of Central Europe, which, as we have seen, pointed to Anatolia rather than the Aegean (in as much as they were foreign at all).

CHAPTER 7

192 1. V. Desborough, *The Last Mycenaeans and their Successors* (Oxford, 1964), *passim*; *Cambridge Ancient History*, revised ed. (fascicles issued in advance), II (1962), chapters XXVII (F. Stubbings) and XXXVI, 1–21 (V. Desborough); *idem*, *P.P.S.*, N.S. XXXI (1965), 213; G. Huxley, *Achaeans and Hittites* (Oxford, 1962); N. Sandars, *Antiquity*, XXXVIII (December 1964), 258.

2. Desborough, *op. cit.* (1964), 241, gives an impressive list of causes of weakness and collapse.

3. W. Kimmig, *Studien aus Alteuropa* (Köln– p. 193
Graz, 1964), 268, particularly valuable on the spread of iron; the interpretation of relations between the Aegean and Central Europe is not that followed here. Also R. Forbes, *Metallurgy in Antiquity* (Leiden, 1964), 181 f., and R. Tylecote, *Metallurgy in Archaeology* (London, 1962), 175 f.

4. T. Powell, *P.P.S.*, N.S. XXIX (1963), 214, with full references; H. Müller-Karpe, *Bayerische Vorgeschichtsblätter*, XXI (1955), 46; also G. Kossack, *Jahrbuch der römisch-germanischen Zentralmuseum, Mainz*, I (1954), 111, and *idem*, *Bayerische Vorgeschichtsblätter*, XX (1954), 1. Early wagon-graves: Hart-an-der-Alz, and Greisbach, Straubing, Bavaria; Standach, Upper Austria; Mengen, Württemberg; and perhaps Saint-Sulpice, West Switzerland, to which add graves with large 'cult-vessels' at Milaveč in Bohemia and Skallerup in Denmark. For the grape see S. Piggott, *Antiquity* (June 1959), 122.

5. E. Sprockhoff, *Jahrbuch der römisch-german-* p. 194
ischen Zentralmuseum, Mainz, I (1954), 61, has the 'razor style' arising at Periods III/IV contemporary with the first 'bossed-style' imports – also probably the first 'boat burials', which are, according to E. Baudou, *Die reg. und chron. Einteilung der jüngerer Bronzezeit im nordischen Kreis* (Stockholm, 1960), 138, *c.* 1000 B.C. or late eleventh century and the beginning of Hallstatt Bi in Germany. Carbon 14 dates are too few to be of much use for this period, but we have Northern Period III 1170 ± 160 and Period IV/V, 815, while for Baudou 'V' only starts at 800; see Table 3.

6. Hallstatt Bi–Bii; H. Müller-Karpe, *Beiträge zur Chronologie der Urnenfelderzeit* ... (Berlin, 1959), 204, figures 41–2, 50–3, to which he gives two centuries, which is generous. The Liptau swords are typical of this decoration, and so is the 'rich style' in Switzerland; for Glasinac see A. Benac and B. Ković, *Glasinac I* (Sarajevo, 1956), plates VI–VII, XXX–XXXII, XLI, etc.

7. The frontier is that between the Nordic Province and the Lausitz in Poland and East Germany, farther west between Nordic and Tumulus-Urnfield groups. E. Aner, *V.I.K. Hamburg* (1958), 17, with distribution maps; also H. Schubart, *ibid.*, 741.

p. 195 8. J. Brøndsted, *Nordische Vorzeit* (Neumünster, 1962), 92 f., and on cremation, p. 104. There is no continuity between these cemeteries and the few sporadic cremations of the earlier Bronze Age; in Period III a quarter of all graves were cremations (see *ibid.*, pp. 92 and 153).

9. J. Coles, *P.P.S.*, N.S. XXIX (1963), 343.

p. 198 10. E. Sprockhoff, *loc. cit.* (Note 5), is the fullest study of 'razor art', perhaps in some of the mythological sections over-speculative; see numerous examples on his figures 6, 9, 15, 16, 23, 30, 32, etc. Also *idem*, *P.P.S.*, N.S. XXI (1955), 257, where Celtic and Nordic patterns are compared side by side.

11. R. Barnett, *Antiquity*, XXXII (December 1958), 225, figure 4, plates XXIA and XXIVB, the Phoenician *hippos*; also R. Lebaron Bowen, *Antiquity*, XXXIV (June 1960), 117, for Egypt. The Greek story of Dionysos' voyage with the vine and his revenge on the sailors is so oriental that it might almost describe an Akkadian sealing.

p. 199 12. R. Hampe, *Frühe griechische Sagenbilder in Böotien* (Athens, 1936).

13. Horse and orb (upside down) on the Vestrup razor (Figure 80A); see also E. Sprockhoff, *loc. cit.* (Note 5), figures 6: 6; 9; 16: 2: 4; 30.

p. 200 14. C.-A. Althin, *Studien zu den Bronzezeitlichen Felszeichnungen von Skåne* (Lund, 1945); see also map in J. Brøndsted, *op. cit.* (Note 8), 127.

15. A. Nordén, *Norrköpingsbygdens Hällristingar* (Stockholm, 1936), *passim*.

p. 202 16. See especially *Guide to National Museum, Ethnographic Dept.* (Copenhagen, 1955), 21; also A. Fredsjö, *Bronze Age Pictures, Gothenburg Art Gallery* (Göteborg, 1956), plate 6.

p. 204 17. See Chapter 6, Notes 12–13, and pp. 160–1 above; C.-A. Althin, *op. cit.*, 196, second half of Northern Period V.

18. R. Loomis, *The Grail from Celtic Myth to Christian Symbol* (Cardiff, 1963), 90–5.

p. 207 19. J. Brøndsted, *op. cit.* (Note 8), 167–9, the latter found together with the great imported amphora with Danubian 'swan-boat' ornament.

20. Compare the metamorphoses of the Etruscan lion, in the seventh century a cheerful dog, that becomes horselike with long ears and face and flat snout; W. Llewellyn Brown, *The Etruscan Lion* (Oxford, 1960), 25. The tassel below the neck on razors (Skivum, Plate 196) may be a memory of the elk's 'bell' (see p. 80 above). In contrast, Central European and southern workshops preferred the water-bird, putting it on weights, ointment boxes, and boats. Isis' swan had a far longer history than the 'hippos' boat, and even Greek geometric horses are a comparatively short episode. During Northern Period V horses begin to turn into birds. They are not easy to distinguish, but roughly, bills turn up at the end, noses down.

21. W. Kimmig, *op. cit.* (Note 3), 274; S. Piggott, *Antiquity*, XXXVIII (December 1964), 300.

22. J. Werner, *Pamatky*, LII (1961), 2, 384, figure 3, shows the whole 'sceptre'.

23. Gundestrup might also give a clue to the odd surrounding 'rays' that could be abbreviations of birds, like bird- or siren-crests on East Alpine helmets of *c.* 600 (Figure 97B) (S. Gabrovec, *Situla*, I (1960), figures 10–14), Vače and Magdalenska Gora, etc.; on the Wismar horns they look like pin-men (E. Sprockhoff, *Jungbronzezeitliche Hortfunde* (Mainz, 1956), 1, figure 60a). Gundestrup is an exotic object that will be discussed below, Chapter 8.

24. Figures from Shercock Co. Cavan, Balla- p. 2
chulish Argyll, Dagenham Essex, Brodenbjerg Mose Denmark, Gorbunovo in the Urals (S. Piggott and G. Daniel, *Ancient British Art* (Cambridge, 1951), plates 30–3; M. Gimbutas, *P.P.S.*, N.S. XXIV (1958), plate XXVI, 2), etc.

25. See Note 3. The appendix gives only nine p.
iron objects between 1200 and 800 B.C. from north of the Alps against close on fifty in the eighth century. See now A. Snodgrass, *P.P.S.*, N.S. XXXI (1965), 229 and see E. Krupnov, *R.I.A.*, *VI C.I.S.P.P.* (Rome–Moscow, 1962). The Assyrians were using iron from the eleventh century but only had it in plenty from the early ninth; K. R. Maxwell-Hyslop and H. Hodges, *Iraq*, XXVIII (1966), 173–5; A. Mnatsakanian, *XXV International Congress of Orientalists* (Moscow, 1960) (Lake Sevan).

26. R. Forbes, *Studies in Ancient Technology*, IX (Leiden, 1964), 186, 195.

27. Used on catch-plates of Boeotian fibulae and on Hallstatt plaques, axes, and pins; P. Jacobsthal, *Greek Pins* (Oxford, 1956), 209 (more are seventh- than eighth-century). The Central European examples seem all to be Hallstatt D and not much earlier than sixth-century; W. Kimmig and H. Hell, *Vorzeit an Rhein und Donau* (Lindau-Konstanz, 1958), plate 97, see p. 163.

10 28. Herodotus, Book IV, 11–13, and Book I, 15–16. M. Gimbutas, *Bronze Age Cultures in Central and Eastern Europe* (The Hague, 1965), 479–517, and T. Sulimirski, *Bulletin of the Institute of Archaeology, London, II, 1959* (1960), 45, both give copious references and the 'classical' invasion view not entirely endorsed here. For cautious and well reasoned arguments see D. Berciu, *Archaeologické rozhledy*, XVI (1964), 264, and G. Gazdapusztai, *Acta Antiqua et Archaeologica*, V (Szeged, 1963), 5.

29. With so many tribes on the move – Medes, Persians, Scyths – most of whom were related to each other and looking much alike, Herodotus's account must be greatly simplified. The Cimmerians are as likely as others to have moved south and west in search of plunder and power; at one time they were allies of Urartu and some became Assyrian mercenaries (B. Piotrovsky, *Vannskoïe tsartstvo Urartu* (Moscow, 1959), *passim*, especially 93–110; R. Ghirshman, *Iranica Antiqua*, II (1962), 165, *ibid.*, III (1963), 60 f.; S. Tolstov summarized in *Soviet Anthropology and Archaeology* (New York, Spring 1964), II, 4). There is no evidence for the date of 'Cimmerian' names in the Crimea except that they must be earlier than the seventh century, when Greek travellers were exploring those parts and the Cimmerians were no longer remembered. Herodotus's 'Cimmerian Land' across the Araxes could as well be the 'Land of Gimirra' in eastern Cappadocia referred to in the Assyrian texts (N. Sandars, *VII Congrès International des Sciences Préhistoriques et Protohistoriques* (Prague, 1966), forthcoming).

30. R. Barnett, *Iranica Antiqua* (1962), 77 f., stresses how far their long connexion with more sophisticated peoples had modified the character of the Scyths. For the later history of the Cimmerians see also H. Kaletsch, *Historia*, VII (1958), 36, and G. Huxley, *The Early Ionians* (London, 1966), 53–4.

211 31. Altin Tepe excavated by T. Özgüc, see Arts Council exhibition catalogue *Hittite Art and Antiquities* (1964), no. 303; seventh century and cf. Jessen's type V (A. Jessen, *Sovetskaja Arkheologija*, XVIII (1953), 49 f.) and cf. Gazdapusztai (Note 28).

32. J. Boardman, *The Greeks Overseas* (London, 1964), 247, 252–3.

212 33. Unfortunately these bronzes are almost all single finds and hence difficult to date; Z. Vinski, *Archiv Orientalni*, XVIII, 4 (Prague, 1950), 341.

34. E. Negahban, *A Preliminary Report on Marlik* . . . (Teheran, 1964), 42 and figure 25.

35. A. Benac, *op. cit.* (Note 6), II (1957), plate p. 213
XXVIII, also plates XVIII, 2, and XXX, 5; see also M. Garašanin, *Atti VI C.I.S.P.P.* (Rome, 1962), 179 f., for chronology. The plainer Phrygian handles are not often illustrated: see however *I.L.N.* (17 May 1958), 830, figure 10, with a bull's head on the 'T' from a cauldron in the Great Tomb at Gordion; also B. Piotrovsky, *Iskusstvo Urartu* (Leningrad, 1962), figures 31–2.

36. F. Maier, *Germania*, XXXIV (1956), 63; J. Alexander, *P.P.S.*, N.S. XXX (1964), 170, who do not give the Anatolian pins; for these see e.g. K. Bittel, *Kleinasiatische Studien* (1942), 62, giving two from Alişar and two from Boghaz Köy, both the Trebenište type (P. Jacobsthal, *op. cit.* (Note 27), 138, with refs.).

37. M. Gimbutas, *Archaeology*, XII (1959), 84, gives a rather early date in the eighth century, but the fibula with shield-shaped catch-plate seems to be a variant of a Balkan type that hardly appears before the seventh century. See also R. Barnett, *loc. cit.* (Note 30), who establishes the Median identity of the *akinakes* sword.

38. V. Mikov, *Le Trésor d'or de Valcitran* (Sofia, 1958); A. Mozsolics, *Mitteilungen der anthropologischen Gesellschaft in Wien*, XCIII/XCIV (1964), 104, argues for a much earlier date. Inlaying with silver is at home in Anatolia, where it is as old as Alaca Hüyük.

39. W. Schmid, *Der Kultwagen von Strettweg* p. 214
(Leipzig, 1934).

40. H. Lorimer, *Homer and the Monuments* (London, 1950), plate XII, 4, and p. 246. Figures of this type are identified as 'Zeus in the character of warrior'. Compare also a provincial geometric figure found near Skopje: M. Grbić, *Choix de plastiques grecques et romaines au Musée National de Beograd* (Belgrade, 1958), 114, and plate I, and the Strettweg figures with the stag.

41. S. Benton, *Annual of the British School at Athens*, XXXV (1934/5), plates 18, 19, 21, etc.; on p. 85 we have the interesting suggestion that tripod vessels on which the 'hurling warriors' stood correspond to Central and North European wheeled vessels, which would ally them in function as well as appearance to Strettweg.

42. T. Powell, in S. Piggott (ed.), *The Dawn of Civilisation* (London, 1961), and M.-L. Sjoested, *Gods and Heroes of the Celts*, trans. (London, 1949), 19–20.

p. 215 43. Quoted in connexion with the Alaca Hüyük stags by H. Koşay, *Les Fouilles d'Alaca Hüyük; Rapport préliminaire* (Ankara, 1951), 186.

44. H. Drescher, *Acta Archaeologica* (Copenhagen), XXXIV (1963); E. and J. Neustupny, *Czechoslovakia* (London, 1961), 140. The technique recalls Anatolian work of the third millennium with bronze and silver. See also W. Llewellyn Brown, *op. cit.* (Note 20), 21, for a rare Etruscan example and references to the Caucasus.

45. K. Kromer, *Inventaria Archaeologica Österreich 2 A II* (Bonn, 1956). Our Plate 220 is reconstructed from several broken pots and should not be taken too literally, but the figures all survive in part, and only the order and division among the pots is arbitrary.

p. 216 46. B. Brea, *Sicily* (London, 1957), 149, 167 (Pantalica I, twelfth century).

p. 217 47. In Italy not till the later eighth century; W. Llewellyn Brown, *op. cit.* (Note 20), 5, 11 f.; K. Maxwell-Hyslop, *Iraq*, XVII, 2 (1956), 150; E. Kunze, *Kretische Bronzereliefs* (Stuttgart, 1931); U. Jantzen, *Griechische Greifenkessel* (Berlin, 1955); and especially useful J. Boardman, *op. cit.* (Note 32), *passim.*

48. M. Guido, *Sardinia* (London, 1963), 192. Recent excavations at Motya off West Sicily and Nora in Sardinia are bringing in more evidence.

p. 219 49. M. Pallottino, *La Sardegna nuragica* (Rome, 1950); C. Zervos, *La Civilisation de la Sardaigne* (Paris, 1954), plate 55; G. Lilliu, *I Nuraghi* (Cagliari, 1962).

50. There is a Carbon 14 date of 1470 ± 200 at Barumini, but also now another of 1820 at Brunku Màdili (*Radio Carbon*, VIII (1966), 128.

p. 220 51. Add to Note 49, G. Lilliu and G. Pesce, *Scultura della Sardegna nuragica* (Cagliari, 1956). The Barumini figure excavated by Lilliu was in his Upper Nuragic I and so is seventh-century. There was an animal-headed boat-vase in the Tomba del Duce at Vetulonia *c.* 650, and another in the Tre Navicelle, also perhaps at Corinth; see *I.L.N.* (28 February 1956) (sixth-century).

52. Compare the Teshub; W. Cullican, in S. Piggott (ed.), *op. cit.* (Note 42), 133, plate 14. Proportions, dress, and gesture suggest the Sardinian figure as a debunked version of this.

p. 221 53. This problem is almost the whole matter of the Gifford Lectures for 1933–4 (E. Bevan, *Symbolism and Belief*) and a warning against facile interpretations.

54. Quoted by E. Gombrich, *Art and Illusion* p.
(London, 1962 ed.), 107, who, however, does not refer to Sardinian art.

55. R. Grosjean, *Études corses* (1955, 1956, et seq.); *idem, La Corse avant l'histoire* (Paris, 1966).

56. Among the earliest appear to be the 'Kurd- p.
Eimer' in the harness grave at Hart-an-der-Alz, Bavaria, and in the hoards of Dresden Dobritz, Saxony (one handle), and Hajdu-Börsömény, Hungary; W. Kimmig, *Bericht der römisch-germanischen Kommission*, XLIII–XLIV (1964), 31; C. Hawkes and M. Smith, *The Antiquaries Journal*, XXXVII (1957), 131, and cf. Note 4.

57. S. Piggott, *loc. cit.* (Note 4).

58. For dating see H. Frey, *Germania*, XL (1962), 56, and XLIV (1966), 48. Also W. Lucke and H. Frey, *Situla in Providence, R.G. Forsch.* (1962); S. Gabrovec, *Situla*, I (1960), 66; and *Najestarejsa Zgodovina Dolenjske*, I (Nove Mesto, 1956), and *Germania*, XLIV (1966), 1.

59. J. Kastelic, *Situla aus Vače: Jugoslavija* (Bel- p.
grade, 1956), perhaps '500 at earliest'. See also W. Lucke and H. Frey, *op. cit.*, 78.

60. S. Piggott, *P.P.S.*, N.S. XXX (1964), 439.

61. K. Maxwell-Hyslop, *loc. cit.* (Note 47) p.
(Khorsabad reliefs, etc.); see also Piotrovsky, *loc. cit.* (Note 35), 42.

62. A. Cook, *Zeus* (Cambridge, 1925), II, 1, 831–3, records that the badge of Thessalian Krannon was two ravens perched on a bronze 'car', evidently a rain and thunder charm. See V. Gordon Childe, *P.P.S.*, N.S. XIV (1948), 185–6 for the Tiryns hoard with tripod. Also E. Kunze, *op. cit.* (Note 47), plate X, and see Note 41 above.

63. The results were astonishingly similar on the eastern as on the western peripheries of the Assyrian–Phoenician–Greek orientalizing world. Scenes of the sacred meal on the Vače situla and on a bronze repoussé bowl with incised decoration from Iran, perhaps eighth–seventh century, treat figures and subject and barbarize both in just the same way; see *7000 Ans d'art en Iran*, catalogue of exhibition, Paris (1961–2), no. 333, not illustrated.

CHAPTER 8

1. J. Filip, *Keltové ve Střední Europě* (Prague, p.
1956), *passim*; C. Hawkes, *Ampurias*, XIV (1952), 81; T. Powell, *The Celts* (London, 1958), 15 f.;

W. Dehn and O. Frey, *Atti VI C.I.S.P.P.*, 197; P. Jacobsthal, *Early Celtic Art* (Oxford, 1944).

27 2. W. Kimmig, *V.I.K. Hamburg* (1958), 75; *idem, Bericht der römisch-germanischen Kommission*, XLIII–XLIV (1964), 31; W. Kimmig and E. Gersbach, *Germania*, XL (1966), 1; W. Dehn, *Neue Ausgrabungen in Deutschland* (1958), 127.

28 3. R. Joffroy, *Le Trésor de Vix, Mon. et mém. Piot 1954* (1958). The crater stands 1·64 m. high, is 1 m. across the mouth, and weighs 208 klg. (5 feet 5 inches; 3 feet 3 inches; 470 pounds).

4. Strabo, *Geographica*, V, 214.

5. The temporary shift to the Rhône in the mid sixth century defines roughly the change from Hallstatt Di to Dii, which in turn overlaps the emergence of Early La Tène. W. Kimmig, *Archaeologische Anzeiger* (1966), 469, and see Table 3.

6. Contrary to some earlier opinions. T. Powell, *op. cit.* (Note 1), map figure 9 and p. 49; W. Dehn, *Reinecke-Festschrift* (1950), 33; W. Kimmig, *Jahrbuch der römisch-germanischen Zentralmuseum, Mainz* (1954), 179. Compare the usual dates for Rodenbach, Rhineland, *c.* 450–400, Dürnberg, Austria, 420, Somme-Bionne (Marne), 430–420, La Motte St Valentin, *c.* 400 (W. Dehn and O. Frey, *loc. cit.* (Note 1)). V. Megaw, *Praehistorische Zeitschrift*, XLIII–XLIV (1965/6), 96.

7. O. Frey in a paper given to the Congress of the Prehistoric Society in London, Easter 1965.

29 8. Herodotus, *Histories*, V, 9; S. Foltiny, *Archaeologia Austriaca*, XXXIII (1963), 23; T. Sulimirski, *V.I.K. Hamburg* (1958), 793; S. Gabrovec, *Germania*, XLIV (1966), 1, but D. Popescu, *Dacia*, N.S. VI (1962), 443, doubts the presence of 'purely Scythian' tribes as far west even as Transylvania.

9. E.g. horse-head ornaments on chains; J. Filip, *op. cit.* (Note 1), figure 51, 3–5.

10. Herodotus IV, 143 and V, 18; see also A. Burn, *Persia and the Greeks* (London, 1962), 134.

31 11. M. Garašanin, *Atti VI C.I.S.P.P.* (Rome, 1962), 179; D. Garašanin, *Katalog Metala* (Belgrade, 1954), plates 22–3, 28–30; the Novi Pazar vase is linked to another in grave 100 at La Certosa di Bologna, also of about 500 B.C. (Garašanin's Iron Age II corresponds to the IVc and Va of Benac and Ćović). For the other brooch with two heads see E. Minns, *Scythians and Greeks* (Cambridge, 1913), figure 61.

12. For the best photographs (without a text) see *Rivista de Preistorie şi Antichităti Naţionale ... Bucureşti* (Bucharest, 1937), plates VII–XXVII; cf. the flying eagle of the Ziwiye gold pectoral (*7000 Ans d'art en Iran* (Paris, 1961), exhibition catalogue, plate 37, no. 500A). The workmen of *Rivista*, plate XXVII, 2, are wearing conical astrakhan caps of the right sort. See also D. Berciu, *Neue Forschungsergebnisse zur Vorgeschichte Rumäniens* (Bonn, 1966); S. Piggott, *Ancient Europe* (Edinburgh, 1965), 226 and plate XL. The Hagighiol grave had a red-figure Attic pot and a silver phiale inscribed with the name Kotys. This was the dynastic name of the kings of a Thracian tribe. A Kotys was active at the beginning of the fourth century and another in A.D. 6–9, so the name does not necessarily carry a fourth-century date (A. Fol, *Neue Beiträge zur Geschichte der Alten Welt*, I (Berlin, 1964), 193, and *Dacia*, O.S., I (1924), 363). Also B. Goldman, *Bull. Detroit Institute of Arts*, XLII (1963), and cf. the Marlik beakers (E. Negahban, *A Preliminary Report on Marlik Excavation* (Teheran, 1964), plates IV, V, VII, XII, etc.).

13. V. Mikov, *Le Tombeau antique près de Kazanlăk* (Sofia, 1954), plates III–V. See the warning by M. Garašanin, *loc. cit.* (Note 11), 191, that even in the late La Tène of the second and first centuries a cemetery near Niš that should have been 'Illyrian' is full of Daco-Getic objects, and in one near Belgrade in what should have been territory of the Celtic Skordi there are again Daco-Getic objects.

14. During Northern Periods III–VI the move- p. 232
ment was on the whole north-south, but especially in V; see maps in E. Sprockhoff, *Jung. Bzt. Hortfunde (Period V)* (Mainz, 1956), I, 41–3, 55–6, and II, maps 17 and 21b, and *Ausgrabungen und Funde*, III (1958), 221 and map 11 (Period II movement) and 231–9 (Periods IV–VI). Also H. Schubart, *V.I.K. Hamburg* (1958), 741; G. Neumann, *ibid.*, 608; W. Kimmig, *loc. cit.* (1958; Note 2).

15. W. Kimmig, *Badische Fundberichte*, XX (1956), 161.

16. D. A. Binchy, in M. Dillon (ed.), *Early Irish Society* (Dublin, 1954), 57; K. Jackson, *The Oldest Irish Tradition* (Cambridge, 1964), 9.

17. J. Filip, *Celtic Civilisation and its Heritage*, trans. (Prague, 1962), 72 f.; T. Powell, *op. cit.* (Note 1), 81.

18. J. Filip, *op. cit.* (Note 1), map figure 17, and p. 233
idem, op. cit. (Note 17), 130, figure 30; S. Piggott, *op. cit.* (Note 12), with refs., 216 f.; W. Kimmig, *loc. cit.* (Note 15).

p. 233 19. M.-L. Sjoested, *Gods and Heroes of the Celts*, trans. (London, 1949), 92.

20. P. Jacobsthal, *op. cit.* (Note 1), will be referred to constantly throughout this chapter and in Chapter 9; only references to tomb-groups *not* found in Jacobsthal will be given here, or special points of interest; for the chronology of La Tène styles, see 135 f., and Notes 1 and 6; for the Early Style, O. Frey, *Ann. Litt. Univ. de Besançon*, Ser. 2, Tom. 2, 1 (Besançon, 1955), and see Note 7.

21. No grave date after Waldalgesheim is really well founded. The Mezek chariot grave near Plovdiv in Bulgaria does not date the *beginning* of the style, though providing a historic event – the defeat of the Celts by Antigonas Gonatas in 276 – as a background for Celtic activity in these parts; see Note 52 below.

p. 234 22. See jewellery from Spina, *I.L.N.* (20 December 1958), 1105, figures 7, 8, and the moustached silenus from Vulci, P. Jacobsthal, *op. cit.* (Note 1), plate 252b. For the date of Rodenbach see Note 6.

23. According to R. Ghirshman, the pointed animal-eared god of Luristan may represent this Iranian deity (*Artibus Asiae*, xxi (1958), 37).

24. J. Keller, *I.L.N.* (3 December 1955), 955–7; *idem*, *Germania*, xxxiii (1955), 33, and *Das Keltische Fürstengrab von Rheinheim* (Mainz, 1965).

25. K. Kromer, *Gräberfeld von Hallstatt* (Florence, 1959), 182 and plate 202.

p. 235 26. See *Sept Mille Ans d'art en Iran* (Paris, 1961–2), catalogue no. 229, plate xx, and no. 282, plate xix; cf. the gold bracelet, O. Dalton, *The Treasure of the Oxus* (London, 1964), plate 1 and p. 212 above.

27. These interesting objects, found in 1962, have received a preliminary publication only: *I.L.N.* (12 January 1963), 48–9, figures 5–8. On Celtic and Luristan parallels see M. Mariën, *Analecta Archaeologica* (1960), 265.

28. Much of the body of the flagon is reconstruction; see W. Kimmig and H. Hell, *Vorzeit an Rhein und Donau* (Konstanz, 1958), plates 116–21. This important grave also held the well-known painted Attic cup with Celtic goldsmith's embellishments and the rich repoussé-decorated gold horn terminals with sheep's heads.

29. I have received help with this find from Professor G. Neumann of Jena.

p. 236 30. *I.L.N.* (20 December 1958), 1105, figure 7, gold earring from Spina etc. See full-face view of head on rim in P. Jacobsthal, *op. cit.* (Note 1), plate 186 top right.

31. I cannot agree with Jacobsthal's contention that the Basse-Yutz and Dürrnberg flagons are 'inseparably connected'. The reason for the late date of the former, given by Jacobsthal and queried by a few writers, is well-founded, as I am advised by J. Boardman. A type of palmette is used that could not have been imitated north of the Alps before the fourth century; *op. cit.* (Note 1), 39, and *Die Antike*, x (1934), 32.

32. Bone wolf from Abramovka in the Urals and p. :
whip-handle from Pazyryk in the Altai Mountains of Central Asia; T. Talbot Rice, *The Scythians* (London, 1957), plate 34 and figure 39.

33. P. Jacobsthal, *op. cit.* (Note 1), 136, also plate 104.

34. P. Jacobsthal, *op. cit.*, plates 230, 234; they are usually silver. There are many silver three- and four-armed whirligigs in the grave (?) found at Craiova in Wallachia, referred to above (Note 8, and D. Berciu, Note 12).

35. S. Marstrander, *Radiologisk datering av arkeologisk materiale* (1956–7), figure 4. There is a Carbon 14 date of 420, but a bowl found with the platter is linked stylistically with Period V, i.e. the eighth century. I owe knowledge of this object to Professor Piggott and further information kindly given by Professor Marstrander. If the 'jaws' of the Cuperly animals are closed, the profile is equally horselike.

36. J. de Navarro, *Germania*, xxxvii (1959), 139; *idem*, *Bericht der römisch-germanischen Kommission*, xl (1959), 79, figure 1, plates 12, 14, 17, 19, etc.

37. The Chi Rho of St Gall and many others. p.

38. P. Jacobsthal, *op. cit.* (Note 1), plate 30, no. 34; 25 and 26 at the bottom are more or less correct, the rest are Celtic. There is no sign of the cow's ears of Hathor, so Astarte is probably the original and could have come from the Phoenicians.

39. P. Jacobsthal, *op. cit.* (breastplate motifs plate 277, PP. 446–7; bracelet plate 45, no. 55).

40. P. Jacobsthal, *op. cit.*, no. 156, plate 99(f).

41. P. Jacobsthal, *op. cit.*, plate 82, 142. p.

42. W. Krämer, *Keltische Gräberfeld von Nebringen* (*Stuttgart*, 1964), 21–2. For a reassessment of dates based on old grave-finds, especially Münsingen, see F. Hodson, *Bulletin of the Institute of Archaeology* (*University of London*) (previously *Annual Report*

and Bulletin), IV (London, 1964), 123. If the abandonment of the Neckarland came at the end of La Tène B (equals IC, early second century), this is roughly between Graves 68 and 79 on Hodson's table, p. 132.

241 43. O. Klindt-Jensen, *Bronzekedelen fra Brå* (Aarhus, 1953); *idem*, *Foreign Influences in Denmark's Early Iron Age* (Copenhagen, 1950).

44. P. Amandry, in *The Aegean and the Near East* (New York, 1956), 239; K. Maxwell-Hyslop, *Iraq*, XVIII, 2 (1956), 150; R. Young, *American Journal of Archaeology*, LXII (1958), plate 25, 15, plate 26, 18; *I.L.N.* (17 May 1958), 830, figures 9–10.

45. From the Býčí-Skála bronze bull through vases with horned handles back to Neolithic pots with heads of oxen (Plates 219 and 217, Figure 44, etc.).

46. K. Willvonseder, *Keltische Kunst in Salzburg* (Salzburg, 1960), figure 9; *idem*, *Beiträge Österreichs zur Erforschung der Vergangenheit und Kulturgeschichte der Menschheit*, *Symposium 1958* (Wenner-Gren, 1959), 75; J. Megaw, *The Antiquaries Journal*, XLII (1962), 24.

47. K. Hucke, *Zeitschrift des Mähr. Landesmuseum*, N.F. II (1942), 87; A. Radnóti, *Germania*, XXXVI (1958), 28; J. Filip, *op. cit.* (Note 1), 49.

242 48. C. Fox, *Pattern and Purpose* (Cardiff, 1958), 23–4 and figure 16; cf. our Figure 99.

49. L. Adam, *Primitive Art* (Harmondsworth, 1949), 199.

243 50. J. Cowen, *Proceedings of the Society of Antiquaries of Scotland*, LXIX (1935), 455; P. Jacobsthal, *op. cit.* (Note 1), 163, 175, and plate 279, PP. 475–6; A. Varagnac, *L'Art gaulois* (La Pierre-qui-vire, 1956), 237, nos. 18, 19, 22.

51. This is as it were a three-dimensional rendering of the 'Scythian' whirligig animal; Jacobsthal's 175a, also based on a face, is much less representational.

244 52. P. Jacobsthal, *op. cit.*, 164, 176; B. Filow, *Bull. Arch. Inst. Bulgare*, XI (1937), 1 f. A La Tène 'egg-bracelet' has been found recently at Delphi, but the type does not allow close dating; see W. Krämer, *Germania*, XXXIX (1961), 32.

53. See for instance P. Jacobsthal, *op. cit.*, plate 276, 432–3.

54. See Note 11 above for Štrpci, Čurug, etc., and *I.L.N.* (31 January 1959), 191, for the El Carambolo gold treasure and (20 December 1958), 1125; also A. Arribas, *The Iberians* (London, n.d.), plates 6, 7.

55. P. Jacobsthal, *op. cit.*, no. 129, and the swords p. 245
nos. 104, 106, 113, etc. For zoomorphic motifs see also J. de Navarro, *B.R.G.K.*, *loc. cit.* (Note 36).

56. H. Zürn, *Germania*, XLII (1964), 27; the date p. 246
is about 500 B.C.

57. T. Powell, *op. cit.* (Note 1), 134, figure 23; p. 247
P. Jacobsthal, *op. cit.*, plate 12 (seventeenth- and eighteenth-century drawings).

58. See Note 38.

59. In the 'Death Tales of the Ulster Heroes', translated by T. Cross and C. Slover, *Ancient Irish Tales* (U.S.A.–London, 1936), 338.

60. Even here there is a suggestion of a face within the pattern. For the Athlone crucifixion see F. Henry, *L'Art irlandais*, I (1963), plate 46; on other stone crosses the abstract language is gradually suppressed (plates 15, 51; p. 73, figure 4; p. 159, figure 14), while the cross that began on coins as a subordinate pagan symbol (Plate 302, bottom right) has now changed places.

61. P. Jacobsthal, *op. cit.*, shows drawings of all four faces on plate 15.

62. N. Sandars, *Antiquity* (December 1964), 306. p. 248

63. Aeneid, VII, 180.

64. Pace Jacobsthal, *op. cit.*, 4 (outlined eye on p. 249
flagon, Plates 241 and 242); notched-outline Spina jewellery in *I.L.N.* (20 December 1958), 1105, figure 7; see the Frontispiece.

65. F. Henry, *op. cit.* (Note 60), colour plate p. 106 and plate 91 from Myklebostad and Oseberg; cf. Jacobsthal, plate 3, top right.

66. A. Mongait, *Archaeology in the U.S.S.R.* (Penguin ed.) (London, 1961), plate 15 and p. 237. For the cross-legged pose see P. Bober, *American Journal of Archaeology*, LV (1951), 13 f., and S. Weinberg, p. 121, plates 1–2 for the Aegean.

67. Map in T. Powell, *op. cit.* (Note 1), 131; P. p. 250
Lambrechts, *L'Exaltation de la tête dans . . . l'art des Celtes* (Bruges, 1954), figures 21–2, 26 ('Jupiter columns', etc.).

68. A. Mongait, *op. cit.*, plate 6b; see also plate 8.

69. E.g. corbel in St Mary, Bedford, *I.L.N.* (10 October 1959), 405, bottom left.

70. J. Camón Aznar, *Las Artes y los pueblos de la España primitiva* (Madrid, 1954), 732, figure 729; 750, figure 754; also figures 731–2. Cf. Iberian

oriental bull, figure 851, and Carrales de Buelna, figures 779–80 (*I.L.N.* (29 June 1957), 1077).

p. 251 71. A. Varagnac, *op. cit.* (Note 50), 147, no. 61, and our Plate 276.

72. A. Varagnac, *op. cit.*, 239, nos. 38 and 41.

p. 252 73. O. Klindt-Jensen, *op. cit.* (1950; Note 43).

74. Not unlike the extra 'tail' of one of the Aylesford horses; see below, p. 270 and Plate 301.

p. 253 75. S. Müller, *Nordiske Fortidsminder*, I (1890–1903), 35 ff.; O. Klindt-Jensen, *op. cit.* (1950), 119, and *Antiquity*, XXX (September 1959), 161, with references to the very extensive literature, since when a lecture by T. Powell to the Easter conference of the Prehistoric Society (London, 1965) has materially strengthened the case for a South-East European source.

76. It is now in the Cluny Museum; see P. Lambrechts, *Contributions à l'étude des divinités celtiques* (Bruges, 1942), 30; P. Bober, *loc. cit.* (Note 66), 14.

77. For the Cave of Magda-Hraškova see E. Vlcek and J. Kukla, *Pamatky*, L (1959), 507; see also V. Mikov, *op. cit.* (Note 13), and M. Grbič, *Choix de plastiques grecques et romaines* (Belgrade, 1958), plates 20–1. These warriors have the same headwear and shields as the Kazanlak pair, but whether they are Celts or not is another matter; see also the engraved bronze sheet from Baratella, Este (*Situla Kunst* (Vienna, 1962), exhibition catalogue, no. 60), of the fourth–third century.

78. S. Piggott, *The Antiquaries Journal*, XXXIX (1959), 19.

p. 254 79. Cf. the Waterloo Bridge helmet, Plate 293. Is it possible that horns like those from La Bouvanderie and Waldalgesheim were mounted on helmets rather than carts? P. Jacobsthal, *op. cit.* (Note 1), plates 96 and 108.

p. 255 80. At the other extremity of the Celtic world the same doubt may be entertained concerning the lion-killer of a granulated gold bracelet in Phoenician–South Spanish style found at Aliseda; D. Harden, *The Phoenicians* (London, 1962), plate 96. T. Powell suggests convincingly that the 'dolphin' may here be a sturgeon.

81. See Note 12 above (Marlik etc.). There is also perhaps a reminiscence of the animal painted on Cucuteni pots (p. 127 and cf. Figure 53 above).

p. 256 82. *Sept Mille Ans d'art* (Note 26), plates VI, VII, and LXI, nos. 67, A and B, and 672; E. Negahban (Note 12), plate V, etc. (Amlash, Mannaean, Median, etc.).

83. O. Dalton, *op. cit.* (Note 26), plate III, and the reference to Voronesh from T. Powell.

84. For good or ill, for it could be the cauldron that renewed life. For reference to this theory and for a new explanation of the scene see W. Kimmig, *Fundberichte aus Schwaben*, N.F. XVII (1965), 135.

85. Like the bull and (very similar) dog at Toprakkale (B. Piotrovsky, *Iskusstvo Urartu* (Leningrad, 1962), 111, figure 75; see also coins of Cyprus and Massilia, Lyon, etc. This pose is so widespread in time and place (it occurs on the Nimrud ivories) that comparison with any single late object, e.g. the Hildesheim cup (O. Klindt-Jensen, *op. cit.* (1950; Note 43), figure 73), has little chronological weight; the same applies to the examples quoted on p. 140.

86. The two silver-gilt phalerae in the Cabinet p. 2
des Médailles 'probably from the Black Sea' and others from Stanitsa, Taman Peninsula, and at Roermond, show a much more conventional composition and varying degrees of provincialism. It may be significant that the base of the Gundestrup cauldron is itself a roundel like the phalerae.

87. Fine examples in the Morel Collection at the British Museum, and see W. Kimmig and H. Hell, *op. cit.* (Note 28), plate 136; for 'Early Style' decoration of pots, O. Frey, *loc. cit.* (Note 20).

CHAPTER 9

1. C. Hawkes and M. Smith, *The Antiquaries* p. 2
Journal, XXXVII (1957), 131; J. Coles, *P.P.S.*, N.S. XXVIII (1962), 156, *P.P.S.*, N.S. XXIX (1963), 326; J. Butler, *Bronze Age Connections across the North Sea* (Groningen, 1965), 211 f.

2. C. Hawkes, *Antiquity*, XXXIII (September 1959), 170, *Ampurias*, XIV (1952), 81; on the linguistic argument, H. Hencken, *American Anthropological Association*, LVII (December 1955), 1.

3. There is still a frontier on the river Parrett in Somerset to the west of which 'village England' is replaced by a landscape of farms, hamlets, winding lanes, and pasture; W. Hoskins, *Provincial England* (London, 1963), 20 n.

4. C. Hawkes, *loc. cit.* (1959), criticized by F. Hodson, *Bulletin of the Institute of Archaeology (University of London)* (previously *Annual Report*

and Bulletin), iv (1964), 123, *P.P.S.*, n.s. xxviii (1962), 140, and xxx (1964), 99. Some of the arguments may be valid, but Hodson underestimates the real extent of La Tène infiltration throughout the British Isles. See p. 273 below for a comment on purely art-historical grounds. For the Belgic invasion see now A. Birchall, *P.P.S.*, n.s. xxxi (1965), 241.

9 5. K. Jackson, *The Oldest Irish Tradition* (Cambridge, 1964), for a convincing demonstration of the relevance of this tradition to the society of the fourth century and even earlier and *vice versa*; he concludes 'if we want to know what it was like to be a late La Tène Celt and what life in the Early Iron Age was like we can get some notion of it by reading the Ulster Cycle of hero stories'. On p. 6, he uses the survival of Celtic art as a valid analogy for literary survival; see also D. Binchy on craftsmen in M. Dillon (ed.), *Early Irish Society* (Dublin, 1954), 57.

6. H. Maryon, *Proceedings of the Royal Irish Academy*, xlix (1938), 204. This is the 'Dowris Phase' of G. Eogan, *P.P.S.*, n.s. xxx (1964), 293.

7. O. Frey, *Ann. Litt. Univ. Besançon*, 2, Tome 2, 1 (Besançon, 1955).

8. G. Eogan, *loc. cit.* (Note 6), 303, figure 15; see also J. Coles etc., *P.P.S.*, n.s. xxx (1964), plates xvii and xix.

0 9. Cf. La Bouvanderie; P. Jacobsthal, *Early Celtic Art* (Oxford, 1944), 171, plate 107 (the border), and M. Jope, *P.P.S.*, n.s. xxvii (1961), 307, plate xxiiie (openwork). For Standlake see M. Jope in S. Frere (ed.), *Problems of the Iron Age in Southern Britain* (Occasional Paper of the Institute of Archaeology, University of London, 1958), 69, plate v. For the Newnham Croft chariot burial etc. see C. Fox, *Pattern and Purpose: A Survey of Early Celtic Art* (Cardiff, 1958), 10; this work is as necessary to any study of British La Tène art as Jacobsthal is to Continental.

51 10. S. Piggott and R. Atkinson, *Archaeologia*, xcvi (1955), 197; C. Fox, *op. cit.*, 22.

11. P. Jacobsthal, *op. cit.*, 107, plate 65.

2 12. In addition to the scabbards illustrated by P. Jacobsthal, *op. cit.*, 113, plate 67, see J. de Navarro, *P.P.S.*, n.s. xxi (1955), 234, plate xxx, 2; on bird brooches W. Dehn, *Helvetia Antiqua* (1966), 137.

13. P. Jacobsthal, *op. cit.*, 156, plate 99 f. (Waldalgesheim bracelet), 129, plates 72–3 (Neuchâtel spear). For the scabbard connexion see M. Jope, *loc. cit.* (1958; Note 9), 80.

14. Folio 202 verso; see also St Mark's throne in the Lichfield Evangeliar. p. 263

15. Quoted by R. Macalister, *The Archaeology of Ireland*, 2nd ed. (London, 1949), 232–3. p. 264

16. M. Jope and H. Hodges, *Ulster Journal of Archaeology*, xx (1957), 98, figure 2; and see F. Henry, *L'Art irlandais*, i (La Pierre-qui-vire, 1963), 298–306, figure 31 (showing the geometric basis from newly discovered pricks and rulings on the Lindisfarne pages), and *Antiquity*, xxxvii (June 1963), 100.

17. The Lattoon disc, the Caergwrle 'boat', etc.

18. C. Fox, *op. cit.* (Note 9), 28, writes of two keels in intimate contact: 'one rises to form the dominant knife-edge while the other slides down the slope to become the bounding line of a terminal "leaf" form, or to broaden the base of the framework of the pattern'.

19. R. Rainbird Clark, *P.P.S.*, n.s. xx (1954), 27 (Snettisham), and xvii (1951), 214 (Ringstead). p. 265

20. Best illustrations of Frasnes-lez-Buissenal in R. Clark, *loc. cit.* (1954). Especially Scythian is the detail on plate vi. The Lough Crew bone slips, as well as giving the patterns and tryouts of intersecting compass-work, show how the whirligig of the Aylesford bucket (Plate 301) could be constructed; F. Henry, *op. cit.* (Note 16), figure 31.

21. I cannot agree with M. Jope, *loc. cit.* (1958; Note 9), 71, on the overriding importance of Waldalgesheim for Britain; it is rather a Waldalgesheim already transformed by the Plastic and Sword Styles. The same writer has proposed placing the Battersea shield at the La Tène I/II horizon, end of third century, which is at least a century and a half earlier than the usual date proposed: *c.* 75 B.C. according to Fox. Perhaps late second century is most likely. p. 266

22. M. Jope, *Ulster Journal of Archaeology*, xvii (1954), 81; S. Piggott, *P.P.S.*, n.s. xvi (1950), 1.

23. P. Jacobsthal, *op. cit.* (Note 9), 105, plate 64 (cf. M. Jope, *loc. cit.*, plate vii left), and Jacobsthal, 103, plate 64 (cf. Jope, figure 1). p. 268

24. Jope finds difficulty in accounting for the 'hourglass junctions' on the Toome scabbard and Lisnacroghera 3, but perhaps these could have been adapted from the hatched triangles that meet, apex to apex, between concentric rings on the Lattoon disc and other Bronze Age gold-work.

25. H. Savory, *Antiquity*, xxxviii (March 1964), 18. The Lambay Island disc and the Elvedon

tankard give as good late parallels for the basic triquetra as the early ones quoted.

p. 268 26. C. Fox, *op. cit.* (Note 9), 84, and *Antiquity*, XXXIV (September 1960), 207, plates XXVI–XXVIII; the mirrors are really confined to Lowland Britain.

p. 269 27. See p. 252 above; also de Navarro, *Germania*, XXXVII (1959), 131 and note 39. For the Aylesford dating, A. Birchall, *loc. cit.* (Note 4); for Marlborough, E. Nylén, *Acta Archaeologica* (Copenhagen), XXIX (1958), 1.

p. 271 28. G. Fabre, in A. Varagnac, *L'Art gaulois* (La Pierre-qui-vire, 1956), 191, plates VI, 3 and X, 5. For the heads of Plate 298 cf. W. Kimmig and H. Hell, *Vorzeit an Rhein und Donau* (Lindau-Konstanz, 1958), 132a (a Nagold coin, end of the second century); also D. Allen, *P.P.S.*, N.S. XXIV (1958), 43, plate IX, 70 (Belgic, Andoco, bronze; the hair has the same stylized locks as the moustached Marlborough profile on Plate 299; for the latter see also T. Powell, *The Celts* (London, 1958), plate 5c, coin of the Carnutes, between Seine and Loire).

29. S. Piggott, *Antiquity*, V (1937), 37. It is 365 feet long and is probably first-century B.C.

30. Many examples in C. Fox, *op. cit.* (Note 9), plates 46, 48, 50, etc. See also M. Jope, *loc. cit.* (Note 22), 92 (Keshcarrigan); J. Megaw, *The Antiquaries Journal*, XLIII (1963), 37 (before giving this Polish find to British workmanship more account should perhaps be taken of Late Plastic Style bronzes from the large *oppida* like Manching; W. Krämer, *Antiquity*, XXXIV (September 1960), 191, figure 6, and *Germania*, XI (1962), 293).

p. 273 31. The Stanwick bronzes, though stylistically pure La Tène, are first-century A.D. and must be left, along with the Deskford boar's head (identified as the mouth-piece of a carnyx), the Easica brooch, and many other first-century A.D. objects. See M. MacGregor, *P.P.S.*, N.S. XXVIII (1962), 17, for the latest account of Stanwick.

32. J. Toynbee, *Art in Britain under the Romans* (Oxford, 1964), 25, for the 'romanists'' opinion not subscribed to here.

p. 274 33. J. Toynbee, *op. cit.*, 13.

34. C. Hawkes, *loc. cit.* (1959; Note 2, see also Note 4).

35. T. Cross and C. Slover, *Ancient Irish Tales* (U.S.A., 1936), 17.

p. 275 36. It survives through the Hallstatt Iron Age, e.g. the belt in Grave 874 (K. Kromer, *Das Gräberfeld von Hallstatt* (Florence, 1959), plate 172). It is still quite geometric-abstract on the chape of a scabbard from the Thames (C. Fox, *op. cit.* (Note 9), plate 10b, and O. Frey, *loc. cit.* (Note 7), figure 3). See also P. Jacobsthal, *op. cit.* (Note 9), plate 271, PP. 296–306; plate 272, P. 335; plate 276, PP. 429–30, etc.; also F. Henry, *op. cit.* (Note 16), plate 8 and figures 24b, 30, 31–4.

37. A. and B. Rees, *Celtic Heritage* (London, p. 1961), 189, note 24, and Note 15 above.

38. P. Jacobsthal, *op. cit.* (Note 9), 390, plate 266, p. PP. 144–6 (with compasses) and 180, 185, plates 113 and 115 (freehand); and O. Frey, *loc. cit.* (Note 7), figures 8 and 9, p. 22.

39. A. and B. Rees, *op. cit.*, 346–7.

40. In 'The Sickbed of Cú Chulainn', Cross and p. Slover, *op. cit.* (Note 35), 182–3. For the motif see T. Talbot Rice, *The Scythians* (London, 1957), plate 2, on the horse both single and double; see also C. Fox, *op. cit.* (Note 9), figure 82: 25; figure 83: 92 etc., and, as a classical lotus, P. Jacobsthal, *op. cit.* (Note 9), plate 263, P. 59 to plate 266, PP. 152–4.

41. A. and B. Rees, *op. cit.*, 346–7; P. Jacobsthal, *op. cit.*, 16 f. A poem of Dylan Thomas has been described in these words: 'The structural elements in it form an irregular spiral which in visual terms could be represented by serpentine lines intersecting at irregular intervals and with no visible end or culmination' (G. Melchior, quoted in *The Times Literary Supplement*).

42. R. Caillois, *The Mask of Medusa* (London, p. 1964), 101 f.

43. M.-L. Sjoested, *Gods and Heroes of the Celts*, trans. (London, 1949), 94. There is a good example of the benevolent bearded type on the Waldalgesheim flagon, and another repetitive type is large-mouthed and smiling; see R. Gensen, *Germania*, XLIII (1965), 49, plate 10 (from Manching, Bad Nauheim, and the Calais museum).

44. T. Cross and C. Slover, *op. cit.* (Note 35), p. 226. The hair and features of the Lindisfarne St Matthew and of St Gall folio 78 are treated in exactly the same abstract decorative manner as many La Tène heads, e.g. Mšecké-Žehrovice. Sausage-like curls and symmetrical beards become standardized. Lindisfarne is roughly contemporary with the recorded descriptions of Cú Chulainn and Conchober. The almost pedantic fascination with numbers crops up in all the stories; there are never

'many' or 'few' men, but five thousand, three hundred, or three; see E. Cassirer, *The Philosophy of Symbolic Form* (Yale and Oxford, 1953–7), I, 226–49, on the magical power of number; also A. and B. Rees, *op. cit.* (Note 37), 59 and 346 f. A particular colour may be linked with a point or direction or part of the body as in ancient Sumer and medieval occultism.

45. P. Lambrechts, *L'Exaltation de la tête dans la pensée des Celtes* (Bruges, 1954), *passim*, exhaustive but occasionally over-ingenious, includes (38 f.) summaries of the relevant classical authorities. Also R. Onians, *The Origins of European Thought* (Cambridge, 1951), 98 f.; T. Kendrick, *The Druids* (London, 1928), *passim.*

46. Cu Roi Mac Dairi in the *Ulster Cycle*, Bran of the *Mabinogion*, the Green Knight of the Gawaine poem are a few. The severed head of Cú Chulainn was able to crack a stone with its magic ardour. Lambrechts, *op. cit.*, distinguishes the monster's paw *on* the head found mostly in the midi, and those with the head *between* the paws found in North-East Gaul; he thinks the former may have been influenced from Etruria, the latter are particularly Celtic. I do not see that coins can be used, as Lambrechts uses them, as evidence for the iconographic importance of the head; they are all Greco-Roman inspired. Some decapitations need have no religious significance.

. 281 47. E. Cassirer, *op. cit.* (Note 44), I, 226–49, with Usener's theory of language, number, and the three persons. For attempts to identify Celtic deities, P. Lambrechts, *Contributions à l'étude des divinités celtiques* (Bruges, 1942), and the cautious approach of M.-L. Sjoested, *op. cit.* (Note 43). See T. Powell, *The Celts* (London, 1958), chapter 3, and now also M. Koenig, *Archaeology*, XIX (January 1966), 24.

48. M.-L. Sjoested, *op. cit.*, 85: heroes 'outside the tribe' with semi-animal nature. Or perhaps we are to suppose, like Cú Chulainn and his hound, alternative animal and human epiphanies of the same god or hero.

49. P. Jacobsthal, *op. cit.* (Note 9), plates 158–9, nos. 312, 313, 315.

50. Cf. Plates 241, 243, and 245 with St Gall, 51 folio 7, top; Kells, folio 247, recto, letter Di; folio 243, letter Di; etc.

51. T. Cross and C. Slover, *op. cit.* (Note 35), 213 ('Cattle-Raid of Ragamna').

52. W. B. Yeats. Empedocles has been compared p. 282
to the Celtic Mongán, doomed to be 'born in all manner of mortal forms'; see F. Cornford, *Principium Sapientiae* (Cambridge, 1952), 122 f.; also p. 109 (Pythagoras and number-mysticism); p. 87 (the prophet, poet, and sage had originally been united in a single figure stemming from the shaman, the wise man).

53. Especially in the Rhineland; see map in T. Powell, *op. cit.* (Note 28), figure 21, and cf. the 'devils' of Stowe 944, folio 7, and Tiberius B.V., folio 87b (T. Kendrick, *Late Saxon and Viking Art* (London, 1949), plates XX, 2 and XXVI).

54. M.-L. Sjoested, *op. cit.* (Note 43), 5 ff. This is still very much the same situation as had faced Neolithic cultivators in the fifth millennium (p. 154 above).

55. *Beowulf*, trans. Gavin Bone (Oxford, 1945), 46.

56. J. Tolkien, *Proceedings of the British Academy*, XXII (1936), 27.

57. The constancy of these types, the identical p. 283
physiognomy, may not be so surprising if we think not of 'a green man' and 'a dragon' but 'the Green Man' and 'the Dragon' or Worm, ancient figures with the accretions of centuries.

58. A. and B. Rees, *op. cit.* (Note 37), 351; M.-L. Sjoested, *op. cit.* (Note 43), 94.

59. There is an interesting and plausible interpretation of the Irish *imrama* or 'voyages' as fragments of a lost *Book of the Dead* with the islands representing abstract and metaphysical qualities: youth–age, masculinity–feminity, white–black and so on (A. and B. Rees, *op. cit.*, 322–5).

60. K. Popper, *The Logic of Scientific Discovery* (London, 1959), 79, and apropos *Gestalt* psychology E. Gombrich, *Art and Illusion* (London, 1962), 231 etc.

61. D. Jones, *Epoch and Artist* (London, 1959), 189.

CHAPTER 10

1. S. Giedion, *The Beginnings of Art* (London, p. 294
1962), 44, 64, etc.

BIBLIOGRAPHY

NOTE

THE materials of prehistory, and therefore of prehistoric art also, are in a continual state of flux due to new discoveries and new techniques, so that works of synthesis are soon out of date in their particulars, though the best, like the works of V. Gordon Childe and P. Jacobsthal's *Early Celtic Art*, retain their value undiminished through the authors' peculiar vision and scope. One result of this continual amendment is that our chief authorities are found in articles, often quite short, scattered through various European specialist periodicals. References to the most important will be found in the Notes. The Bibliography gives a selection of titles of general surveys of countries, periods, or particular sites which are still (1966) in whole or in part essential to the study of prehistoric art in Europe. Apart from the General Works, they are listed under the chapter on which they have most bearing, though often applying to others as well.

GENERAL WORKS

ALMAGRO, M. *Ars Hispaniae*, I. Madrid, 1947.

CAMÓN AZNAR, J. *Las Artes y los pueblos de la España primitiva*. Madrid, 1954.

CASSIRER, E. *The Philosophy of Symbolic Form*. Yale and Oxford, 1953–7.

CHILDE, V. G. *The Danube in Prehistory*. Oxford, 1929.

CHILDE, V. G. *What Happened in History*. Harmondsworth, 1946.

CHILDE, V. G. *Prehistoric Communities of the British Isles*. 2nd ed. London, 1947.

CHILDE, V. G. *The Dawn of European Civilisation*. 6th ed. London, 1957.

CHILDE, V. G. *Prehistory of European Society*. Harmondsworth, 1958.

CLARK, J. G. D. *Prehistoric Europe: The Economic Basis*. London, 1952.

CORNFORD, F. *Principia Sapientiae*. Cambridge, 1952.

EHRICH, R. (ed.). *Chronologies in Old World Archaeology*. Chicago, 1965.

ELIADE, M. *The Myth of the Eternal Return*. Trans. London, 1955.

ELIADE, M. *Myths, Dreams and Mysteries*. Trans. London, 1960.

ELIADE, M. *Shamanism*. Trans. London, 1964.

GIEDION, S. *The Eternal Present, Part One: The Beginnings of Art* (The Mellon Lectures for 1957). London, 1962.

GOMBRICH, E. *Art and Illusion*. London, 1959 and 1962 (new ed., reset).

HOERNES, M. *Urgeschichte der bildenden Kunst*. Vienna, 1898.

KIMMIG, W., and HELL, H. *Vorzeit an Rhein und Donau*. Lindau-Constance, 1958.

KÜHN, H. *Die Kunst Alteuropas*. Stuttgart, 1958.

MONGAIT, A. *Archaeology in the U.S.S.R.* Trans. Harmondsworth, 1961.

MYRES, J. L. *Mediterranean Culture* (Frazer Lecture). Cambridge, 1943.

ONIANS, R. *The Origins of European Thought*. Cambridge, 1951.

PIGGOTT, S., and DANIEL, G. E. *A Picture Book of Early British Art*. Cambridge, 1951.

PIGGOTT, S. (ed.). *The Dawn of Civilisation*. London, 1961.
Some of the individual contributions have since appeared enlarged as separate books.

PIGGOTT, S. *Ancient Europe*. Edinburgh, 1965.

POULÍK, J., and FORMAN, B. *Prehistoric Art*. Prague–London, 1956.
A high quality picture-book relating to Czechoslovakia only.

POWELL, T. *Prehistoric Art*. London, 1966.
This excellent and richly illustrated concise study has appeared too late for more than mention in this bibliography.

SHETELIG, H., and FALK, H. *Scandinavian Archaeology*. Oxford, 1937.

VERNON, M. *The Psychology of Perception*. Harmondsworth, 1962.

ZEUNER, F. *A History of Domesticated Animals*. London, 1963.

CHAPTERS 1 AND 2: PALEOLITHIC

BANDI, H.-G., and MARINGER, J. *Kunst der Eiszeit*. Basel, 1952.

BATAILLE, G. *Lascaux; or The Birth of Art*. Lausanne, 1955.

BREUIL, H. *Four Hundred Centuries of Cave Art*. Montignac, 1952.

GJESSING, G. *The Circumpolar Ice Age*. Copenhagen, 1944.

GRAZIOSI, P. *L'Arte della antica età della pietra*. Florence, 1956; English ed. London, 1960.

An essential work with very full documentation.

HERBERTS, K. *The Complete Book of Artist's Techniques*. Trans. London, 1958.

Describes experiments with supposed prehistoric techniques.

KLÍMA, B. *Dolní Věstonice*. Prague, 1963.

KÜHN, H. *Die Felsbilder Europas*. Zürich–Vienna, 1952.

The English translation, London, 1956, is less well illustrated.

LAMING, A. *Lascaux*. Harmondsworth, 1959.

LAMING-EMPERAIRE, A. *La Signification de l'art rupestre paléolithique*. Paris, 1962.

This includes a full and discursive bibliography.

LEROI-GOURHAN, A. *Préhistoire d'art occidental*. Paris, 1965.

Magnificently illustrated and well documented, this volume appeared too late for detailed discussion here but the main lines of the author's thesis had already been made known in notes and articles which have been considered in this text. In spite of its critical apparatus, this volume does not give sufficient statistical material to carry agreement with all the author's contentions.

MORRIS, D. *The Biology of Art*. London, 1962.

OAKLEY, K. *Frameworks for Dating Fossil Man*. London, 1964.

SIEVEKING, A. and G. *The Caves of France and Northern Spain: A Guide*. London, 1962.

WINDELS, F. *Lascaux, chapelle sixtine de la préhistoire*. Montignac, 1948.

CHAPTER 3: MESOLITHIC

ALMGREN, O. *Nordische Felszeichnungen als religiöse Urkunden*. Frankfurt-am-Main, 1934.

BÖE, J. *Felszeichnungen im westlichen Norwegen*. Bergen, 1932.

CLARK, J. G. D. *The Mesolithic Settlement of Northern Europe*. Cambridge, 1936.

LAJOUX, J. *The Rock Paintings of Tasili*. Trans. London, 1963.

LHOTE, H. *The Search for the Tasili Frescoes*. Trans. London, 1959.

MCBURNEY, C. *The Stone Age of North Africa*. Harmondsworth, 1960.

PORCAR, J.-B. *Excavaciones en la cueva Remigia (Castellón)*. Madrid, 1935.

RAUDONIKAS, W. *Les Gravures rupestres des bords du lac Onega*, I and II. Leningrad, 1936 and 1938.

For this chapter see also H. Kühn (with good bibliography to 1952) and J. Camón Aznar under Chapters 1 and 2 above.

CHAPTER 4: NEOLITHIC EASTERN AND CENTRAL EUROPE

BERCIU, D. *Contribuții la problemele Neoliticului în Romînia în lumina noilor Cercetări*. Bucharest, 1961.

DUMITRESCU, V. *Habașești*. Bucharest, 1954.

GALOVIĆ, R. *Predionica*. Priština, 1959.

GARAŠANIN, D. *Starčevačka Kultura*. Ljubljana, 1954.

GIMBUTAS, M. *The Prehistory of Eastern Europe*, Part I, *Mesolithic, Neolithic and Copper Age Cultures in Russia and the Baltic Area*. Cambridge, Mass., 1956.

KANDYBA, O. *Schipenitz*. Vienna, 1937.

KOROŠEC, J. *Neolitska Naseobina u Danilu Bitinju*. Zagreb, 1958.

MELLAART, J. *Earliest Civilisations of the Near East*. London, 1965.

NEUSTUPNY, J. and E. *Czechoslovakia before the Slavs*. London, 1961.

NOVAK, G. *Prehistorijska Hvar*. Zagreb, 1955.

RADIMSKY, W., and FIALA, F. *Die neolitische Station von Butmir bei Sarajevo in Bosnien*. Vienna, 1895, 1898.

SCHMIDT, H. *Cucuteni*. Berlin–Leipzig, 1932.

VASIĆ, M. *Prehistoriska Vinča*, I–III. Belgrade, 1932–6.

VULPE, R. *Izvoare*. Bucharest, 1957.

CHAPTER 5: NEOLITHIC SOUTH-WEST AND NORTHERN EUROPE

BREA, B. *Sicily before the Greeks*. London, 1957.

EVANS, J. *Malta*. London, 1959.

GIOT, P.-R. *Brittany*. London, 1960.

GUIDO, M. *Sardinia*. London, 1963.

HENSHALL, A. *The Chambered Tombs of Scotland*, I. Edinburgh, 1963.

KLINDT-JENSEN, O. *Denmark before the Vikings.* London, 1957.

LEISNER, G. and V. *Die Megalithgräber der Iberischen Halbinsel,* I, *Süden.* Berlin, 1943.

O'RÍORDÁIN, S., and DANIEL, G. *New Grange and the Bend of the Boyne.* London, 1964.

PIGGOTT, S. *Neolithic Cultures of the British Isles.* Cambridge, 1954.

POWELL, T. G. E., and DANIEL, G. *Barclodiad y Gawres.* Liverpool, 1956.

ZERVOS, C. *Naissance de la civilisation en Grèce.* Paris, 1963.
Includes much Balkan material.

CHAPTER 6: METALLURGY AND THE BRONZE AGE TO CIRCA 1200

AITCHISON, L. *A History of Metals.* London, 1960.

ALTHIN, C.-A. *Studien zu den bronzezeitlichen Felszeichnungen von Skåne.* Lund, 1945.

ATKINSON, R. *Stonehenge.* Harmondsworth, 1960.

BROHOLM, H. *Danmarks Bronzealder,* I–IV. Copenhagen, 1943–9.

BRØNDSTED, J. *Danmarks Oldtid,* II. Copenhagen, 1938–40. German ed., *Nordische Vorzeit,* II, Neumünster, 1962.

BUTLER, J. *Bronze Age Connections Across the North Sea* (Palaeohistoria, IX). Groningen, 1963.

COGHLAN, H. *Notes on the Prehistoric Metallurgy of Copper and Bronze in the Old World.* Oxford, 1951.

DUMITRESCU, V. *Necropola de incinerație . . . de la Cîrna.* Bucharest, 1961.

ELIADE, M. *The Crucible and the Forge.* Trans. London, 1962.

FINLEY, M. *The World of Odysseus.* Harmondsworth, 1962.

FORBES, R. *Metallurgy in Antiquity,* I–IX. Leiden, 1956–64.
An invaluable study, especially vol. IX.

GIMBUTAS, M. *Bronze Age Cultures in Central and Eastern Europe.* The Hague, 1965.
With Professor Piggott's rather differently orientated *Prehistoric Europe,* the only recent work of synthesis on a large scale.

HACHMANN, R. *Die frühe Bronzezeit im westlichen Ostseegebiet.* Hamburg, 1957.

KALICZ, N. *Die Péceler (Baden) Kultur und Anatolien.* Budapest, 1963.

OTTO, H., and WITTER, W. *Handbuch der ältesten vorgeschichtlichen Metallurgie in Mitteleuropa.* Leipzig, 1952.

POPESCU, D. *Die frühe und mittlere Bronzezeit in Siebenbürgen.* Bucharest, 1944.

STENBERGER, M. *Sweden.* London, 1963.

TYLECOTE, R. *Metallurgy in Archaeology.* London, 1962.

CHAPTER 7: THE LATE BRONZE AGE

ALTHIN, C.-A. *See* Chapter 6 above.

ARRIBAS, A. *The Iberians.* London, n.d.

BENAC, A., and COVIĆ, B. *Glasinac I–II.* Sarajevo, 1956–7.

BOARDMAN, J. *The Greeks Overseas.* Harmondsworth, 1964.

BRØNDSTED, J. *Nordische Vorzeit,* II (Chapter 6 above).

DESBOROUGH, V. D'A. *The Last Mycenaeans and Their Successors.* Oxford, 1964.

GROSJEAN, R. *La Corse avant l'histoire.* Paris, 1966.

GUIDO, M. *See* Chapter 5 above.

HARDEN, D. *The Phoenicians.* London, 1962.

KOSSACK, G. *Studien zum Symbolgut Urnenfelder- und Hallstattzeit Mitteleuropas.* Berlin, 1954.

KROMER, K. *Das Gräberfeld von Hallstatt.* Florence, 1960.

KROMER, K. *Hallstatt: Prähistorische Kunst.* Vienna, 1963.

LILLIU, G. *I Nuraghi.* Cagliari, 1962.

LILLIU, G., and PESCE, G. *Scultura della Sardegna nuragica.* Cagliari, 1956.

LUCKE, W., and FREY, H. *Die Situla in Providence, Röm-Germ. Forschungen,* XXVI (1962).

MÜLLER-KARPE, H. *Beiträge zur Chronologie der Urnenfelderzeit.* Berlin, 1959.

PALLOTTINO, M. *La Sardegna nuragica.* Rome, 1950.

SPROCKHOFF, E. *Jungbronzezeitliche Hortfunde, Südzone des nordischen Kreises, Period V.* Mainz, 1956.

ZERVOS, C. *La Civilisation de la Sardaigne.* Paris, 1954.

CHAPTER 8: IRON AGE CONTINENTAL

CROSS, T., and SLOVER, C. *Ancient Irish Tales.* U.S.A.–London, 1936.

FILIP, J. *Keltové ve střední Europě.* Prague, 1956.

FILIP, J. *Celtic Civilisation and its Heritage.* Trans. Prague, 1962.

JACOBSTHAL, P. *Early Celtic Art.* Oxford, 1944.
The outstanding work on this subject.

KELLER, J. *Keltische Fürstengrab von Rheinheim.* Mainz, 1965.

KLINDT-JENSEN, O. *Bronzekedelen fra Brå.* Aarhus, 1953.

KLINDT-JENSEN, O. *Foreign Influences in Denmark's Early Iron Age.* Copenhagen, 1950.

LAMBRECHTS, P. *Contributions à l'étude des divinités celtiques.* Bruges, 1942.

LAMBRECHTS, P. *L'Exaltation de la tête dans la pensée et dans l'art des Celtes.* Bruges, 1954.

LANTIER, R., and HUBERT, J. *Les Origines de l'art français.* Paris, 1947.

MINNS, E. *Scythians and Greeks.* Cambridge, 1913.

MINNS, E. 'The Art of the Northern Nomads', *Proc. Brit. Acad.*, XXVIII (1942).

POBÉ, M., and ROUBIER, J. *Kelten-Römer.* Olten–Freiburg im Breisgau, 1958.

POWELL, T. G. E. *The Celts.* London, 1958.

REES, A. and B. *Celtic Heritage.* London, 1961.

TALBOT RICE, T. *The Scythians.* London, 1957.

VARAGNAC, A., and FABRE, G. *L'Art gaulois.* Paris, 1956.

CHAPTER 9: IRON AGE BRITISH ISLES

DE NAVARRO, J. 'The Celts in Britain and their Art', in *The Heritage of Early Britain*, ed. Knowles. London, 1952.

FOX, C. *Pattern and Purpose.* Cardiff, 1958.
The outstanding work on British La Tène.

HENRY, F. *L'Art irlandais*, I–III, especially I. La Pierre-qui-vire, 1963.
Takes the place of the same writer's *Irish Art*, London, 1940.

JACKSON, K. *The Oldest Irish Tradition.* Cambridge, 1964.

POWELL, T. G. E. *See* Chapter 8 above.

ROSS, A. *Pagan Celtic Britain.* London, 1967.
Appeared too late for inclusion.

TOYNBEE, J. *Art in Britain under the Romans.* Oxford, 1964.

VARAGNAC, A., and FABRE, G. *See* Chapter 8, especially Fabre on coinage.

THE PLATES

1. Solutrian 'laurel leaf'. Flint.
Paris, Musée de l'Homme

2. (left) Man from Brno, Czechoslovakia. Gravettian. Ivory. *Brno, Moravian Museum*
3. (above) Woman from Willendorf, Lower Austria. Gravettian. Limestone. *Vienna, Naturhistorisches Museum*

4. Animals from the Vogelherd cave, Württemberg, Germany. Gravettian. Bone and ivory. *Tübingen, Institut für Vor- und Frühgeschichte*

5. Woman's torso from Ostrava Petřkovice, Czechoslovakia. Gravettian, *c*. 25,000. Haematite. *Brno, Academy of Sciences, Archaeological Institute*

6. (left) Woman's head from Dolní Věstonice, Czechoslovakia. Gravettian, *c.* 23,000. Ivory. *Brno, Moravian Museum*
7. (above) Bear from Dolní Věstonice, Czechoslovakia. Gravettian, *c.* 23,000. Baked clay. *Brno, Moravian Museum*

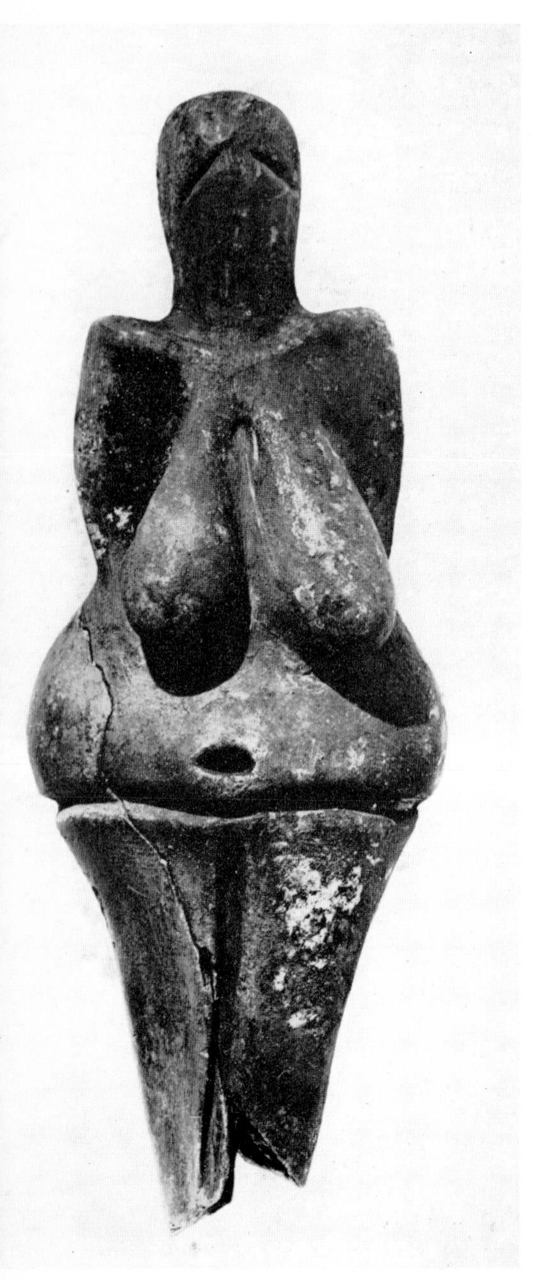

8. (above left) Woman from Dolní Věstonice, Czechoslovakia. Gravettian, *c.* 23,000. Baked clay. *Brno, Moravian Museum*

9. (above right) Breasts from Dolní Věstonice, Czechoslovakia. Gravettian, *c.* 23,000. Ivory. *Brno, Moravian Museum*

10. (right) Woman's head from Grotte du Pape, Brassempouy, Landes, France. Gravettian, *c.* 22,000(?). Ivory. *Saint Germain-en-Laye, Musée des Antiquités Nationales*

11. Woman's torso from Sireuil, Dordogne, France. Gravettian. Calcite. *Saint Germain-en-Laye, Musée des Antiquités Nationales*

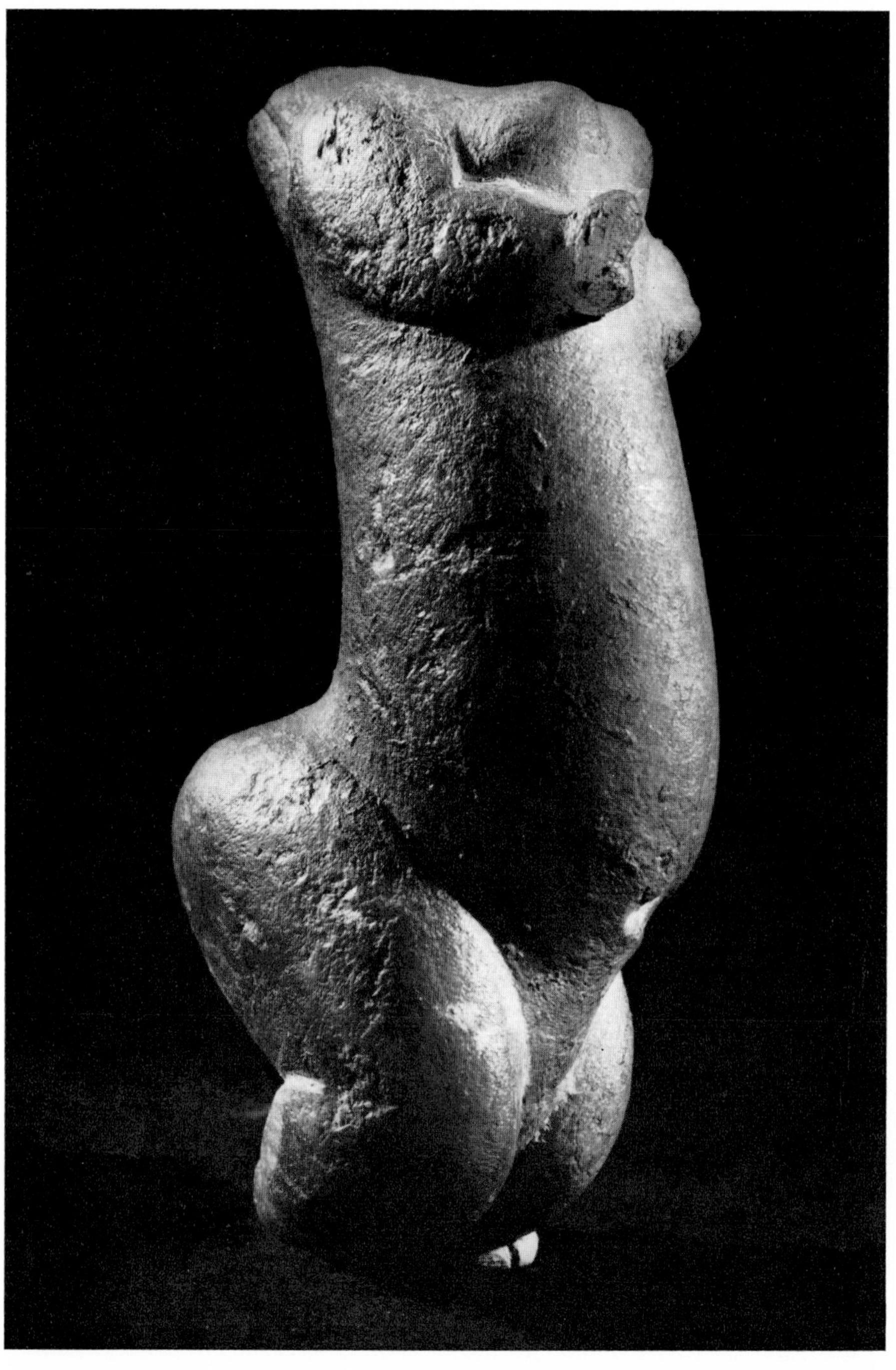

12. (left) Woman's torso from Savignano, Italy. Gravettian. Serpentine. *Rome, Museo Pigorini*
13. (right) Woman from Lespugue, Haute-Garonne, France. Final 'Perigordian' or Gravettian (?). Ivory. *Paris, Musée de l'Homme*

14. (top) Engraved vulvae from La Ferrassie, Dordogne, France. Aurignacian. Rock. *Musée des Eyzies*

15. (bottom) Engraved 'macaroni' at Pech-Merle, Dordogne, France. Solutrian (?). Hardened mud

16. (top) Bison engraved in the cave of La Grèze, Dordogne, France. Gravettian
17. (bottom) Horses engraved in the cave of Pair-non-Pair, Gironde, France. Proto-Magdalenian(?)

18. (left) Relief of a man from Laussel, Dordogne, France. Gravettian, *c.* 19,000(?). Stone. *Bordeaux, Charon Collection*
19. (above) Relief of a woman from Laussel, Dordogne, France. Gravettian, *c.* 19,000(?). Stone. *Paris, Musée de l'Homme*

20. (above) Bison at Tuc d'Audoubert, Ariège, France. Magdalenian, after 15,000. Modelled clay

21. (top right) Relief of cows at Fourneau du Diable, Charente, France. Solutrian(?)

22. (bottom right) Relief of ibexes at Roc de Sers, Charente, France. Solutrian(?)

B

23. (below) Ivory tusk with female figure from Předmostí, Czechoslovakia. Gravettian. *Brno, Moravian Museum*

24. (middle right) Spear-thrower carved with a fawn or young ibex from Mas d'Azil, Ariège, France. Magdalenian III or IV. Bone. *Saint Brieuc, Péquart Collection*

25. (far right) Spear-thrower carved with an ibex from Mas d'Azil, Ariège, France. Magdalenian III or IV. Bone. *Saint Germain-en-Laye, Musée des Antiquités Nationales*

26. (bottom right) Bison from Mas d'Azil, Ariège, France. Magdalenian. Bone. *Saint Germain-en-Laye, Musée des Antiquités Nationales*

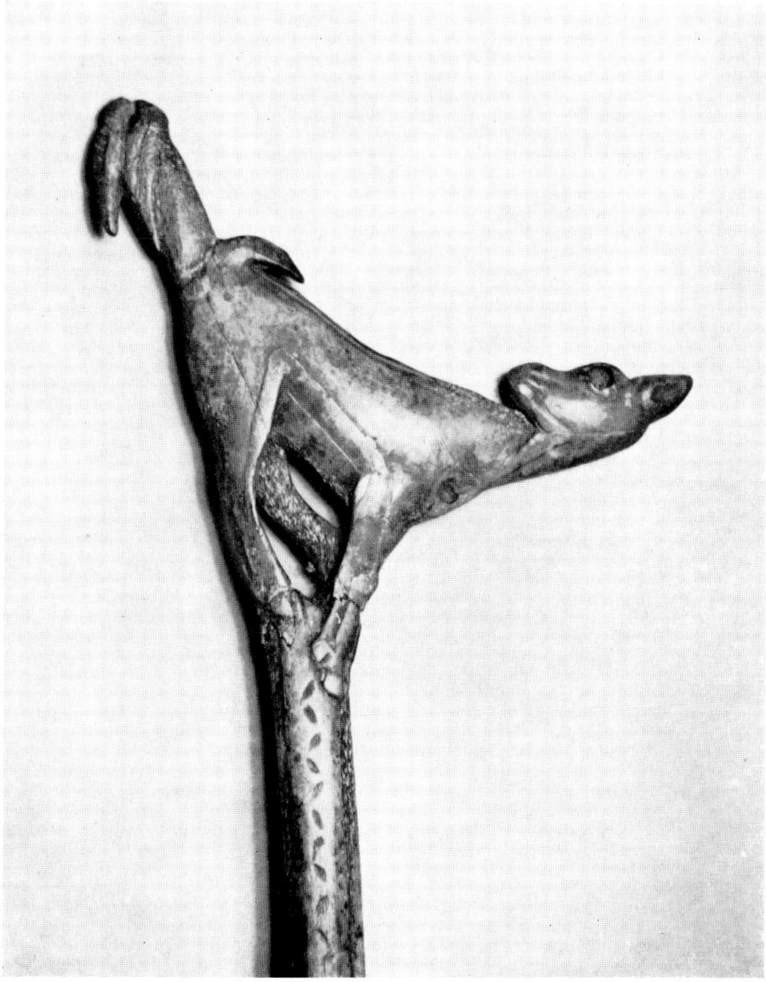

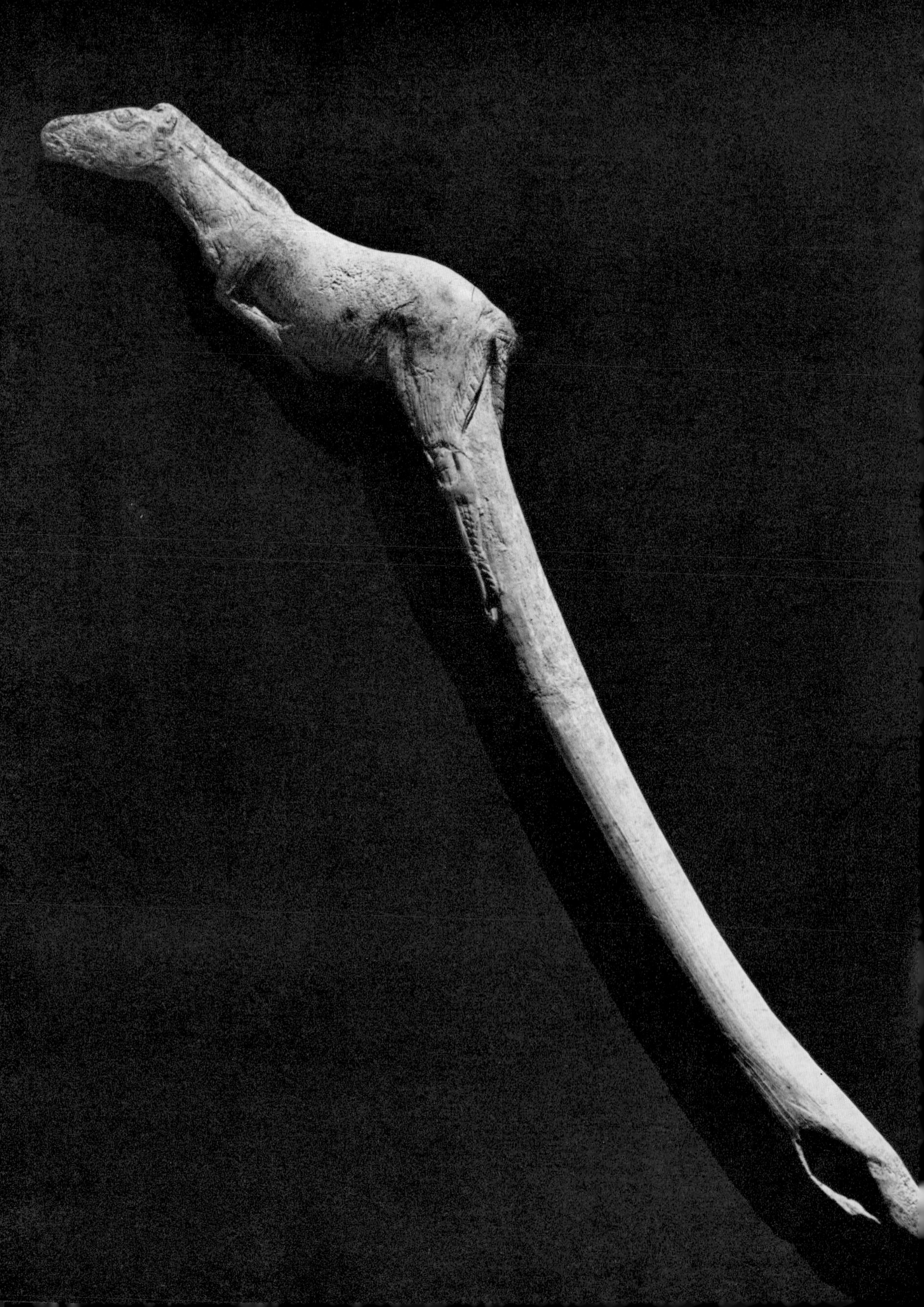

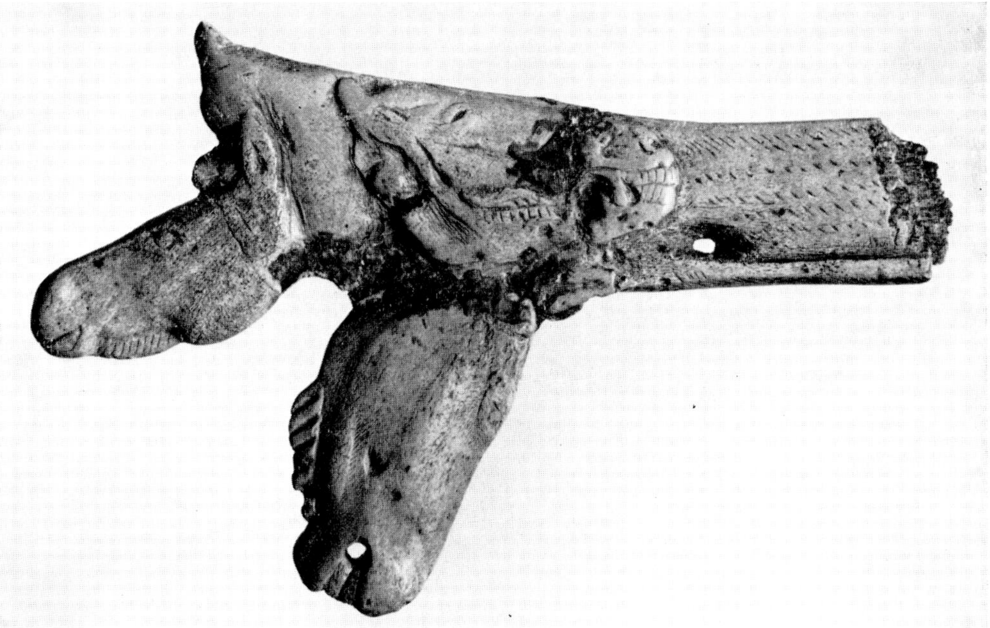

27. (left) Spear-thrower carved with a horse from Montastruc, Tarn-et-Garonne, France. Magdalenian III or IV. Bone. *Montauban, Bétirac Collection*

28. (top right) Engraved silhouettes at La Roche, Dordogne, France. Magdalenian(?). *Musée des Eyzies*

29. (bottom right) Spear-thrower carved with three horse-heads from Mas d'Azil, Ariège, France. Magdalenian. Bone. *Saint Germain-en-Laye, Musée des Antiquités Nationales*

30. (top left) Relief of reclining woman at La Magdeleine, Tarn, France. Magdalenian III–IV(?)
31. (bottom left) Relief of reclining woman at La Magdeleine, Tarn, France. Magdalenian III–IV(?)
32. (above) Relief of horse at Cap Blanc, Dordogne, France. Magdalenian III–IV
33. (below) Relief of three women at the Roc aux Sorciers, Angles-sur-l'Anglin, Vienne, France. Magdalenian III, *c.* 12,000.

34. (top left) Horse from Schweizersbild, Switzerland. Magdalenian. Engraved bone. *Zürich, Schweizerisches Landesmuseum*

35. (bottom left) Horse's head engraved at Lascaux, Dordogne, France. Magdalenian

36. (top right) Painted outline of horse and deer at Niaux, Ariège, France. Magdalenian

37. (bottom right) Painted outline of a stallion at Niaux, Ariège, France. Magdalenian

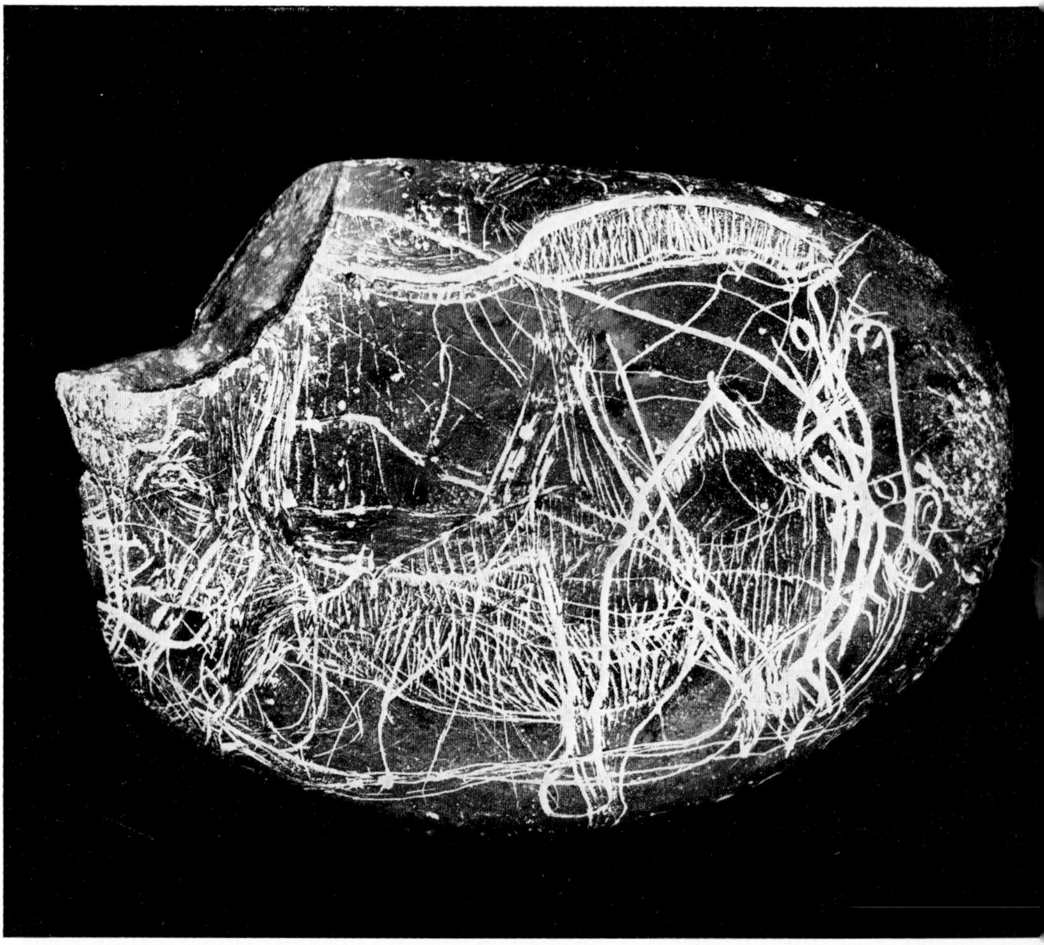

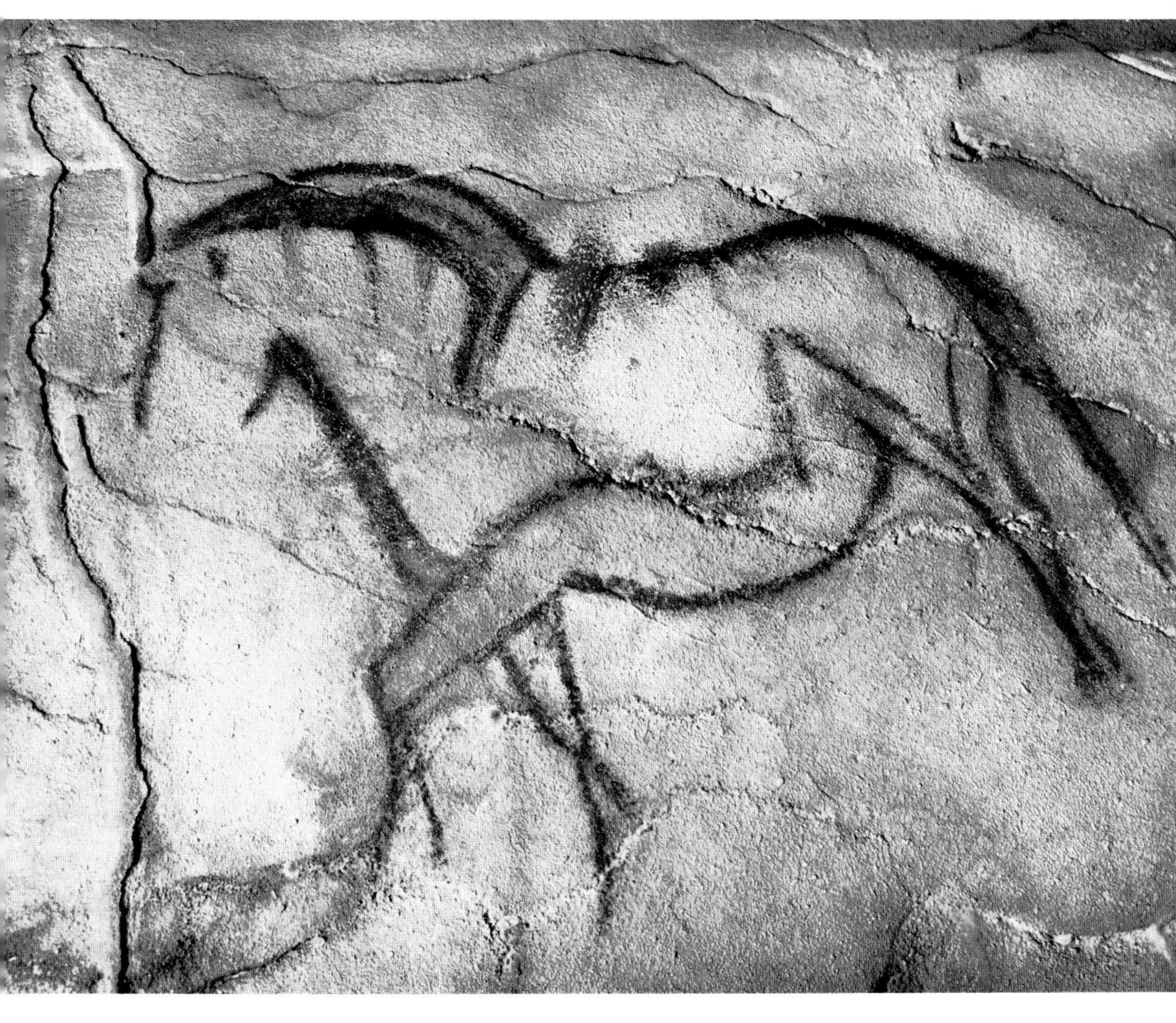

38. (top left) Pebble engraved with animals from La Colombière, Ain, France. Magdalenian or late Gravettian(?). *Cambridge (Mass.), Harvard University, Peabody Museum*
39. (bottom left) Bone engraved with deer and salmon from Lortet, Hautes-Pyrénées, France (development). Magdalenian. *Saint Germain-en-Laye, Musée des Antiquités Nationales*
40. (above) Painted horse on rock at Le Portel, Ariège, France. Magdalenian III–IV

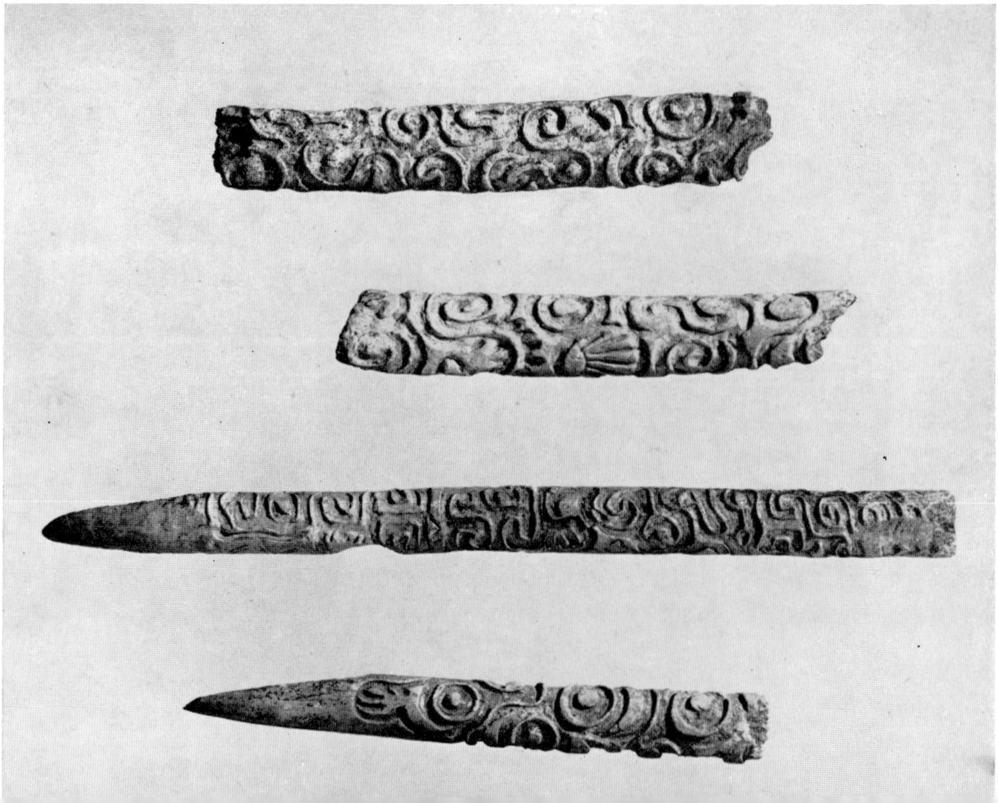

41. (top left) Painted signs at El Castillo, Santander, Spain. Magdalenian
42. (bottom left) Carved bones from Isturitz and Lespugue, Basses-Pyrénées, France. Magdalenian. *Morigny, Saint-Périer Collection*
43. (top right) Dagger carved with a horse from Pekarna, Czechoslovakia. Magdalenian. *Brno, Moravian Museum*
44. (bottom right) Large black cow and horses at Lascaux, Dordogne, France. Early Magdalenian I–II

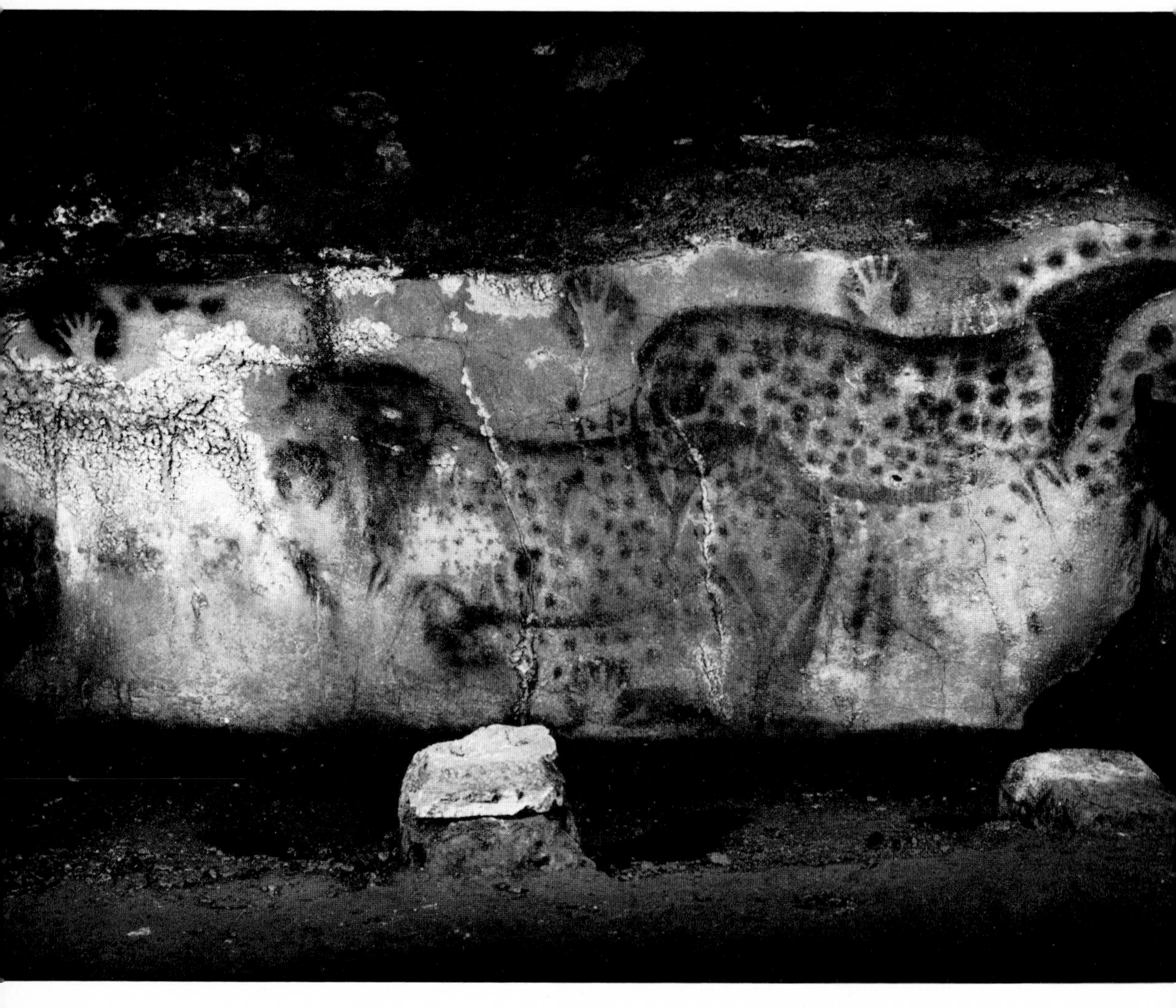

45. (above) Painted 'circus horses' at Pech-Merle, Dordogne, France. Magdalenian
46. (top right) Painted bison at Marsoulas, Haute-Garonne, France. Magdalenian
47. (bottom right) Painted bull's head at Lascaux, Dordogne, France. Early Magdalenian

48. (top left) Painted deer at Covalanas, Santander, Spain. Magdalenian
49. (bottom left) Painted bison at Marcenac, Lot, France. Magdalenian
50. (above) Two painted bison, back to back, at Lascaux, Dordogne, France. Early Magdalenian

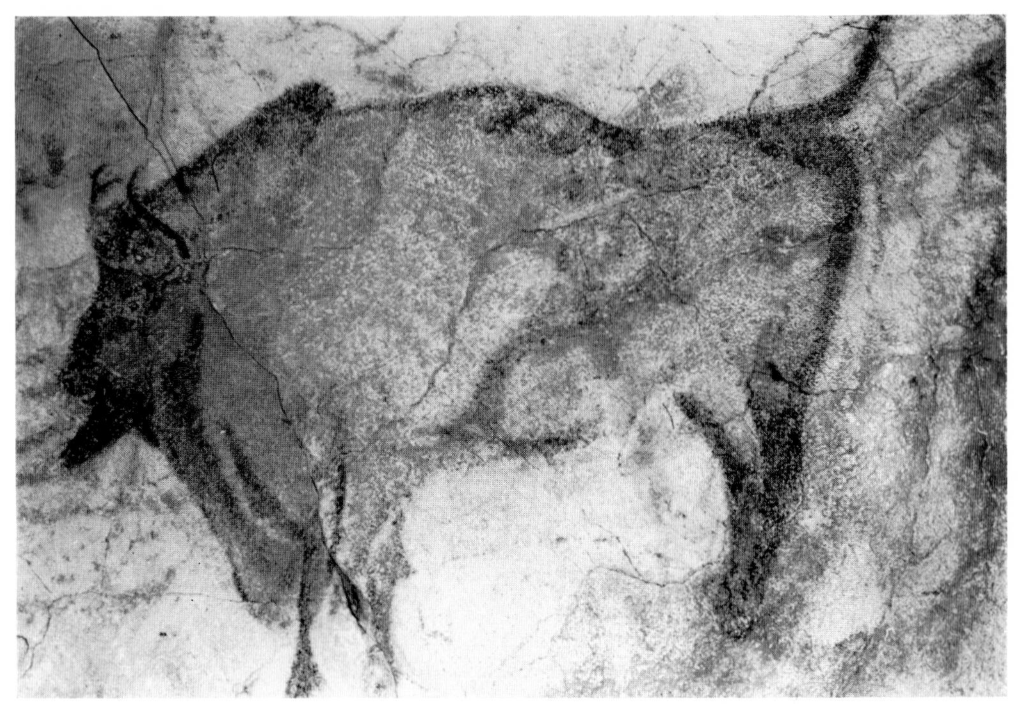

51. (top left) Painted bison at Altamira, Santander, Spain. Magdalenian
52. (bottom left) Bone engraved with cows from Mas d'Azil, Ariège, France. Magdalenian. *Saint Germain-en-Laye, Musée des Antiquités Nationales*
53. (right) Three painted cows and a horse at Lascaux, Dordogne, France. Early Magdalenian

54. (above) Painted 'leaping' cow and small horses at Lascaux. Early Magdalenian

55. (below) 'Hall of Bulls' at Lascaux. Early Magdalenian

56. (left) General view of ceiling of axial gallery at Lascaux. Early Magdalenian
57. (top right) Painted bison at Niaux, Ariège, France. Magdalenian
58. (bottom right) Engraved horses behind a large cow at Lascaux. Early Magdalenian

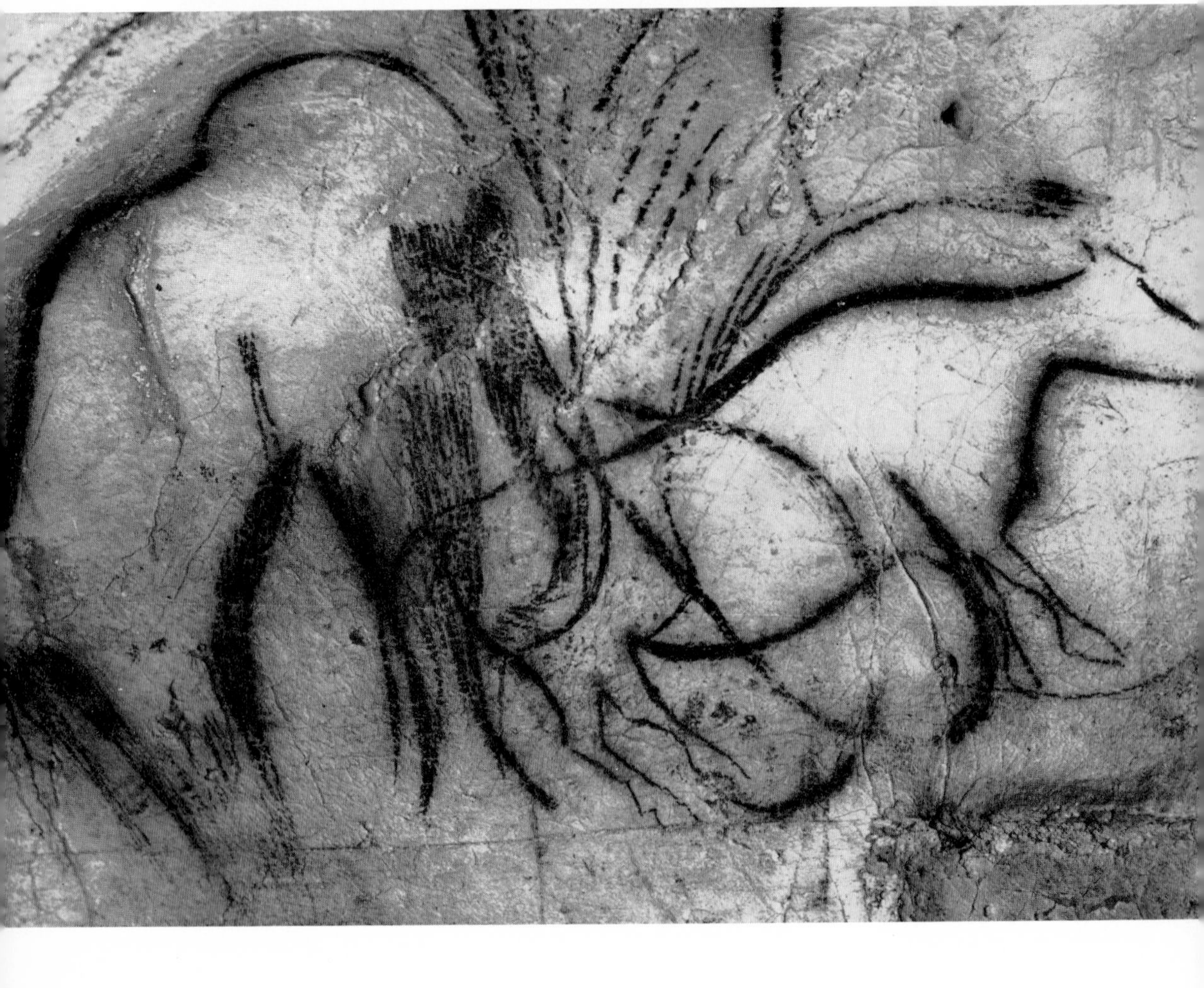

59. (top left) Painted deer at Altamira, Santander, Spain. Magdalenian
60. (bottom left) Mammoth, cow, and unfinished outlines at Pech-Merle, Dordogne, France. Magdalenian
61. (below) Horse and unfinished outlines at Pech-Merle, Dordogne, France. Magdalenian

62. (below) Bison stalagmite at El Castillo, Santander, Spain. Magdalenian
63. (top right) Engraved bison with natural hollows at Niaux, Ariège, France. Magdalenian
64. (bottom right) Stags' heads at Lascaux, Dordogne, France. Magdalenian

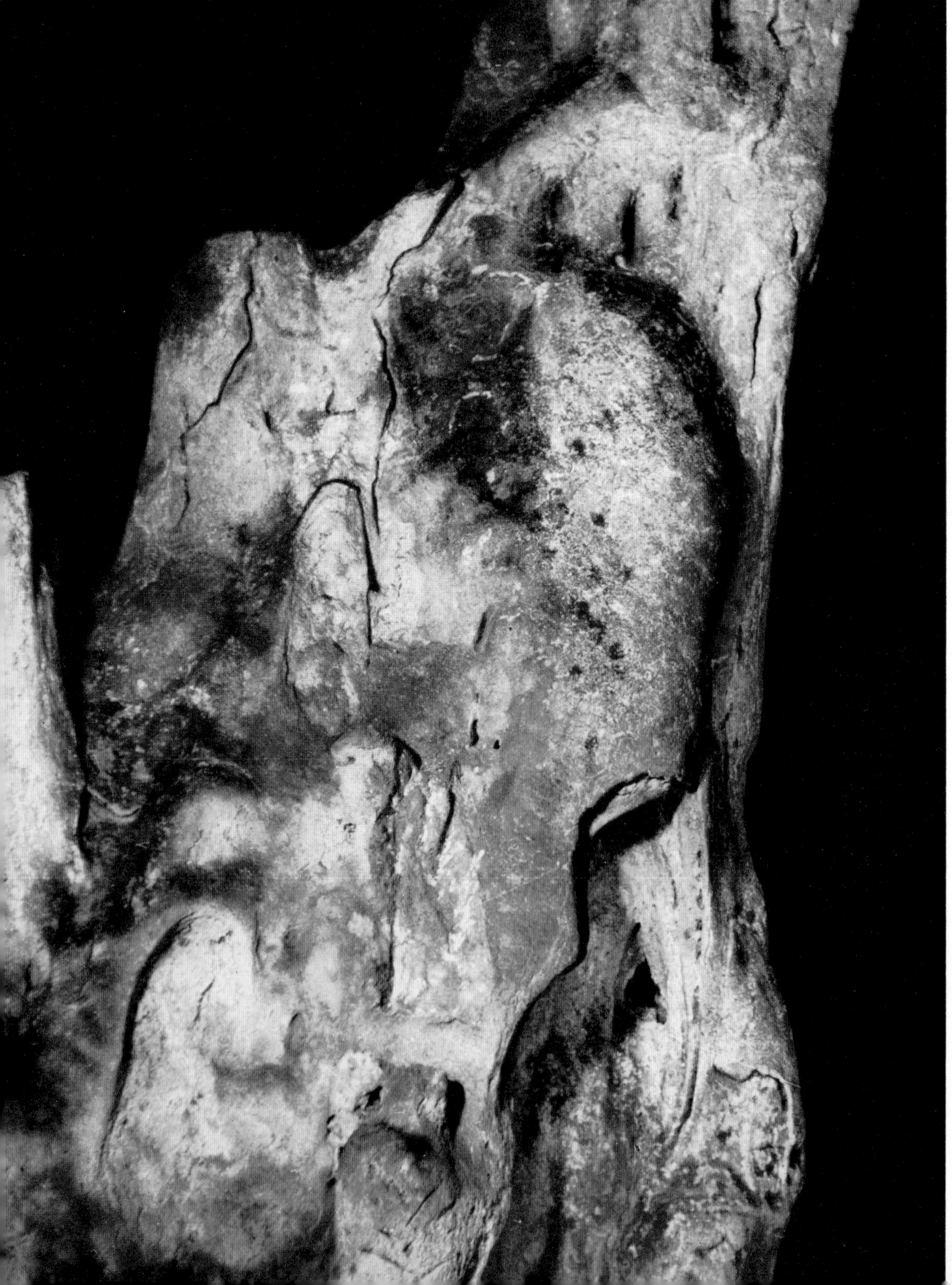

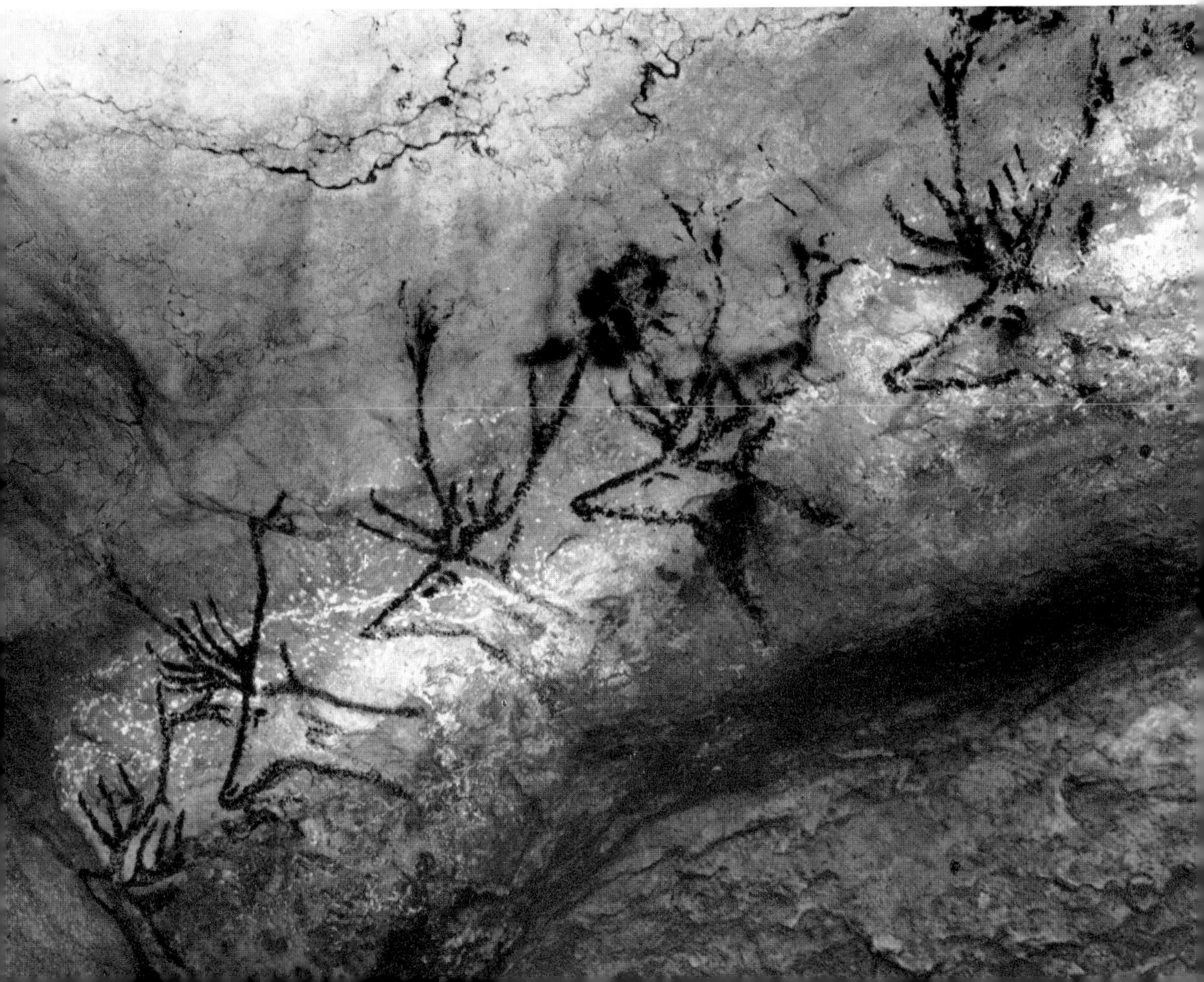

65. (top) Engraved bone with chamois heads from Gourdan, Haute-Garonne, France. Magdalenian. *Saint Germain-en-Laye, Musée des Antiquités Nationales*
66. (bottom) Engraved bone with wolves from La Vache, Ariège, France. Magdalenian. *Tarascon, Robert Collection*

67. (top) Engraved bone with bison from Pekarna, Czechoslovakia. Magdalenian. *Brno, Moravian Museum*

68. (bottom) Engraved bone with scene from Les Eyzies, Dordogne, France. Magdalenian. *Musée des Eyzies*

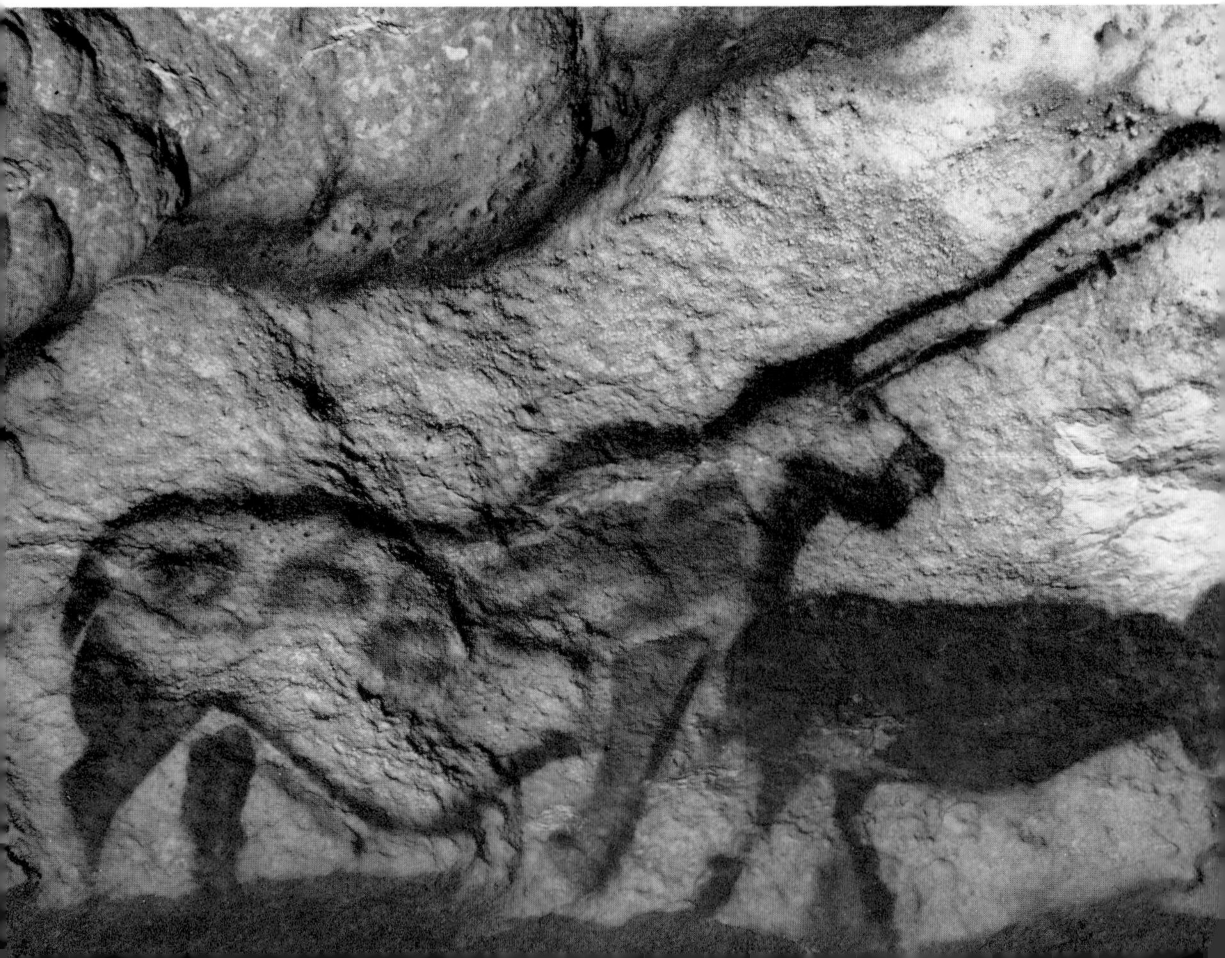

69. (top left) The 'dead man' at Lascaux, Dordogne, France. Early Magdalenian
70. (bottom left) 'Monster' with long horns at Lascaux, Dordogne, France. Early Magdalenian
71. (top right) Engraved bone with man and (?) woman from La Colombière, Ain, France. Magdalenian or late Gravettian
72. (bottom right) Engraved stone with human (?) figures and bear from Péchialet, Dordogne, France. Magdalenian. *Saint Germain-en-Laye, Musée des Antiquités Nationales*

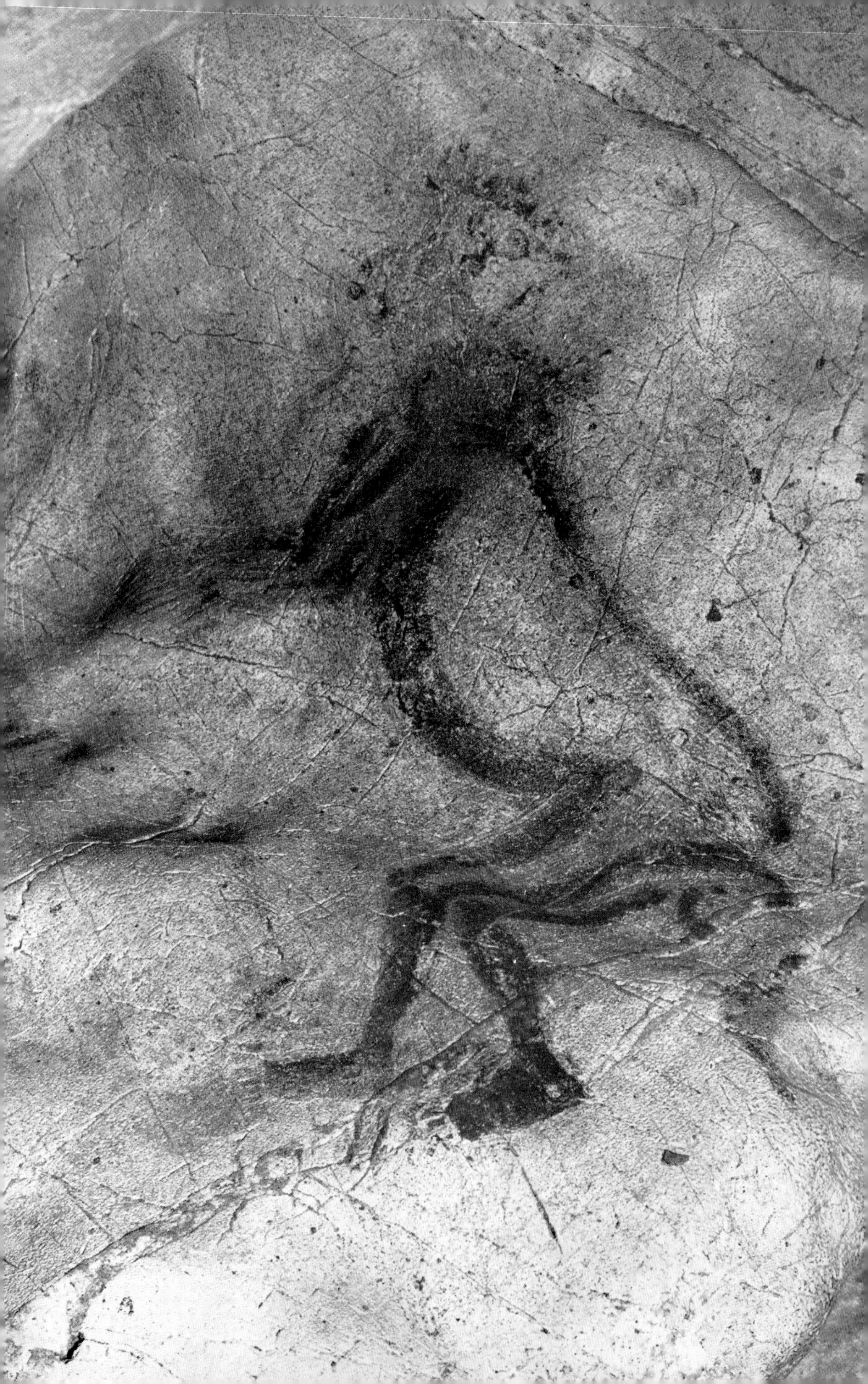

73. (left) Painted 'sorcerer' at Trois Frères, Ariège, France. Magdalenian
74. (above) Engraved bison and bison-man at Trois Frères, Ariège, France. Magdalenian

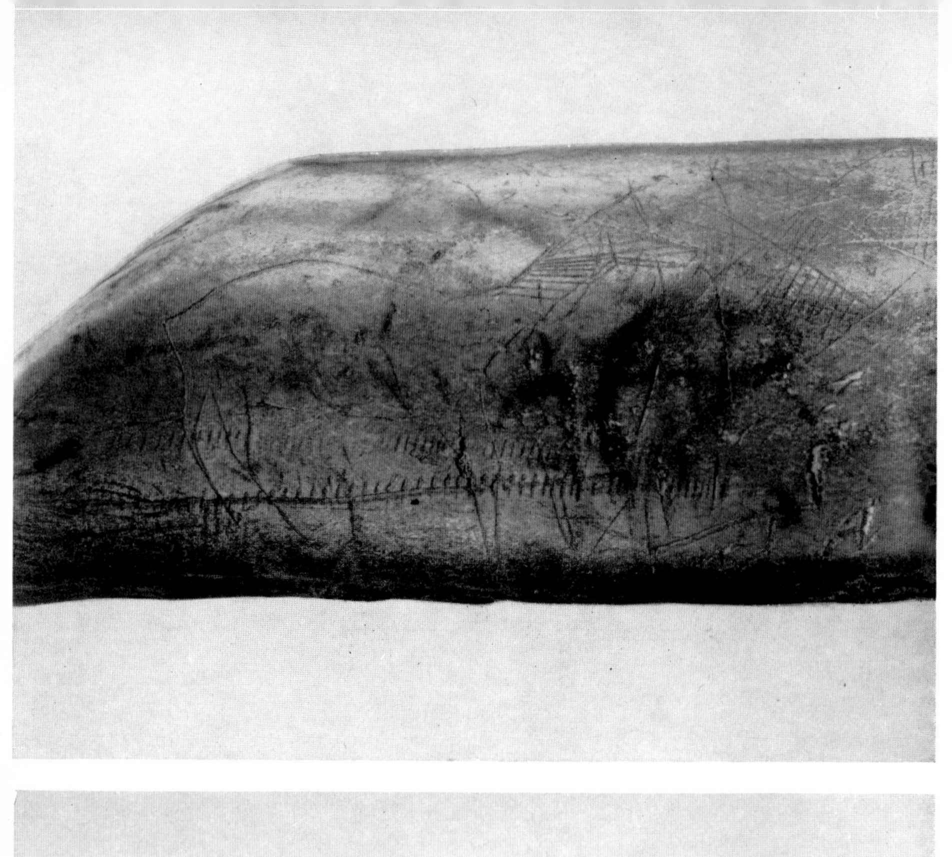

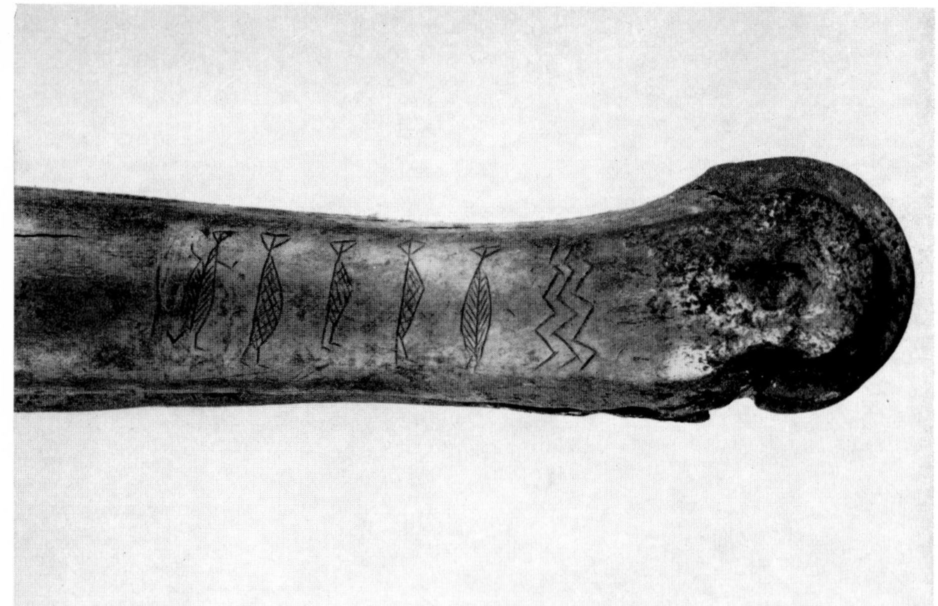

75. (top left) Engraved antler haft with two deer from Ystad, Skåne, Sweden. Maglemosian. *Stockholm, Museum of National Antiquities*
76. (middle left) Engraved aurochs bone club from Rymarksgård, Zeeland, Denmark. Maglemosian. *Copenhagen, National Museum*
77. (bottom left) Spearhead from Bjernede, Sorø, Holbaek, Denmark. Maglemosian. Bone. *Copenhagen, National Museum*
78. (above) Carved animals from Resen and Egesvang, Viborg; and Egemarke, Holbaek, Denmark. Maglemosian (?). Amber. *Copenhagen, National Museum*

79. (top left) Elk and bear (?) engraved on rock at Landsverk, Jämtland, Sweden
80. (bottom left) Elk engraved on rock at Adalsliden, Nämforsen, Ångermanland, Sweden. Style B
81. (above) Engraved rock with three men on skis at Zalavruga, White Sea, Russia

82. (top left) Man walking to the left, detail of Addaura engravings (cf. Plate 84)

83. (bottom left) Deer and woman with a sack, detail of Addaura engravings (cf. Plate 84)

84. (right) Engraved rock with figures at Addaura, Sicily. *c.* 8000

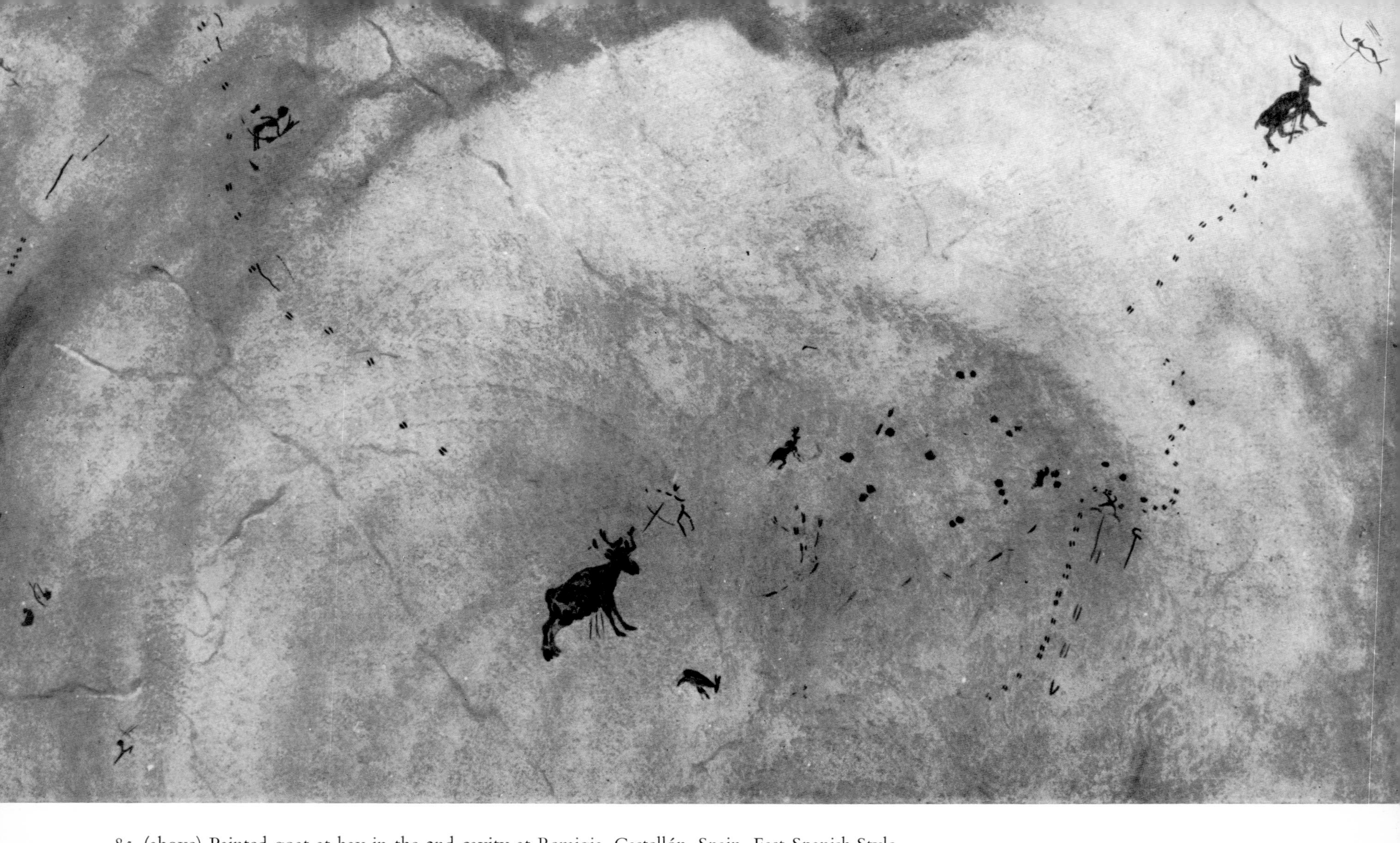

85. (above) Painted goat at bay in the 2nd cavity at Remigia, Castellón, Spain. East Spanish Style

86. (below) Painted galloping goat and bowman in the 4th cavity at Remigia, Castellón, Spain. East Spanish Style

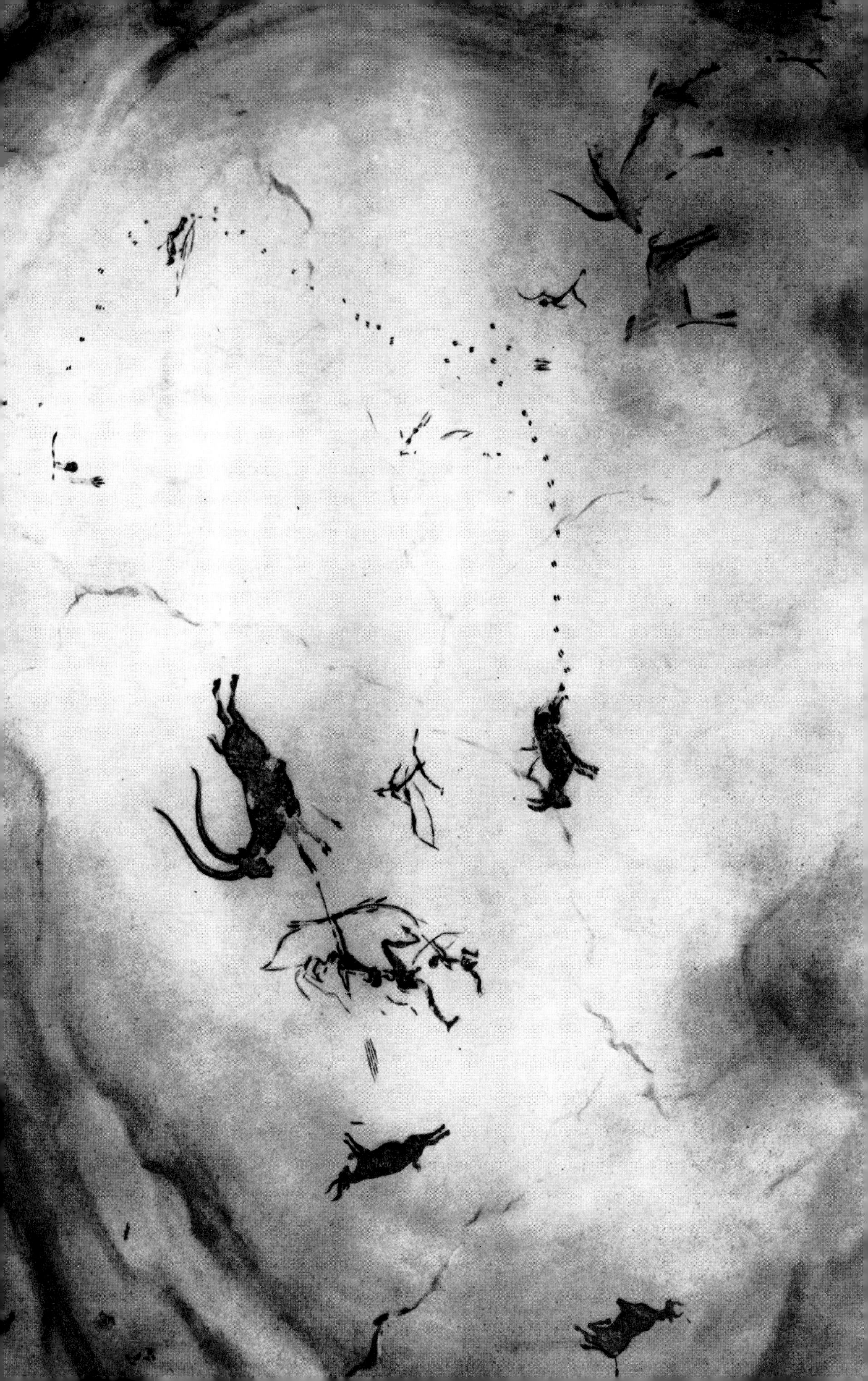

87. Painted battle scene at Civil, Valltorta, Castellón, Spain. East Spanish Style

88. (top left) Painted running spearman at Garroso, Alacón, Spain. East Spanish Style

89. (bottom left) 'Execution group' in the 5th cavity at Remigia, Castellón, Spain. East Spanish Style

90. (right) Head from Starčevo, Serbia, Yugoslavia. Starčevo culture, fifth millennium. Clay. *Belgrade, National Museum*

91. (top) Head in pointed cap from Vinča, Serbia, Yugoslavia. Vinča-Tordos, fifth-fourth millennium. Clay. *Belgrade, National Museum*

92. (bottom) Head from Vinča, Serbia, Yugoslavia. Tordos/Pločnik, fourth millennium. Clay. *Belgrade, National Museum*

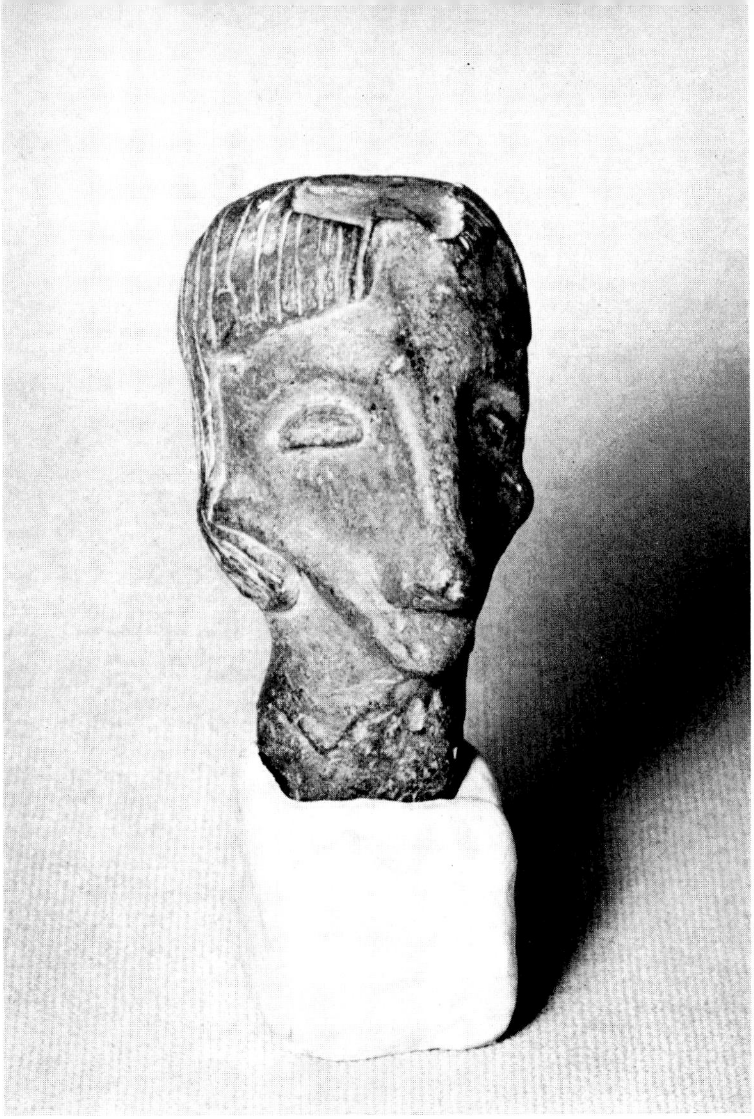

93. (top) Woman's head from Predionica, Serbia, Yugoslavia. Vinča-Pločnik, fourth-third millennium. Clay. *Kosova-Metohije*

94. (bottom) Head from Predionica, Serbia, Yugoslavia. Vinča-Pločnik. Clay. *Kosova-Metohije*

95. Large stylized head from Predionica, Serbia, Yugoslavia. Vinča-Pločnik. Clay. *Kosova-Metohije*

96. Large stylized head with chignon from Predionica, Serbia, Yugoslavia. Vinča-Pločnik. Clay. *Kosova-Metohije*

E

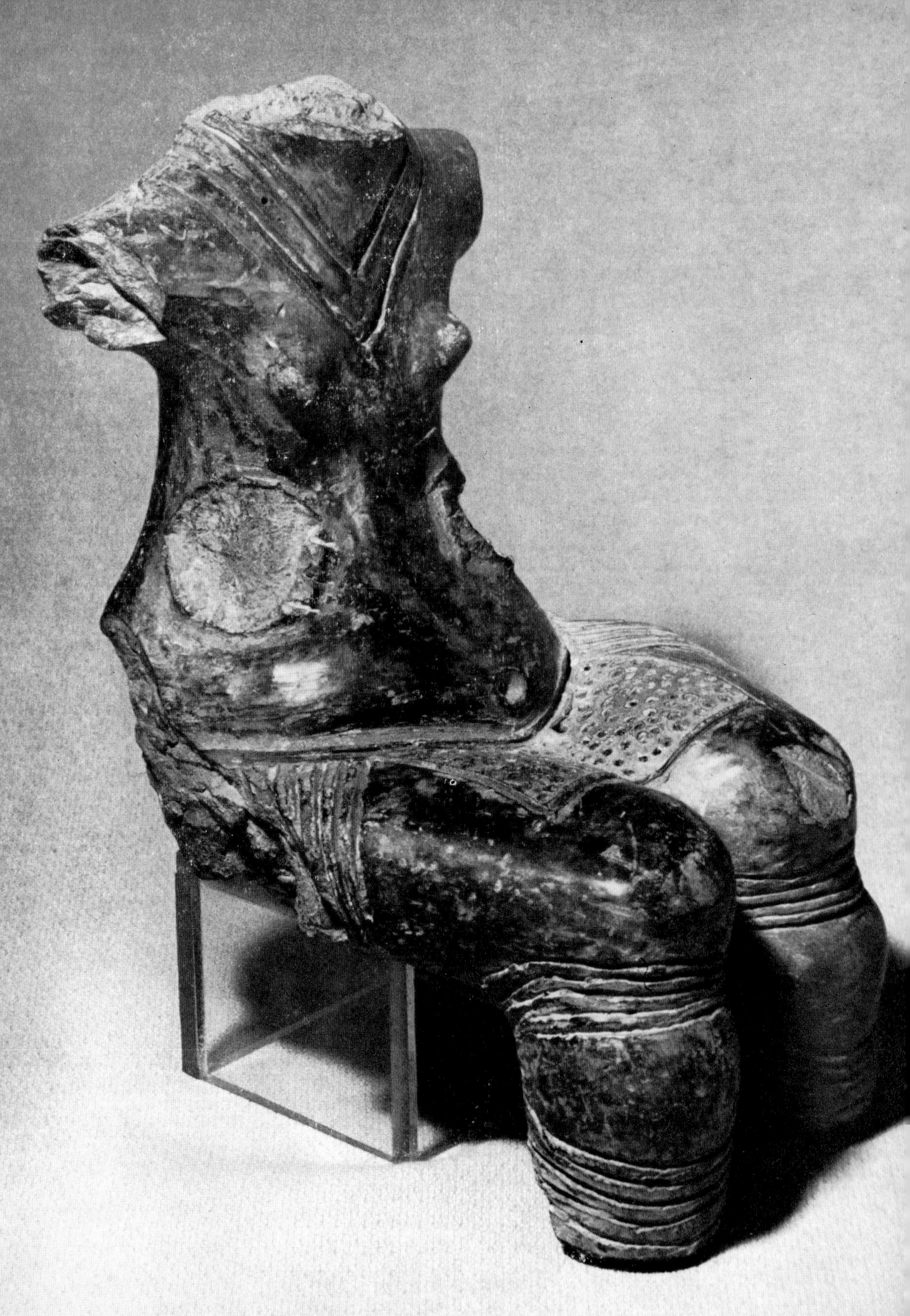

97. (left) Seated woman from Čaršija, Serbia, Yugoslavia. Vinča-Pločnik. Clay. *Belgrade, National Museum*

98. (top right) Squatting figure from Vinča, Serbia, Yugoslavia. Vinča-Tordos (?). Clay. *Belgrade University, Faculty of Archaeology*

99. (bottom right) Seated figure from Predionica, Serbia, Yugoslavia. Vinča-Pločnik. Clay. *Kosova-Metohije*

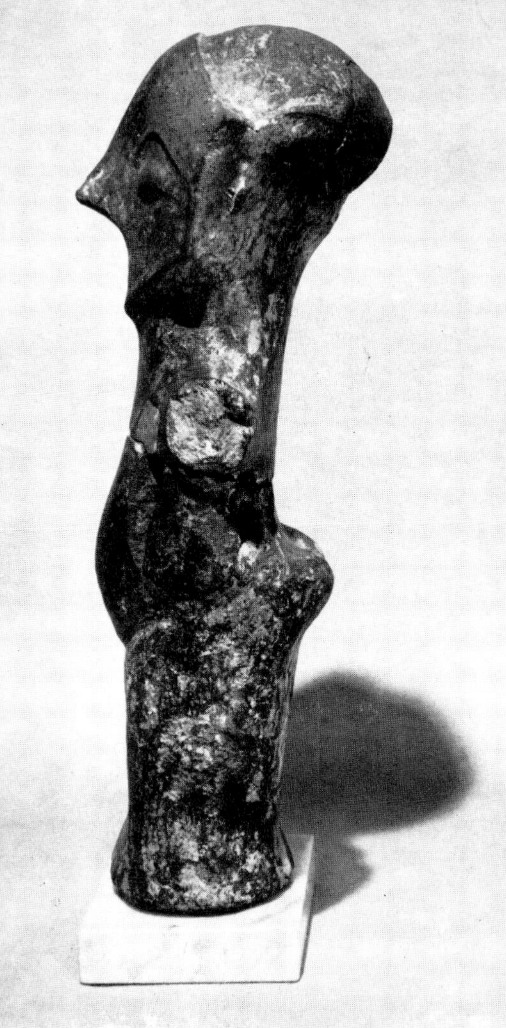

100. (left) Fragmentary figure from Gradac, Serbia, Yugoslavia. Vinča-Pločnik. Clay. *Belgrade, National Museum*

101. (above) Side and front view of 'Vidovdanka' from Vinča, Serbia, Yugoslavia. Vinča-Pločnik. Clay. *Belgrade University, Faculty of Archaeology*

102. (right) Standing figure from Vinča. Vinča-Tordos (?). Clay. *Belgrade University, Faculty of Archaeology*

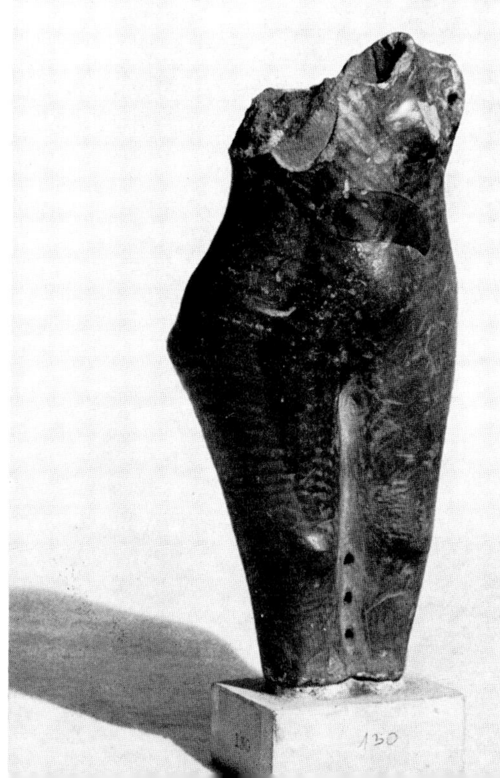

103. Standing figure, as a pot, from Vinča. Vinča-Pločnik. Clay. *Belgrade, National Museum*

104. 'Crusted' torso from Vinča. Vinča-Pločnik. Clay. *Belgrade University, Faculty of Archaeology*

105. Head of classic type from Butmir, Bosnia, Yugoslavia. Fourth-third millennium. Clay. *Sarajevo, Archaeological Museum*

106. 'Expressionist' head from Butmir. Fourth–third millennium. Clay. *Sarajevo, Archaeological Museum*

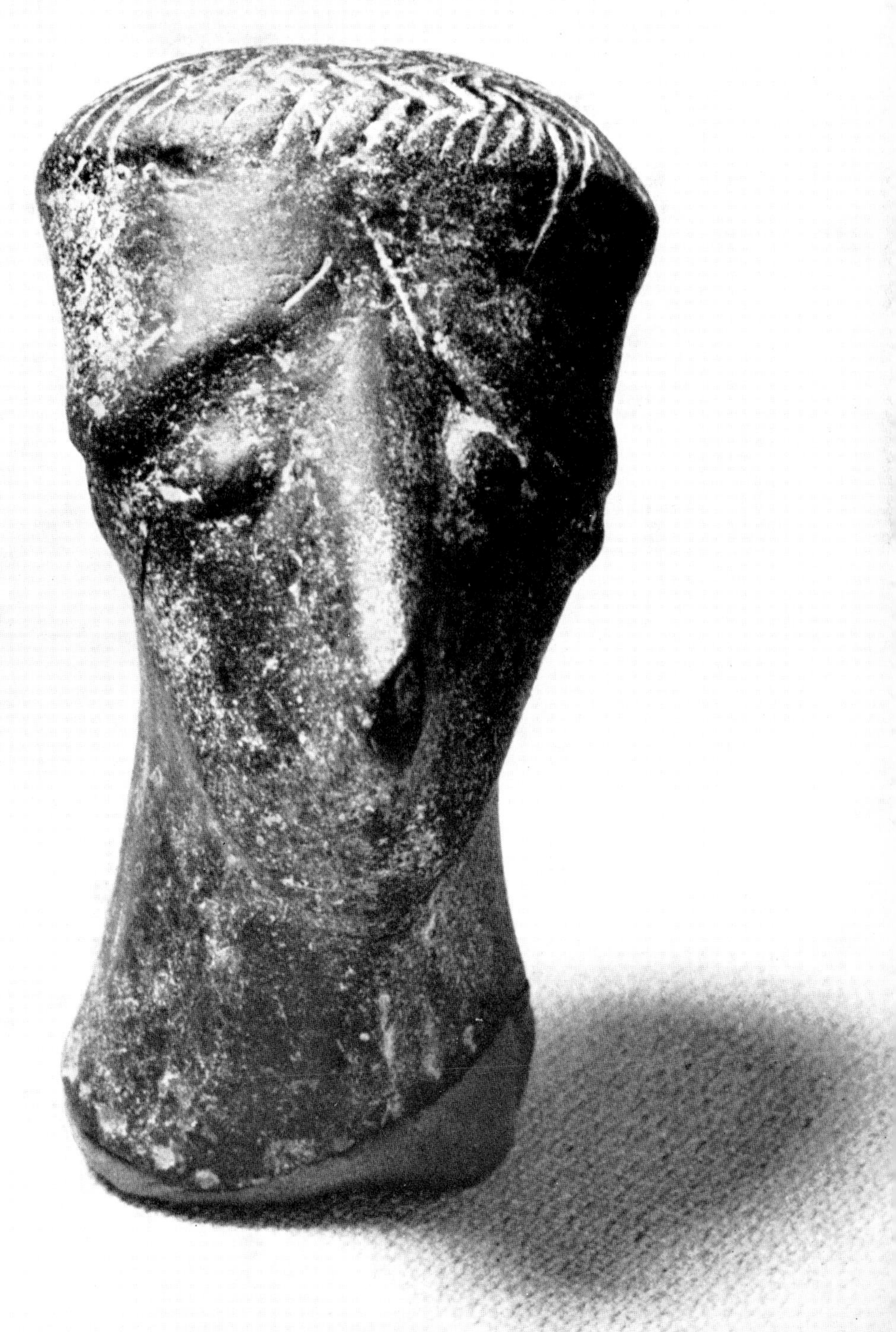

107. (top left) Head with large eye from Butmir. Fourth-third millennium. Clay. *Sarajevo, Archaeological Museum*
108. (middle) Woman from Blagoevo, Bulgaria. Gumelnița, fourth millennium (?). Marble. *Sofia, National Museum*
109. (right) Seated woman with bowl from Bordjos, Serbia, Yugoslavia. Tisza culture, fifth-fourth millennium (?). Clay. *Belgrade, National Museum*

110. Side and front view of seated man from Szegvár-Tüzköves, Hungary. Tisza culture, fifth-fourth millennium. Clay. *Szentes, Czalog Collection*

111. Man (right) and woman from Cernavoda, Dobrogea, Rumania. Hamangia culture, later fourth millennium. Clay. *Bucharest, National Museum of Antiquities, Institute of Archaeology*

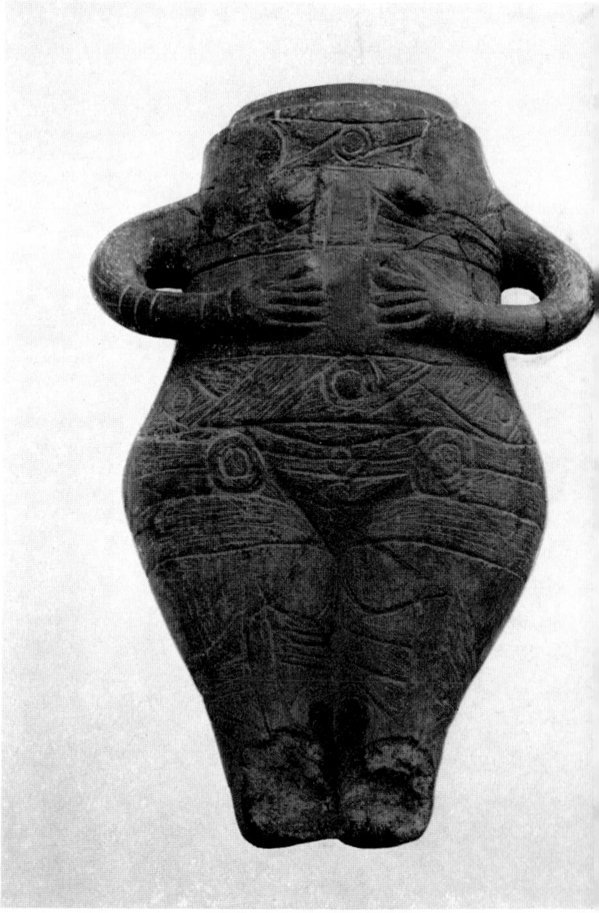

112. (left) Side and front views of standing figure as a pot from Vidra, Rumania. Fourth millennium (?). Clay. *Bucharest, Historical and Town Museum*

113. (below far left) Torso from Boskovštýn, Moravia, Czechoslovakia. Moravian Painted Ware, fourth-third millennium. Clay. *Brno, Moravian Museum*

114. (below left) Head from Jaroměřice, Moravia, Czechoslovakia. Moravian Painted Ware, fourth-third millennium. Clay. *Brno, Moravian Museum*

115. (right) Woman from Hluboké Mašůvky, Moravia, Czechoslovakia. Moravian Painted Ware, fourth-third millennium. Clay. *Brno, Vildomec Collection*

116. (above) Mother and child from Zengövarkony, Hungary. Lengyel, fourth-third millennium. Clay. *Pecs, Janos Pannonius Museum*

117. (middle) Standing incised figure from Cucuteni, Moldavia, Rumania. Cucuteni A, later fourth millennium. Clay. *Bucharest, National Museum of Antiquities, Institute of Archaeology*

118. (right) Bear rhyton from Abrahám, Slovakia, Czechoslovakia. Moravian Painted Ware. Clay. *Pieštany, District Museum*

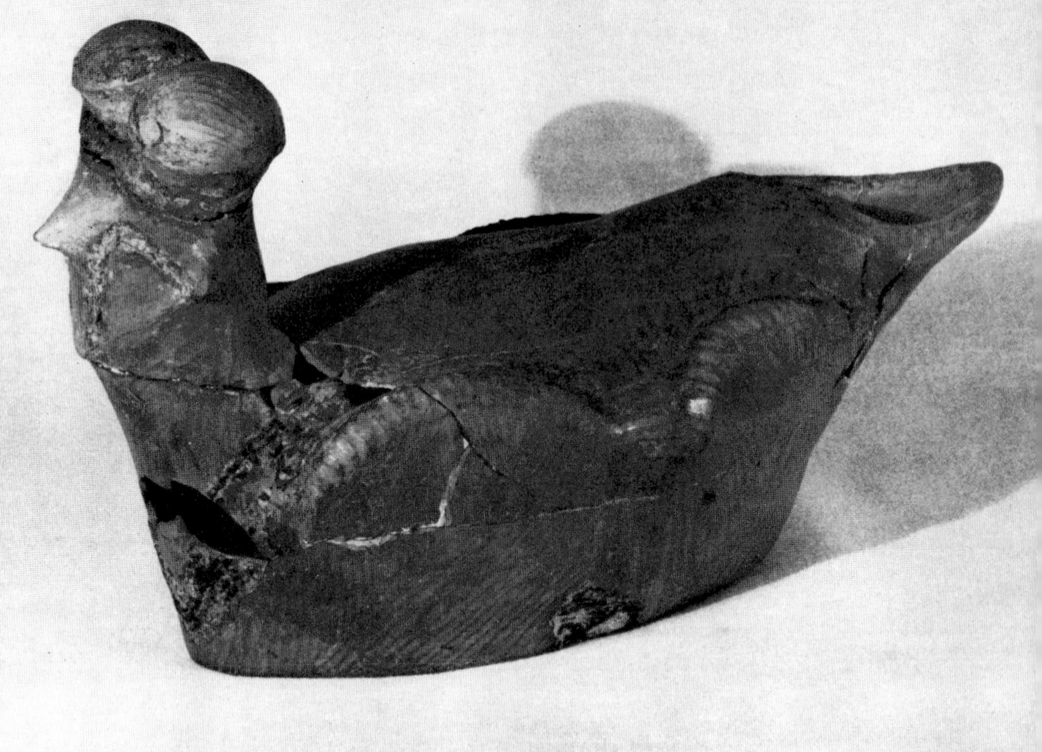

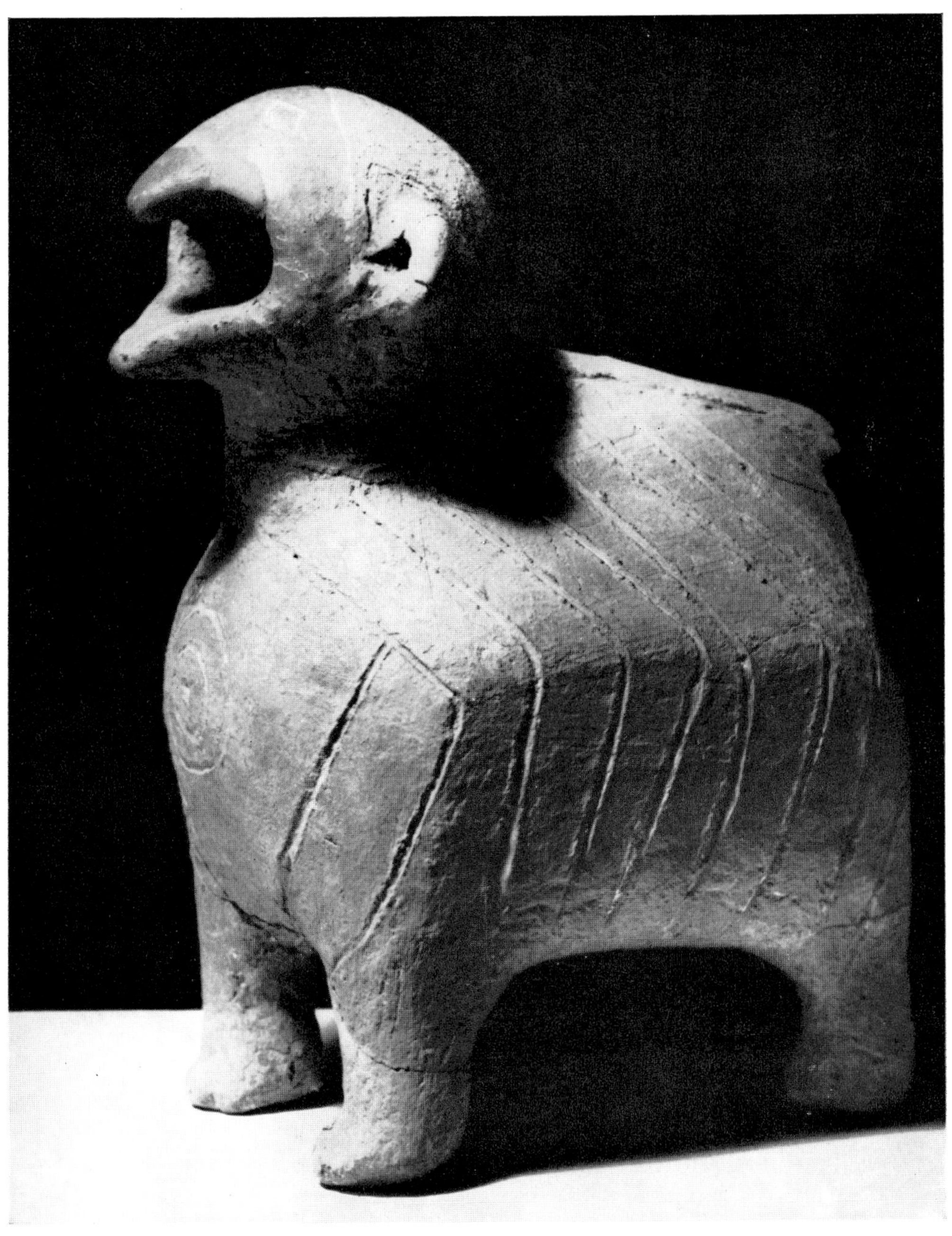

119 (top left) Bird pot from Vinča, Serbia, Yugoslavia. Vinča-Tordos (?). Clay. *Belgrade University, Faculty of Archaeology*

120. (bottom left) 'Altar' with three calves' heads from Vinča, Serbia, Yugoslavia. Vinča-Tordos. Clay, red paint on buff. *Belgrade, National Museum*

121. (above) Animal pot from Kodjaderman, Bulgaria. Gumelnița. Clay. *Sofia, National Museum*

122. (left) Pot from Střelice, Moravia, Czechoslovakia. Moravian Painted Ware. Clay. *Boskovštýn, F. Vildomec Collection*

123. (top right) Anthropomorphic pot from Svodín, Slovakia, Czechoslovakia. Lengyel, fourth-third millennium. Clay. *Prague, National Museum*

124. (bottom right) Animal lid from Vinča, Serbia, Yugoslavia. Vinča-Tordos, fifth-fourth millennium. Clay. *Belgrade, National Museum*

125. (top left) Bowl on foot from Starčevo, Serbia, Yugoslavia. Starčevo culture, fifth millennium (?). Clay. *Belgrade, National Museum*
126. (bottom left) Chalice from Karanovo, Bulgaria. Karanovo II, early fifth millennium. Clay. *Sofia, National Museum*
127. (above) Bowl from Skarpsalling, Denmark. Passage Grave Period, third millennium. Clay. *Copenhagen, National Museum*

128. (top left) Two bowls from near Domäne-Viesenhäuserhof, Stuttgart, Germany. Rössen, fourth millennium. *Stuttgart, Württembergisches Landesmuseum*

129. (bottom left) Two pots from Hluboké Mašůvky, Moravia, Czechoslovakia. Moravian Painted Ware, fourth-third millennium. Clay. *Prague, National Museum, and Boskovštýn, F. Vildomec Collection*

130. (top right) Pot from Butmir, Bosnia, Yugoslavia. Late third millennium. Clay. *Sarajevo, Archaeological Museum*

131. (bottom right) Cucuteni pot, Rumania. Cucuteni A, late fourth millennium. Clay. *Bucharest, National Museum of Antiquities, Institute of Archaeology*

132. (top left) Pot from Traian, Moldavia, Rumania. Cucuteni AB, third millennium. *Bucharest, National Museum of Antiquities, Institute of Archaeology*

133. (bottom left) Pot from Traian, Moldavia, Rumania. Cucuteni A, later fourth millennium. *Bucharest, National Museum of Antiquities, Institute of Archaeology*

134. (top right) Pot from Valea Lupului, Moldavia, Rumania. Cucuteni B, third millennium. *Iaşi, Historical Museum of Moldavia*

135. (middle right) Pot with graphite paint from Karanovo, Bulgaria. Karanovo VI, fourth millennium. Clay. *Sofia, National Museum*

136. (bottom right) Cucuteni pot, Rumania. Cucuteni B, third millennium. Painted clay. *Bucharest, National Museum of Antiquities, Institute of Archaeology*

137. (above) Tarxien temple, Malta. Late third millennium
138. (right) Figure from Hağar Qim, Malta. Late third millennium. Clay. *Malta, Valetta Archaeological Museum*

139. (top left) Impressed pot from Comiso, Sicily. Fifth–fourth millennium. *Syracuse, Museo Nazionale*

140. (middle left) Painted pot from Megara Hyblaea, Sicily. Stentinello, fifth–fourth millennium. *Syracuse, Museo Nazionale*

141. (bottom left) Stentinello pot from Matrensa, Sicily. Fifth–fourth millennium. *Syracuse, Museo Nazionale*

142. (top right) Diana style pots from釋Paternó, Sicily. Late fourth–third millennium. *Syracuse, Museo Nazionale*

143. (bottom right) Serra d'Alto pot handle from Paternó, Sicily. Late fourth millennium. *Syracuse, Museo Nazionale*

144. (top left) Castelluccio painted pot from Monte Tabuto, Sicily. Third–second millennium. *Syracuse, Museo Nazionale*

145. (bottom left) Monochrome red-ware cup from Malpasso, Sicily. Third millennium. *Syracuse, Museo Nazionale*

146. (top right) Woman from Senorbí, Sardinia. Ozieri culture, late third–early second millennium. Marble. *Cagliari, Museo Archeologico Nazionale*

147. (bottom right) Bossed plaques from the Cava della Signora, Castelluccio, Sicily. Third–second millennium. Bone. *Syracuse, Museo Nazionale*

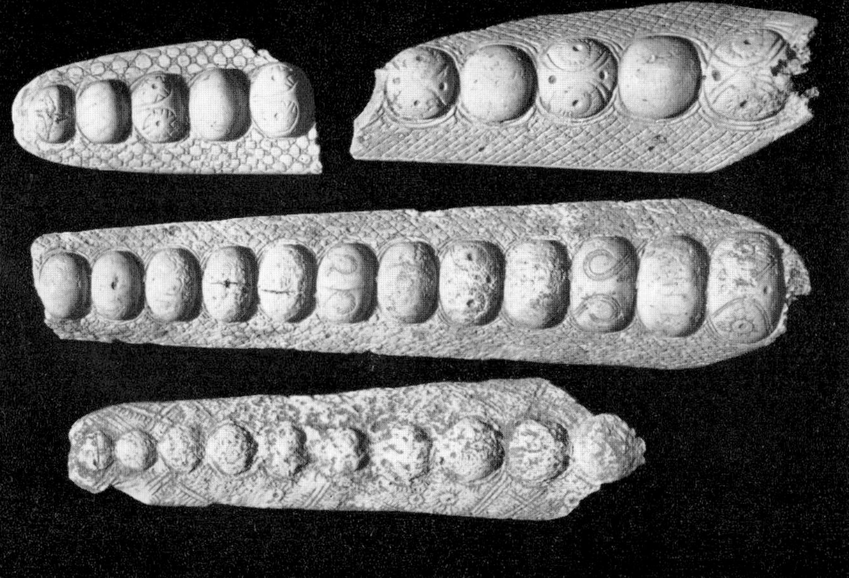

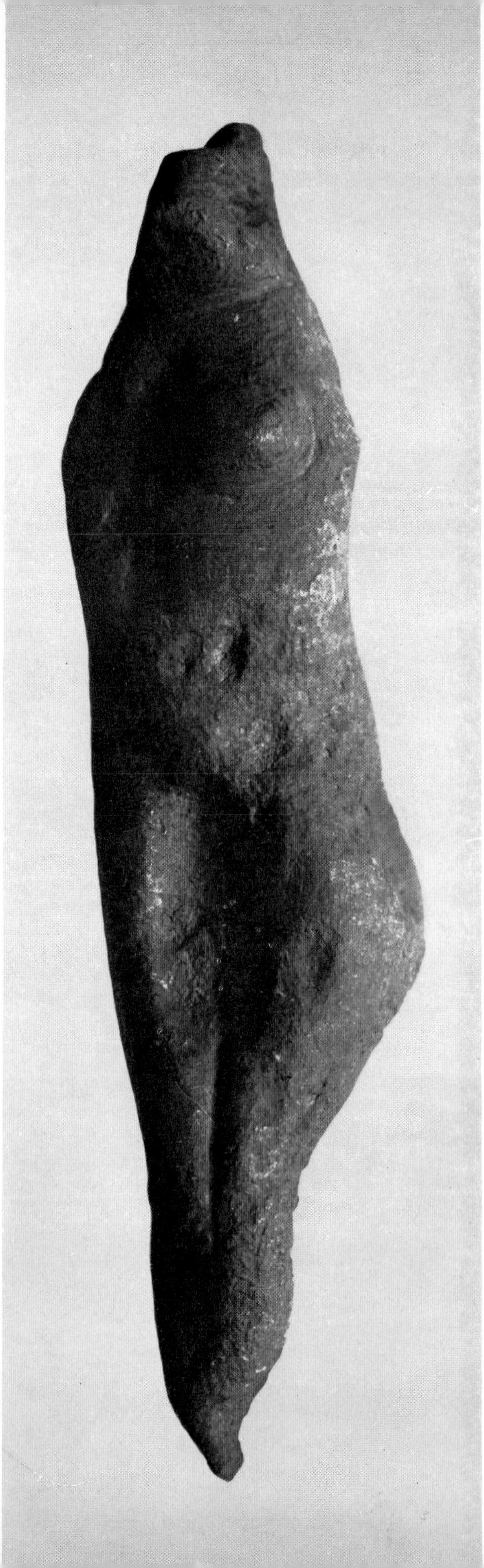

148. (above) Tomb door slab from Castelluccio, Sicily. Third-second millennium. *Syracuse, Museo Nazionale*

149. (middle) Woman from S'Adde, Macomer, Sardinia. Neolithic (?). Basalt. *Cagliari, Museo Archeologico Nazionale*

150. (right) Tomb chamber of passage-grave at Maes Howe, Orkney. *c.* 2000

151. (above) Ball from Glas Towie, North-East Scotland. Late third millennium (?). Stone. *Edinburgh, National Museum of Antiquities*
152. (right) Stone tomb slabs at Gavr'inis, Brittany. Passage Grave, third millennium (?)

153. Stele from Mas Capelier, Aveyron, France. *c.* 2000 (?). Stone. *Saint Germain-en-Laye, Musée des Antiquités Nationales*

154. (top) Decorated grave slab from Leuna-Göhlitzsch, Merseburg, Germany. Saale Corded Ware, end of third millennium. Stone. *Halle, Landesmuseum für Vorgeschichte*

155. (bottom) Face-pot from Svinø, Denmark. Passage Grave Period, third millennium. *Copenhagen, National Museum*

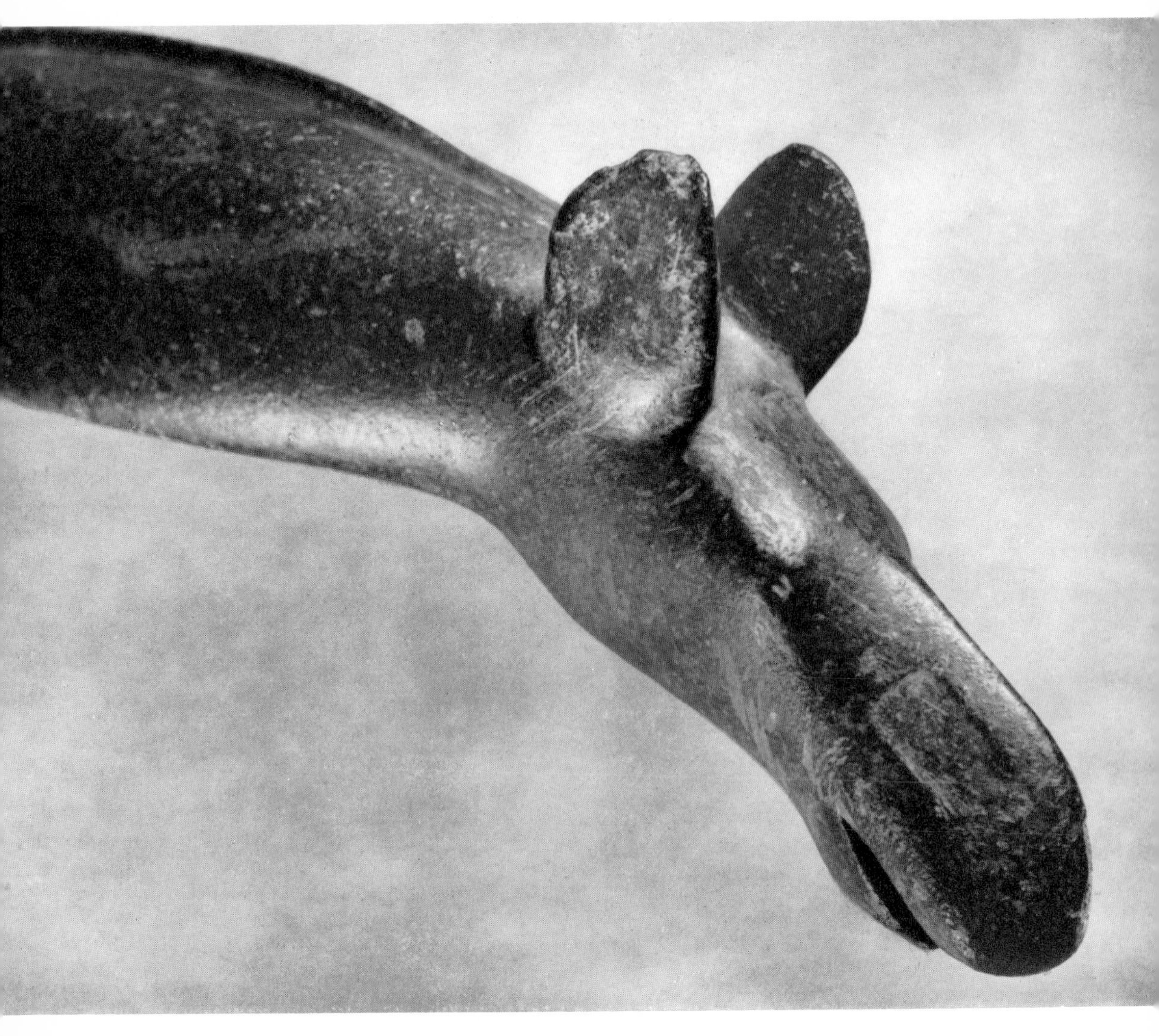

156. (above) Axe with elk's head from Alunda, Uppland, Sweden. Neolithic, third millennium (?). Stone. *Stockholm, Museum of National Antiquities*
157. (top right) Flask from Mokrin, Yugoslavia. Perjamus, early second millennium. Clay. *Belgrade, National Museum*
158. (bottom right) Cup from Ruma, Yugoslavia. Baden culture, *c.* 2000. Clay. *Zagreb, Archaeological Museum*

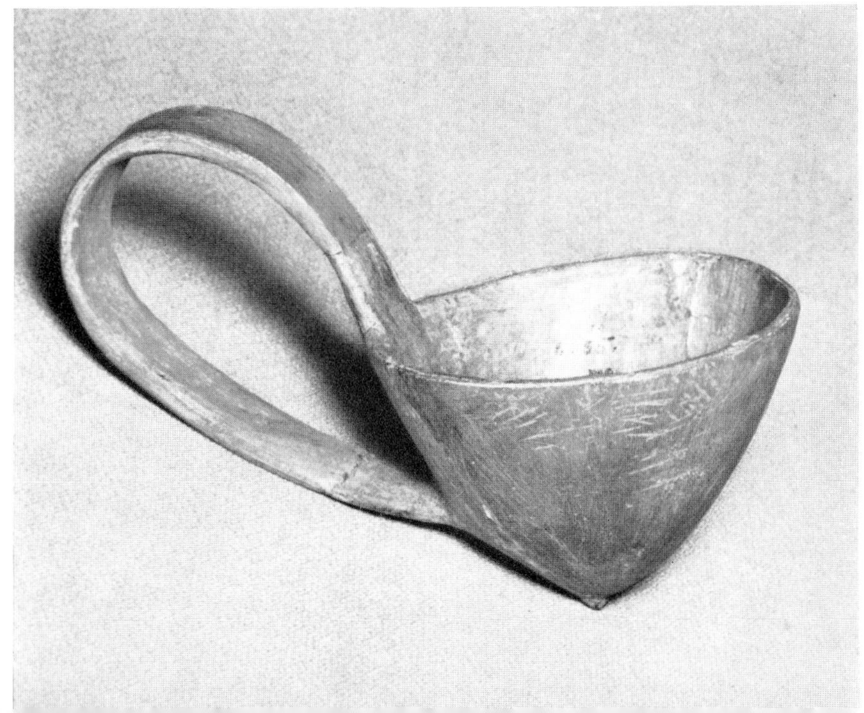

159. (left) Funeral vase from Patince, Slovakia, Czechoslovakia. Pannonian Crusted Ware, first half of the second millennium. Clay. *Nitra, Archaeological Institute of the Slovak Academy of Sciences*

160. (right) Three white-encrusted pots from Sarvaš, Yugoslavia. Vučedol, early second millennium. Clay. *Zagreb, Archaeological Museum*

161. Amphora from Omoljica, Yugoslavia. Vattina type, second millennium. Clay. *Belgrade, National Museum*

162. (top) Funeral vase from grave 54, Cîrna, Oltenia, Rumania. Mid second millennium. Clay. *Bucharest, National Museum of Antiquities, Institute of Archaeology*
163. (bottom) Funeral vase from grave 48, Cîrna, Oltenia, Rumania. Mid second millennium. Clay. *Bucharest, National Museum of Antiquities, Institute of Archaeology*

164. (above) Handled pot from Barca, Slovakia, Czechoslovakia. Otomani culture, mid second millennium. *Nitra, Archaeological Institute of the Slovak Academy of Sciences*
165. (top right) Base of cup from Hungary. Füzesabony type. Clay
166. (bottom right) High-necked pot from Barca, Slovakia, Czechoslovakia. Otomani culture, mid second millennium. Clay. *Nitra, Archaeological Institute of the Slovak Academy of Sciences*

167. (left) Figure from Kličevac, Yugoslavia (destroyed). Mid second millennium. Clay
168. (above) Figure in wheeled vehicle from Dupljaja, Yugoslavia. Mid second millennium. Clay. *Belgrade, National Museum*

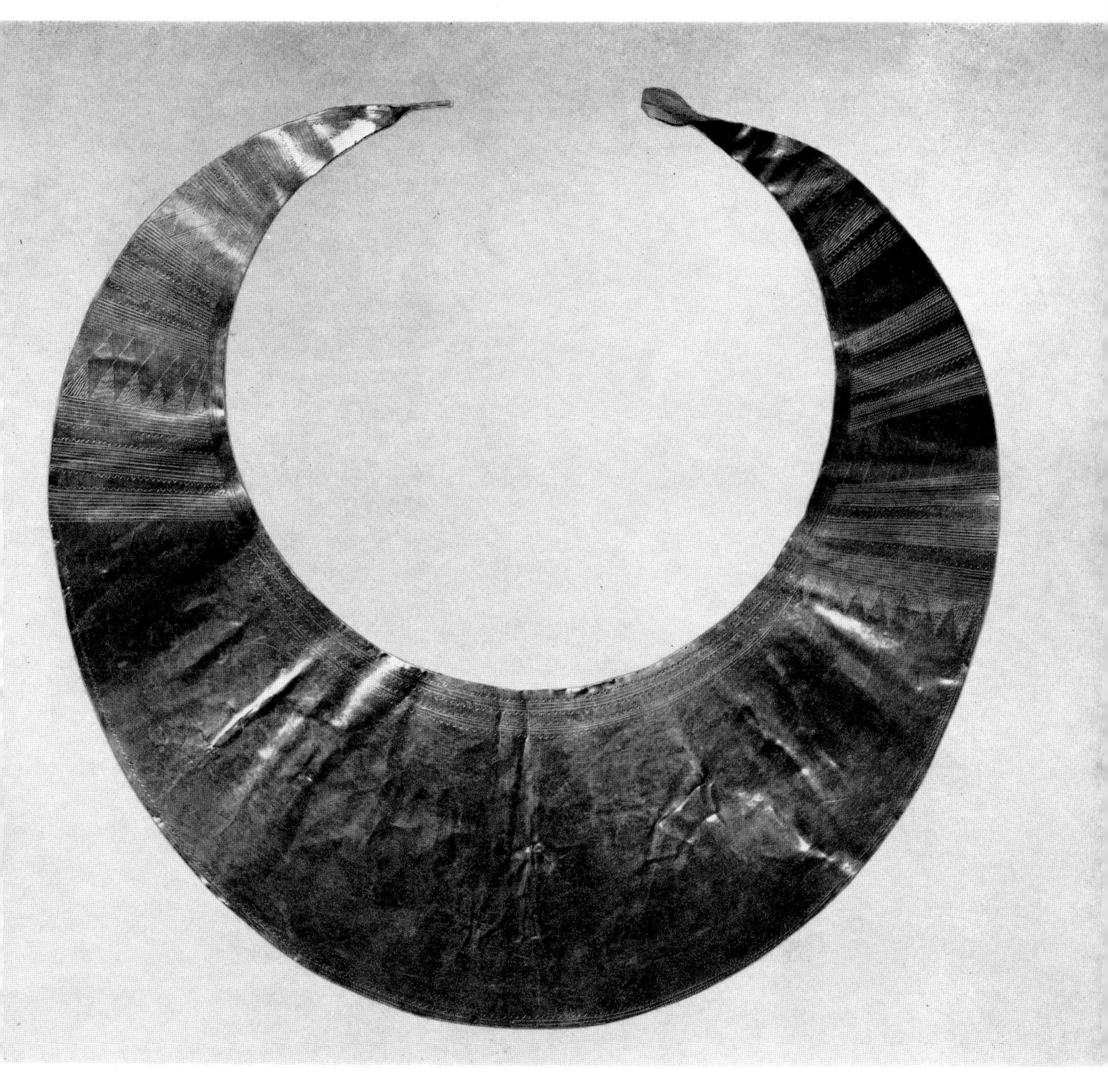

169. (left) Woman from grave 10, Cîrna, Oltenia, Rumania. Mid second millennium. Clay. *Bucharest, National Museum of Antiquities, Institute of Archaeology*
170. (above) Lunula from Ireland. Early second millennium. Gold. *London, British Museum*

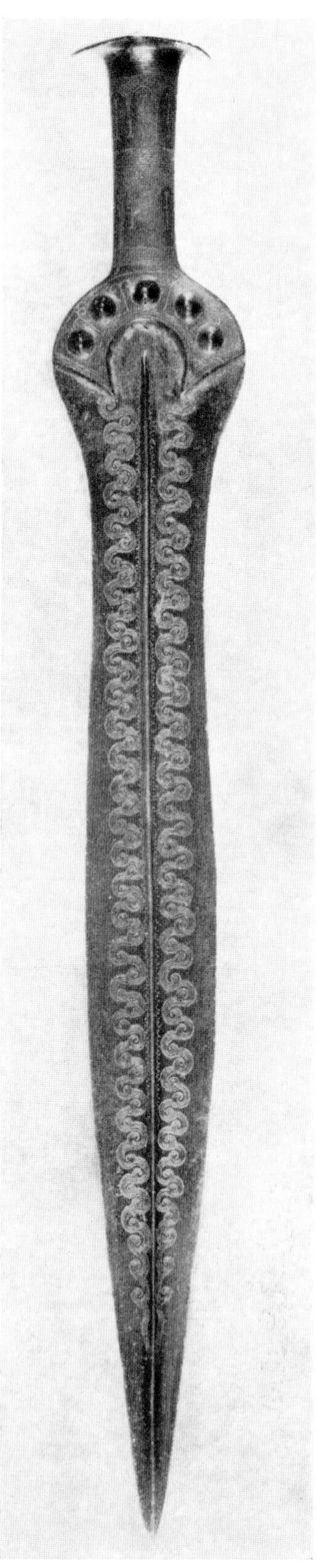

171. (left) Sword from Hajdusámson, Hungary. Second millennium. Bronze. *Debrecen, Déri Museum*
172. (right) Butt of axe from Apa, Rumania. Second millennium. Bronze. *Bucharest, Museum of Antiquities, Institute of Archaeology*

173. (top) Axe from Hajdusámson, Hungary. Second millennium. Bronze. *Debrecen, Déri Museum*

174. (bottom) Axe from Hajdusámson, Hungary. Second millennium. Bronze. *Debrecen, Déri Museum*

175. (left) Bracelet from Bellye, Hungary. Second millennium. Gold. *Vienna, Naturhistorisches Museum*

176. (bottom left) Tubes and disc from Nitriansky-Hrádok, Slovakia, Czechoslovakia. Mid second millennium. Bone. *Nitra, Archaeological Institute of the Slovak Academy of Sciences*

177. (below) Lid from Surčin, Croatia, Yugoslavia. Mid second millennium. Marble. *Zagreb, Archaeological Museum*

178. (right) Swords from Stensgård and Torupgårde, Denmark. Period I/IIa, mid second millennium. Bronze. *Copenhagen, National Museum*

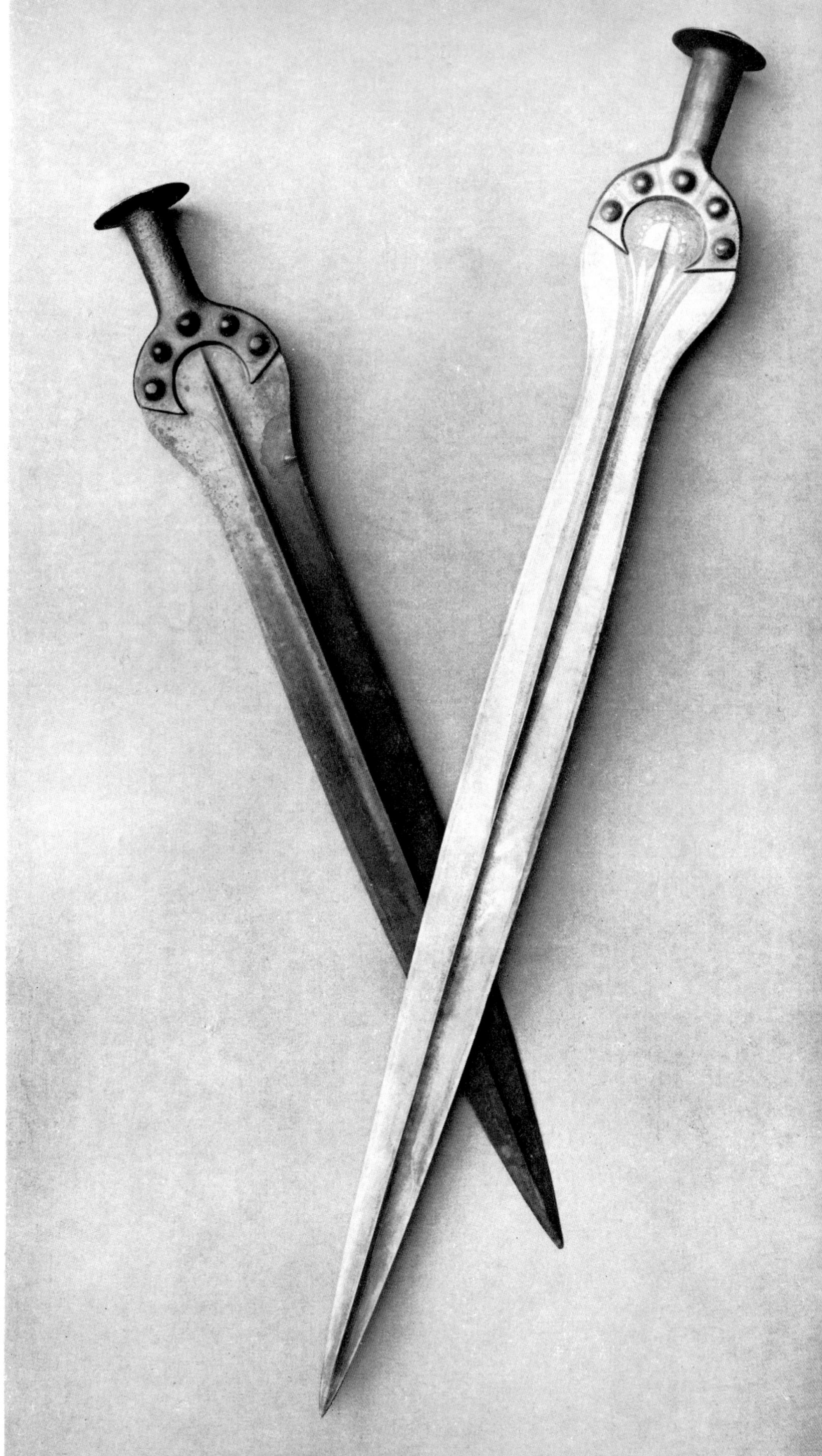

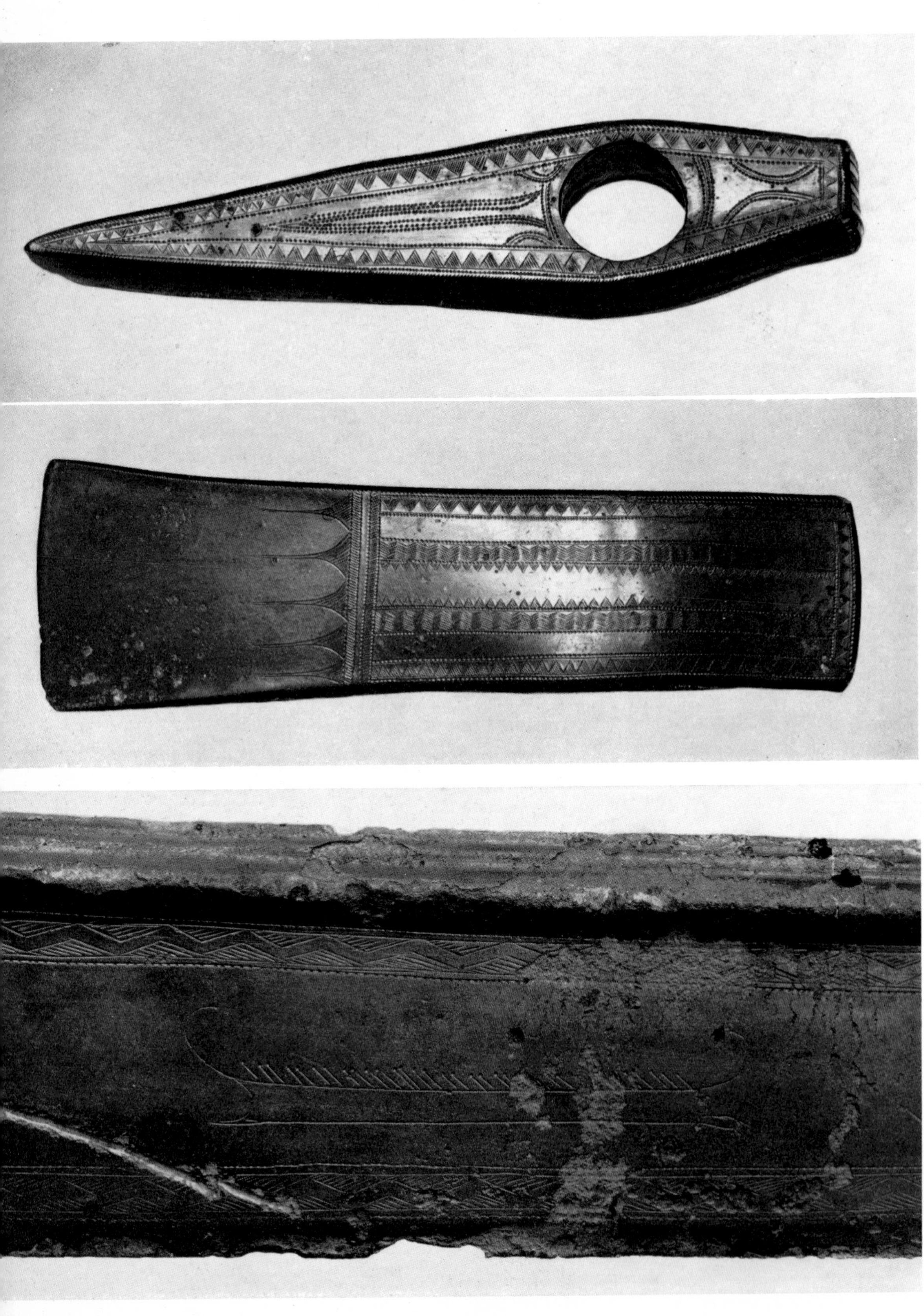

179. (top left) Two views of axe from Fårdrup, Denmark. Period I/IIa, mid second millennium. Bronze. *Copenhagen, National Museum*

180. (bottom left) 'Scimitar' with incised boat from Rørby, Denmark. Period I/IIa, mid second millennium. Bronze. *Copenhagen, National Museum*

181. (right) Dagger from Hindsgavl, Denmark. Mid second millennium. Flint. *Copenhagen, National Museum*

182. (left) Tutulus from Langstrup, Denmark. Period IIbc, second half of the second millennium. Bronze. *Copenhagen, National Museum*

183. (top right) Axe from Brondsted, Denmark. End of second millennium. Bronze. *Copenhagen, National Museum*

184. (bottom right) Gorget from Gleninsheen, Co. Clare, Ireland. Dowris Phase, eighth century (?). Gold. *National Museum of Ireland*

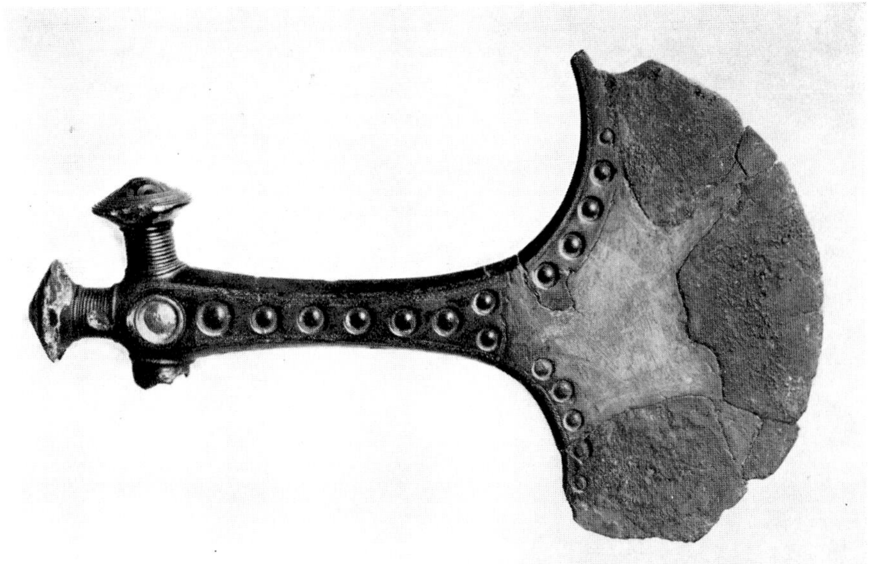

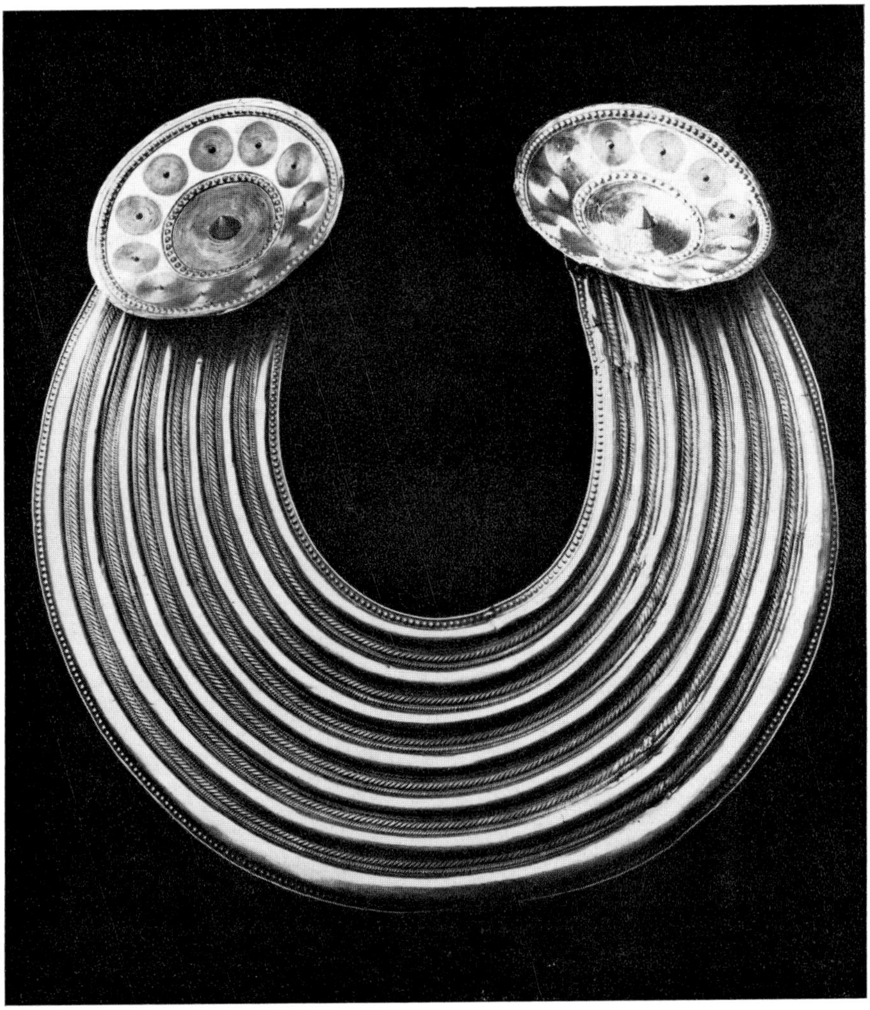

185–6. (above and left) Horse and car with 'sun-disc' from Trundholm, Denmark. Thirteenth century (?). Bronze and gold. *Copenhagen, National Museum*
187. (top right) Grave slabs at Kivik, Skåne, Sweden. Thirteenth-twelfth century (?). Stone
188. (bottom right) Detail of grave slab at Kivik, Skåne, Sweden. Thirteenth-twelfth century (?). Stone

189. Stonehenge, Wiltshire. Sarsens first half of second millennium

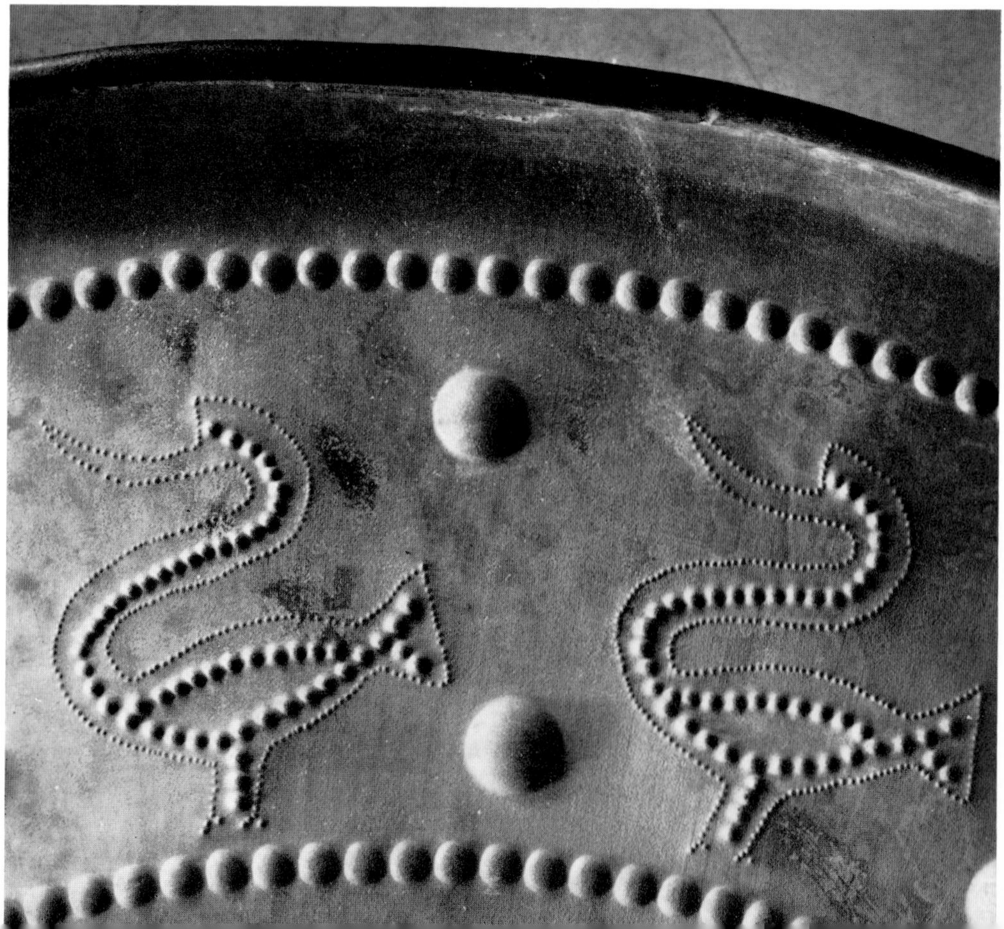

190. (top left) Embossed shield from Denmark. Early first millennium. Bronze. *Copenhagen, National Museum*

191. (bottom left) Embossed shield (detail) from Nackhälle, Sweden. Eighth century. Bronze. *Stockholm, Museum of National Antiquities*

192. (above) Embossed and other beaten bronze vessels from Ronninge, Siem, Dienmose, and Birkendegård, Denmark. Period IV–V, tenth–eighth century. *Copenhagen, National Museum*

193. Necklet from Svrabljivac, Glasinac, Yugoslavia. Early first millennium. Bronze. *Sarajevo, Archaeological Museum*

194. Lur from Tellerup, Denmark. Ninth-eighth century. Bronze. *Copenhagen, National Museum*

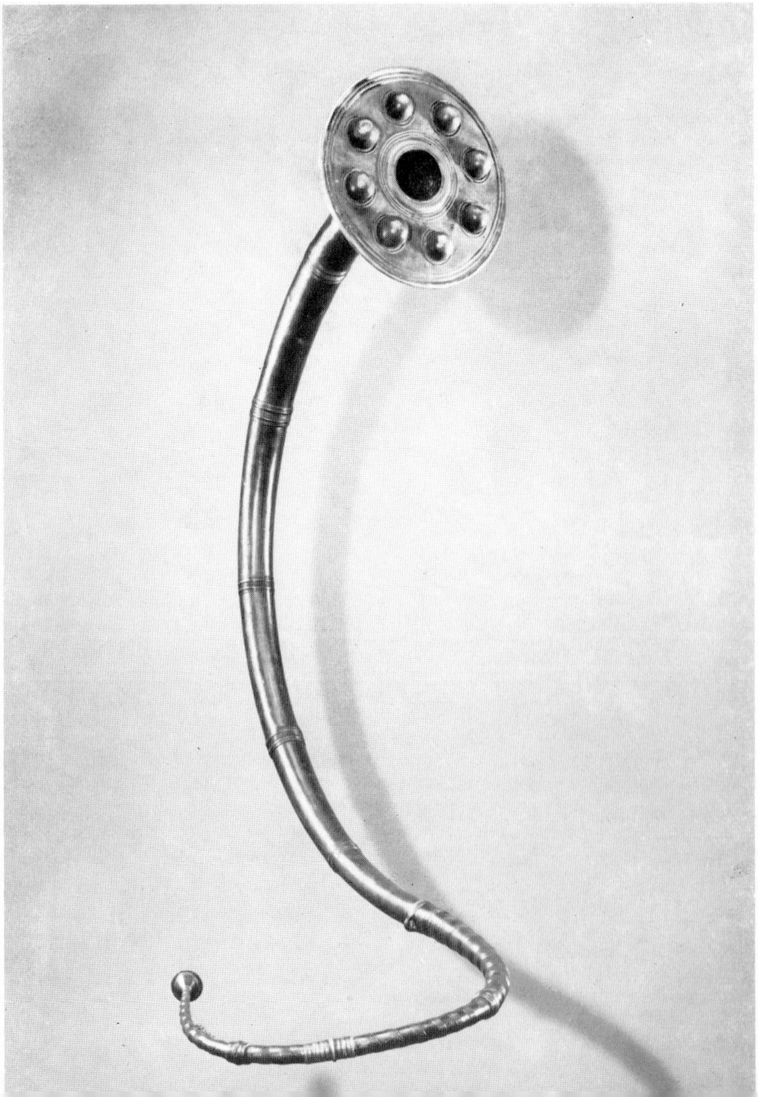

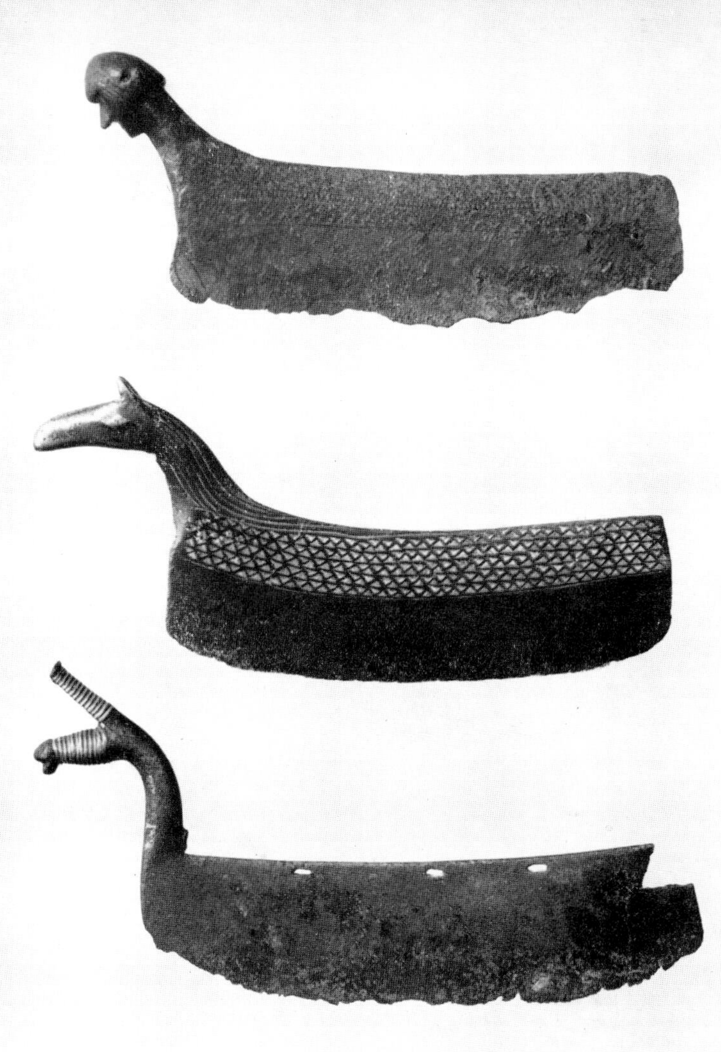

195. Razors from Gerdrup, Darup, and Fordlose, Denmark. *c.* 1100–700. Bronze. *Copenhagen, National Museum*

196. Razors from Magleby and Skivum, Denmark. Period V, eighth-seventh century. Bronze. *Copenhagen, National Museum*

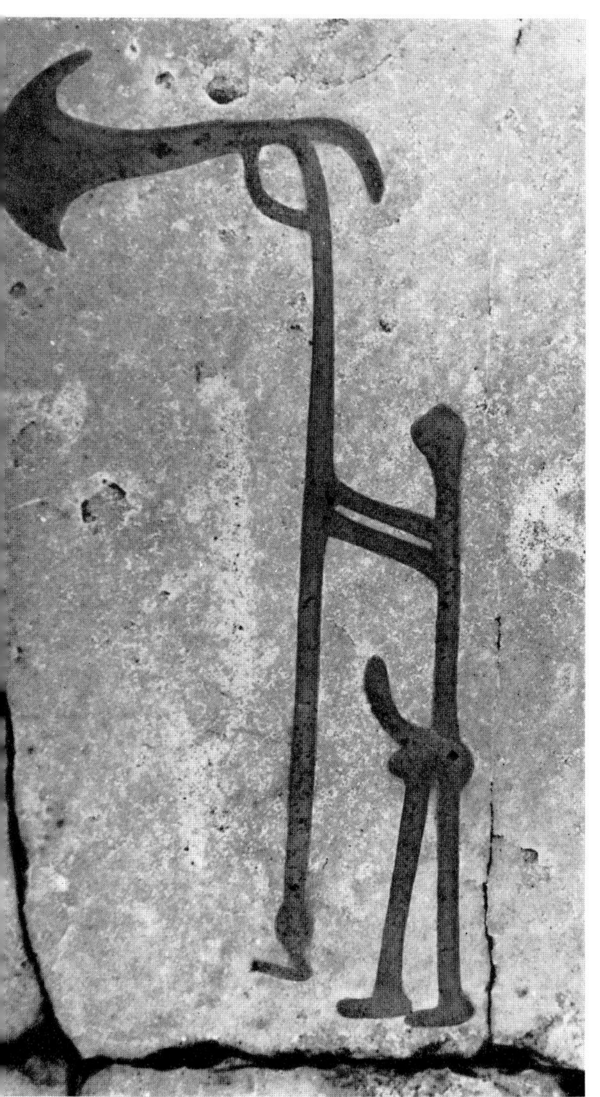

197. (top left) 'Belt-box' from Stevneskov, Denmark. Period V, eighth-seventh century. Bronze. *Copenhagen, National Museum*
198. (bottom left) 'Belt-box' from Billeberga, Skåne, Sweden. Period V, eighth-seventh century. Bronze. *University of Lund, Historical Museum*
199. (above left) Rock engraved with man and axe, touched up with paint, at Simris, Skåne, Sweden. Early first millennium (?)
200. (above right) Rock engraved with 'sorcerer' at Järrestad, Skåne, Sweden. Early first millennium (?)

201. (top left) Engraved rock at Fossum, Bohuslän, Sweden. Early first millennium

202. (bottom left) Rock engraving at Vitlycke, Bohuslän, Sweden. Early first millennium

203. (top right) Rock engraving at Kalleby, Bohuslän, Sweden. Early first millennium

204. (right) Rock engraving of giant with spear at Tanum, Bohuslän, Sweden. Early first millennium

205. (left) Front and back views of a vase-bearer on a knife handle from Itzehoe, Holstein, Denmark. Eighth-seventh century. Bronze. *Copenhagen, National Museum*

206. (bottom left) Front and side views of a kneeling figure from Fårdal, Viborg, Denmark. Eighth century. Bronze. *Copenhagen, National Museum*

207. (top right) Horned helmets from Viksø, Denmark. Eighth century. Bronze. *Copenhagen, National Museum*

208. (bottom right) Pinhead with human and goat's head from Rovalls, Vänge, Gotland, Sweden. Eighth-seventh century. Bronze. *Stockholm, Museum of National Antiquities*

209. (left) Sceptre (?) from Rolkegärdet, Svartarp, Västergötland, Sweden. Eighth–seventh century. Bronze. *University of Lund, Historical Museum*

210. (bottom left) Dippers from Vimose, Overdrev, and Borbjerg, Sorø, Denmark. Tenth century. Gold. *Copenhagen, National Museum*

211. (left) Side and front views of knife handle from Simris, Skåne, Sweden. Eighth-seventh century. Bronze. *Stockholm, Museum of National Antiquities*

212. (below middle) Goat from Sisak and animal from Prozor, Bosnia, Yugoslavia. Mid first millennium(?). Bronze. *Zagreb, Archaeological Museum*

213. (bottom) Stag from Surdak, Yugoslavia. Mid first millennium (?). Bronze. *Zagreb, Archaeological Museum*

214. (left) Figures in animal-ended boat from Roos Carr, Holderness, Yorkshire, England. Late first millennium (?). Pinewood. *City and County of Kingston upon Hull Museums*

215. (bottom left) Bull from Spjuterum, Sweden. First half of the first millennium. Bronze. *University of Lund, Historical Museum*

216. (right) Figure from Roos Carr, Holderness, Yorkshire, England. Late first millennium (?)

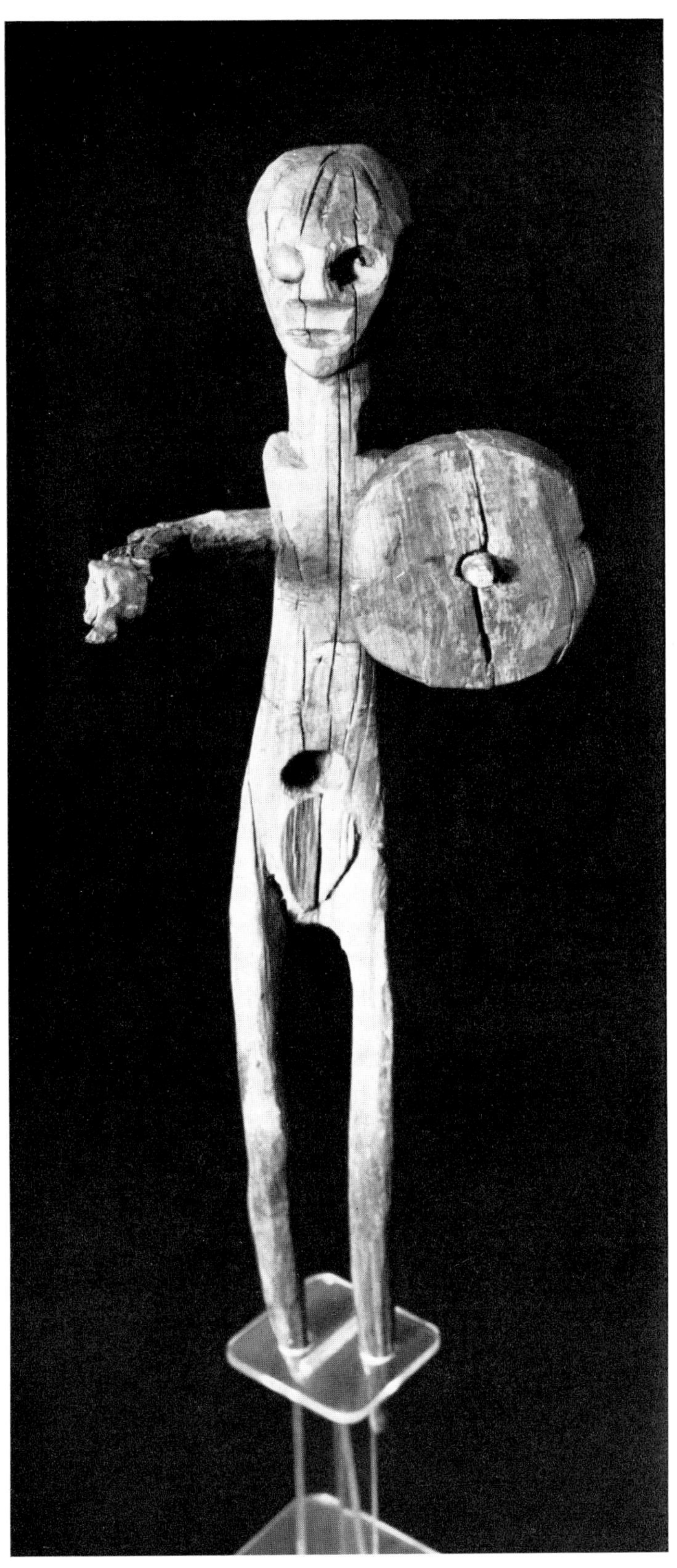

217. (above) Animal rhyta from Dalj, Yugoslavia. *c.* seventh century. Clay. *Zagreb, Archaeological Museum*
218. (below) 'Cult-wagon' from Strettweg, Austria. Seventh century (?). Bronze. *Graz, Landesmuseum Johanneum*

219. (left) Bull from Býčí Skála, Moravia, Czechoslovakia. Sixth century (?). Bronze. *Vienna, Naturhistorisches Museum*

220. (bottom left) Pot with figures from Gemeinlebarn, Austria. Seventh century (?). *Vienna, Naturhistorisches Museum*

221. (right) Impressed dish from 'Sternberg', Gomadingen, South Germany. Seventh century. *Stuttgart, Württembergisches Landesmuseum*

222. (left) Bowl on high foot from Pantalica, Sicily. Twelfth century. Clay. *Syracuse, Museo Nazionale*

223. (above) Su Nuraxi, Barumini, Sardinia. Principally eighth–sixth century

224. (top) Two wrestlers from Monte Arcosu, Sardinia. Eighth–sixth century. Bronze. *Cagliari, Museo Archeologico Nazionale*

225. (left) Archer from Santa Vittoria de Serri, Sardinia. Eighth–sixth century. Bronze. *Cagliari, Museo Archeologico Nazionale*

226. (left) Man from Sardinia. Eighth-sixth century. Bronze. *Cagliari, Museo Archeologico Nazionale*
227. (right) Woman in a cloak from Coni or Santu Millanu Nùoro, Sardinia. Eighth-sixth century. Bronze. *Cagliari, Museo Archeologico Nazionale*

228. (left) Situla from Vače, Slovenia, Yugoslavia. Fifth century. Bronze. *Ljubljana, Archaeological Museum*
229. (above) Situla from Vače (detail)
230. (right) Mother and child from Santa Vittoria, Sardinia. Eighth-sixth century. Bronze. *Cagliari, Museo Archeologico Nazionale*

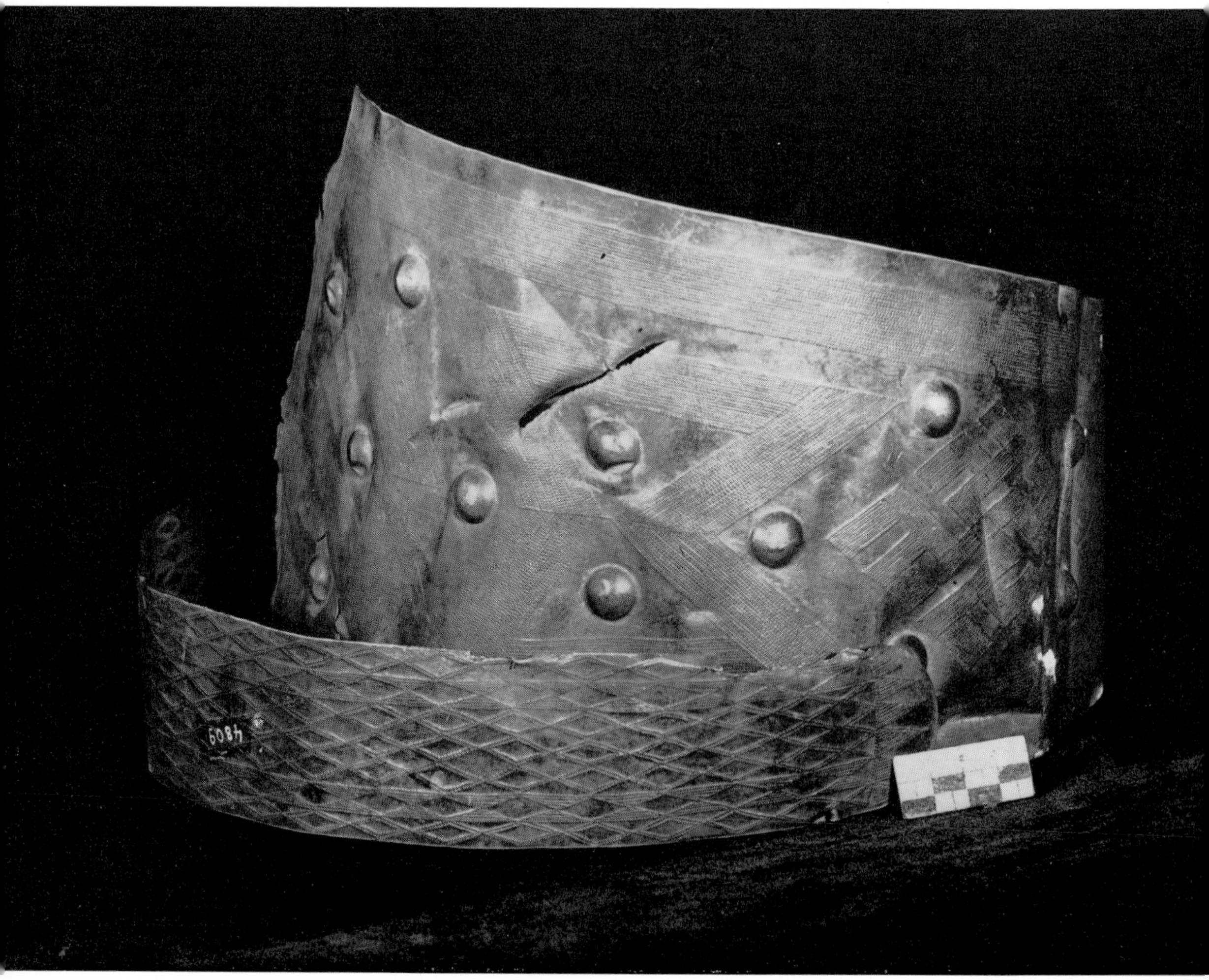

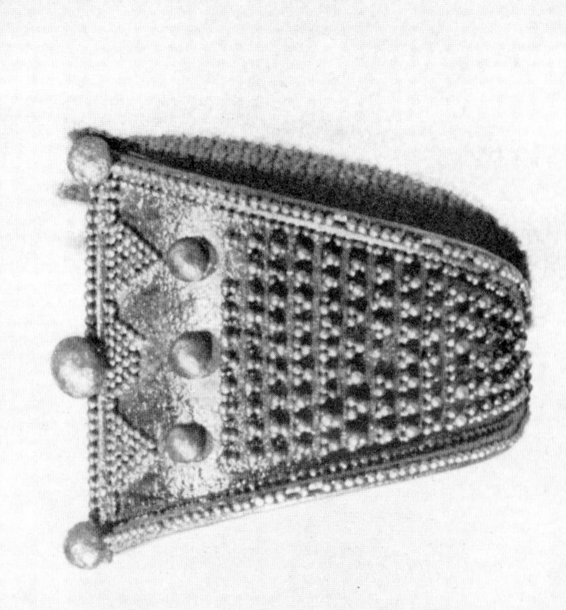

231. (top) Belt from Mramorac, Serbia, Yugoslavia. *c.* 500 (?). Silver. *Belgrade, National Museum*

232. (left) Earring from Čurug, Serbia, Yugoslavia. Sixth–fifth century. Silver. *Belgrade, National Museum*

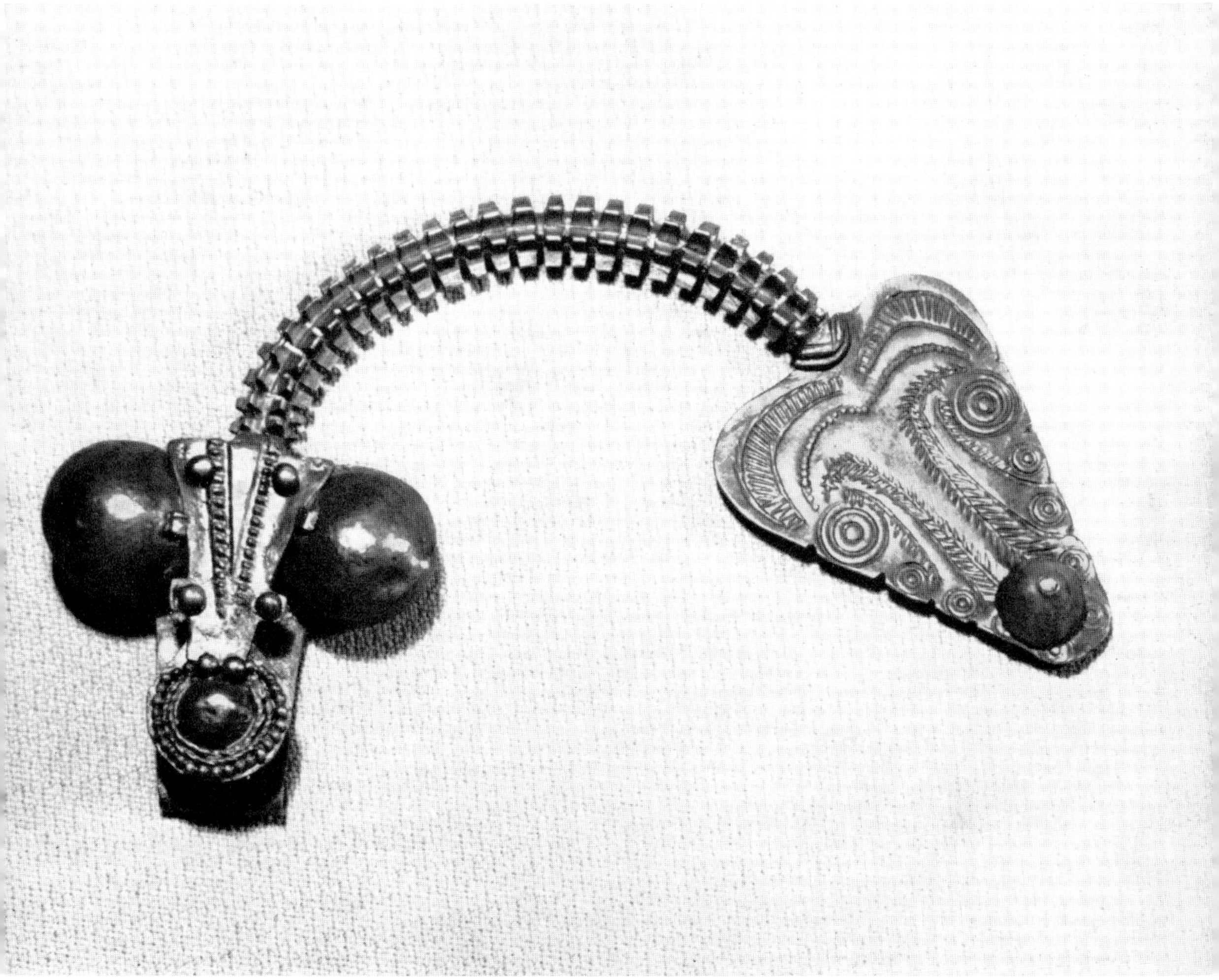

233. (top) Brooch from Čurug. Serbia, Yugoslavia. Sixth-fifth century. Silver. *Belgrade, National Museum*
234. (right) Brooch from Bulgaria. Fifth century (?). Bronze. *Sofia, National Museum*

235. Tiara from Poiana-Coţofeneşti, Rumania. Fourth century (?). Gold. *Bucharest, National Museum of Antiquities, Institute of Archaeology*

236. Ring and bracelet from Rodenbach, Rhineland, Germany. Fifth century. Gold. *Speyer, Historisches Museum der Pfalz*

237. (above) Necklet and bracelet from Rheinheim, Saarland, Germany. Fourth century. Gold. *Saarbrücken, Museum für Vor- und Frühgeschichte*

238. (left) Bracelet from Rheinheim (detail)

239. (top right) Cock on a brooch from Rheinheim, Saarland, Germany. Bronze and coral. *Mainz, Romanisch-Germanisches Zentralmuseum*

240. (bottom right) Belt-buckle from Weisskirchen, Saarland, Germany. Fifth century. Bronze and coral. *Trier, Landesmuseum*

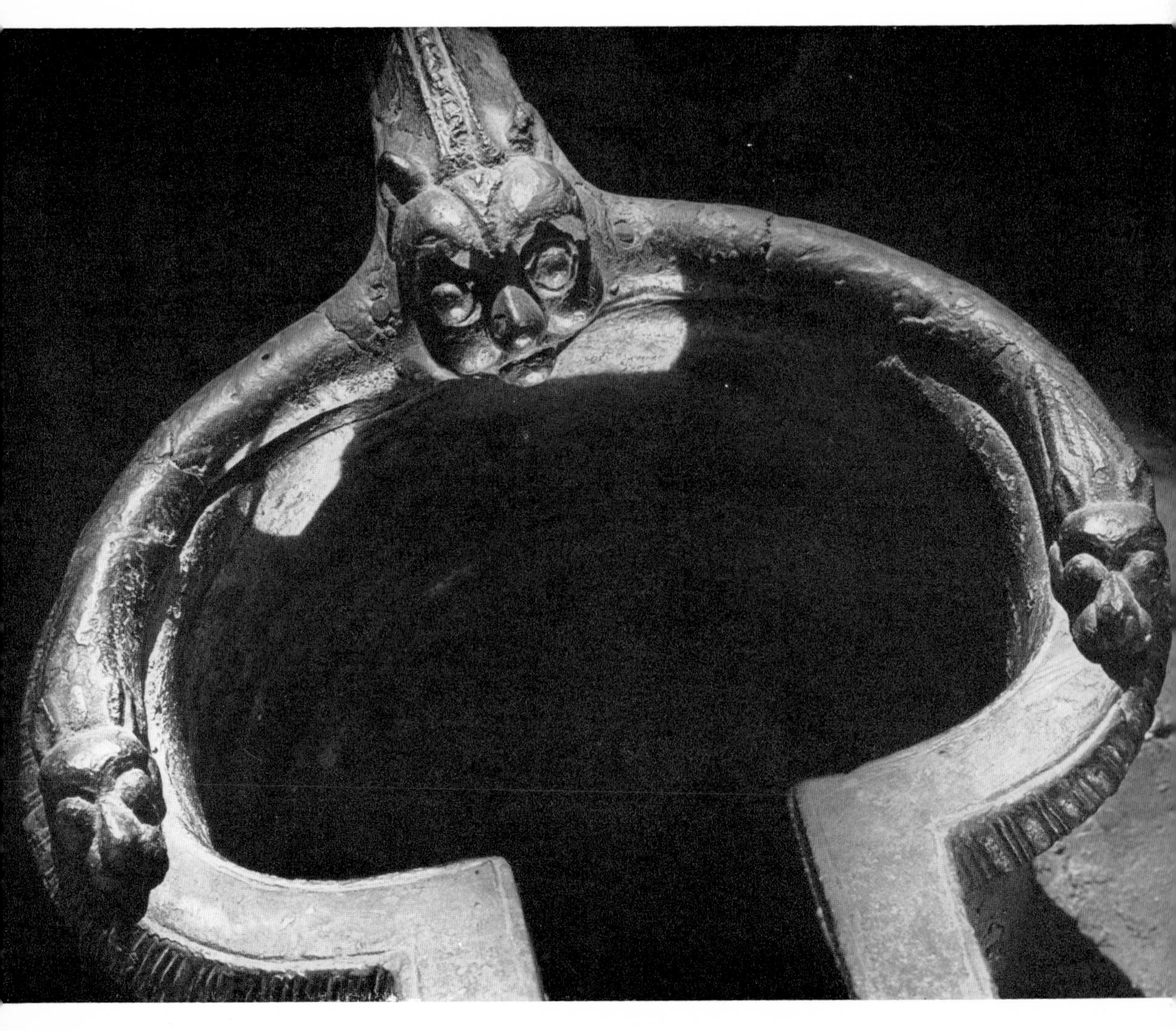

241. (above) Flagon from Klein Aspergle, Württemberg, Germany, detail of rim. Early-mid fifth century. Bronze. *Stuttgart, Württembergisches Landesmuseum*
242. (right) Flagon from Klein Aspergle, detail of base of handle

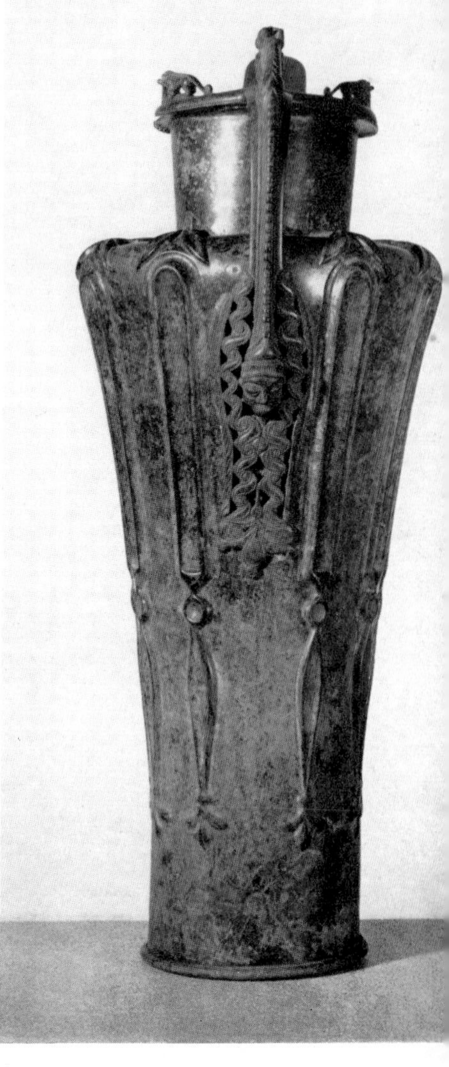

243. (top left) Flagon from Borsch, Bad Salzungen, Thuringia, East Germany. Late fifth century. Bronze. *Jena, Vorgeschichtliches Museum der Friedrich-Schiller-Universität*

244.(above) Flagon from Dürrnberg, Austria. *c.* 425. Bronze. *Salzburg, Carolino Augusteum*

245. (left) Flagon from Dürrnberg (detail)

246. (right) Flagon from Basse-Yutz, Lorraine, France. Early fourth century (?). Bronze, coral, and enamel. *London, British Museum*

247. (far left) Brooch with heads from Oberwittighausen, Baden, Germany. Fifth-fourth century (?). Bronze. *Karlsruhe, Badisches Landesmuseum*

248. (left) Brooch from Parsberg, Oberpfalz, Germany. Fifth-fourth century (?). Bronze. *Nuremberg, Germanisches National-Museum*

249. (bottom left) Openwork ornament from Cuperly, Marne, France. Late fifth century. Bronze. *Saint Germain-en-Laye, Musée des Antiquités Nationales*

250. (top right) Wooden stand or platter from Høstad, Norway. Fifth century (?). *Trondheim, Videnskapsselskapets Oldsaksamling*

251. (bottom right) Cast of pot from La Cheppe, Marne, France. Fifth century (?). *Saint Germain-en-Laye, Musée des Antiquités Nationales*

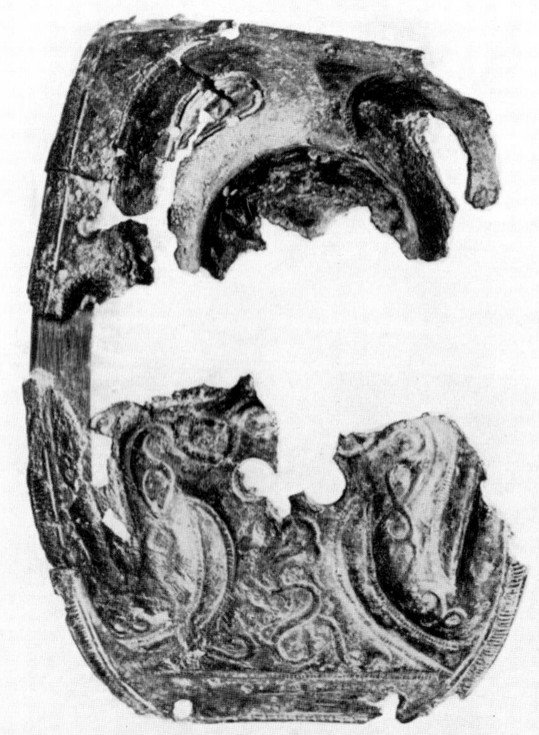

252. (top left) Discs from Saint Jean-sur-Tourbe, Marne, France. Late fifth century (?). Bronze. *Saint Germain-en-Laye, Musée des Antiquités Nationales*

253. (bottom left) Busts from Waldalgesheim, Rhine, Germany. Mid fourth century. Bronze. *Bonn, Rheinisches Landesmuseum*

254. (above) Necklet and bracelets from Waldalgesheim, Rhine, Germany. Mid fourth century. Gold. *Bonn, Rheinisches Landesmuseum*

255. (right) Handle with bulls' heads on cauldron from Brå, Jutland, Denmark. Third century (?). *Aarhus, Museum*

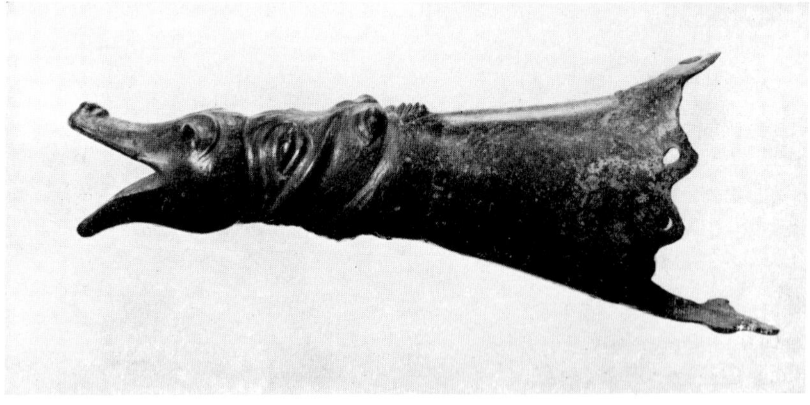

256. (top left) Owl from Brå cauldron (cf. Plate 255)
257. (bottom left) Spout with back-to-back heads from Dürrnberg, Austria. Third century (?). *Salzburg, Carolino Augusteum*
258. (top right) Openwork ornament from Brno-Maloměřice, Czechoslovakia. Third century (?). Bronze. *Brno, Moravian Museum*
259. (bottom right) Openwork ornament from Brno-Maloměřice, detail of Plate 258
260. (bottom far right) Two heads from openwork ornament from Brno-Maloměřice. *Brno, Moravian Museum*

261. (left) Linch-pin from Champagne, France (?). Third century (?). Iron plated with bronze. *Saint Germain-en-Laye, Musée des Antiquités Nationales*

262. (bottom left) Tube with faces from Champagne, France (?). Third century (?). Iron plated with bronze. *Saint Germain-en-Laye, Musée des Antiquités Nationales*

263. (top right) Bracelet from Tarn, France (?). Third century (?). Bronze. *Saint Germain-en-Laye, Musée des Antiquités Nationales*

264. (below right) Bracelet from Aurillac, Tarn, France. Third century (?). Gold. *Paris, Bibliothèque Nationale*

265. Detail of Aurillac bracelet

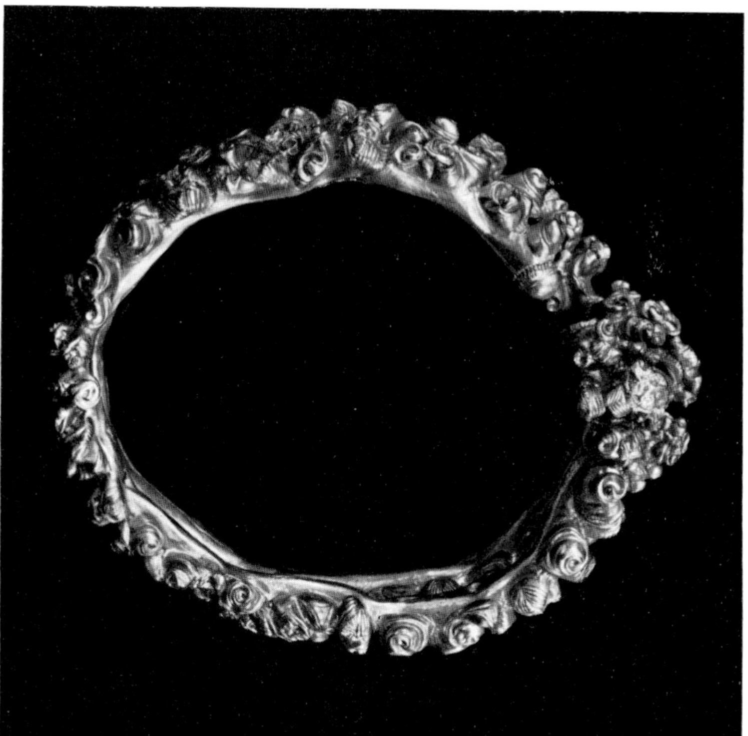

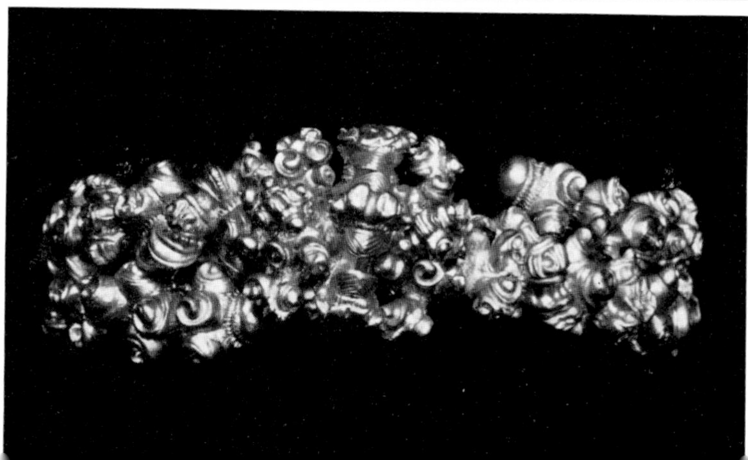

266. (left) Head from Heidelberg, Germany. Fourth century (?). Sandstone. *Karlsruhe, Badisches Landesmuseum*
267. (above left) Pillar from Pfalzfeld, Rhineland, Germany. Fourth century (?). Stone. *Bonn, Rheinisches Landesmuseum*
268 (above right) Pillar from Waldenbuch, Württemberg, Germany. Fourth-third century. Sandstone. *Stuttgart, Württembergisches Landesmuseum*

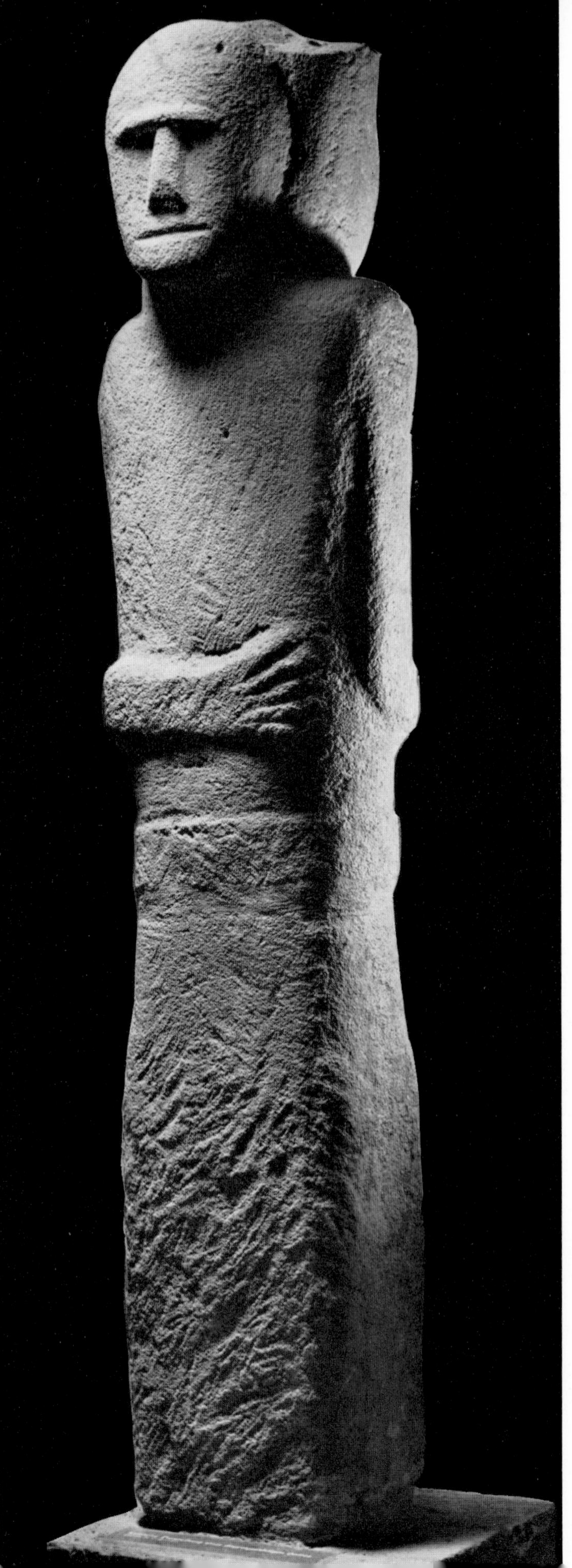

269. (left) Figure from Holzgerlingen, Württemberg, Germany. Third-second century (?). Stone. *Stuttgart, Württembergisches Landesmuseum*

270. (top right) Janus heads from Roquepertuse, Provence, France. Fourth-second century. Stone. *Marseille, Musée Borély*

271. (bottom right) Seated figure from Roquepertuse, Provence, France. Fourth century or later. Stone. *Marseille, Musée Borély*

272. (far left) Figure from Euffigneix, Haute-Marne, France. First century B.C. (?). Sandstone. *Saint Germain-en-Laye, Musée des Antiquités Nationales*
273. (middle) Side view of figure from Euffigneix
274. (above) Head from Mšecké-Žehrovice, Bohemia, Czechoslovakia. Second century (?). Ragstone. *Prague, National Museum*

275. 'Tarasque de Noves' from Bouches-du-Rhône, France. First century B.C. (?). Sandstone. *Avignon, Musée Calvet*

276. Mask from Tarbes, Hautes-Pyrénées, France. Third century (?). Bronze. *Musée de Tarbes*

277. (top left) Boar from Neuvy-en-Sullias, Loiret, France. First century B.C. (?). Bronze. *Orléans, Musée Historique*

278. (bottom left) Cock from Bussy-le-Château, Marne, France. 'La Tène'. Bronze. *Saint Germain-en-Laye, Musée des Antiquités Nationales*

279. (top right) Small cock probably from France. First century B.C./A.D. (?). Iron. *Saint Germain-en-Laye, Musée des Antiquités Nationales*

280. (bottom right) Dancing woman from Neuvy-en-Sullias, Loiret, France. First century B.C./A.D. Bronze. *Orléans, Musée Historique*

281. (top left) Cauldron with human head and bulls from Rynkeby, Denmark. First century B.C. (?). Bronze. *Copenhagen, National Museum*

282. (bottom left) Bowl from Gundestrup, detail of bull from base (cf. Plate 283)

283. (top right) Bowl from Gundestrup, Jutland, Denmark. Second-first century B.C. (?). Silver. *Copenhagen, National Museum*

284. (bottom right) Bowl from Gundestrup, detail of panel with goddess

285. (top) Inner panel of cauldron from Rynkeby (cf. Plate 281)
286. (bottom) Pony-cap and horns from Torrs, Kirkcudbright, Scotland (as restored incorrectly). Third century (?). Bronze. *Edinburgh, National Museum*

287. (left) Scabbard mount from the river Witham near Lincoln. Third century (?). Gilt bronze. *Alnwick, Duke of Northumberland*
288. (right) Long shield boss from Wandsworth, London. Third century (?). Bronze. *London, British Museum*

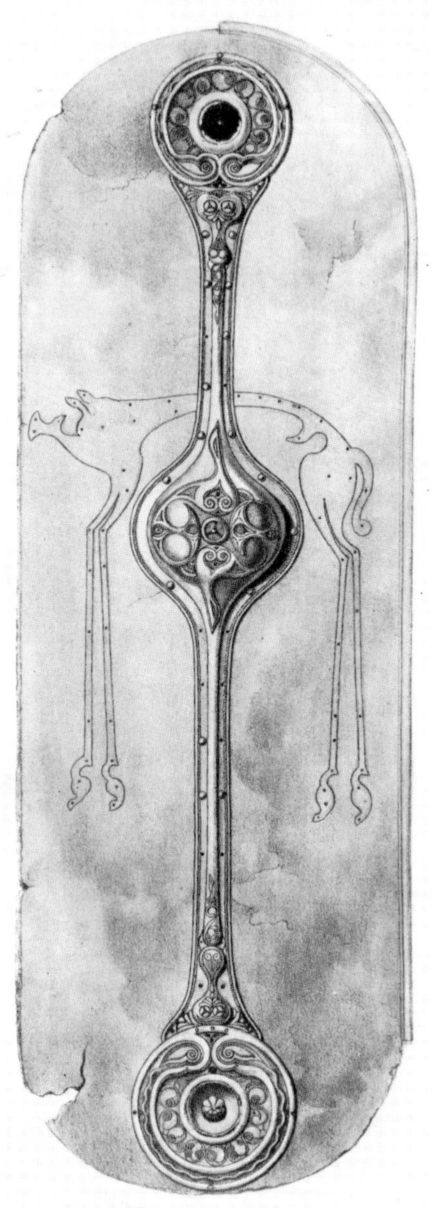

289. (top left) Round shield boss from Wandsworth, London. Third century (?). Bronze. *London, British Museum*
290. (bottom left) Detail of one end of the Witham shield (cf. Plate 291). *London, British Museum*
291. (above left) Drawing of the Witham shield. Third-second century (?). Bronze
292. (above right) Shield from Battersea, London. Second century (?). Bronze, originally gilt. *London, British Museum*

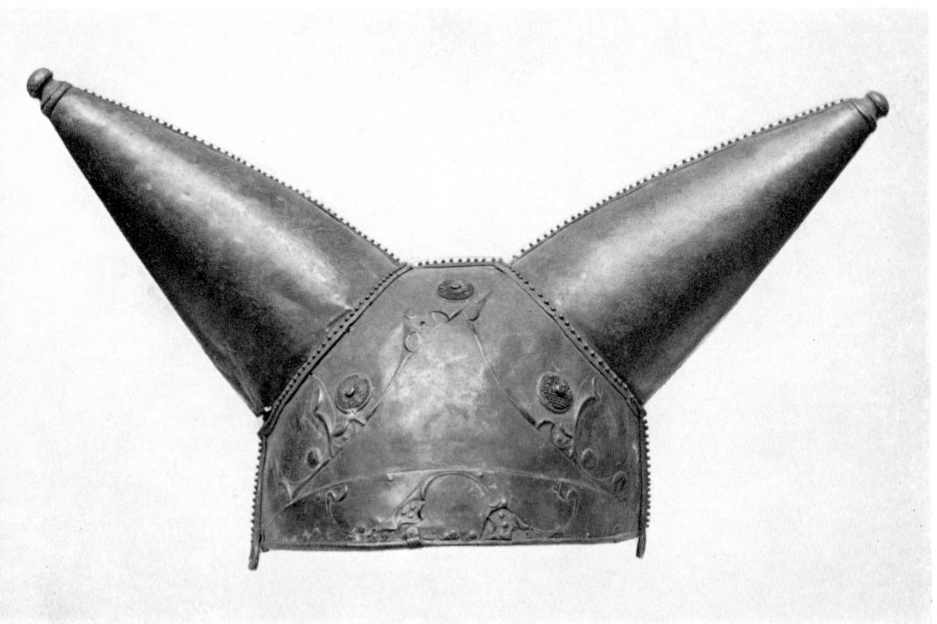

293. (above) Helmet from Waterloo Bridge, London. Second-first century (?). Bronze. *London, British Museum*

294. (middle) Scabbard 3 from Lisnacroghera, Co. Antrim, Northern Ireland. Third-second century. Bronze. *Ulster Museum*

295. (top right) Painted vase from Prunay, Marne, France. Fourth-third century. Clay. *London, British Museum*

296. (bottom right) Torc from Snettisham, Norfolk. Late first century B.C. Gold. *London, British Museum*

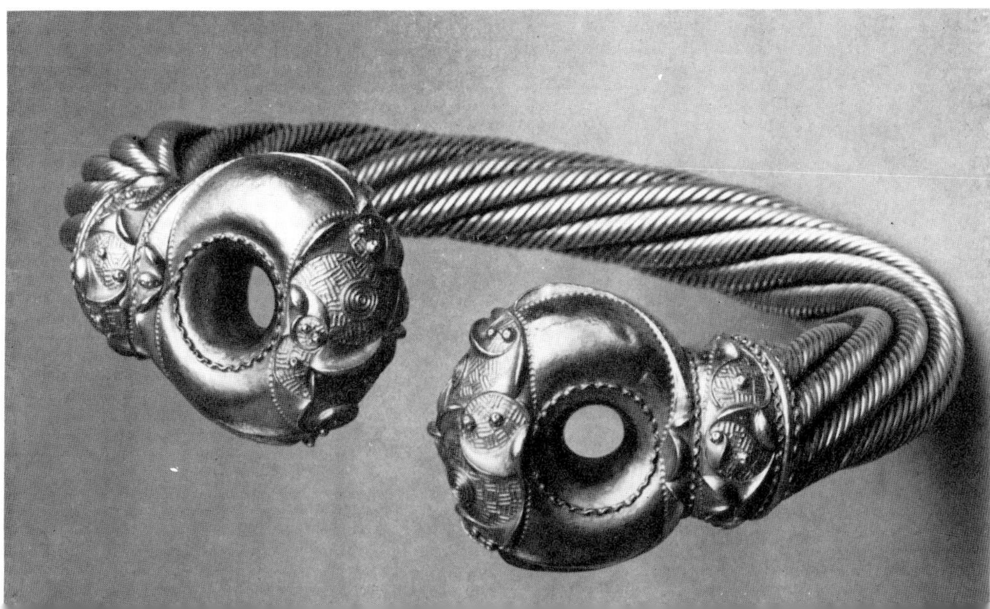

297. (top) Panel with head and horse from tub from Marlborough, Wiltshire. Bronze. *Devizes, Museum*

298. (bottom) Panel with profile heads from Marlborough tub (cf. Plate 297)

299. (top) Panel with moustached profile from Marlborough tub (cf. Plate 297)
300. (bottom) Panel with opposed horses from Marlborough tub (cf. Plate 297)

301. (above) Bucket from Aylesford, Kent. Late first century B.C. Bronze. *London, British Museum*

302. (left) Staters of the Parisii, obverse (head) and reverse (horse with canopy), of the Andecavi (human-headed horse and giant), and of the Virudini (horse and cross) from France, various sites. Gold. *Paris, Cabinet des Médailles de la Bibliothèque Nationale*

303. (right) Mayer Mirror, provenance unknown, probably southern England. Late first century B.C. (?). Bronze. *City of Liverpool Museums*

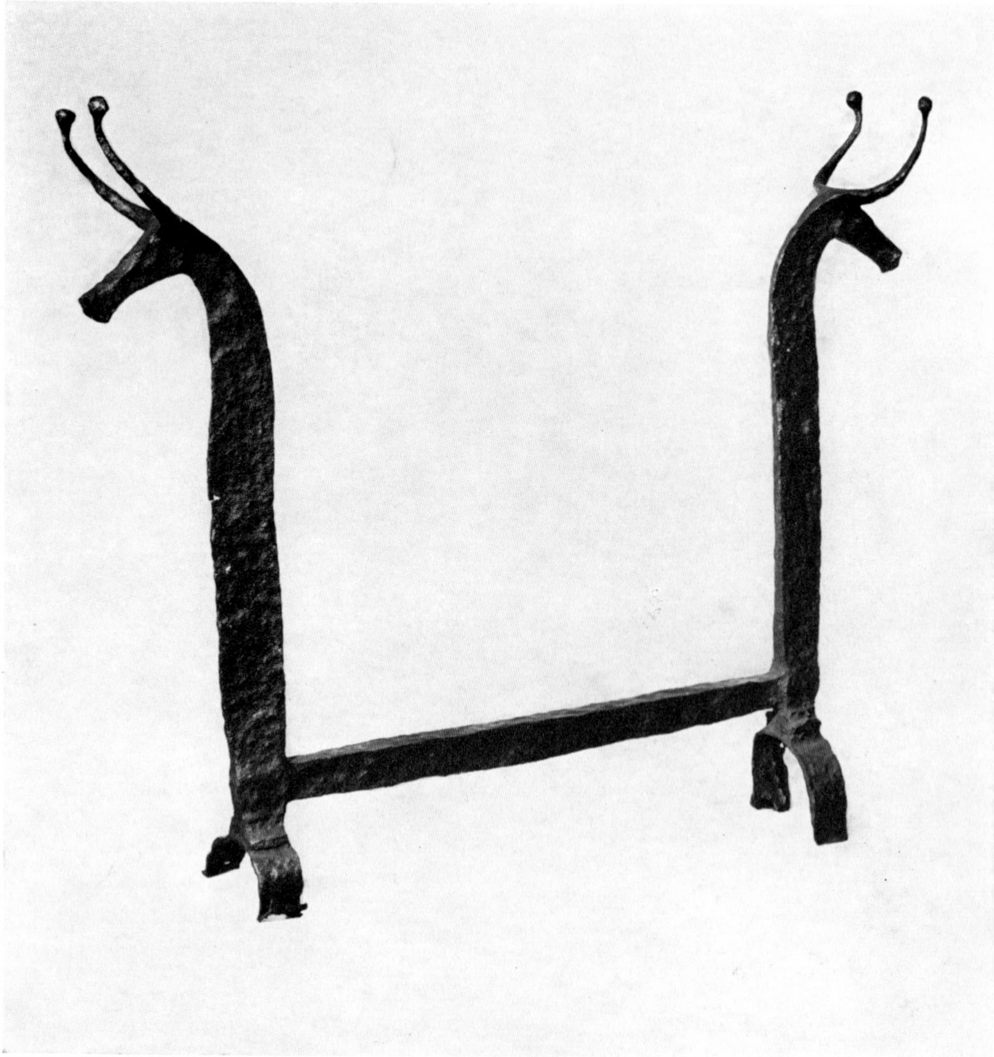

304. Fire-dogs from Lord's Barton, Cambridgeshire. First century B.C. (?). Iron. *Cambridge, Museum of Archaeology and Ethnology*

INDEX

Numbers in *italics* refer to plates; numbers in **bold** type indicate principal entries. References to the notes are given to the page on which the note occurs followed by the number of the note; thus 309[40] indicates page 309, note 40. Only those notes are indexed which contain matter to which there is no obvious reference from the text. In the case of general subjects (e.g. Animals, Animal representation), only the most important references are given.

A

B

INDEX

D

F

G

H

M

W

X

Y

Z

709
P384
V.30

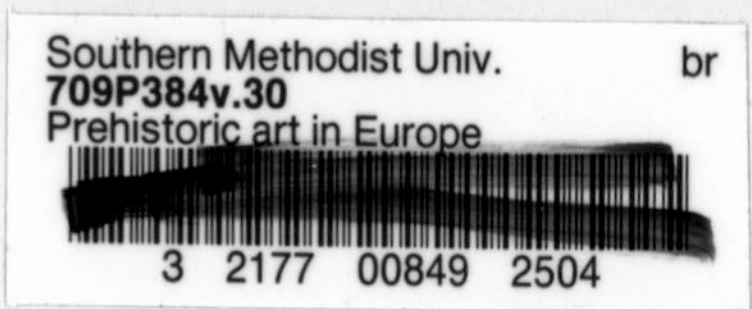
Southern Methodist Univ. br
709P384v.30
Prehistoric art in Europe
3 2177 00849 2504

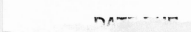